PERSON TO PERSON

Positive Relationships
Don't Just Happen

Fourth Edition

Sharon L. Hanna
Southeast Community College

Prentice
Hall

Upper Saddle River, New Jersey 07458

Library of Congress Cataloging-in-Publication Data

Hanna, Sharon L., 1940-
   Person to person: positive relationships don't just happen/Sharon L. Hanna.—4th ed.
      p.cm.
   Includes bibliographical references and index.
   ISBN 0-13-099586-X
   1. Interpersonal communication. 2. Self-actualization (Psychology) 3. Interpersonal relations. I. Title.
BF637.C45 H32 2002

158.2—dc21   2002024300

VP, Editor-in-Chief: Leah Jewell
Senior Acquisitions Editor: Stephanie Johnson
Managing Editor: Sharon Rheinhardt
Editorial Assistant: Katie Fox
VP, Director of Production and Manufacturing: Barbara Kittle
Production Editor: Randy Pettit
Prepress and Manufacturing Manager: Nick Sklitsis
Prepress and Manufacturing Buyer: Tricia Kenny
Director of Marketing: Beth Mejia
Senior Marketing Manager: Sheryl Adams
Cover Design Director: Jayne Conte
Cover Design: Joseph Sengotta

To Bob Dinkel, my husband and
very best friend, with whom I have
grown in love and intimacy, and to
whom I owe so much.

This book was set in 10/12 Palatino by TSI Graphics
and was printed and bound by R. R. Donnelley.
The cover was printed by Phoenix Color Corp.

 © 2003 by Pearson Education
Upper Saddle River, New Jersey 07458

Printed in the United States of America
10 9 8 7 6 5 4 3 2 1

ISBN: 0-13-099586-X

Pearson Education LTD., London
Pearson Education Australia PTY, Limited, Sydney
Pearson Education Singapore, Pte. Ltd.
Pearson Education North Asia Ltd., Hong Kong
Pearson Education Canada, Ltd., Toronto
Pearson Education de Mexico, S.A. de C.V.
Pearson Education – Japan, Tokyo
Pearson Education Malaysia, Pte. Ltd
Pearson Education, Upper Saddle River, New Jersey

Contents

Section Two   Communication: The Key Relationships   167

Preface

Person to Person: Positive Relationships Don't Just Happen, Fourth Edition is intended to encourage and guide you on a journey, first within yourself and then into the world of positive interactions and relationships. Ann Landers once wrote: "Life is peculiar. It waits until we flunk the course and then it teaches us the lesson." All of us will make mistakes during our lives; however, the fewer "courses we flunk," the better. This book, whether you read it as part of your formal education or just for personal reasons, can help you make wise choices and live a happier, more fulfilling life.

Building a positive relationship isn't an accident; each one requires understanding and effort. Relating with people is an art to be learned and practiced. Because the self is the foundation of all relationships, the goals of the first part of the book are self-discovery and self-satisfaction, with an emphasis on heightened self-esteem, ability to make wise choices, and increased happiness and well-being. Because through interpersonal communication human beings interact and relate to one another, it is essential to learn how to communicate in a positive way—the objective of the second part of this book. Only after you have learned to love yourself and then develop effective communication skills is success in relationships probable. The last part of this book teaches about various interactions and all kinds of relationships. Career, love, couple relationships, marriage, and family are given special emphasis. More than ever, the workplace demands interpersonal and communication skills. This book can assist its readers in all walks of life and can help us live positively in a world of diversity.

Sadly, yet importantly, the incomprehensible tragedy involving the terrorist hijacking of airliners and the subsequent attacks on the World Trade Center in New York City and the Pentagon in Washington, D. C., on September 11, 2001, occurred while I was working on this edition. Even more than ever I am convinced that the world needs acceptance and appreciation of diversity, love and respect for human life, and the finest of interpersonal relations skills. Remember that each of us can be a candle that enlightens the world.

Features of this book include: "Looking Ahead" objectives so that you know what is important; "Reflect and Apply" mini-sections to stimulate thoughts and actions that will make the learning more personal; "Looking Back" summaries and listings of resources for your use; suggested readings marked in the References to encourage further exploration; Reflections and Applications, a separate section at the back of the book that you are encouraged to complete.

Edmund Burke, a philosopher, said, "To read without reflecting is like eating without ingesting." Please read and reflect! The more you "get into it," the more you will gain.

At the end of the book you can be satisfied that you have become better educated about yourself and life. Hopefully, you will have a clear vision of what you want, a realistic idea of how to satisfy your goals, and the positive attitude and high self-esteem needed to achieve harmony and happiness. The realization that life has an ebb and flow can enable you to live life to its fullest with purpose and meaning and to reflect on your past while looking forward optimistically to continued growth and achievement.

If the book does for you what it has for others, I'll be delighted. Several people have credited the book for making their lives much more positive. A student commented: "Thanks so much for my first real lessons about life. I'll never forget it. Now to put it all into practice . . . I can't wait!" I hope that you, too, will learn, grow, and benefit, and then put all you have gained into practice. Do experience joy along the way!

ACKNOWLEDGMENTS

Appreciation and praise are vital to positive human relationships. Although acknowledging by name everyone who has contributed to this book isn't possible, I want to express special thanks to the following people:

- My husband and best friend, Bob, who at times thought he had lost his wife (and then found her in the den in front of the computer) . . . for his deep love, affirmation, and encouragement, for back rubs and hugs, for taking over so many responsibilities along with running his own demanding business, and for always "being there" for me.
- My family members and friends . . . for their understanding and support.
- The thousands of students, colleagues, and friends who have contributed to my personal growth as well as to this book by sharing their lives with me.

My deep appreciation also goes to the following people, who gave their time and talents behind the scenes:

- Pat Peterson, reference specialist at Southeast Community College's Learning Resource Center, who was outstanding in her research of numerous sources of information. She was exceptionally positive and encouraging and made my job so much easier.
- Staci Dittmer McMahon, whose positive attitude and willingness to do whatever was asked were greatly appreciated as she typed countless entries for the References section plus helped in several other necessary tasks.
- Trish Reimer and Ceil King, who cheerfully and efficiently conducted important research for this edition.
- My daughters, Lisa and Lyn Patterson, deserve recognition for their unconditional love, understanding, and support.

Special acknowledgment goes to those whose work appears in the book: Greg Dinkel, photographer; Roberta Sward, artist; Ben Thomas, cartoonist; and to those special professionals who kindly offered their personal opinions and advice to readers: Sue Frahm, Larry Frahm, Carlton Paine, Andrea Sime, Jeanne Baer, and Don Collins.

I would like to thank the Prentice Hall reviewers: Joan H. Rollins, Rhode Island College; Fay A. Gentle, Chemeketa Community College; Nancy Koschmann and Candace Widmer, both of Elmira College. Reviews are not always fun to read; however, these were constructive and useful, and many of the reviewers' ideas were incorporated.

And to the wonderful people at Prentice Hall, especially Sharon Rheinhardt, Managing Editor, who in her warm, encouraging, and helpful way made my work easier and more enjoyable; Randy Pettit, Production Editor, who solved problems and provided help in numerous ways; and all the hardworking publisher's representatives who market this book. My questions and concerns were always addressed in the positive ways emphasized in *Person to Person: Positive Relationships Don't Just Happen*. At Prentice Hall they make positive relationships happen!

—*Sharon L. Hanna*

ABOUT THE AUTHOR

Sharon L. Hanna is Chair of Social Sciences, Academic Education, at Southeast Community College in Lincoln, Nebraska. Having been an educator in Nebraska, New Jersey, and Illinois over a period of several years, she remains enthusiastic about teaching and her students. She has received both faculty achievement and outstanding teacher awards. Her research on the strengths of stepfamilies was published in academic journals, and she served as national president of the Stepfamily Association of America. She is the author of *Career by Design*, Second Edition, published by Prentice Hall in 2002. Married to Bob Dinkel, she has two daughters, two stepsons, a granddaughter, and a grandson.

Section One
Relating: Beginning with the Self

LOOKING AHEAD

After completing this section, you will be able to:

- Describe a positive relationship, define interpersonal relations, and tell how they are related to each other.
- Explain how people learn interpersonal skills.
- Contrast personal and professional lives with those in the past and explain why interpersonal skills may be needed even more in today's world.
- Describe personal and professional benefits of interpersonal skills.
- Recognize that the characteristics desired in employees are those that are important in living a happy, satisfying life.
- Realize that people with a desire can learn interpersonal skills.

The journey to the development of positive relationships begins within.

—Sharon Hanna

Do you feel a need to relate to others? Hopefully, your answer is "yes," because contact and connection enhance human development. Personal growth and happiness are by-products of positive relationships.

What are positive relationships? A **positive relationship** is one in which individuals experience the following reactions:

- Significantly more pleasure than pain
- General feelings of satisfaction and happiness
- Personal growth grounded in a genuine regard for self and others

Other criteria to be discussed in this book will enrich a relationship.

In order to develop positive relationships, we engage in **interpersonal relations**, an ongoing interactive process that includes initiating, building, and enriching relationships with different people in a variety of situations. At times, ending a relationship is involved. If the process goes well, we are likely to live happier lives. Because nobody is born knowing how to relate, interpersonal skills must be learned.

You can use this book to develop a deeper understanding of human interactions and relationships. The beginning of this understanding is within each of us. Knowing and loving yourself helps you reach out positively to others. The foundation of respect for others is self-respect (Branden, 1992).

Be gentle with yourself.
Learn to love yourself, forgive yourself.
For only as we have the right attitude toward ourselves,
can we have the right attitude toward others.

—Author unknown

Unfortunately, individuals do not always understand the need to learn to relate.

> The expression on Rodney's face during his first interpersonal relations class ranged from a sneer to a glare. After class he came to me and said, "I want you to know that I shouldn't have to take this class. I've been around the horn and seen everything, so I don't need it. What's more, I don't think this stuff can be taught. You either have it, or you don't!" I was taken by surprise at his outburst. I said that I hoped he would give the course a chance. Rodney, a defiant man in his late thirties, seemed to say, "I dare you to try to teach me anything."

Rodney's resistance was the greatest challenge of my teaching career. His comment that he had been "around the horn" implied that just living one's life leads to interpersonal skills. Is experience enough? As an employer, would you hire applicants for important positions who had learned only from their life experiences? Because relationships are so important and, usually, are complex and unpredictable, specialized training in interpersonal relations can make a significant difference in the quality of our lives. In a national study (Packard, 1992), 66 percent of family relations teachers identified interpersonal relationships or communication skills as essential.

A strong case can be made that adjustment and relating skills are even more necessary today than they were in the past. See how many examples you can think of for the descriptors in "Comparisons to Yesteryear."

Comparisons to Yesteryear

Today's life is more:

- Populated and mobile
- Diverse
- Full of choices
- Fast changing
- Complicated

Years ago, divorce, suicide, drug use, and violence weren't occurring in the numbers they are today. Let's look at what's happening.

- Every 17 minutes another life is lost to suicide. Suicide takes the lives of more than 30,000 Americans every year. More teenagers and young adults die from suicide than from cancer, heart disease, AIDS, birth defects, stroke, pneumonia and influenza, and chronic lung disease combined (National Strategy for Suicide Prevention, 2001).
- Arrest rates for aggravated assault remain almost 70 percent higher than they were in 1983 (Youth Violence: A Report of the Surgeon General, 2001).

Figure I-1

- Neither nonfatal violence nor the percentage of students injured with a gun at school declined from the peak years of the early 1990s, according to self-reports of young people (Youth Violence: A Report of the Surgeon General, 2001).

Undoubtedly, the single most deadly, hateful event occurred on September 11, 2001, when over 3,000 people were killed in terrorist attacks in the United States. The unspeakable tragedy and other violent incidents call for massive changes in the ways people think and live plus continued efforts to teach people how to handle stress and frustration without hurting others.

Another reason for the need for interpersonal skills relates to gender and family roles that are so different from the past. Are children seen and not heard as they were expected to be in the past? Are they obedient at all times? How do females and males decide who does what and how their lives will be structured? Finally, even if life were no different from yesteryear, individuals today experience many more interactions and relationships because of longer life expectancy. Interpersonal and communication skills are needed more than when roles were clearly established and people were limited in the number of relationships.

Today, formalized training is available, yet frequently overlooked or avoided. A logical learning environment is the educational system. Yet, how many classes have taught you specifically about yourself? For most people, the answer is none. Leo Buscaglia (1982), who taught college classes about love and relationships, questioned an educational system that has a worthy goal of self-realization and then doesn't teach it.

Let's consider the benefits of interpersonal training. First, doesn't it seem likely that individuals who feel positive about themselves and others would do better educationally? Self-esteem building and interpersonal training are related to enhanced academic performance (Clark, 1997). In a study, 5-year-olds who felt more positive about themselves were also more competent, adjusted better to school, and enjoyed higher levels of social acceptance (Verschueren, Marcoen, & Schoefs, 1996). In spite of the perceived benefits, courses about self and relationships are limited because of an overloaded curriculum and lack of awareness of their value. Even if such courses exist, they are rarely required. Think of people you know who could benefit from such courses. Would they voluntarily take them? One student said, "If only my husband would take this relationships course! But I couldn't drag him here!"

If courses are not required, most people will continue to learn from experience and untrained teachers. The home is the first learning environment; our ideas about self and relating to others are formed in the cradle. A sad truth is that families may teach negative ways of interacting. Humans learn in many ways. Among them are:

- Direct instruction ("Don't hit your sister.")
- Modeling (watching a parent hit your sister, which is confusing if you've been told not to hit!)
- Experience (hitting someone and receiving encouragement or discouragement for doing so.)

In addition to family members, we learn from friends, school experiences, the media, and other sources in the world. What have you learned about love? For many, their training about relationships comes from television soap operas. What is learned is often neither helpful nor adequate. Having "been around the horn" just isn't enough.

What are other benefits of learning about self and relations? A basic one is understanding of self and heightened self-esteem. Rodney, the reluctant student, did not truly know or like himself, and his lack of self-worth created a fear of self-discovery. For every Rodney, however, there are many others who eagerly anticipate the journey within. Most are pleasantly surprised with what they find. Karen wrote on a self inventory: "I've learned so much since I came back to school, but I never expected to learn about me. I never knew how much I was or how much I had the power to be. I never knew how interesting I was. I'm not so bad. I'm okay! No one ever taught me that." Her lovely poem follows.

> At first I was afraid to meet her . . .
>   But you know
>   The more I got to know her
> To accept and understand her
>   The more I grew to love her.
>   She is me.

Additional benefits are taking charge of your own life, being motivated to change, gaining insight into how to adjust, and learning coping strategies. Have you ever heard anyone say, "I can't help it; I just can't change?" Some changes may be impossible, yet the self can be improved in a number of ways. Usually, limitations exist only in the mind. The belief that you can change is one result of interpersonal relations training.

> I believe that wherever you are in life, and however you learned it, that if you want to learn it differently, anything that can be learned can be unlearned and relearned. (Buscaglia, 1982, p. 66)

Even when you want to change, you may still do nothing. The "how-to" component is missing. Personal growth consists of both thought and behavior change. Insight without change is self-defeating.

Interpersonal relations training can also help you cope with stress and crisis. Feeling a heavy burden of guilt, a young student wrote:

> When my cousin was dying of leukemia, I didn't go to see her. I didn't think I could face it. Now she's dead, and I never told her how much I cared.

This student was comforted somewhat when she realized that most of us have not been taught how to handle the illness and death of loved ones.

Coursework can produce what seems like a miracle. One example was Vernon, a 35-year-old who reflected deep depression and low self-esteem on his first class assignment. He wrote: "Sometimes I feel so totally worthless since I was injured and lost my job that I think my wife and kids would be better off without me." A few months later a transformed Vernon wrote in another paper:

> I'm beginning to love myself, not in a self-centered, conceited sort of way but that deep down, good kind of feeling that makes me glad I'm me. I'm ecstatic that this course was required. It has helped lift my veil of depression and allowed me an inner calm that has not been mine for some time.

Vernon had learned to deal with crises and depression and, most important, how to change his thoughts about himself. His successes in college and his positive attitude empowered him to change. Today he is a successful restaurant manager.

Do you know that people can develop unhealthy relationships as well as healthy ones? How productive we become and the extent of meaning in our lives are influenced by the quality of our relationships. As interpersonal knowledge and skills are improved, direct benefits are healthy relationships and enrichment of personal and professional lives.

Too often, couples who don't know what to do about their problems either end their relationship or settle for an unhappy one. If people learn to relate, problems can be avoided or solved. Remember Rodney? Toward the end of the course, he came into my office and announced, "I have to hand it to you. You've finally taught me something I can use. My wife and I have been having problems, and the stuff about fighting fair just might help." I was elated! Along with couple relationships, parenting is easier and more enjoyable after training. The probability of raising well-adjusted children is higher if parents learn how. It is reasonable to expect that those who learn relationship skills will be better parents.

How can positive interpersonal skills benefit your career?

- Knowing yourself will help you choose a satisfying career and rewarding jobs.
- Having a high level of self-esteem will increase the chance to get the job you want.
- Using people skills enhances your value as an employee.

In a study of corporations, the two most desired capabilities were communication skills and interpersonal skills (Daniel, 1998). Interpersonal and communication abilities are rated as essential in both the United States (Carrig, 1999) and Canada (*Canadian Manager*, 1999). Interpersonal and communication skills will either make or break a person's career success (Carrig, 1999).

Employers often remark that they can teach technical skills; however, new employees are expected to be able to communicate and relate positively to others. This doesn't stop at the beginning of a career path. Many executives who failed did so most often because of an interpersonal flaw, not technical inability (Gibbs, 1995). According to Jeanne Baer, president of a business consulting firm, "People skills are essential. If you're a manager who likes and is liked by your people, you're a valuable asset to your organization."

Employees are viewed as representatives of the employer. An owner of a fabricating company remarked, "I have a few employees I try to keep hidden from the public, yet it's become increasingly difficult to do that." A truck-driving student announced, "I'm going into trucking because I just like to be alone." He learned quickly that he had chosen the wrong field. Unless you are training to be a hermit, ability to get along with people is a necessity.

A final beneficial, and often overlooked, result of interpersonal relations training is a potential reduction in tragedy. As noted earlier, violence is a fact of life. Two young men, both former students, lost their lives because others lashed out savagely. One was burned to death in a fire set by an angry stranger. Another was bludgeoned to death by two teenagers. Violence, suicide, alcoholism and other drug abuse, job failure, and poor academic performance can result from lack of interpersonal skills. What can help? One of the most effective ways of preventing youth violence is social skills training (Youth Violence: A Report of the Surgeon General, 2001). Not all tragedy can be prevented; yet a dramatic decrease in tragic incidents is possible.

The story of Rodney ends here. He called me at home one night after completion of the course. Obviously distraught, he said:

> I need to talk to you. I fell off the wagon and started drinking again today. I've just called my AA sponsor, and the only other person I want to talk to is you.

I continued to listen, and one point was especially poignant.

> I know now that if I had been raised differently and had understood myself better, I probably wouldn't be like this today. I could have used the interpersonal relations course years ago. In fact, I know now that I would have gotten a lot out of it back when I took it with you, but I was afraid and closed my mind to it. I wish I could take it again.

That was the last word from Rodney. My sincere hope is that he has found a way to turn his life around. It was encouraging that he realized the necessary first step—that he could change.

What Rodney indicated is that a desire to learn and willingness to change are all a person needs to improve interpersonal skills. You might question the necessity of other criteria. Don't you have to be physically attractive or smart to relate to others? Isn't it necessary to have an outgoing personality? The answer is no. Even though certain characteristics are advantageous, there are no physical, mental, or personality requirements beyond basic abilities, as shown in the following profiles.

- Julie, by society's standards, is unattractive, yet her self-esteem is high. She is a sincere person with compassion for others and is successful in her career.
- Verleen sometimes describes herself as a "chubbette." She handles it with humor, never as a drawback! She is generous and caring, a joy to be around. Those extra pounds are no obstacle.
- Bill has spent his entire 38 years in a wheelchair. He was born with cerebral palsy. Cheerful and friendly, he enjoys communicating. He is concerned about others and has a positive attitude.

Figure I-2   Verleen is a delight-ful person who has learned to re-late positively to others.

- Chris is in his thirties; however, he has the mental ability of a much younger person. He was born with Down syndrome. His IQ is not high, yet his SQ (so-cial quotient) would be hard to surpass! He is conge-nial, genuinely concerned about people, and praised for his attitude and determination.
- José is introverted and prefers to be with just a few people at a time. He is not a party-goer. He is sup-portive to his friends, a great listener, polite, and fair-minded.

These individuals lack what are considered the ideal ba-sics for interpersonal relations; yet each has succeeded because of a desire to relate in a positive way.

This book will help you gain insight into yourself and others, learn to communicate in a positive way, and discover how to develop healthy relationships. Take the time to complete the self-appraisal at the beginning of Reflections and Applications (page 413). Even if you al-ready interact in a positive way and enjoy fulfilling rela-tionships, new interpersonal challenges will appear as you grow and change. And, our present level of interpersonal skills can be im-proved. You can appreciate the goodness of life as you learn, grow, and relish the joys and rewards of positive relationships. The interpersonal journey can be inter-esting and highly rewarding, and it begins with you!

I am convinced that much human misery is rooted in ignorance of self and relationships.
—Teresa Adams

1

Knowing and Valuing Yourself

LOOKING AHEAD

After completing this chapter, you will be able to:

- Explain the concept of self.
- Discuss the benefits of self-knowledge and understanding.
- Name and describe the four developmental areas of the self.
- Define attitude, optimism, and pessimism; compare a positive attitude with a negative one; list benefits of a positive attitude.
- Relate the four developmental areas of the self to each other.
- Explain self-concept, self-esteem, and ideal self.
- Describe the concept of wellness and list ways to improve one's health.
- Cope with stress more effectively.
- Give reasons why high self-esteem is important and identify its sources.
- Discuss ways to build self-esteem.
- Use cognitive restructuring.
- Define self-fulfilling prophecy and recognize its existence in your own thinking.
- Define self-efficacy expectations and discuss the importance.
- Raise your own self-esteem level.

The unexamined life is not worth living.

—Socrates

How would you reply to the question, "Who are you?" An off-the-top-of-my-head answer is, "I am Sharon Hanna." Yet you and I are much more than names. Each of us is a unique whole self, an integrated human being.

What is the self and why is it important in the development of positive relationships? Think of the **self** as a separate being within an environment. Early in life, humans distinguish their selves from others. Self-knowledge continues throughout life. "The greatest joy in life is to know oneself from the inside out. Such knowledge enables us to know another and be known" (Adams, 1987, p. 1).

An early pioneer in understanding the self was George Herbert Mead, a sociologist. Mead believed that social experience shapes the self. Selves only exist in relationships to other selves (Mead, 1934). Psychologists, too, have a keen interest in the self. The humanistic approach, which is emphasized in this book, features a complete, or holistic, view of self. The focus is not on selfishness; instead, self-discovery, self-awareness, and self-fulfillment are its goals. Humanistic psychology seeks to help people become fully functioning and achieve their full potential so they have more to give to others.

Although learning about the self can be fascinating, reluctance to seek insight is common. Initial pain may be the price. If you are hesitant, push yourself to learn more. The rewards are many, and as the process continues, the discomfort becomes less. Maturity comes from self-discovery even though one's self isn't a quick study, nor is it one that is ever finished. The *self*, as described by Branden (1983), is a "vast continent whose exploration we can never complete" (p. 173).

EXPLORING DEVELOPMENTAL AREAS OF SELF

Recognizing that the self is whole, human development researchers pay attention to four developmental areas of the self: physical, mental or intellectual, emotional, and social. Let's take the self apart and concentrate on one area at a time, with the assurance that it (and we) will come together again!

Physical Self

Condition of the body and appearance are included in the physical self. Characteristics such as race, sex, hair texture, the natural color of hair and eyes, bone structure, height, and size of feet are either determined or greatly influenced by heredity. On the other hand, we have more control over other physical aspects such as weight, hairstyle, and muscle tone. Accepting what cannot be changed is wise. For example, your age was determined by others—your parents. It does no good to bemoan the fact that one is 20 years old, or 30, or—for some the worst of all—40! Each of us will age—as long as we are alive! Viewing the aging process as depressing, so common in the American society, is setting oneself up for despair. Similarly, wishing to be another race or 4 inches taller is self-defeating.

Health.   How do you define health? For many, being healthy means being free of disease, yet is that all there is to it? Think of **health** as a general feeling of physical and mental well-being. A realistic picture places health on a continuum.

Very ill → Ill → Feeling OK or fine → Well → Very healthy

Very healthy is synonymous with **wellness**, a high level of physical and mental well-being. Total wellness includes the following (Bloomfield, 1978).

- Trim and physically fit
- Full of energy, vigorous, rarely tired
- Free of minor complaints (such as indigestion, constipation, headaches, insomnia)
- Alert, able to concentrate, clearheaded
- Radiant, with clear skin, glossy hair, and sparkling eyes
- Active and creative
- Able to relax easily, free of worry and anxiety
- Self-assured, confident, optimistic
- Satisfied with work and the direction of your life

- Able to assert yourself, stand up for your rights
- Satisfied with your sexual relationships
- Free of destructive health habits, particularly smoking, overeating, and excessive drinking
- Fulfilled and at peace with yourself

Sounds ideal, doesn't it? Even though few people possess every characteristic, wellness is possible; the closer you come to it, the higher your chance for a fulfilling life. Try thinking of the body as a machine. How well are you taking care of it? Machinery can be replaced; whole bodies cannot. Unfortunately, most people treat machinery better than they do their own bodies.

Even though most people consider their health to be of high priority, a large number admit that they don't practice health-enhancing behaviors, and several even pursue unhealthy lifestyles, especially during high school and college years. Do you take your health for granted? Any disregard for health in the present has ramifications for the future. Former governor of Colorado Richard D. Lamm stated:

> The single most important factor determining our quality of life is our health, and the single most important factor affecting our health is the degree to which we as individuals are willing to take responsibility for our own diets and exercise, no matter what age we are at the present time. (Carlson & Seiden, 1988)

In thinking about your health, which of the following three categories best describes you (Crose, 1997)?

Health gamblers: They take their health for granted and assume that there is little they can do about changing the way they are. "My dad died at a young age of lung cancer so I'm expecting that will happen to me, too," said a 30-year-old man as he smoked another cigarette.

Health mechanics: They are willing to tend to their health when illness strikes, yet do little to promote wellness. "I figure if it isn't broken, why do anything?" was how one woman described her attitude.

Health gardeners: They are mindful of their physical and mental health, take steps to prevent illness, and are active in promoting wellness. "I eat sensibly most of the time, use supplements to elevate my health and protect my body, exercise regularly, and get sufficient rest. I feel absolutely great most of the time!" commented a woman.

Are you satisfied with your category? Later in this chapter you will read about several ways to become a "health gardener."

Appearance. A strong point could be made that Americans pay too much attention to one part of the physical self: the outer shell. Body image, defined as a perception of one's appearance, is strongly correlated with regard for the self, and females are significantly less satisfied than males (Stowers & Durm, 1996). Many people, seemingly obsessed with appearance, work hard to achieve high standards of beauty. Women, especially, may not even consider comfort when just to look attractive, they squeeze their feet into pointed-toe, spiked heels.

How can a desire for attractiveness interfere with good health? Achieving the "thin look," so prevalent in the media, can become all-important. Unhealthy ways to lose weight such as using laxatives, taking diet pills, inducing vomiting, and restricting caloric intake to under 1,200 calories a day were commonly used by high school female students, especially those who were frequent readers of beauty and fashion magazines (Gorrell, 2001). Putting such a high premium on weight, especially if it endangers health, is alarming. **Anorexia nervosa** is a life-threatening disorder that includes a distorted body image, refusal to maintain a healthy weight, and an intense fear of being overweight. A realistic attitude about weight is worth seeking. Being considerably overweight is a health hazard, and attempting to achieve close to an ideal weight and a fit body is highly recommended. How to lose weight in a healthy way is covered later in this chapter.

Men, too, can feel pressured to achieve a "look," so they may use steroids for purely cosmetic reasons. Side effects are common. Steroid users often develop mood disorders that may be accompanied by violent or aggressive behavior (*Menninger Letter*, 1994). Shockingly, a survey found that 2.7 percent of 965 middle school athletes, some as young as 10, used steroids and that girls' involvement was about the same as boys (*Lincoln Journal Star*, 1998a). The desire to be muscular isn't worth the price, especially since other ways to achieve that look are available.

Individuals continue to take health risks because they believe that a tan look is attractive in spite of conclusive research on skin cancer. Across cultures, young people who are highly concerned about physical appearance are more likely to sunbathe and not take proper precautions (Prentice-Dunn, Jones, & Floyd, 1997). Excessive sun exposure puts a person at risk for melanoma, a serious type of skin cancer that claimed an estimated 7,700 lives in the United States in 2000 (Cowley, 2001). The annual number of new cases has more than doubled since 1973, according to the National Cancer Institute. This could partly be due to the introduction and use of tanning beds. Exposure to sunlamps and sunbeds plus all types of solar radiation are identified as known human **carcinogens**, substances that tend to cause cancer (U.S. Department of Health and Human Services, 2001). Ironically, sun exposure leads to skin wrinkling which is not a standard for attractiveness. Proper use of sunscreens and asking the question, "Is a tan worth it?" are highly recommended. Additionally, a change in this standard of attractiveness would be most beneficial.

Judging others only on their looks can limit possibilities and lead to unhealthy relationships. People often miss opportunities to meet less attractive, yet wonderful, individuals. Those who evaluate themselves only on the basis of appearance put their self-esteem at risk. Trying to look as attractive as possible can be an enjoyable expression of how we feel about ourselves as long as appearance isn't the yardstick by which our self-worth is measured.

Mental Self

The mental self is fascinating. Learning abilities, thought-processing patterns, as well as attitude and motivation are facets of this important area of the self. Cognitive (thought) development occurs throughout one's life.

Mental abilities.   How mentally able are you? What intelligence means and how to assess it are controversial issues. For years **intelligence** was considered to be an intellectual capacity or potential. Recently, attempts have been made to broaden this definition. Believing that a narrow scholastic definition of intelligence can cause children with abilities to think they are stupid, Howard Gardner (1983) introduced the concept of seven **multiple intelligences**. More recently he has expanded the number of possible intelligences and emphasized the abilities to solve problems and to create products that are of value in a culture (Gardner, 1999).

Which of the Multiple Intelligences Do You Possess?

- Linguistic (related to language)
- Logical-mathematical (related to problem solving, mathematical operations, and scientific investigation)
- Musical (related to performance, composition, and appreciation)
- Bodily-kinesthetic (using the body and handling objects skillfully)
- Spatial (related to manipulation of space)
- Interpersonal (related to understanding and working with others)
- Intrapersonal (related to understanding oneself)

Regardless of definition or number of intelligences, wouldn't you agree that everyday competence, problem solving, display of curiosity, and ability to get along with others are as important as academic intelligence?

Intelligence is believed to be a complex result of the interrelationship between heredity and environment (Singh, 1996). The prenatal environment probably plays a significant role (Devlin, Danieis, & Roeder, 1997). An IQ (intelligence quotient) test is typically used to measure intelligence. A score indicates a person's level of ability and potential mainly in the areas of language and mathematics. Other tests such as the ACT and SAT measure academic aptitude and play a major role in college admission and financial aid. Caution is advised because low achievement can be caused by other factors such as cultural bias in testing, test anxiety, or **learning disabilities**, a group of related and often overlapping conditions that lead to low achievement by people who have the potential to do better (Smith, 1993). Most people with learning disabilities are talented and bright; however, traditional schooling is often challenging. The educational system has found ways to recognize and help those who learn differently. Reading a book such as *ADD and the College Student* (Quinn, 2001) and also seeking help from a specialist can make a great deal of difference. College students with learning disabilities who ask a lot of questions and seek support are more likely to graduate than those who don't. Learning disabled students can acquire a better way to learn and realize their potential.

No matter how one learns, achievement and grades in school are usually a reflection of how much effort a person is willing to make. A study of high school valedictorians revealed that they were not always the brightest students; they were, however, the hardest working (Arnold, 1995). Whatever your measured degree of intelligence or your style of learning, you can choose how to use it.

Learning readiness and strategies. Willingness and eagerness to learn are valuable traits, and employers view them as assets. Curiosity about a number of subjects can result in a well-rounded person who is both interested and interesting. You may be surprised to realize that being confused can set the stage for learning. Students confess that they are afraid to ask questions, citing situations in

Figure 1-1   Reading is a favorite way to improve mentally.

which they were put down or laughed at because they did so. This is unfortunate. What is often the case in classrooms is that only the teachers ask questions. If you are reluctant to ask or answer questions, try to overcome the hesitancy. Regard both as an indication of some knowledge and a desire to learn.

How do you learn most easily? Individuals typically learn from their experiences, so actual hands-on, or **experiential learning** is effective. For example, you may have been instructed as to how to set a videocassette recorder. Wouldn't it have been better to have actually gone through the motions as well? You have probably learned through traditional methods, and, hopefully, you have found one or more that works well for you. Generally, learning is most effective when it involves several of our senses.

Critical and creative thinking.   How much have you ever thought about thinking? Where did you learn to think? Or were you ever taught actual thinking skills? **Thinking** is the ability to activate and then pursue mental activity. For years our educational system presumed that if students were reasonably intelligent, they were able to think and didn't need training. Educators only gave information and told students about ideas. The same practices exist today and do not encourage thinking. Too often, only memorization skills are needed, and those who have difficulty memorizing don't do well. Ability to think is rarely assessed. Years ago, von Oech (1983) criticized our educational system. Unfortunately, what he wrote still applies.

> Much of our educational system is geared toward teaching people the one right answer. By the time the average person finishes college, he or she will have taken over 2,600 tests, quizzes, and exams. Thus, the "right answer" approach becomes deeply ingrained. This may be fine for some mathematical problems where there is only one right answer. The difficulty is that most of life doesn't present itself in this way. Life is ambiguous; there are many right answers—all depending on what you are looking for. But if you think there is only one right answer, then you will stop looking as soon as you find one. (p. 21)

Being "right" or certain can stop us from being curious, and curiosity is the basis of learning. As you read this book, you will see how important thought processing is. The ability to think is the foundation of human accomplishments. Each person develops methods of processing information and acquires a number of beliefs. These ideas are beneficial only if they aren't so rigid that they limit a person's ability to discover, think, and learn.

Taking nothing for granted is one aspect of **critical thinking**. Do you believe everything you read or hear? If so, you aren't using critical thinking. Do you dig deeper, challenge assumptions, and examine the logic of differing points? If so, you are thinking! Try to develop a "working knowledge" of material by thinking, talking, and actually using what has been read or presented.

You employ **creative thinking** when you think about ideas in different ways and generate a variety of solutions to problems. The basis of creativity is mental flexibility. Try creative thinking and come up with different uses for common objects such as a brick. A problem that isn't too difficult (although you may be surprised how many times individuals don't seem to be able to solve it) is that it's 7:30 in the morning, and your car won't start. You have a class in an hour. What can you do? Creative thinking is liberating and can solve many problems in your life!

Why are different types of thinking so important? First, new facts and opinions bombard us, and we are faced with numerous decisions. Too often, people depend upon so-called experts and accept all that they see and hear. Using our brains in critical and creative ways is excellent mental exercise! A middle-aged student commented at the end of a sociology course, "I don't know for sure how much I've learned, but the course really taught me to think." I told him that learning how to think was the most valuable lesson of all.

Limiting oneself by lack of curiosity, fear of questioning, and lack of confidence is a waste of human potential. As you read this book and participate in discussions, use your wonderful mind to ask questions, present alternative ideas, and generate thoughts! Be like Carolyn, a middle-aged student, who wrote: "My mind has been resting on a shelf for too long, and now it's ready to apply its power!"

Attitude.   Undoubtedly, an extremely influential aspect of the mental self is **attitude**, a state of mind that is reflected in how a person approaches life. In referring to the future, **optimists** have positive thoughts, while **pessimists** view life as negative. As a humorous contrast, think of optimists as thinking that they'll never die or if they do, they'll wake up to the glory of heaven, while pessimists are certain that they won't live much longer and that if they wake up in heaven, they won't like it (Chapman, 1993). In a study of college students, high optimists enjoyed the highest overall quality of life satisfaction while low optimists were dissatisfied and used more alcohol in an attempt to cope (Harju & Bolen, 1998). Optimists and pessimists interpret the same experiences very differently and live opposite lives. Which do you prefer?

Quite a Contrast

Optimists
- Protected their personal health (Greenberg, 1997)
- Coped with extremely difficult situations through activity (Greenberg, 1997)
- Had fewer serious disease and health problems (Goleman, 1997)

Pessimists
- Discontinued their medicine and reported poorer health (Aversa & Kimberlin, 1996)
- Had a higher risk for death from cancer (Schulz, Bookwala, Knapp, Scheier, & Williamson, 1996)

Some people have been "attituded" excessively, with such common statements as "Your attitude stinks," "If you'd only improve your attitude," or "You've got an attitude." Yet, its effects on the self and others are so powerful that they cannot be disregarded. Incidentally, we all have an attitude!

> If you can create and keep a positive attitude toward your job, your company, and life in general, you should not only move up the ladder of success quickly and gracefully, you should also be a happier person. If you are unable to do this, you may find many doors closed to you on the job, and your personal life less than exciting. (Chapman, 1993, p. 20)

Attitude is described as positive or negative; it usually varies between these two extremes. A positive attitude is not the same as a "Pollyanna" way of looking at life. That is, you can have a positive attitude and realize that life is not absolutely wonderful all the time. Being positive means that you look on the brighter side of events, that you are more "up" than "down," and that you usually feel responsible and in control of yourself. Positive people are generally energetic, motivated, and alert. With a negative attitude the world almost always appears bleak, a "down" feeling is apparent, and blaming and excuse making are common. Think of someone you know whose attitude is negative. Any of these descriptions may come to your mind: fault finding, irresponsible, lazy, apathetic, complaining, or gloomy. An individual who fits this description is likely to be avoided by others. "Misery may love company, but company doesn't love misery" (Myers, 1992, p. 20). Employers want employees with positive attitudes.

> Attitudes are caught more than they are taught. Both negative and positive attitudes are transmitted on the job. A persistently negative attitude, like the rotten apple in the barrel, can spoil the positive attitudes of others. (Chapman, 1993, p. 23)

Think about those who influence you, and, most importantly, those who look to you for guidance. The tone of a day can be set by one person. Attitudes are truly contagious!

In specific situations, employees can especially benefit from positive attitudes. Pretend you are a supervisor. You have two employees who have a disagreement, and they come to talk to you. Carlos is a positive person, and he rarely complains. Sean's attitude is generally negative, and this is not the first gripe he has brought to you. The two tell different versions of the same event. Which one will you believe? Even if Sean's version is accurate, the odds are that Carlos will be believed.

A positive attitude is also highly desirable beyond the workplace. Ask athletic coaches, teachers, and others who work with people about the advantages of a positive attitude. Positive individuals are better competitors and give up less easily; they try harder in the classroom and use their mistakes to improve; they are enjoyable people, and interactions with them are more productive. Think about individuals you know. Don't you prefer to be around those who are more "up" than "down"? An outstanding example of a positive attitude maintained against all odds was Mike, a student who wrote as a description of himself: "I have a slight health problem—cystic fibrosis, but I don't let it get me down." Cystic fibrosis is much more than a *slight* health problem; however, Mike has never let it change his marvelous attitude.

Examine your way of approaching life. You have an opportunity to rate your attitude in Reflections and Applications and compare it with what others think. Remember that attitude is always a choice; the key is to change both thoughts and behaviors. The book *Learned Optimism* (Seligman, 1998) is an excellent guide with ideas on how to become more positive. Coursework can also help. I was delighted when a student wrote on a paper, "After only two interpersonal relations classes, I have a better attitude about life!" Reading and putting into practice the ideas and methods presented in this book can empower you to develop an even more positive attitude.

You have probably heard about the power of thought. Norman Cousins (1979, 1983, 1989) told remarkable stories of his recoveries from a serious illness and a heart attack and of research showing that intense determination and hope influences the course of disease. Others believe that pain can be caused by belief or attitude and that a person's way of thinking can decrease or eliminate pain (Benson, 1987). In this book you will learn more about the power of belief and how to change your thoughts.

Emotional Self

A third part of the self is emotional; it is composed of feelings and ways of expressing them. Human beings are often unaware of their emotions. For example, when asked, "What are you feeling right now?" a person commonly answers, "I don't know," "Fine," or "Okay." Rarely are emotions identified. Human beings are emotional; that is, we have feelings that color our lives. Personal expressions of emotions vary considerably. Because of its importance, Chapter 5 is devoted to the subject of the emotional self.

Social Self

"How do you get along with other people?" This question relates to the social self. Important aspects are **statuses**, defined as what we are or our social positions and **roles**, the behaviors that are a part of those statuses. For example, some of Bob's statuses are son, father, husband, employee, and friend. Within each status, he performs certain roles such as provider and nurturer. Consider your own statuses and roles. Other parts of the social self are relationships and social behaviors. Humans require social exchanges with others in order to be loved and to learn to love. Nobody can survive in a vacuum, and social relationships are vital to our well-being!

A primary objective of this book is to guide you in the development of relationships. A beginning step is to understand how you have socially developed. Personality, covered in Chapter 2, plays a major role in the social aspects of life.

INTEGRATING YOUR WHOLE SELF

Fortunately, you aren't like Humpty-Dumpty, who couldn't be put back together again! The parts make up a whole, and examining your integrated self is fascinating. "Every

Figure 1-2

Developmental Areas of Self

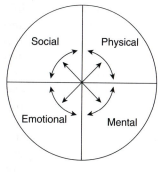

Figure 1-3

baby born into this world is a living question mark. The first question is about the self: "Who am I?" (Powell, 1976, p. 47). Humans continue to search for the answer. By discovering and valuing your own self-identity, you can have a positive relationship with yourself.

Coming together, or integration of the self, is illustrated in Figure 1–3. The arrows indicate that the parts are interrelated, and they influence each other both negatively and positively. Recall a time when you were not feeling well physically. What were you like mentally, emotionally, socially? Even if you didn't realize it, you were probably diminished in these other areas, too. The good news, which has already been mentioned, is that a positive spillover also occurs. For example, attitude can make a positive difference in the physical, emotional, and social parts of life. Studies indicate how important it is to pay attention to a patient's emotional distress and social support along with the physical. From his work with support groups for breast cancer patients, David Spiegel (1996) of Stanford University School of Medicine found that social contact not only had positive emotional effects but also reduced the death risk. He also discovered that a reduction in depression and anxiety seemed to increase the activity of natural killer cells in the body. Thus, a positive emotional state was related to improved physical health.

Improving yourself physically, mentally, emotionally, or socially will create benefits in the other developmental areas. Pat was unhappy and shy. She started on an exercise program and had her hair cut and styled. She reported how much better she felt physically, mentally, and emotionally and described a definite improvement in her social relationships. An activity in Reflections and Applications gives you an opportunity to describe yourself in all areas. Checking to see that you are balanced in the four areas is also important. Some people devote a great deal of time and energy to their mental self and exclude their social development. Others build their bodies and are strangers to their feelings. Jack was happy-go-lucky and sociable. He left home to attend college. He became depressed and sought counseling. He had been concentrating on social activities and found himself failing in school and feeling ill, he slept minimally, his diet was poor, and he drank excessive amounts of alcohol. He learned the hard way that he was an integrated being.

DISCOVERING YOUR SELF-CONCEPT

When you consider who you are, what do you perceive? Whether we realize it or not, each of us carries about with us a mental blueprint or image of ourselves. How this self develops is of interest to both sociologists and psychologists. Influential is the **generalized other**, which Mead (1934) described as the organized community or social group. Thinking of a whole community's attitude gives you a concept of the generalized other. Have you ever thought, "I can't do that. What would *they* think?" If by "they," you don't mean specific people and are describing a collective attitude, you are tapping into the generalized other. Think about how this guides our behaviors and development of self.

What are your ideas, mental representations, and understanding of your own self? The **self-concept** is the totality of your thoughts and feelings with reference to yourself and is the foundation on which almost all your actions are based (Rosenberg, 1979). When does self-concept form? During infancy, emotional experiences form the basis for its development (Eder & Mangelsdorf, 1997). Carl Rogers (1961) wrote about self-concept and how it develops. As a psychotherapist, he believed that at the heart of most of his clients' problems was a search for self. Fulfillment of self means that one is basically positive, open to experience, trustful of one's own thoughts and feelings, self-valuative rather than at the mercy of others' approval, and willing to be a process rather than a product. Rogers, a humanistic psychologist, was optimistic about human potential.

The self-concept consists of self-descriptions, ideal self, and self-esteem or self-worth. Use the key word "like" to help conceptualize self-concept. Think of it as: (1) what I'm like, (2) what I'd like to be like, (3) how much I like what I'm like. Your current self descriptions and your **ideal self**, the image of what you would like to be, may be similar or quite different. Because of external standards, you may have an unrealistic ideal. If so, that image is more hurtful than helpful. Amy described herself as overweight, short, average in intelligence, shy, and unhappy much of the time. Her ideal self was slim, at least 4 inches taller, brilliant, friendly, and always happy. Which descriptors of her ideal can help her improve and which would just be hurtful? As was mentioned earlier, knowing what you can change and what you cannot is valuable. Amy has formulated an ideal self that, in some respects, is not possible and is likely to lead to dissatisfaction and frustration.

In addition, people can be absorbed with their ideal selves to such an extent that they are at risk. A study of college students found that preoccupation with the ideal self was correlated with anxiety, self-consciousness, and vulnerability (Bybee, Luthar, Zigler, & Merisca, 1997). Balanced thinking is essential. Also important is to realize that achieving one's ideal self is not a requirement for high self-esteem or happiness. Instead, if your ideal is reached, set your sights even higher. Rather than ideal, try thinking of this image as your **desired self**. Then use it to discover ways to improve in realistic ways. Realize that if you want the best possible relationships, you will want to create the best possible "you." Striving for improvement makes life interesting as well as challenging. Regardless of your level of self-satisfaction, positive changes can be made. Awareness of self followed by a sincere desire to change are the forerunners of personal growth. Throughout this book, you will be encouraged to improve in each of the developmental areas; later in this chapter, you will read more about self-esteem.

Figure 1-4

IMPROVING YOUR HEALTH

An obviously important beginning is in your degree of wellness. Remember the earlier description of the "health gardener"? This section will emphasize ways you can become an active participant in your own health. Think of any possible physical, health-enhancing changes. Check "Tips to Wellness" to see how many came to your mind.

Tips to Wellness

- *Increase physical activity.* For most, the easiest is to walk more. The key is to find activities that you enjoy and will do on a regular basis, then move your body!
- *Improve your nutrition.* Learn what is healthy and then put it into practice. Realizing that you will have only one body, care for it better than you do a vehicle or other material object.
- *Maintain a healthy body weight.* Set a realistic goal. People feel and look better when their weight is "right" for them. If you are obese, aim for 5 percent to 15 percent weight reduction and notice a dramatic difference.
- *Get adequate sleep.* Being well-rested improves all areas of the self.
- *Effectively cope with stress.* You can't escape stress; however, you can manage it and make it beneficial in your life.
- *Eliminate unhealthy behaviors and habits.* Choices that subtract from the quality of life are yours to make. Chapter 3 describes these.

Now let's consider why putting the wellness tips into practice will enhance your life and learn ways to do so.

Physical Activity

Did you know that physical activity is related to:

- Living longer (Fozard, 1999)
- Lower risk of heart disease (Lee, Rexrode, Cook, Manson, & Buring, 2001)
- Decreased risk of both colon cancer (Batty, 2000) and breast cancer (Verloop, Rookus, van der Kooy, van Leeuwen, 2000)
- Prevention and better management of diabetes (Folsom & Kushi, 2000)
- Lowered blood pressure (*Harvard Health Letter*, 1999)
- Relief of stress (Bartolomeo, 2000) and of depression (Mangum, 2000)
- Increased cognitive skills especially in older adults (Larkin, 1999)
- Protection against and better management of Alzheimer's disease (Friedland, 1998)
- Fewer chronic medical problems, higher levels of functioning, and greater strength in older adults (Fozard, 1999)
- Lowered risk of osteoporosis (Adler & Raymond, 2001)
- Healthy weight maintenance (Anderson & Wadden, 1999)
- Smoking cessation (Aschwanden & Cederborg, 1999)

Becoming more active seems to benefit all areas of self. How much activity is healthy? An American study showed that the risk of death can be reduced 19 percent by adding just one mile to an ordinary daily walk (Hakim et al., 1998). An important point is to be sensible about exercise, as intense long-duration exercise can depress the immune system (Pedersen, Rohde, & Zacho, 1996).

Reasons for not becoming more physically active are often heard. "I can't afford to join a health club right now" or "I don't have time" are among the most

Figure 1-5   Enjoyable physical activity contributes to wellness.

common. In Chapter 4 you will see how excuses can block happiness. Be honest with yourself. If you sincerely want to add physical activity to your life, you can. Simple ways are to just walk farther and to climb stairs instead of using an elevator or escalator. To motivate you, read what a well-known authority on wellness (Weil, 1995b) says:

Human beings are meant to walk. We are bipedal, upright organisms with bodies designed for locomotion. Walking exercises our brains as well as our musculoskeletal systems. When you walk, the movement of your limbs is cross-patterned. This type of movement generates electrical activity in the brain that has a harmonizing influence on the whole central nervous system—a special benefit of walking that you do not necessarily get from other kinds of exercise. (p. 188)

It is no wonder that enthusiastic walkers talk as much about the psychological benefits as they do the physical gains. Another benefit is a more pleasing appearance. When asked to identify the everyday hassles in life, middle-aged people listed weight as their main concern (Lazarus, 1981). Doesn't it seem likely that exercise would do much to alleviate this problem, thus reducing stress? A medical examination before you begin any strenuous program is suggested. Realize that you can feel better, have more energy, and save money on medical bills. The time spent in physical activity could be the wisest investment you'll ever make.

Nutrition

Would it surprise you to know that many people know little about this subject? Do you know what foods contain certain vitamins and minerals and how much is healthy? What about the foods that are definitely unhealthy and which make up a large portion of the typical American diet?

Are you aware that:

- Food and supplements can be used to maximize brain power, boost memory, elevate mood, improve IQ and creativity, and prevent and reverse mental aging (Carper, 2000).
- Diet is related to the most common chronic diseases including coronary heart disease, hypertension, cancer, and osteoporosis (Shikany & White, 2000).
- Calcium deficiencies lead to osteoporosis (Cromer & Harel, 2000). Calcium saves bones, relieves premenstrual symptoms, helps prevent colon cancer, and fights fat (Carper, 2000). Yet, of those over 50, only 60 percent of men and less than 50 percent of women consumed the recommended daily allowance; for teens it was far worse with only 25 percent of boys and 10 percent of girls getting enough calcium. (Raloff, 2000). Do you consume enough calcium?
- Antioxidants in several foods are associated with a decreased risk of cardiovascular disease and cancer (Agarwal & Venketeshwer Rao, 2000).

These facts will come as no surprise if you consider that your body uses what you put into it to build cells and strengthen your immune system. What quality of a body do you desire? Unless you are certain that you are taking in the amount of nutrients not only to stay relatively healthy but also serve as a potential preventive force, you will not achieve a high level of wellness. Even a small increase in fruit and vegetable intake has the potential to prevent disease (Khaw et al., 2001). Unfortunately, half of us don't get the minimum of three vegetable servings a day; three-fourths don't eat the suggested two servings of fruit. In fact, no fruit whatsoever passes the lips of half of American adults on any given day (Jaret, 1998).

Even government experts say that a good diet may not be enough. Scientists at the Institute of Medicine recommend supplements to get enough B vitamins, which appear to play an important role in prevention of heart disease and birth defects (*Health*, 1998). Other recommended supplements are calcium and vitamins such as E if you aren't getting enough from your diet. Even though a person can overdo with supplements, this is rare. Rather than being overly concerned about getting too much, you would benefit by getting the proper amounts of nutrients.

By learning about nutrition from reliable sources and then by practicing better eating habits most of the time, you can fuel your body in healthy ways. One reliable source is *Your Miracle Brain* (Carper, 2000). The author, a noted health journalist, recommends how to optimize your health with nutrition as well as what not to do. For example, she offers compelling evidence that eating breakfast can boost brain functioning while starting the day on an empty stomach leaves the body short on fuel and more vulnerable to failure. Citing research at Harvard Medical School, elementary school students who ate breakfast had 40 percent higher math grades and were less likely to be absent or tardy from school than those who rarely ate breakfast. Much can be learned about the fascinating field of nutrition. Challenge yourself to be among those who are "in the know" and use the power of nutrition to enhance your health. Not only are healthy foods important, water is essential to balanced health. Why not have a glass right now?

Weight Maintenance

Practicing healthier eating habits and being physically active lead to an added bonus of weight maintenance which is a health issue as well as one of attractiveness. What is a healthy weight? A simple answer is a weight at which a person's health is not at risk and at a level that feels good. A measure that more accurately reflects healthy weight is body mass index (BMI). Values of 19.0 to 24.9 fall in the desirable range (Anderson & Wadden, 1999). A calculator comes in handy as you figure BMI. Multiply your weight in pounds by 703 then divide by your height in inches squared.

Obesity, defined as a BMI of 30 or greater, kills 300,000 Americans prematurely each year by contributing to heart attacks, high blood pressure, strokes, diabetes, and many other serious diseases. "The fatter you are, the sicker you will be and the earlier you will die" (Fumento, 1998, p. 36). Evidence suggests that obesity can increase the risk of dying from certain cancers by up to 50 percent. (American Cancer Society, 2001). Of all behaviors leading to illness, only smoking takes more lives than obesity (Fumento, 1998). On the positive side, being at a healthy weight contributes to overall good health and lessens the risk of disease.

Reflect

- What physical improvements would you like to make?
- Do you wear a seat belt when riding in a vehicle? If not, use critical thinking and find comparison figures regarding fatalities and serious injuries.
- In what ways has self-esteem affected your life?
- Recall one "message" that you have received about yourself.

Apply

- In the next week or so, improve your physical self.
- Demonstrate a positive attitude the next time you face an adverse situation.
- Use one word or phrase to describe yourself in each of the four developmental areas.

How are we doing? Not well at least in the United States, according to many experts. In fact, American society has the dubious honor of being the second fattest society in the world with first place going to a tribe in the South Pacific (Butler, 2001). A recent national survey found that 59 percent of adults are overweight, and 23 percent of those are obese (Sturm, 2000). Sadly, children are three times as likely to be overweight today as they were 30 years ago (Wingert, 2000). Generally, the reasons are evident. Eating too much high-calorie, fat-laden junk food and drinking sugar-filled beverages while sitting in front of a television screen or computer monitor is the culprit. That is the bad news. The good news is that even modest weight losses (5 to 10 percent of initial weight) can result in substantial improvements.

How do you achieve and maintain a healthy weight? Wise choices regarding nutrition and physical activity are necessary. Going on a diet isn't the answer. People who do this often end up in repeated cycles of weight loss and gain. Called **yo-yo dieting**, it is unhealthy and doesn't work. Instead, the key is to eat sensibly and healthfully most of the time and increase physical activity so that you increase metabolic rate and decrease body fat. Remember a simple bit of mathematics: Weight loss comes from burning off more calories than you take in. Walking, which is easy for most people, burns calories. Most experts recommend 45 minutes a day in order to lose and keep weight off (Bilyeau, 1998). The top fat-burning exercises are bicycling, jogging, and swimming (Napier, 1998). Enjoyable physical activity, along with better nutrition, does away with the idea of dieting and becomes a way of life.

Because most people will consider weight loss at some time in their lives, education is a practical idea. A misconception is that not eating is the way to lose weight. When the body is deprived of food, energy level is low and metabolism slows down so you don't burn off fat nearly as efficiently. Breakfast, by the way, wakes up your metabolism. According to a Mayo Clinic study, people who chronically skip breakfast burn an average of 150 fewer calories a day than those who eat breakfast even when both groups consume the same amount of daily calories (Thornton, 2000). Eliminating most junk foods and those high in fat (remembering that we need some fat in our diets) and, instead, eating fruits, vegetables, and foods that contain fiber, controlling portion sizes, and eating at regular intervals are highly recommended. Because extreme overweight is likely related to genetics as well as environment and is such a serious health challenge, obese people are advised to seek the help of a professional in developing a successful weight management plan. Being realistic about your weight, learning all you can about weight loss, and making it part of a total wellness program are the answers to a challenge faced by many Americans.

Adequate Rest

How much rest do you get? Seven to eight hours of sleep in a 24-hour period is recommended. Teenagers require approximately 9 1/4 hours of sleep to maintain optimal alertness, and most are sleep-deprived (Black, 2000). Sleep serves many functions so it seems obvious that not getting enough would affect health. Think of how you feel when you are very tired. Even more serious are the other consequences of sleep deprivation.

- impaired cognitive and motor performance equivalent to alcohol intoxication (Williamson & Feyer, 2001)
- decrease in learning abilities (Segall, 2001).
- heightened risk of accidents (Libbon, 2000).
- reduced memory abilities (Butcher, 2000)
- negative effects on health especially metabolism and hormone production, according to *Current Health* 2 (2000).

College students were studied to see what accounted for grade point average differences. Sleep habits led the list (Trockel, Barnes, & Eggert, 2000). As is obvious, sleep rejuvenates the body. Making a choice to get enough sleep is undoubtedly in your best interest.

Stress Management

How well do you handle stress? Stress management deserves special attention. **Stress** is what the body experiences when there is a perceived demand to adjust. One point is clear. Stress cannot be avoided; it is a by-product of life. **Stressors,** the conditions that cause stress, are numerous and never ending. Instead of life being a bowl of cherries, one could say that life is a bowl of stressors!

Effects of stress. The "father of stress research" Hans Selye (1976) described the body's stress response as a sequence of three stages called the **general adaptation syndrome**. In the alarm stage, the body mobilizes itself to defend; if stress continues, the body draws on its resources during the resistance stage; and if there is no relief, during the exhaustion stage, a person is susceptible to illness. Stress that is either not handled or mishandled is related to numerous problems, including poor health conditions. This has been recognized for several years. "Stress may be the greatest single contributor to illness in the industrialized world" (Eliot & Breo, 1984, p. 14). Approximately 60 to 90 percent of doctor visits are for conditions related to stress (Benson, 2001).

Stress appears to be involved in cardiovascular disease and cancer (Senior, 2001) along with high blood pressure, pain, insomnia, allergies, and infertility (Benson, 2000). After being exposed to viruses, 47 percent of individuals under high stress came down with a cold compared to only 27 percent under little stress (Goleman, 1997). How can stress be involved in such diverse physical conditions? The common thread appears to be the immune response which can be lowered by chronic stress (Senior, 2001).

The other areas of self can also suffer. Mismanaged stress contributes to relationship or social problems, emotional distress, and severe mental challenges. When you consider how unmanaged stress affects your life, it is no surprise to know that stress is connected to mental concentration (Vernarec & Phllips, 2001), depression (Evans, 2000), and anger in the workplace (Calabrese, 2000).

Even with its potentially high cost, stress is not necessarily negative. Certain types and degrees of stress can be motivating and healthful. Equate stress to the strings on a violin. If they are stretched tightly, the tone of the violin is sharp; too loose and the sound is flat and lifeless. Either way beautiful music is not possible. The key is to adjust the strings to a desirable degree of tightness. Similarly, individuals can benefit from knowing how much and what type of stress is good for them. Each person is different. For example, you may be one who feels quite relaxed sitting in a boat all day fishing. Another person would be bored and actually experience stress engaging in the same activity.

Stress that is good for you is called **eustress**. In its positive form, stress is motivating and contributes to an interesting life. "Stress is the spice of life. Who would enjoy a life of no runs, no hits, no errors?" (Selye, 1974, p. 85). How do you know when your level of stress is unhealthy? There will be clues. Are you experiencing frequent headaches, stomach distress, minor aches and pains, muscle tension, or fatigue for no apparent reason? Do you feel uneasy, tense, or irritable? Are you having difficulty sleeping or concentrating? Even apathy may be a sign. Learning about stress—what is an optimal level for you and how to handle it in a positive way—is a "must" in terms of self and relationships.

Sources of stress.   What are the stressors in your life? Most of us have long lists. Anyone who denies having stress is probably unaware of what it actually is. Researchers have uncovered many sources of stress. In one of the first studies, participants identified major changes in their lives. Each event was then given a value based on its magnitude or effect. The top five stress-producing events then were (1) death of spouse, (2) divorce, (3) marital separation, (4) jail term, and (5) death of close family member (Holmes & Rahe, 1967). I jokingly ask my students how they could avoid the top three. Not getting married would seem to do it! Both positive and negative events if they prompted some type of coping or adaptive behavior were stressful. The study indicated that when too many events happen in succession, the strain can produce unhealthy effects. Because change results in stress, you are advised to regulate your stress by not attempting too many changes at one time.

Another study (Lazarus, 1981) dealt with minor irritants, or the hassles of everyday life. Viewed as ongoing stressors, these are often left unattended because they occur so often and are seemingly routine. Lindsey was annoyed by a tiny squeak everyday as she drove to work. She kept telling herself that some day she would get it fixed. That day never seemed to come until she realized that her irritation at work and at home might be related to the annoyance she experienced each day. "The petty annoyances, frustrations, and unpleasant surprises that plague us every day may add up to more grief than life's major stressful events" (Lazarus, 1981, p. 58). College students were asked to identify stress sources. Overall, 81.1 percent of these were daily hassles. The top five stressors were a change in sleeping habits, vacations/breaks, change in eating habits, new responsibilities, and increased class workload (Ross, Niebling, & Heckert, 1999). Adult female community college students identified child care concerns as their greatest stressor (Johnson, Schwartz, & Bower, 2000). What everyday hassles bother you? What are you doing about them? If your answer is "nothing," the accumulative effects of stress may be harmful.

Stressors are either external or internal. **External stressors** are demands from outside of self. Other people, events beyond your control, and the environment deliver daily doses of stress. Can you name some? **Internal stressors** are those we create or magnify. One of the more common ones is **worry**, a process of involving negative thoughts and uneasy feelings. How is worry different from concern? Concern stems from actual events while worry is rooted in relatively uncontrollable images and thoughts usually about future negative possibilities. Certain unrealistic myths such as "If I worry, the negative event won't happen," "Events and people make me worry," and "Worrying shows that I care" perpetuate worry (Goulding & Goulding, 1989). Worriers usually do nothing about their feelings which contributes to a feeling of powerlessness.

The reality is that if you are a worrier, you manufacture stress and waste a great deal of time. Compared to nonworries, chronic worriers spend up to 8 hours a day fretting, which disrupts their lives (Kelly & Miller, 1999). A worrier also increases the risk of illness (Michaud, 2000). Sorting out real concerns from the mass of imaginative and insignificant worries is a worthy challenge. Ninety percent of what we worry about never happens. "Worry never robs tomorrow of its sorrow: it only saps today of its joy" (Buscaglia, 1992, p. 182).

The book *Worry: Controlling It and Using It Wisely* (Hallowell, 1997) suggests several ways to avoid turning minor problems into potential disasters. Other tips are to change "what if" to "so what if," set aside a short period each day to really worry and refuse to do so at other times, keep a worry journal so that the thoughts are put on paper and then check to see how many worries even materialized, use deep breathing, and definitely *act* on your worry. Exercise and a technique discussed later called *thought-stopping* can also help.

Also falling into the category of internal stressors are irrational thoughts, unrealistic expectations, inability to express emotions in a healthy way, an overload of tasks, neglect of physical health, negative self-talk, and boredom. An awareness of the sources can enable you to analyze, possibly decrease the numbers, and reduce the impact of stressors.

Coping with stress.   The subject of handling stress is well covered in a variety of books and articles, and the number of suggestions is mind-boggling. Yet many people still do nothing about stress. You may be one who already copes well because of **psychological hardiness** (Kobasa, 1979). In a classic study of executives who experienced high stress, those who didn't get sick had personality characteristics of hardiness: strong commitment to self and various areas of life, a sense of meaningfulness or purpose, the attitude that change is challenging, and an internal locus of control. If these descriptors don't sound like you, consider what you can do to become hardier!

What else can you do? When faced with a stressor, you can either face the problem directly or avoid it. Withdrawing may involve getting out of a stressful relationship or getting rid of other people's problems and returning them to their rightful owners. Even if a stressor is not apparent, you are wise to employ regular stress management strategies that protect you from the effects of daily stressors. Each of the wellness tips offered earlier are excellent strategies. Several other practical stress-reducing suggestions follow. The challenge is to put them into regular practice.

- Whenever possible, reduce or wisely schedule major life events. For example, don't begin college, start a job, get married, quit college, and get divorced in the same year!
- Prioritize hassles in your life. Take action to eliminate or reduce the most annoying ones. If a messy desk is bothering you, take the time to clean it. Carry extra keys in case you lock one inside the car or house.
- Challenge worrisome or anxiety-provoking thoughts. When faced with physical pain or other symptoms, pay attention and seek information. Ask questions so that you feel in control. Learn techniques to eliminate unnecessary worry and anxiety.
- Use cognitive techniques to change stress-producing thoughts. Much unnecessary stress is manufactured by the ideas we have. Try asking, "What's the worst thing that can happen here?" Many times the worst isn't so awful. Or if you think that saying no isn't a nice thing to do, change your thinking to, "Nice has nothing to do with this."
- Develop a decision-making process. Don't be hasty, yet remember that "staying on the fence too long" is stressful.
- If you feel frustrated or worried, ask yourself what you can do about it. Either act or let go of the feeling. Be realistic about what is possible and realize that some things are beyond your control.
- If you truly don't want to do something, say no and stick with it. Pent-up resentment is stressful.
- Learn to manage time and to schedule so you aren't rushing through life. Make time for pleasurable activities. If you are a workaholic or a person who is always in a hurry, attempt to change. Add variety to your daily routine.
- Escape periodically. Physical and mental changes of scene offer temporary respite.
- Express your feelings and begin to communicate more with others.
- Find a reliable support system.
- Write in a journal or diary. Studies confirm the value of expressing stressful thoughts to others or getting them down on paper (Stone, Smyth, Kaell, & Hurewitz, 2000).
- Have a good relieving cry.

- Find someone to hug. Have a relaxing massage.
- Laugh and enjoy life. Don't take most things so seriously. Engage in an enjoyable hobby or diversion.
- Breathe deeply. Deep breathing is a full, deep expansion of the lungs followed by complete expiration. The rhythm of the breath is slow and quiet (Weil, 1995a). Proper breathing involves the diaphragm, the thin muscle that separates the lung and abdominal cavities. Breathing properly is not only relaxing; it facilitates health by increasing the amount of oxygen in the blood (Williams and Harris, 1998). See directions for deep breathing in Reflections and Applications (page 413).
- Use a deep relaxation technique and meditation. Consider the use of biofeedback.

The last suggestion may be the most effective in lowering the stress response. In 1985, a friend who is a biofeedback and stress management specialist, Andrea Sime, said to me, "Give me an hour of your time because what I want to show you could make all the difference in the world." This was after I learned that I was facing surgery for removal of what would, in all probability, be a cancerous eye tumor. I gave her the hour and am tremendously grateful to her for introducing me to biofeedback and deep relaxation techniques and teaching me that I can change my physiological reactions to stress.

Deep relaxation is a profoundly restful condition in which one feels physically relaxed, somewhat detached from the immediate environment, and usually to some extent even from body sensations. It involves a feeling of voluntary and comfortable abandonment of one's conscious control and stewardship over major body functions—a distinctly passive attitude in which one simply turns over control of the body to its own built-in "autopilot." (Albrecht, 1979, p. 191)

Besides a wonderful feeling, deep relaxation allows the body to become balanced, or homeostatic, and, thus, work as it is intended to. One of the first to enlighten society about protection from "overstress" was Herbert Benson (1975), a physician and associate professor of medicine at Harvard Medical School, who taught and wrote about the relaxation response.

Meditation can be thought of as a physical act of remaining quiet and focusing on one's breath, a word, or a phrase. The actions quiet "inner chatter" and reduce stress (Barbor, 2001). Meditation and other relaxation techniques helped elementary school students score higher on standard achievement tests (Benson, 1987) and college students attain significantly higher GPAs (Hall, 1999). Other dramatic results from ongoing meditation programs include a 40 to 45 percent reduction in medical symptoms and psychological distress (Salzberg & Kabat-Zinn, 1997).

In addition to deep relaxation and meditation, methods that produce similar results are self-hypnosis, yoga, guided imagery, and autogenic training. Individuals remain awake and alert and remember all that occurs; the control of the person is in his or her own hands (Miller, 1978). Employing a technique for only 15 to 20 minutes on a regular basis can produce astonishing results, including increased energy, optimism, contentment, and reduction in pain. The effects of stress on the body seem remarkably diminished.

Relaxation exercises are used in **biofeedback training**, a series of steps by which a person learns to regulate physiological responses such as muscle tension, skin temperature, and heart rate. Through the use of monitoring equipment, an individual becomes aware of changes within the body and then discovers how to control them using relaxation. In addition to lowering stress reactions, there are biofeedback treatments for a variety of problems including anxiety disorders, depression, alcoholism and addiction, attention deficit hyperactivity disorder, migraines, hypertension, asthma, chronic pain, and rheumatoid arthritis (*Patient Education Management*, 2001). If an organic basis for an ailment has been ruled out, a strong recommendation is to see a stress management specialist.

Technology has ushered in EEG (electroencephalogram) biofeedback also known as neurofeedback or brainwave training. Neurofeedback is a specialized kind of biofeedback that involves operant conditioning of the brain's electrical activity in order to improve brain function. This, in turn, impacts emotions and behavior (Othmer, Phillips, & Roos, 2001). According to Andrea Sime, a specialist in biofeedback training, "Research in neurofeedback has demonstrated positive results especially with epilepsy and attention deficit hyperactivity disorder. Neurofeedback has also been used successfully with anxiety and panic disorders, sleep disorders, chronic pain, posttraumatic stress disorder, alcoholism, and numerous other conditions. Many athletes, performers, executives, and others are using neurofeedback to promote peak performance."

Both biofeedback and neurofeedback are based on the mind-body connection that is used in healing. Based on the idea that stress that leads to depression and despair can set the stage for cancer growth, a research team (Simonton, Matthews-Simonton, & Creighton, 1978) used psychological interventions with medically incurable patients and noted that a number of them improved and were living longer and better lives. Psychological intervention (relaxation, visualization techniques, and perception changing) reduced stress, decreased feelings of depression, and helped patients feel more hopeful. This made cancer regression possible.

Several recommendations in this book are related to the mind-body connection and to stress reduction. Stress will be a part of your life; by learning about it and taking charge, you can make a positive difference in your health and well-being. Wellness choices reflect how much you care about yourself and affect your present and future health. We will never be perfect; nonetheless improvement in physical and psychological well-being is worth pursuing.

VALUING YOURSELF

Another critical part of self-concept is **self-esteem**, the value that we place on ourselves. It is indicative of a positive or negative orientation toward the self (Rosenberg, 1979), an overall self-evaluation or degree of self-worth. Whether you perceive yourself to be competent to cope with life's challenges and to be deserving of happiness is a reflection of your self-esteem (Branden, 1992). Think of it as a point on a scale ranging from very low to very high; this self-respect goes beyond acceptance of self and is virtually self-love. You may be thinking, "Love myself? That's selfish!" Such a notion was disputed by (Fromm 1956), who asserted that a selfish person does not possess true self-love. Fromm's belief that self-love is necessary in order to love others is now widely accepted. If you are a loving individual and care about yourself, then you can be of value to others.

Can you think too highly of yourself? What is the difference between self-love and vanity or conceit? Vain individuals do not truly love themselves. Self-inflation is typically a sign of self-doubt. A person whose self-esteem is low may try to mask inadequate feelings with a false show of pride (May, 1953). Genuine love for self is a feeling of worth and dignity. Branden (1983) makes a sensible point: "No one would ask, 'Is it possible to enjoy too high a level of physical health?' Health is an unqualified desirable. So is positive self-esteem" (p. 15).

An important note is that esteem for the self that is unwarranted (Seligman, 1998) or what could be described as a false sense of self-worth is not conducive to living a productive, worthy life. Self-esteem that is earned by one's own efforts is, however, of utmost significance. One of our primary needs as humans is to feel worthwhile (Glasser, 1965; Maslow, 1968).

Effects of Self-Esteem

What specific areas of life are affected by self-esteem? A quick and wise response would be, "All areas." Specifically, note the following.

Academic success.   Studies have found a significant positive correlation between self-esteem, grade point average, and positive classroom behavior (Baker, Beer, & Beer, 1991), as well as academic achievement and intrinsic motivation (Skaalvik, 1997). In terms of potential academic performance, a student's IQ score may not be as important as the self-esteem rating. "Self-confidence permits a child to perform; whereas brilliance may be trapped in low self-esteem" (Briggs, 1970, p. 270). Although individuals with low self-esteem can achieve, the path is usually more difficult.

Emotions and behaviors.   Low self-esteem, loneliness, and depression are often connected (Bothwell & Scott, 1997). After controlling for depression, a study showed that self-esteem was associated with thinking about, threatening, and attempting suicide (Vella, Persic, & Lester, 1996). Low self-esteem was found to be a factor in abnormal eating behaviors (Button, Loan, & Davies, 1997) and children's use of tobacco and alcohol (Jackson, Henriksen, Dickinson, & Levine, 1997). "Self-esteem is the armor that protects kids from the dragons of life: drugs, alcohol, delinquency, and unhealthy relationships" (McKay & Fanning, 2000, p. 279). A search for markers of happiness found that self-esteem definitely mattered. "When the going gets tough, those with strong feelings of self-worth keep going" (Myers, 1992, p. 108).

Relationships.   Friendships and love relationships thrive in the presence of high self-esteem. Feeling liked and loved by others isn't possible until you believe you deserve it. A study revealed that socially uncertain college students had lower levels of self-esteem as well as higher levels of depression, stress, and loneliness (Salmela-Aro & Nurmi, 1996). How you treat others is related to self-worth. "You will do unto others as you do unto yourself" (Briggs, 1977, p. 4). High self-esteem encourages us to seek out others and to develop healthy relationships enhanced by caring, democratic behaviors. According to Maslow (1968), the best helpers of others are those who feel positive about themselves. "So often the sick or inadequate person, trying to help, does harm instead" (p. iii). One student, Debra, expressed a benefit of self-love beautifully, "My self-nurturance is my gift of love to others."

Long-term relationships are more likely to succeed if both people feel self-love. Falling in love is easy; sustaining love over time requires high self-esteem. Parenting is one of the most critical responsibilities in life. A classic study found that parents with high levels of self-esteem have a better chance of raising children with high levels of self-worth (Coopersmith, 1967). Relationships built on high levels of self-esteem are more likely to be nourishing. When you love yourself, you are not going to deliberately hurt yourself or anyone else (Hay, 1991).

Career success.   A job seeker with high self-esteem will almost always achieve better interview ratings and receive more job offers than those with low self-esteem. Because employees' work will reflect the degree of their own self-worth, employers seek applicants who value themselves. As one advances, self-worth continues to pay off. Managers with high self-esteem have less trouble giving up control and delegating. Qualities such as innovation, personal responsibility, self-management, and self-direction are all by-products of high self-esteem (Branden, 1992). "In the workplace self-esteem is a survival requirement" (p. 77). Additionally, a higher level of self-esteem helps in assessing ourselves realistically and making desirable changes. When faced with choices and decisions, a feeling of self-worth is a powerful ally.

A benefit to those with high self-esteem is the ability to recognize self-improvement possibilities and the tendency to view criticism as constructive. They do not interpret a *no* as an assault or a rejection; instead, they usually learn from mistakes and have more energy to begin anew. Both Lisa and Jessica were criticized by their track coach for not pacing themselves over a long race. Lisa accepted the criticism and changed her pattern. Jessica, whose self-esteem was below average at the time, became disheartened and quit the team. Self-worth allows people to view difficulty as a challenge, choose wisely, and engage in positive personal growth.

In its influence on all aspects of life, self-esteem is the foundation upon which happiness and well-being are built. Nathaniel Branden (1983), who has studied and written extensively about self-esteem, express it well: "Of all the judgments that we pass in life, none is as important as the one we pass on ourselves, for that judgment touches the very center of our existence" (p. 1).

Sources of Self-Esteem

Human beings are not born with self-esteem. You have learned who you are and how worthy you feel from internalized messages and a variety of experiences. Four broad contributors can be identified (Baron, 1990): (1) social interaction, (2) social information, (3) social comparison, and (4) self-observation.

The first two categories have to do with relationships. How people reacted and treated you in social interactions and their valuative comments about you have had much influence, and they still do. An early, well-researched study found that the quality of the relationships between children and significant adults in their lives laid the foundation for self-love (Coopersmith, 1967).

Babies and young children are especially vulnerable in terms of the actions of others; parents usually serve as the most significant influences. An essential behavior is holding a baby in a loving way (Josselson, 1992). Children learn they are lovable by being treated as if they are special. A tragic price of low self-worth or worse is paid if there is a lack of warmth, love, care, and attention.

Parenting effects remain influential throughout a child's life. A detrimental parental message is that a child is not good enough. Sometimes the messages are blatantly negative such as "You'll never amount to anything," or "What did I do wrong to deserve you?" Without a doubt, these do grave damage. Others are more subtle or underlying and are still injurious.

> "Can't you ever do something different with your hair?"
> "When I was your age, I had a full-time job and still got good grades in school."
> "You could do a lot better if you'd just try."

Several of my students have identified the last message as common. "No matter what grade I brought home, short of 100 percent or A+, my dad told me I could have done better," a troubled young woman shared. Can you think of similar messages you received? The underlying theme is that something is missing or wrong.

Parents' opinions usually continue to have an impact after a young adult leaves home. A 25-year-old confessed:

> I don't know why I care what my parents think of me anymore. Most of what they did was criticize me, and that's what they still do. But I care so much, it hurts. I'm still trying to be the way they want me to be.

Opinions of other family members can diminish self-worth. Students often mention siblings who teased and ridiculed them. "I am convinced that there are no genes to carry the feeling of worth. It is learned. And the family is where it is learned" (Satir, 1972, p. 24).

Joyce, a middle-aged student, remembered her childhood and a negative family environment. She wrote of feeling clumsy, skinny, and not as smart as her siblings. Those feelings came from her own parents. "My dad said until the day he died that I was the clumsiest kid he had. When Mom made clothes for me, she said I was so straight that nothing fit me. They both told me I should do better in school because the other kids did." Sadly, she could not recall any positive messages. In fact, she said that any pride in accomplishment was frowned upon. Her parents thought that pride was the same as bragging. When Joyce was 40, she finally came to grips with her feelings of low self-esteem. The pain resurfaced when she prepared a childhood analysis for extra credit. She wrote: "I didn't want to do this paper, and I did want to. I knew I didn't have to. But something kept pulling me to do it. I realize now I needed to unload some more, and I felt better afterwards." Her postscript was: "This has been a painful experience for me. Lots of feelings that I didn't want to deal with came back. Not one of us kids came out of that family with anything but low self-esteem." Today Joyce feels positive about herself. I smiled as I read: "I am respected by my classmates, I am a good person, and I will make a success out of despair." And she has!

Figure 1-6

Another student, Linda, optimistically wrote:

A self-esteem tip that hit home with me was not to belittle or label your children negatively which is what happened to me. Unfortunately, my own parents' self-esteem was negative, and it was passed on to me. *But cycles can be broken, and this one is already beginning to crumble.*

Incidentally, self-esteem can also be damaged by being ignored and neglected. "I just felt it didn't matter whether I was alive or dead, there or not there," said a young man. "I still have a hard time thinking that I matter to anyone."

In addition to family contributions, interactions with and information from others were and continue to be influential. Various groups impact on self-descriptions whether we are aware of what these are or not. Children learn to tease others usually because of physical appearance. Another source of ridicule is perceived or actual knowledge of a gay male's or lesbian's sexual orientation. A review of studies indicated difficulty for gay adolescents in achieving healthy levels of self-esteem as a result of stigmatization (Radkowsky & Siegel, 1997).

Think back to school experiences and relationships with teachers and peers. For some, school is a nightmare. I remember a junior high teacher who delivered a daily assault of putdowns to a timid boy. "Can't you write any neater than that?" "Hurry up. You're so slow!" "That's a dumb question." One day he announced that the lowest grade in the class was Gary's—as usual! Several students followed the teacher's lead, and Gary became the object of many cruel tricks and insults. That Gary survived is remarkable; the damage to his self-esteem is hard to imagine. As a warning, Ellen Rosenberg, author of *Growing Up Feeling Good* (1983), told an audience of teachers, "Self-esteem may not be a separate subject in school curriculums, but children's self-esteem is being chipped away or built up at every minute at school or elsewhere." If educators understand this, fewer children like Gary will suffer.

Once self-esteem is high, input from other people is less influential. Nevertheless, students remind me how rewarding it is when instructors praise their work, and I, too, relish favorable comments. One way to assess whether a relationship is healthy is to ask if it enhances feelings of self-worth. We may be secure, yet replenishment is invaluable!

How often do you compare yourself to others? Social comparison is a powerful source of ideas about self. People tend to measure themselves against other individuals often based on physical appearance, talent, and popularity. Comparisons within the family are common. When I ask students how many were compared to their siblings, almost every hand goes up. Generally, they acknowledge that the comparisons weren't motivating or helpful and could be harmful. One young man realized why he harbored negative feelings about his older brother: "I was never as good as Scott. He was better-looking, smarter, and athletic. I was nicer, but that didn't seem to matter to Dad." Any comparison can diminish your uniqueness if you try to be someone you are not. Keep in mind that someone better-looking, smarter, friendlier, or more popular likely exists somewhere so what difference does it make? Individual comparisons are helpful only if you learn constructively from them.

Broader comparisons can also be damaging. Members of a **minority**, a disadvantaged group that lacks power within a society, are frequently and unfairly perceived of as inferior. People who differ from the majority group in race, ethnicity, or sexual orientation often face self-esteem challenges. For example, gays and lesbians are raised in a society oriented toward **heterosexism**, the belief that anything other than a heterosexual orientation is wrong. Do you think that what was written years ago is still true today? "Homophobia, a fear or hatred of lesbian women and gay men, is so interwoven in society that lesbian and gay youth face especially difficult struggles for self-esteem, emotional security, and a sense of a caring community" (Whitlock, 1989, p. 1). Even though racism and heterosexism are rooted in ignorance and untruths, individuals can be immeasurably damaged.

Culture, which consists of behaviors, values, beliefs, and lifestyle that are characteristic of a particular social group and which distinguish it from other groups, is a key factor in self-esteem. Any group or individual difference can be either ridiculed or looked at with positiveness. Aspects of self, when affirmed rather than condemned, bolster self-esteem. **Multiculturalism**, a movement that recognizes cultural diversity, appreciates everyone's "roots," and promotes equality of all cultures, can yield high rewards for everyone.

Do you realize that it's possible to compare yourself to a person who does not exist—your ideal self? If your self-description and ideal self are very different, self-esteem will be low. You may be underestimating your actual self or harboring an unattainable self-fantasy. **Perfectionism** is having an inflated and impossible ideal self. Perfectionists believe that they must set the highest performance standards or be second-rate. No matter what, they aren't good enough. In a study of college students, a high level of perfectionism was associated with a low level of self-esteem (Flett, Hewitt, & DeRosa, 1996). A step in increasing self-esteem is to create a realistic ideal or possible self then use it as a friendly guide, not as an enemy.

The fourth category, self-observation, comes from one's own actions, interpretations, and feelings. Picture two young children on a playground. Haley successfully climbs the ladder of the slide and glides down. Melissa stands at the bottom, fearful of the ascent. After working up the courage to mount the steps, she sits frozen at the top and begins to cry. Haley comes to her rescue by sitting behind her and helping her down. Can you see how Haley's and Melissa's self-observations were quite different?

Adults continue to be self-observant. Mike and Angela are newly hired firefighters. Angela has been involved in two heroic rescues. Mike has spent most of his on-duty time cleaning the station, playing cards, and keeping in shape. He has participated in a few minor fire calls and is feeling frustrated. In the two situations the four individuals have different self-observations that increase or decrease self-esteem. Self-observation becomes increasingly important as you mature. Are you aware of yourself? What are you doing with what you observe? At this point in your life, you have a great deal of control over your level of self-esteem.

Part of self-observation, and of utmost significance, are your thoughts. Consider two young men who are insulted by a coworker. Tim thinks, "I must be a hard person to work with if that's what he thinks of me." Greg's thoughts are: "I don't know what his problem is. He must be having a bad day." How will the two thoughts differ in their effect on self-esteem? Do you see how powerful your thoughts are? They, in essence, create your reality.

Figure 1-7

Self-Esteem Building and Strengthening

What is your current level of self-esteem? You can use the rating scale in the self-concept inventory in Reflections and Applications to measure it. For those with healthy levels, self-esteem strengthening is a wise investment. If yours is low, you can do much to change it! Beginning to realize your sense of worth is a vitalizing experience. "You literally uncover the hidden jewel of your own value" (Mckay & Fanning, 2000, p. 89). Use the following suggestions in your building or strengthening process.

Heal psychological pain.   One day Teri, one of my outstanding students, came to see me. In her forthright manner, she said, "Sharon, your ideas on developing self-esteem are great, but I don't think they will work for anyone who feels terribly wounded. They wouldn't have worked for me years ago." Our discussion clarified why individuals can fail in their attempts to develop self-esteem. At fault could be severe psychological pain, which is "like a dragon that keeps growing heads as long as you do not deal with it" (Stone & Stone, 1993, p. 5). Teri referred to it as a wounded "inner child," a term used by some counselors and authors (Chopich & Paul, 1990; Whitfield, 1987). Teri's story vividly describes the pain.

> I have personally experienced the inner torment, mental confusion, and negative physical results of a damaged and hurting inner child. To the outside world I had it all! Inside I was miserable, wasn't "together," and was lonely and hurting. I was so good at hiding my real self that I didn't know myself nor recognize my feelings. I divorced and then dealt with my mother's illness and death. The one coping skill I had was to ignore my feelings, and I was left very vulnerable. My second marriage was a dreadful descent into my husband's world of alcoholism, drug addiction, and domestic violence. The day he literally picked me up and flung me through our sliding glass door I realized I needed intense professional help. A first realization was that I'd always "been there" for a multitude of people, but no one had been there for me.

Teri's story had a wonderful ending that turned into a new beginning. She changed her life with the help of counseling and the book *Healing Your Aloneness* (Chopich & Paul, 1990).

> The effects of all those years of frustration, ineffective coping skills, inner pain, mental confusion, and unhappiness began to fade away. I began to establish personal boundaries, I demanded respect for myself as a person, and I respected other's boundaries, too. I built my self-esteem. Life is now fun, challenging, and easier. I make positive choices and look upon each new experience as a challenge and opportunity to learn and grow.

Another major stumbling block in terms of self-esteem is extreme depression. Anyone suffering from untreated clinical depression lacks the energy and willpower to build self-esteem. Depression must be alleviated before the self can be elevated. Ways to do this are covered in Chapter 5.

Perhaps, it's a matter of **self-verification**, an intriguing theory which maintains that individuals have a strong desire to preserve their self-concept even if it is a negative one (Andrews, 1989). Jenni wrote in her journal: "I think sometimes I'm afraid to feel good about myself—to not be insecure. It sounds so odd, but it's almost like letting go of something you know so well and for so long for something you have never known." Paul expressed it as "just too afraid to feel good." Self-verification by confirming what a person already believes may make the world seem safe and predictable. Yet another possibility is **self-handicapping**, which refers to actions taken to sabotage performance and increase the opportunity to excuse failure (Berglas & Jones, 1978). Self-handicappers appear to have a valid reason for not succeeding other than their lack of ability. When self-sabotaging was discussed in the classroom, a young man said, "That sounds like me. What can be done?" Awareness is the first step. The enlightening book *Making Peace with Your Past* (Bloomfield, 2000) focuses on identifying and healing a painful past by coming to grips with shame, guilt, regret, blame, and unresolved grief.

If you think you are beset by self-handicaps or might be in need of healing, explore the avenues for healing that have been discussed in this section and then take steps to change your life. You deserve it! As Debra, a vibrant student, expressed it, "I found that a decision that you are *for* yourself is the beginning of an entirely different life."

Choose healthy, conscious living. Increasing your level of wellness, as discussed earlier, is basic to self-esteem development. Existing in a mental fog, even partially, limits potential for self-love. Think about how often you choose the level of consciousness at which you function. The choice may be between habitual drug use and alertness, or between fatigue and getting enough sleep. Lack of alertness is not conducive to creating a positive self-image. The visibly alive, bright-eyed students I see each day have made a wise choice and are completing the first step toward building high self-esteem. Others are severely limiting themselves.

Set priorities. Think about where you rank yourself in comparison to others. Generally, those with low self-esteem place others ahead of themselves. While being self-centered or selfish is not recommended, making yourself a priority is. You will then have more to offer the world. After a relationship in which she described herself as totally dependent, Faith, a young woman, said, "I finally learned how to put my love into myself rather than in someone else. Since I did this, my relationships have been much better, and a love relationship will just add more beauty to the life I already have."

Concentrate on your strengths. What do you like about yourself? Even the simplest positive quality is significant. Do you listen well? Are you considerate? What are your talents? You can make a list of strengths and post it where you will notice it. Positive statements about self are called **affirmations**. Ones such as "I am worthy" and "I deserve happiness" are powerful tools. More specific ones reflect unique positive aspects such as, "I am kind." Easy to repeat frequently, they empower the self. A woman working on self-esteem started each day by repeating to herself three affirmations and ended the day with three others. She reported a positive outcome: "I've become a much better friend to myself." In addition to writing, reading, and thinking affirmatively, you can visualize yourself in a positive light.

There is a tendency to focus on weaknesses and become bogged down. All of us have drawbacks. The key is to be aware of positive characteristics and appreciate yourself as you are. Concentrating on your potential, not on limitations, is a way to build self-confidence and self-esteem.

Demonstrate your strengths.   Acting on your strengths is even more affirming. **Self-enhancement** is the process of finding and interpreting situations that result in a positive view of self. College students experienced enhanced self-esteem after receiving high grades; they believed that this reflected their abilities (Woo & Mix, 1997). Whatever you already do well, do! If you have musical talent, join a performing group. If you're a whiz in the kitchen, cook a meal for someone. Accept positively any compliments. Contributing to worthwhile causes can also be a tremendous boost. Tina volunteered to accompany elderly people on shopping trips. Brad became involved in an environmental clean-up project. Each reported heightened feelings of self-worth. One of the surest ways to sustain a change is self is by helping someone else. Giving to others is a gift to yourself!

Make positive changes.   Constructive changes improve your present self and ensure future well-being. Create an attainable, yet challenging, ideal self. Then choose an improvement area and set up an action plan. Chapter 3 suggests ways to achieve a goal. Express the change in a positive way. Say, "I will become assertive" rather than, "I don't want to be passive." Emphasize self-directed action. Instead of, "I hope I improve my grades," think and say, "I am studying so I can improve my grades." Think, "When I lose weight, I will feel better," not "*If* I lose weight" (Canfield & Siccone, 1993).

Allowing yourself to make mistakes along the way is healthy. High self-esteem does not mean that you never make errors. Instead, regardless of mistakes, accept yourself as a worthy human being. Feel good about yourself in spite of mistakes; don't wait until all has been corrected (McKay & Fanning, 2000). Use mistakes as helpful information and change your course of action. Of utmost importance is to give yourself many "hurrahs" along the way!

Seek positive relationships.   Building self-esteem is easier with the help of positive, supportive people. Cassie, who had low self-esteem, said she was bothered by a friend who was critical. She was advised to seek new relationships with individuals who feel positive about themselves. These people don't need to put others down, and modeling after them is beneficial.

Evaluate sources.   Analyzing how your self-esteem developed can be helpful. All of us have been criticized or put down. Instead of accepting negative assessments from others at face value, you might ask, "For what reason did they say or do that? Could it have been because they felt inferior or lacked self-esteem? Were they taking their frustrations out on me? Were they just being hateful? Did they just not know better and even think they were helping me?"

Parents raise children with the resources they possess, and they almost never intend to harm their offspring. If you understand that your parents probably did the best they could do within their limitations, you can free yourself to repair self-esteem. Extreme cases of psychological or physical abuse can be helped with therapy. The helpful book *Making Peace with Your Parents* (Bloomfield, 1996a) gives reasons and methods for releasing resentments. When we hold on to past resentments toward parents, current peace of mind and the ability to experience satisfaction in our here-and-now relationships are in jeopardy. Take responsibility for your own self-esteem. I love the simple, true statement: "You make up your adulthood" (Spezzano, 1992, p. 17).

Perhaps you weren't criticized by others, yet your self-esteem has suffered because you think you have disappointed someone. Troy berated himself about his career choice. "My folks want me to go to law school, and they think I'm crazy for deciding to be a teacher. Dad said I'm afraid to use all my abilities, and he's disappointed. I'm at the point of believing him." Children often feel forced to live according to their parents' expectations and to reach for unrealistic standards of excellence.

Can you think of some areas in which you didn't measure up? A frequent one is tidiness. Some parents demand perfection in bed-making, cleaning, and organization of belongings. "No matter how hard I tried, I couldn't make my bed to please my mother," said Ashley, "so I finally quit trying. It's only been recently that I can challenge the importance of being perfect at bed-making!" Breaking away from others' expectations is liberating. "If your life is a continual assessment of whether or not you please others, you are having your buttons pushed from behind" (Satir, 1978, p. 90). Caring what others think about us can be beneficial; however, we may pay a price in decreased self-esteem for trying to satisfy someone else. Similarly, taking responsibility for ourselves is affirming. This is covered more in Chapter 4.

Change your thoughts.   Let's continue the esteem-building process by taking a close look at **cognitive restructuring**, or thought changing. The first step is to tune in to **self-talk**, your thoughts. "The practice of self-love begins in your mind. You must learn to control your thinking" (Dyer, 1976, p. 54). What do you think about yourself—your appearance, behavior, and impact on others? Self-talk can be pictured as drops of water that become either a clear, unpolluted body of water or a toxic one. Do you hear critical remarks? To decrease the criticisms, follow a valuable suggestion: "I live by a helpful little motto, 'I won't criticize myself—there are more than enough people willing to do this for me'" (Glasser, 1984, p. 165).

Most of us find it virtually impossible to eliminate all negative thoughts. Yet restructuring an unrealistic self-thought is useful. **Irrational beliefs**, unreasonable and exaggerated thoughts, are at the heart of negative feelings about self, and people who persist in such thinking make themselves miserable, according to Albert Ellis (1977), a well-known cognitive therapist. You can debate irrational thinking in regard to yourself just as you probably would do with a loved one. Try using these four steps:

1. Identify an irrational thought, exaggeration, or belittlement about yourself.
2. Determine the truth and the facts by asking: "What is the reason for the original thought? What is the truth?"
3. Then use this way of restructuring: "Just because (*the truth as identified in Step 2*) doesn't mean (*the irrational thought in Step 1*)."
4. End with an affirmation related to the specific situation or use a general one.

Pretend you have been told that you are no longer loved by someone. Following are the four steps:

1. "Nobody will ever love me." *This is an irrational thought (Step 1).*
2. A significant other has told you he or she doesn't love you. *This is the truth (Step 2).*
3. "Just because this person doesn't love me doesn't mean that I'll never be loved." *This is the actual cognitive restructuring (Step 3).*
4. "I'm a loving person and deserve someone special." *This is the affirmation (Step 4).*

If you don't succeed in switching to positive self-talk using these steps, try a cognitive technique called **thought-stopping**. Mentally, you can say any of the following loudly, clearly, and angrily: "Stop thinking this way!" "This is unrealistic." "I won't think it!" or just "STOP!"

Drawing on all the self-esteem recommendations, individuals can overcome the past and build and strengthen self-worth in the present. One basic question has to do with whether you are as kind and supportive to yourself as you are to a good friend. If you aren't, why not become your own best friend?

CREATING A FRIEND OR FOE: SELF-FULFILLING PROPHECY

Predicting the future is usually the work of astrologers or those who claim to be prophets. In reality, each of us predicts what will be, and we also make it come true. A **self-fulfilling prophecy** is a thought or expectation that helps bring about a predicted event or behavior which then strengthens the original thought. The concept was introduced by Merton (1948), who used it to refer to situations in which false beliefs become true. A classic study by Rosenthal and Jacobson (1968) demonstrated that teacher expectations could influence student achievement.

Examples of the self-fulfilling prophecy are easily found. A youngster who is labeled a brat is likely to believe and, thus, become one. I remember my first year of teaching. Jimmy, a sixth grader, suffered from an eye disease. I had been told that he could not be expected to do what other students did, neither in quantity nor in quality. Being new to teaching and optimistic, I asked Jimmy how he felt. He said he wanted to be treated like the others and expected to handle it." We spent hours after school; his own determination made the difference. He left sixth grade with average grades; the next fall he strutted into my classroom with a beautiful smile on his face. "Guess what?" he said. "I made the honor roll in junior high!" Jimmy provided a wonderful lesson. What others believe can become internalized and then actually create one's reality. An expansion on this concept is a self-created prophecy.

Relationship Between Thoughts and Behaviors

Behaviors are usually the demonstration of thoughts. Let's say that you think of yourself as shy. **Shyness** involves a feeling of discomfort and usually apprehension in a social setting. Listen to your self-talk:

> I'm a shy person. I've always been that way. I was born shy. And because I am, I don't like to be around people. I can't talk to them, and I'm always uncomfortable. I will go through the rest of my life being shy, and that's it.

Powerful thinking, right? A friend (you have one, even though you're shy!) invites you to a party. What is your reaction?

> I don't want to go. I never have a good time at parties. I'm shy, so I can't look at people or talk to them. I'd just have a terrible time because I'm the way I am.

In this case your friend persuades you to attend the party. "I know I won't have any fun because I'm shy," you tell yourself. How will you act at the party? You stand next to the wall away from the others and you look up, down, at the wall. You appear unapproachable and don't smile because shy people act this way! After a miserable evening, a strong confirming thought surfaces:

> See, I knew I wouldn't have any fun. Nobody talked to me, and I couldn't talk to them. I never enjoy myself at parties because I'm shy.

As illustrated in Figure 1-8, this type of self-fulfilling prophecy becomes a vicious circle. A thought about self is carried out in behavior, which then brings about an even stronger confirming thought. You, the shy person, have fulfilled your own prophecy. If the descriptor is a positive one and increases your self-esteem, the self-fulfilling prophecy is a friend. Too often, though, thoughts are limiting or berating and serve as our enemies.

Self-fulfilling prophecies are powerful. A story is told of two brothers, one who was alcoholic and one who hardly drank liquor. A psychologist wondered why they differed. One brother said that because his father was an alcoholic, he had become one, too. The other explained that because his father was an alcoholic, he learned the horrors of the habit and decided to abstain (Branden, 1983). Clearly, two people with the same background are capable of forming opposite prophecies with different outcomes and, thus, create their own unique realities.

Changes in a Self-Fulfilling Prophecy

Examination of self-fulfilling prophecies is valuable. If you want to change any of yours, two avenues are possible. Psychologists who emphasize cognitive techniques would tell you to change your thoughts. Learning theorists would have you alter your behavior. I recommend, as do many in the cognitive-behavioral area, changing both.

Let's go back to the example of shyness. An unrealistic thought would be, "I am no longer shy." However, you could use cognitive restructuring and think, "Just because I've been shy in the past doesn't mean I have to continue. I don't like it, and I am going to change." One authority on shyness says that you are shy if you think you are (Zimbardo, 1977). Empowered with a different belief, you can attend another party and change your behavior. As difficult as it may be, you position yourself near people. A next step is to look at others with an open expression. You may even smile! If you are not approached, you can muster your courage and go up to someone and say hello. In almost all

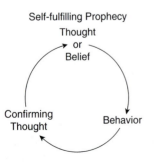

Self-fulfilling Prophecy

Thought or Belief

Behavior

Confirming Thought

Figure 1-8

For Better or For Worse®   **by Lynn Johnston**

Figure 1-9

cases, the person you approach will respond positively. At that point you have broken out of the vicious circle.

   With success, new ways of behaving become easier. For a class self-improvement project, an overweight female student decided to change. In the process, she learned an invaluable lesson as she recalled the pain of her self-fulfilling prophecy.

> I felt so insecure, as a teenager. I felt I was being judged because I was fat so I wouldn't give people the chance to reject me; I rejected them first. It was a perfect example of a self-fulfilling prophecy. I mourn all the friendships I missed out on. With the help of this course I see that when most people look at me, they see *me*, not an overweight person, and when I look at them, I see them as they are and not just as individuals who could hurt my feelings.

Examining all of your self-prophecies is wise. As a way to strengthen self-esteem, keep the ones that are friends; work on the foes!

> *The greatest discovery in our generation is that human beings, by changing the inner attitudes of their minds, can change the outer aspects of their lives.*
> —William James

INCREASING YOUR CAPABILITIES: SELF-EFFICACY

Whether you have the confidence to improve yourself will depend on what was defined by Bandura (1977) as **self-efficacy**, "the conviction that one can successfully execute the behavior required to produce the outcomes" (p. 79). Self-efficacy expectations are beliefs regarding capability or competence related to a particular task or activity (Bandura, 1986). Notice the difference between thinking, "I can handle this task," rather than, "I can't do it." You may remember the story of the little engine who succeeded in ascending a mountain by saying, "I think I can, I think I can." People who have self-efficacy expectations think they can handle the task.

How positively you assess your capability in a specific situation influences success in several ways. First, you are more likely to attempt a particular task if you think you can do it. Second, if you expect a positive outcome, you will exert more effort, and, finally, you will persist much longer. Success is then likely to occur.

Extensive studies have shown that self-efficacy is a primary factor in behavioral change (Cervone, 2000) and can improve outcomes in a number of important areas. Self-efficacy is related to the following.

- Prevention of and adaptation to cancer (Lev, 1997)
- Better outcomes for smoking cessation (Etter, Bergman, Humair, & Pernegeri, 2000) and for alcohol dependence treatment (Allsop, Saunders, & Phillips, 2000)
- Continuation in exercise programs (Sullum & Clark, 2000)
- Higher grades (Jinks & Morgan, 1999)

Even though perceptions of self-efficacy are likely to be generalized across situations (Cervone, 2000), believing that you can handle any and all tasks is unwise. One reason is that this is impossible. Then, if you are perceived as being capable of everything, others may not think you need any help. After my surgery for cancer in 1985, my husband and I participated in a two-week program to learn how to deal with emotions and thoughts about the disease. An important realization was that because I appeared to be capable and strong, others were less likely to provide support. The program helped me admit that I didn't want to always handle things without help and encouraged necessary support. We all need to lean at times!

Think of times in your life when your own self-efficacy has motivated you. Has a lack of self-efficacy ever hindered you? Take the opportunity to describe self-efficacy and one of your self-fulfilling prophecies in Reflections and Applications. Building and strengthening self-esteem, creating empowering prophecies, and increasing self-efficacy expectations are wise investments in yourself. Each bolsters the others.

Reflect

- Identify a negative self-fulfilling prophecy from your past or present. Then determine how it could have been or can be changed.
- Think of a recent task in which your self-efficacy expectations were high. Then think of a skill you lack or a task in which your self-efficacy expectations are low.
- Recall a time your "I can" belief was beneficial.

Apply

- Behave differently from a past or present self-fulfilling prophecy.
- Act on a skill or expertise in order to demonstrate high self-efficacy expectations.
- Try something new!

LOOKING BACK

- Awareness of self is at the heart of interpersonal relations, and self-understanding is an ongoing process.
- Each of the four developmental areas (physical, mental, emotional, and social) influences the others, and together all four form an integrated, whole self.
- Self-concept is a collective view of self including self-description, ideal self, and self-esteem. Ideal self is an image of what one wants to be and is most helpful when it is realistic and attainable. Self-esteem is the value placed on self.
- Improving one's physical and psychological health requires wise choices in the areas of physical activity, nutrition, weight, rest, and stress management.
- Because high self-esteem has numerous advantages, learning to value yourself is highly recommended.
- Self-esteem develops through feedback and interactions with others and through one's own observations and judgments.
- In order to build self-esteem, it may be necessary to first heal psychological pain.
- Self-esteem can be built and strengthened by conscious living, prioritizing, concentration on and demonstration of strong points, positive changes, healthy relationships, cognitive restructuring, and evaluation of self-esteem sources.
- Self-fulfilling prophecies can be helpful or damaging. A way to improve one's life is to examine, evaluate, and change negative prophecies.
- Self-efficacy is the sense of competence in the face of a particular task. Many studies have shown that self-efficacy expectations are related to well-being and success in life.

I am convinced that the crucial factor in what happens both inside people and between people is the picture of individual worth that each person carries around.

—Virginia Satir

RESOURCES

Learning Disabilities Association of America (LDA), 4156 Library Road, Pittsburgh, PA 15234. Toll-free: (888) 300–6710. www.ldanatl.org

Parents and Friends of Lesbians and Gays (PFLAG), 1101 14th Street NW, Suite 1030, Washington, DC 20005. (202) 638–4200. www.pflag.org

Overeaters Anonymous. (505) 891–2664. www.overeatersanonymous.org.

Counselors in educational institutions can help with learning disabilities as well as personal problems.

Self-esteem classes are often offered through wellness centers at hospitals, social service agencies, colleges, and organizations.

2

Understanding Yourself
Throughout the Life Span

LOOKING AHEAD

After completing this chapter, you will be able to

- Discuss what is meant by and known about personality.
- Describe psychological theories of personality development and explain how socialization influences behavior.
- Explain Erikson's psychosocial theory of personality development and relate it to your life. Recognize challenges to development.
- Discuss transactional analysis and use your understanding of ego states, life positions, scripts, and strokes.
- Understand personality typing and describe eight preferences.
- Distinguish between extraversion and introversion and note advantages and disadvantages of each.
- Accept personality differences in a positive way.
- Define gender role, summarize how it is learned, and discuss its influences.
- Identify disadvantages of stereotypic gender roles for both sexes.
- Define androgyny and describe its potential benefits.
- Contrast assertiveness with aggression and nonassertiveness.
- Understand yourself and others better.

When one is a stranger to oneself, then one is estranged from others, too.
—Anne Morrow Lindbergh

How well do you truly know yourself? Because self-understanding is the foundation of healthy relationships, it deserves attention throughout life. In Chapter 1 you were asked to think about yourself and your sense of self-worth. From this chapter you will gain deeper self-understanding.

Begin to describe yourself. If you are like many people, you start with physical descriptors. Some people have difficulty going further. **Personality** is the "unique you." It consists of characteristics or traits related to how one thinks, feels, and acts. The combination of these qualities that only you possess is the cornerstone of your separate identity. Have you ever heard someone say, "She has no personality"? This usually means that the person is extremely reserved or dull. The personality may not be projected, but one does exist!

HOW DOES PERSONALITY DEVELOP?

With a perfect memory, you could describe the numerous experiences that have influenced your personality. Even that would not tell the entire story. Identical twin and adoptive studies seek to discover how heritable is personality. The findings vary although most agree that heredity and environment each account for 50 percent (Harris, 1998). This means that within a group of individuals, genetic differences account for about half of the variation in personality traits. Parents may wonder about their children's personalities and ask, "How can they be so different? We raised them the same." First, raising children the same isn't possible nor advisable. Then, they are forgetting about other important factors such as genetics, sex, physical and mental abilities, birth order, and, most importantly, other people's influences and the unique experiences of each individual. You may have heard this referred to as the interaction between **nature** and **nurture.**

Influences on Personality

An early pioneer in personality development was Sigmund Freud. His theories dealt with early childhood influences, the role of the unconscious, psychosexual stages of development from birth through adolescence, and a structure of the personality made up of three parts (id, superego, and ego). Later in this chapter you will learn about ego states based on Freud's concept. The **psychodynamic** perspective and its theorists continue to contribute to the ongoing study of personality, emphasizing the influence of the unconscious on personality development and human behaviors.

Another perspective is **learning.** Divided into behaviorism and social-cognitive theory, it focuses on environmental influences, observational learning, and cognitive processes in the development of personality. B. F. Skinner (1953, 1987) showed that personality develops in response to stimuli in the environment. Rewards and punishments strengthen and weaken behavior. Any characteristic that has been **reinforced**—made stronger—is probably recognizable in your personality. Social-cognitive theorist Albert Bandura (1977, 1986) credits **modeling** as a strong influence on personality. If your personality is similar to a family member's, observational learning undoubtedly played a part.

Social-cognitive theorists point out how a person's mental processes affect behavior as well as the contribution of variables within each person. **Expectancies,** one of these variables, are predictions about the outcome of behaviors. They, along with the perceived value of behavioral choices and outcomes, have an influence on personality (Rotter, 1972; Rotter, 1975). For example:

> Binh, a recent Vietnamese immigrant to the United States and a college student, is deciding how to spend his weekend. He has an important examination on Monday. He wants to do well because of self-pride and future career opportunities along with the realization that his parents have high expectations for him. He also wants to go out with friends. He thinks: "I will feel great if I do well and terrible if I don't. My parents will be so disappointed if I get a low grade, and I'm happiest when I please them."

Can you see how the way he is thinking about his behaviors and what he eventually decides reflects and influences his personality? Learning theory is especially useful in helping to make desired changes using behavior modification and cognitive principles.

Humanism, often combined with existentialism, is a major personality perspective. Emphasis on the development of the self-concept and the use of individual choices in improving personality are central points. Healthy personal growth includes openness to experience, responsibility, and trust in the self. Developing one's full potential is an ideal goal (Rogers, 1961). Because humanism focuses on choices and self-control, its ideas are emphasized throughout this book.

The **trait** perspective identifies key aspects of personality. A trait is a relatively stable quality. When you describe yourself as trusting or suspicious, you are making use of a trait theory. This perspective helps to describe and compare individuals as well as to predict behavior. Personality theorists generally accept the "Big Five" factor model (Jang et al., 1998) which are: (1) extraversion, (2) agreeableness, (3) conscientiousness, (4) openness to experience, and (5) emotional stability. Each dimension has a wide range. For example, in emotional stability, a person could be poised and calm at one extreme or anxious and excitable at the other. Interestingly, cross-cultural research has identified these five dimensions throughout the world (Benet-Martinez & John, 1998).

Cultural psychology looks at how individuals develop as they participate in particular cultural contexts (Markus & Kitayama, 1998). Consider the following:

> Elvira, a Mexican-American, and Sarah, a Jewish-American, were 21-year-old college students who lived with their parents. At 11:30 P.M. Saturday at a party, Elvira was preparing to leave because she was to be home by midnight. Sarah said, "I don't see how you stand having a curfew." Elvira replied, "I don't mind. As long as I'm living at home, I do as my parents want. I don't want to worry them."

Both young women care about their parents: yet, how and why are their personalities different? Think of a person raised in a different society and consider aspects of personality that are different from yours because of cultural influences.

Like psychologists, sociologists too, are interested in personality development and emphasize **socialization,** a process of learning how to behave according to the requirements of our society. Personality is developed gradually as an individual comes into contact with others (Mead, 1934). Various sources or **agents of socialization** such as family, education, religion, and the media teach the culture and, in doing so, encourage us to form basic personality characteristics. We learn to follow **norms,** those behaviors expected of us as contributing members of society. In Reflections and Applications, you can describe your own personality and compare it to family members. Undoubtedly, you are the product of both nature and nurture!

Stages of Development

Personality develops in a series of stages, according to Erik Erikson, an influential theorist in the fields of psychology and human development. Using Freud's psychoanalytic theory as a basis, he emphasized social interactions and the influence of social development and believed that personality formation continued throughout one's lifetime.

Erikson (1963) described eight psychosocial stages throughout the life span. Each stage has a crisis or challenge to be resolved in order for a personality strength or virtue, as Erikson called it, to be developed. These virtues are the result of a favorable balance between two possible outcomes at each stage. Successful resolution at each stage helps a person meet future developmental challenges and build a healthy personality. According to Erikson (1963, 1968), each item of personality is related to all others, and they all depend on proper development in a particular sequence. Think of a set of blocks and imagine trying to build a tower. Maybe the first block isn't on a solid surface. Or maybe the second block is not centrally placed, so the tower falters a bit. Another poorly placed block will surely cause the blocks to topple. Just as the tower can be rebuilt at any point, a person can later work to develop a favorable balance (Erikson, 1963).

The stages are related to chronological age, yet Erikson (1963) wrote that there could be variations in the timing and intensity of each stage. Order and timing can be affected by historical and cultural conditions. Understanding Erikson's theory can help identify your developmental stage as well as show how you can assist others in resolving the challenges. In the following descriptions, the strength or virtue that emerges is identified after the two possible outcomes. Remember that ages may vary.

I. (Birth–1 year) Trust versus Mistrust [Hope].   A newborn needs to feel secure in the environment. Trust develops when a baby is loved. What are the behaviors that demonstrate love? Parents or other primary caregivers who respond to the baby's needs and express caring by holding and touching are helping the baby develop trust. The opposite is a stressful, unpredictable, and unloving environment that can lead to a higher degree of mistrust. Holding during this stage is of utmost importance. "Based on early good-enough holding, children reach out for experience with the expectation that the world will not let them fall" (Josselson, 1992, p. 33). If there is not a healthy balance between trust and mistrust, hope is at risk, and all stages after this will be more challenging.

Jason cried often, and his parents believed that they would "spoil" him if they responded. When he was only a few months old, a sitter began to spank him for crying and when he didn't respond to what was said. Jason became detached and mistrustful of people. In contrast, Kevin received loving attention on a regular basis including when he cried. He was often cuddled and felt secure and loved.

II. (1–3 years) Autonomy versus Shame and Doubt [Willpower].   A typical 2-year-old is learning about independence. The toddler has developed a measure of control over the environment, and a show of defiance is common. The "terrible twos" are normal! Yet parents who don't realize this often respond with force and a suppression of any attempt at autonomy. A constant barrage of "No," "You can't do that," and "You're naughty" upsets the balance between autonomy and shame and doubt.

Kristen was a clinging toddler. Her mother bragged about how much the little girl depended upon her. She was so attached to her mother that she cried whenever she was left with a relative or sitter. An interesting addendum to this story is that when

Kristen was 13 years old, her parents divorced, and she chose to live with her father. She had finally achieved independence from her mother! One of her playmates, Lisa, was encouraged to play by herself and praised for certain independent behaviors. She enjoyed the attention of others, but didn't require it.

III. (3–6 years) Initiative versus Guilt [Purpose].
Initiative is developed when a child undertakes, plans, and proceeds with a task or uses creativity. Children at this stage often have their first experience with a nursery school or day care center. Wise parents will check to see what the facility does to encourage initiative. For example, beware of perfect artwork: it is probably the product of the staff, not the children. Adults who criticize or deprive children of opportunities to engage in appropriate activities are not contributing to a child's healthy development.

Tony was a curious child who wanted to try new things. His mother was a perfectionist who wanted the house to be immaculate. She seldom let him do any-

Figure 2-1   Life can be fearful as a young child develops autonomy.

thing that might make a mess. He also liked to put on his own clothes and button his coat but was rarely allowed to do so. "I'm in a hurry. Let me do it for you," his mother would say. Tony struggled in trying to develop self-direction or purpose. Compared to Tony, Luis engaged in a variety of activities both at home and at his preschool. He was praised for his creativity and developed a sense of pride in what he did.

IV. (6–12 years) Industry versus Inferiority [Competence].
During this stage, children want to develop skills and complete tasks. They like to help and may even ask to stay after school to assist the teacher! At this stage, they are ready for household chores, paper routes, and various projects. Think of the eager Girl Scout selling cookies at your front door. Praise at this stage is so important. A young woman wrote: "I didn't have any encouragement. I cried for attention at this time, but the only person who heard me was me."

Jodi wanted to help her dad with yardwork. She was 8 years old and so enthusiastic. Her dad was in a hurry and thought she would just be in the way. He told her to go inside and watch television. Seven years later Jodi was lying in front of the television when her dad asked her to help him outside. She said she didn't want to miss her favorite program. "When you were young, you wanted to help, and now that you're old enough, you won't. I don't understand." No, Dad didn't understand!

V. (12–19 years): Identity versus Ego Diffusion [Fidelity].   The critical task of this stage is to determine one's ego identity. Calling this a formidable task, Erikson (1968) conceptualized optimal **identity** as a sense of psychosocial well-being, which includes "a feeling of being at home in one's body, a sense of 'knowing where one is going,' and an inner assuredness of anticipated recognition from those who count" (p. 165). As adolescents seek identity, they will "try on many hats" and probably take risks. Extremely influential is the peer group. Can you think of some crazy things you did during these years? This can be an exasperating time for both teenagers and parents as separation begins to occur. The trauma of this stage is influenced by successful development of earlier strengths.

> Chris had been a passive child who seemed to change dramatically after puberty. His parents divorced when he was 14, and he and his mother moved to a different city. Chris started running around with a gang that had a reputation for drug use. He became surly and quiet. When he was home—which wasn't often—he stayed in his room and played loud music. Inwardly, he struggled with mixed feelings of rebellion versus love for his mother. He felt conflicted and wasn't sure who he really was. His older sister Jessica's story was quite different. She seemed to handle her teen years without a great deal of turmoil. At each stage she had seemingly developed the strengths required to help her adjust to adolescence.

VI. (20–40 Years) Intimacy versus Isolation [Love].   After a successful resolution between identity and ego diffusion, which may or may not be completed during adolescence, an individual can strike a balance between intimacy and isolation. This means developing a close, meaningful, and stable relationship with another person while continuing to feel inwardly secure. In most societies this type of relationship leads to marriage. Erikson's theory can explain why teenage marriages are much more likely to end in divorce (Strong, DeVault, & Sayad, 1998). Tammy wrote: "I married too young and never developed my own identity. I had children while I was still a child myself. Instead of growing and learning about myself, I became 'Mommy' and nothing else. My divorce has brought me to college. I need to learn professional skills and, most importantly, about myself. Losing a husband is hard, but finding myself is wonderful."

Figure 2-2

Eric was 19 years old when he entered the U.S. Army. He had been struggling with identity questions for years. He had not successfully completed several of the earlier psychosocial stages, and his adolescence was troubled. The army was helping him find who he really was. He received orders to go overseas, which prompted a threat from his 17-year-old girlfriend. "Marry me so I can go with you, or I won't be here when you return." Against the wishes of family, Eric and Teresa married. They had numerous disagreements and power struggles. Their relationship was a classic example of a union between two people who hadn't resolved their identity crises and weren't ready for intimacy. Within a year they divorced. In actuality, this freed them to discover who they were.

Many individuals remain within a marriage for years unable to achieve intimacy; instead, they feel isolated. The importance of finding out who you are is illustrated in Linda's story. She recalled that the identity stage was extremely difficult for her. She had come shakily through the earlier stages feeling inferior for being "the kid with red hair, freckles, buck teeth, and used clothes." She used alcohol and drugs excessively, engaged in promiscuous sex, had a horrible relationship with her mother, and quit school at 16. She got married at 17 and ended up in a disastrous marriage. Several years later she realized that she wanted to grow. Counseling and college helped her discover who she truly was, and, as she puts it, "I'm rebuilding my block tower, it's going well, and I feel great!"

VII. (40–65 Years) Generativity versus Stagnation [Caring].   Looking beyond one's self rather than remaining inwardly focused is one way to describe what is needed at this stage. Erikson (1963, 1968) viewed it as a desire to guide the next generation and identified parenthood as a common avenue. He did acknowledge that not everybody progressed through this stage by raising children and included the possibilities of productivity and creativity in other realms. For most parents, this time of life includes children leaving home, which can result in what is called the *empty nest syndrome*. Pursuing a purpose beyond self and family would likely diminish any sense of emptiness.

> Margaret's marriage was an unhappy one. She tried to compensate by devoting her time and energy to her two children. After her younger daughter was married, Margaret lapsed into a severe depression; she felt worthless. She became preoccupied with her health and was frequently ill. She described herself as "stagnant and bored." Quite different was Susan's generativity stage. Feeling secure in herself, she had a satisfying relationship with her partner. She held a top position with an accounting firm and involved herself in meaningful volunteer activities. She felt she was making a difference in the world.

VIII. (65 years–death) Integrity versus Despair [Wisdom].   The last stage of life is one of acceptance and satisfaction. If all the preceding crises have been successfully resolved, Erikson (1968) believed that in this person "the fruit of the seven stages gradually ripens" (p. 139). Acceptance of one's life and others in it and acknowledgment that no other path would have served one as well are hallmarks of integrity. Contentment and peace are possible if memories are meaningful and fulfilling. Strength at this stage takes the form of wisdom.

Harvey, a 70-year-old man, had periods of irritability and bitter nostalgia. He often spoke of what he wished he had done and of how life had cheated him. He had retired from a long career and had developed no hobbies. He spent many hours alone watching television. In contrast to Harvey and his despair is a dear friend, Marilyn Wyman. A wonderful parent and grandparent who does so much for others in her work as a therapist and volunteer, Marilyn believes that it is vitally important that she contributes something of value to the world. Describing herself as somewhere between generativity and integrity, she says:

I love stumbling upon new insights. I will be looking and learning until my last breath if I'm lucky. The integrity stage can go on and on and never get boring. I think beauty is innate, that somewhere within each of us lies the ability to discover beauty, and that truth is what we search for all our lives. My world is made up of many truths and each one holds a special beauty of its own. I feel more connected with life each time I share what I have discovered. Not to share would be to die.

Think about your life up to this point. Answer the questions about your developmental stages in Reflections and Applications. If desired, you can concentrate on working through unresolved stages, keeping in mind that neither of the extremes (e.g., trust vs. mistrust) is ever totally developed and that the conflicts are present throughout life. For example, what could happen that would cause a weakened sense of identity? Any dramatic change may necessitate a new struggle. Familiarity with the psychosocial stages is like a road map for your life as long as you realize there may be detours. This book can help you discover what is missing and give you the tools to develop the virtues Erikson deemed important.

Challenges to Personality Development

At any stage of life, dysfunctional family experiences and psychological trauma will likely hinder positive growth. Low self-esteem and depression can block substantial progress at any stage.

Challenges can also stem from issues related to adoption and minority status. For example, an adopted child often feels a need to locate biological parents or at least learn about them. Racial and ethnic minorities can go through a period of questioning their "roots." Kaili, a biracial student, said, "I have struggled with the difficult identity question of being a part of two racial groups. I would be happy with a biracial identity if society would be more accepting."

Sexual orientation also poses a challenge. The American society is predominantly heterosexual. The prevalence of gay male or lesbian sexual orientation appears to be less than 10 percent of the population and varies depending on whether a study is measuring behavior, desire, or identity. A conservative estimate is that 5 million Americans have a same-sex orientation (Blum, 1998). What causes sexual orientation has not been determined for either heterosexuals or homosexuals. Most scientists believe that there is no single cause, that reasons for sexual orientation may vary among individuals and that biology, cultural influences, and experiences can all be factors (Wade & Tavris, 2002; Yeoman, 1999). Whatever the reason, professionals including the American Psychological Association do not consider same-sex orientation to be a deviance, illness, or psychological disorder.

Most lesbians and gay males begin to realize their sexual orientation during or shortly after puberty, although hints of it may have been there earlier. When gay males and lesbians discover this uniqueness, choices have to be made. Most feel forced to hide an important part of themselves out of fear. They feel "different" and in a heterosexist society are condemned solely on the basis of sexual orientation. Obviously, this is a challenge in achieving a positive identity. Self-esteem can be a major help. Even though the researchers acknowledged that gay and lesbian young people often experience isolation and emotional stressors related to harassment and abuse, self-esteem was strengthening, especially for females (Grossman & Kerner, 1998).

Gays and lesbians who are hiding their identity may feel unauthentic. They live a lie, fearing that they won't be accepted if people know the truth (Herek, 1996). Risk of negative reactions by parents is of major concern. Mike, a young male student, talked candidly about his pain at keeping his sexual orientation hidden from his parents. "I think they suspect because they make remarks. Dad said once, 'If I ever found out you were queer, I'd kill you.' It really hurts to not be able to be who I am with people I love." Hopefully, Mike and others can be helped by the book *Mom, Dad, I'm Gay: How Families Negotiate Coming Out* (Savin-Williams, 2001), designed to help bridge the gap between gay and lesbian youth and their parents.

Being *who I am* is vital to living a happy, satisfying life, and it is tragic that individuals are deprived of this right. Gay male or lesbian sexual orientation, like a heterosexual orientation, is not a matter of wanting only a sexual relationship. Just as heterosexuals are attracted to a special person to share deepest thoughts and feelings, to have fun with, and to devote time and energy to, so are gay males and lesbians. Close relationships between two gays or two lesbians are as loving, close, healthy, and nourishing as those developed by heterosexuals (Peplau, Cochran, & Mays, 1997).

Forcing anyone to live a life of denial is cruel. One young man explained that sexual orientation is not a choice any more than race or sex is, and added, "Think about it folks, with homophobia, AIDS, discrimination, hate crimes, what sensible teenager would make a choice like that?" (Minton, 1993). During a discussion of sexual orientation, one student suggested that being gay or lesbian may not be a choice, but acting on it was. She thought a gay male or a lesbian *should not* act like one. A simple question is an effective response: "Would you want to be told you couldn't act on your sexual orientation?"

According to Jim, a gay adult, the decision to "come out" or stay closeted is an extremely difficult one for most because of the risks involved with family, other relationships, and career. If they want to live open and truthful lives, extreme courage is required. One such person is Amy, who wrote me a wonderful and motivating note at the end of an interpersonal relations course concerning the first edition of this book.

> I think your book is wonderful. As I read it, I noticed that it is very heterosexually focused as are most textbooks. I have to switch things around to make them apply to me. Can you imagine how it feels to read and read and never see yourself in words? I had such a hard time dealing with my sexuality when I was younger. I thought I was the only one who was having these feelings, and I found nothing to validate that what I was feeling even existed. I remember my feelings the first time I read a book that dealt with a homosexual relationship. It was only a brief mention, but my feelings were so intense, I almost cried. I know that human relationships are all basically the same, yet I think there are enough differences to at least warrant a mention. I think if nongay people had to read chapter after chapter about relationships from a gay point of view, they would have a hard time relating. I don't want to sound as if I'm jumping on my soapbox, but I get so frustrated at never being validated or placed first. I know you are a very open-minded and understanding person, and I also know you are in a tough position, but I would like you to at least give thought to what I've said. Maybe sometime in the future you can make a difference to someone like me who wanted to kill myself because I never had any positive re-

inforcement or situations I could relate to about the way I was feeling. Thanks. I feel lucky that I am able to be comfortable in sharing my thoughts with you.

As I read those words, tears came to my eyes, and I decided to try to help someone else. After assuring her that she would see herself in future editions, I asked permission to use her note. I hope Amy's words will touch you, as well. Acknowledging that misunderstanding, prejudice and social stigma regarding sexual orientation creates major developmental challenges for most gay and lesbian adolescents, researchers offer a heartening note that the majority of sexual minority youth lead healthy, productive lives (Tharinger & Wells, 2000).

Predictions about Personality

What will you be like in 20 or 30 years? Obviously, you do not know for sure. Those who believe that there is consistency of personality over a lifetime point out that even though there is likely to be some change, general personality, especially those traits identified in the "Big Five" factor model, is stable in most people (Costa & McCrae, 1997). Changes in single traits are more likely; after age 30, women's personalities seem to change more than men's (Ardelt, 2000). Benefits of having a good idea of what you will be like in the future are predictability and reassurance in who you are.

Class reunions are enjoyable to me because of both the similarities and differences in people from years past. When someone says, "Sharon, you haven't changed a bit," I know they are talking about my personality, not my appearance. Some changes in personality are inevitable, and a gentle transition has occurred in my classmates and myself. Occasionally, someone seems to have a new, dramatically changed personality. Remember Gary from Chapter 1, who was berated by a junior high teacher? During high school he was quiet and somewhat odd. At our twenty-fifth reunion, he was a totally different person—outgoing, confident, and demonstrative. When I talked with him, he confided: "I think this was the real 'me' back then, and I just couldn't let it come out. I felt that I needed a cocoon around me then, and I don't now." This satisfied my curiosity about what seemed to be his dramatic personality change. I did experience some sadness, though, as I thought about individuals who feel a need to wrap their personalities in cocoons.

UNDERSTANDING THROUGH TRANSACTIONAL ANALYSIS

Of help to people in comprehending why people would feel compelled to hide their true personalities is **transactional analysis** (TA). Described as a system for understanding human behavior and as a personality theory, it provides insight into self-awareness and personal growth (Clarkson, 1992).

Eric Berne, a psychiatrist who developed TA, used it to help his clients. The general public learned about the theory and methods when the book *I'm OK, You're OK* (Harris, 1969) became a best-seller. Other books, seminars, and classes teach practical applications. This section will describe the basics of TA and show how to use them in your own life.

Ego States

Basic to TA are **ego states,** which are facets of personality and related patterns of behavior. Serving as the model for ego states was Freud's personality structure of id, ego, and superego. Berne's names for them are related to actual life figures, and personality consists of all three.

Impulsive, spontaneous, emotional, and creative are words that describe the child ego state. It was so named because this part is childlike (like a child between the ages of 2 and 5, according to Berne) and acts on feelings. In the "child" are "the countless, grand 'a-ha' experiences and feelings of delight" (Harris, 1969, p. 27). People of all ages have a child ego state, although it varies in how noticeable and freely expressive it is. Your "child" is the part of you that loves and hates, feels exhilarated or completely miserable, relishes ice cream and pizza, laughs and cries, and can enjoy life.

Figure 2-3   The child ego state can be alive and well at any age!

Imagine a wild colt with no restraints. A person's "child" could resemble one.

The child ego state did not develop freely, however. As soon as you were able to understand parental figures in the environment, another ego state began to develop. This part consists of verbal and nonverbal messages you received. Think of it as a collection of recordings in the brain that function as a conscience. This ego state contains rights and wrongs, "shoulds," "oughts," and strong ideas of what to do and not to do.

The messages poured in during your early years and were largely unedited; that is, you didn't question or reject them (Harris, 1969). And no matter how old you are, you continue to receive directive messages that can sound like commands. These opinions, judgments, values, and attitudes are recorded and automatically play back in your mind. Or you have a visual image of a nonverbal message. A good example came from Lisa: "When my mother was watching television, she usually ignored me when I'd ask her a question. As a kid, I'd always feel as if I'd done something wrong. And when I'm ignored today, I tend to feel that way, too." Even though these messages come from a variety of sources, because so many came from actual parents, this is called the **parent ego state.**

Remember that the messages originally came from an external source and are now internalized. A partial list of some hilarious messages contributed by students follows. Can you think of any of your own that strike you as ridiculous?

- Benjamin Franklin took a bath every day of his life, and he was never sick. So be sure to bathe daily.
- Lift your feet off the floor of the car when you cross over railroad tracks.
- Swallowed gum will stick to your spine, and you won't be able to stand up straight.
- Nice girls don't wear red fingernail polish or pierce their ears.
- Masturbation will cause blindness.
- Clean the house before you leave in case of a fire.

Incidentally, wise and useful "parent" messages such as, "Look both ways before you cross the street" and "Don't drive if you've been drinking" also exist and are worthy of attention!

Often, when you are in your parent ego state, you feel, think, and act like one of your own parents. If this has not yet happened, you will probably have the experience of saying something to one of your own children that has a familiar ring to it. Ironically, it is often exactly what you vowed you would never say! Even though "parent" messages affect your parenting behavior, ideally you will parent from all ego states. By the way, if you have children, you can even receive "parent" messages from them!

Before we discuss the third ego state, imagine this scenario. It's 7:00 on a cool, rainy morning. The alarm clock rings, and you hit the snooze button. You feel warm and happy lying in bed, and your child ego state is enjoying it immensely. "Ohhh, to just stay here and sleep, skip class. This feels so good." Then another voice penetrates your relaxed state. "Get up! You shouldn't miss school! Don't be so lazy!" It sounds like Mom or Dad, but it isn't because you don't live at home anymore. You're hearing your own parent ego state. What a dilemma—the struggle between "child" and "parent" continues in your mind.

How fortunate that you have another ego state that can enter the picture at this point. "Let me think—I haven't missed that class yet, and I remember the instructor saying there was going to be a film. I could watch that at another time. I haven't been getting enough rest lately. I think I will sleep this morning." This is one possible resolution. A second one is, "I've missed that class several times, and I don't think it's wise to be absent that much. Besides, the lecture is always full of important material! I think I'll go to class." Other creative solutions—which I hesitate to mention—are possible from this ego state: sleeping in for a while and going to class late, going to class and leaving early to head back home to bed, or going to one class and skipping another.

This part of the personality thinks and is able to logically and objectively analyze. It sees alternatives and acts as a decision maker using facts in a cool, calm way. The name **adult ego state** is quite appropriate. Like a computer, the "adult" gathers information from the three sources of "parent," "child," and stored "adult" data as well as new evidence in the present (Harris, 1969). The "adult" can find either the "child" feelings or the "parent" messages appropriate and allow them to prevail. Also possible is to strike a balance between the two or gather additional information and make an original decision. The "adult" begins to develop at about 10 months of age (Harris, 1969) as an infant assumes some control over the environment; choices are then possible!

Each ego state has its positive and negative qualities. The "child" is exuberant, enjoys life, and readily expresses affection; yet, it also can be depressed, fearful, wounded, and defeated. The "parent" has useful knowledge and reacts quickly. How fortunate we are that our parent ego state tells us to be on time for work. Unfortunately, the "parent" contains some outdated and negative information, can be close-minded, and passes on potentially damaging messages. The "adult" is a necessity in most situations; however, it can be programmed with detrimental or inaccurate information and be a stranger to emotionality.

A well-adjusted individual uses all three ego states. In some cases, an ego state is more powerful and overwhelms or contaminates the others. An overpowering "child" is what Kushner (1986) cautioned against: "Fun can be the dessert of our lives but never its main course. It can be a very welcome change of pace from the things we do every day, but should it ever become what we do every day, we will find it too frivolous a base to build a life on" (pp. 69–70).

Which of the three ego states is dominant in the following examples?

> Joan is aloof and reserved. She does well at her accounting job and finds it easy to analyze data. She is a calm person who rarely shows emotions.
> Kim is a 12-year-old who has strong convictions about many issues. She tends to be domineering and judgmental.
> Paul is a twinkly-eyed 80-year-old. He enjoyed a raft trip down a rushing river as a way of celebrating the event. He is witty, enthusiastic, and readily shows his feelings. However, he often acts on impulse and can be moody.

If you named "adult" for Joan, "parent" for Kim, and "child" for Paul, you are correct. An imbalance can occur regardless of age. Even a 4-year-old can exhibit an expanded "parent."

Adults are wise to ask themselves if they have a healthy child ego state. Do you ever act on impulse? When were you last spontaneous? Can you wonder and dream? Do you truly feel your emotions, and do you express them? When did you last really laugh? Are you a hugger; do you enjoy being hugged?

Leo Buscaglia, who was widely known as a big hugger, encouraged people to "let down their hair" and be a little crazy once in a while. He told of coming home from Wisconsin on a late-night flight. He carried gifts he couldn't check in as luggage: a large pumpkin, leaves (which he loved), cheese, and homemade bread. When airborne, he impulsively spread the gifts across several seats and pushed the call button. The tired flight attendant was quite surprised and, amazingly, reenergized by the craziness. She called the other attendants; they brought wine and had a party! A potentially boring flight was special because of someone's "child." A class viewed a videotape of Buscaglia in which he talked of his passion for leaves. One autumn day, a student told me he wished he could give all his raked leaves to Leo Buscaglia. Spontaneously, I said, "Let's do it!" We collected beautiful Nebraska leaves (the Prairie State really has them!) and mailed them in a large cardboard box with love to Leo. His thank-you note reflected his joy at our craziness. One student, however, asked in a bewildered voice, "Why would we send him leaves?" I patiently explained as I wondered about her "child."

Some do not notice that they are not using their child ego state until it is too late. In a live presentation, Leo Buscaglia described an 85-year-old reflecting on life.

> If I had my life to live over again, I'd dare to make more mistakes next time. I'd relax. I would limber up. I would be sillier than I have been this trip. I would take more chances. I would take more trips. I would climb more mountains and swim more rivers. I would eat more ice cream and fewer beans. I would perhaps have more actual troubles, but I'd have fewer imaginary ones. You see, I'm one of those people who lived seriously and sanely hour after hour, day after day. Oh, I've had my moments, and if I had to do it over again, I'd have more of them. In fact, I'd try to have nothing else, just moments, one after another, instead of living so many years ahead of each day. I've been one of those people who never went anywhere without a thermometer, a hot water bottle, a raincoat, and a parachute. If I had to do it again, I'd travel lighter. If I had my life to live over, I'd start barefoot earlier in

the spring and stay that way later in the fall. I'd go to more dances. I'd ride more merry-go-rounds. I would pick more daisies. If I had my life to live over again, but I don't.

Think of all the "parent" messages that restricted her "child." Can you think of any "child" wants and wishes you are denying yourself? If you were 85 years old, what would you wish for yourself? What can you do about it now? Remember, an 85-year-old doesn't have life to live over, and neither will you.

A problem lies with inconsistent messages. Did you have a parental figure who said one thing and did just the opposite? Did anyone say, "Don't drink and drive," and then proceed to do exactly that, or, "Religion is important, so go to Sunday School," yet who rarely went to church, or a significant person who maintained, "All people are equal," then said, "I don't welcome one of those people in this house"? A sad "parent" message is, "Do as I say, not as I do."

"Parent" messages can be retrieved by thinking about why you do what you do, why you have certain beliefs and ideas, and where they came from originally. A major task of healthy adulthood is to process "parent" messages through the adult ego state. Getting rid of extremely harmful and hateful messages is highly recommended. Buscaglia (1982) revealed that he has been more involved in unlearning than in learning during various stages of his life. "I'm having to unlearn all the garbage that people have laid upon me" (p. 147). That "garbage" consists of "parent" messages. With each discarded piece he became freer. As you process messages through your "adult," you become more your own person. Use Reflections and Applications to describe your ego states.

Recognizing your own ego states can be beneficial in making decisions.

Ryan is a 36-year-old factory worker who quit high school to marry and get a job. He realizes he is going nowhere with a career and is considering quitting and going back to school. Of value to Ryan would be awareness of the role of each ego state. His "parent" has such messages as, "A man is supposed to support his family," "You're too old to go back to school," "Everyone will think you're dodging responsibility." The "child" in him is frightened by risk yet somewhat excited at the prospect of a new experience. Ryan will benefit from "plugging into" his adult ego state. This ego state will gather more information about costs, management of the family's financial situation, and benefits compared to losses.

A goal of TA is to encourage freedom of choice—the freedom to change (Harris, 1969). This can happen if you, like Ryan, become aware of each ego state and use your "adult" in the decision process.

Life Positions

The book title *I'm OK, You're OK* (Harris, 1969) came from the preferred life position in the TA framework. A **life position** is a perspective on the world based on feelings about self and others. Berne, (1962) identified four positions. The preferred, or healthy, position, **I'm OK, you're OK,** is based on equality and positiveness. In one's initial approach to people and situations, hope and optimism are present. "Persons in this position are winners. They reflect an optimistic and healthy outlook on life and freely relate with others" (Woollams & Brown, 1979, p. 107). This position requires self-love and esteem. The "I'm OK" belief is followed by toler-ance, equality, and acceptance of others.

The **I'm not OK, you're OK** position is not unusual. In fact, some consider it to be the most common one (Woollams & Brown, 1979). Self-esteem is low; the in-dividual feels inferior. "I'm unworthy, and everyone else has it together" would be a typical thought. These people appear defeated; they usually have difficulty accepting compliments or communicating positive self-talk.

Several years ago a man by the name of Patrick Sherrill committed a violent crime; he killed several coworkers and then himself. The headline read, "Gunman Hated the World and Himself." This is an extreme example of the position **I'm not OK, you're not OK.** The position reflects an extremely negative, pessimistic atti-tude. These people seem to hate themselves and the world. They can behave in various ways, and most are not criminals. Some retreat from the world and be-come loners, and others simply give up and just manage to survive. The frighten-ing ones are those, like Pat Sherrill, who take out their self-hatred on others. Sometimes, identifying this position is difficult because those who occupy it may come across as cocky and self-assured. Beneath this "I'm something" facade, how-ever, is probably an "I'm not OK" person.

An annoying and potentially damaging position is **I'm OK, you're not OK**. People in this position feel superior to others. They show it in annoying ways by maintaining that they are always right, judging or patronizing others, and telling others what to do.

What position are you occupying? The question is frequently asked, "Can you be in more than one?" You may have characteristics that fit more than one position; however, view yourself in a general way. What orientation do you usually take to-ward others and the world? If it's not **I'm OK, you're OK,** decide to work toward it!

Life Script

Think of a script for a play. A life script is similar. A **script** is an ongoing program, first developed in early childhood, that directs behavior (Berne, 1972). The TA framework does not suggest that your life is predetermined or that you simply read lines and play a role; however, unless you become aware of your life script, you may be play-ing it out without realizing it. Self-fulfilling prophecies serve as powerful directions within your script. Julie could be counted on to be late to class. She explained:

> I'm late to everything, including work. I've always been this way. Mom told me I wasn't organized, and Dad said I had no concept of time. My friends just expect me to be late and wouldn't believe it if I were ever on time. I'm just a "flake."

Julie played the part of the always-late, disorganized "flake," and she played it well.

Does Julie have to continue playing this part? The TA framework provides a technique called **script analysis**, a way of becoming aware of how your script de-veloped. You then can decide to take different courses of action. Julie did not have to continue in her role, but the decision to change had to be hers. After college she landed a job. A few months later she was fired; you guessed it—chronic tardiness. She rationalized that it wasn't her dream job anyway. Within a short period of time she was hired as a fashion buyer—an ideal position for her! When she was warned about lateness during her first evaluation session, she made an attempt to be on time, yet it was short-lived. Losing that job was depressing for Julie, yet it proved to be the jolt she needed. She resolved to change her script, and with the help of a counselor, set up a behavior modification program. She rewarded herself for each on-time experience and relished the praise of others. The always-late, disorganized Julie is different, and part of her new script is, "I can make positive changes if I really want to!" She proved what Nathaniel Branden, (1992) wrote, "We need never be the prisoner of yesterday's choices" (p. 73).

Scripts are based on the past. Even though you cannot change your past, learning from past experiences in invaluable. Ask yourself, "Is my past illuminating my present or contaminating it?" (Satir, 1976). The present is where change is possible, and you can rewrite your future script if you choose to do so. Can you think of some changes you would like to make in your script? Taking charge of your own life and destiny isn't necessarily easy, but being your own scriptwriter is very rewarding!

> *We are not prisoners of the past. We are pioneers of an exciting future.*
> —John Powell

Strokes

"I enjoy having you in class." "I like you." "You did a great job." These phrases, along with a smile, a hug, and a friendly wave, are special verbal or nonverbal behaviors called **strokes.** Usually, these feel good to the receiver; if so, they are positive strokes. Negative strokes do not feel good and are generally meant to be hurtful. Think of some negative verbal and nonverbal strokes. See Table 2–1 for examples of each type. Human beings need recognition, and positive stroking is an effective way of letting people know that they count. Strokes can be *conditional* (based on certain behaviors or conditions) or *unconditional* (given simply because the receiver is alive). A mother commented, "I realize that I've been giving positive strokes but only under set conditions. I decided to tell my son that I appreciated him simply for being here—to stroke his person." She had realized the beauty of unconditional strokes! Can you add others to the lists in Table 2–1?

TABLE 2-1   Strokes

Verbal Positive	*Verbal Negative*
"I love you."	"I don't like you."
"I like your smile."	"Get lost!"
"You're a great employee."	"You're so lazy."
"Hello, how are you?"	"You look awful!"

Nonverbal Positive	*Nonverbal Negative*
A pat on the back	A shake of the fist
A wink (if it feels good!)	A hit or a slap
A back rub	A frown
A special card or gift	Inattention
A hug or kiss	Laughter at someone

Young children definitely can learn about the nature of strokes. When directing an early childhood center, I used the program "TA for Tots." Positive strokes were called "warm fuzzies," while negative ones were "cold pricklies." The children soon recognized how much more comfortable the atmosphere was when "warm fuzzies" were being given and received. In our "warm fuzzy" circle, the children gave and received positive strokes. In the beginning, several were hesitant—an indication that "warm fuzzies" weren't too familiar to them. Gradually, verbal strokes seemed easier. Two boys interacted during this time. Danny was a spontaneous and expressive boy with a healthy child ego state. Tim was reserved and unexpressive. On this particular day, when it was Danny's turn, he did something out of the ordinary. He gave Tim a big hug and kiss on the cheek. The others seemed embarrassed, and I quickly said, "I really like that 'warm fuzzy.' I'd like to see more of those!" Because young children look upon teachers as a final authority, they reacted in a positive way—all except Tim. I was saddened that this boy, at the age of only 4, recoiled from his friend's gesture. For whatever reason his script included, "I don't want to be touched." During the course of the year he became more open to expressiveness.

Strokes, or lack of them, influence scripts and life positions. An all too common scenario goes like this: A child makes the bed and completes assigned tasks each day, but receives no recognition, no positive stroke. One day the bed is not made! What happens? A negative stroke is delivered immediately: "You're irresponsible and lazy!" This scenario is played out frequently in the home, at school, and even at work. Even though evidence shows that positive strokes are powerful motivators, negatives are more common.

When people don't receive positive strokes, they tend to settle for negative ones. "Taking negative strokes is like drinking polluted water; extreme need will cause us to overlook the harmful qualities of what we require to survive" (Steiner, 1974, p. 127). A child who is misbehaving or an adolescent who "acts out" may be deprived of positive strokes and willing to settle for any kind. One student remarked that we give pets more pats than we do human beings. Positive strokes can be lacking in marriages. A young married female wrote:

> Sometimes I feel as if I'm dying of lack of attention. We've been married only 5 years, and the only time he touches me is in bed. I haven't heard a positive word from him in a long time. I feel dried up and starved for affection, and I don't know what to do.

For Better or For Worse   **by Lynn Johnston**

Figure 2–4 Copyright 1981 Universal Press Syndicate. Reprinted by permission. All rights reserved.

I suggested she start by asking for positive strokes.

In your life, monitor the strokes you receive and record them in the personality activity in Reflections and Applications. Ask, "Whom do I receive them from? What kind are they? Under what conditions do I receive them? What do I want?" Also, become aware of the strokes you give by asking the same questions. My husband and I tried a stroke-monitoring experiment with our four children, keeping track of numbers and types of strokes given and received. The one who was receiving the fewest positives and the most negatives from us was, in turn, sending the same back. At that time he was also "acting out" more than the others. We can all influence the quality of our own lives and of those around us by increasing the number of positive strokes and decreasing the number of negative ones.

The TA framework has much to offer. Only the basics have been presented here. If you want to learn more, read any of the books cited in this section. Transactional analysis can be used to enrich your life.

WHAT IS YOUR PERSONALITY LIKE?

Carlos is miserable at work. He enjoys being around people, yet his job demands that he analyze data in a back office. Connie is frustrated in a certain classroom situation. The instructor doesn't seem to be organized, and the class discussions focus more on possibilities than on realities. Rich and Jamie had been so happy when they first married. Three years later, they both feel dissatisfied. Rich doesn't like the way Jamie seems to make irrational decisions, and she finds him too analytical and inconsiderate of others' feelings.

An understanding of personality types can help each of these individuals. Psychological typing categorizes several related personality traits. Carl Jung (1921), an early psychologist, believed that behavioral differences are based on the ways people prefer to approach life (Jung, 1968). Based on Jung's typology with some of their own refinements, Isabel Myers and her mother, Katharine C. Briggs, developed the Myers-Briggs Type Indicator (MBTI). It achieved widespread acceptance in the 1970s and has remained a popular instrument useful in career selection and satisfaction, education and learning preferences, and interpersonal relationships. A study confirmed that the MBTI reliably measures personality characteristics associated with Jungian theory (Wheeler, 2001). Intended for use with "well" people, the indicator focuses on positive aspects. You can use it to make life decisions, gain personal insight, understand differences, and learn how to work well with others.

Originally published in 1980s, the book *Gifts Differing* (Myers, 1995) describes personality preferences as well as ways in which people can use their own strengths and understand the differences of others. The author explains:

All too often, others with whom we come in contact do not reason as we reason, or do not value the things we value, or are not interested in what interests us. The merit of the theory is that it enables us to expect specific personality differences in particular people and to cope with the people and the differences in a constructive way. (p. 1)

Personality Preferences

Following is a brief summary of the four pairs of personality preferences. The MBTI will show your inclination for one or the other.

- **Extraversion-Introversion** (type E or I). Relates to an inward or outward orientation and to life energy sources. (*Note*: The spelling extraversion is used in this book to correspond to the MBTI. The spelling extroversion is also common.)
- **Sensing-Intuition** (type S or N). Pertains to the preferred ways of taking in information as well as what is of interest.
- **Thinking-Feeling** (type T or F). Indicates whether one prefers to use thought or personal values in decision making and judgments.
- **Judgment-Perception** (type J or P). Shows how one deals with the outer world and the type of environment that is preferred.

Understanding their meanings and knowing that we don't have absolute preferences are important. A common misconception is that an extraversion preference means being totally extraverted. Instead, individuals are both extraverted and introverted, yet in differing degrees.

The meanings of extraversion and introversion are typically misunderstood. Unfortunately, this confusion has led to an assumption that a person needs to be extraverted in order to be successful and happy. Western culture seems to more strongly reward the outgoing, sociable person (Keirsey & Bates, 1978). While introversion is often associated with such descriptors as shy, lonely, and snobbish, these do not define introversion. This inaccuracy is unfair, and a true understanding can correct these misconceptions.

Let's look at what these preferences really are. Think in terms of life energy or force. What charges your battery? If your preference is **extraversion,** you get much of this force from external sources, including other people, and you probably project energy outward. Extraverted behavior is outgoing, showing an outward orientation and a preference to operate in the outer world of people and things. **Introversion** means an inner orientation and having an interest in the inner world of concepts and ideas. If there were such a word as "ingoing," it would describe an introverted preference well. The source of energy is within and comes from solitary experiences. Thus, those with a preference for introversion can reenergize themselves and don't rely on external stimuli. In fact, interaction drains their energy, and they need to spend time recharging themselves.

People who prefer extraversion will usually behave in a friendly fashion, and they appear to be open. They are not necessarily any more emotional, caring, or loving. Those with an introversion preference will generally be more reserved in a social setting, and they do not usually seek out others. This does not mean that they are uncaring, snobbish, lonely, or shy. They are often skilled in working with people; however, their preference is for smaller numbers and an opportunity to know the people well. People who are described as shy, lonely, and uncaring are lacking in social skills and may be either introverted or extraverted.

Another difference is that extraverts will usually respond more quickly than introverts. Introverts think about what they are going to say; extraverts tend to think out loud. In fact, extraverts commonly talk their thoughts! If you often "put your foot in your mouth," extraversion could be a partial reason. However, talkativeness is not necessarily an exclusive characteristic of either. Because introverts prefer smaller groups, you could be sitting next to a person on a bus or airplane who talks and talks in a one-on-one situation and be surprised to know he or she has an introverted preference. Similarly, in classrooms introverts may participate often and surprise their classmates when their personality preference is identified.

Both preferences have advantages. Extraverts frequently report greater happiness and satisfaction with life. Reasons could be the experience of more potentially positive interactions, ease with affectionate behaviors, more acceptance by society, and greater social support (Myers & Diener, 1995). Extraverts are usually eager to interact. Does it surprise you, though, to know that extraverts can behave in a shy manner? **Shyness** is timidity and a feeling of unease in a social situation. As an extravert, I have felt and acted shyly at some social activities because I didn't feel at ease or wasn't in the mood to talk. The dissatisfaction I felt after the event came from not using my extraverted preference. If I were an introvert, I probably wouldn't have been bothered. That leads to one distinct advantage for introverts. They don't require social exchange and can get along just fine alone for long periods of time. In addition, introverts are often thought of as sincere people and good listeners even though they may be neither. Can you think of other advantages for each preference?

What about disadvantages? Extraverts can be overwhelming in social settings and be perceived as obnoxious loud-mouths. If extreme in their extraversion, others may see them as superficial or phony. Another potential problem for an extraverted person was expressed by Jodi.

> I'm quite extraverted, but there are still times when I am quiet. If that happens around friends, they act upset with me and ask, "What's wrong with you anyway?" I find it hard to have any quiet time when I'm around others. They expect me to be the life of the party.

Introverts are frequently criticized for their lack of conversation and what is often interpreted as aloofness. They may be perceived as uncaring or uninterested. If an extreme introvert does go to a party, the stay will likely be short. The accusation of "party pooper" is inaccurate; in actuality, the party "pooped" the introvert (Keirsey & Bates, 1978). How might a person with an extraverted preference (E) and one with an introverted preference (I) seem to each other? Without understanding their differences, an "E" can seem shallow to an "I," and an "I" may seem withdrawn to an "E." After a program I gave on preferences, a woman in her sixties approached me and laughingly asked, "Where were you three years ago when I got divorced? I thought I was married to a 'dud,' someone who just didn't know how to have fun. Now I realize he was just introverted, which to me seemed terrible. This could have saved my marriage!"

Extraversion and introversion were looked upon as valuable opposites by Carl Jung. He believed that most individuals use both preferences but not with equal ease (Myers, 1980). The most important points are that both extraversion and introversion include positive behaviors and advantages, and we have preferences in varying degrees for both.

All categories and preferences are important, and if their meanings are not clarified, confusion and misunderstanding are probable. The other three pairs of preferences can be understood as follows:

- **Sensing and Intuition:** When you want to find out something, your preference may be sensing (S) which means a preference for gathering facts through the senses. "You tend to be realistic, practical, observant, and good at remembering a great number of facts and working with them" (Myers, 1980, p. 2). If you prefer **intuition** (N), "you tend to value imagination and inspirations, and to be good at new ideas, projects, and problem solving" (Myers, 1980, p. 2). In perceiving reality differently, sensors are concrete and attuned to details, and intuitives are visionary and ablaze with possibilities and ideas. Any successful business needs people with both preferences. When working on a task, sensors prefer a systematic step-by-step procedure and don't seem to be bothered by repetition. Intuitives often devise their own methods, will work on several steps or projects at once, and prefer variety. An intuitive preference gets restless with "sameness," has an appreciation of new and different experiences, and wants to modify life.

Can you see how these preferences can affect job satisfaction? Think of jobs that a intuitive would dislike. What would bother a sensor in a work situation?

- **Thinking and Feeling:** Once you have found what you want to know, you may have a decision to make. If your preference is for **thinking** (T), you will predict the logical results of your actions and decide impersonally. The other way to decide is through **feeling** (F). You will consider anything that matters or is important to you or to other people (logic is not required) and decide according to personal values (Myers, 1980). Those who have a clear thinking preference view emotions as more of a problem than as part of a solution (Keating, 1984). This person can be oblivious to other people's feelings, while the opposite (a strong feeling person) can bend over backward to avoid hurting anyone. Either can become a problem. In one study (Shermis & Lombard, 1998), thinkers had lower test anxiety scores than feelers. Can you see why? Both preferences can care a great deal about people and believe that their decisions are based on the "right" motives. Caring from a "T" is more apt to be sympathy and from the "F" empathy (Jeffries, 1991). The two preferences can clash or complement each other. Clashing is probably more common.

A crucial difference between a "T" and an "F" that isn't easily bridged is how issues are perceived. A "T" prefers to deal with them in a detached manner outside of self, while an "F" takes them to heart and thinks in terms of everyone involved.

- **Judgment and Perception:** The descriptors judgment (J) or perception (P) reflect one's orientation toward the outer world. **Judgment** means that you prefer living in a "planned, decided, orderly way, wanting to regulate life and control it" (Myers, 1980, p. 6). Planning and preparation are typical behaviors. A judging person seeks closure and prefers to reach a decision or judgment quickly. If instead you like living in a "flexible, spontaneous way, wanting to understand life and adapt to it," (Myers, 1980, p. 6), your preference is **perception.** You often "go with the flow" and prefer to delay closure and continue perceiving. Key words are *organization* and *order* for the judging preference and *flexibility* and *adaptability* for perceivers.

Keep in mind what judging means. I remember one student who was upset to discover he was a "J." He said, "I'm not a judgmental person!" I quickly assured him that "J" doesn't mean that.

I laughed when I read a comment written by Paul, a strong judger. "I like the idea of someone throwing me a surprise party, but I want to be prepared for it." He also wrote, "I live by my planner. I take it everywhere, even parties." In contrast to Paul, a perceiver probably wouldn't have a planner or like Kari, who said, "I bought a calendar diary but just don't bother to use it!" In the workplace, colleagues of these two extremes can have difficulty getting along. The judging person would probably view the perceptive individual as disorganized or flighty, while the perceptive one could become frustrated with a perception of an overly organized and inflexible coworker. I appreciate both in the classroom. Judgers remind me of due dates, time, and schedules, and perceivers readily adjust to any deviation!

Think about which of the preferences in each of the four categories sounds like you and then elaborate on these in Reflections and Applications. Combining two or more preferences provides even more insight. For example, you can come up with your temperament type (Keirsey & Bates, 1978) by doing the following.

1. Determine your preference in the second category (either S for sensing or N for intuition.)
2. If it is S, pair it with your preference in the fourth category (either J for judgment or P for perception). Your temperament type is either SJ or SP.
3. If it is N, pair it with your preference in the third category (either T for thinking or F for feeling). Your temperament type is either NT or NF.

See if the following description of your temperament type is accurate.

- SJ is orderly, dependable, realistic, expects others to be realistic, strives to belong and contribute, conservative, well-organized, can easily be critical of mistakes.
- SP is flexible, open-minded, willing to take risks, highly negotiable, hungers for freedom and action, can be indecisive, lives for the moment, does not like to plan or be hemmed into a definite plan.
- NF is empathic, highly responsive to interpersonal relations, keeps in close contact with others, sees possibilities, searches for meaning and authenticity, gives and needs praise, and may be overly swayed by feeling.
- NT is responsive to new ideas, hungers for competency and knowledge, works well with ideas and concepts, is not always aware of others' feelings, likes to start projects but may not follow through.

Learning styles can also be examined using other combinations (McClanaghan, 2000). Which style seems most like you?

- ST wants specific information, knowledge of what's right and wrong; does better in a structured environment and learns best from repetition, drill, memorization, and actual experience.
- NT wants solid evidence and reason; does better when challenged and allowed to be creative; is skeptical, analytical, and logical and learns best when allowed to be independent.

- SF wants material to have personal relevance; does better in a harmonious setting where there is cooperative learning; learns best by talking and being involved in group activities.
- NF wants to see the "big picture" as well as possibilities, patterns, and connections; does better in a flexible, innovative setting; is bored by routine and established learning procedures.

Obviously, how strong your preference is will affect how closely you match any of the preceding descriptions. For example, if you have a strong preference for both sensing and thinking, the ST learning style will likely sound just like you.

Interesting research is conducted with the MBTI. A study revealed that even though women in the general population tended to be feeling, women in executive-level positions often had a thinking preference usually combined with intuition; however, "NFs" made up 31 percent of the group (Daugherty, Randall, & Globetti, 1997). Can you think of reasons why an "N" preference would be useful?

A college library or counseling service may have a version of the MBTI you can take, or you may have an opportunity in a class or workshop. The book *Please Understand Me* (Keirsey & Bates, 1978) offers a questionnaire that yields scores in the four categories. Remember that with any measurement, the results may vary for a number of reasons. Taking the test more than once and being honest in answering the questions will give you a more reliable profile. The four preferences together become a **psychological type.** Remember that being an "ENFP" doesn't mean you don't have and won't use the other preferences of "ISTJ." For example, you may have a strong preference for using your right hand, yet you can also use your left.

Personality typing indicates your strengths and comfort zones; in certain situations, you are wise to use the lesser preference. For example, in the world of work, you will likely use more thinking and judgment, and in your personal life, the feeling and perceiving preferences lend themselves to warmth and enjoyment. The extent of difference between the two will influence your degree of ease in various personal and professional situations. If the two preferences are close, you probably are comfortable using either one. In some cases, all four preferences will be extremely strong as in the case of Chad, a definite "ISTJ." He agreed to share the following.

All clothes in my closet hang in a particular order on white plastic hangers. Dress pants, because they are worn the least, hang together followed by sweat pants, then jeans. In the center of the bar are empty hangers separating the pants from the shirts. I have exactly as many hangers as I do articles of clothing. There would be no point in having extra hangers in my closet. Next to the empty hangers are white T-shirts, then casual shirts and dress shirts. At the bottom of the closet are two laundry baskets; one is for colors, and the other is for whites. I also have a system for clothes that aren't in my closet. All my boxer shorts are numbered on the inside tag. I wear them in the right order so they will wear out evenly and can be replaced at the same time.

Even if this sounds unlike you, what thoughts and behaviors are indicative of strong sensing, thinking, and judging preferences? Chad also said that he can't believe many of the "stupid" things people do, then added, "It's a good thing I'm so introverted because I just think this and don't say it!"

Remember that the MBTI is not intended to pigeonhole people or arm them with excuses for certain behaviors (e.g., "I can't help that I'm disorganized. I'm a 'P'" to which I would respond, "You also have a 'J' preference into which you can shift".) Reading books on the subject will give further ideas for using this understanding in career, marriage, parenting, and leadership situations. Can you recognize how personality was creating hardships for the individuals in the examples at the beginning of this section? Carlos is extraverted, and his job doesn't allow him to be in contact with people. Connie is more sensing, while her instructor appears to be intuitive. The marriage is in trouble because Rich, who has a thinking preference, and Jamie, who prefers feeling, don't understand each other. Knowing more about your personality can help you make wiser choices and maximize your potential. By understanding your own personality type and that of others, you can draw on your strengths and appreciate and grow from the differing gifts of others. Remaining open to and understanding differences leads to enrichment.

HOW DOES GENDER INFLUENCE YOUR LIFE?

How would your life be different if you had been born the opposite sex? This may be difficult to imagine and, possibly, even distasteful. Years ago when I asked students to react to this, I received a quick, loud response from a 37-year-old man: "It makes me sick to think about it!" His reply demonstrated an attitude I was planning to discuss later with the class and made a salient point more dramatically than I could have—that a perception exists that being male is preferable to being female.

Reflect

- How is your personality similar and/or different from five years ago?
- Recall two "parent" messages, a time when you acted from your "child," and a decision you made through your "adult."
- Think of an acquaintance, friend, or family member who has a personality different from yours. Does it bother you? If so, can you relate it to the personality preferences identified in this chapter?

Apply

- Ask a friend or family member to describe your personality. See how it compares to your description of yourself.
- Give two positive strokes to someone within the next 24 hours.
- Shake hands with your less preferred hand. How does it feel? The feeling is somewhat like you probably feel when behaving according a weaker personality preference.
- Try to think or act in an opposite way from one of your personality preferences.

Gender Differences

Over several years, I have asked more than 3,000 students the question, "How would your life be different if you had been born the opposite sex?" An interesting pattern emerged; but, in recent years, the differences have not been as acute. Following are the categories most often mentioned, with a general explanation of the differences imagined by the men and women.

Career choice.   This area was by far the most commonly mentioned. When considering being raised male, women would have made a different career choice, had an earlier pursuit of career, put more emphasis on career, and realized a definite increase in financial assets. Some felt they would be more restricted: "I would have been forced to take over the family farm or business." Men indicated that, as women, they would either have a different, stereotypic female career, slow advancement, or no career at all! "I'd be more sheltered and let others take care of me" and "I'd just go out and trap a rich guy!" were two male observations. One man said, "Maybe I'd really do something different and be a doctor!"

Education.   Women said they would have gone to college earlier, finished earlier, attended a more prestigious college, and planned their education based on future earning power. One woman said, "I would have been forced to achieve more from my education all the way through because I'd need it to earn a living." Men mentioned not going to college, and a few said that, if female, they couldn't have afforded further education.

Sports and other activities.   Although opportunities in women's athletics have increased since 1970s legislation, women still said that they would have been involved in a wider variety of sports. Men, conversely, would have been less involved. One outstanding female basketball player remarked, "I may have taken a shot at playing professionally. As a female, there wasn't much of an opportunity for that." Another woman said that, as a boy, she would not have been a cheerleader. She added, "But I would have had to really be 'into' sports." A distinct difference was mechanical. Women were sure that they would know more about automobiles and other machines. And a young man said, "As a female I wouldn't know anything about a car. I would just expect a man to handle it!"

Household tasks.   A definite difference was clear in this category. Males, if raised female, would do more housework and cooking and no outside chores. Women would move out of the kitchen and into the garage and yard. Most females said that they would be paid more for allowances. One man stated, "I got more money for mowing the yard than my sister did for doing dishes."

Marriage and child raising.   Several women said that they would have married later or not at all if they had been men. The men envisioned being married, having the role of housewife, and being the primary parent. One male reply was, "I'd probably have married young, been married two or three times, have lots of kids, and be looking again for someone to support us!" "If male, I wouldn't have custody of my children," said a divorced woman.

Self-esteem and self-efficacy.   Both sexes viewed women as placing a lower value on themselves and having less confidence. An older female student said that she would have had higher self-esteem earlier in life and wouldn't have wasted her talent. Another woman reported that her family favors boys: "Boys are very special, and they know it." However, a disadvantage to men was also noted. A woman said, "I'd be under a lot more pressure and have more stress. I'd probably die younger thinking I had to handle everything."

Independence and assertiveness.   Both sexes perceived men as more independent, self-sufficient, assertive, and in control of their lives. One woman said, "I'd have more 'guts.'" Two other comments from women were, "I wouldn't be taken advantage of" and "My needs would come first." A disabled female said, "I would have a harder time being handicapped because as a female, it's easier to ask for help." More evidence of the stereotype of the nonassertive female is a book first published in 1975 *The Assertive Woman* (Phelps & Austin, 2000). Can you imagine a similar book written for men? As you will learn later, both sexes can benefit from assertiveness; yet, the attention is usually on women.

Emotions.   The stereotype of men as unemotional, unfeeling, and in control came through repeatedly. Both sexes mentioned that being female meant being more sensitive, aware of feeling, and expressive. One man said, "I wouldn't have gotten spanked for crying when I was young." Women were seen as more fearful by both sexes.

Gender-Role Stereotypes and Development

If a woman has difficulty imagining any difference in her life, I ask, "Do you plan to marry?" Most say they do. "Will he take your name?" I have yet to hear a "yes." Most individuals haven't given the question much thought; after they do, this difference is apparent. Because of a desire to keep a family name alive, for professional reasons, or simply because of personal preference, women may want to keep their birth name, yet few do. In a national sample of married persons and of their married offspring, only 1.4 percent in the main group and 4.6 percent of the offspring made a nonconventional last name choice. Those who did were ones who married later in life, were better educated, were more career oriented, and held more liberal gender-role values. Additionally, the marital naming choice of the mother had a strong effect on her daughter's choice of names (Johnson & Scheuble, 1995). Whether female or male, if you were the opposite sex; Would name changing make your life different?

Name changing came up in a sociology class. Impatiently, a young man asked, "What's the big deal anyway? It's just a name." Yet, when asked, "Then would you take your wife's name?" he quickly shook his head and said a definite, "NO." Another student interjected, "Then it *is* a big deal, isn't it?" Calling the name problem for married women a clumsy mess, Lance Morrow, 1993 noted that if men were to wake up one morning and find themselves transformed into married women, most would insist on continuation of their name. Hyphenation maintains both names; however, men do not usually use a hyphenated name. Gloria Steinem (1992) comments on the path from "Mrs. John Smith" to "Mary Smith" to perhaps "Mary Jones" as becoming independent much like slaves became free and gradually assumed different names from their masters. The practice of women taking the husband's name does come from a **patriarchal** (male-dominated) marital history. The tradition is still strongly supported in actuality, although attitudes are more flexible. One can question whether the sexes are equal until couples at least seriously consider this issue.

Other differences are in the areas of finding an intimate partner and physical attractiveness. Women pay far more attention to both. Romance novel readers are predominantly women. Magazines for teenage girls have almost no articles on career success and financial independence; instead, the themes are beauty and dating. In a study, half of the fourth-grade girls said they were dieting. One girl said, "We don't expect boys to be that handsome. We take them as they are." Another added, "But boys expect girls to be perfect and beautiful. And skinny" (Kilbourne, 1995, p. 395). An observational question regarding a difference: "Have you ever seen two heterosexual females dancing together? What about heterosexual males?" We do tend to make distinctions in appropriate behavior on the basis of biology alone. A logical "why" remains a mystery.

Avenues to Prestige—Does Biological Sex Matter?

What are the leading avenues for prestige? Significant gender differences emerged for 14 out of 15 (Suitor & Carter, 1999). The main findings were:

- **Males**: Sports, grades, intelligence
- **Females**: Physical attractiveness, grades, intelligence

Turn to the personality activity in Reflections and Applications and answer the questions related to gender role. You may be surprised that your life, too, would have been different.

Thinking about how one's life would be different reveals a great deal about perceptions and the limitations created by stereotypes. A **stereotype** is a preconceived idea or belief, often a generalization, about an identifiable group. Stereotypical expectations and behaviors related to being female or male have influenced your life and continue to do so. Some of these are so subtle that they go unnoticed and yet have an impact.

Studies of male-female differences have been numerous in the last 30 years. A classic one (Maccoby & Jacklin, 1974) addressed both actual and perceived differences and encouraged researchers to explore gender, an aspect of self that had been virtually ignored. Gender-role development is covered in most introductory psychology and sociology courses and is frequently offered as a separate course in colleges and universities. **Gender** refers to the meanings that societies and individuals attach to being female and male. Even though popular and research-based usage suggests that gender and sex are synonyms, social scientists separate the two and define **sex** as the biological division of humanity. **Gender identity** is an individual's emotional and intellectual awareness of being either male or female, while **gender role** consists of personality characteristics, attitudes, behaviors, and expectations about femininity and masculinity. Even though our images of feminine and masculine typically are physical ones, when thinking about gender, femininity and masculinity refer to personality traits and behaviors that are culturally determined. Gender is best thought of as independent of a person's biological sex (Doyle & Paludi, 1998). This is sensible because both feminine and masculine traits make up a well-adjusted personality.

Generally, explanations of gender differences focus on learning. Sociologists believe that *socialization*, the process by which individuals learn their culture, is instrumental. See "Socialization and Sex Differences" regarding two recent versions of the socialization explanation. Psychologists also credit the environment as a source of learning through observation and conditioning. Sandra Bem (1993), in explaining gender-schema theory, says that we view the world through "the lenses of gender" and develop cultural female or male scripts. As an example, in a study of professional men, Hispanics had significantly higher masculinity scores than non-Hispanics which coincides with the Mexican and Latin American value on self-confidence, courage, and masculinity or what it means to be macho. Interestingly, the Hispanic males had self-acceptance scores that were significantly lower than other males (Long & Martinez, 1997).

Encouragement and discouragement regarding emotional behaviors and the tasks/activities of children play an important role in gender-role development. One student said her brother's only household task was to take out garbage. "My mother even cleaned his room, and now his wife does it!" Humorous or pathetic? Clearly, parental influence is of utmost importance. A recent study found that girls devote more time to household tasks while high school males spend more time on extracurricular and leisure activities. Girls work longer hours in both unpaid and paid labor (Gager, Cooney, & Call, 1999). The field of cognitive psychology emphasizes thoughts and processing of information. Young children begin to make distinctions between what is masculine and feminine and then act upon these distinctions. Years ago, I taught in a preschool language-development program and knew little about gender roles. One of the activities involved categorizing toys into a boys' and girls' pile. Almost every child by the age of 3 could do so without hesitation. This grouping carried over into their actual activities. Seldom did a little boy venture into the play kitchen, and then it was usually to ask what was for dinner! Have things changed? Certainly children are being exposed to a wider variety of toys and activities today. Yet notice how toys are categorized and even how greeting cards are displayed in stores. Gender stereotypes are reinforced in a variety of ways.

Socialization and Sex Differences . . . Two Newer Versions

Why is he less emotionally supportive than she? Could it be?

- *Different cultures account:* Because of socialization, women and men end up in two different emotional worlds or cultures. He may not offer emotional support in the same way; however, he and his male friends are satisfied and feel "comforted."
- *Skill specialization account:* Women and men share one culture. Because of differences in socialization, females develop emotional support skills. He is lacking in skills that lead to emotional support. (Kunkel & Burleson, 1999)

Any difference between females and males is more pronounced if children are raised stereotypically. For example, consider two young children with skinned knees. Both begin to cry. Terri is hugged and consoled, while Terry is scolded for not being brave. Learning theory emphasizes rewards, punishments, encouragements, and discouragements humans receive. I once asked a young man in class what his parents' reactions would have been if he had come home and announced that he was going to try out for cheerleading. "Mom would have been embarrassed and disappointed; Dad would have killed me!" was his honest reply.

The Way It Was

Which of these norms described by a 50-year-old still exist?

- For school dances, the girls made the decorations while the boys got on the ladders to put them up.
- At the dance, the boys were expected to risk rejection when they requested a dance while the girls waited and tried to look appealing, yet uninterested.
- At church events, only women worked in the kitchen.

Controversy exists as to the influence of biology on gender. Studies of cognitive skills yield certain "on average" differences between females and males that do not point to a smarter sex or to the fact that such contrasts are permanent (Halpern & Crothers, 1997). As in all of human behavior, biology has a role. Gender behaviors are undoubtedly the result of an interplay between nature and nurture. Important to keep in mind is that studies indicate only generalities and do not take into account the variations within large groups of males and females. Differences resulting from social and cultural expectations tend to fade if individuals aren't bound by stereotypic gender roles and, in fact, there are more similarities between men and women than there are differences. No matter how gender role developed, your personality, behavior, and aspirations have been influenced by it. Of value now is to become aware of your thoughts about your own gender role and that of the opposite sex. How have perceptions influenced expectations of yourself and your behaviors? How do they affect your relationships? Are you stereotypic or not?

Disadvantages of Stereotypic Gender Roles

Conforming to gender-role stereotypes has several disadvantages. Both men and women suffer from a rigid perception of roles. As evidenced by the earlier student responses, men are generally regarded in a more positive light by both sexes. Thus, many women may behave like the weaker sex and feel inferior. When asked what sex they would prefer if they could have only one child, 42 percent of Americans said a boy compared to 27 percent who indicated a girl. This preference for boys has not changed much over a 60-year period and is even stronger than it was in 1997 (Simmons, 2000). Surveys taken by my students include reasons for a sex preference that follow stereotypic thinking. "I want a girl because they're so cute and cuddly" compared to a boy preference because "He would carry on the family name and be a protector to his siblings." The book *Reviving Ophelia* (Pipher, 1994) is an excellent wake-up call regarding adolescent females and our "girl-poisoning culture."

Girls today are much more oppressed. They face incredible pressures to be beautiful and sophisticated, which in junior high means using chemicals and being sexual. America today limits girls' development, truncates their wholeness and leaves many of them traumatized. (Pipher, 1994, p. 12)

Cases of wasted female talents are evident at all ages. Skills are not used because of lack of confidence or reluctance to move beyond the stereotype. A bright young female student disclosed that she had always wanted to become a physician. She was settling for a career as a medical assistant, she said, because her fiancé was in school too, and she needed to work to help pay his tuition. "He doesn't really want me to go to medical school," she reported. This reluctance to develop a self-supporting career puts women at risk during each stage of life. Only 50 percent of working women have retirement plans, and more than 80 percent of retired women are not eligible for pensions. Is it any wonder that 75 percent of the elderly poor are women? (*Women in Business*, 2000). The **feminization of poverty,** the increase in the number of women and often their children who are poor, is a tragic result of relying on someone else to take care of them, as women have traditionally done. A woman may not end up among the poor; however, hundreds of thousands of divorced women in their sixties are forced to stay in the work force because they cannot afford to retire, according to the *New York Times* (*Omaha World-Herald*, 2001).

- Women earn less than men—76 cents to the dollar.
- Women spend 11.5 years out of the work force caring for children.
- Only 30 percent of women are in jobs that earn pensions.
- Women live longer.
- Women are most of the low-income or no-income population. (Goodman, 2001).

Even when women excel, they have found it difficult to achieve top positions. In 2000, women made up only 12.5 percent of top positions in Fortune 500 companies. Ironically, bosses rated female managers higher than male managers in 16 of the 20 skills areas (Choi, 2001). A male author (Farrell, 1986) warned women: "The beauty-focused woman who depends on men to 'tow my car,' 'pick up my packages,' and 'pay for the dates' pays a high price for her dependence on men and becomes less happy the older she gets" (p. 76).

Men, too, have suffered. Pressures to achieve and to be the primary breadwinner have caused undue stress. In a tragic situation in Lincoln, Nebraska, a middle-aged man killed his family and himself. He had been depressed because of his financial difficulties and what he perceived as his inability to support his family. "Men pay dearly for the privilege of dominating" (Keen, 1991, p. 42). Depression in men often is ignored because it is perceived as unmanly; then, without treatment, it leads to extreme individual and relationship pain (Real, 1997).

Although the exact cause is unclear, men have shorter life expectancies. In the United States, a woman can expect to live about 5.7 years longer than a man (National Center for Health Statistics, 2001). Two enlightening books, *Why Women Live Longer Than Men . . . and What Men Can Learn from Them* (Crose, 1997) and *How Men Can Live As Long As Women* (Goldberg, 1993), explain reasons for this, ranging from biological theories to stereotypic behaviors. Do you know men who resist help until their symptoms or pain are acute? Women visit doctors 30 percent more often than men (Swartzlander, 1998). Stereotypic men if they view health-giving behaviors as feminine would seemingly be at higher risk. Women tend to be more in tune with their bodies, seek more professional help, engage in more preventive health measures, have less destructive health behaviors, and take less risk (Crose, 1997). More men than women get cancer; they also more often die from cancer and adapt less favorably to a cancer diagnosis (Nicholas, 2000).

Another reason for an earlier death stems from aggression. Male violence, which is frequently depicted as noble and brave, is destructive and clearly poses a threat to physical and emotional health. The common message for "real" men to be tough, physically aggressive, and violent when necessary damages psychological health (Brooks, 2001). "The blueprint for masculinity is a blueprint for self-destruction" (Farrell, 1986, p. 17).

Aside from health and mortality, men, like women, can be restricted and limited. In certain situations, they feel forced to behave not as they want to but to satisfy the stereotype. They go into unsatisfying careers and are deprived of certain activities for fear of ridicule. One man said that he was an excellent volleyball player and would have liked to have been on the high school team. "It never went beyond a secret desire. Volleyball was considered a girl's sport, and I would have been the laughingstock of the school." A good point to consider is that women who increasingly take on additional roles in their personal and professional lives have an advantage over a stereotypic male who lives only a provider role. Multiple roles allow us to be productive throughout our lives, which is conducive to sound health (Crose, 1997). In contrast, a stereotypic man is ill prepared for retirement because it denotes the end of productivity.

In addition, men generally are not raised to be nurturing and expressive, which can lead to physical and psychological problems and deprive them of close relationships with others. A stereotypic man is much less likely to be comforting, to value comforting skills, or to be emotionally supportive (Kunkel & Burleson, 1999). Men generally do not create adequate emotional intimacy when they are not in partnership with a significant other; because of this, they can suffer from lack of social support (Vandervoort, 2000). One woman shared her greatest wish as wanting to be close to her dad and to have him verbalize and show his love. "He keeps saying that he just can't show it. He doesn't know how because men aren't like that." The belief that "men aren't like that" plays itself out in repressive behaviors that can be destructive. Anger and despair that build up in men can result in both homicide and suicide. Men who cling to macho images of invulnerability, power, violence, and dominance are at risk (Crose, 1997). The typical male way of coping with stressful events appears to increase their risk for coronary heart disease (Weidner, 2000).

As long as stereotypic differences are emphasized, equality isn't possible. Being pampered and allowed to go first (a "lady's" traditional right) aren't conducive to equal rights and treatment. Similarly, viewing the sexes as extreme opposites is an enemy of equality. Because men have long been dominant, what is considered masculine is viewed as worthy. In higher prestige occupations, masculine personality attributes were found to be necessary (Cejka & Eagly, 1999). By contrast, feminine traits are devalued. For example, women who develop stereotypic masculine personality traits such as independence are praised; not so for men who reflect the softer feminine side of nurturance and warmth. This leads to a devaluation of what is considered female. Wendy wrote in a paper on gender: "As a girl, at times it was 'cool' to be a tomboy; other times we learned it was better to dress up. We could show both sides and be accepted; that was not the case for boys."

Her point that males have fewer socially approved gender-role choices is well taken. In addition, as times have changed, men have become targets of negative stereotyping and "male bashing." One young man commented, "It's considered out-of-line to put women down but really funny to degrade men." While "turning the tables" may please some, such behavior only polarizes the sexes and will not bring about gender equity. William Pollack, author and faculty member of Harvard Medical School, stated, "The stereotype of men as bad without any virtuous pieces is not right. It's time to stop arguing about which is the better half and to look for what is good in both" (Rios, 1993, p. 6).

Does it seem reasonable to continue gender stereotyping? The answer would seem to be a resounding "no". Assigning people to roles because of their sex makes no more sense than assigning them to play positions on a football team based on their shoe size (Worchel & Shebilske, 1989). Because bipolarity and stereotyping ultimately hurt everyone, what is fair and reasonable is to recognize that, psychologically, we are much more similar than dissimilar and to proclaim and live our full human potential.

Benefits of Androgyny

Androgyny, a blend of positive masculine and feminine personality traits, allows us to be free as human beings. Sandra Bem (1974) challenged the idea that a person has to be either masculine or feminine in personality traits and behaviors and suggested that strongly sex-typed individuals might be seriously limited. Her research indicated that stereotypically feminine women were limited by being less independent and assertive, while masculine men were less playful, warm, and responsive. Even though stereotypic individuals would have benefited from different behaviors, they resisted. In contrast, androgynous men and women coped more effectively with diverse situations (Bem, 1975). Androgynous (from *andro,* "male," and *gyne,* "female") behavior allows for flexibility. Responding to the demands of a situation is more practical than the restrictive behaviors of a stereotype, and valuing all positive behaviors regardless of their appropriateness for one sex or the other is advantageous to society (Doyle & Paludi, 1998).

Androgyny in early research was found to be related to a number of positive qualities and outcomes. For example, in love relationships, androgynous individuals scored higher on verbal expressions of love and nonmaterial evidence of love and were more tolerant of their loved ones' faults and more likely to express their feelings than feminine or masculine individuals (Coleman & Ganong, 1985). "It is not macho men and feminine women who make the best lovers, at least not as love is measured in this study" (p. 174). Families with one or more androgynous parents scored highest in parental warmth and support, and the researcher (Witt, 1997) maintained that parents who wish to be gender-fair and encourage the best in both their sons and daughters would benefit from an androgynous personality.

In recent years, androgyny and how it is measured have been challenged mainly because to name polar opposites as masculine and feminine may defeat androgyny's original purpose which was to promote a blend of characteristics (Hoffman & Borders, 2001). Instead, researchers are now focusing on concepts of **instrumentality**—traits related to competence, accomplishment, and self-sufficiency—and **expressiveness**—traits associated with warmth, nurturance, and communication. A cross-cultural study conducted in Singapore supported the value of both instrumentality and expressiveness in human beings (Ward, 2000). Another demonstrated that the use of qualities associated with both reported more positive outcomes (Stake, 2000).

A female student described her own path to androgyny.

> Self-doubt came from years of my mother's coaching: "Stephanie, get a job in a hospital so you can marry a doctor or Stephanie, become a stewardess so you can find a pilot to marry, or Stephanie, put on your makeup because your looks are all that count." My response today: Well, Mom, I'm going to be the doctor or the pilot. I'm not going to watch others achieve while I sit on the sidelines and put on makeup!

Good news for androgyny is a study in which 60 percent of the males and 63 percent of the females identified with nontraditional gender roles (Dawson, Threat, & Huba, 1996). To make positive changes, a person needs to realize how stereotypic or androgynous she or he is. Check yourself by responding to the personality questions in Reflections and Applications. "We are all pioneers in this era of loosening and changing gender definitions to fit human needs rather than to reinforce masculine and feminine stereotypes. It is both an exciting and a threatening time" (Goldberg, 1979, p. 275).

BECOMING ASSERTIVE

Because nobody is born assertive, we all share the challenge of developing a learned set of behaviors. **Assertiveness** includes maintaining one's legitimate rights, choosing for self, and expressing genuine thoughts and feelings in nonthreatening ways. Assertive behavior promotes equality, and people can exercise their personal rights without denying the rights of others (Alberti & Emmons, 1995). In contrast, **nonassertive** or **passive behaviors** allow others to be in control and always choose. Essentially one denies the self. Also opposite of assertive are **aggressive behaviors** where a person tries to control and choose for others. An aggressor enhances the self at another's expense.

How does one develop assertiveness? You can begin with attention to body language. Do you sit, stand, and walk with assurance? The way that you listen and speak indicates a great deal about your level of assertiveness. You will learn communication skills in later chapters of this book. Deciding that saying no is healthy is a primary step. Other cognitive techniques are also helpful. Ask yourself, "What's the worst thing that will happen if I say no? How does that compare to what happens to me when I say yes and resent it?" Then continue to think, "What if the person is angry with me because I say no? How bad will that be?" Keep telling yourself that you have the right to say no. Once you have decided to learn to say no, behavioral techniques are useful. Practice how you will say it. Of course, you can just say the two-letter word, but most people feel more comfortable with other kinds of statements, such as these.

- I have decided not to take on any more obligations.
- I would like to say yes; however, this time I'm not going to.
- I want to spend more time with my family, so I'm not going to get involved with any more outside activities right now.
- I've been doing some time management work and prioritizing, and right now other things are more important to me.
- Thanks for asking; however, I'm not going to participate now.
- Believe it or not, I'm really going to say no.

Note that you aren't using the word "can't," which is usually inaccurate. Making up an excuse is generally not as convincing as the truth. It's your choice as to how much to explain. You don't owe anyone a reason, although offering a statement of fact can make saying no easier. "I haven't felt well lately, and I'm not taking on any additional responsibilities" is brief and clear. By speaking the truth—saying that you don't want to or you won't—you are being assertive. A primary key to assertiveness is the use of "I" statements. Do you see how each way of saying no clearly speaks for itself and is not hostile or aggressive? Effective assertiveness is usually courteous, kind, and gentle. At times saying no can be the greatest act of love (Buscaglia, 1992).

You can decide to give an indefinite or a limited no. Limited means that you are saying no now and might reconsider in the future. "I don't want to have any responsibility in the fall fund-raiser; however, I may help out next spring." If possible, anticipate the other person's response. You probably know some people who will accept your reason without argument. On the other hand, you may have relationships with people who have a hard time accepting no for an answer. With this latter group, you are wise to fortify yourself. One idea is to acknowledge their persuasive abilities and still be firm. "I know you're a hard person to say no to, yet I'm going to do it this time."

Check your own assertive behavior by responding on the personality activity in Reflections and Applications. Assertiveness may not be one of your

---

Reflect

- How would your life be different if you had been born the opposite sex?
- What is the first stereotype that comes to your mind for females? Males? Come up with an example of a female and a male who don't fit these stereotypes.
- Do you posses any andrognynous behaviors? If yes, what are these?
- Are you generally aggressive, nonassertive, or assertive? In what way?

Apply

- Observe examples of stereotypic and nonstereotypic gender-role behaviors.
- Ask some engaged couples if they have discussed name changing after marriage. Whether they have or haven't, ask what they plan to do in this regard.
- Behave assertively in a personal or professional situation.

needed changes, although professionals agree that because no one is born as-sertive, almost everyone can benefit from skills training. Whatever you desire, within reasonable parameters, can be accomplished. Understanding what you are all about, how you developed to this point, and what you can do to improve can turn a desire into reality. The choice is yours!

LOOKING BACK

- The core of self is your personality, the unique combination of qualities and behaviors that only you possess.
- Personality is influenced by both heredity and environment.
- Major theories in both psychology and sociology explain personality development.
- Erik Erikson linked personality to social development and identified eight psychosocial stages.
- Challenges to personality development are possible for a number of rea-sons that include being a racial/ethnic minority or an adopted child. Especially challenging because of heterosexism is to forge one's identity as a gay male or lesbian.
- Personality over a life span is marked by both consistency and variation.
- The TA framework can help to understand yourself, others, and your in-teractions. Three ego states compose the personality. The four life posi-tions are perspectives on life, with the preferred I'm OK, you're OK seen as a healthy orientation. A script is a personal design of life. Strokes are positive or negative, verbal or nonverbal behaviors. Types of strokes in-fluence one's script and life position.
- The MBTI can be used to understand personality by identifying prefer-ences in four areas. One deals with extraversion and introversion, which are important in social interaction. The other areas are related to gather-ing information, making decisions, and dealing with the world. The four combine to form a personality type.
- A perception of your gender role and how you view the opposite sex are valuable. Masculinity and femininity are learned as part of one's culture. One's gender role influences personality, behavior, and expectations. Stereotypic behaviors are disadvantageous for both sexes.
- Androgyny, a blend of positive feminine and masculine traits and be-haviors, has positive effects. Instrumentality and expressiveness are es-pecially useful to well-adjusted human beings.
- Assertiveness is a set of learned behaviors that help people maintain their legitimate rights and express thoughts and feelings in nonthreaten-ing ways. Being assertive can improve self and relationships.

3

Exploring Values and Making Wise Choices

LOOKING AHEAD

After completing this chapter, you will be able to

- Define values and list sources.
- Describe how the ego states can be involved in values.
- Explain why it is wise to evaluate your own values.
- Identify and give examples of the methods and influences in receiving and learning values as described in values programming analysis.
- Explain the decade theory of values development and relate it to at least two decades.
- Describe and give examples of reasons for a change in adult values.
- Evaluate your values and recognize healthy values criteria.
- Define morals and discuss Kohlberg's theory of moral development.
- Name and describe two ways of transmitting values and tell why they are not recommended.
- Discuss recommended ways to impart values.
- Develop an effective way to make decisions.
- Discuss reasons for ridding oneself of poor health habits and engaging in safe, sound practices.
- Make a commitment to choose wisely in terms of health.
- Define goals, explain their importance, and relate the three ego states to goals.
- Ask questions to check the likelihood of achieving a goal.
- Achieve goals by using goal-completion criteria.
- Explain and use effective time management strategies.

All values, when pushed too far, become demonic and destructive. Beliefs not examined, as the life not examined, are hardly worth having. Values held thoughtlessly are without substance.

—Charles Stephen

Would you lie to another person?
Would you withhold hurtful information from a loved one?
How much time do you spend with family members?
Do you want high grades?
If a cashier gave you too much change, would you say anything?
How often do you do favors for friends?
Would you break a law?
Have you exceeded the speed limit?
If under age, would you drink alcohol? (Note that the last two are lawbreaking behaviors!)

Your answers to these questions reflect **values**, which are qualities, conditions, and standards that are desirable, worthy, and important. Values are directly related to the kind of person you are and will be, as well as to your goals and aspirations, beliefs, behaviors, and the quality of your relationships. Even though choices, decisions, and courses of action are based on them, rarely are values examined. You may know your values. Do you also know how they came to be and how they may change? Are your behaviors in harmony with what you value? Do you realize the impact that values and relationships have on each other? This chapter will offer insight and suggest ways to clarify your values and to achieve wellness and success.

WHERE DO VALUES ORIGINATE?

You and I were not born with a set of values. They were given to us; we learned what was important. Remember "parent" messages from transactional analysis? Most values originate as verbal or nonverbal messages from others. Families play a dominant role, and other agents of socialization and institutions in society such as peers, schools, religion, government, and the media contribute. We learn the values of our culture through socialization. Parents' values determine both the outcomes they want for their children and their parenting behaviors. Your values will affect your parenting behaviors just as your parents' values influenced how you were raised and what kind of person you are today. Obviously, parental attitudes and values reflect the culture.

Values vary from one culture to another and are fascinating to explore. Obviously, in a diverse world, individuals benefit from understanding the values of other cultures. For example, in China and other Far East societies, what is known as "face" is of high value. This refers to an individual's reputation, self-respect, and family honor. In order to increase "face," a person is patient, gracious, and generous. Embarrassment causes a loss of "face" while respect adds to it. In the culture of most Latin American countries, personal relationships and mutual trust are highly valued and are important to develop before business dealings are completed (Axtell, Briggs, Corcoran, & Lamb, 1997). Are you aware of other cultural values?

Institutions within a society are other sources of values. Although some people oppose formal instruction regarding values in the classroom, the education system is influential. Even if no values development programs exist, teachers, counselors, and coaches do impart values. If you were brought up in a home where religion was valued, your beliefs and values were molded by its tenets. A societal function of religion is to convey values. Another powerful source of values is the media. Messages from television programs and advertisements bombard us. An example is a value on youth. Is it any wonder that, unlike other societies, American society devalues aging? In addition, your experiences have influenced your values and will continue to do so. For example, if you frequently seek and receive the support of friends, you likely place a high premium on friendship. If you have been hurt by dishonesty, you probably value honesty.

After looking at "TA Revisited," think of some times in your life when your behavior did not reflect the values in your parent ego state. For Julio, religion was

TA Revisited

"Parent" messages did and continue to tell you what is of value. For example, "A dollar saved is a dollar earned," "Take your vitamins," "Get good grades," and "Work hard and play later" are value-laden messages. Nonverbal messages also were and are influential. Did your parents always buckle their seat belts? Did they attend church? Were your friends accepting of others who were different? What messages regarding values do you receive from the media?

"Child" can motivate you to act according to your values. For example, the value you place on friendship is usually expressed emotionally from your "child." It can also tempt you to act against your values. The passionate "child" in each person can put sexual morals to the test. "Child" also feels guilt when values are not acted upon and pride when they are.

"Adult" plays an essential role by questioning values embedded in the "parent," looking at alternatives, and making choices based on your own thinking process. "Adult" can choose to retain, modify, or reject a value.

an important value as it had been for his parents and other influential people in his life. One week he was exhausted from a full schedule of work and classes; he overslept and missed the worship service. He could hear an inner voice admonishing him for sinning. The "parent" essentially serves as a conscience; as such, it is capable of creating guilt or in directing us in positive ways. Can you think of times when your "child" helped you act on your values? How about situations where you were greatly tempted by the wants of the "child"?

Have you used your "adult" to question and evaluate the values you have? You may be wondering why that is important. Let's assume that many of your values reflect those of your parents. Their values were possibly acquired from questionable sources and definitely developed during an earlier time in different environments and situations. Also, conflicting ideas can come from "parent" messages. "Our family values human equality and goodwill toward all people," you may have been told. Then you came home with a new friend of a different race and received a different message. Little wonder that you were confused. Because personal values direct your life and could possibly influence the next generation, taking a critical look at them is advisable.

> Maybe one of the kindest things we can do for ourselves at this moment is to take a look at everything we believe in and ask ourselves if it really fits or is it something that we were told should fit. Is it a carryover from the past that we have accepted without any critical investigation? (Satir, 1978, p. 113)

Another critical answer to "why" is that values only become your own after "adult" evaluation and processing. How do you know when this occurs? A way to check is to ask yourself, "Why do I believe or value this?" Henry, at age 75, attends mass every week without fail. One of his grandchildren asked him why he went to church even when he wasn't feeling well. He replied, "You're supposed to, so I do." Henry's value on religion and church attendance is based in his "parent." His wife, Helen, goes to church regularly, and she explains, "I value my religion and enjoy going to mass because I feel spiritually fulfilled afterward. I can miss and feel fine, too; however, I prefer to attend." Do you see the difference? Helen's is an "adult" value. When values become yours, they feel comfortable and are easier to act upon.

Any evaluative process can be challenging, and people typically experience discomfort when confronted with possible change. If your values came from someone whose support is important, any deviation is difficult. Processing, however, is in your best interest. "Neither pride nor self-esteem can be supported by the pursuit of second-hand values that do not reflect who we really are" (Branden, 1992, p. 41). New thoughts and beliefs expand your horizons and encourage you to become your own person.

HOW DO VALUES DEVELOP?

After recognizing the source of values, the next step is to look at the ways values are acquired and transmitted. Think of your life as you read this section.

Receiving and Learning Values

In the videotape "What You Are Is What You Were When," Dr. Morris E. Massey points out methods and influences at different age periods. He calls this **values programming analysis**. Think about your own life as you look at Table 3–1 and read about his ideas.

Early Years.   The first stage reveals the importance of early childhood. The earliest method of receiving values is **imprinting**. Think of making an imprint of your foot in wet sand or imprinting a design on a shirt. Imprinting of values means that young children do almost no editing and receive values as absolutes.

You may be thinking of a 2-year-old who balks at what you say. "Eat your vegetables. They're good for you," a parent says. "No," is the typical reply. "I hate vegetables." Is the child rejecting the idea? Follow that same child to the day care center and listen as he or she tells others, "You're supposed to eat your vegetables. They're good for you. My daddy says so." The message registered. Do you know people who eat everything on their plate even if they aren't hungry? Ask them why, and the response may be, "I was told to do it. I've done it all my life. You're supposed to." They're hanging onto a powerful early idea.

Little children are open to the values of people they trust and love. Think about this when you choose caregivers outside your family. Of all considerations, one of the most significant is the values these caregivers can instill. Preschool

TABLE 3-1   Receiving and Learning Values

Chronological age (approximate)	Method	Influence (who/what is most influential)
1–6	Imprinting	Family, especially parents and significant caregivers
7–12	Modeling	"Heroes" and "stars," usually those in the media
13–19	Socialization	Peers

children look upon their teachers as "supreme beings." "Teacher says—that's why" is a frequent comment. Try to recall early messages related to values. "Our first map is usually made up of the one right way" (Satir, 1978, p. 112).

Middle Years. The second stage is **modeling**. The family remains influential; however, the child is looking outward, away from home. The role models could be older children, teachers, and local sports leaders; however, the primary influence comes through the media. Because of the popularity of television, this stage may begin earlier than age 7 and overlap with the first. The principal role models are those in the movie and television industries and the sports world.

In 1982, Sydney J. Harris, a columnist, wrote about these models. He described a study in which 2,000 eighth-grade American students were asked to name their top 30 heroes—the people they most admired and would want to be like when they grew up. Their leading role model was the screen actor Burt Reynolds, followed by entertainers and actors Richard Pryor, Alan Alda, Steve Martin, Robert Redford, and the late John Belushi, who died from complications of a drug overdose. All 30 were entertainers or sports figures. Harris wrote the column because he was concerned that not one of the 30 had made a humanitarian contribution to the world (although some had been involved in worthy causes). He said, "Our heroes and heroines are not people who have done big things, but people who have Made It Big" (p. 6).

In a survey replicating Harris's, Trish Reimer, Ceil King, and I asked the same question of 114 Nebraska elementary school students in 2001. Even though they most often named athletes (32) and entertainers (15) for a total of 47, family members were listed by 41 children. Parents led the family list. Of the "stars," Sammy Sosa was named most often. The obvious and most common reason was his ability to play baseball. However, one child added: "He seems nice and respectful." Other answers given for admiring an individual are worth savoring.

- I admire my mom because she doesn't smoke or get drunk so I hope I don't when I grow up. I admire my dad because he wants to keep our family safe and cares about us.
- Jesus because he is nice and does not sin. He is a very good person who didn't like killing or violence. I am kind of like that. I hope I will be nice and go to heaven like him.
- I'd want to be myself because I don't want to act like someone else. I want to be my own person.

The survey reveals that children admire family members and others, yet continue to be enamored with "stars." As a parent, I watched my children go through idolization phases, and I recall a few of my own. My philosophy was usually, "This, too, will pass," as the various posters showed up on walls and bulletin boards. And it always did, even though the star-struck stage sometimes continued into high school days. Knowledge of "star power" can be used in positive ways. "It's a good idea to use important people to deliver messages. Parents tell us this all the time, and we don't listen," said one young girl. Can you remember some of your own idols from the preteen years? What did they represent, and how much influence did they have?

Teen Years.   "Everyone else is doing it, so I want to do it too" typifies the next step in values programming analysis. The stock answer from generations of parents is, "If everyone else jumped off a cliff (or bridge), would you do it too?" Frankly, a teenager might! Encouragement, discouragement, and modeling are included in this method called **socialization**, the same term sociologists use for the lifelong process of learning the culture.

The adolescent period is a time of searching for an identity. Feeling a part of the group is critical. A **peer group**, composed of people of similar age with whom one identifies, has great influence. In a review of research about antisocial behavior and social failure, peer affiliations during childhood appeared to be related to choices during adolescence (Henry, 2000). This period of life can be a frightening, stressful time for both teenagers and parents. The young person will likely experiment with "in-vogue" behaviors and attitudes. Cigarette and alcohol use is strongly related to peer norms, substantially more so than with parental involvement (Olds & Thombs, 2001). Not surprising, 89 percent of adult smokers began in their teens (*Health*, 1997). Perceptions of whether their peers are sexually active appears to be related to teenagers' engagement in sexual intercourse. Adolescents have a strong preference to either act like their peers or believe that their friends are like themselves (Nahom et al., 2001).

If the peer group reflects most of the parents' values, this period can be relatively easy. Usually, though, at least some parental values are challenged. Parents can make this an easier time by being understanding and flexible. If the request is reasonable, parents who say emphatically, "I don't care what anyone else does. You aren't going to, and that is that," are setting the stage for added problems. Expecting a teenager to uphold all parental values and ideas if they are opposite those of a normal peer group is asking for supreme sacrifices and potential damage to self-esteem and the sense of belonging. According to at least two experts (Steinberg & Levine, 1997), adolescents generally choose friends whose values, attitudes, tastes, and families are similar to their own. They rarely go "bad" just because of their friends. A study of adolescents showed that academic success and intelligence are their most important life concerns (Tiggemann, 2001). Also helpful is to be aware of the findings from "The State of Our Nation's Youth" (2001) survey. A majority of teenagers said that there is no pressure to look a certain way, have sex, use drugs, or drink alcohol. Instead the pressure was to get good grades. Future success was defined by 84 percent as having close family relationships, and nearly all said they could confide in a family member. Today's youth seems to be grounded and striving was the conclusion of the report.

Parents who remember the issues and problems in their own teenage years are more apt to be understanding and supportive as their children seek their own identity. Teenagers can help by understanding themselves and their parents and by being reasonable. Parental values are not necessarily wrong just because of their ownership, and rebelling just for the sake of being a rebel is neither mature nor healthy. Open communication and democratic discipline techniques (covered in later chapters) can make a major difference during this challenging time. Adolescents are more likely to make wise choices if they have parents who practice the values development techniques described later in this chapter.

Societal Influences.   According to values programming analysis, children at about the age of 10 become more aware of events, issues, and trends in the world and begin to incorporate these into their value systems; these continue to influence values throughout life. Because the model is divided into 10-year periods, think of it as a **decade theory**. Table 3–2 outlines one decade and one event. Think about issues during and since your 10-year-old decade. Do you recognize how they have affected you? Looking at various decades will also help you understand why people of other ages have dissimilar viewpoints. "Now I know why my grandmother does some of the crazy things she does!" exclaimed one student. Her grandmother might say the same about her granddaughter if she knew about the decade theory.

Comparing specific decades is interesting. For example, the major event of the 1940s was World War II. People who were 10 years old and older then are usually patriotic and, in many cases, fairly definite about right and wrong. The war demanded a united national effort, and almost all U.S. citizens had no question about the justness of their cause. Quite the opposite is true of the 1960s and 1970s, when the Vietnam conflict and the civil rights movement split the nation, followed by a sense of disillusionment resulting from the Watergate scandal and the resignation of President Richard Nixon. Thinking more in "gray" than in "black and white" and doubting the absolute rightness of a country or philosophy are more characteristic of individuals influenced by those decades.

What about 10-year-olds today? How might current issues influence their values? Because the world is figuratively at their fingertips due to mobility and the media, few happenings escape the minds of young people today. Unexplainable violence in schools and elsewhere, AIDS, controversy regarding abortion, concerns of minority groups, and equal rights are some that will probably have effects. Undoubtedly, the most influential event will be the horrific terrorist attacks on the World Trade Center and the Pentagon and the incomprehensible loss of lives that occurred on September 11, 2001. The graphic displays of this international tragedy impacted all of us. Truly, our lives are forever changed. Pause and reflect on the different possibilities in regard to values. One can be pessimistic or view this and other challenges as opportunities.

Young people have several alternatives. They can "cop out" and value only their self-interests, or they can decide to take action and do what they can to solve widespread problems. Being actively involved in society is as important today as it ever was. However, a 1998 national survey of first-year college students by UCLA found that just 27 percent believe that keeping up with political affairs is important, a decrease from 58 percent in 1968. One speculation is that students have a feeling of

TABLE 3-2   Decade Theory of Values Development

Birth decade	10-year-old decade	Significant events	Influence on values
1920s	1930s	The Great Depression	Conservation of money and resources
			Strong work ethic
			Government seen as an aid to the citizens

powerlessness. In comparing the 1960s to the 1990s, another possibility is that people get involved in politics when things are bad, not during times of relative contentment (Greene, 1998). Interestingly, an Internet search via Google of college students and apathy came up with 23,800 "hits." Perhaps, the threats posed by terrorism will activate many people. Regardless, a wise course for each of us is to value the moment because the future is unsure and then to take action to make the tomorrows better.

Altering Your Values

After adolescence, values are established from imprinting, modeling, socialization, and societal influences. Other general influences explained in this section could also have been involved. Values could remain similar throughout the rest of life, yet most people's will change. Let's explore the general influences on values that are most likely to occur from young adulthood through old age.

Major Life Change. Just as stress is related to a major life event and change, so is an analysis and possible alteration of values. At age 23, Joe valued health, sports, and bodybuilding. One summer day he was riding his motorcycle and had a terrible accident. He was left paralyzed from the waist down and confined to a wheelchair. After soul-searching and values analysis, he altered his emphasis on sports and bodybuilding so that he could participate, yet in a different way. Other values became important, and he began to help individuals with special needs.

An accident or injury is one type of major change. Others are the birth of a child, loss of a job, divorce, or death of a loved one—any of the crises that will be discussed in later chapters. A change can motivate you to develop worthier values. Melanie was an adolescent, unmarried mother. She candidly talked about her values.

> At 16 I valued friends and good times. I partied a lot and didn't care much about school or working, I just wanted to have fun. After Jason was born, I changed my whole way of thinking, Because of him, I realized how important it is to take care of my health, get some education, and learn to support us. I'm a new person, and I like who I am.

Mental Unrest. Exposure to new ideas can cause you to think more deeply about your beliefs. You may question them and experience mental unrest. This can happen within a formal learning experience. Tony took a sociology class and became aware of different ideas regarding equal rights. Kelly began to question her strict religious upbringing after studying philosophy and religion in college. In informal ways such as reading a book, talking with people who have different beliefs, traveling, and watching television you glean new information. Having a closed mind to new ideas will make learning less likely; however, most people are open enough to at least wonder.

Changes in Wants. Values will probably be altered as you and what you desire changes. If you just want to have fun during a particular phase of life, your values will be different from those you need to succeed in a career. Values can vary as statuses and roles change. A business owner is apt to adjust values and think differently than he or she did as an employee. New parents almost always alter some values. Mike told his classmates, "If you don't believe that having kids won't change

Figure 3-1   Having a baby is likely to change one's values

your values, just wait. Their presence just forces you to change." Commonly, one value will take precedence over another. Sara had always valued her social life, then she was diagnosed with an autoimmune disease that required long-term rest. She put her own health ahead of her desire to go out with friends. A change in priority doesn't mean a rejection of a value; the emphasis has just shifted.

Evaluating Your Values

The likelihood that you will experience a major change, mental unrest, and different wants during a lifetime is extremely high. For this reason, flexibility is necessary. Having a strong value system does not mean upholding the same ones throughout a lifetime. Instead, it includes the ability to process and evaluate. Well-adjusted people understand that they may discard, modify, add, and change values themselves or their ranking.

Sherri, who had valued marriage, traditional suburban life, and a lovely home, found her life dramatically changed when her husband divorced her. She was no longer married, was no longer a part of traditional, couple-oriented suburban life, and was unable to make house payments. Flexibility allowed her to change her priorities and to develop new values in order to survive. Independence, education, and career emerged as high values.

Lack of flexibility has definite drawbacks. Inflexible values tend to make individuals judgmental.

> The more we adhere to any system, the more this belonging will be limited to others who believe as we do. We even see our children as "bad" if they don't follow "our" way (Glasser, 1984, p. 85).

Close relationships have been threatened and even destroyed by people's unwillingness to adjust their thinking. Inflexibility and certainty can also stifle learning.

> When we think we are absolutely right, we stop seeking new information. To be right is to be certain, and to be certain stops us from being curious. Curiosity and wonder are at the heart of all learning. The feeling of absolute certainty and righteousness causes us to stop seeking and to stop learning. (Bradshaw, 1988, p. 8).

Practicing flexibility rather than rigidity seems justified.

If you were asked to assess a value, what criteria would you use? Even though values are not necessarily positive or negative, it's helpful to evaluate yours as healthy or unhealthy (McKay & Fanning, 2000). What's the difference?

Healthy Values Are. . .

- Owned
- Realistic
- Behaviors that promote positive outcomes
- Life-enhancing

After you have read through the words that describe healthy values, think deeply about each one. Do you own your own values or are you living by someone else's? Ask yourself why you chose the career field you did. Why did you marry, or why will you marry? Usually, until a careful analysis is done, people are unaware of how their behavior might be based on someone else's "should." This is the reason that processing values through your "adult" is so essential.

Are your values in touch with reality and apt to foster positive outcomes? One student wrote on an assignment, "I don't believe in divorce, no matter what." I posed some questions to her such as, "Even if you were being abused? Even if your children were being abused? Even if the person became a despicable individual who was involved in all kinds of unethical behavior?" She thought and then replied, "I hadn't even considered those possibilities, and in those cases, I certainly wouldn't hold fast to that value." She was able to realistically look at situations and understand that her value could result in negative outcomes. Then flexibility allowed her to change her mind.

If a value does not enhance life, it likely restricts it. An example would be to value another person in such a way that you allow him or her to rule your life. "I won't go back to school because he wants me to stay home" is life-restricting. Conversely, life-enhancing values encourage you to do what is nourishing.

Freedom is destroyed by restrictive, rigid values. Adopting a broad-based approach to values is advisable. This means that instead of having set answers to all moral dilemmas, an evaluative process is used. Ask questions such as, "Are the behaviors I choose likely to harm others or myself? What are the probable consequences? If pain is a possible side effect, does the outcome warrant it?" Critical thinking about values is healthy.

Also helpful is to consider each dilemma on its own merits. A value on human life may mean that capital punishment is always wrong, but could there be justifiable cases? If you believe that life begins at conception, a value on human life translates into an antiabortion belief. Could any situation warrant an abortion? For example, a news story told of a 12-year-old girl who had been raped and became pregnant. Carrying the baby meant a 50–50 chance of death for both her and the fetus. The girl's mother, because of her religious views, forbade an abortion— an absolute stance. What do you think about this particular situation? "Although it takes more effort you will be more in control of your life if you evaluate each situation at the time you encounter it rather than rely too much on any value system" (Glasser, 1984, p. 85).

Values are personal, and you may be more comfortable with absolutes. If so, at least consider options and the healthy values criteria that have been recommended. Being flexible allows you to accept different ways of thinking and to develop respectful relationships with people who are different from you.

HOW DO MORALS DEVELOP?

Morals are related to rightness or wrongness and are more specific than values. Because values and morals essentially guide your life, you can benefit from knowing how they evolved. **Moral judgment,** or a sense of right and wrong, was traced by Kohlberg (1963), who presented short stories with moral dilemmas to individuals and then asked them what they thought the characters should do. Kohlberg was more interested in the reasoning behind the answers. One of his classic stories follows.

> In Europe, a woman was near death from a special kind of cancer. There was one drug that the doctors thought might save her. It was a form of radium that a druggist in the same town had recently discovered. The drug was expensive to make, but the druggist was charging ten times what the drug cost him to make. The sick woman's husband, Heinz, went to everyone he knew to borrow money, but he could only get together $1,000, which is half of what it cost. He told the druggist that his wife was dying, and asked him to sell it cheaper or let him pay later. But the druggist said, "No, I discovered the drug, and I am going to make money from it." So Heinz got desperate and broke into the man's store to steal the drug for his wife.

Consider how you would respond to questions such as, "Was Heinz justified in stealing the drug? Why?" "Should the druggist have been charging that much? Why?" "Which is worse—to steal or to let a loved one die? Why?" The *why* is the key.

The results led Kohlberg to identify three levels of moral development, each composed of two stages. Your ability to process, evaluate, and possibly modify your values is related to the level at which you make moral judgments. The first possibility is *preconventional,* when rewards and punishments are most impressive. This is obvious in ideas expressed by young children: "I won't take her toy because the teacher will send me to the 'time-out' area." *Conventional* is the second level; individuals at this level conform because of social disapproval from peers or authorities. "I'll take her book because the other kids think it's funny to tease her." Many adults are still at the conventional level. "I laughed at the racist joke because I wanted to be a part of the group" is an example of this kind of thinking. Authority is respected, and a law is a law and should be obeyed. Research shows that most people never progress beyond the conventional level (Conger & Peterson, 1984). Using the healthy values criteria discussed in the last section requires a person to move beyond this level.

The highest level, *postconventional,* is based on moral principles. Those at the first stage of this level follow democratic laws. They generally behave according to societal rules, yet see the arbitrary nature of laws. If they see a law as unfair, they usually work to change it. At the highest stage, which few people reach, individual principles take precedence; universal ethical ideas can supersede a law. Examples are Mahatma Gandhi and Martin Luther King, Jr. who followed their own consciences and defied laws that they considered unjust.

Even though Kohlberg's theory is widely accepted, it has critics. Noting that his study participants were all men, Gilligan (1982) broadened the concept of morality to include meeting the needs of others and caring—behaviors more associated with females. Another limitation to Kohlberg's study is that the participants only represented one culture (Baron, 1998). A strong value in other cultures is obedience to authority. Moving beyond this way of thinking is extremely challenging and Kohlberg's theory would not necessarily be a fair way to assess moral development in those cases. Nevertheless, think about yourself in relation to these levels and, especially, ponder the "why" of your moral decisions.

HOW ARE VALUES TRANSMITTED?

While it's interesting to examine how values and morals are received, it is just as valuable to examine transmission of values. As you read this section, ask yourself:

- How did your family convey its values?
- If you are or become a parent, how will you transmit yours?

Traditionally, adults have used two distinctly different ways of imparting values, neither of which is recommended. **Moralizing** is the direct, although sometimes subtle, transmission of the adults' values to young people (Simon, Howe, & Kirschenbaum, 1991). Based on the assumption that the adult has experienced life and knows best, moralizing is telling others to believe and value what the moralizer believes and values. Delivery of values comes from the parent ego state. The controlling "parent" states definitely what is of value and how life should be lived. "A well-paying job is essential, so go out and find one" is the command. The nurturing "parent" delivers essentially the same message in a different manner: "Now, honey, you know how nice it is to live comfortably, so you really need to find a well-paying job." Indirect messages are also possible: "I'll bet John's parents are really proud of him. He got a well-paying job last week."

Moralizing is common. Parents, teachers, members of the clergy, and administrators are among those who use direct, commanding statements to tell others what is important. Even friends can moralize: "Jessica, you should break up with Jacob. He isn't going to amount to anything." As common as it is, moralizing is

Figure 3-2

things." In contrast, I enjoyed what a newly divorced student wrote, "I think that some people believe I need to rely on my family because they are all I have now. I have news for them—I have ME, and that sounds good!"

The opposite means of transmitting values is by a **laissez-faire** method, which means hands off (Simon, Howe, & Krischenbaum, 1991). The young person is left to discover values without leadership or guidance. "Go out and find your own way" is the message. For what reasons isn't this recommended? Simply put, children need guidance. Young people do not want adults to run their lives; what most youth seek is help. Children who learn from a values vacuum float at the mercy of circumstances and situations (Eyre & Eyre, 1993).

Recommendations for Values Development

What does work? Most agree that a warm, stable, and loving family setting is most conducive to values development and controls (Megargee, 1997). The following suggestions are likely to lead to worthy values and specific behaviors that enable an individual to make life-enhancing decisions.

Set a Positive Example. The message of "Do as I say, not as I do" is not likely to produce desired results. People are more influenced by behavior than words. Modeling the values you want to see is extremely important. This means that if you want someone to value health, first examine your own health habits. If education is of value, make sure you are broadening your own level of knowledge. Parents who are pursuing college degrees are sending powerful messages to their children of the values of education, hard work, and pursuit of worthy goals. Be aware that modeling can work in a negative way. A study of children showed that children's tobacco and alcohol use was associated with parental use (Jackson, Henriksen, Dickinson, & Levine, 1997). What you do definitely makes a difference.

Encourage the Values You Think are Important.   Offer praise when someone demonstrates one of your values. **Positive reinforcement**, presenting a pleasant stimulus that strengthens a response or behavior, is not used nearly as much as it could be. Instead of waiting to criticize when others don't measure up, give credit or praise when they do. "I'm proud of you for telling your teacher the truth," "I like it when you share your possessions," and, in the workplace, "I appreciate your loyalty to the company" are powerful motivators. Give rewards to show your approval. Even though you may simply expect others to behave morally, showing appreciation doesn't hurt and is usually reinforcing.

Teach and Guide.   Instead of teaching and guiding, moralizers tell individuals what to value—a much less effective technique. Teaching opportunities regularly present themselves. For example, watch a television show with children and then discuss situations that require moral reasoning and judgments. Ask questions and encourage them to express their opinions. "The lyrics of that song are immoral, and I won't let you listen to it," says a moralizer. A teacher or guide would ask, "What do you think about those lyrics? Do you see any potential harm from listening to them? What do they say to you? What do they say to younger children?" You can eventually express your own opinions *after* encouraging an open, free discussion. Chapter 7 presents a positive way to do so.

Giving options to younger ones and explaining why other choices are not allowed is instructive. With adolescents, rather then telling them what to do, first discuss the situation and then guide them toward understanding the values you think are important. They may persist in different ideas, yet your chances as a teacher and guide are better than as a moralizer. At times you may feel compelled to try to prevent certain behaviors by children; however, do so only *after* you have been open to their opinions.

> Children need limits. They need guidelines. They need them for their security, and they need them for their survival. One can teach with respect, or one can teach with intimidation. One can speak to a child's intelligence or to his or her fear of punishment. One can offer a child reasonable choices within sane and comprehensible ground rules, or one can lay down the law (Branden, 1983, p. 136).

Allow a Person's Own Experiences to Teach.   Do you remember learning from your mistakes? Consequences of behavior are among the best teachers in the world. As difficult as it may be for a loving parent, "letting the chips fall" can lead to effective results. Michelle was slow and nonchalant about getting ready for school. After weeks of begging and nagging Michelle to be ready, her parents, who took turns driving her to school, left the house one morning at 8:00 A.M. Michelle walked to school in a rainstorm, was late, and suffered the consequences. The problem was solved because she discovered firsthand the value of punctuality. If she had not gone to school, other consequences would have taught the lesson. Most individuals are influenced by consequences.

Instill a Value of Self.   Of all the values a parent can inspire in a child, a most important one is the value placed on self. Parents don't help children by doling out false messages and treating them in ways that unwarranted self-worth develops. Instead, motivating children so that they develop healthy self-esteem is a precious gift. Already covered in Chapter 1, the value of this type of self-esteem cannot be overemphasized. Although most students acknowledge this, "self" rarely appears when they are asked to identify their five top values, whereas friends, family, and others are listed by almost everyone. You may need to remind yourself how important it is to value yourself so you can show genuine and healthy regard for others. "Self-esteem is one of the most powerful forces in the universe. Self-esteem leads to joy, to productivity, to intimacy. That's why I advocate a value system that promotes self-esteem. Self-esteem is like faith: it can move mountains!" (Burns, 1989, p. 115). Cheri, a student in her late thirties, wrote about her values:

> When I was younger, I devoted my time and energy to my family and home. I got lost somewhere in the shuffle. My insistence on working outside the home has helped me to grow. I like myself more than I did in those earlier years. My education has always been a dream, and it took a lot of courage for me to return to school. I know now that I'll always be in pursuit of knowledge. What I'm learning is helping to open my eyes to new ideas. I feel like a little bird that has just begun to stretch its wings. Everything I am learning and all the new people I am coming in contact with are the wind beneath my wings.

Valuing herself made this possible. Another student, Deborah, mentioned that she had valued others before herself for most of her life. After elevating her self-esteem, she said that she still valued her family; however, now she valued and relied on herself even more. This allowed her to "be there" for her parents and siblings, when needed, as they had been there for her.

Emphasize Universally Acceptable Values. Throughout history and in almost every society, humane values such as honesty, integrity, kindness, generosity, and love have proven their worth. Today's world cries for values of freedom, peace, and diversity. Children and adults can learn to assess their values in terms of outcomes. Does a value spawn behaviors that are beneficial both to the practitioner and to those on whom it is practiced?

Encourage Thinking for Oneself. Critical and creative thinking require a questioning mind. Parents too often stifle children's questions either because they don't want to answer or because they just don't like being questioned. Children who are fearful about questioning a parent grow into adulthood afraid to ask, which interferes with learning and the ability to make wise decisions. Often, parents react negatively when a child disagrees with their opinions. Rather than rigidity in thinking, a realization that life is full of many rights and numerous ways of thinking, not of absolute sets of right-wrong options, is beneficial. "Things are not usually all good or all bad, all right or all wrong. Life is just not that simple. The answers and solutions we seek usually lie somewhere between the opposites" (Buscaglia, 1992, p. 9).

Figure 3-3   Learning to value differences is highly desirable in a diverse society

Reflect

- Think of some "parent" messages you have received that are related to values.
- Come up with an example of how and by whom you were influenced in each of the three values programming analysis stages.
- What are some recent events, issues, and trends that will probably influence the values of young people?
- Recall a moralizing statement you have received or given.

Apply

- Look through a newspaper or newsmagazine and find an example of a story that can influence values.
- In Reflections and Applications for Chapter 3, answer questions about your own values development.
- Use one or more of the recommendations for values development with a friend or family member.
- List two or more of your values, then check each in terms of the criteria discussed in this chapter: ownership, realism, promotion of positive outcomes, and life enhancement.

LEARNING TO CHOOSE WISELY

Choices set the stage for decisions. **Decision making** means to select one alternative from various possible courses of thought or action. Because change is involved, decision making is usually stressful, and some people resist or have difficulty making decisions. Keep in mind that indecision, or not making a decision, is a decision. Seeking closure too early may be problematic; however, at some point, decisiveness is in order. Knowing how to make any decision has value in reducing stress and putting you in charge of your life.

Understanding your MBTI personality preferences, as covered in Chapter 2, helps to know your strengths and weaknesses in making decisions. Combining two preferences can be used to describe decision making as follows.

- Sensing-thinking (ST) focuses on verifiable facts, then makes judgments by impersonally evaluating the facts. Decisions are usually practical and matter-of-fact.
- Sensing-feeling (SF) focuses on verifiable facts, then makes decisions by weighing values and considering others. Decisions tend to be sympathetic and friendly.
- Intuition-thinking (NT) prefers a variety of possible solutions, then selects by impersonal analysis. Decisions are likely to be logical and ingenious.
- Intuition-feeling (NF) recognizes a wide range of possible solutions and decides by weighing values and considering others. Decisions are generally enthusiastic and insightful.

In some cases, you may want to call upon others who are strong in your weak area. For example, because Jessica's personality preference was "feeling," she had

Steps in decision making	What steps must be taken to yield the highest probability of successful decisions? The acronym ACTION indicates six fundamental ones:
	A ANALYZE the problem and gather data.
	C CONSIDER the alternative solutions.
	T TAKE action—select a solution.
	I IMPLEMENT the solution.
	O ONGOING EVALUATION. Conduct an ongoing evaluation of the solution: encourage feedback from employees.
	N NEED for change. After you have tried the solution, consider the need for modifications of the original decision.

Figure 3-4
From Halloran and Benton, (1987), *Applied Human Relations*, p. 372, Prentice Hall.

difficulty keeping her personal values detached from business decisions. A colleague with "thinking" strength provided logic. The preferences may annoy one another. Those with a judging preference are apt to experience stress until a decision is made therefore often decide or press for a decision fairly quickly, while perceivers enjoy keeping options open and will change their minds more easily. Those who are both intuitive and perceiving will have numerous ideas and will delay making a final choice. This can be interpreted by others as stalling or being wishy-washy.

Regardless of personality preferences, we can all benefit from learning a process in decision making. Six steps can be spelled out with the acronym ACTION (Halloran & Benton, 1987). See Figure 3–4.

Any decision has a risk factor. Most people worry about making a wrong choice. Should I take this job or wait for a better offer? Would going to a community college be better than attending a university? Consider that for most decisions, there is no absolute right and wrong. Whatever you decide will merely be a different course of action. When a mistake is made, you are wise to accept it and realize that this is necessary in any learning process. If you're not failing occasionally, you may not be taking any risks and charting new territory. View mistakes as information about what worked and what didn't and as errors that can be corrected. You won't want to make mistakes on purpose; however, do regard them as valuable insight.

TA Revisited

"Parent" is full of shoulds, shouldn'ts, do's, and don'ts and often tries to push for quick decisions.

"Child" has its wants that influence decisions and will be swayed by emotions.

"Adult" analyzes the issue, sees and considers alternatives, and decides based on reason and logic.

Decision making deserves attention and study. As with other life skills, you have probably received little formal training in how to evaluate choices and make decisions. Because we must make so many decisions in life, an essential choice is basic: Do you want to take charge of life or let life be in charge of you?

Taking Control of Your Health and Well-Being

Choosing wellness is the first step in getting rid of unhealthy behaviors and in preventing disease. Motivation comes from being informed on health issues. Then, if you truly value yourself, you can make wise choices. Ask yourself how healthy you want to be then educate yourself.

Smoking Cigarettes.   If you smoke, you inhale several potentially dangerous substances, including the most potent cancer-causing substances known as **carcinogens**. A number of substances in tobacco smoke cause cancer in human beings (Centers for Disease Control, 2001a). The high risks have been apparent for years, and the future for a smoker is bleak. Nearly 5 million children living today will die prematurely because of a decision they will eventually make—to smoke cigarettes (CDC, 2001a). Tobacco use worldwide, which causes nearly 4 million people to die in a year, is the leading preventable cause of death (Satcher, 2001).

The death rate in the United States alone is equivalent to two jumbo jets colliding in midair every day over a year's time with all passengers being killed (Rathus, 1999). Consider these research-based facts about smoking:

- Kills more people each year than AIDS, alcohol, drug abuse, car crashes, murders, suicides, and fires combined (CDC, 2001a).
- Results in more than 5 million years of potential life lost each year (CDC, 2001a).
- Causes heart disease, lung and esophageal cancer, and chronic lung disease, and leads to a high likelihood of dying of these diseases as well as emphysema, other respiratory diseases, and various types of cancer (CDC, 2001a).
- Is related to erectile dysfunction and general sexual fitness (Wuh & Fox, 2001).
- Puts babies at risk for sudden infant death syndrome (SIDS), poor lung development, asthma, and respiratory infections and increases the risk of stillbirths, premature births, low weight babies, and a higher rate of infant mortality (CDC, 2001a).

Think of 24 hours ago. During that time, there have been over 10,000 tobacco-related deaths (*Pediatrics*, 2001).
A smoker loses 11 minutes of life per cigarette (*Health*, 2000).

If health isn't that important, other reasons may be. As employers become more aware of the relationship between health and cigarette smoking, smokers may find it difficult to get jobs. Typically, smokers average more sick days. Another reason is skin aging. A student said, "I've heard it all, and nothing has jolted me to quit smoking until I heard about wrinkling. That did it!" She was referring to research which found that those who smoke have much more prominent wrinkling (Lauerman, 2001). Or perhaps a smoker will consider money. Jon figured how many dollars he would save in a year and was motivated to quit. And cigarettes aren't the total cost. Smokers spend more on cold remedies, health care, and life insurance. Tobacco addiction is a major economic handicap.

Knowing all this the obvious question is "Why do people take up smoking?" Again, look at research-based facts.

- Approximately 80 percent of adult smokers started smoking before age 18 (CDC, 2001a). Individuals at young ages are more suggestible and tend to conform.
- Many start because their peers and family members smoke (Williams & Covington, 1997).
- Smokers are significantly less knowledgeable about smoke-related diseases than ex-smokers or nonsmokers (Najem, Batuman, Smith, & Feuerman, 1997).

Obviously, after a habit is established, nicotine, the stimulant in cigarettes, creates an **addiction**—a physiological dependence (Kessler, 1995). If you have not started smoking, the obvious wise choice is to never start. If you have, are you willing to risk years of life or experience a low-quality existence? Having emphysema and depending upon an external breathing device that you may have to drag around is a pathetic state of being. Hopefully, you will place more value on health and quality of life and want to quit. How does one do this? The two current strategies are just quitting immediately or gradually or using pharmacologic agents (Mocharnuk, 2001). Medications can double your chances of quitting (CDC, 2001a). Help is readily available. One easy source is the Web site of the Centers for Disease Control (see Resources at end of chapter). The following guidelines are offered.

You Can Quit!

(Tips from the Centers for Disease Control, 2001a)

- Prepare by setting a quit date. Get rid of all cigarettes and ashtrays. Stay away from others who smoke in your presence.
- Announce your intentions and get support.
- Replace smoking with other activities such as taking a walk. Refrain from environments and activities associated with smoking.
- Get medication and use it correctly.
- Be prepared for a relapse usually within the first 3 months. If you smoke again, set a new goal and be even more determined. Keep your "eye on the prize."

Because environmental tobacco smoke (ETS) is a critical factor in health, a person might decide to quit out of love. Passive smoking, as ETS is called, kills more Americans than either auto accidents or AIDS (*The Futurist*, 1999). An alarming study concluded that environmental smoke has all the cancer-causing substances contained in tobacco smoke (Anderson et al., 2001). ETS, which is completely preventable, is a significant predictor of increased disease and ill health among children including sudden infant death syndrome (SIDS), asthma attacks, chronic ear infections, and lower respiratory tract infections (CDC, 2001a).

Environmental tobacco smoke is a serious health risk to children (Ferrence & Ashley, 2000).

Children aren't the only potential victims. Research reveals higher risks in non-smoking spouses and fellow employees for lung cancer (World Health Organization, 1998), heart disease (Wells, 1998), and atherosclerosis (Howard et al., 1998).

Nonsmokers have choices. Opting not to breathe someone else's smoke may require assertiveness; however, if you value health, the choice is clear. If you are a smoker, you can show consideration by checking with nonsmokers about smoking and then understanding and accepting their wishes. Your choice to quit smoking may well be the best health decision you will ever make. Thousands have quit; you can, too!

Drinking Alcohol   Alcohol, the most widely used and abused drug in many societies, has wreaked havoc on health and personal lives. About 14 million people in the United States are alcoholics or abuse alcohol (Brink, 2001). Alcohol abuse is frequently at the root of domestic violence, child abuse and neglect, crime, lost productivity, chemical dependency, and fatal accidents and injuries. In excess, alcohol and other drugs are "truly the crutch that cripples" (Eliot & Breo, 1984, p. 200). Alcohol is linked to violence and aggression (White, 1997) and to risky sexual behavior (Poulson et al., 1998). The innocent suffer, too. Each year babies are born with fetal alcohol syndrome (FAS) which often results in impaired intellectual functioning; difficulties in learning, memory, problem solving, and attention; and also problems related to mental health and social interactions (*Alcohol Research & Health*, 2000).

Without a doubt, alcohol affects all developmental areas of the self and overall health. Heavy drinking and alcoholism can seriously affect the functioning of the entire nervous system, especially the brain. Impairments in perception, learning, and memory are likely. Studies have found alcohol use to be associated with a heightened risk of large-bowel cancer (Baron et al., 1998), cirrhosis of the liver, and cancers of the mouth, esophagus, pharynx, larynx, and liver (Thun et al., 1997). Studies in four countries involving over 300,000 women associated alcohol consumption with breast cancer in women (Smith-Warner et al., 1998). Intensity of drinking is a higher risk factor than the number of years a woman consumes alcohol (Bowlin et al., 1997).

Sadly, choices are made at young ages. Underage drinking is described as epidemic. At least once a month, over five million high schoolers engage in **binge drinking,** defined as four consecutive drinks for a female and five for a male. Consider that those who begin to drink before age 15 are four times more likely to become alcohol dependent than those who begin after 21, and a tragic road to addiction becomes apparent. Besides the damage to health, alcohol is the major factor in the three leading causes of teen death—accidents, homicide, and suicide (Center on Addiction and Substance Abuse, 2002). Wiser choices are definitely needed.

While health definitely suffers from heavy consumption, a few benefits are associated with light to moderate use, and a panel of experts even advocate moderate alcohol consumption at meals (de Gaetano & Simini, 2001). A study found that moderate wine consumption was associated with decreased odds of developing age-related macular degeneration, a serious threat to vision (Obisesan, Hirsch, Kosoko, Carlson, & Parrott, 1998). Because alcohol is a depressant, it can also relieve stress. It's important to know how much changes the balance from benefits to risks. Based on results from the Physicians Health Study, that amount is quite small—one drink a day for men and a little less for women (Brink, 2000).

Myths and Facts about Drinking Alcohol

(Kowalksi, 2001)

Myth: I can think clearly when drinking.

Fact: Alcohol targets the brain and interferes with judgment and motor functions.

Myth: I can handle alcohol.

Fact: When drinking heavily, a person can't judge the effects of alcohol.

Myth: Drinking will make me popular.

Fact: Alcohol use often causes problems in social interactions and relationships.

Myth: I'm not an alcoholic so I don't have a problem.

Fact: Any kind of alcohol use that leads to problems is a problem.

Myth: Underage drinking is "cool."

Fact: The earlier a person starts drinking, the greater the chance of becoming an alcoholic.

Myth: Everybody drinks.

Fact: Many people do not drink at all, and most do not drink excessively.

Most researchers agree that both environmental and genetic factors are involved in susceptibility to alcoholism (Anyanwu & Watson, 1997). Regardless, of the cause, wise choices are more likely to be made by those who are informed and don't try to fool themselves into thinking that no harm can come from drinking alcohol. All of us know that irresponsible drinking has disquieting effects. A person may not be an actual alcoholic, yet still have a problem. A definition of a "problem drinker" is anyone who causes problems because of drinking. If an individual becomes extremely obnoxious, abusive, or hurtful, it's time to modify habits.

The potentially devastating effects of drinking and driving are unquestionable. Every 30 minutes, someone in the United States dies in an alcohol-related crash. Even though alcohol-related fatalities have decreased in recent years, 41.7 percent of 18-, 19-, and 20-year-old crash fatalities are still tied to alcohol use (National Highway Traffic Safety Administration, 2001). If you have not been affected by someone's death from a drunk-driving incident, you are lucky. Keep in mind that you or someone you love could be.

Kristi went home one weekend during her first quarter of college. She made an unwise decision and rode with a friend who had been drinking. For months after a serious accident, Kristi lay almost completely paralyzed in a hospital. A year later she had some mobility; however, her life has been tragically changed. In another situation, Scott came to tell me that he was quitting school. "I'm going into a treatment program to get control of my drinking," he said. "I was the drunk driver who hit and killed the pedestrian last weekend. I'll be facing criminal charges, too, and I'm really scared." Sue tearfully told a class about an accident in which a drunk driver hit a crowd of pedestrians. Her sister is now paralyzed. My nephew Steve Hanna and a friend were victims of a drunk driver whose blood-alcohol level was over .20; he was sentenced to prison, released after a number of years, and was again at fault in an alcohol-related accident.

Remember these stories and others when you consider getting behind the wheel of a car after drinking or riding with a driver who has been drinking. The best course of action is to make a conscious decision that you will not combine drinking and driving, program your mind when completely sober, and then let others know of your decision. This is important because drinking can diminish moral maturity and judgment. Do whatever works for you so you won't be responsible for injury and potential tragedy. Also, in an assertive way, refuse to allow others to drive if drinking or other drug use will impede their abilities. Alcohol use numbs thinking processes and physical abilities. Accept that it will.

Your personal support for and involvement in organizations such as Mothers Against Drunk Driving (MADD) and Students Against Drunk Driving (SADD) can show that you act on your values and will help decrease the number of tragedies. Candy Lightner started MADD in 1980 after her daughter was killed by a drunk driver. By 1985, that same driver had been arrested six times for drunk driving, and in one accident injured another young girl. Lightner says, "We've kicked a few pebbles, we'll turn a few stones, and eventually we'll start an avalanche" (Lee, 1985, p. 77). Most of the strides against drunk driving are the results of efforts by MADD and other activist groups.

For those who are addicted to alcohol or even have problems with its use, support groups such as Alcoholics Anonymous and treatment programs are available in most communities. Because individuals are unique, no one program works for all. People are advised to try a different one if there is no improvement. For many, personal counseling is necessary. The focus on alcohol is not intended to lessen the tremendous amount of damage suffered from other drugs. Learning about the long-term effects of all of them is the first step in taking control of your own use. Then, if you continue to have a problem, seek help for yourself and for all those who care about you.

Engaging in Risky Sexual Activities. Sexual behavior in today's society can pose a dire health risk. **AIDS, acquired immune deficiency syndrome**, is a fatal condition resulting from an extremely weakened immune system. First identified in 1981, it is caused by HIV, human immunodeficiency virus, that is transmitted by exposure to infected blood, semen, and vaginal secretions usually through sexual activities or the sharing of hypodermic needles and other drug paraphernalia by injection-drug users. Transmission from mother to her newborn is also possible (Jemmott & Jemmott, 1996). In 1981, fewer than 100 people in the United States had died from AIDS. Between then and the end of 2000, 448,060 deaths have been reported. About 40,000 new HIV infections occur in the United States ever year (Centers for Disease Control, 2000).

AIDS should be a household word; the good news is that 90.6 percent of students nationwide have been taught about AIDS and HIV infection (Centers for

Disease Control, 1999). This is fortunate because HIV-positive symptoms usually do not materialize for years, and teenagers would not otherwise know that they can be infected (Kassin, 1998). "It's the worst feeling to be 26 years old and hear a doctor say you have AIDS. Then I thought about all my sexual partners during the past 10 years," lamented a young man.

Accurate information is available, and anyone who values health will seek it. AIDS is not curable, but it is preventable. Recommendations are to become well informed, either abstain or practice only safe sex, and avoid multiple sexual partners. Continue to ask yourself about the value of your own life and use your mind to protect your life.

> Other than abstinence, the best way to avoid getting HIV and other sexually transmitted diseases is to use a latex condom whenever you have sexual intercourse. Remember: Whenever you have sex with someone, you're also having sex with everyone they've ever been sexually active with (Altshul, 2001).

Education about AIDS can also help to change people's attitudes and feelings about victims of the disease. Fear of HIV victims and homophobia among college students lessened over an 8-year period; those with the least knowledge had the greatest fear of victims (McCormack, 1997). Blaming a certain group of people for a disease is ridiculous. For example, decades ago polio was a serious, often fatal disease. Polio, like AIDS, was caused by a virus. Who were its victims? For the most part, they were children. Wouldn't it have been ridiculous to harbor and voice such thoughts as, "Those children caused polio," "We should get rid of all those kids, and that would take care of polio," and "They deserve what they're getting"? Yet uneducated people blame the victims of AIDS who, initially, were at one time mostly gay males and intravenous drug users. Today, AIDS is every group's potential disease.

Risks related to sexual behavior are of special concern because of the activities of increasingly numbers of younger people. Generally, teenagers lack complete, accurate information and following a developmental norm, believe that nothing bad will ever happen to them. Almost 3,000 children were followed over a 7-year period. In the 8th grade, 18 percent had engaged in sexual intercourse, in 9th grade the number increased to 30 percent, and in 10th grade, 43 percent were sexually active (Nahom et al., 2001). The societal messages in the United States are confused and confusing to young people. At the same time they are being told to abstain, they are bombarded with thousands of sexual encounters from television alone. This has resulted in what is described as *nonchalance* and the presumption that relationships will inevitably lead to sexual intercourse. Some even see sex as an entitlement; this attitude breaks down respect for self and others (Stodghill, 1998). "I don't think it's as special for many of us as it was for our parents. Too much exposure takes away any sense of mystery and most anticipation," was how an 18-year-old expressed it.

Being sexually active and not using birth control often leads to teenage pregnancy. The United States has the highest teenage pregnancy rate of all developed countries. About 1 million become pregnant each year, and 95 percent of those pregnancies are unintended (Centers for Disease Control, 2001b). The costs in terms of health and well-being are high. Hardships for young mothers include discontinued education and reduced employment opportunities leading to social service dependence, repeated child births, increased health and developmental risks to the children, and a greater likelihood that these "children of children" will repeat the cycle. In a comparison of teen mothers who kept their babies compared to those who placed them for adoption, giving up the baby resulted in more favorable outcomes (Namerow, Kalmuss, & Cushman, 1997).

On a positive note, birthrates among American teenagers has reached a 60-year low due mainly to a decline in sexual activity and improved contraceptive use (Davis-Packard, 2000). As many as two-thirds of sexually active teenagers now use condoms, three times as many as in the 1970s (Stodghill, 1998). Parents can make a difference. Warm, supportive parent-adolescent relationships are essential in the sexual well-being of teenagers (Meschke, Bartholomae, & Zentall, 2000). Could it also help to teach young people how to make responsible decisions based on healthy values? All through life, decisions about sexual behavior will be required. Choosing wisely is essential to well-being and, perhaps, a matter of life or death.

Growing Older.   Even though you can't escape growing older, you may have an unhealthy attitude about aging. Essential to your well-being is to recognize you also have many choices. Many have bought into the media messages that extol the virtues of staying young. Old age is not considered of value and, in fact, is actually looked down on and thought of as a dreary wasteland. Attacking what she calls the mystique of age, Betty Friedan (1993) contends that almost all images of older people are bleak. Consider the absurdity of such an attitude. As long as you live, you age. If you don't want to grow old, you will have to die young. If aging continues to be viewed as negative, anyone who remains alive is heading for depression and despair.

Getting rid of inaccurate stereotypes about old people would be beneficial to everyone. Common beliefs are that memory will be lost and that elderly people will become seriously impaired both physically and cognitively. One-half of Americans incorrectly believe that forgetfulness is by itself Alzheimer's disease (*Geriatrics*, 2000) when, in fact, there can be many reasons. Interestingly, when young people are asked, "Do you ever forget things?" the answer is almost always yes. Yet, it carries no meaning of losing mental capacities. Even though unfortunately, 4 million Americans suffer from Alzheimer's, only half of people over the age of 85 are affected, according to the Alzheimer's Association (2001).

A review of "normal" changes reveals a great deal of diversity among older adults with many individuals maintaining high levels of functioning into very advanced age (Carman, 1997). A final blow to the "woe-is-me" stereotype comes from a survey of 1,200 individuals 100 years of age and older. Reporting themselves to be in good to excellent health were 82 percent, 75 percent were fully mobile, and 30 percent were still doing some work. After we have broken the stereotypes of what older people cannot do, a floodgate of opportunity opens (Bortz, 1991). Having examples of positive aging helps. Can you think of any? I'm fortunate to have several, including both my parents whose mental states and physical levels of agility and energy were high until right before their deaths.

In addition to changing our picture of old age, we can realize that there are advantages to aging besides the obvious one of continuing to be alive! For most people, stress declines because of fewer daily hassles and upheavals, short-term illnesses are not common, and frustrations are less because of added realism. Many report newfound sources of pleasure. Leisure time is usually more plentiful. The successful completion of Erikson's seven preceding stages leads to an old age of fulfillment and the achievement of integrity.

Sage Advice about Growing Old

- A mind at rest is likely to remain at rest (Bortz, 1991).
- Retiring from life will cause life to retire from us (Bortz, 1991).
- The more you don't walk, the less you will be able to walk so it's important to keep moving (LeShan, 1997).
- Don't think about how old you are; think of how you are old (Bortz, 1991).

Wise choices help to bring about a high quality of life throughout the life span, so taking care of yourself while still young is important. Analysis of a 60-year-long study showed that men younger than 50 who developed good health habits fared much better physically and mentally than those who didn't (Bower, 2001). It's truly a case of use it or lose it, and this is a choice. Most of what contributes to healthy, positive aging is within a person's control. Experts identify the following as significant (Hensrud, 2001).

- Physical activity and fitness
- Mental activity such as reading, doing crossword puzzles, and playing cards
- Healthy nutrition
- Nonsmoking and no more than small amounts of alcohol
- Proper weight maintenance
- Active lifestyle with involvement in activities
- Optimistic attitude

Other identified factors in living a higher-quality life as an older person are engagement in activities with a meaningful purpose, continued curiosity and a desire to learn, a sense of humor, and close social ties. Love and intimacy tend to protect us from disease (Ornish, 1998). What is tragic is to stagnate, to pull away from activities, and to allow negative thoughts to prevail. If you continue to value yourself throughout life, you will value aging, because to age is to live.

Choices reflect how much you care about yourself and affect your present and future health. We will never be perfect; nonetheless improvement in health and well-being is worth pursuing.

Achieving Goals

In order to have a successful life, the first question is how you define success. If you describe yourself in the future as "a success," what will you be like and what will you have done? Then it's time for decisions and choices regarding what you want and how you become successful. A **goal** is a specific and measurable accomplishment to be achieved (Rouillard, 1993). Nobody doubts that in order to do much of anything, a person has to be motivated. **Motivation** is the energy or force that activates and propels an individual in the direction of activity or a particular goal.

Decades ago, three social motives were identified (Murray, 1938). **Achievement** is accomplishment or carrying through to a successful end. Achievement motivation is highly correlated with grades and grade point averages (Chiu, 1997). Even though achievement is typically related to education and career, in all endeavors, individuals vary considerably in their motivation to achieve. A coach described a female basketball player as "the most determined person I've ever worked with" and "an individual who with less ability than many has achieved more than most." Who or what has been influential in terms of your achievement motivation? The other two social motives are **affiliation**, associating or connecting with others, and **aggression**, defined as behavior designed to intimidate or harm. Obviously, connecting with others in a positive way is a motivation that is strongly encouraged and emphasized in this book. Similarly, learning to channel your aggressive tendencies into constructive actions and more desirable behaviors is a worthy goal of interpersonal relations.

An employer speaking to a career development class said, "Human beings will if they want to and won't if they don't. I want employees who are motivated to work and will be enthusiastic about it." Thinking about what motivates you is worthwhile, and you might be asked about this in a job interview. If you are one who is self-motivated by the thrill of accomplishment or the pride of achievement, you're ahead of the rest. Once a person is motivated, a major decision is in order: How do I get what I want?

Jason stifled a yawn in the career planning class. "We're going to discuss and set goals," the instructor had announced. Several other students looked bored. Jason thought, "If I've heard this once, I've heard it a thousand times. I'm only 20, and I'm already sick of goals. Isn't there a new way to approach this?" Jason would be pleased to know that there is by using the transactional analysis ego states. Did you receive messages about goals from your parents, teachers, and counselors? The idea of even having goals was originally a "parent" message: "You should have goals." "You'll never amount to anything without goals." A student put it so well: "When I got out of high school, all I knew was that I had to get 'there,' wherever 'there' was, and it didn't sound like fun." Although their importance is realized, goals may seem tedious.

Even the language underlying most goals is "parent." How many of these sound familiar? "I should lose weight." "I ought to be on time." "I must get a job." Is it surprising that so many goals are not achieved or even acted upon? Restricting them to the parent ego state makes them boring and dreadfully task-laden. Harris & Harris (1985) wisely recommend that getting the child ego state involved makes a positive difference. A first step is to allow yourself to dream; let the "child" out without restrictions from "parent" or "adult." Get rid of the "parent" language and let the wants flow! A want is fun and spontaneous. The emotion within the "child" is motivating and energizing. The "icing on the cake" is enthusiasm.

Enthusiasm is one of the most powerful engines of success. When you do a thing, do it with all your might. Put your whole soul into it. Stamp it with your own personality. Be active, be energetic, be enthusiastic and faithful, and you will accomplish your objective. Nothing great was ever achieved without enthusiasm.

—Ralph Waldo Emerson

How does the adult ego state get involved in goal achievement? Remember that the "adult" is the thinker that processes information and makes decisions. Your "adult" can look at your wants, determine how realistic they are, put them into order of importance, and then direct you in the process of achieving. It also helps in evaluating your goals and in changing them, if necessary. A goal may not be achievable, so the "adult" adapts and selects an alternative. It can also make sure that your goals enhance personal growth and well-being. What you become as you work toward a goal is of utmost importance.

Assess the Goal.   Through your "adult," you can ask specific questions based on goal criteria (Walker & Brokaw, 1998).

- *Is the goal mine and not someone else's?* Can you think of some examples of trying to live another person's goal? Do you know anyone who is in college pursuing a degree only because a parent wants it? A characteristic of self-actualization, the pinnacle of human achievement, is to make growth choices rather than fear choices. Values based on what someone else wants are usually based on fear.
- *Is the goal in accord with my values?* Because values are powerful motivators, you will find the path difficult if you don't feel in harmony with what you believe.
- *Is the goal a priority of mine?* Goal overload is suffered by people who don't recognize honest human limitations. Can you achieve high grades, work full time in order to advance in your career, be an outstanding parent, build a successful marriage, develop close friendships, and serve as an organization's leader at the same time? A study showed that compared to students who worked 10 or fewer hours a week, those who worked 10 to 20 hours had lower GPAs and attendance, and those who put in over 20 hours a week were lower in GPAs, attendance, and test accuracy (Lenarduzzi & McLaughlin, 1996). Human beings do have limits. The key is to concentrate on what you specifically want at any given time.
- *Is the goal realistic?* Sometimes the answers are obvious. Trying to lose 25 pounds in 1 week is not realistic. You could want too much or be shortchanging yourself. Look for challenges that you can manage.
- *Is the goal specific?* A common problem is to have a vague goal such as, "I want to be rich," "I want to travel," or "I want to be thin." Identify how rich you want to be, where you want to travel, and how thin you want to be. Then add a "by when" date to each.

If the answer to each of the above questions is "yes," you are ready to move ahead with enthusiasm.

Write the Goal.   Of benefit is to put your specific goal in writing and post it where you will look at it daily. Goals that are floating around in your head stand little chance of being acted upon. Katerina wrote, "I want to send out 10 résumés and cover letters during the month of October" and tacked it to a bulletin board above her desk. She also wrote notes in the form of questions and placed them in strategic spots—on the refrigerator door and inside her briefcase: "What about the résumés?" "How many résumés have you sent so far?" "RÉSUMÉS?"

> A goal shapes the plan.
> The plan sets the action.
> Action achieves a result.

Determine Specific Action Steps.   People often do not get what they want because even a realistic goal can seem overwhelming. The first way to change this is to **pinpoint**, or set goals with realistic numbers attached (Schmidt, 1976). Instead of, "I want to quit smoking by the end of January," you would say, "I want to decrease my cigarette smoking to one pack a day by January 15." One pack a day can be measured so you can see whether you succeed. Pinpointing helps you to break your goal into specific action steps with time deadlines attached to each. This practice can be thought of as making molehills out of mountains (Schmidt, 1976). The value of a deadline is that it serves as a target and a motivator. If you miss a deadline, just set another target date.

Take Action.   The keys to accomplishment, initiative and action, separate successful people from others. Doing something every day in the direction of a goal is important. If weight loss is a goal, instead of a simple, " I will lose 5 pounds by May 7," think of the extremely important question "HOW?" A first action step is to find out how much you weigh. Then note the specific action steps in "Losing Weight Step by Step."

Losing Weight Step by Step

- I will walk two miles each day starting May 1.
- I will buy a calorie counter on May 1.
- I will learn how to calculate healthy levels of fat intake by May 1.
- I will decrease my intake of calories to 1,400 and my fat intake to 40 grams or less per day beginning May 2.
- I will not skip any meals and will try to spread my intake of food throughout the day beginning May 2.
- I will eat three servings each of fresh fruits and vegetables a day beginning May 2.
- I will decrease my intake of cola to two cans a week beginning May 2.
- I will eat a dessert only once a week beginning May 2.
- I will write down everything I eat or drink beginning May 2.
- I will evaluate my weight loss program on June 15.

The chance of successfully achieving the desired weight loss with a pinpointed plan is much higher than it would be with the typical "I should lose weight" or "I'm going to try to lose weight." Being specific about each step is the difference. Instead of "I will exercise daily," write down exactly what and how many exercises you will do for how long and when. Then you will know whether you have accomplished what you intended.

Another advantage of taking small steps is that you can acknowledge each minor success, which converts into the energy to continue. The good feeling of accomplishment you get every time you complete a small task will sustain you through a lot of drudgery. What if you don't succeed with a certain action step? Check to see whether it's realistic. You can then decide whether to change it. A temporary problem with one step won't defeat you unless you let it. A worthwhile goal now is to do the activities related to getting what you want in Reflections and Applications. Consider a goal related to interpersonal skills and meaningful relationships. Happiness is created and esteem is built by striving toward worthwhile, reasonable goals with first-rate efforts.

> *Either you let your life slip away by not doing the things you want to do, or you get up and do them.*
>
> —Roger von Oech

MANAGING YOUR TIME

Too much to do in too little time is a common challenge for almost everyone. The benefit of effective time management was evident in a study of college students as it had a greater positive effect on academic stress than did leisure time activities (Misra & McKean, 2000). A fallacy in thinking is that we either don't have time or we will accomplish our tasks and goals when we have more time. The reality is that we will never have more time available than we have right now, which is 86,400 seconds each day. The key to achievement is time management.

How to Find Time

A constructive action is to keep track of exactly how your time is spent over a week. Angela's reaction was: "I was amazed at how much time I spent on the telephone with unimportant calls!" You will probably find small segments of time that can be saved and used differently. At work, can you spend a few less minutes at lunch or on break? Can you consolidate trips from one part of the building to another? Is it possible to shorten your telephone conversations? At home, can you give up a television program? How much time are you actually using for pleasure? Even though enjoyment is necessary, you may be indulging yourself more than you realize. Consider that just 30 minutes of time a day gains you about 183 hours a year, and by the time you are 70, cutting out those wasted minutes gains you over a year's time!

Even consciously increasing your rate of speed can save precious time. Rick walked to different parts of a college campus. "I doubled my walking speed, saved time, and, in the process, probably did something good for my health." In other activities, without realizing it, you may be taking longer than necessary. Becoming aware of this and then deciding that you can easily increase your speed are precious time savers.

How to Eliminate Time Wasters

Do you spend a lot of time looking for misplaced items such as papers? Over a lifetime, the average person spends an entire year searching for misplaced objects (*Lincoln Journal Star*, 1998b). We benefit by being more careful about where things are placed. Taking precious time to organize a desk and file cabinet and then making sure to put items away can increase the amount of time you have later. Your own personality may be responsible for wasting time. Each of the preferences identified on the Myers-Briggs Type Indicator (Myers, 1980) has its own potential drawback, as follows:

- *E (extraversion):* Because energy is drawn from human interactions, those with a strong extraverted preference may spend far too much time connecting with others. Also, the individual may be easily distracted by the activities of others.
- *I (introversion):* Living in an inner world and relishing introspective activities may result in time passing with no observable accomplishments.
- *S (sensing):* The strong sensor can become immersed in details and needless facts and figures and let a great deal of time go by.
- *N (intuitive):* Endless possibilities are usually in the mind of a person with a definite intuitive preference. Mulling over endless ideas can become overly time-consuming.
- *T (thinking):* Deep analysis is not usually done quickly. Strong thinkers weigh facts objectively and then apply reason to their decisions. These behaviors take time.
- *F (feeling):* Because they want to make everyone happy, people with strong feeling preferences agonize over any choice that might upset another person. Also, individuals with definite feeling preferences have a hard time saying no to requests, and doing for others does take time.
- *J (judging):* While these people are usually well organized and skilled in scheduling, they may spend more time than necessary figuring out how to accomplish a task and not enough time actually doing it.
- *P (perceiving):* "Going with the flow" has its advantages; yet a strong perceiver is typically a procrastinator. Being laid back can mean that time passes, and when a deadline is on the horizon, these people are in trouble.

Being aware of potential pitfalls that stem from personality preferences allows you to use your weaker preference when that's in your best interest. A perfectionist is an expert time waster and is bound to be frustrated because no matter how hard he or she tries and regardless of the amount of time spent, perfection is impossible.

How to Use Time Wisely

What else can be helpful? You can find practical ideas in the book *Take Back Your Time* (Jasper, 1999). Experts in time management offer the following tips.

Make Use of Self-Knowledge.   Are you more energetic in the morning, afternoon, evening, or late at night? Unless you are getting adequate rest, this answer may not be obvious. "I'm just not a morning person. Of course my going to bed at 1:00 or 2:00 A.M. may explain that!" said Jennifer laughingly. With enough rest, you will feel more energetic at all hours yet still have more productive times of day. Tackling the most difficult tasks during this time makes sense. Self-knowledge will tell you whether or not you work better according to a fairly rigid time schedule or rather you favor flexibility (Knaus, 1998). If you have several tasks which one do you undertake first? If you are energized by doing the easiest ones, that's the best choice. Conversely, you might opt to begin with the least pleasant or difficult ones in order to get them out of the way.

What physical environment works best? You may require a quiet atmosphere with few distractions or be more productive in the middle of noise and activity. What skills can you utilize to increase your productivity? For example, can you save time by typing a memo rather than handwriting it? What tasks are time-consuming for you? If you are slow at some tasks and speedier at others, you may be able to do some trading. For example, in their shared apartment, Chris cooked and Nate cleaned. Why? Each was more efficient at his designated task, and this saved time.

Use Planning and Scheduling to Your Advantage.   You may be well organized and an excellent planner. If so, you have probably already discovered what method works best, and if it's effective, you may skim this part! If you are lacking in this area, read on.

- *Decide whether to develop a schedule that is macro (bigger picture and longer span of time) or micro (more focused over a shorter time frame).* You can also create a schedule for both. For example, you may want to look at what to accomplish during a month (macro) or decide to focus on one day at a time (micro). Often, people opt to maintain a weekly schedule. You can use a planner, a simple calendar, or just make a list.
- *Categorize what you want to do.* You may have "must-do" activities such as meeting with your supervisor or paying a bill. Other activities could be classified as either moderately important or unnecessary but nice to accomplish. Once you have the lists, you can select appropriate days and times. Other ways to categorize are by type of activity, goal, or subject such as school, work, and household.
- *Plan efficiently.* If you take time to plan, you can often save both energy and time. Either the night before or early in the day, time spent looking ahead can reap benefits.
- *Be realistic and flexible.* A major problem stems from planning to accomplish too much. Having a reasonable perspective on task completion alleviates frustration and stress.
- *Reward yourself.* We typically forget to give ourselves a pat on the back for completion of tasks. Instead, we fret about what didn't get done. Emphasizing our lack of accomplishment creates the illusion that our time management efforts didn't work.

People who are effective time managers avoid a great deal of stress. In order to succeed and enjoy the process, what is most useful is to manage time in a way that works for you.

Reflect

- Think of examples of people whose wellness level is lower because of a poor health habit.
- Pretend you are a parent of a young teenager. What information related to smoking, alcohol use, and sexuality would you give?
- Using a past or present decision, check yourself using the ACTION steps in Figure 3–4.
- Think of recent situations in which better time management would have really helped. Which tips would have been useful?

Apply

- If you can "see" yourself in terms of the unwise health choices, make at least one positive change.
- Look for examples of positive aging in the media or as demonstrated in people you know.
- Set a goal to become healthier. First, ask the questions based on the criteria given in the book. Use action steps and pinpointing.

LOOKING BACK

- Values are top priorities in life—qualities, conditions, and standards that are desirable, worthy, and important. They motivate behavior and affect all aspects of life.
- Assessing what you value and why you do are important in self-understanding and achieving your own identity; this is a lifelong process.
- Values originate from external sources. The three ego states play principal roles in values development and implementation.
- The ways in which values are received can be traced by values programming analysis. Imprinting, modeling, and socialization are three methods of receiving values from different influences. Societal events and issues in various decades also affect values.
- During adulthood, values may alter because of a major life change, mental unrest, and a change in wants.
- Flexibility and ability to adjust are encouraged. Other characteristics of healthy values are ownership, realism, and life enhancement. Restrictive and absolute values can destroy individual freedom of choice
- Morals are standards reflecting right and wrong. Your morals and values develop in stages.
- Values are transmitted by parents and other authority figures. Two methods, moralizing and laissez-faire (or hands-off), are not recommended because of their ineffectiveness and potential problematic results. Several other methods are more likely to produce well-adjusted individuals capable of making healthy decisions.
- Choices are a part of a free society. Making responsible decisions is a learned process, and decision-making models are useful.

- The quality of our health is largely determined by choices. Behaviors and certain habits impair health and can be destructive.
- Increased life satisfaction comes from wise choices related to sexuality and aging.
- Goals help us to act on our decisions and get what we want in life.
- All ego states are involved in goal achievement. Our "adult" can check a goal for possibility of success and help determine the "how" of accomplishment.
- Effective time management improves many aspects of life.

RESOURCES

AIDS Hotline. Toll-free: (800) 342-AIDS (2437).
Project Inform: www.projinf.org
Al-anon Family Group Headquarters, Inc. (for friends and relatives of someone with an alcohol problem), 200 Park Avenue South, Room 814, New York, NY 10003. (800) 344-2666. www.al-anon.org

Alcoholics Anonymous. www.alcoholics-anonymous.org
American Cancer Society. Toll-free: (800) 227-2345. www.cancer.org.
American Society of Addiction Medicine. www.asam.org
Center for Substance Abuse Treatment Hotline. Toll-free: (800) 662-4357. www.samhsa.gov
Centers for Disease Control. www.cdc.gov

Mothers Against Drunk Driving. www.madd.org
National Council on Alcoholism and Drug Dependence Hotline. Toll-free: (800) 622-2255. www.ncadd.org
National Institute on Alcohol Abuse and Alcoholism. www.niaaa.nih.gov.

4

Achieving Happiness and Satisfaction

LOOKING AHEAD

After completing this chapter, you will be able to

- Describe a general concept of happiness.
- Discuss factors that contribute to happiness and recognize the role of needs satisfaction and the influence of culture.
- Explain how expectations can be obstacles to happiness and change your expectations to realistic ones.
- Tell why dependency on external sources of happiness is inadvisable.
- Identify and act on ways to create your own happiness.
- Differentiate between an excuse and a reason and realize that excuses do not promote long-term happiness.
- Reduce the uses of the words can't, couldn't, should, and shouldn't in your thinking and speaking.
- Be positive, use alternative thinking, and act on desired changes.
- Concentrate on the present and enjoy life's pleasures more.
- Appreciate more fully what is worthwhile in your life.
- Recognize the joy of giving.
- Realize that you can create happiness by developing healthy relationships.

Happiness is having a sense of self—not a feeling of being perfect but of being good enough and knowing that you are in the process of growth, of being, of achieving levels of joy. It's a wonderful contentment and acceptance of who and what you are and a knowledge that the world and life are full of wondrous adventures and possibilities.

—Leo Buscaglia

What do human beings desire and seek? You may think: health, wealth, relationships, success, and love. Each is a probable avenue to what is sought by nearly everyone and crucial to psychological well-being—happiness. We think better, perform better, feel better, and are healthier when we are happy (Maltz, 1960). In developing healthy, nourishing relationships, a happy person has definite advantages.

As valuable as happiness is, not much is done to help people learn to be happy. Don, a troubled 19-year-old student, wrote in a paper:

> I've spent a large part of my life in mental health facilities. The personnel there teach us that we have problems but don't direct us the right way. They prevent suicides, but don't give reasons to live. I think I'm finally finding it here.

Sadly, his therapy sessions and the class discussions on happiness weren't enough. Don's body was found in his apartment a few weeks after the term ended. What appeared to be a suicide is another tragic reminder that we are not doing enough to help people live happy, satisfying lives.

What is happiness? How does one become and stay happy? These important questions are easy to ask; the more significant answers are difficult. This entire book provides insight. Specifically, this chapter will provide a basic overview of the concepts of happiness and satisfaction and will suggest ways to achieve them.

WHAT IS HAPPINESS?

A starting point in any search is to know what is being sought; however, defining happiness is difficult. First, happiness, like trust and love, is intangible. It can't be seen, heard, or touched. Abstract words aren't easy to define. Another challenge comes from our own uniqueness; what is happiness for one person may not be so for another. Mary found satisfaction in creating beautiful paintings in art class. Beth was unhappy trying to achieve even average work in the same class. Each has a slightly different path to follow. For the purpose of clarity, think of **happiness** as a general sense of well-being that can range from contentment to ecstasy. Happiness is a state of mind that is not determined by one's circumstances. Adult happiness stems more from honor and integrity of the self than from simply an experience of pleasure (Pittman, 1998). Even when you aren't excited about anything special, happiness means that we will like ourselves and appreciate life.

SATISFYING ONE'S NEEDS

Related to happiness is satisfaction. Satisfaction can precede or follow happiness and almost always accompanies it. One way of looking at both is to equate them with the fulfillment of needs.

Figure 4-1   What is enjoyable for one may be boring for another.

Hierarchy of Needs

Abraham Maslow's (1968) **hierarchy of needs** has become a standard in outlining human motivation. He identified five levels of needs. The first four are *survival*, *safety*, *love* and *belongingness*, and *self-esteem*. Before a person can begin to satisfy higher needs, the basic or survival needs must be met. For example, "If you spent a long time without water in the desert, you would feel that you were the happiest person in the world if you found an oasis. Even the word *ecstasy* might not adequately describe your feelings as you took your first sip of water" (Williams & Long, 1983, p. 339). After thirst has been quenched, extreme happiness will probably not persist; then a higher need will take precedence, and you will be motivated to strive for something more.

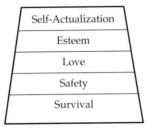

Even though the order of the levels is not exactly the same for everyone and for all conditions, satisfaction is achieved by fulfilling needs at each stage. The highest and most difficult to attain is self-actualization. Individuals do not even work at this level until the previous four stages are completed. To Maslow, self-actualization meant achieving one's full potential, fulfilling a mission, possessing fuller knowledge of and accepting one's self, and feeling unified or integrated. Self-actualizers want to become all they are capable of becoming. Maslow described self-actualization as full humanness. After satisfying their needs in the previous four levels, people who are unhappy and dissatisfied with life would benefit from asking themselves, "What can I do to become a self-actualizer?" Self-actualizing individuals are striving to achieve the following characteristics.

- Fully experiencing life in the present
- Searching for self-knowledge on an ongoing basis
- Assertively expressing feelings and thoughts
- Making growth choices instead of fear choices
- Being honest and genuine in interpersonal relationships
- Setting and achieving goals of excellence
- Becoming involved in meaningful life activities

other people is essential in satisfying two basic needs: the need to love and be loved, plus the need to feel that we are worthwhile to ourselves and to others. As a psychiatrist, Glasser felt that people had to learn how to fulfill their own needs without depriving others of the ability to fulfill theirs—what he called *responsibility*. He identified the following additional needs.

- Surviving and reproducing
- Belonging—loving, sharing, and cooperating
- Power, which includes recognition and influence
- Freedom
- Fun

Fun, Glasser believed, is an integral part of life and, as such, needs to be incorporated into our learning experiences and work. People can be happy if they spend their time and energy working on fulfilling their needs instead of choosing to be miserable. Think of your own needs. Doesn't it make sense that fulfilling your needs could lead to satisfaction? Then it's logical that happiness would be the result. Quite often, the quest for one leads to the other.

REMOVING OBSTACLES TO HAPPINESS

In the pursuit of happiness several obstacles can hinder a person. Before you can create happiness and become satisfied, eliminating the barriers is essential.

Unrealistic Expectations

Expectations often set up a roadblock. Far too many people expect happiness to just happen. "They don't see it's something they have to do. People will go to a lot of trouble to learn French or physics or how to operate a car, but they won't be bothered learning how to operate themselves" (Newman & Berkowitz, a pleasant experience. Check your own "happiness pulse" in the activity "Happiness—It's Up to Me!" in Reflections and Applications.

The realization that all people go through unhappy times can help us accept trials and tribulations and appreciate the many positives in life. In fact, unhappiness can be a forerunner to happiness. Buscaglia (1982) was a firm believer in the value of unhappiness: "Joy is a great teacher, but so is despair" (p. 74). A widow in a workshop on coping with crisis shared her personal experience with the participants and me.

> My husband died 18 months ago. I loved him, and I miss him. It was painful. However, a few months ago I realized that I felt reborn. While married, I didn't take classes or use talents outside the home. I've been doing so lately; from my loss has come happiness.

Accepting pain and allowing the reality of unhappiness to contribute to learning and growth translate into long-term happiness.

Searching Outside of Self

Where is happiness found? How can satisfaction be achieved? Too often people engage in a frantic, fruitless search for these elusive feelings, usually in the wrong places. Looking outside of ourselves is common. What are some external sources? A partial list includes material possessions, money, a certain person, a job, marriage, a baby, drugs, the weather, activities, and even a day of the week (maybe Friday?).

How often do you think that a particular person or a specific thing can make you happy? This belief carries grave risks. One of these is dependency. Relying on an external source for happiness puts control of your life outside yourself. If externals make you happy, they can also make you unhappy. And expecting happiness from things or others often means that we do little about our own happiness except just depend.

We further risk losing happiness by putting all our happiness "eggs in one basket." Reliance upon only one source is dangerous, and dependency upon a person is a mistake. Julie believed that her fiancé made her happy. She was devastated when he broke their engagement, and she believed she could never be happy again. She became severely depressed because she did not recognize other potential sources of happiness. Her pathetic situation illustrates the importance of being responsible for one's own happiness.

People may equate a certain achievement with happiness. While satisfaction and temporary happiness accompany a successful experience, the achievement is not the answer.

> We constantly tell ourselves such things as, "If I could just go back to school and acquire more knowledge—perhaps get a master's degree—then I will be happy." But are people with master's degrees or Ph.D.'s any happier than the rest of us? It is beautiful to acquire knowledge, but it is misleading to expect it to bring us peace, love, and happiness (Keyes, 1975, p. 5).

Another problem is that this "mad search" is unending. Happiness is always at the next turn or over the hill ahead. For example, those who seek money to make them happy, once one plateau is reached, will simply want more and continue the endless quest. We all are so busy chasing after external objects of one kind or another that we have no time left for enjoying our lives (Dyer, 1990). Even though finding satisfaction outside ourselves is impossible, unhappy people persist in trying to do so.

Because advertisers realize that people desire happiness and have a tendency to look for it externally, they use it to sell products. Look through any magazine or watch television commercials; an ad may show the merits of a product, but what is enticing is the subtle message that the product will bring happiness. Alcoholic beverages are sold almost exclusively with this theme. Picture the scene: A group of young people are playing volleyball on the beach with a cooler of ice-cold beer near at hand. The play is often interrupted for one guzzle after another. Each beer seems to increase their skill level—amazing! They seem ecstatic. What is the message? Drink beer and be happy. The tragic side of alcohol abuse will never be shown in the product's advertisement, and usually the taste is not the point. The sales pitch is concentrated on consumer happiness.

The same could be said for clothes, cars, and other material goods. Even, as shown in Figure 4–3, toilet-bowl cleaners have happy users! Research shows that the relationship between consumption of products and personal happiness is weak. Neither is happiness correlated with age, being female or male, nor money. Once people can afford the necessities of life, increasing levels of wealth matter little, and having money is no guarantee of happiness (Myers & Diener, 1995). Think about your ancestors. You may have or will have more spending power, yet are you happier just because of it?

Advertisements also persuade parents to buy products to make their children happy. This is potentially damaging. Because children learn from parents, the message that happiness comes from things is perpetuated. "We are raising the next generation of frustrated consumers (who may face house prices double or triple what they are today) on a steady diet of television ads. Most children have fantasies of desire long before they have fantasies of achievement" (Spezzano, 1992, p. 170). Also, by relying on a happiness-producing product to entertain, parents may deprive their children of valuable personal attention and meaningful parent-child interaction.

It is always a by-product, never a primary goal. Happiness is a butterfly—the more you chase it, the more it flies away from you and hides (Kushner, 1986, p. 23).

Although the media and general public have many ways of creating the illusion that happiness is out there "somewhere" and can be sought and bought, the belief is a fallacy. You don't become happy by pursuing happiness. What does make a difference? Factors include culture, specific aspects of self, and individual actions. Agreeing that national and cultural factors are involved, Myers & Diener (1995) named four traits of most happy people: self-esteem, a sense of personal control, optimism, and extraversion. In terms of the latter, one can speculate that extraversion helps people make social contacts that increase happiness or that being

Figure 4-3

happy encourages outgoing behaviors. Happy people also are able to filter out ideas that others are better; they pay more attention to their own internal standards of performance and don't use how well others do as a measure of success (*Health*, 1998a). Without a doubt, what people do is critical. Individuals of all ages who continue to use their brains to think and their bodies to move are happier. Older people who keep mentally active are most likely to maintain their intellectual abilities and to be generally happier and better adjusted than those who don't. Importantly, the source is not outside waiting to be discovered. *Potential happiness is inside waiting to be created.*

Reflect

- What do you need? Relate this to your degree of happiness in the past and present.
- Where would you place yourself on Maslow's hierarchy of needs?
- Think of examples of unrealistic expectations or searching outside of self for happiness.

Apply

- Ask other people what they consider to be their greatest needs. Note how similar these are to your needs.
- Check with friends and family members. What factors do they relate to their personal happiness?
- Identify some advertisements that try to sell happiness.

CREATING HAPPINESS AND WELL-BEING

Developing an inner reservoir or base of happiness is something only you can do, and from that, you can derive even more happiness from externals. Without this solid foundation, positive feelings are fleeting. Think of this reservoir as an "inner joy," which is a power source—not something that happens to you but something you create (Bloomfield, 1980).

A fine-line difference exists between someone or something making you happy and your using externals to increase a personal store of internal happiness. For example, with self-satisfaction and a general sense of well being, becoming happier because of another person, material possessions, and the like is possible. However, *they do not make you happy.* Happy people become happier from outside sources; unhappy people continue to seek in vain. How, then, can a person create this reservoir and add to it? No magic formula exists, and no one way is right for everyone. Consider the suggestions in this chapter and the rest of the book as building blocks and action steps that can empower you to create your own happiness.

Cultivate Self-Knowledge, Self-Esteem, and an Optimistic Attitude

A basic recommendation is to know yourself well. This will enable you to determine what happiness and unhappiness mean to you. Nothing is more destructive to the human spirit and to personal happiness than never quite knowing who you really are, what you really want, and what you were put here on earth to accomplish (Bloomfield, 1980). Developing self-esteem is essential. Generally, people with low self-esteem put themselves into situations that perpetuate unhappiness. "If we care little for ourselves, we are likely to end up as someone's doormat" (Buscaglia, 1992, p. 285). Years ago, "women who love too much" were described as not believing that they deserved to be happy, tending to depend on others for their sense of self-worth, and believing that they must earn the right to enjoy life. At the crux of their unhappiness was critical low self-esteem (Norwood, 1985).

Mary Hollins, an insightful young woman whose self-esteem had been low, shared some of her writing.

> You cannot live for or be another person. The joy and the happiness is to know, accept, and grow, becoming uniquely you.

Mary made a conscious effort to build her self-esteem, as can each of us. Closely related to self-esteem is an optimistic attitude, and both are characteristic of happy individuals (Myers & Diener, 1995). Unhappy feelings follow a pessimistic way of thinking. Optimism lends itself to endless choices and opportunities to make the most of and enjoy all of life.

Have Realistic Expectations

People who create happiness have a realistic self-appraisal and accept their true potential. They do not live their lives at one extreme, where they require perfection, or at the other extreme, where they allow themselves to "just get by." A student, for example, would be unrealistic to expect all top grades if she or he were not capable of them. Yet the thought "Just so I pass," if a person can do better, is self-defeating. In the first case, failure and unhappiness could result; in the latter, not giving oneself the opportunity to feel proud and satisfied isn't a way to happiness. "It is well to challenge ourselves with dreams of what we would like to be, but it is wiser to stay within the realistic realm of who we are" (Buscaglia, 1992, p. 285).

The deadly "perfectionist trap" isn't conducive to happiness. Wanting to do well is one thing; thinking that one must be perfect is another. A perfectionist is someone who thinks that anything short of perfection in performance is unacceptable (Hendlin, 1992). Often, the obsession with perfection stops people from trying and robs them of potentially rewarding activities. Hannah believed that she had to be a perfect golfer. She took lessons and became quite skilled. Then one day she "whiffed." Having missed the ball completely, she knew she wasn't going to play a flawless game. She left the course and decided that she was through with golf! She gave up hours of potential pleasure because she couldn't be perfect. Her case is an exaggerated one, yet many persons who participate in sports do not truly enjoy themselves unless they are performing almost perfectly. The happiness comes not from playing but only from superb performance. Perfectionistic people frequently avoid challenges and do not comprehend the value of failure. Perfectionists do not welcome mistakes as sources of learning, and this deprives them of helpful information. "The dream of perfection turns mistakes from warnings into sins" (McKay & Fanning, 2000, p. 135).

More common is to receive the message, "Whatever you choose to do, do your very best." Does that sound familiar? Most of us heard it from parents, school

Baseball and Perfection

A perfect batting average is 1.000 which means that a hitter always gets on base. Nobody expects this out of baseball players. In fact, an average of .400 (4 hits out of 10 times at bat) is outstanding and rare. As in baseball, it is neither possible nor wise to expect perfection in life.

personnel, coaches, and friends who had well-meant intentions. Allow yourself to challenge this belief. Think of at least five of your statuses such as student, employee, parent, son or daughter, friend. In order to do your very best, what is required of you in any one status? Time, energy, effort, commitment, and determination certainly are necessary. Is it possible, then, to do the very best you can in all statuses at the same time? Buying into the belief of having to be the best in all we do and then kicking ourselves when we do not succeed leads to unhappiness. Fully enjoying what you are achieving is impossible if you're carrying around the guilt from not performing the best in everything. Nobody has or can have unlimited power.

Ann was a full-time student, mother, wife, friend, member of her original family, and church member. She didn't seem to be satisfied with anything in her life as she kept thinking, "I must be the best student I can be, the best mother, wife, friend, family member, and church member." One day she came to an important realization. "It's not realistic for me to expect to be the best in each of these. Right now being a student is primary, and I think I can still do a better than average job as mother and wife. I'll just put the others on the 'back burner' and learn to feel okay about that." She freed herself to be happy. This liberation is difficult for those of us who have been led to believe that we must excel in all endeavors.

As long as this "be-the-best" belief persists, happiness is not possible. Instead, happiness can be created, as Ann did, by prioritizing your statuses and deciding that you will do the best you can in each one—under your present circumstances. Creating happiness means looking for challenges that are reasonable.

At the extreme opposite of overly high self-expectations are those who are apathetic about life and accomplishments. They seem to lack self-pride and any hint of motivation. For whatever reason they have little direction and seldom try to achieve. They pretend that they are happy just getting by, and perhaps they feel as happy as they want to be. Sadly, they may be depriving themselves of the potential for much greater life satisfaction.

Do not be timid and squeamish about your actions. All life is an experiment. The more experiments that you make the better. What if you are a little coarse, and get your coat soiled or torn? What if you do fall, and get fairly rolled in the dirt once or twice? Up again. Never be afraid of a tumble.

—Ralph Waldo Emerson

Initiate Activity and Pleasure

Satisfaction eludes many people because they do not take the initiative in bringing about pleasure. They play a waiting game. It's as if they believe that there is a "happiness godmother" who will invite them to participate in life.

Conversely, those who create happiness realize that there is much they can do for their own well-being. Happy people are active in life. They know what can add pleasure to their lives, and they go for it. They are willing to take risks. Carolyn, a middle-aged woman who was just starting college, wrote, "I've been taught to take a 'better safe than sorry' approach to life. I'm now throwing that safety role out the window and taking chances. It's really invigorating!" The fully alive person asks, "How can I enjoy this person, place, situation, or challenge?" This requires a positive, creative mental attitude.

How alive do you feel? How often do you seize the moment and create delight? "Mentally healthy people keep a vital forward thrust through life until death" (Adams, 1987, p. 198). In contrast, noninitiators are inactive and wait for a "bolt of happiness" to strike them. They put someone else in charge.

> Most of us do not "sculpt" our lives. We accept what comes our way, then we gripe about it. Many of us spend our lives waiting—waiting for the perfect mate, waiting for the perfect job, waiting for perfect friends to come along. (Jeffers, 1987, p. 63)

Julie was a divorcée who talked about her desire for a social life. On Monday mornings she would usually say, "I had a boring weekend. I wanted to go out, but nobody called. After you're divorced, couples don't want you around, you know, so I sat home. I could not call them." Laura, a widow, said, "I get so tired of sitting home, and I wish my family would come visit more often and take me places." Julie and Laura are not incapacitated; they just do not initiate. You may want to look at pleasure in your life and ask what you are doing to bring it about.

> *For those of you wondering what to do while waiting for your prince to come, I say, "Enjoy the frog!"*
>
> —Ric Masten

Take Responsibility

Excuse making, a common way of not taking responsibility for one's happiness, can create dissatisfaction and misery. In order to avoid the harmful excuse-making habit, it helps to recognize the difference between an excuse and a reason. A reason is a statement of fact usually offered with acceptance of responsibility and control. An excuse can consist of facts; however, responsibility for behavior is lacking. Instead, an excuse usually includes a "that-should-get-me-off-the-hook" presumption. Contrasting excuses with reasons is helpful in distinguishing between the two. For example:

I couldn't go visit him because it was raining.	versus	I didn't go visit him. I don't like to drive in the rain so I decided not to go.
I didn't have time to study.	versus	I didn't take the time to study. I chose to use my time to do other things.

Lack of time is a common excuse. When I remind students that they really did have time to complete a paper or study for an exam, I can get indignant protests. There wasn't *any* time, I hear. How much time do we literally have? The answer is that each of us has 24 hours in every daylong period, 8,760 hours each year. In reality, we do have time; we just may not have time left over. "We always have time, if we but use it aright (sic)," said the German poet and dramatist Johann Wolfgang Goethe, who died in 1832. This is still true today.

When we persist in thinking that we don't have time, it really does seem to be nonexistent. Potentially satisfying experiences can be delayed or never accomplished. Melissa insisted that she wanted to "work out" regularly, but she just didn't have time. So she didn't exercise. One day she decided to awaken earlier and exercise. She found time that had actually always been there!

Another common excuse and a definite obstacle to happiness is age. "I'm too old" is a phrase that, if recognized as an excuse, can be eliminated. When exercising, I sometimes feel winded. It's tempting to think, "It's my age." My preferred thought is, "I'm just not in shape yet!" Do you see the beauty of thinking the latter? In doing so, I can change my physical condition and stamina; my age is unchangeable.

Certain obstacles exist if you have some type of disability. Having an artificial eye has been challenging for me, and using it as an excuse is occasionally tempting. I recall trying to do so once when discussing a tennis match with my daughter Lisa. She showed up with a patch over her eye and proceeded to win the set and remind me of the senselessness of excuse making! A more dramatic example is an amazing man who calls himself Mitchell. He describes himself as someone who could be called the unluckiest man alive because of two devastating accidents that left him badly scarred and disabled from severe burns and paralyzed from the waist down.

> With my scarred face, my fingerless paws, my wheelchair and real, genuine happiness in my heart—I want to be your mental image of the power of the human mind to transcend circumstances. *It's not what happens to you, it's what you do about it.* (Mitchell, 1997)

Having read his book and heard him speak, it is obvious that because he refused to make excuses, Mitchell has overcome immense obstacles and has taken responsibility for his own life.

Sources for excuses are bountiful. Passage of time, people, the weather, a car, and even the dog can be at fault. Another convenient scapegoat is an emotion. Have you ever thought or said something like, "I was so angry that I just had to honk my horn," "I was so frustrated that I couldn't help screaming"? Ask yourself what part of that statement is true. You were angry (even *so* angry) and frustrated; the rest is inaccurate. You did not *have* to honk the horn or scream. A young woman said, "I was so depressed, I couldn't go to work." Have you ever gone to work or to classes when you were depressed? Obviously, she could have gone to work, but she did not. Taking control of her life would mean thinking, "I was depressed, and I chose (or decided) not to go to work." Then she is free in the future to be depressed and go to work if she chooses. Certainly, emotions are important influences in our lives; however, they do not have to control or justify behavior. "I couldn't help it" usually means "I didn't help it."

Excuses limit choices. Blaming outside forces takes away freedom and power. "This class is boring," someone might say, and then the class or the instructor is at fault. This blaming could prevent a person from ever enjoying the class because the responsibility is elsewhere. Don complained that he was unable to study for a test because his roommate was talking on the phone. He blamed his roommate for his poor test score. Who was actually responsible for his score? As long as Don continues to blame others, he will be at their mercy and will be unable to change his life. Responsibility gives us the power to make changes and to create the kind of life we want.

As an instructor I have heard almost every excuse. One of my favorites was, "My dog 'diddled' on my paper, and that's why I'm not handing it in on time." This was clearly an excuse; a reason, on the other hand, would have been, "I left my paper on the floor, and my dog 'diddled' on it. I realize it's late, and I'll take the responsibility for it." Stating reasons and then verbalizing your responsibility is like a breath of fresh air!

Excuses are like antacids; they can bring temporary relief but do not contribute to long-term happiness. Excuses decrease self-control and dim feelings of success. For example, how can you feel proud about a high grade if you don't take responsibility for the low ones? Even though it may be temporarily upsetting to realize that you have created pain for yourself, this realization is your biggest blessing. When you take responsibility for your own misery, you discover you have the power to find pleasure and create happiness.

People who take responsibility either have or develop an **internal locus of control**, the belief that they are in control of their own lives. The opposite, a perception that outside-self factors control one's life, is **external locus of control**. Over the years there has been increasing interest in whether individuals believe that outcomes of their behaviors are due to their own actions or personal characteristics or due to chance, luck, fate, or under others' control (Rotter, 1972, 1990). People recognized as being psychologically hardy (Kobasa, 1979) have an internal locus of control, and one of the traits of happy people is a sense of personal control (Myers & Diener, 1995). Think about your own locus of control and strive to empower yourself by taking responsibility. Happy individuals welcome control over their lives. Ultimately, excuses prevent present happiness and block potential well-being.

Change Can't and Couldn't Thinking

Excuses frequently include the words *can't* or *couldn't*. People think and verbalize in these terms. Have you ever said or heard this common expression: "I *couldn't* get up this morning"? Really? Picture what would be necessary for this to be true. Perhaps you were lying there in a full-body cast? Usually the person means "I didn't get up because I decided not to," "I had a hard time getting up," or "I didn't want to get up." Often, a person doesn't mean *can't* or *couldn't* in actuality, yet without realizing it, potential happiness can be jeopardized. Analyze *can't* and *couldn't* messages, and then challenge them. Read the following thoughts and then reflect on what a person will likely miss by thinking and then behaving accordingly.

I just *can't* ski.
I *can't* talk to people.
I *couldn't* ask her to go to the party with me.

Do you see how limiting such thinking is? Think of as many literal uses of the words as you can, and you'll discover that the words are correctly used in only a few instances such as, "I *can't* live forever." Even if you can't do something now, in most cases, you could eventually! A wise decision would be to stop using the negative words unless they are entirely accurate. "Adulthood is the time for doing what you can and not talking about what you can't" (Spezzano, 1992, p. 20).

Obviously, life has circumstances or external forces that cannot be changed. You can't control the weather, many tragedies, and other people's behavior. You do, however, control your reactions and future actions regarding these uncontrollable events. Thus, learn to recognize your own internal power and avoid thinking *can't* when you actually have control.

Can't may be a cover-up for fear. Other times use of such words is just wishful thinking. A student wrote on an evaluation form, "I liked this class. I wish I could have put more into it." She *could* have put more into it. Replacing the word *could* with *would* means she can be more involved in future classes and have a happier experience. How frequently do you say, "I can't," or "I couldn't"? To create happiness, eliminate as many as possible and think, "Yes, I can."

Rethink Should and Shouldn't

Closely related to *can't* and *couldn't* are *should* and *shouldn't*. Perhaps you are not feeling happy or satisfied about what you do because you think in these ways.

I should study more.	I should lose weight.
I should visit my grandparent's more often.	I shouldn't waste time.
I should work harder at my job.	I shouldn't ever be late.
I should exercise more.	I shouldn't get angry.

What emotions are likely to follow a thought of should when it is not acted upon? What feelings do you have when you believe you *shouldn't* and then do it anyway? Guilt, frustration, or anger are common responses, and these emotions go hand in hand with unhappiness. "Shoulditis" is what Briggs (1977) calls this. She points out that "should-ought-must-have-to" messages lower self-esteem and lead to unhappiness. Also, an expression of *should* doesn't sound like fun. When

Figure 4-4

someone says, "We should go to lunch" or "We should get together," does it sound inviting? Wouldn't it be more positive to hear, "I'd like for us to go to lunch" or "I want us to get together"? Part of being fully alive is to enjoy activities and want to participate rather than think you have to. Other forcing words similar to *should* that, also, are best to avoid are *must, have to, need to,* and *ought.*

So what is better to think and say? Happiness is more likely if, whenever possible, you replace these words with *want* or *don't want.* Consider first the activity or task. You probably do want to spend more time with friends so instead of "I should spend more time," you can think, "I want to spend more time." Wanting to do something may not be the case. Then you can focus on the outcome. For example, you may not want to study, yet you do want better grades. You can think, "I want better grades so I will study more." If you honestly don't relish doing the task and you don't want the outcome, either finish it anyway or get rid of the thought and move on with enjoyable living! Reword the other forcing words, as well. When a student says, "I have to leave class early to visit a friend in the hospital." I reply, "Remember that you don't *have* to. You want to and have decided to leave, and it's fine."

Generally, these forcing words are used in **irrational beliefs**, unreasonable and exaggerated thoughts identified by Albert Ellis (1977), a well-known cognitive therapist. Some of these include "I can't help it," "I can't stand it when things don't go well," "I should be liked by everyone," and "I must be perfect." Ellis explained that people who carry around such overgeneralizations end up making themselves miserable. Challenging irrational beliefs is necessary for mental health. You can begin by changing the forcing words and, thus, chalk up another step in creating happiness!

Concentrate on Positives

Personal put-downs are also obstacles to happiness. "I'm no good." "I can't do anything right." "I can't make friends." "I'm not attractive." A most devastating example of negative self-talk is, "I can't change."

Consider the following damaging thoughts.

We don't like the way we look. We can't stand our bodies. We think we're stupid, incompetent, untalented, and, in many cases, unlovable. We think our thoughts are wrong and inappropriate, our feelings are wrong and inappropriate. We believe we're not important, and even if our feelings aren't wrong, we think they don't matter. We have never come to grips with ourselves, and we look at ourselves not through rose-colored glasses but through a dirty, brownish-gray film. (Beattie, 1987, p. 109).

Other thoughts are less blatant. "She's smarter than I am," "My brother was more popular," "I wish I were prettier," or "I could have done better." Because they are subtle, you may not even recognize their damage. Any time you use a qualifier and think or say, "I'm *only* a kid," "I didn't do *much* in high school," or "I've *just* had work experience on a farm," you are taking away from your sense of self-worth and well-being. During job interviews, many applicants who make the mistake of emphasizing what they lack lower their chances of getting the job.

People who engage in negative self-talk and see the worst in everyone and everything seem addicted to negativity and can be called *negaholics*. Those who suffer from negaholism limit their own abilities, convince themselves that they can't have what they want, and sabotage their wishes, desires, and dreams (Carter-Scott, 1989). They also dampen the spirits of others. Qualifying thoughts and comments can emerge even under positive circumstances. A clerk said, "Even when I feel proud, I qualify it by thinking that we were so busy at work that anyone could have made as many sales as I did." After recognizing this, she began to challenge such thoughts by telling herself, "Even though we were busy, I don't know that anyone else could have done as well as I did. I made the sales, and that's great!" Whenever you hear yourself saying something like, "I received a good grade, but it was an easy test," rephrase the thought. Thought-stopping, explained in Chapter 1, can also be useful here.

Why would anyone use negative self-talk instead of positive? Such a person might have had well-meaning parents who didn't want their children to seem conceited or vain. They might have encouraged them, instead, to be modest and not to think too highly of themselves. For an unfortunate few, it's the result of direct put-downs that they have internalized. Negaholism is frequently handed down from generation to generation (Carter-Scott, 1989). Julie spoke of her mother's emphasis on negatives. "I was excited about a piece of pottery I had finished and told my mom to come see it. She walked in, and the first thing she said was that the table where I had placed it needed dusting!"

Thinking and speaking negatively about yourself lowers self-esteem and leads to unhappiness. What about other negativism? Interestingly, the use of what are called "bummer" words (Buscaglia, 1982) can depress your spirits. Try saying these words aloud slowly.

no	never	gloomy	bored	hate
not	ugly	dumb	bleak	wrong
negative	sick	bad	worthless	awful

Did you notice any change in your feelings? Most people become aware of how depressing both the sounds and the images of the words are. Depressing, by the way, is a "bummer" word. Now do the same thing with this list.

yes	laugh	fun	able	love
cheerful	right	smart	great	excited
super	well	good	wow	alive

A fascinating study showed that higher use of positive emotion words relative to negative ones was associated with better health (Pennebaker, Mayne, & Francis, 1997) and that people who used more positive emotion words and fewer negations were perceived more favorably by others (Berry, Pennebaker, Mueller, & Hiller, 1997). Just by using different words, you have more control over your mood, health, and interactions. Imagine going through life thinking and verbalizing in "bummer" language. Instead, think differently and increase the number of positive words you use.

After you rid yourself of negatives, remarkable things can happen. When you employ positive self-talk, your mental image will focus more often on what is good about yourself, what you can do, and what you have done well. Most important, you will know that you can change if you want. You will no longer put yourself second or third in all aspects of life. If someone is truly better looking or more talented, you can acknowledge this as a reality yet understand that it is only as important as you make it. Concentrating on positives in yourself and others creates a happier reality.

Be not afraid of life. Believe that life is worth living and your belief will help create the fact.
—William James

Seek Alternatives

An important part of the thinking process, and essential for achieving happiness and satisfaction, is the ability to recognize alternatives. "Locked-in" thinking can be depressing, as it limits you to only one way of viewing life; it can also be tragic. The story is told of a woman who is waiting for a phone call from her boyfriend, Buster. The call does not come, and, in despair, she kills herself (Buscaglia, 1982). This tragic and desperate behavior, as in most suicides, is the result of an inability to think of any possible alternative. In contrast, my students suggest several. First, they let Buster off the hook by giving reasons for his not calling. A unique one is that he hadn't paid his phone bill and found that his line was dead. If, in fact, Buster no longer loves the woman, alternatives are still possible. "Find a better Buster!" is a common recommendation. "Maybe the truly mentally healthy individual is the one who has the most alternatives, the most viable alternatives" (Buscaglia, 1982, p. 108). Remember that any problem has more than one solution.

The happiest people are those who don't limit their choices. Being confident that you can solve your problems by thinking of several options is a sign of maturity and strength. Critical and creative thinking skills, discussed in Chapter 1, emphasize unlocking people's minds, seeing a multitude of possibilities, and then exploring alternatives.

Certainly, choices are more difficult for some people. Because of our original socioeconomic status and upbringing, the concept of alternatives may not be easily grasped, or effective decision-making skills may be lacking. In addition, life delivers some devastating blows, and we may feel trapped by circumstances. Education about choices is a necessity, and society can be instrumental in providing encouragement, training, and resources related to bettering one's life. This book encourages individuals to learn how to make wise choices.

Take Positive Action

Seeing alternatives isn't beneficial if you don't act. In fact, understanding what to do and then not doing anything can be stressful. A frustrated student came to me one day after reading several self-help books. She said, "I'm so upset because now I know what to do, but I'm not doing it!" I reminded her that human beings are not perfect, helped her plan some action steps, and encouraged her to continue to work on desired changes. Taking action and taking responsibility for outcomes are signs of a mentally adjusted person. Lack of action often leads to unhappiness.

It costs far more not to change than to change. The alternative to change is stagnation. To stagnate is to die while still breathing (Adams, 1987, p. 206).

Looking for what can be done in any circumstance is happiness producing, and you can be proud of any positive action. Cheri is unhappy about her sloppy roommate. What can she do about it? If she does nothing, is she pursuing happiness? Cheri can start with the easiest possible solution and act on it. If it doesn't work, she can go to the next one. If she exhausts all the alternatives, she still has a choice. She can accept what she has not been able to change, or she can remove herself from the depressing situation. A story is told of a man who prayed everyday that he would win the lottery. One day, he heard the thunderous voice of God: "If you want to win the lottery, at least buy a ticket!" Wasting precious time and energy bemoaning your plight in life is draining and not conducive to happiness. Instead, do something constructive, learn from mistakes, and avoid negative situations in the future. Then pat yourself on the back for taking action and enjoy the energizing feelings from taking even a small step!

> *Life is in your hands. You can select joy if you want or you can find despair everywhere you look. Kanzantazkis says, "You have your brush and colors. You paint paradise, and then in you go."*
>
> —Leo Buscaglia

Avoid Chronic Procrastination

Putting off activities, which is known as **procrastination**, can deprive you of a more positive future. Interestingly, procrastination can be used in a creative way. You can, for example, choose to postpone a tedious task in order to engage in a pleasurable activity. You may decide to put something off because it's low on your priority list or because you want to allow time to make a thoughtful decision. In that case, delay can work in your favor.

In contrast, **chronic procrastination** is the habit of postponing, and it blocks happiness. If you want and plan to complete a task, putting it off delays the happiness of achievement and creates stress in the meantime. Eventually, it becomes a major obstacle to happiness. "The demands and responsibilities of adult life are much greater, and procrastination begins to feel more like a prison than a game" (Burka & Yuen, 1983, p. 15). Despite the difficulty, when the consequences of procrastination are faced, most people want to change. Consider the costs (LeBoeuf, 1979).

- *Waste of the present:* I'll do it tomorrow, but tomorrow may not come.
- *An unfulfilled life:* Today won't count for anything if nothing is accomplished.
- *Boredom:* Life can become dull and flat when filled with things undone.
- *Anxiety:* Working under pressure at the last minute is a stressor.
- *Impotent goals:* Goals not acted upon are like hot air, one "I'm gonna" after another with no results.
- *Unsolved problems:* A constant plague of these is like vermin, one breeding another and another.
- *Continuous frustration:* Not getting any "wants" becomes disheartening.
- *Poor health:* Putting off taking care of self or maintaining safety can be harmful.

- *A mediocre career:* Delay and inaction lead to nonproductivity, and even though most procrastinators claim that they will be different at work, the habit lingers.
- *A life of indecision:* Becoming a slave to the future instead of the master of it is a heavy price.
- *Fatigue:* Putting things off takes energy.

A study of college students showed that procrastinators reported higher stress and more illness late in the term; overall, they were ill more often. They also received lower grades on all assignments. Procrastination of this type was a self-defeating behavior marked by long-term costs (Tice & Baumeister, 1997). Anyone who wants to live a happy life would adopt the worthy goal of defeating procrastination.

Discovering why you procrastinate can help you find another way to satisfy your need or to decide whether the reason is worth the costs. Ask yourself:

1. Do I procrastinate because the task seems overwhelming or unpleasant? In Chapter 3 you learned how to break a goal into smaller action steps. This puts an end to initial procrastination and motivates you to take the second step. Unpleasant tasks can be evaluated. (1) How important is this? (2) How bad will it be if I don't do it? (3) What are the rewards? For example, cleaning toilet bowls is not high on most people's lists of desirable tasks. Next time you are faced with the chore, apply the three questions. If you honestly decide that cleaning the toilet is unimportant, that it won't be so bad left undone, and that the rewards aren't worth the effort at the time, you aren't procrastinating!
2. Is procrastination an excuse for a poor performance? If so, this is like trying to make two wrongs into a right. Most students who leave major projects to the last minute do poorly.
3. Are you waiting for more time? Ironically, people will say, "I didn't do well because I ran out of time," and they will expect to be excused because of lack of time. Another procrastinating message about time is, "I'll do it when I have more time." We will never have more time, and allowing too many demands on our time leads to pressure. Procrastinators are often time-wasters who don't use small time segments. Even though enjoyable activities are important, people who say they don't have time are often using a great deal of it for enjoyment. If you aren't an effective time manager, review the time management section in this book.
4. Do you use procrastination to gain sympathy? Donna played the "poor-me" game to explain why things didn't get done. "I wanted to be a good mother and take the kids to the zoo, but too many other things came up" and "I have more things to do than most, and I can't afford to take time for myself" were some of her pleas for sympathy. When a friend told her that she was tired of hearing all her tales of woe, Donna maturely took a look at herself and decided to end the game.
5. Are you defending against blows to self-esteem by putting things off? "I didn't get it done" may be a cover-up for "I was afraid it wouldn't be good enough." Perfectionists tend to procrastinate for this reason.

Check your behavior. If you have a pattern of procrastination, do something about it now!

Live in the Present

When are you living your life? This may sound like a senseless question, yet asking it *is* sensible! Do you harbor thoughts such as, "I'll be happy when I graduate" or "I can't wait until I get to move away from home and be on my own"? Describing this type of thinking as "futurizing," Dyer (1990) calls it a most destructive habit.

> Your life is not a dress rehearsal for the future. It is right here and now (Carlson, 1999).

In the book *Making Peace with Yourself* (Bloomfield, 1996a) a chapter is devoted to "I'll be happy when." It is interesting that many of the events are opposites (when I get married, when I get divorced; when I have children, when the children leave home). All are excellent examples of "The grass is always greener on the other side of the fence." Many of us live the first half of our lives postponing satisfaction and the last half with regrets. Fulfillment is just over the hill (Bloomfield, 1996a). When I hear people say, "I can't wait until the weekend," I often reply, "I hope you can, and I certainly hope you enjoy each minute from now until then!" Too many people seem to be focused on endings—the end of the week, the end of the day, the end of the school term and then want time to go even faster. Happy, satisfied people create happiness by an ongoing process of living *now*.

Another habit is one I somewhat jokingly call "pasturizing"—mentally living in the past. "If only I had married John instead of Jim" and "I wish I had started college right out of high school instead of later" are examples of wishful thinking that destroy opportunities for present happiness. People who converse only about accomplishments or problems from the past are not living in the here and now.

Well-adjusted people accept and appreciate the past and can enjoy nostalgia. Wise individuals use the past as a series of vast learning experiences to make their present more rewarding. Happy people plan for their future and anticipate to a certain extent, yet they keep focused in the present. Obviously, what is happening now can be unpleasant, and you will, at times, hope tomorrow comes quickly. Nevertheless, if you make a habit of living elsewhere, you'll realize too late that you haven't really lived. Focusing on life as a journey, not a destination, is helpful.

Recognize that "now" is the only time you ever really have. An example I wish I didn't have available to use is that of Lynn Hansen, a student who was the daughter of a couple from my hometown. Lynn graduated from college and began her career full of excitement and hope. That same month a malignant brain tumor was discovered and removed. Lynn survived the delicate surgery and the cancer treatment and spent several months in a rehabilitation center. When I visited, I was impressed with her positive attitude and hope for the future. Nine months after the tumor was found, Lynn was buried in the local cemetery, leaving behind many who loved her—a terrible loss. Nobody is guaranteed a future. It's a depressing thought, but one that can keep us focused. Happiness must be practiced in the present. A consolation is that Lynn created and experienced happiness in the "now" of a short life before her illness.

> The only reality is the now. Yesterday is gone, and there's nothing you can do about it. It's good because it brought you to where you are right now. It isn't real any more. And tomorrow? Tomorrow is a wonderful thing to dream about, but it isn't real. And if you spend your time dreaming about yesterday and tomorrow, you're going to miss what's happening to you and me right now. (Buscaglia, 1982, p. 75)

Enjoy Life's Pleasures

"Stop and smell the roses." What a delightful idea! How often do you do it? "Roses" can be anything as long as pleasure is felt. Sensory delights are everywhere. Do you see sunsets? Do you feel awe when viewing nature's treasures? Do you smell the scents of the seasons? Do you marvel at a snowflake? Do you hear the delightful songs of birds? Positive feelings are generated by pleasurable sensory stimulation. **Peak experiences** are brief moments of extreme pleasure (Maslow, 1968). Often, these come from the simpler pleasures of life. Being open to new experiences allows us to create happiness. "Fully alive people are aware of the thorns but concentrate on the roses" (Powell, 1976, p. 57).

Why wouldn't people take the time to marvel at life? "I'm too busy. I don't have time" is a common excuse. Ask yourself when will you have time and when will you not be busy? "If we wait for everything we want accomplished to be completed before we celebrate, we will miss the party of life" (Pearsall, 1988, p. 61). "But I have to clean the house" and "I can't stand it if the yard isn't in good shape" are detriments to enjoyment (unless you enjoy cleaning the house and doing yardwork, that is!) Joys are missed when we are rushing through life. Be sure to slow down and experience joy—over and over!

One of the most treasured memories in my teaching career is of a lovely 29-year-old woman named Dawne. The single mother of two children, she had a great desire to better herself and make a happy life for her family, and she was thrilled that she had returned to school. She was bright, articulate, and enthusiastic—a joy to teach. One spring she brought her completed final examination to my desk and said, "Sharon, all quarter we've been talking about hugs, and I want to give you one!" That was so like her. I happily agreed, and we embraced warmly. It was the beginning of the summer break, and as Dawne walked out of the room, she reminded me to "practice what I preach" and enjoy my few weeks of vacation. She smiled and was gone. The next day she and her daughter were killed in a car-train accident—a horrible, unexplainable tragedy. As I grieved, I remembered that last loving encounter and the poignancy of what she wrote to me at the end of her test: "Now remember, Sharon, to stop and smell the roses." Whenever I forget to do so, I think of Dawne, a lovely person who followed her own advice so well. Ways of creating happiness by "smelling roses" are everywhere. Don't miss them!

Figure 4-5   Take time to enjoy the beauty of nature.

Count Your Blessings

One day a student remarked, "Sometimes it helps when I stop and think of what isn't wrong with me and then I feel grateful." Too often, we forget how fortunate we are. Think right now of how many blessings you have. Are you healthy? Do you have loving relationships? Can you see and hear? Consider what life would be like without one or more of your senses. A remarkable blind woman, Peggy Shald, told of overhearing a person complain about having to take a bus. Peggy's thought was: "I wonder how she would feel if she always had to walk 10 blocks to a bus stop even on the coldest day, and she was also blind." In the process of creating happiness, it can help to experience an occasional reminder of how bad things could be and be reminded of our blessings. Equally affirming is to keep in mind that for every act of unkindness, there are a million kind acts, a network of good (Dyer, 1992).

Give to Life

Happy people not only take in the wonder and beauty of life, they also give back to life and pursue a meaningful existence. Self-centered people tend to be unhappy, while those who contribute develop a positive legacy that will remain after they have died. Self-actualization, the pinnacle of the hierarchy of needs, is more likely for those who are reaching beyond self and contributing to the greater good of humankind. Joy comes from giving, not getting; from contributing, not acquiring (Dyer, 1992).

Giving to life doesn't necessarily mean great works. You can create satisfaction by doing worthwhile and purposeful deeds. Possibilities are all around. When was the last time you visited someone in a hospital or a nursing home? Have you recently volunteered to help in a worthy cause? Have you taken the time to do a favor for anyone? When did you last send a "just thinking about you" card or note? Have you even smiled at someone recently? Buscaglia (1982) underscored this point, "Every day you take from the ground, you take from the air, you take from the beauty—what are you giving back?" (p. 82). Even the smallest gesture can do wonders for another, and, in return, for you. In the depths of the tragedy of the terrorist attacks on the World Trade Center and Pentagon in 2001 came countless expressions of generosity and giving that shed some light on the anguish. A major reason for enhancing self-esteem is to have something to offer. We can only give what we possess, and the more we have, the greater our capacity to give. Choose to give of yourself.

> Each of us can make a difference. We can choose to live a life in which we can say, when we die, that the world is a better place for our having been here (Jampolsky, 1990, p. 5).

Develop Nourishing, Rewarding Relationships

A primary objective of this book is to help you learn to develop positive relationships. Their value in the creation of happiness is unquestionable. Love and belongingness are human needs. Enjoying a supportive network of close relationships is associated with happiness (Myers & Diener, 1995). Would you prefer to be remembered for your punctuality and success at earning money, or because of your loving relationships? Most would agree that what really matters are the interpersonal connections and the love we share with others. Even though intimacy demands a high risk, it yields the richest rewards (Adams, 1987). Many of the guidelines presented in this book can help you develop nourishing relationships. Self-satisfaction and happiness are the rewards. The reservoir of happiness and satisfaction within you is unlimited; happy people replenish theirs often by living life to its fullest.

Reflect

- Think of a "can't" statement you have used or heard. Then reword it.
- If you have a "should" in your life, change the thought to a "want" in one of the suggested ways.
- Select one of the ways to create happiness and use it.

Apply

- Practice saying both "bummer" and "positive" words, then compare your emotional reactions.
- Make a list of your blessings.
- Do something positive for another human being.

LOOKING BACK

- People yearn to be happy. Not knowing what happiness and satisfaction are, having unrealistic expectations, and looking for happiness outside of self are three obstacles.
- Having realistic expectations about happiness is wise. Realizing that unhappiness is a part of life is realistic and can help you appreciate your happiness even more.
- Happy people learn from their misfortunes and grow from adversity. They know that happiness does not magically come from external sources. One must be happy inside; if not, all the outside sources in the world will bring only temporary happiness at best.
- Happiness is within reach, yet it does not automatically fall into anyone's lap. Initiative and effort are necessary. A reservoir of internal happiness must be created. Externals then can add to what is already there.
- Creating happiness means developing a high degree of self-worth, a positive attitude, and an internal locus of control.
- Happy people rarely use excuses and negative words. They look for possibilities, not limitations.
- Happy people see alternatives. Negative self-talk is avoided, as is chronic procrastination.
- Individuals who create their own happiness are active and do what is best for them. They do not "futurize" or "pasturize." They make good use of the past and strive for a happy future, yet they live in the present.

Figure 4-6   A headstone of a young man who is still alive. Think about all you've read so far and speculate about the meaning of this headstone (photo courtesy of Greg L. Baker).

- Happy people are seekers in life who enjoy discoveries and simple pleasures. They stop to "smell the roses" and count their blessings. Because they are truly happy within, they tend to reach out and provide happiness for others.
- Satisfied, happy people are nourished and rewarded by positive relationships.

Alas for those who never sing but die with all their music in them.

—Oliver Wendell Holmes

5

Experiencing and
Expressing Emotion

LOOKING AHEAD

After completing this chapter, you will be able to

- Realize that emotions are a complex and important part of the self and of relationships.
- Give a general description of emotion and explain three components.
- Name at least six different emotions.
- Describe ways in which emotion can be expressed.
- Name and describe influences on emotional expression.
- Relate the transactional analysis ego states to emotional expression.
- List benefits of expression in each of the four development areas.
- Realize that you can become more demonstrative.
- Express emotions such as anger in appropriate, constructive ways.
- Describe ways to change your feelings.
- Use rational emotive behavior therapy and control theory to change what you feel.
- Differentiate between mild feelings of sadness and major depression; name symptoms of and explain treatment options for major depression.
- Use knowledge of suicide in preventive ways.
- If needed, be able to wisely select a therapist or counselor.
- Describe and use coping methods.

Emotions can be viewed as the spice of life; they give our lives character and pizazz.
—Stephen Worchel and Wayne Shebilske

A letter arrives congratulating you on a scholarship that will pay a full year's college expenses. Your supervisor refuses to give you a day off to attend a wedding. You and a family member disagree, and your reasonable suggestions are being misinterpreted. An automobile coming toward you seems to be out of control. What do these situations have in common? All usually bring about an emotional response.

Were you able to predict what feelings would probably be present in the examples? The emotions of joy, disappointment, frustration, and fear come readily to mind and, in most cases, would be accurate predictions. As you will discover, however, these particular feelings do not have to occur; you may respond with different emotions, depending on several factors.

Emotions make up a most interesting and important developmental area of self. Human beings are emotional, and our feelings both enrich and disturb our lives. Feelings bring texture, color, and sensitivity to life. Without them, we would be robots (Satir, 1988). If you stop to consider how drab life would be without emotions, you will begin to grasp their value.

Emotions are very important, and have been researched; yet, much is still to be learned. Emotion is a feeling state that involves certain components. The complexity of emotions frequently creates problems in individual lives and within relationships. Check yourself to see how puzzling the elements of your emotional self can be.

1. Are you in touch with your feelings? It can be difficult to decide if a state of being is an emotion or some other aspect of self. For example, confused indicates a mental lack of understanding, not an emotion. "I feel tired" is a physical description.
2. Can you identify what emotion you are experiencing at any given time? Most people will typically reply that they feel fine, good, or bad rather than naming a specific emotion.
3. Can you pinpoint the reason for your feelings? Several emotions are situational, which means they are preceded by an event. Others seemingly come from "out of the blue," and the cause is not apparent.
4. How accurate are your predictions of emotions? Do you know how you will feel under certain circumstances? Nisha was shocked to discover on her wedding day that she felt sad. She loved Matt and wanted to marry him. What would cause this?
5. Can you tell by behavior what emotion is being experienced? Picture this scene. Three individuals are waiting in line to go on a thriller ride at an amusement park. All three are smiling, laughing, and pacing. What are their emotions? Possibly one person could be excited, another mildly anxious, and the third terrified!

In recent years **emotional intelligence** has been conceptualized (Goleman, 1995; 1998). The cornerstones are having an ability to recognize the meaning of emotions and to use them in thinking and problem solving (Mayer, Caruso, & Salovey, 1999). Benefits include being attuned to the feelings of others and being able to handle disagreements. This chapter will clarify the mysterious emotional self. Developing emotional well-being and emotional intelligence can lead to meaningful interactions and positive relationships.

IDENTIFYING AND CATEGORIZING EMOTIONS

How do you understand your feelings? Three components of emotion—physiological changes, subjective cognitive states, and expressive behaviors (Tangney, Miller, Flicker, & Barlow, 1996)—can provide insight.

The component called **physiological arousal** refers to biological reactions and activities of the nervous system, various glands, and organs within the body. If frightened, your glands secrete hormones into your bloodstream, causing your heart rate to quicken and your pupils to enlarge. You may or may not be aware of the arousal. In some cases, the reactions are observable. Have you ever blushed? The redness was caused by what was going on inside your body. Many of these responses can be measured by medical monitoring devices and biofeedback equipment.

A second component is **subjective cognitive state**; this can be thought of as awareness and appraisal. For example, how do you know you are happy? You may identify an experience with happiness because of your thoughts. Cognitive appraisal, according to one theory (Schachter & Singer, 1962), is largely responsible for the label we give to emotion. Any physiological arousal could be labeled anger, fear, jealousy, or even love, depending on the circumstances.

The third component is **expressive behavior**—observable verbal or nonverbal actions. How do you show happiness? Sadness? Anger? Sometimes expression is confused with the feeling state itself. For example, crying is expression, not emotion. Have you ever heard someone say, "I was so angry I just had to scream"? In reality, the person did not have to scream. Expressive behavior is the one component over which we have the most control. In the following, see if you can identify the three components.

> Joan continued to cry. She had received a letter telling about the death of a close friend. She was shocked and extremely sad. She felt numb. "Why did this happen?" she asked her husband. He reassuringly took her hand in his and noticed how cold it felt. Joan gulped and said, "I feel almost dead, inside, too."

Physiologically, Joan's hand temperature reflects a reaction to the shock. Her numbness is probably also due to physiological changes. The realization that her friend had died and her description of "feeling almost dead inside" make up her subjective cognitive state. Her expressive behaviors are crying, talking, and gulping.

Researchers, in an attempt to clarify the emotional self, have identified and categorized possible feelings. One model identifies six major clusters or groups (Shaver, Schwartz, Kirson, & O'Connor, 1987). These clusters were love, joy, surprise, anger, sadness, and fear (see Fig. 5–1). Although several emotions fit within one of the clusters (e.g., anxiety is a type of fear), the researchers pointed out that some emotions are blends or combinations. Sympathy, for example, can be a mixture of sadness and love. Even categorizing an emotion is a challenge.

Emotions can vary in intensity. For example, you may be mildly annoyed if a friend is 5 minutes late meeting you for lunch, upset after a half-hour, and outraged when you discover that she or he has deliberately avoided you because of a preference to have lunch with someone else. The underlying emotion is anger. Regardless of how emotions are described and categorized, the realization that they are an integral part of you is basic to self-understanding. Because the component of expressive behaviors influence relationships to such an extent, it deserves special attention.

Emotion Clusters

Figure 5-1

EXPRESSING FEELINGS

Abby dramatically explained, "I'm an emotional person. I cry at weddings, funerals, movies—you name it. I let people know when I'm mad or happy. But that's just the way I am." In contrast, Shamiso said, "I'm a controlled person. I don't let others know my feelings. But that's just the way I am." Is it just the way Abby and Shamiso are? Opinions and theories vary. Expressiveness likely has a genetic base (Ekman, 1994), yet because our emotional socialization and experiences are different, much of "if, what, how, and to whom" we express has been learned and strongly influenced by other factors that will be covered later.

> **TA Revisited**
>
> "Child" is the home of all emotions, the feeling part of personality.
> "Parent" contains messages that tells you to express feelings and how to do so; it can also tell you not to express.
> "Adult" is unemotional yet is involved as it can decide to permit or deny emotional expressions; it also can help you change what you feel.

Expression occurs verbally and nonverbally. For what reason would you suspect that another person is upset? She or he may tell you, "I'm upset because you borrowed my book and didn't return it right away." Or the words could be less direct and might even deny the feeling: "I just don't understand why some people do things like that, but I guess it's really nothing." Other possibilities are profanity or hostile insults. One of the problems with verbal expressions is that people may not accurately state what they are feeling. Perhaps the person doesn't really know, feels embarrassed, or simply doesn't want to share feeling. Individuals may worry about hurting someone's feelings. Generally, we have not been trained to express our emotions assertively, and, obviously, this can easily create relationship challenges.

More commonly, individuals reveal feelings through what is called body language. Facial expressions, changes in voice, behaviors such as laughing and crying, and posture offer glimpses into the emotional self. It is best to be cautious, when you try to interpret others' nonverbal expressions. For example, why does a person cry? An obvious answer is because of sadness. Can you think of other emotions that may result in crying? Even at a wedding, interpretations can be inaccurate. Mark shed a tear at his daughter's wedding. Monica, the mother of the bride, sniffled into a handkerchief. Another young woman sobbed. Mark's tears were the result of pride and happiness. Monica was sad and somewhat regretful that her daughter was old enough to be married. What about the young woman? She had once been engaged to the groom and was feeling resentful and jealous!

Feelings can often be gleaned from facial expressions, and this ability is found in different cultures (Jolley, Zhi, & Thomas, 1998). However, emotion can be disguised. You may have heard the expression "It's written all over your face"; but true feelings can be masked. "Facial expressions are imperfect communicators of emotional states" (Plutchik, 1980, p. 268).

Influences on Emotional Expression

Remember the ways that we learn? Whether and how to express ourselves are acquired through direct instruction, modeling, and experiences. Think of some messages about emotions. A partial list follows:

Keep a stiff upper lip.	Don't wear your heart on your sleeve.
Don't be a crybaby	Don't be a 'fraidy cat.
She's too emotional.	You'll get over it in time.
Cheer up.	Cool it.
Others have it worse than you.	Shut up or I'll give you something to cry about!

Do you see a common theme among them? "Keep your feelings to yourself" is the underlying message. Using the TA framework, you can see that there is often a conflict between "parent" messages and the expressive desires of our "child."

Emotional expression is greatly influenced by one's culture. The North American message has generally been one of control. The strong, silent type is heralded as a hero. Even in extremely sad situations, you may hear someone being praised for being "strong," which means that grief isn't being shown. Other societies also can be restrictive. A student from Kenya described how horrified her mother was when she came to the United States for a visit. "Those people were actually hugging each other in public. Shameful!" she said. Emotional crippling is being afraid to feel, afraid to express, and afraid to have others feel (Rubin, 1998). Other cultures encourage expressiveness. A Chinese student, Anh, told the class: "At Chinese funerals everyone is encouraged to cry and cry because it shows you really care and will miss the person; it reveals the extent of your love."

Expressiveness is also related to gender role. In general, men are given the "don't express" message more than women. As pointed out in Chapter 2, boys and girls are often socialized differently, and the skill specialization account (Kunkel & Burleson, 1999) can explain how they develop different ways of handling emotions. Even though male infants are as emotionally expressive as females, a crossover at later ages occurs because male emotionality is suppressed by parents and peer groups. Boys experience sharp limitations especially when it comes to the expression of caring/connection emotion (Levant, 1997).

Many societies are in a transitional stage, and gender differences are far less extreme than they were. Yet, as long as males and females are given opposite messages, differences in actual expression are inevitable. Can you name emotions that men are allowed or encouraged to feel more than others? Over the years the typical first response in my classes has been **anger**, a feeling of strong displeasure because of an actual or perceived wrong. On the other hand, **fear**, an emotional response to a perceived threat or danger, is customarily off-limits for men. Women are allowed to be afraid of spiders, mice, the dark, and strange noises. Can you picture the reactions if a man demonstrated the same fears? Some examples of stereotypic differences in encouragement and allowance for women and men are shown in Table 5–1.

A list of discouraged or not allowed emotions could be made just by switching the male and female columns. For example, women traditionally have been

TABLE 5-1   Emotional Expression and Gender Role

Encouragement and Allowance

Men	Women
Anger	Sadness, depression
Bravery	Fear
	Hurt
	Love, affection
	Worry, anxiety
	Disappointment

discouraged from awareness and expression of anger. In fact, a fairly recent study, which found no significant variations between boys and girls in total anger level, did reveal significant differences in expression of anger. Boys had higher levels of aggressive responses (Buntaine & Costenbader, 1997).

These differences are not "cast in stone." A Central-American student expressed amazement during the discussion of gender-role differences. "In my culture the men are usually the expressive ones, and women are expected to be more controlled," she said. Within the world of athletics, changes in expressiveness have definitely occurred. Males are given permission to show more emotion and even engage in behaviors commonly off-limits such as hugging and shedding a few tears. Female athletes are encouraged to display anger and aggression.

Changes are desirable because stereotypic masculine nonexpressiveness can create problems. Expressive behavior has its benefits, as the next section will show. Does it make sense to restrict these benefits to one sex? And is it fair when innocent people pay a price for stereotypic toughness? An account of an airline crash in Washington, D.C., during a blizzard illustrates this. Judging from the tape-recorded conversations of the crew, the pilots' attitude about the buildup of ice on the wings of the airplane was casual. With what seemed like an air of bravado, he decided to just "go for it." The jet slammed into a bridge and plunged into the Potomac River, killing 72 passengers, 4 passing motorists, and the pilots (*Time*, 1982). How tragic that individuals not wanting to display even legitimate fear frequently take unnecessary risks with their own and others' lives. After being asked about bravado David Spiegel, M.D. pointed out another potentially dangerous unemotional reaction: "Some men, when they start having chest pains with a heart attack, get down on the floor and do push-ups to prove to themselves that it's not happening" (Moyers, 1993 p. 167). Obviously, this could have serious effects.

Are you aware that lack of expressiveness causes male-female relationships to suffer? Ironically, when women are asked to identify characteristics they would like in a man, they mention ability to express emotions such as fear and sadness. "I wish he would just cry sometimes," one young woman said. On the other hand, men can be confused about women's expressiveness and feel frustrated when they are accused of not understanding. Heterosexuals might benefit from understanding and adopting certain dynamics of gay and lesbian relationships, which tend to be more emotionally revealing (Huston & Schwartz, 1996).

Another powerful influence in emotional development is the family. Which sounds more like a description of your family?

- Almost no emotions are expressed. Parents are controlled. They rarely touch others or express warm, loving feelings. Neither do they display anger or frustration. Relationships are rather businesslike.
- Some emotions are encouraged. Occasionally, the parents show love and warmth. They express anger at times; however, the children are scolded if they behave angrily. A common command is, "Go to your room and don't come out until you're over it." Children are not supposed to cry often or loudly, and praise is given for being brave and strong.
- Several unpleasant emotions are acted upon. Parents let the children know when they are angry, frustrated, disappointed, depressed, and hurt. The children react with displays of negative feelings. However, almost no expressions of warmth and affection are present.

- All emotions are present. Parents express feelings and let the children do so. The household is emotionally charged, and many hurtful behaviors can be observed. A verbal or physical assault almost always follows anger.
- Emotional expression is encouraged. Parents try to model constructive ways of dealing with feelings. Open communication allows for discussion of emotions. When a person hurts others with emotional expression, an apology is given.

Variations of the five models are possible. If your family sounds like the last one, you are fortunate. Most families either suppress emotional expression or allow hurtful behaviors. Few make the attempt to model and teach constructive emotional expression.

Other agents of socialization play a prominent role in expressiveness. From childhood through adolescence, the influence of the **peer group** (those of similar age and interests) is strong. Peers may demonstrate warmth and affection, or they may be more reserved. Young people may openly cry and hug each other in support, or they can be uncomfortable with displays of sorrow. Additionally, the media and religion present standards of emotionality. From all of the external sources, if your models of expressiveness encouraged constructive behaviors and if you were generally accepted and praised for showing feelings, your emotional self is likely to be healthy.

Figure 5-2

Internal reasons and experiences also influence expression. Difficulty could come from perception of your social role or a fear of disclosing. Certain people believe that they must be controlled in their professional positions, and they become almost emotionally sterile. Protection may be a reason. If you have been hurt as a result of expressing, you may have built a wall around your emotions. Jeff told another firefighter how apprehensive he felt at an accident scene. The fire captain heard about it and cautioned Jeff about his fear. Jeff resolved to keep future emotions hidden. Dave expressed his love for Kelli; in return, she said that she preferred just being friends. His hurt led to a layer of defensive inexpressiveness.

A major barrier lies in what expression means. Many people equate emotional suppression with self-control. If you are one who believes that any show of feeling means you are weak and not in control, you will probably suppress rather than express. With pride, a woman said, "I never get angry." What she meant and eventually said was that she didn't show her anger, and to her, this was a virtue. Did her anger disappear? As Rubin (1998) describes it, her anger probably went into a slush fund only to surface in other ways.

Of benefit would be a change to a different belief: *Showing feelings requires strength, and expressing doesn't mean lack of control*. In fact, control could be defined as deciding whether, when, and how to express. Andrew, a man not used to expressing his feelings, heard a rumor at work that he had been passed over for promotion. He seethed all morning, then stormed into his supervisor's office and announced loudly that he was quitting, and walked out. He stopped to pick up his mail and found a memo congratulating him on his promotion. His display of emotion was not only inappropriate but also disastrous. Sometimes you are wise to wait before venting a feeling. A well-adjusted person can choose to express, can select from any number of responses depending on the situation, or can decide not to show a particular feeling. Use "Emotional Monitoring and Learning" in Reflections and Applications to gain personal insight.

Constructive behaviors can be developed at an early age or learned later. Sadly, when individuals tell how and what they were taught about expression, a fairly predictable response is, "You have no right to feel that way!" Instead, we have every right to feel what we feel and then express it in an appropriate way. Healthy messages would be:

- Experiencing all feelings is acceptable.
- Any way of expressing feelings that is not intended to hurt would be allowed.

Is lack of expressiveness related to health problems? Research has focused on this question. The calm that can come from suppression is bought at a price—a higher risk for asthma, high blood pressure, colds, and overall ill health. Female suppressors with breast cancer may be more likely to have future tumors (Goleman, 1997) and could be at greater risk for early death (Pennebaker, 1997). Are you aware of times when your suppressed emotions seemed to play havoc with your physical condition? Anxiety often leads to headaches and stomach distress. I love John Powell's (1969) quote: "When I repress my emotions, my stomach keeps score" (p. 155).

Emotion and biology appear to be closely connected. Years ago, a type of personality was identified as cancer-prone; it combined two major features: an inability to express emotions such as anger, fear, and anxiety and an inability to cope with stress with a tendency to feel hopelessness, helplessness, and depression (Eysenck, 1988). On a positive note, a fighting spirit and emotional expressiveness are associated with better adjustment to breast cancer (Classen, Koopman, Angell, & Spiegel, 1996). The message seems to be that constructive outlets are preferable to lack of expressiveness.

Benefits of Constructive Expression

Constructive emotional expression is a way of behaving that provides a healthy, nonhurtful outlet for feelings. A person can learn, model, and teach positive expressive behaviors and reap many benefits. Let's look at benefits in the four developmental areas.

Physical self.   Does it seem possible that emotions in early life might have an effect on a person's life span? A study of Catholic nuns revealed an association between positive emotions in their early life stories and longevity 60 years later (Danner, Snowdon, & Friesen, 2001). Emotional expression and health are also related. Allowing patients to express their feelings seemed to improve their health (Spiegel, 1999). On the positive side, the following expressive behaviors are health producing.

Touching   Both hugging and therapeutic touch can relieve aches and pains and alleviate muscle tension. For most people, a hug is both soothing and energizing. In babies it appears to ease pain (Motte, 2000). Therapeutic touch is recognized as a valuable medical tool, as it can relieve pain, speed healing, and clear energy blockages that may be interfering with healing (Weil, 1995b). Studies have shown that therapeutic touch and massage therapy relieve pain (Moore, 1999) and decrease levels of anxiety and depression (Diego & Field, 2001). Premature infants who were massaged gained significantly more than that of a control group and showed far fewer stress behaviors (Field, 1996). Massage has even proven to enhance immune function (Diego & Field, 2001). Human touch is essential for our well-being.

A hug is a great gift—one size fits all, and it's easy to exchange.

—Anonymous

Figure 5-3   A hug is healthful and feels so good!

Laughing   When people laugh, muscle tension is relieved. Body movements related to laughter are physical exercise. More importantly, laugher is associated with stimulation of the immune system, reduction in stress hormones, pain reduction, decrease in blood pressure, and improved respiration (Berk, 1996). Researchers conclude that humor therapy and related laughter may have both preventive and healing effects

(Berk, Felton, Tan, Bittman, & Westengard, 2001). A study revealed that people with heart disease were 40 percent less likely to laugh than healthy individuals (Hickling, 2000). This could be a result of laughter's ability to reduce stress. When did you last really laugh?

Amazing Story of Laughter and Healing

Believing that laughter contributed to his miraculous recovery from what was thought to be an irreversible, crippling disease, Norman Cousins (1979) described laughter as a form of inner jogging and a behavior that creates a mood in which other positive emotions can more easily function. "Laughter helps make it possible for good things to happen" (p. 146). Infection in Cousins's body was measured before and after a few minutes of robust laughing. The amazing results showed a decrease in inflammation that held up over time. Years later when much more had been learned about the biology of the brain, Cousins (1989) speculated that laughter had helped to activate the release of endorphins, neurotransmitters in the body that act as painkillers. He cautioned not to substitute laughter for medical care but to use it to bring forth love, hope, festivity, determination, will to live, and purpose. "The positive emotions can be no less effective in bolstering the immune system than the negative emotions are in weakening it" (p. 91).

The most wasted of days is that during which one has not laughed.
—Sebastian Chamfort

Crying   Most people feel psychologically and physically better after crying, and it has long been recognized as a way of releasing feelings. How is crying related to physical health? Interestingly, a laboratory test revealed that the chemical composition of emotional tears differs from that of irritant ones (induced with freshly cut onions). Thus, shedding tears may be a way of ridding the body of substances that build up in response to stress (Levoy, 1988). Making a strong case for emotional release is a cardiologist who believes that crying also opens the chest and enhances healthy breathing. He advocates crying as protection against heart disease and contends that next to love, crying is perhaps the most healing activity for the heart (Sinatra, 1999).

Stereotypic gender role behaviors can negate the physical benefits of emotional expression. In most societies, boys are typically ridiculed for crying and discouraged from doing so. Males may actually have to give themselves permission to cry.

> A good healthy cry can be a sign of maturity. We've got it all wrong if we still believe that crying is a sign of weakness. Real weakness is in not allowing ourselves access to the emotions expressed through tears (Buscaglia, 1992, p. 280).

The restrictions can be prevented from the beginning. If you have input into a child's life, avoid the common message "Don't cry" or "Boys don't cry."

Men are also given less freedom to hug than women are. Watch men interacting with others. Typically, they will just shake hands. Only in recent years have genuine hugs been exchanged between men. Perhaps as we learn more about the benefits of behaviors such as hugging, laughing, and crying, all human beings will become freer in their expressions.

Mental self.   Not recognizing or experiencing what you are feeling can cloud your thinking. Greg was considering a job change and a move to another city when his fiancée ended their engagement. Even though he showed little emotional reaction, his thinking abilities seemed impaired; he was confused and indecisive. He talked to a friend of his who was a counselor. With a great deal of encouragement, he began to talk about feelings of shock, hurt, and anger. The breakthrough in his seemingly blocked mental state came after an intense session of physically working out his feelings. After beating on a stack of large pillows with a tennis racket, he felt absolutely cleansed of negative feelings. "It was a cathartic experience, and I felt as if a weight was lifted from my body. It's hard to really describe." His reward was renewed ability to think about himself and his life. "As feelings are experienced, the mind clears" (Branden, 1983, p. 155).

Being overly concerned and anxious can affect mental performance. Emotional expression can lead the way to resolving a mental block. Test anxiety is a good example. Britt found that if she expressed her feelings before an examination, she could think in a calmer, more organized manner. In a similar vein, relaxation therapy and intensive physical exercise are used to reduce test anxiety (Burke, 1999). An interesting study suggests that emotional suppression can impair memory. The researchers conclude that "keeping a stiff upper lip" decreases recall of the details of an emotional situation (Richards & Gross, 2000). As more is learned about cognitive processes, a clearer link between emotion and cognition is forged.

Social self.   Communicating emotions forms a bridge between two people. If you want to develop close relationships, being able to express feelings is a necessity. Two robotic persons may not notice how colorless their relationship is. Yet, when one robotic person interacts with a functioning emotional being, neither feels fulfilled. And the emotional individual is apt to be frustrated. The closest, healthiest, and most meaningful relationships are between two emotionally expressive individuals.

Expression has long-lasting effects. A study showed that adults who had experienced expressions of warmth and demonstrated affection as children enjoyed happier and more well-adjusted lives as adults (Franz, McClelland, & Weinberger, 1991). Even expressing unpleasant feelings can lead to loving feelings. When my husband talks about the closeness between himself and my two daughters (his stepchildren), he gives credit to honest emotional expression. "We had some verbal battles where anger was genuinely expressed," he says. "Then, we talked and really got to know each other. Love grew as a result."

Think of emotional expression in relationships as a positive circular effect. As you feel and express genuine feelings, you learn about yourself. Others get to know who you truly are and are apt to appreciate knowing a whole person. Then it is likely that they will feel free to share feelings with you leading to close relationships.

The price of not expressing can be high. A letter to Ann Landers from No Name, No City, No State is quite moving.

A few weeks ago I kissed my son for the first time and told him I loved him. Unfortunately he did not know it because he was dead. He had shot himself. The greatest regret of my life is that I kept my son at arm's length. I believed it was unmanly for males to show affection for one another. I treated my son the way my father treated me and I realize now what a terrible mistake it was. Please tell your male readers who were raised by "macho" dads that it is cruel to withhold affection from their sons. I will never recover from my ignorance and stupidity.

On a positive note, a study of fathers and preadolescent sons showed that intimate and nurturing types of touch were a frequent and important part of their relationship (Salt, 1991). Expressing your feelings gives nourishment to relationships.

Emotional self.   Doesn't it make sense that the expression of feelings enhances the emotional self? Kimberly felt resentful because she thought her mother favored her sister Kris. She bottled up this feeling for years and found herself becoming angry and even hostile. One day she told Kris a lie about their mother and then suffered from guilt. She became depressed and went for counseling After a period of time, she realized that the initial resentful feeling had led to several others. She decided to express in writing her true feelings to her mother and sister and acknowledge the lie she had told. The three of them came together and honestly expressed their emotions; relief followed. "I felt as if the clouds had lifted, and my only regret is that I didn't do it sooner," said Kimberly.

Emotional relief is stymied by stuffed feelings. Expressing one emotion often reveals the presence of another. During a cancer-coping session, Marian went through a process that stripped away one emotion after another. She began by expressing depression, which was covering fear. Underneath all this was intense anger. She had felt emotionally drained; after the expressive experience, she was energized. People risk the experience of joy when they have too much control of their emotions (Pearsall, 1988). Suppression inhibits all feelings. As Marlon, a young student from Jamaica, expressed: "Having feelings and not showing them is like having a bird that doesn't sing!"

Honest emotional expressions help people feel authentic. Individuals who do not express can feel phony, frustrated, and depressed. Especially damaging is to not express resentful feelings which are like tiny pockets of venom that never disappear (Bloomfield, 1996b). Even when one has awareness of resentment, expressing it is difficult. "It's easier to keep quiet," said one woman. After she was encouraged to let her resentment be known in a nonthreatening way, she admitted, "I feel so relieved now. Keeping a lid on resentment was causing me frustration and unhappiness. Being assertive has made all the difference in how I feel about myself."

In all developmental areas, positive growth is a benefit of genuine emotional expression. True sharing of feelings usually leads to heightened self-esteem and a healthier life style.

Steps to Expressiveness

"I realize that I could benefit from becoming more expressive, but how do I go about it?" is a common question. As with any change, the primary step is desire. Telling yourself, "I want to express my feelings more, and I'm going to try," begins the process. Being determined, yet patient, is good advice. Just as you couldn't expect to lose 30 pounds in a short period, you won't become expressive overnight. We can, however, act ourselves into a new way of thinking and think ourselves into a new way of acting. "We may be products of the past but are also architects of our future" (Myers, 1992, p. 122). Concentrated effort and practice are required, and you can expect to feel uncomfortable at first as you face challenges involved in expression. As with other behaviors, repeated expressiveness becomes a part of who you are.

If you aren't what I call a naturally warm, demonstrative person, use your adult ego state in permitting the "child" to act. Stephanie had a life-threatening accident from which she recovered. She decided that she wanted to become more affectionate and demonstrative. She told her husband, children, and friends, "I want to give and receive more hugs and pats on the back." She actually had to tell herself in the beginning, "Go give Michael a hug," and she kept track of how many she gave and received. Anyone in the family could request a hug. They treated it as somewhat of a game until they found that hugging had become second nature.

I cherish a note from a student: "Sharon, I am so thrilled to tell you about this. Yesterday, I hugged my grandma and for the very first time told her I loved her. She looked so surprised, and tears came to her eyes. She seemed to like it. I didn't think I could just go do that, but, thanks to your class, I got up my nerve!" I smiled as I thought to myself that hugging hadn't been one of my typical behaviors until I began to teach about relationships, and now others were learning from me. Because we are unique, you may prefer to express affection in other ways such as words, writing, gifts, favors, helpful behaviors, and just by listening.

Anger Management

Few people have received constructive modeling or advice on expressing anger. Remember the three components of emotion? Physiological arousal is usually a clear sign of anger. Typically, blood pressure rises, and the heart may seem

---

Reflect

- Think of a time when you were aware of physiological arousal due to an emotion.
- On a scale of 1 to 5 (5 being almost always): How often do you recognize your feelings? How often do you express emotion?
- Identify an emotion you usually express as well as one you often don't express.
- Considering each developmental area of self, how have you benefited (or not) from emotional expression?

Apply

- Keep a one-day log of your emotions. Include all three components that you recognize.
- Observe facial expression and guess how the person feels. If you feel comfortable doing so, verify your guess.
- Engage in any or all of expressive behaviors. Hug or touch someone in a loving way. Laugh! Have a good cry.

to beat harder or faster. Cognitively, angry people believe that they are being mistreated and can experience frustration. Behaviorally, they have a tendency to lash out at others. However, a person can also cry, become very quiet, and even act in constructive ways.

Most people describe anger as unpleasant although it can be a positive motivating force. Anger itself is neither good nor bad. How it is expressed is where to focus our attention. Too often, anger leads to negative behaviors. In relationships, the emotion can erupt in violence. Additionally, one of the risk factors for alcohol, tobacco, and other unhealthy drug use is **trait anger**, defined as a state of general hostility (Thomas, 1997). Rather than accept the idea that very little can be done about your angry expressions, decide to become an effective anger manager. Becoming aware of how anger affects people and why anger is experienced can lead you into making wise choices about expressing.

Effects of anger.   Although being angry doesn't have to cause problems, not constructively expressing the feeling can damage individuals and relationships. Anger appears to be related to risk for heart attack and death because the emotion is likely to raise blood pressure, speed up the heart, and narrow blood vessels (*Consumer Reports on Health*, 2001). Researchers at Harvard Medical School found that the most common emotion experienced in the 2 hours before a heart attack was anger (Goleman, 1997). Another study showed that an increased risk of heart disease is related to proneness to anger (Ahmad, 2000). In fact, coronary heart disease risk is related to both heightened expression and inhibition of anger (Stoney & Engebretson, 2000).

In *The Angry Book*, (Rubin 1998) points out many "assorted poisons" related to repressed anger: anxiety, guilt, depression, overeating, high blood pressure, self-imposed starvation, sleep problems, psychosomatic illnesses, obsessions, and compulsions. He also identifies a serious side effect of what he calls the "freezing" of anger which is the stifling of all emotions, including love. Just as a person cannot feel with a frozen finger, he or she cannot feel with frozen emotions. Is it any wonder that anger management is needed?

Understandably, anger and love occur in the same relationships. Expressing your anger can be a sign that you care and want a change for the better. However, too much anger in a relationship is unhealthy, and negative ways of handling it will definitely erode loving feelings. Teresa Adams (1987), a therapist and author, writes: "In every divorce, the mishandling of anger is a major cause of the failure of a marriage" (p. 151). Continually stuffing your anger is a way of mishandling it.

A dangerous type of anger mismanagement is the use of aggression and violence. Obviously, too many individuals vent their anger in violent, abusive ways. Random assaults and killings have become far too common. Since 1990 what have been termed "road rage" cases have increased by 51 percent. (Stephen, 1999). Certainly, one does not drive today without feeling frustrated and even angry at times. Yet, to allow such feelings to escalate into violent acts is alarming and demands concerned attention and intervention.

Reasons for anger.   Recognizing the sources of anger can be instrumental in bringing it under control. Annoyance and hostility can result from an inability to accurately make **attributions**, deductions about the causes of behavior or events; in other words, you may have difficulty determining the correct reason for a behavior. Biases in attribution generally lead to problems. For example, if individuals in an automobile wrongly believe that another driver with bright headlights is just trying to make them mad, hostility is highly probable. In relationships, attributions play a significant role. Consider the following incident.

> At a class reunion Katrina danced with a former boyfriend.
> Her husband Ryan thought, "I know that she's doing that just to make me jealous."
> He became angry.

Could Ryan's attribution been incorrect? What effect would this likely have on their relationship, at least for this period of time? Can you come up with a different attribution?

Believing that others make you angry and not feeling in control of your feelings makes you a victim. If anger is appropriate, use it as a "call to action" and make the situation better. If the anger doesn't make sense, decide to release it in a constructive way and use cognitive restructuring to "talk yourself out of" the anger. Taking pride in yourself means that you don't just respond; instead, you decide. Responding to hate with hate, or anger with anger, is not because of what was directed your way; it's because of what's inside of you (Dyer, 1992). Ask yourself, "Why am I angry and what can I do to change that?" Use anger in a productive way to make your life better, not worse!

Choices in expressing anger.   Beyond understanding the effects and determining the reasons for anger, what can help? The issue becomes one of discovering constructive ways to express. Following is a partial list of possibilities.

Walk, jog, swim, engage in any type of physical exercise.
Hit a pillow, punch a punching bag or stuffed object.
Talk to someone who is trusted.
Scream (in a private place), write angry thoughts, cry.
Clean house, pull weeds.

A physical act seems to be especially relieving. However, if you find that your actions serve to escalate anger, another method is advisable.

Thought-changing, covered in the next section, can be helpful especially in situations where you may be misinterpreting another's behavior. An excellent technique is to look at anger-provoking events from different perspectives and not personalize everything that happens. If you are angry with an individual, try to let him or her know. The key is to use assertiveness and positive communication techniques covered in this book rather than to engage in unbridled expressions of anger.

After awareness of the problems of suppression and the benefits of expressiveness, the next steps become obvious. Select behaviors that seem to fit you and even experiment with some that at first seem uncomfortable. Continue to practice your new expressive actions and monitor yourself to see how you're doing. Have you hugged anyone recently? When was the last time you really laughed? What did you do or not do the last time you felt angry? What could you have done? Are you allowing any tears? Keep in mind what most people do not realize: suppressing any emotion will affect total expressiveness. Negate anger and you also negate love (Rubin, 1998). In an emotionally healthy climate, feelings are not labeled good or bad, and all are given ample play and freedom.

> It is all right to feel love, and it is all right to feel anger. It is all right to express love, and it is all right to express anger. Your feelings are welcome here, and we would like to know what they are. You are loved and accepted and safe with all your feelings. You needn't stifle any of them to please us. (Rubin, 1998, pp. 21–22)

CHANGING WHAT YOU FEEL

Being an expressive person does not mean that you are at the mercy of your feelings. A significant way of taking charge of your life is to be able to change what you feel. Being more in control of emotions can also improve health. Negative feelings of anger, anxiety, and depression, if strong and prolonged, can make us more vulnerable to disease, worsen the symptoms, and get in the way of recovery (Goleman, 1997). Doesn't it make sense to know how to eliminate or at least diminish the intensity of these emotions?

The Power of Your Thoughts

A **cognition** is a thought. Often a person's thoughts about an event determine the particular emotion. If your interpretation of the event is accurate, any emotion will be normal and appropriate (Burns, 1980). Thoughts can create pleasant or unpleasant emotions and can also relieve unpleasant ones. For example, pretend that you are driving a car and are stopped at a red light. The instant the light turns green, you hear a horn honking behind you. Do you feel surprised, concerned, angry, annoyed, or calm? Whether you realize it or not, how you feel depends on your thought about the honking, not the event itself. "Oh, I wonder who is honking at me. Maybe it's someone I know" would elicit surprise and possibly even delight. "The person must have an emergency to be in such a hurry" is a thought that could result in concern. "How dare anyone honk at me! I know what a green light means" would spark anger or annoyance. "Somebody likes to use their horn. I'm glad I'm not that stressed," you think and then feel nothing but calmness. We actually can create our own emotional reality.

What you think and feel then guides your behavior. You may turn around, scowl, and shake your fist—or worse. Or you may turn around, smile, and wave, or choose to do nothing. You have the choice. Cognitive therapy trains people to change the way they interpret and look at things so that they can experience different emotions, feel better, and act in a positive, productive way.

Rational emotive behavior therapy.   One of the best known and applicable cognitive systems, rational emotive behavior therapy, or REBT, was developed by Albert Ellis (1977, 1984). The central theory of REBT is that events or situations do not upset you; instead, it is your belief about what has happened that does. Irrational beliefs, discussed in Chapter 4, are responsible for unpleasant or negative consequences. The approach uses the letters "ABC."

A stands for *activating* event, situation, or experience.
B represents *beliefs* or thoughts about the activating event.
C means *consequences* (emotions, further thoughts, and behaviors).

Ellis (1993) points out that cognitions, emotions, and behaviors are interactive in that each influences the other. According to him, REBT is opposed to rigidity, "must" thoughts, one-sidedness, and strongly favors openness, alternative seeking, and flexibility. REBT helps people challenge irrational beliefs and change their lives.

Let's put REBT into practice. You receive a failing grade on your first college examination. This is the activating event (A). Your initial belief or thought (B): "That's it. This proves I can't handle college-level coursework. I might as well quit right now." Can you see that your initial belief is irrational? These thoughts would probably lead to emotions of disappointment, depression, and hopelessness followed by actions to quit school (C).

Instead, REBT changes the belief and alters the consequences. Remember the cognitive restructuring formula from Chapter 1? Consider this alternative:

> Just because I received a failing grade on the first exam doesn't mean I can't handle college-level work. I didn't perform as well as I wanted to; however, one grade does not mean I will fail this course.

You have now eliminated the irrational thought. How would the consequences be different? Your initial emotion may still be disappointment, yet you would then feel hopeful, your thoughts and behaviors would be more positive and directed to doing what you could to improve. You would not quit school on the basis of one examination grade!

Cognitive techniques work best for those who have the ability to reflect on their own thoughts. Individuals with a thinking preference in decision making as shown on the MBTI (Chapter 2) may have an advantage over feeling types. However, if you are inclined to "think with your heart," you can especially benefit from the use of REBT.

REBT is not useful when your thoughts are rational and suitable to the occasion. You do not want to create unpleasant emotions by thought-changing. For example, Mike had been invited to go out of town for the weekend with friends. His original thought was, "It was neat that they asked me, and it sounds like a good time." His feelings were anticipation and happiness. Later he found himself thinking, "I wonder why they asked me. I'll bet they needed another car, and I have a nice one." Do you see how quickly his feelings would then change? Be careful that you don't replace pleasant, realistic thoughts with unpleasant, irrational ones.

The Power of Your Behavior

Closely related to REBT is **reality therapy** developed by William Glasser (1965). According to him, rational thought and behavior are both necessary as is the ability to think of several possibilities. Glasser (1984) has also taught and written about **control theory**. In the earlier example of failing your first examination, control theory would say you are depressing yourself. If you want to feel different, first change your behaviors. Instead of moping around, you can choose to socialize with friends, go to a movie, or do whatever is pleasurable. You can alter your thinking, too, as suggested before; however, more emphasis is placed on changing the behavior. When people who are miserable do something different, they invariably change their, feelings. Have you ever whistled or hummed cheerily and then recognized a slight mood elevation? If so, you were using basic control theory.

A fascinating idea is that facial expressions can change feelings, at least to a modest degree (Averill, 1997). People have been able to feel fear and disgust by creating the related expression on their faces. Studies have shown that a particular type of smile, one in which the eye muscles are active, is associated with enjoyment and reports of positive emotions (Ekman, Davidson, & Friesen, 1990). Simple experiments in my classes indicate that happy facial expressions and positive behaviors can pleasantly affect feelings. Try putting on a happy face and see what happens!

Cognitive and behavioral techniques can be used effectively to change most emotions, including minor depression or a "down" feeling. Experiencing a "blue mood" once in awhile is common, and to feel better, you can use any of the ideas for creating happiness covered in Chapter 4, plus thought and behavior changing. Exercise, which has been already highly recommended in this book, has definite mood-lifting benefits (Jaret, 1999). Other ideas include engaging in enjoyable activities such as reading, shopping, going to a movie, or watching television. We really do have control over those brief occasional bouts with the "blues." Another option is simply to allow yourself to feel mildly unhappy for a brief time! An underlying theme of this book is that human beings have numerous choices, one of which is deciding to change what you are feeling.

SEEKING PROFESSIONAL HELP FOR DEPRESSION

Certain emotional states do not lend themselves exclusively to self-help. A common psychological disorder that affects thoughts, feelings, physical health, and behaviors is **major** or **clinical depression**. Far different from just a "down" feeling, it is characterized by a depressed mood or loss of interest or pleasure in most activities for a period of at least 2 weeks. Other symptoms are diminished ability to think, concentrate, or make decisions; feelings of worthlessness; recurrent thoughts of death or suicide; increase or decrease in appetite or weight; insomnia or sleeping too much; fatigue; and loss of energy. "Passive negativity—being stuck—is the hallmark of depression" (Baumel, 1995, p. 5).

Often called the "common cold" of mental illness, major depression along with other types of mood disorders is suffered by one out of every seven people. Many do little or nothing to alleviate their pain. Nearly 60 percent of people who score positive for depression have never been treated (Screening for Mental Health, Inc., 2001). Yet of those who seek help, approximately 80 percent respond well to treatment and go on to lead productive lives, according to the National Depressive and Manic-Depressive Association (2001).

Not only is clinical depression a dreadful feeling that impinges on quality of life, it is related to health. A study showed that chronically depressed older people had a significant 88 percent excess risk of developing cancer when compared to those who weren't depressed (Penninx et al., 1998). Because treatment of depression in cancer patients leads to better patient adjustment and reduced symptoms, it appears to influence the course of disease (Spiegel, 1996). People with depression also have an increased risk for coronary heart disease (Henderson, 2000). The *British Medical Journal* (2001) called depression the largest determinant of disability in the world. In addition to decreasing the potential for disease, successful treatment usually helps a person resolve additional psychological and relationship problems.

Why is help not sought? Often a person may be aware of the symptoms but not suspect depression as a cause. Other factors are the continuing stigma attached to any type of psychological problem and gender role socialization. The revealing book *I Don't Want to Talk About It* (Real, 1997) focuses on depression in males and maintains that men, more easily than women, "get depressed about being depressed and allow their pain to burrow deeper and further from view" (p. 35). Depression in men is often hidden, which may be one of the reasons that depression appears to affect nearly twice as many females as males. Females are more likely to seek help. Three to four million men in the United States have major depression (National Institute of Mental Health, 2001), and they usually pay a high price: an inability to develop and maintain intimate relationships (Real, 1997). A medical doctor who suffered from depression expressed a reason for seeking help. "With the right guidance and the right support, a breakdown can become a breakthrough" (Ornish, 1998, p.76).

What causes major depression? The general consensus is that genetic, biochemical, and environmental factors can all be involved (National Depressive and Manic-Depressive Association, 2001). According to the National Institute of Mental Health (2001) major depression presents itself in generation after generation in some families; yet, it also occurs when there is no family history. One type of depression, **seasonal affective disorder (SAD)**, stems from lack of sunlight and is usually experienced only in the fall and winter. In many cases, light therapy, which involves the use of a special light box or visor, brings relief.

Proper diagnosis is extremely important in determining treatment. If the cause is biologically based, antidepressant drugs are usually prescribed and work for about 70 percent of people (*Harvard Health Letter*, 2000). "But I don't want to use drugs" is a common protest. It can help to realize that the proper prescription of an antidepressant merely restores the functioning of the brain. The medications "fix" what's in need of repair and do not create something artificial or unnatural (Podell, 1992). Antidepressant medicines are not addictive or habit forming according to the National Institute of Mental Health, although there can be side effects (*Harvard Health Letter*, 2000).

Taking the best drug in the correct dosage is essential. A person is advised to carefully select an experienced psychiatrist or, ideally, a psychopharmacologist whose specialty is drug therapy. Then, being carefully monitored and following the treatment plan in its entirety will make the difference in the degree of success (Preboth, 2000). The results of successful drug therapy seem like miracles. "I feel like a completely new person," said Mark, as he walked confidently into the classroom.

When medication can ameliorate the symptoms of a chemical imbalance, why should we be made to feel that taking it is somehow irresponsible? Do we condemn those with hypertension for their dependence on medications that lower blood pressure? (Dowling, 1991, p. 25).

A depressed person typically needs more than just drugs to eliminate depression (Trickett, 1997). Combining drug and psychological therapy has significant advantages over just one or the other (Keller, et al., 2000). Even therapy alone is successful. A program of cognitive-behavioral therapy significantly reduced depressive symptoms and negative thinking while it increased self-esteem (Peden, Rayens, Hall, & Beebes (2001). Cognitive-behavioral therapy seems to be especially helpful in preventing future depression (Fava, Rafanelli, Grandi, Conti, & Belluardo, 1998). Physical activity is again beneficial. Among clinically depressed older people, was associated with fewer depressive symptoms regular physical activity (Moore et al., 1999).

A most compelling reason for seeking professional help is that suicide is often an answer for a severely depressed person. More than 90 percent of people who kill themselves have a mental disorder which is commonly one of depression, according to the National Institute of Mental Health (2001). Regardless of the cause, suicide is a tragedy that affects many. In the United States, more than 30,000 deaths—more than 80 per day—are because of suicide (Screening for Mental Health, Inc., 2001). In a 17-year period, the rate of suicide among 10–14-year-olds has increased by 109 percent; and 11 percent for 15–19-year-olds. Tragically suicide is the leading cause of death in the older adolescent group (Stanard, 2000). Probably because of social stigma, gay and lesbian young people are at a higher risk than heterosexuals (Hartstein, 1996).

An excellent book I would like to see in the hands of anyone even remotely considering suicide is *A Reason to Live* (Beattie, 1991). The book gives many ways to feel in control of life again, suggestions of options to suicide, and numerous resources. One strategy is to imagine how devastating your death would be to someone with whom you are not angry and for whom you care deeply, such as a grandparent. "Anytime the idea came into my mind, I saw my grandma's face and knew I would never do that to her," said one young man. Remember if you ever consider suicide: "Keep it a question. It's not really an answer" (Colgrove, Bloomfield, & McWilliams, 1991, p. 69).

Ideally, a depressed person will seek help. However, because lack of motivation or energy is usually present, this may not happen. An estimated 70 percent who commit suicide tell others of their intentions (Baron, 1998); yet, 79 percent of youth who killed themselves had never seen a mental health counselor (Standard, 2000). If you know someone who has any of the depression symptoms, displays drastic changes in his or her behaviors, or talks about death or suicide, do all you can to get him or her to a professional. Selecting a professional can begin with a licensed or certified counselor or therapist or a physician who knows enough about depression to refer the person to a specialist in mood disorders. Or one can get references from hospitals, universities, or professional associations (see Resources at the end of this chapter).

Hopefully, the stigma attached to depression and all types of therapies will be eliminated and the future will be bright for those who suffer from major depression as

Figure 5-4   Severe depression can be difficult and dangerous.

well as for their families and friends. Having the proper diagnosis, using drug therapy if needed, enhancing one's physical health, and then working with an effective therapist can make the difference between living in the depths of despair or enjoying the beauty of life.

COPING WITH EMOTIONAL CRISES

My sister-in-law sounded numb when she called at 3:30 in the morning. "Steven was killed in an automobile accident about midnight. A drunk driver going over 80 miles an hour on the wrong side of the highway hit his car head-on." I managed to gasp, "Oh, no," as a jolt of disbelief and horror hit. Steve, my beloved 22-year-old nephew, was dead. The grieving began at that moment, and years later the sorrow remains, diminished somewhat by time, coping strategies, and beautiful memories. Emotions run rampant when a crisis occurs.

The death of a loved one is a profound tragedy. Losing a child is the ultimate crisis. Not only is there a loss of a precious life, but a young person's death seems so unfair and unthinkable. It was supposedly Albert Camus who explained: "The order of nature is reversed. Children are supposed to bury their parents" (Stearns, 1984, p. 15). A child's death is not only the pain of losing a person; it means a loss of parents' dreams, a part of themselves, and a part of their future (Davis, 1991). "A child's death is like having part of ourselves sliced away" (Sanders, 1992, p. 120). One study had hopeful findings in that bereaved parents reported slightly higher levels of marital satisfaction and expressed different sources of life satisfaction and sources of worry (deVries, Davis, Wortman, & Lehman, 1997). A bereaved father said, "I truly don't 'sweat the small stuff' anymore, and I'm satisfied with a lot of little stuff." In a book designed to help cope with the loss of a child, the author (Donnelly, 2001) assures parents that recovering doesn't mean forgetting.

Steven's tragic death began a series of crises for my family. Within a little over a year I underwent cancer surgery and was fitted with an artificial eye, my 16-year-old daughter experienced a prolonged illness and surgery as a result of an autoimmune disease, and my father died unexpectedly. I was beginning to believe what I had read on a greeting card: "Into every life some rain must fall" and on the inside: "followed by large hail and damaging winds." On a positive note, these crises led to personal learning and can now provide hope, encouragement, and suggested coping strategies to you.

The Path of Life

Life isn't easy. "The farther one travels on the journey of life, the more births one will experience, and therefore the more deaths—the more joy and the more pain" (Peck, 1978, p. 75). As an introduction to an interpersonal relations course, I draw on the chalkboard a line depicting life. What do you think it looks like? It's not a straight line, nor is it vertical or horizontal, and neither does it go up for a period of years (maybe 40?) and then head downhill. The "dip 'n doo" line, as I call it, goes up and down like a series of peaks and valleys. The drawing reveals the certainty of change. Life has both positive and negative experiences from which we can't escape.

What can the line teach? The word *choice* comes to mind. All of us will spend time in the valleys. What are your choices? One is to make the situation worse. Tragedy can become more tragic because of one's thoughts or actions, or both. Kurt was badly injured in an accident. He had not used alcohol much before; now its effects seemed to lessen the hurt. He was frequently verbally abusive to his family. Another possibility is to remain stagnant, do little, and maybe wallow in self-pity. The thought "There's nothing I can do about this" is common. The best choice is to gather your resources and strength and begin to ascend from the valley. Recognizing the pattern of the lifeline reminds you that dips eventually curve upward.

Another relevant point has to do with learning. Joyful and peaceful times are too often unappreciated. "I look back on those days before I was ill and kick myself for not enjoying them more," reported a cancer patient. "Now I am grateful for each minute of life." Because we often take the peaks for granted, generally, less learning is experienced there. Valuable lessons are learned in the trenches, the dips of life. Also, the variety of life's experiences adds depth and meaning to existence.

> A full life will be full of pain. But the only alternative is not to live fully (Peck, 1978, p. 133).

Without a doubt, the terrorist attack on the World Trade Center and the Pentagon on September 11, 2001, was the greatest collective crisis in recent history. The tragic loss of so many lives and the damage to property and the economy were devastating. The following is both poignant and meaningful.

> Grief and love, rage and vengefulness, pride and defiance—a volatile set of emotions was let loose in America. They can be dangerous, but they can also be constructive. It hardly seems possible, or even fitting, to imagine that some good could come out of such horror. But the best memorial to those who perished would be the achievement of a safer, saner world. And it is not out of reach (Auchincloss, 2001).

Crises of this magnitude as well as all others are traumatic, yet the possibility of positive change offers a beacon of hope.

> *Sometimes when the bottom falls out of our lives, we are set free. Loss can make artists of us all as we weave new patterns into the fabric of our lives.*
> —Charles Stephen

Any unexpected negative or positive event that dramatically changes your life is a **crisis**. Loss is commonly experienced directly such as losing a job, a loved one, a personal possession, or a dream and indirectly in cases of rape, chronic illness, or the birth of a disabled child. Answers to how long is the path to recovery and how much time will it take are only speculative.

> When a significant loss has us in its grip, a minimum of six months to a year is usually required for healing. Some aspects of the process continue into the second year. Resolution may not come until even later. (Stearns, 1984, p. 19)

When a crisis of loss isn't resolved or healed, problems can emerge later. "Unresolved grief haunts us" (Kennedy, 1991, p. 12).

How to Cope

The coping mechanisms that will be most effective in a situation depend on the nature of the crisis. Often we are wise to do what the title of a helpful book suggests: *Hoping, Coping, and Moping.* (Jevne, 2000). Whenever a loss is involved, the following coping behaviors make the going easier, perhaps faster, and increase the possibility for growth.

Feel your feelings.   An emotional response is inevitable in any crisis. Keep in mind that suppressed feelings can cause unwanted problems and almost never help the situation. You may be reluctant to express, especially if the feeling is an uncomfortable one for you. Depression is one of my least favorites. Going through an unwanted divorce was depressing, and the accompanying feelings of hopelessness and helplessness made it worse. Wanting to appear strong, I seldom let anyone see how I felt and even believed that I was doing a good job denying my feelings to myself. Knowing what I do now, I'm convinced that my body wasn't fooled.

> Any emotion that is repressed will eventually seek manifestation at a later date. What you resist emotionally, persists. And by experiencing the emotion I don't mean you need to act out the emotion. Simply feel the emotion fully (Ellsworth 1988, p. 77).

Feeling the emotion goes beyond naming or talking about it. During my first cancer-center session I eagerly volunteered to be the first to tell my story. The leader stopped me after a few minutes and asked, "How did you *feel* about losing your eye?" I glibly put names to the feelings: anxious, sad. When she pressed me to actually feel what I felt, I found myself resisting. She said, "I don't think you have really dealt with that loss." To my surprise, I felt the tears coming. She asked me why losing an eye was so sad. Without thinking, I blurted out, "Because I have always been complimented on my blue eyes. My husband said it was one of the first things he noticed about me, and now one is gone." Both my husband and I cried then—a welcome release and a sure sign that until then we hadn't truly experienced the pain of the loss.

> Lean gently into your pain. You won't find it bottomless. Let yourself be with the pain. When it is at its worst and you feel it all, you're already starting to heal. (Bloomfield, 1980, p. 268)

Release feelings.   In any crisis, emotional expression can be extremely therapeutic. Crying, deep breathing, and hugging are appropriate behaviors intended to relieve tension. Being touched is reassuring. I remember the horrible night I was told that there was a 98 percent probability that my eye tumor was cancerous. Crying was a welcome release; being held by my husband got me through the night. Relaxation techniques described in Chapter 3 can be quite soothing. Some audiotapes are designed to help people release feelings and then move on with their lives. Another possibility is to keep a journal. I remember feeling a release during several crises as the feelings seemed to move from inside me onto the paper. Often, when thoughts are put on paper, a person can begin to see "form in the chaos" (Kennedy, 1991, p. 29). Another benefit may not be so obvious. One Sunday I wrote about my pleasant feelings and positive attitude. I noticed that on the previous Sunday I had been depressed. I thought, "It's hard to believe I felt that down." I was left with the assurance that more positives lay ahead.

Research supports the benefits of writing (Smyth, 1998). Writing about emotional upheavals improved the physical and mental health of grade-school children, nursing home residents, asthma and arthritis sufferers, college students, maximum security prisoners, new mothers, and rape victims (Pennebaker 1997; Suedfeld & Pennebaker, 1997). Recommendations are to focus on current issues and explore both the objective experience and your deepest feelings about it. Talking into a tape recorder can be substituted for writing.

Take charge of your thoughts. Thoughts can help or hurt. The cognitive techniques, explained earlier, are especially beneficial. Be aware of what you are thinking during a crisis. Is it realistic? If not, remember that you can change it using a method such as rational emotive behavioral therapy. Cognitive restructuring, discussed in Chapter 1, helped breast cancer patients shift to problem-focused coping that resulted in positive life changes (Spiegel, 1996). The doctor who led support groups for these patients offers recommendations in an inspiring book *Living Beyond Limits: New Hope and Help for Facing Life-Threatening Illness* (Spiegel, 1993). Sustaining positive thoughts is critical. In both crises of divorce and cancer, I found books about and living examples of people who had survived those experiences, and I filled my mind with hope. At times, discrediting someone else's opinion is necessary. One day I heard someone say, "The weeds in my yard are like a cancer. They just spread and spread, and there's absolutely nothing you can do about it." I said to myself, "Oh, yes, there are many things you can do about cancer." Thought-stopping becomes a lifesaver. When a dreary, anxiety-provoking thought appears, tell yourself to stop and replace it with a positive one.

Acceptance of reality and realization of what you cannot change are healthy. "My husband no longer loves me and wants a divorce," "My child is addicted to drugs," "I have a serious disease," "My mother is dead" are difficult to think about; yet, as facts, they need to be acknowledged so they can be dealt with. Denial is usually a first reaction, and it helps absorb the shock. After a time, denial is unhealthy. A challenging question may be advisable. I remember standing in front of a mirror and saying, "OK, you are going to be divorced. What are you going to do now?" The statement freed me to move on with my life, and the question forced me to take action. Recognizing and then acting upon what you can do makes any crisis easier to bear.

Become educated. Educating yourself about any topic related to the crisis can make a positive difference. Libraries and bookstores contain many resources on coping and offer positive examples of those who "have gone before you." For example, the book *Just Get Me Through This!* (Cohen, 2000) is highly recommended by Emily, a friend of mine, as an excellent tool to help deal with breast cancer. Decide how much you want to know, ask questions, and reframe your thinking in a positive direction. It's important to note, though, that too much obsession isn't advisable. Thinking and talking only about your crisis is not only unhealthy, it is likely to "turn off" others.

Seek support.   Isolating yourself for a long period of time during any crisis is not a good idea because, more than ever, support is necessary. Social networks and support have been shown to reduce mortality rates, to improve recovery from serious illness, and to increase the use of preventive health practices (Hurdle, 2001). Who can provide support? Family and friends can be comforting and helpful; in some cases, they are not. A life crisis can overwhelm loved ones and erode their abilities to be supportive. Typically, other people need for you to them know what you need and want as well as what you don't want. A woman in a cancer support session reported that her family had descended upon her when they learned of her diagnosis. They were overly helpful and refused to let her do anything, even though she could. She decided to tell them to stop doing certain things for her because feeling helpless and out of control could make her condition worse. The book *The Healing Family* (Simonton, 1984) is an excellent resource for families. The author writes: "So often family members, even those with the best intentions, give the wrong kind of support, which sometimes hurts more than it helps" (p. 2). Likewise, the book mentioned earlier *Just Get Me Through This!* (Cohen, 2000) enlightens potential supporters. Friends and family can be asked to carry out tasks, talk, listen, touch, or just be there. Tell them what you want.

Support groups made up of others who have had similar crises can be invaluable. If you have any reservations about seeking support, you are probably equating it with being weak. Instead, believe that you *deserve* help and that you are showing internal strength by seeking and responding to external support. An immediate benefit is the realization that you are not "different" and weren't singled out for this particular hardship. Education and a safe place to vent feelings are necessary ingredients of worthwhile groups. What isn't helpful is a group that dwells only on problems and offers little that is positive. A partial listing of resources is given at the end of this and other chapters. Most telephone directories list support groups in a special section. You may need courage to pick up the phone or attend a meeting, yet the benefits almost always outweigh any initial discomfort. "Buried feelings fester. Shared feelings enrich and lead to growth and healing" (Smolin & Guinan, 1993, p. 164).

Professional help is frequently needed, and you don't have to be feeling desperate to seek it. Any one of several reasons could motivate you. You may not be receiving needed support from family, friends, and groups. Therapy could move you along faster in a healing process and can certainly enhance the quality of life. In cases of sudden, traumatic death of a spouse or a child, grief is never "normal," and mental health treatment is almost always warranted (Wortman, Battle, & Lemkau, 1997). Words of caution about selecting a counselor are in order. Be as careful as you would in choosing any medical specialist. Don't just pick a name out of the yellow pages. Use suggestions given in the earlier discussion about depression. Ask people for recommendations. Feel free to interview a few counselors and find out their level of expertise, their degree of familiarity with your particular crisis, and, most important, how much rapport you have with them. Then, if you aren't satisfied with the counselor, find another one.

Be extra kind to yourself.   Taking good care of yourself is good advice any time; during a crisis, it is of utmost importance. Because ordinary stress affects us physically, it stands to reason that during periods of unusual strain, our bodies will suffer. Eating well even if you don't feel like it, exercising, and getting plenty of rest become even more important. You can also pamper yourself without feeling guilty. Those ice cream cones I ate during my cancer recovery I deserved!

Stay active and set goals.   Even though a crisis generally saps motivation, activity is a reassuring measure. Even simple tasks such as showering, brushing your teeth, and making coffee can be energizing. Staying involved with your work, if possible, is highly recommended. Pleasurable activities divert your thinking temporarily and convince you that life can still be enjoyed. A change of scene is especially refreshing. A few months after my first husband asked for a divorce, my daughters and I traveled to San Jose, California, to visit my sister. The trip itself and the time I spent there bolstered my spirits immensely. I thought, "There's a big world out here just waiting for me to explore, and it's filled with beautiful people and enjoyable activities."

Sometimes a crisis opens doors. Widowed at 54, Bernice decided to attend college and acquire career skills. She discovered a new person within herself and thoroughly enjoyed her learning experiences. Others do volunteer work, refresh their talents, learn skills, and acquire new hobbies and interests. Setting goals says that you can move beyond the crisis, your thinking becomes more directed, you are acting upon life rather than being acted upon, and you are sending positive messages to your body. Goals stimulate feelings of hope and anticipation and are a reinvestment in life. Delaying major decisions, however, is wise, as your judgment will probably be clouded for awhile.

Death: A Universal Crisis

Any crisis is challenging; however, the death of a loved one is most stressful. This could be because death is often so unexplainable. Judy Mize, a dear friend whose husband died unexpectedly, expressed it so well. "It's so hard. Relationships don't die with death. I still have a relationship with Paul; yet Paul isn't here to have a relationship with." Rita, a widowed student, reflected on additional reasons for pain:

> I have come to realize there are many more losses tied to John's death. I lost my husband, my lifetime partner, my best friend, and my son's father. Resulting losses from his death included leaving my job and moving from Virginia. I felt I had lost myself along with John. The "me" that was, was no more. She was gone forever.

Rita's words remind us that death usually precipitates another crisis—one of identity.

Death is a universal crisis because all of us, unless we die before every other person we care about, will face a loss. "One out of one dies. Nothing, no one, lives forever. All things end at some point (Sims, 1985, p. 1). Death is especially painful because each loss is connected to all loss, and every death reminds us of our own death. Because dying is considered such a taboo subject, most people try to avoid it in their thinking and talking. Unfortunately, this avoidance means that coping strategies are not being developed.

> Americans tend to have a negative attitude about grieving, feeling that it is something we should get over with as soon as possible. Grief, whether our own or that of

someone in our social or business life, is an inconvenience, an interruption in our hectic schedules. We harbor many misconceptions about the grief process and scarcely comprehend or appreciate its value and purpose. (Vail, 1982, p. 52)

Grief is an emotional, physical, spiritual, and intellectual response to loss (Edwards, 1989). In addition to sorrow, a person can experience anger, relief, frustration, guilt, and self-pity (DeSpelder & Strickland, 1999). Even though grief is the hardest work we will ever have to do, it's a way to heal from pain, and we must "go through to get through" (Edwards, 1989, p. 16).

Stages of death and grieving.   Five stages associated with acceptance of death were identified by Elisabeth Kübler-Ross (1969). These are:

denial → anger → bargaining → depression → acceptance

Her theory has led to a closer look at the grieving process and, like other stage theories, suggests that acceptance of death is a series of somewhat predictable thoughts, feelings, and behaviors that are subject to individual differences.

Each stage has its challenges and its usefulness. Denial, the instant shock and disbelief in the face of tragedy, is initially a protector. Judy, after the sudden, unexpected death of her husband, Paul, said, "I am so grateful for denial." The next stage of anger, even if incomprehensible at the time, may allow a bereaved person to vent deep feelings. If the death was untimely and/or perceived as preventable, anger will likely be the dominant feeling (Wortman, Battle, & Lemkau, 1997). Bargaining is an attempt to change the circumstances. Often, the attempted "deal" to not let this happen is proposed to a supreme being, and disappointment is a definite possibility. The next stage of depression, which is so unpleasant, can indicate that one is approaching the acceptance stage. Obviously, a survivor experiences sadness throughout every stage; the throes of agony are more apparent during this stage. The final stage of acceptance does not mean that the pain is over; however, it is not as acute, and one can move on.

Understanding the basic stages can help you see where you are in the process and why you feel as you do. A student read a book about dealing with death for a class project. Her comment was, "Until now I didn't understand what I went through when my mother died. It was over a year ago, and the book still helped me see that what I feel is normal." A college classmate of mine hinted at the stage process in a lovely book she wrote for her two children before her untimely death in 1976.

> When you are very close to someone who dies, there will be sadness. You won't be sharing your life with that person anymore. Sadness hurts. You may feel as though a big hole has been torn in your life. And there will probably be feelings of loneliness as you remember the good times you had with the person you loved. Sometimes it takes a very long time for the sadness to melt away, but slowly you will begin to remember important shared times without the hurt tugging at your memories. (Potter, 1979, p. 12)

Thinking only in terms of stages has some disadvantages. People can get discouraged if they believe they should progress in a certain order and time frame. More helpful is to think of the process as a "fluid experience of a variety of emotions with one underlying theme: coming to terms with the loss" (Davis, 1991, p. 13). Do you ever get over the death of a loved one? Most experts say that you don't. Most people will never reach a time when they completely stop grieving; however, the feeling is less intense and not as frequent. As one bereaved mother expressed, "You don't get over it; you get used to it" (Wortman, Battle, & Lemkau, 1997). Recovering doesn't mean forgetting, and a sense of acceptance can be reached.

> The rainbow hues of your grief—the red-yellow anguish, the blue-green questions, the purple confidence—are woven permanently into the tapestry of your life. Grief invariably leads to new strengths. When you allow yourself to experience fully the subtle gradations of its colors and textures, grief adds to your personal richness and depth. (Tubesing, 1981, p. 57)

Behaviors of grief.   Has anyone said to you, "Don't grieve when I'm gone. I don't want you to mourn my death"? Although the remark was well meant, the person isn't doing you a favor. Grieving serves as a natural and necessary path to healing. A young mother tried hard to block the process: "Crying would be good for me, but my children have lost a father, and I have to be strong for them." She and her children would be better served by getting rid of the equation between strength and suppression of feeling. Her children could benefit from her sharing her sorrow and modeling grieving behaviors.

Grief is invariably unsettling. Many times death is irrational, illogical, and crazy, so a reaction that can feel like the "crazies" is normal (Donnelley, 1987). "Significant emotional loss is an abnormal event in a person's life, and there is no normal way to react to an abnormal event" (James & Cherry, 1988, p. 11). Even though grief is painful, like death, it is a part of life. Experiencing all of life means that you and I will grieve.

> I don't like being hurt. I don't really enjoy experiencing pain. But I believe that I become less of a human being if I learn the art of detachment so well that I can experience the death of a friend or relative and not be emotionally affected by it. To be alive is to feel pain, and to hide from pain is to make yourself less alive. (Kushner, 1986, p. 89)

Grieving behaviors vary from one person to another. Stereotypic gender differences may emerge. Men and women share equal feelings of pain and grief, yet women seem to use a social support system while many men either do not have one or don't use it. During times when partners need each other's support, the differences can cause relationship problems. Honest communication can bridge the gap and lessen the pain.

Other differences have to do with cause of death. Suicides appear to be the most difficult. In addition to depression, guilt is the most intense emotion for parents. They first blame themselves (Smolin & Guinan, 1993). In a study of adult next-of-kin who were mourning a suicide, the participants either didn't ask for support or encountered barriers when they sought it. Professional help was identified as the most pressing need as well as what was most wanted (Provini & Everett, 2000). Because so little had been written for survivors, two authors wrote a book in which they point out that for every suicide about seven to ten others are intimately affected. Immediately finding a therapist who is an excellent listener is strongly recommended. It can also help parents to keep in mind that they can do a thousand things for a child but perhaps not a thousand and one (Lukas & Seiden, 1997).

Grieving and Healing

- Let loose of feelings.
- Don't isolate yourself. Stay engaged in activities and involved with people.
- Tell people what you want and don't want.
- Ask for help and also insist on doing for yourself, if that is what you feel.
- Create a sanctuary for grief, a place where you can be alone with your feelings
- Spend focused, yet brief, times in this sanctuary and focus on memories and personal grief.
- Give yourself a "vacation" from pain whenever possible. Focus on diversions.
- Set up or donate to a worthy cause in the person's memory.
- Create a new nonphysical relationship with the deceased.
- Write to the person and/or about the person.
- Stay involved with family and friends.
- Engage in something that has a meaningful purpose.
- On a regular basis, manage your personal stress.

Recommendations for grieving.   When you are in the throes of deep despair, realize that "Grief is the price we pay for love. Though death comes, love will never go away" (Sims, 1985, p. 6).

Writing about the deceased is therapeutic. After my nephew's death, I asked for contributions to a booklet in his memory. One classmate, in praising Steve's lust for life, his caring, giving ways, and his accomplishments, offered solace with: *The donation of life, more than the duration, is significant; length of one's life is less important than the beauty of one's life.* I completed the project a year after his death, experiencing further emotional release because of it, and at the end wrote:

> Because of Steve, we have all loved, cried, shared, and grown. Our lives are all the better for his having lived. I continue to grieve because Steve deserves each tear I shed.

More recently, my uncle wrote and then put together a beautiful book of tributes and photographs of his beloved wife. Each family member received one—a cherished gift that is so meaningful and comforting.

Writing a tribute to the person who has died can serve more than one purpose. Amy Sheil used an original poem to release her feelings and extol her father after he died.

I Love You, Dad

> Theodore Alan Sheil was my Father.
> I think he was the greatest man to ever be on this earth.
> He was kind, considerate and he always
> wanted to do things for other people.
> I wish he was here now
> to see what I am doing with my life.
> Sometimes I feel cheated,
> I didn't get to know him as long as everybody else did.
> He was very strong, and this was probably
> the time when I learned the most

about how special he was and also how strong.
I tried to be there for him as much as I could,
But it scared me to think of losing him, so I ran away from it.
All I did was try to have fun with my friends
and try to still be there for him some of the time.
It seems so empty now without him.
It's like a part of the family died with him.
I thought he was so handsome and so special.
I thought he would never die.
It's unfair to Mom, too.
They were married for a long time
and they still acted like they were on their honeymoon.
I hope I have a marriage like that one day;
at least they gave me a good example.
Now, my thoughts are all jumbled
But I want to put my feelings on paper,
so I can read this years from now
and know how I felt in my 18th year of life.

I hope Amy and all of us who have grieved remember:

We never lose the people we love, even to death. They continue to participate in every act, thought, and decision we make. Their love leaves an indelible imprint in our memories. Memories make us immortal (Buscaglia, 1992, p. 230).

Other creative talents such as composing a song or just singing one in memory or tribute, painting, sculpting, or drawing are all ways of releasing.

A tragedy can lead to worthwhile actions, and becoming involved in a cause related to the death is an excellent idea. Mothers Against Drunk Driving (MADD), an organization that has made a significant difference, was started by a woman whose daughter was killed by a drunk driver. My nephew Steve's death launched a campaign at Bowling Green State University called "Never Again" to combat drunk driving. Grief can be channeled into positive energy. To gain insight into crisis and coping, use the activity in Reflection and Applications.

Reflect

- Recall an activating event, your beliefs about the event, and the consequences—the ABCs of rational emotive behavioral therapy.
- What do you do when you're in a "blue mood"?
- Think of what you would say or do if someone you know talks of suicide.

Apply

- In the Reflections and Applications section for Chapter 5, fill in the boxes showing that you can use rational emotive behavioral therapy.
- When you experience an unpleasant emotion, use control theory and change the "doing" part of your behavior. Be aware of what happens.
- If you feel comfortable doing so, tell a friend how you have effectively coped with a crisis

At some point—and only the grieving person can decide when that point has been reached—moving on with life is essential. You then may be able to see that death can be a teacher helping us appreciate each other, ourselves, and life itself. You may become closer to loved ones, share feelings more, tell people that you care, take extra safety precautions, become healthier, and contribute to a worthwhile cause. "An awareness of death increases my appreciation of the preciousness of life. The glory of life is inseparable from the fact that it is finite" (Branden, 1983, p. 200).

Life—a lovely, lively flame dancing inside us. At death, the dancing stops. But the special feeling for the person we loved never stops.

—Linda Lytle Potter

LOOKING BACK

- The emotional self is interesting, complicated, and challenging; confusion about emotions is common.
- Researchers identify and categorize emotions. Combinations of the basic emotions make up other feeling states.
- An emotion has three components: physiological arousal, subjective cognitive state, and expressive behavior. The behavioral component is the most controllable.
- Expression is learned from a variety of sources. Men, especially, receive restrictive messages.
- All four developmental areas are strengthened by constructive emotional expression; self-esteem is also bolstered. Relationships thrive on open, honest, and constructive expression. For many, demonstration of feelings is not easy, yet can be developed.
- Anger will occur, and the key is to learn to manage the emotion so that interactions and relationships are not damaged.
- Emotions can be changed by altering thoughts and behaviors through rational behavioral emotive therapy and control therapy. This is beneficial when emotions are unpleasant and causing harm.
- Clinical depression, different from minor mood changes, is serious, and therapy is highly recommended. Suicide is the tragic outcome of many cases of deep depression.
- Crises of any kind create stress and can wreak havoc on the emotional self. Specific strategies can lessen the impact and help resolve the crisis faster, reduce the harmful effects, and use the situation for positive growth.
- Death, which affects everyone, is the ultimate crisis. Grief, while not welcome, is necessary. You can cope and, in some cases, use the tragic event to improve your own life and make needed changes in society.

The full and free experience and expression of all our feelings are necessary for personal peace and meaningful relationships.

—John Powell

RESOURCES

American Psychiatric Association, 1400 K Street NW, Washington, DC 20005. (202) 682–6000. www.psych.org

American Psychological Association, 750 First Street NE, Washington, DC 20002–4242. Toll-free: (800) 374–2721. www.apa.org

Center for Healing & Wellness, 2235 Grant Road, Suite 6, Los Altos, CA 94024. (650) 625–1987. www.healingandwellness.org

Compassionate Friends (support for bereaved parents), P.O. Box 3696, Oak Brook, IL 60522–3696. Toll-free: (877) 969–0010. www.compassionatefriends.org

Emotions Anonymous International (for anyone wanting to learn to deal with emotions), P.O. Box 4245, St. Paul, MN 55104. (651) 647–9712. www.mtn.org/EA

Heartbeat (support for survivors of suicide victims), 2015 Devon Street, Colorado Springs, CO 80909. (719) 596–2575. www. codenet.net/suicideprevention/ HEART.html

Heartbeat Suicide Hotline: (719) 596–5433.

Menninger Clinic (mental health), P.O. Box 829, Topeka, KS 66601–0829. Toll-free: (800) 351–9058. www.menninger.edu

National Association of Social Workers, 750 First Street NE, Suite 700, Washington, DC 20002. Toll–free: (800) 638–8799. www.socialworkers.org

National Depressive and Manic- Depressive Association, 730 North Franklin Street, Suite 501, Chicago, IL 60610. Toll-free: (800) 826–3632. www.ndmda.org

National Institute of Mental Health, 6001 Executive Blvd., Room 8184, MSC 9663, Bethesda, MD 20892–9663. (301) 443–4513. www.nimh.nih.gov

Rainbows for All God's Children (support for children and adults who have experienced death, divorce, separation, or abandonment). 2100 Golf Road, #370, Rolling Meadows, IL 60008. Toll–free: (800) 266–3206. www.rainbows.org.

Human Service Directories (included in most telephone directories) list agencies and support groups dealing with almost all situations.

Section Two
Communication: The Key to Relationships

LOOKING AHEAD

After completing this section, you will be able to

- Define communication and describe its process.
- Discuss the importance of communication.
- Explain how and where people learn to communicate.
- List ways in which family communication could be improved.
- Give reasons for formal training in interpersonal communication.
- Describe characteristics helpful in being a positive communicator.

I see communication as a huge umbrella that covers and affects all that goes on between human beings—the largest single factor determining kinds of relationships and individual happenings in the world.

—Virginia Satir

"We don't communicate," was the couple's agreed-upon answer when asked why they wanted a divorce. "Oh, but you do," came the surprising reply from the counselor. The couple did not realize that whenever two people occupy the same environment, communication is taking place. Although people can stop talking, they continue to communicate with body language. An accurate reason for wanting to end a relationship is "We don't communicate well" or "The way we communicate has caused problems and damage."

Whether intentional or not, communication influences all relationships. Without communication, interaction would not occur. **Interpersonal communication** is a complex process of mutually exchanging messages between two or more individuals. Models of communication are not simple diagrams. When verbal exchange is taking place, what exactly is happening? Speaking and listening are two necessary parts of the process. Nonverbal behaviors accompany both. A communication interaction is an encompassing process in which:

- A message is sent verbally and nonverbally.
- The message is received and interpreted.
- Verbal and nonverbal feedback is usually given.
- Feedback is offered by sender.

As you can see, the individuals in the exchange are simultaneously sending and receiving messages.

A major purpose of interpersonal communication is to share a common meaning. Both the sender and receiver are responsible for clarity. When different meanings come from messages, the outcome can be negative. "But that's not what I meant" is far too common. What is worse is not being aware that you have been misunderstood. What was true years ago is probably still accurate: As much as 70 percent of our communications efforts are probably misinterpreted, misunderstood, rejected, disliked, or distorted (Donaldson & Scannell, 1986).

Communication is the foundation for all relationships and the primary cause of their success or failure. Ineffective or faulty communication is at the root of most interpersonal difficulties. Conversely, effective communication is necessary to develop and maintain any positive interpersonal relationship.

> *Human communication is the most awesome force in the world. It can be directly responsible for peace or war, love or hate. Communication is unavoidable, and our communication skills are directly related to the quality of life we experience.*
> —Jacquelyn Carr

Most of the research on communication has focused on couples. Leo Buscaglia (1984) conducted a study in which he asked couples about problems and strengthening factors in their relationships. The same factor was identified as being both the most problematic and the most strengthening. Not surprisingly, it was communication. More than 85 percent of the hundreds of respondents said that the most essential quality for a lasting relationship was the ability to communicate (Buscaglia, 1992).

In assessing a premarital course, couples reported that the communication skills part was the most helpful (Scott et al., 2001). When asked in an informal survey to list the three most important factors necessary for a good marriage, 81 percent of respondents named communication and placed it ahead of love and friendship. Couples who desire satisfying long-term relationships are wise to invest time and energy into improving their communication skills. Studies conducted by colleagues and myself indicated that positive communication contributed to the strength of the stepfamily (Hanna & Knaub, 1981; Knaub, Hanna, & Stinnett, 1984). When stepchildren were asked to identify areas of concern, communication was frequently mentioned (Knaub & Hanna, 1984). One girl offered this response: "The worst thing about my stepfamily is that my stepfather thinks he's always right and we're always wrong—what he says goes" (p. 87). She suggested that he listen and show a willingness to compromise, two important ingredients in positive communication.

Being able to communicate effectively benefits you in everyday situations, in a job search, in the advancement of your career, and in all types of relationships. When you think of your friendships, doesn't communication strike you as an essential component? It is highly unlikely that you will remain friends with someone with whom you have difficulty communicating. Between patient and physician, full communication is indispensable because communication can be as important to healing as medicine (Cousins, 1989). Strong communication skills were listed as one of the top three aptitudes that employers want (Fisher, 2001).

How well we communicate affects how others perceive us and all aspects of interpersonal relationships.

> All communication is learned. Every baby who comes into this world comes only with raw materials—no self-concept, no experience of interacting with others, and no experience in dealing with the world. Babies learn all these things through communication with the people who are in charge of them from birth on. (Satir, 1988, p. 52)

Realizing how important communication skills are, one could assume that they would be taught as systematically as other valuable behaviors. Are they? How did you learn to communicate? Were you taught by trained professionals? Almost everyone learned by observation, modeling, and feedback; teaching came from untrained individuals. If communication skills are left to amateurs who learned from untrained people, is it any wonder that communication difficulties are plentiful?

> Effective communication makes life work. But where can you learn it? Parents are often dismal role models. Schools are busy teaching French and trigonometry. Communication skills have been known and available for years. They can and should be taught right along with the three R's (McKay, Davis, & Fanning, 1983, p. 8)

A survey of psychology students at Southeast Community College assessed family communication on a 5-point scale ranging from excellent to poor, first within the family as a whole and then separately with their fathers and mothers. The results were interesting.

- Almost 50 percent rated overall family communication as good or excellent. About 20 percent placed it below satisfactory, and 30 percent rated it as satisfactory.
- A definite difference between fathers and mothers was noted. Thirty-five percent said their fathers needed improvement compared with 14 percent for mothers. Excellent were 28 percent of the mothers and only 8 percent of the fathers. If males are not raised to be communicative, they will be less capable as parents—another unfortunate outcome of gender-role stereotypic training.

Figure II-1   Copyright King Features Syndicate. Reprinted with permission

Several suggestions for improvement were offered.

- Set aside time to talk and listen. Be sure that communication takes place daily. Statistics revealed that mothers on a typical workday spent only 11 minutes in focused conversation with their children, and fathers spent just 8 minutes (Cutler, 1989)
- Talk about everything, not just gripes and problems. Include as many or more positive subjects than negative ones.
- Allow and encourage everyone to talk. Consider all points of view and don't judge.
- Be sincerely interested and show this by actively listening.
- Ask questions, especially those that require more than a one-word answer: not, "How was school today?" but, "What class did you like (or not like) today and for what reason?"
- Be open, honest, and flexible when you communicate. Open communication is covered in Chapter 7.

Do you see how much is involved in communication? If you've followed the suggestions offered in this book, you have a head start in becoming an excellent communicator. Several attitudes and behaviors are important in the communication process.

- A life position of I'm OK, you're OK is at the heart of positive communication. Participants have high self-esteem, and they treat each other with respect.
- Honesty in communication means authenticity. Communicators do not play games, mislead, and try to manipulate each other. Knowing that another person will be up-front with you creates a positive atmosphere.
- Openness is a necessity. A closed person who isn't interested in learning and growing is a poor interpersonal communication candidate. You are likely to be enjoyed as a conversationalist if you are open.
- Willingness to share means that you are able and willing to disclose about yourself and to express your ideas. Listening is a valuable skill; however, if you only listen, you aren't completely participating in an exchange.
- Expressiveness has been praised in terms of health and well-being. Willingness and ability to show your feelings also help you to be a better communicator.
- Appropriateness relates to the content of a message. An effective speaker knows what is suitable to say and what is not.
- Flexibility is needed in positive communication. Being closed-minded is detrimental to a give-and-take communication process.
- A sense of humor, while not a necessity, separates good communicators from excellent ones. Having a sense of humor does not mean telling one joke after another. Instead, you see humor in life, add a witty spark to conversations, don't take yourself too seriously, and appreciate others' humor.
- Understanding and the ability to interpret are needed in order to achieve a shared meaning. Being a critical thinker with the ability to process and see

alternatives can solve communication problems caused by locked-in thinking.

- Patience, often referred to as a virtue, is extremely helpful. Impatient communicators are typically poor listeners.

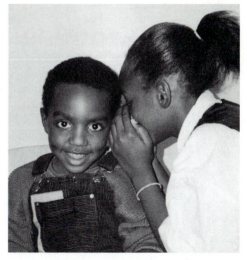

Figure II-2   Communication can be a joyous experience!

Healthy communication is gratifying to the participants. During an exchange, each may experience frustration; however, gratification often comes with the outcome. The outcome *could* be a realization that you misunderstood the other. If you learn from mistakes, you can still feel satisfied. Rewards of affirmation, understanding, and intimacy are viable products of healthy communication.

If you and I can honestly tell each other who we are, what we think, judge, feel, value, love, honor, and esteem, hate, fear, desire, hope for, believe in and are committed to, then and then only can each of us grow.

—John Powell

6

Becoming a Positive Listener

LOOKING AHEAD

After completing this chapter, you will be able to

- Define listening and recognize what is involved.
- Differentiate between hearing and listening.
- Give reasons why listening is important.
- Identify barriers to positive listening.
- Understand the importance of body language and verbal responses.
- Describe negative listening behaviors.
- Name and give examples of the types of listening.
- Become a better listener!

Listening is the most profound ingredient of communication. Listening is a hallmark of loving another.

—Teresa Adams

The day care director spoke to an excited group: "Children, you need to listen to your teachers and me." The bright-eyed children nodded. They had heard about listening at home and knew that it was expected. If we could follow each child from that time until adulthood, we would find that a few had somehow learned to listen well, several had an average skill level, and others were poor listeners. They were told to listen yet not instructed in how. What is often not realized is that good listeners are made, not born.

UNDERSTANDING THE ART OF LISTENING

Listening is not a given. Instead, listening well is an art. Positive listening is made up of skills; each is learned and can be improved. **Listening** is an active process of paying attention, hearing, interpreting, and then acknowledging. **Hearing**, using the auditory sense to take in a message, is the first step in the process. Understanding, which comes next, depends on an accurate interpretation of both the content and nonverbal clues. Acknowledgment requires activity. If you are a good listener, you are not passive. When you listen positively, you are attentive, involved, stimulated, and animated. The next time you are in the listener's role, ask yourself, "Am I truly listening? Do I give the impression that I am?"

The Why of Listening

Listening has purpose. You may listen for any of these reasons.

Enjoyment: Of particular pleasure are the times spent in enjoyable listening. Examples are daily conversations at work and home, the radio, television, and movies.

Information: People seek information from the media and in conversations. Students in the classroom listen primarily to become informed. Enjoyment and information listening can coincide; often the best listening situations are those that include both. Isn't a classroom more interesting when you are engaged in both informational and enjoyable listening?

Help: You will receive and provide help by listening. Relationships thrive on a positive listening environment.

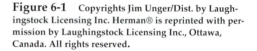

"I really look forward to your visits."

Figure 6-1   Copyrights Jim Unger/Dist. by Laughingstock Licensing Inc. Herman® is reprinted with permission by Laughingstock Licensing Inc., Ottawa, Canada. All rights reserved.

Whatever the purpose, positive listening in relationships will help you to understand another person's thoughts, feelings, and actions.

The Importance of Listening

Listening is basic to learning, and people who cannot hear must employ other means to receive messages. Because listening is the first language skill developed by those who hear, all other skills are dependent upon it. Yet listening is often the most neglected subject taught in school. Consider the amount of time students spend listening in classrooms alone and how essential it is that they have good listening skills. If you want to succeed academically, good listening is a "must!"

The workplace, too, demands good listening skills. Initially, you will receive information and directions during the job interview. Demonstrating good listening skills to get a job is only the beginning. Besides helping employees learn required technical skills, positive listening builds satisfactory customer relations and enriches work relationships. Inefficient or poor listening becomes costly to both businesses and consumers.

Listening creates and improves personal relationships. Being a good listener is a frequently mentioned characteristic of a cherished friend. A person who has difficulty listening may be avoided by others. Satisfying communication in love relationships requires excellent listening skills.

> True listening is love in action. Yet most couples never truly listen to each other. Consequently, when couples come for counseling or therapy, a major task is to teach them how to listen. (Peck, 1978, p. 128)

In creating and preserving intimacy, listening is the most important of all the communication skills (McKay, Fanning, & Paleg, 1994). Listening has significance throughout the world. In Turkey, a person shows respect by not interrupting; in fact, the longer, he or she listens, the more respect is shown. In Japan listening is a sign of authority (Axtell, Briggs, Corcoran, & Lamb, 1997).

> Good listeners stand out in a crowd.
> They are cherished by family, friends, teachers, and employers.
> Good listeners get hired, they get promoted, and they are more informed (Petress, 1999)

A common complaint in families is that nobody listens. Parents lament that their children don't listen to them (usually because the child has not completed a task or followed a command) and children complain that their parents don't listen. Listening is a sign of affirmation. When family members truly listen, they contribute to one another's self-esteem. When they don't, the interpretation is frequently negative.

If you are a parent, you undoubtedly realize that total listening to a young child is impractical, especially if she or he is talkative. However, even a small amount of time devoted to true listening yields invaluable rewards. One of the most rewarding rituals my husband and I established even before we became a stepfamily was to have an evening out with each of the four children. Once a week, we two adults went out with one child for dinner, and the focus of attention was on the child. One evening I started to chat with my husband about a business matter, and my 8-year-old daughter, Lyn, assertively said, "Hey, remember that this is my time." She and the others, when it was their turn, came ready to talk, and we truly listened. I treasure those precious evenings when we learned and shared so much.

How and Where Listening Is Learned

When you entered school, if you could hear, you were expected to know how to listen. Listening skills activities may be included as a part of a class; however, a specific course on how to listen is a rare offering even today. The executive director of a banking association commented:

> I spent years in school learning about history, math, and science. In my career I spend most of my time communicating, much of which is listening. How much training did I get in listening? None. If they taught it, I missed it.

He probably didn't miss it; the skills just weren't taught. If you are like most, you'll need to learn the art of truly listening. "Most of us are poor listeners if we actually listen at all. But there is hope because listening is learned" (Buscaglia, 1992, p. 167).

REMOVING BARRIERS IN THE LISTENING PROCESS

If you are planning a trip by automobile, you can make it more pleasant by knowing about any road construction, poor weather conditions, or detours along the way. Then you can avoid them or at least be prepared to face the delays. Recognizing barriers in the listening process will definitely help you to avoid or decrease their negative effects.

Preoccupation or Lack of Interest

A major obstacle is preoccupation or lack of interest. If you aren't interested, you will not want to listen. You have at least three choices. You may listen anyway and attempt to develop an interest. You might pretend to listen, or you can be honest and tell the person you aren't interested. The decision would be based on the situation and your feelings at the time.

Besides disinterest, preoccupation can be caused by other factors. Have you ever said or heard someone say, "I can listen to you while I'm reading the newspaper (or watching television)"? People can do more than one thing at a time; however, they aren't doing any with complete concentration. Full attention is required if you are going to do your best listening. Carefully listening to someone is a precious gift that communicates care and concern (Miller, Nunnally, & Wackman, 1979). Chronic preoccupation is sure to deaden a relationship. A study designed to predict marital success identified a pattern of listening called stonewalling, a behavior in which the listener presented a "stone wall" to the speaker—not moving the face very much, avoiding eye contact, holding the neck rigid, and not using any listening response. Husbands used this more than wives, and over time it led to marital dissatisfaction (Gottman, 1991).

Environmental Factors

Think about barriers in the environment. Noise detracts, and even with the best intentions, listening is difficult in the middle of an explosion of sounds. Have you ever tried to communicate when a television set is turned on somewhere in the room? Even if nobody is actively watching, or even if the sound is turned off, the set attracts attention. Visual distractions, temperature, and lack of airflow can be just as bothersome as auditory ones. The extent of listening I can expect from students is directly related to the climate of the classroom. Important listening situations deserve an environment free of distractions.

Psychological Filter

Of prime importance in the listening process is the listener's psychological filter, which is composed of preconceived ideas, moods, assumptions, labels, stereotypes, past experiences, hopes, memories, and our own self-concepts. We form impressions of a speaker quickly, and our filters influence what those impressions are. Attitudes predispose us to respond positively or negatively. For example, if you know that you do not agree with a speaker and there will be no opportunity to respond, you will probably not listen well. Also, a negative self-fulfilling prophecy may keep you from even trying to listen. John commented that he has been told so often by teachers and parents that he is a poor listener, he believes it and continues the inactive listening behaviors he developed early in life.

As selective listeners, we are capable of filtering out anything we consider unimportant. Obviously, we can miss important and interesting information. Just as a homeowner checks a furnace filter periodically, examining your psychological filter is a good idea. You may not be able to eliminate it entirely, yet being aware of clogging elements and discarding whatever you can will help you become a better listener.

Emotions

A challenging obstacle arises from the listener's emotional state. Think of a heated discussion between you and another person. Any frustration and anger undoubtedly interfered with positive listening. Immediately after Holly saw the low grade she received on an examination, she became extremely depressed. "I totally 'tuned out' everything the professor said about the test and had no idea why I had done so poorly. I didn't learn anything that could help me next time." Listening, and thus our perceptions, in general, are altered by emotion.

Rate Differences

A person talks at a slower rate than the listener thinks. The average rate of speech is about 125 to 175 words a minute, whereas the brain can think at the rate of 500 to 1,000 words a minute. This means that you, as a listener, are ahead of the speaker! You might think of the speed of an automobile compared to that of a jet airplane. The span of time can hinder your continued concentration, and the mind can wander. Positive listeners remain focused.

Negative Intentions

Although they may not realize it, listeners can have negative intentions. Do you know people who almost always want to lead the conversation? They listen briefly and then jump to conclusions, interrupt to disagree, and attempt to impose their perspective or solution on the speaker. They don't truly listen; instead, they are thinking about and rehearsing what they will say. Because of this, they frequently interrupt. A similar style of nonlistening comes from wanting always to be right which can result in lying, shouting, changing the subject, justifying, quibbling, making excuses, and accusing (McKay, Fanning, & Paleg, 1994)—everything, it seems, except positive listening.

Other negative intentions are listening only enough to gain an advantage or to win, to devise a way to manipulate another, to use the information in a harmful way (as in the case of gossip) or to feign an interest that doesn't exist. Just as insincere or phony talkers eventually reveal their true colors, listeners with negative intentions generally end up losers in interpersonal relationships.

IMPROVING LISTENING BEHAVIORS

Eliminating any of the barriers sets up a positive listening atmosphere. Then, being aware of your own behaviors, improving your skills, and becoming active will lead to positive listening.

Open and Attentive Body Position

Do you appear to be listening? The way you position yourself in relation to the speaker makes a difference. Establishing a comfortable distance apart is basic. Physical space zones are covered in Chapter 7. Being on the same level sets the tone for the interchange because if one stands and the other sits, the person seated can feel at a disadvantage. Facing the speaker is essential. Turning your body away carries a message of disinterest and lessens your involvement, while facing the speaker squarely and leaning slightly forward demonstrates attentiveness.

Adopting an open, attentive posture indicates interest, openness, and involvement. Sitting with legs and arms crossed, slouching, or leaning away from the speaker is likely to give negative impressions. Instead, you can sit with your hands at your sides or on your lap. In situations such as a job interview, you appear more professional if you keep your feet together on the floor. A slumped posture may be comfortable, yet if you are truly interested, your body reflects it by an upright position. Having attentive posture does not mean being rigid and tense. A relaxed position of openness and attentiveness is ideal.

Positive Eye Contact

Maintaining eye contact in American society is expected. In fact, conversation usually doesn't even start until eye contact is made. A person who does not look at you or who often avoids eye contact can cause discomfort. Employers will likely have negative impressions of applicants who don't keep their eyes on the interviewer. Poor eye contact may be interpreted as a lack of confidence or as indicative of dishonesty or lying. Knowledge of various cultures is important. For example, a student from the Middle East commented that direct eye contact is discouraged in his society. In other societies looking down rather than at the speaker is respectful.

Knowing how important eye contact can be and being able to actually maintain it may be altogether different. A student said, "Sharon, I hope in your book you will do more than just say, 'Have good eye contact.' I already know that, but how?" First, realize that eye contact is almost never a direct meeting between sets of eyes. You don't have to look squarely into a speaker's eyes; you can focus anywhere on the face, including the nose, mouth, or ear. As long as you are at least 18 inches away from the speaker, the person usually can't tell that you aren't maintaining exact eye contact.

A recommendation is to look at the speaker's face for roughly three quarters of the time, in glances lasting from 1 to 7 seconds. A speaker will look at a listener for less than half the time, and these intermittent glances rarely last for more than a second (Marsh, 1988). Staring is definitely not recommended. Knowing that you can look elsewhere and keeping a relaxed frame of mind make it easier to maintain eye contact.

Facial Expression

To a great extent, feedback is delivered by changes in facial expression. A "poker face" is helpful in a card game; it is generally useless, and often demeaning, in the listening process. A positive listener reacts to what is being said by registering thinking and feeling responses. Avoiding inappropriate facial expressions is also very important. A smile, a frown, or a look of bewilderment or surprise are just a few of the expressions your face can make. Actually, about 20,000 different facial expressions are possible (Carl, 1980). Changing your facial expression isn't that difficult! Look into a mirror and actually practice changing your expressions. Joel said, "I know it's important to smile, but I hate the way my teeth look." He finally decided that getting his teeth fixed was worth the price he had been paying in decreased relationship skills.

Head and Body Movements

One of my favorite listening behaviors is nodding the head. An affirmative nod shows the speaker not only that you have heard but also that you agree. A nod can motivate and energize a speaker. "Nodders" are worth their weight in gold! Even a side-to-side nod indicating confusion or disagreement can be helpful in arriving at a shared meaning. Nodding can be developed. You may want to tell yourself to do so until the behavior becomes natural. Since it is possible to nod too much, be sure to use the movement moderately and when appropriate. Other body movements such as tilting the head to one side or shrugging the shoulders also provide feedback to the speaker.

Touching

Depending on your relationship with the speaker, listening can be improved by an appropriate touch. One day a student came in to talk about a personal conflict and was having difficulty expressing herself. I reached over and touched her hand, and the words poured out. The touch had evidently reassured her that she could speak freely. The arm is generally considered to be a neutral or nonvulnerable area. Vulnerable areas are comfortably touched only by intimates. Even though touching can serve as a positive listening behavior, be sure that it is appropriate and acceptable to the other person.

Verbal Responses

Listening is usually a nonverbal activity; however, verbal responses are also included in positive listening. These can vary from a simple "Oh" or "Hmm" to "I see" or "That sounds interesting." You can, however, use too many responses and literally interrupt the speaker's flow. "Really," "I know," or "I understand" stated after each comment is distracting and annoying. A question that encourages the speaker to continue is an excellent response. Some possibilities are: "How do you feel about that?" "What are your alternatives?" "What happened next?" If you are an attentive listener, your question will not move the conversation away from the point. Note the difference in these two examples.

1. SPEAKER: I'm upset with my supervisor. She scheduled me to work this weekend after I told her I wanted the time off.

   LISTENER: Did she just get mixed up?

2. SPEAKER: I'm upset with my supervisor. She scheduled me to work this weekend after I told her I wanted the time off.

   LISTENER: Well, did you hear that she fired Joe?

Open questions requiring more than a simple yes or no answer are preferred because they are encouraging and move the conversation forward. You are telling the speaker, "What you are saying is of interest, and I want to hear more."

Verbal responses can involve more than short reactions or questions. **Paraphrasing** is restating in your own words what you think the speaker said. Here is an example of paraphrasing.

SPEAKER: My kids have been driving me crazy.

LISTENER: It sounds like you are really bothered by them.

When you paraphrase, you don't add to the message; instead, you repeat the meaning you received. This shows that you received the message and want to be sure the meaning is shared. You can use such lead-ins as, "It sounds like," "You mean that," or "Let me make sure I understand what you mean." Paraphrasing may seem clumsy at first; yet once you find and practice a few phrases that sound natural, using them will become easier.

The benefits of paraphrasing are worth the initial discomfort. They include:

- People appreciate that they were heard.
- The possibility of misinterpretation is greatly reduced because errors can be corrected immediately.
- Anger and other emotions can be defused.
- What was said is more likely to be remembered.

Paraphrasing can work beautifully with children, who often just want to know that their message was received. For example, picture a 4-year-old girl who tearfully tells you that an older brother has yelled at her. "It sounds like you didn't like him to yell at you" is the parent's paraphrase. In most cases, the child will nod and return to whatever she was doing.

Gaining a clear understanding of the speaker's emotions is also helpful. Jason tells Anja that he is "down in the dumps." She says, "It sounds as if you are really depressed." Jason can then think about her impression. He may respond, "I'm not really that unhappy," or he can say, "Yes, I am really down." When the listener provides an idea of the feeling that is sensed, the speaker receives valuable information. The speaker may also feel free to elaborate further about the feeling and even express other emotions. A listener who echoes a feeling is essentially saying, "I'm here for you."

Clarifying goes just a little further than paraphrasing. You not only restate; you also ask questions to get more information and background. Your questions are genuine attempts to ensure that the two of you are sharing the same meaning. In doing so, both the exchange and the relationship are enriched. Even if you don't agree with the speaker, positive listening means that you first do everything possible to understand the other's perception.

Feedback, the last step in the listening process, comes after other listening behaviors. **Feedback** is responding with what you, as the listener, think, feel, or sense. You may still clarify with questions such as, "Is this what you meant?" or "Is this the way you feel?" Then you respond with your perspective or point of view. A few tips for engaging in feedback are:

- Provide input in a timely way.
- Be honest, yet react in a nonhurtful way. Avoid beginning your response with the word "you." Instead of "You would be crazy to take a job for that kind of pay," say "I think you'd be wise to consider how satisfied you'll be with that pay."
- Support the speaker. Do not put the speaker down. If you are entrusted with thoughts and feelings, handle them with care.

Feedback is more accurate if you have paid attention to the speaker's nonverbal behavior, voice, and words. For example, my stepson Greg responded to a question of where he was going with, "Over to my friend's house for a while." I noticed his facial expression, which appeared hostile. My thought was that he really didn't like me, and I was glad I clarified by asking him whether I had done something to offend him. He looked genuinely surprised and said, "No. What makes you think that?" I gave him feedback by describing what I thought his face was saying and how I felt. He laughed and said, "I probably looked mad because I was thinking about my car's empty gas tank!"

Tone of voice can be confusing to a listener, and again, feedback is appropriate. Judy said to her friend, "I'm just fine. I don't need any help." The words said one thing, and her weak, quivering voice revealed another meaning. Her friend responded with concern. Usually, the quality of voice is more honest; however, a good listener will check to make sure. Are you surprised by the number and complexity of listening behaviors? Can you see why listening is considered active and animated? Good listening is not for the lazy.

Elimination of Negative Listening Behaviors

Knowing what to do is essential; knowing *what not to do* is equally important. The opposites or extremes of the behaviors just described are obvious negatives. For example, have you ever tried to describe a serious incident to a listener who is slightly grinning?

Interrupting, unfortunately, is common and is one of the surest signs that a person isn't truly listening. Individuals who enjoy talking have more difficulty with this bothersome behavior. Families composed of outgoing, talkative members can have frustrating scenes. My brother Dave once commented about an unusually boisterous exchange among our family members, "Sometimes being in this family is like being in an echo chamber!" He was absolutely correct! Interrupting can be a part of another disaster in listening: a two-way conversation. A conversation starts. Instead of remaining attentive, the listener begins to speak about a different topic. The speaker can either stop, continue with the original topic, or switch to accommodate the interrupter. If the speaker stays with the first topic, a two-way conversation results and shared meaning is completely lost.

Certain listening gestures and sounds can bother the speaker and create a negative communication climate. Several are identified by Ernst (1973).

- Cheek puffing and corners of mouth going down
- Eye rolling
- Shoulder shrugging to indicate an I-don't-care attitude
- Foot or leg bouncing up and down at high speed
- Drumming the fingers or thumping the hand or arm
- A "tsk"ing sound made by the tongue, or sighing

Students in role-playing activities have added a few of their own such as loud gum chewing, yawning, and knuckle-cracking. Can you identify the negative messages these behaviors might communicate? If you recognize any of the behaviors in yourself, try to eliminate or at least decrease them.

Figure 6-2   Positive listening is an art.

USING DIFFERENT TYPES OF LISTENING

All listening is not the same, even though the active listening behaviors described earlier are essential ingredients in all positive communication exchanges. Different types of listening are most effective in certain situations.

Empathic Listening

Empathy—being able to put yourself in another's place and see and hear from that person's perspective—is a quality to be treasured. **Empathic listening** means that you first become aware of the speaker's experiences and feelings. Then you communicate this. A comment such as, "I can see why you feel (or think) that way" makes an exchange more pleasant and positive.

Because emotional expression is beneficial, an empathic listener has a worthwhile role. As was pointed out in Chapter 5, people can have difficulty verbalizing feelings. A safe, comfortable climate for communication encourages expression, and an empathic listener sets the tone. Instead of just reacting to the words you hear, listen with concern and caring. For example, when a mother says, "I wish you just weren't so busy," she may sound critical and angry; however, she could be feeling disappointed, hurt, and sad. An empathic listener is likely to recognize the difference or probe to discover the underlying emotions. Listening in depth and with empathy makes it easier to effectively help others and is an appreciated skill.

A communication empathy scale, proposed by Messina (1982), is a good way to check your empathic listening. Pretend that a friend has just told you that he has lost his job. Following are descriptions of four levels and examples of responses.

Level 1: Listener misses the facts and the feeling—"Let's go get a bite to eat."
Level 2: Listener grasps facts but misses the feeling—"It's too bad you lost your job, but something else will come up."

Level 3: Listener understands the facts and realizes that the speaker has a feeling but isn't empathic enough to be correct about which one—"It's too bad you lost your job. I'll bet you're really mad."

Level 4: Listener correctly understands both—"I realize that losing a job is a bad deal. It sounds like you're upset and depressed, and I can see why."

The fourth level is a worthy goal. Notice that the use of the word "but" in Level 2 seems to negate the speaker's situation.

Empathic listeners express empathy by tone of voice and body language. In addition, they can use short verbal responses. Some listeners are quick to say, "I know just how you feel"; such a response is not recommended. Even though people can empathize, they do not know just how another feels. A better response would be, "I have a strong sense of how you feel." Can you detect the use of empathic listening in the following?

> SPEAKER: I was trying to lead the group discussion, and she kept interrupting. I felt like she thought that I wasn't handling it right.
>
> LISTENER: It sounds like you were in a difficult spot.
>
> SPEAKER: I tried to politely tell her to quit distracting us, but she kept doing it.
>
> LISTENER: I would have been frustrated.
>
> SPEAKER: I was really frustrated, and by the time the evening was over, I was ready to scream.
>
> LISTENER: I can almost feel what you were going through. It sounds like it kept building up until you were really angry.
>
> SPEAKER: That's right. I'm glad you understand.

Note that the listener expressed a personal sense of frustration and then picked up on the escalation to anger. The "I can almost feel" phrase is much more honest than "I know exactly how you feel."

Empathic listening is desirable in most exchanges. Once in a while, however, you can better serve the speaker by being objective and honest. If the person is in a rut or is demonstrating inappropriate feelings, first express your understanding. Then, because empathizing would validate the person's inappropriate emotional reaction, use feedback to express your true reaction in a nonthreatening way.

Receptive Listening

All listening is receptive; however, **receptive listening** is a specific type with certain restrictions placed on responses. In some cases, silence is best if accompanied by appropriate nonverbal behaviors. Perhaps it is no coincidence that "silent" and "listen" contain the same letters (Wolvin & Coakley, 1988). When using receptive listening, you will do the following.

Listen without interrupting.   Except for preventing an injury, nothing justifies interrupting, and it is extremely annoying in a conversation. Keep silent, and if you do interrupt, apologize and let the speaker continue.

Listen without judging or "putting down".   People seem to have great difficulty keeping critical, judgmental, and admonishing reactions to themselves.

> SPEAKER: I charged over $1,000 on my credit card bill this month.
>
> LISTENER: Oh, no! (in a horrified tone of voice)
>
> SPEAKER: I have a budget, but I just couldn't pass up buying stuff and going away for a weekend.
>
> LISTENER: That's crazy. You know better than that.

What do you think the speaker's reaction would be? Most people would react defensively and, usually, the interaction would end on a negative note. Note the following improvement.

> SPEAKER: I charged over $1,000 on my credit card bill this month.
>
> LISTENER: Oh. (In a neutral, somewhat concerned tone.)
>
> SPEAKER: I have a budget, but I just couldn't pass up buying stuff and going away for a weekend.
>
> LISTENER: That's too bad. Are you going to be able to pay for all of it?

Listening openly is not easy and requires patience. Later, in the feedback stage, the listener can express any concerns. Being judgmental will only cut off further communication.

One reason that individuals don't express their feelings is that judgments are frequently leveled at emotions. "How could you be angry about that?" "That's stupid," "I wouldn't have let that bother me," or one of the worst, "You have no right to feel that way," are almost sure to prevent further disclosures of emotion. Ironically, judging can be so ingrained that we tend to use it even in simple exchanges. Have you ever told someone you enjoyed a movie and been told, "Oh, I don't see how anyone could like something like that?" In Chapter 7 you will learn ways to voice an opinion that doesn't sound like a judgment.

Listen without one-upping.   When I present this in class, the reactions clearly indicate how common this response is. "One-uppers" have a definite intent which is to tell their own story because it is more dramatic, more interesting, better, or worse than yours. In some cases, one-uppers just react from habit or because they want to relate to the speaker's experiences. Whatever the reason, to be one-upped is annoying.

> SPEAKER: I went fishing yesterday and caught two bass. I—
>
> LISTENER: (interrupting) That's nothing! I caught six last week.

> SPEAKER: I've been really depressed because my favorite aunt died a few days ago.
>
> LISTENER: I know just how you feel. My grandmother died a few months ago, and I'm still trying to get over it. She was such a wonderful person, and we all loved her. Why, just before she died, she was helping my cousins settle an argument. . . (Story would continue!)

> SPEAKER: I'm really excited. We're leaving for Mexico next week.
>
> LISTENER: You're going to Mexico? I'm going to Europe. I'll be in England a few days, then on to Scotland, then to France. I'll be gone for at least four weeks, then I'm going to . . .

When role playing the last conversation, after the listener stopped, the speaker said loudly, "And I hope your plane goes down!" The laughter indicated that any of us would probably harbor similar thoughts! Notice the lead-in of "That's nothing!" in the first example. Besides preceding a one-upping comment, the phrase is negating and is one to avoid.

Do you recognize anyone, even yourself, as a "one-upper"? Awareness can eliminate or decrease most of its use. Remember not to jump in too quickly and sound as if your story is better. If you slip, acknowledge that you took over the conversation and lead the speaker back to the original story.

Listen without advice-giving and problem solving.   Caring individuals have difficulty with this one. They want to be helpful, so they are quick with advice, not realizing that it can stop the exchange prematurely. Either feeling or thinking MBTI personality preferences can respond too quickly. Thinkers do so because they enjoy problem solving, and it's logical to do so as quickly as possible. Feelers can experience so much empathy, they just feel compelled to help.

> (*Advice-giving*)
>
> SPEAKER: I'm having trouble communicating with my parents.
>
> LISTENER: I can suggest several good books for you to read.

> (*Problem solving*)
>
> SPEAKER: I'm upset about my relationship with him.
>
> LISTENER: I think you should just call it quits.

Can you see how the quick response can end the exchange or steer it in another direction? A better response would be to paraphrase or express understanding of the feeling when appropriate or show that you are receptive just by body language. In most cases, the speaker has more to express verbally, nonverbally, or both.

I was reminded of the importance of listening without attempting to problem solve when one of my students stayed after class. She looked sad, and I asked her how she was. She replied, "Just terrible. I've been sick, and now my husband has started drinking again." I stifled a strong urge to tell her about support groups for families of alcoholics and books she could read. Instead, my facial expression was one of concern. I said, "Oh," and because she looked so forlorn, I put my arms around her. She started to cry, and we stood there for about two minutes while she sobbed. Afterwards, we talked, and I eventually made some suggestions. If I had responded immediately with my well-meaning advice, the opportunity for her to release stress and genuine emotion would have been lost.

Receptive listening means that you remain in the listening role longer and don't jump in too soon. Think of it as keeping an invisible piece of tape over your mouth for awhile. Show encouragement nonverbally or with short responses.

Directive Listening

This type of listening is more controlling than either empathic or receptive, and the listener is more verbal. Asking questions is the key technique. Five different types of questions can be used; they are listed here in the order of most to least effective (Miller, Wackman, Nunnally, & Miller, 1988)

Open questions: These usually begin with who, what, where, when, or how, but not why. Open questions allow the speaker choices and encourage longer responses.

Multiple questions: These ask for more than one answer at a time. They flood the speaker, and the questioner often doesn't get the desired information. For example, a job interviewer who asks, "What are your strengths and weaknesses and how might you improve?" is unlikely to get complete responses in each area.

Closed questions: These are questions that can be answered with just one or a few words.

Leading questions: These are designed to get a certain response. For example, "Don't you think you'd be wise to check the benefits they're offering?" is a disguised way of telling the other person what to do.

"Why" questions: Reactions of defensiveness and tension are typical when confronted with "why?" Instead of using "why," try: "How did you go about making that decision?" or "What reasons did you have for that choice?"

Directive listening is appropriate when one wants to resolve issues efficiently or make decisions quickly. Job interviews, other business exchanges, and consultations employ directive listening. And, at times, parents feel a need to use it as well! Knowing how to direct conversations with effective questions is a practical skill.

Listening is of great significance in the communication process. Take the opportunity to check your own listening on a scale in Reflections and Applications. Then use positive listening to create an open communication climate that leads to healthy relationships.

Reflect

- Think of examples of when you listen for enjoyment, for information, or for help, plus situations in which you listen for more than one reason.
- Select a particular barrier and think of the last time it hindered the listening process.
- Recall a situation in which empathic listening was used. Do the same for directive listening.

Apply

- With a partner, practice both negative and positive listening behaviors.
- Use receptive listening when someone shares an experience with you.

When I ask you to listen to me and you
start giving advice,
you have not done what I asked.
When I ask you to listen to me and you
begin to tell me why
I shouldn't feel that way, you are
trampling on my feelings.
When I ask you to listen to me and you
feel you have to do
something to solve my problems, you
have failed me,
strange
as that may seem.
So please, just listen and hear me.
And if you want to talk,
wait a few minutes for your turn and
I promise I'll listen
to you.

—Author Unknown

LOOKING BACK

- Listening is an active process of attending, receiving, and interpreting auditory stimuli and then providing feedback. Listening well includes observing and interpreting nonverbal behaviors and reacting to a speaker. Listening goes beyond hearing because it involves interpretation and responding. Listening skills can be learned and improved.
- Individuals listen for various reasons. Three purposes are to enjoy, to become informed, and to help. A goal of listening is to share a common meaning with another person.
- Positive listening cannot be overemphasized. In work situations, friendships, and family relationships, listening is the key to healthy interactions. Poor listening creates problems.
- As important as listening is, almost everyone learned to do it informally. Little, if any, formal instruction is offered in school curriculums. Becoming a positive listener is an individual's responsibility.
- General barriers to listening are preoccupation, environmental factors, psychological filters, emotions, rate difference between speaking and thinking, and negative intentions.
- Improvement comes from eliminating barriers and demonstrating positive nonverbal and verbal behaviors.
- Paraphrasing, clarifying, and delivering feedback are important skills. Negative listening behaviors can be identified and eliminated.
- All listening is active. Specific types of listening include empathic, receptive, and directive.

7

Improving Communication: How to Send Messages

LOOKING AHEAD

After completing this chapter, you will be able to

- Explain the importance of how messages are delivered.
- Contrast the open and closed styles of verbalizing.
- Discuss the benefits of open communication.
- Describe and give examples of three types of closed verbalization.
- Recognize dogmatic, commando, and grandiose wording.
- Use "I" statements, tentative words and phrases, and qualifiers to change the closed style to an open one.
- List and describe dimensions of effective expression.
- Recognize metamessages.
- Reduce the number of fillers in your speech.
- Provide an explanation and description of paralanguage.
- Define body language and describe three aspects of it.
- Realize the importance of both paralanguage and body language.
- Be an open, effective communicator.

The "how" of communication is as meaningful as the "what."

—Sharon Hanna

In all interactions, information and meaning are communicated. What is communicated is of utmost importance and will be covered in Chapter 8. Often overlooked are the manner and method of delivery, yet they are equally critical in the communication process. This chapter will focus on improving how messages are delivered both verbally and nonverbally. Specifically covered will be openness, effectiveness, paralanguage, and body language.

IMPROVING YOUR VERBALIZING STYLE

Have you ever thought about the way you deliver your thoughts, feelings, and needs? **Style** refers to how a person verbalizes. A particular style influences how the speaker comes across and usually elicits a certain response. Communication styles can be identified and changed.

Pretend you are the listener in the following conversations and assess each one in terms of your reactions:

1. The supervisor doesn't care how well I do my job. The only thing she thinks about is how much money the company makes. She puts so much pressure on everyone and never says we're doing good work. You're crazy to ask to be transferred over here.
2. I get the impression that the supervisor isn't very interested in how well I do my job. It seems to me that her major concern is how much money the company makes. We feel a lot of pressure from her, and I hardly ever hear her tell us we're doing good work. I don't think you'd like to work here.

Essentially, the same message was delivered. Yet, if you are like most people, your reaction to each would have been different. In the first one, the speaker is using the **closed style of verbalizing**. This means that the comments are definite and if the listener disagrees, leave little opportunity for a reasonable response. The closed style, because of its absoluteness, finality, forcefulness, and all-inclusive/exclusive language, stifles positive exchange. A student once commented about a friend, "I cannot win his kind of conversation, so I just keep my mouth shut." The closed style fosters a negative communication climate. Opinions stated as inflexible truths invariably close the door to healthy communication.

In the second example the **open style of verbalizing** is used, and discussion is encouraged. A point of view is stated in a flexible manner. Because the expressed ideas sound open, they invite a reasonable, positive response. Open communicators are refreshing! Rather than offending or turning others off, open communicators attract people and are more likely to develop and maintain healthy relationships. The old adage "It's not what you say, but how you say it" has a great deal of merit.

Closed and Open Communication

Awareness of the closed style and recognition of its use is the first step toward becoming an open communicator. Following are descriptions of three types of closed communication and ways to change to the open style.

1. *Dogmatic*—"definitely definite," rigid, absolute, and inflexible. When verbalizing, a dogmatic communicator sounds like the final authority. A key measure of dogmatism is closed-mindedness (Vogt, 1997), and in verbalization this comes across as *expression of opinion as fact or truth*. Here are some dogmatic statements:

"The weather is lousy" or "It's a beautiful day today."
"Valentino's has the best pizza in the world" or "Valentino's has the worst pizza in the world."
"He has been a very poor president" or "He has been an excellent president."
"Religion is necessary for a happy life" or "It isn't necessary to be religious to be happy.".

How a comment is stated, not its content, makes it dogmatic. Each example expresses an opinion; yet it comes across as the "way it is."

TABLE 7-1   Actual "I" Statements

I think	I like	I want
I believe	I consider	I feel
I feel that	I prefer	I am or was

Note: An opposite could be made of each by inserting don't or another appropriate word.

Using "I" statements.   The basic technique of open style communication is to rid yourself of dogmatic comments by the use of "I" statements. Because you are speaking for yourself, "I" statements are also regarded as assertive language and are self-empowering. "I" statements are less inflammatory, put responsibility on the speaker, and are much more likely to be heard (McKay, Fanning, & Paleg, 1994).

"I" statements can be divided into two categories. The first group consists of phrases known as actual "I" statements. The word "I" is said first or begins a phrase used elsewhere in the sentence (see Table 7–1). The second category is made up of phrases that give an "I" meaning. These, too, demonstrate that the speaker's opinions do not necessarily take precedence over others (see Table 7–2).

A common error is to use "I know" for "I think" such as "I know students do better in smaller classes." The speaker does not *know* this. Only when a fact is being stated would "I know" be correct.

Following are rewordings of the dogmatic statements on page 193.

"I like (or don't like) the weather."
"As far as I'm concerned, Valentino's has the best (or worst) pizza in the world."
"I think he is a terrible (or excellent) president."
"In my opinion, religion is necessary (or not necessary) for a happy life."

Remember that "I" statements are not necessary in all verbalizations. When you express facts, they certainly aren't. My dad expressed many of his opinions in a dogmatic way. I suggested that others would react much more positively to him if he used "I" statements. He "leaped" into this in his usual enthusiastic fashion, and it was as if the three words "in my opinion" gave him freedom to say anything. In his zeal, he used the phrase frequently. One day he came into the house and said, "It's raining outside," and then, looking directly at me, added, "In my opinion." I hurriedly explained that when expressing a fact, "I" statements aren't necessary! Also, simple dogmatic observations such as "That's interesting" are seldom considered offensive.

To become an open communicator, listen for your dogmatic statements and concentrate on using "I" statements. A world of difference exists, *in my opinion*, between saying, "College doesn't prepare you for the real world" and "I think that college experiences rarely prepare you for what goes on in the world." Remember that you affirm yourself when you express opinions in an open style.

2. *Commando*—forcing, pressuring. This category includes words and phrases such as "should," "have to," "must," "ought," and "need to" that leave little, if any, opportunity for alternatives. Note the authoritarian, commanding nature of these statements:

TABLE 7-2   Phrases Conveying "I" Meaning

In my opinion	In my way of thinking
As far as I'm concerned	My thoughts are
It seems to me	To me it appears

"You should get a job."
"She has to listen better."
"You had better take my advice."

Consider how you react to forcing words, especially when they are preceded by the word "you." Defensively? In a study, adolescents described accusatory "you" statements as likely to evoke stronger antagonistic responses than assertive "I" statements. The teenagers reported that the use of "you" with angry messages increased their hostile responses and provoked resistance and rebellion (Kubany, Richard, Bauer, & Muraoka, 1992). When people speak in a "commando" way, reactions of defiance, resentment, or passivity are possible; none would appear to be healthy and positive. The "commando" type is usually expressed dogmatically as well, which obviously makes such statements sound even more closed. This style may remind you of moralizing, which was discussed in Chapter 3. Moralizers make use of commando-type words.

Being tentative and flexible.   When the "commando" type has been used, first check to see whether the statement is also dogmatic. If so, create an "I" statement and then replace the forcing part with a flexible and tentative phrase. See Table 7–3 for examples.

Following are changes in the examples of commando statements.

"I think it would be a good idea for you to get a job."
"I believe she would benefit from listening better."
"It seems to me that my advice could be helpful to you."

The forcing words "should," "must," "has to," and "had better" were replaced with tentative phrases, and "I" statements were used. The same point is made in a less demanding way.

TABLE 7-3   Some Tentative Phrases

It would be a good idea if
He or she, they, or you could benefit from
It could be helpful if
It seems important that
He or she, they, or you might be wise to

3. *Grandiose*—exaggerated, all-inclusive or all-exclusive, and often dramatic. The use of this type can lead to inaccuracy or a distortion of the facts. Following are examples of grandiose words and statements in which they are expressed:

everyone—no one
everybody—nobody
all—none
always—never
everything—nothing—anything
only
every

"All kids today are disrespectful."
"He doesn't do anything except lie around."
"The only way to become skilled in word processing is to take a class."
"I don't have anything to wear."

Consider a statement such as: "Everybody's having kids." My quick reaction is, "I'm not!" Note that grandiose statements are almost always (not always) dogmatic.

A statement that contains grandiose words is usually inaccurate. How often is "always" correct? Be careful you don't answer that with "never."

At times, "always" is accurate. Years ago I suggested the possible elimination of the words "always" and "never" from the language until Ed, a good friend, reminded me of their accuracy in certain statements. He noted that the Pope is always Catholic and never Jewish! In most cases, grandiose words are used only for their dramatic effect. Yet, because they usually create an inaccurate statement, the point can be lost. Parents are advised to not say to a child, "Your room is always a mess" or "You never clean your room." Why? The child can clean once in a 5-year period and prove that you are wrong!

Listening for examples of the grandiose style from others as well as yourself can actually be fun. Keeping a sense of humor, one can challenge the obvious inaccuracy of such comments. Try inwardly responding to the suggestions in parentheses when you hear these types of statements:

"All men are that way." (All? Really?)
"You never do anything right." (Surely once in a while the person does!)
"All he does is eat." (That's all he does? Amazing!)
"I'm always late." (Not even once are you on time?)

Depending on your relationship with the grandiose speaker, you may be able to verbalize these questions. When students say, "There was *no* way I could have come to class," I try to humorously challenge them! Awareness is the first step toward improvement.

Adding or replacing with qualifiers.   To correct the "grandiose" type, an "I" statement may be needed to get rid of dogmatism. Then replace or modify the grandiose word with a qualifier (see Table 7–4). For example, if "always" or "never" has been used, ask. "Is the word correct?" If not, select a qualifier that does not change the meaning to any extent. In the statement "She's never on time," what word could be used to qualify "never"? Some possibilities are "rarely" or "hardly ever" as replacements or adding "almost" in front of "never" as a modifier. Be careful that you don't change the meaning to any great extent. For example, if you are rewording "Everyone is so rude," the meaning would be significantly changed if you

TABLE 7-4   Words Useful as Qualifiers

almost	quite a few	frequently	infrequently
nearly	probably	often	rarely
many	possibly	usually	seldom
most	some	generally	sometimes
several	few	in general	hardly ever

replaced "everyone" (the grandiose word) with "someone." Instead, use "many people" or add "almost" to "everyone." Some possible open statements are "I've noticed that she is rarely on time" and "It seems to me that most people are rude."

Using qualifiers makes statements accurate and less hurtful. A young man said that his father repeatedly told him, "You'll never amount to anything." "Never" and "anything" felt like arrows accentuating the attack on his self-esteem. Qualifiers decrease the sting of a critical remark. Again, compare the statements that follow with the ones given in the description of the grandiose type on page 196.

"In my opinion, many kids today are disrespectful."
"It seems to me that he spends a lot of time lying around not doing much."
"I found that taking a class in word processing really improved my skill, and I would recommend it."
"I don't have many things to wear.".

These reworded statements are accurate, less dramatic, and open. Note that each is an "I" statement.

All three types of the closed style set up obstacles to honest interactions. Either they stop communication or, if exchange does take place, disagreement or combativeness is apt to occur. Statements that contain all three types aren't unusual. In a book written for teenagers in stepfamilies (Getzoff & McClenahan, 1984), closed communication, called aggressive language, is associated with responses of defensiveness, attack, or resentment. None solves a problem.

Figure 7-1

Can You Find All Three Closed Types?

"Politicians should tell the truth, and they never do."

"You ought to save part of your paycheck."

"Students need to study hard to get good grades."

How well did you do? All are dogmatic because they express opinion as fact. Did you find the forcing words (*should, ought,* and *need to*)? In addition, politicians and students with an implied "all," and the word "only" are grandiose. Don't the following reworded statements sound open and positive?

Can You Create Open Communication?

"In my opinion, most politicians hardly ever tell the truth, and I think it would be much
   better if they did."

"I believe that it's a good idea to save part of your paycheck."

"I think that most students who study hard can get good grades."

Open communication is worth the time and effort spent in developing the techniques. By the way, this type of dogmatic statement is permitted in a textbook! The first step in becoming an open communicator is a desire. The second requires listening to your usual style. Then, rewording mentally and restating aloud will complete the process. Accomplishment comes from practice and more practice! To help, Reflections and Applications asks you to identify and rewrite closed statements. Eventually, open communication will become easy and natural.

BECOMING AN EFFECTIVE COMMUNICATOR

In addition to using an open style, you can improve communication by expressing yourself effectively. This can be accomplished by paying attention to certain guidelines (McKay, Davis, & Fanning, 1983).

Directness

Being direct means stating what you want to say. You don't assume that others know what you are thinking or feeling, and you don't hint. People, often those with a feeling personality preference, may not say what they mean because they don't want to offend others. Yet indirectness can cause deeper hurt. For example, since her parents' divorce, Tiffany had spent 2 months each summer visiting her dad. One summer she didn't want to stay the full time, yet she was concerned about hurting his feelings. Because she wasn't direct with her dad, she stayed and felt resentful, causing their relationship to become distant. This hurt both of them. Other reasons for indirectness are indecisiveness, shyness, and nonassertiveness. "We cannot hear what the other is not saying; and, sometimes, when we finally do, it's too late" (Buscaglia, 1992, p. 152). A message worth sending deserves to be delivered directly.

Straightforwardness

Related to directness is straightforwardness, which means being honest and not disguising information or intention. A **metamessage** is one in which the true meaning is not openly expressed. Instead, an underlying message is transmitted by accenting a word, changing the tone of voice, or making suggestive comments. For example, if a person says, "*Obviously,* you're right," the real meaning probably is, "You act like you're always right." A metamessage is often sarcastic. Note the following metamessages and the possible intended meanings.

"She must have really been an interesting conversationalist."
(Meaning: I was hurt that you spent so much time talking to her.)
"Don't worry about being out of town when we have the graduation party. We'll manage without you."
(Meaning: I'm unhappy that you won't be here.)

Instead of using a metamessage, either be straightforward and say what you mean or just keep silent. In the next chapter you will learn how to respond to metamessages effectively; you undoubtedly know someone who uses them!

Clarity

Effectiveness calls for the delivery of a clear message. Individuals who say "I feel funny" or "There's something wrong" aren't being clear. Another example is the practice of asking a question when a statement would be more effective. For example, "Why don't you try harder?" would be much clearer as: "I've noticed you haven't been turning in as many projects of high quality lately, and I'd like you to try harder." My husband reminds me to be clear whenever I ask, "Are you planning to get yourself more coffee?" He responds, "Does that mean you would like me to get you some?" Sheepishly, I realize that I'm being neither clear nor direct.

Simple requests may be harmless; however, lack of clarity and confusion can lead to serious relationship problems. For example, what does "I'll call you later" mean? It could be 15 minutes in one person's mind and a week in another's. Abstract words such as love, trust, loyalty, and honesty often have different meanings for people. What does respect mean to you? Ask a few others and see if meanings are the same. A couple was having an argument. She said, "I just wanted you to be honest with me." He replied, "I was honest. I didn't lie to you." Her comment was, "You may not have lied; however, you didn't tell me all about it, and that's dishonest!" Do you see how their meaning of honesty was different? To avoid this, effective communicators do more than use a word; they describe, behaviorally if possible, exactly what they mean.

Another problem with clarity comes when someone says one thing and indicates another with body language. "I'm listening!" she says as she continues to write a letter. How do you know which to believe? Effective communicators strive for clarity. "A message clearly given that is clearly received is a rare and beautiful phenomenon" (Adams, 1987, p. 135).

Immediacy

Waiting too long to express can be ineffective and also lead to frustration and resentment. More effective messages are often immediate ones. For example, imagine a passenger in an automobile who delays saying anything about the recklessness and speed of the driver even though he or she feels a great deal of anxiety. Because nothing was said, a tragic accident could occur. Similarly, individuals may hesitate to deal with conflict and make matters worse. Each situation requires an assessment of the ideal degree of immediacy.

Supportiveness

Effectiveness is not enhanced by hurting someone or trying to appear superior. Nonsupportive communication includes using sarcasm, calling attention to past errors and problems, comparing others unfavorably, attacking in a judgmental way, and delivering threats. Effective communicators are not out to prove points or win; instead they want to be supportive and promote understanding and goodwill.

Efficiency and Sharing

Finally, effective communication is damaged by using fillers, adding unnecessary details, meandering, and monopolizing the conversation. What creates a barrier in the following?

> "Well, you know—I go to college—you know—and—a—it's been a good experience—you know. I've really—you know—learned a lot—you know—and I think you—uh—oughta—well basically—you know—try it!"

Is there any doubt? The filler "you know" is heard in all walks of life from the playground to the corporation boardroom. A **filler** is a word, phrase, or sound used for no reason except to replace silence. Other common ones are "basically," and saying "right?" after every statement such as "I went to the movies last night—right? There was this guy there—right? And he struck up a conversation with me—right?" An odd one that I used at one time is "Believe you me" at the beginning of a statement. One day a student asked me what it meant. I replied, "I have no idea," as I vowed to rid myself of that habit. How many other fillers can you identify? Overuse of any word or expression gives people a reason to not listen. An effective communicator eliminates fillers. A speech class can do wonders in this regard. Another idea is to ask someone else to catch you using the filler.

An efficient speaker reaches the point with only interesting details so that listeners aren't frustrated or bored. For example, let's listen to two people tell about their vacation.

> SPEAKER 1: We left last Monday morning.
> SPEAKER 2: No, it was after lunch.
> SPEAKER 1: No, it was morning because it was before the mail came.
> SPEAKER 2: I know we left in the afternoon. Don't you remember that we got an invitation to a wedding reception and knew we couldn't go because we'd be on vacation?
> SPEAKER 1: No, we got that invitation the day before. We stopped for lunch in Platte City—or was it North Platte? I think it was North Platte. Do you remember?
> SPEAKER 2: No, I just know we left after lunch!

If you're smiling, this probably reminds you of someone. The disagreement is annoying, as is the length of the story with the unnecessary details!

Have you ever been engaged in an interaction in which the other person did almost all the talking? People who monopolize conversations by either telling one story after another, repeating stories, or giving you endless accounts of themselves and others they know are ineffective and annoying. In fact, such an individual could rightly be described as a poor communicator. Efficiency and a give-and-take in conversation are most appreciated.

Effective communication takes practice. To achieve your purpose, follow the guidelines of effective expression and use open communication.

RECOGNIZING THE IMPORTANCE OF PARALANGUAGE AND BODY LANGUAGE

The "how" of communicating is greatly influenced by other factors. In fact, about 93 percent of an expression is conveyed by vocal changes and nonverbal behaviors, and not by the words alone (Mehrabian, 1968, 1981). Becoming aware of paralanguage and body language and learning how to use yours effectively are valuable tools in communication.

What Is Paralanguage?

A vital part of meaning is conveyed by **paralanguage**, the vocal changes or variations in the human voice. Paralanguage has several components.

Rhythm.   When emphasis or accent is placed on different words, rhythm varies. In the phrase "It seems to me," if you accent *seems*, you are giving the impression of openness; if you emphasize *me*, you have defeated that purpose. Rhythm can be used in a negative way to convey sarcasm and criticism. For example, "Oh, no. You didn't say *that!*" can sound critical.

Inflection and pitch.   Inflection is a change in pitch or in tone of voice. Pitch ranges from low to high, and people have varying degrees of natural degrees. In normal conversation, positive communicators will vary their pitch purposefully; for example, when asking a question, pitch usually rises. Depression or physical fatigue can create a lower voice. Altering rhythm, inflection, and pitch can make a major difference. Note the variations that change the meaning of the same series of words.

You received an award.
You received an *award*!
You received an award?

Robert Frost, the famous poet, said, "There are tones of voice that mean more than words." Listening to the variations in your own voice and, at times, recording yourself can be very helpful. You may be expressing more than you realize!

Volume.   Loudness or softness of speech changes the meaning and can create a dramatic effect. A professor told a group of aspiring teachers that in order to get the attention of noisy students, they should whisper; this, she contended, would quiet them faster than a loud voice. I can honestly report that whispering has worked for me—and then again, it has not! It depended on the group of students and the specific situation. Regardless of its effectiveness in quieting others, varying the volume of expression can add interest and meaning to your speech.

Speed.   The rate at which one speaks makes a difference in the degree of understanding as well as the interest level of the receiver. People who talk very fast are often misunderstood, or they tend to overwhelm the listener. In contrast, a slow speaker can easily put others to sleep or create a great deal of frustration! Again, variety and appropriateness are important.

Articulation.   "What did you say?" The question is often asked because of poor articulation. A speaker mumbled and was not understood. Enunciation, or distinct pronunciation, is a necessary element in delivering a clear message; however, you can overenunciate and give an unfavorable impression. If problems exist in this area, awareness and practice can be beneficial.

Effects of Paralanguage

Paralanguage adds meaning to what you say and makes you a more interesting speaker. Because of paralanguage, you can seem insensitive or be hurtful. You can also sound warm and caring. If you want to realize the profound effects of paralanguage, try expressing a few thoughts or feelings without any variation in your voice.

At times, certain paralanguage usages are demeaning. You probably will, or already do, engage in conversation with elderly people in a work or personal setting. Speaking softly and slowly and articulating dramatically, as if the receiver were incapable of understanding, is unnecessary in many cases and can diminish the self-esteem of the elderly person. I was delighted one day when an older friend of mine told a young receptionist, "I am quite capable of understanding you if you speak to me exactly as you did to the last patient!" You may not be made aware of this habit as the receptionist was; it's up to you to become more aware of how you sound to others.

Components of Body Language

Body language consists of nonverbal communication and, by itself, may make up as much as 55 percent of the meaning of a message (Mehrabian, 1968, 1981). Think of times when what was expressed by body language carried more impact than the person's words. Misinterpretation is common. For example, Steve was surprised and dismayed when Melissa frowned, tossed her head, and turned away. "Why are you mad?" he asked. Her reply was, "Mad? I just remembered a phone call I was going to make." Three areas of body language can be monitored and analyzed.

Body movements.   Facial expressions, eye contact, gestures, and other body parts can vary immensely while verbalizing. Animated is a positive way to describe a face. I received a wonderful compliment when I asked my class how they could tell that I enjoyed teaching (expecting to get a reply related to a particular comment I had made earlier). One student quickly replied, "It shows all over your face during class."

How often have you "read" someone's eyes? They, too, are capable of expression. The eyes have been called "the mirror of the soul." "I could always tell from the look in her eyes," said one man. According to one expert on body language, it is not the eye itself that creates expression but the length of the glance, the extent of the opening of the eyelids, and the manipulations of the skin around the eyes (Fast, 1970). Yet some eyes do seem to dance and sparkle while others look vacant or like lumps of coal.

Even less expressive eyes can be a positive factor if the person maintains direct eye contact, at least in American society. Not doing so can cause others to doubt the words or to feel uncomfortable. In other societies, direct eye contact is not necessarily viewed as positive. In most Asian cultures, eye contact is limited. Incidentally, in all cultures, direct eye contact is generally more difficult when speaking than it is when listening.

Gestures are movements of the hands and arms. As an accompaniment to speech, they help to convey meaning and, even with no verbalization, can send a message. Gestures are symbols; their meanings vary across cultures, and the differences are worth learning. For example (Axtell, Briggs, Corcoran, & Lamb, 1997):

- The OK sign (index finger forming a circle with the thumb with the other three fingers extended) is a rude gesture in Germany and Greece.
- The "hook 'em horns" gesture (index and little fingers extended from an upheld fist commonly used at the University of Texas) means in Italy: "Your spouse is having an affair."
- In Italy, if a man twists his index finger into his cheek, it is a compliment meaning, "That woman is beautiful."

The meanings of gestures can also vary from time to time so you are wise to stay informed especially if you travel to other countries.

As helpful as they can be, gestures can be overdone, as in the case of people who "talk with their hands." Cultural differences are apparent in this regard, too. For example, Italians are generally quite animated and active in their use of hand movements.

An ordinatry gesture can express negativism. Think about how you react to a finger pointed at you to emphasize a statement. Defensive or resentful? These are common reactions even though the "pointer" may just be doing so from habit. Clearly, these behaviors are learned. In your gestures, aim for the "happy medium" between enough movement to add interest and emphasis and too much motion, which detracts. Do avoid potentially annoying gestures.

Body position.   Another element of body language has to do with how you sit or stand because you create an impression. Expression of agreement, disagreement, interest, boredom, respect, affection, dominance, and harmony are possible. Degree of self-confidence is often indicated. Positioning yourself at a different eye level than another is not recommended. Try sitting and carrying on a serious conversation with another person who is standing. "I don't like it at all!" is a common comment. A tall young man in a stepfamily success class my husband and I were teaching said, "I've never had kids, and my fiancée's little boy acts scared of me." My husband suggested that he get down to the 3-year-old's eye level the next time he talked with him. "Wow!" he said the next week, "What a difference that made."

Closed positions include crossed arms and legs, the head turned slightly away, and a slouched posture. Open positions are achieved by just the opposite. A relaxed position, as opposed to a rigid, tense one, generally creates a positive atmosphere. The situation will influence body position. Your position when conversing with a friend in a home setting will usually differ from your posture during a job interview. In the classroom, others, including the professor, assess students' body position. How would you describe yours? In all situations, appearing open and interested is positive.

Spatial relationships.   Where you position yourself in terms of distance from another reflects spatial relationships. Four distinct zones have been identi-fied (Hall, 1969).

Intimate—actually touching to 18 inches apart
Personal—1 $\frac{1}{2}$ feet to 4 feet apart
Social—4 feet to 12 feet apart
Public—12 feet or more apart

Individuals vary in their personal-space preferences. Generally, the closer the prox-imity, the more intimate the relationship. For most people, conversations within the personal zone are comfortable. The social zone is used more in business or other formal interactions. Again, cultural differences are important to note. For ex-ample, in most Latin cultures, people stand closer when engaged in interactions.

Often, an attitude or emotion is communicated simply by the amount of per-sonal space. Standing close to someone could imply invasion or domination or could signify dependence. Keeping your distance may indicate disinterest, dis-comfort, or dislike. Being aware of the appropriate physical space distances and placing yourself accordingly are advantageous behaviors.

Importance and Interpretation of Body Language

Nonverbal behaviors can express emotions, communicate messages, and control human beings; both individual preferences and cultural influences are involved (Scheflen, 1972). Because body language transmits more than half the meaning in most messages, its influence is immense. Body language is also used in what is called **presentation of self**, the attempt to present ourselves to oth-ers so they will see us as we wish to be seen (Goffman, 1959). Think of appear-ing capable your first day of work or so-ciable at a party. How many ways can you communicate these traits through body language? Joshua came to an in-terview in a nice-looking dark gray suit,

Figure 7-2   What nonverbal message is being communicated?

Figure 7-3   People usually feel comfortable conversing within the personal spatial zone.

white shirt, and a fashionable necktie. From his polished shoes to his neatly combed hair, he looked the part. He smiled confidently, looked directly into the interviewer's eyes, and responded to the outstretched hand with a firm handshake. He was off to an excellent start!

Nonverbal behaviors also indicate aspects of personality. "He's so rude," was the comment. Why? "Because he just stared fixedly at me when I talked to him." One could also be considered rude for not looking directly at a speaker. Aggressive, shy, and confident are just a few of the personality traits that may be assigned to individuals because of their body language. Those skilled in sign language certainly understand the power of body language. The impression you make and the ones you receive, as well as the health of your relationships, are greatly influenced by nonverbal behaviors.

Entire textbooks have been written on the subject of body language. The science of body language is called **kinesics** (Fast, 1970). After learning about body language, one student said, "I never thought about it like that. I've become much more aware of how I may appear to others." If you are in the presence of others now, ask yourself, "What impression am I giving right now with my body language?" Throughout your personal and professional life, this question is a crucial one. How your body language is interpreted will make a marked difference in how you are perceived by others.

Some caution regarding body language is recommended because a few simplistic interpretations have emerged. One seminar leader tried to convince participants

Reflect

- How often do you use forcing words? Grandiose words? Start paying attention to your style of verbalizing and reword when necessary.
- Think of some words that have different meanings for various people.
- Think of a recent conversation. About what percentage of time were you talking? About what percentage of time were you listening? If the two percentages aren't about the same (50–50, 60–40, 40–60), evaluate the interaction closely. If you were doing far more talking than listening, change this in future conversations. Or you may want to increase how much you contribute verbally.
- Give a negative, then a positive example from each of the three areas of body language.

Apply

- Listen for the three types of closed communication, then inwardly reword them.
- Tune into any words or phrases you use as fillers, then eliminate them.
- Answer the question under the photo (Fig. 7–2) using an "I" statement.
- Using the following statement. See how many different ways you can change the meaning using paralanguage; "That's really funny."

that all behaviors carry deep psychological meanings. When he said that stirring an iced drink with the tip of one's finger always has a sexual meaning, I reacted with nonverbal behavior—a shake of my head, which meant "I don't agree!" He seemed to be using imagination in his interpretation. Experts in the field say that most body language is learned and then develops into habits (Scheflen, 1972). Stirring with a finger usually comes from convenience or habit rather than from deep sexual longings.

Videotape can be used to see how you appear to others. As students in a career development class watch themselves during a mock interview, the amazed reactions are predictable: "I didn't know I did that," "I'm going to have to sit on my hands," "I sure looked a lot more confident than I felt." If you have an opportunity to see yourself as others do, take advantage of a unique learning experience. Even though it may be a jolting experience, it will undoubtedly be well worth it if you make necessary changes. An activity in Reflections and Applications lets you work with both paralanguage and body language.

Are you recognizing that communication is complicated? Its many dimensions can be somewhat overwhelming, yet awareness of all aspects is needed to understand and improve interactions and relationships. Be patient. Positive communication techniques, in the beginning, can be awkward and difficult. Start listening to yourself and others, and, if necessary, reword, add, subtract, and modify in an attempt to improve. Clear, effective, and open verbalization, combined with positive uses of paralanguage and body language, are rewarding interpersonal skills. Remember that you learned how to communicate, and you can unlearn and relearn.

LOOKING BACK

- How people communicate is an area not often analyzed and is as important as what information and message are given.
- Open and closed are the two verbalizing styles; they usually result in quite different reactions and responses.
- People commonly express their ideas and feelings in a closed style using dogmatic, commando, or grandiose expressions instead of being open, flexible, and accurate.
- Open communication consists of "I" statements and tentative words and phrases and qualifiers. Because this style is likely to result in positive relationships, developing the skills is a worthy goal.
- Effective verbal communication is a worthy goal. Being direct, straightforward, clear, timely, supportive, and efficient are beneficial.
- Paralanguage, the variations in voice, adds depth and meaning to expressions.
- Body language, the nonverbal behaviors related to movement, position, and spatial relationships, is of utmost importance in communication.

Positive communicators lift us by their warmth; their eyes light up in response to us, showing their openness. They refresh our spirit, making us glad to be around them. Negative communicators repel us and arouse feelings of uneasiness within us. We feel lonely, shut out, or attacked around them. Even if they are in our families, we want to avoid negative persons because they zap our energy.

—Teresa Adams

8

Improving Communication: What to Say

LOOKING AHEAD

After completing this chapter, you will be able to

- Discuss how people verbalize on different levels.
- Name and give examples of the four levels of self-disclosure.
- Recognize appropriateness of self-disclosure.
- Describe benefits of healthy self-disclosure.
- Give and receive compliments in a positive way.
- Explain perception and ways in which perceptual errors can be made.
- Use perception checking and dimensions of awareness in order to express clearly.
- Respond positively to criticism, metamessages, and bothersome language patterns.
- Improve the quality of what you say.

Only if we honestly reveal ourselves, can we truly know and appreciate each other.
—Sharon Hanna

"Yackity-yack, yackity-yack" is a recurring phrase in a light, popular song of years ago. **Content** consists of the words and sentences uttered during the communication process. "Yackity-yack," composed of idle comments, makes up the content of many conversations. However, content also includes words that go down in history such as President John F. Kennedy's famous lines, "Ask not what your country can do for you—ask what you can do for your country." Examining what you say and finding positive ways of expressing yourself will help you become a better communicator, which leads to positive relationships.

UNDERSTANDING CONTENT

Think of all the topics you cover during the day. "What time is it?" "How are you?" "Nice day, isn't it?" "I got a speeding ticket on the way to work!" "I don't like greasy food." "I'm feeling depressed." "I think that employees deserve more input into company policy." These are just a few pieces of possible conversation. Although some comments lack depth and may even be trivial, talking with others is important.

Levels of Content

Categorization of content is useful. Five levels identified by Powell (1969) are related to an individual's willingness to share parts of the self. The levels are listed here in order of least revealing to deepest sharing.

Cliché conversation. This is made up of superficial and conventional comments such as "How are you?" and the predictable response of "Fine," "What do you think of the weather today?" "Nice party," and "Have a nice day." Sometimes called cocktail-party talk, such comments are usually safe, with no sharing of self. This type serves its purpose, however, and life would be dreary without it.

Reporting the facts about others. Just a step above a cliché is a comment about a neighbor, friend, coworker, or family member. Whether positive or negative, nothing is revealed about the speaker except that she or he can talk about other people.

My ideas and judgments. This is riskier because the speaker reveals thoughts and opinions. Fearing rejection, the usual pattern is to say only so much and retreat if any adverse reaction is noted.

My feelings (emotions) or "gut level." Because of emotional suppression, this level is difficult for most. Verbalizing what is felt, however, is essential if one is to live as an authentic human being.

Peak communication. Openness, honesty, and complete willingness to share occur at this level. For most, this level is achieved only with close friends and loved ones. Sadly, too often what would seem to be a close relationship lacks this level of communication.

Excellent communicators use all of the levels in appropriate situations and in reasonable amounts. People who discuss only the weather or similar superficial topics, those who spend an unreasonable amount of time at any level, or individuals who use the deepest levels with mere acquaintances are not effective communicators. Those who are effective disclose deeply to close friends and family members and appropriately reveal themselves to others.

Awareness of Content

The words we use reveal a great deal about our attitudes and personalities and directly influence the effect we make on others. Based on the premise that we create and shape our relationships through talk, the book *I Only Say This Because I Love You* (Tannen, 2001) is a useful guide in helping people become more aware of content. A positive communicator wants to avoid potential pitfalls in the communication process. Specific areas of possible difficulty follow.

Semantics.   A major common problem is a difference in **semantics**, the meaning of words. In a career development class, I noticed a puzzled and disturbed look on the face of a Vietnamese man as I talked about the need to sell oneself in order to get a job. Later, he told me, "Selling myself is bad." Understandably, he had literally interpreted the word "sell." After I explained another meaning, he was reassured and said, "Yes, that's good."

Even if people share the same native language, misunderstanding can occur. As discussed in Chapter 7, abstract words such as "trust" can be especially difficult. Using clear expressions, stating your own meaning, and then using examples that are concrete or describing behaviors will decrease the opportunities for semantics problems. Feedback by listeners is helpful in this regard. "If verbal communication is to be reasonably clear, both the sender of a message and the receiver have the responsibility to make it so" (Satir, 1983, p. 88).

Dialect.   Related to semantics is **dialect**, a variety of a language that differs from other varieties of the same language, including distinct pronunciations, unique meanings, and different words altogether. Dialect often reflects differences in region and culture. When I lived in New Jersey, it surprised me that they didn't know what I meant by "pop" (any soft drink). "The word 'pop' appears on Midwest menus," I explained. Differences in dialect can be interesting and fun and only disconcerting when some people insist that their way of speaking is the only way.

Bias-free language.   Awareness is necessary in order to avoid the use of **biased language**, words and statements that are insensitive and demeaning. Sensitive people do not want to offend, and in the workplace, using biased language will keep you from being hired or could get you fired. Certain examples related to race, religion, gender, disabilities, and ethnic background are obvious. Derogatory labels such as "broad," "retard," "nigger," "honky," "spick," or "fag" and words that historically are demeaning such as "boy," "colored people," "little woman," "deaf and dumb," "poor white trash," "illegitimate child" are degrading and are to be avoided.

People may use biased words because they forget or are unaware of the meanings. As a teacher of a sixth-grade class years ago, I responded to a comment about a "colored" kid by asking the young boy, "What color do you mean?" He looked surprised, glanced at his bare arm, and said, "Hey, I guess we're all colored!"

A challenge in using bias-free language is that meanings change. Sex-equality consciousness has challenged language that denotes male dominance. For years the use of male pronouns and other words did both openly and in subtle ways deliver messages of superiority and exclusion. Fortunately, sexist language is becoming almost extinct. Subtle examples of undermining females that in many cases have no overt sexist intention are references to a woman as "honey," or "sweetie" and to women as "girls" or "gals." We seldom hear a group of professional men referred to as "boys" or "guys." What one is called is significant.

Nonsexist language is now taught and its use encouraged in classrooms, the work environment, and within the mainstream of society. For example, the word "chairman" is more appropriately "chairperson" or "chair," and because women have established nontraditional careers, firemen and policemen are now firefighters and police officers. Fair-minded men recognize that they wouldn't like it if things were reversed and are positive about elimination of outdated sexist speech. Since anyone can suffer from biased language, its elimination is definitely necessary.

One difficulty in sensitivity is that individuals have various preferences and attach personal meanings to words. You may not know, for example, whether to refer to a person as Hispanic or Latino; white, Caucasian, or European American;

black or African American. Students in a diversity class were enlightened when they were told by a female panel member: "My family and I live in the United States. I prefer to be called Mexican because I was born in Mexico. My children are Mexican Americans because they were born in the United States." If you want to know a racial or ethnic designation for someone, a wise solution is to ask an individual what she or he prefers.

College students sometimes struggle with what to call an instructor or professor and wonder whether one title is better than another. For example, some women professors prefer Dr. Smith; others want to be called "Mrs. Smith," while others are irritated with the "Mrs." title and prefer "Ms.," even if married. Still others solve the problem by telling students to address them by a first name. Your best course of action is to let others know your preferences and to ask about theirs. A person who is skilled in interpersonal relations will keep abreast of new developments and be sensitive to all human beings.

English as a second language (ESL).   As a result of significant increases in immigration among people who speak other languages, many are in the process of learning English. Rather than criticize or ridicule anyone, consider that English is a difficult language filled with as many exceptions as rules. Then admire those who are working hard to master it. How many languages do you speak? Learning a second one is a definite asset.

Emotion-packed phrases.   Inadvertently, you may use what are called **emotion-packed phrases** (Walker & Brokaw, 1998), groups of words usually said as lead-ins to statements that carry an emotional punch. Some of these follow.

After all I've done for you
When I was your age
You should know better
After you've worked here as long as I have

Note that many emotion-packed phrases begin with "you" and can easily be reworded. Listen to yourself and to others. How many such phrases do you hear? They can turn off the listener or sidetrack a positive exchange, so try to eliminate as many as you can.

Disclaimers.   An expression that denies or shrinks from responsibility is a **disclaimer**. A common one is "Not to change the subject, but." The speaker has said that the intention is not to change the subject; however he or she will do so anyway! Confusing? Instead, why not say, "I'm going to change the subject," or "I'd like to change the subject for the moment." Disclaimers may seem easier and less offensive; however, others can become annoyed or resentful of the indirectness. The key word in disclaimers is "but," which is a way of saying yes and no in the same sentence (Satir, 1976). Here are some examples:

I love you, but I wish you would take better care of yourself.
I'm sick, but don't worry about me.

These statements often leave the listener feeling uneasy and confused. A definite improvement is to substitute the word "and" for "but."

Another example of a disclaimer is the "just in jest" remark. If there is negative reaction to a comment such as, "You're so slow, a turtle could get there faster," the disclaimer is, "Just kidding." Yet the person probably wasn't kidding. Disclaimers are ineffective ways of verbalizing.

Slang, colloquialisms, and vulgarity.   **Slang**, consists of terms that are popular at a given time. They are usually interesting and fun to use, yet become a problem if they are misinterpreted or overused. A job interviewer wrote on an evaluation form: "I don't like the company referred to as 'you guys'" as in, "What kind of products do 'you guys' sell?" Incidentally, the applicant did not get the job. Monitor your use of slang and be aware that it can cause problems. Informal folksy words and phrase are **colloquialisms**. They can add color to expressions, yet can also be overused and misunderstood. An added problem is that they can create an unfavorable impression. For example, in the Midwest, the word "yes" is commonly replaced with "yeah." In formal situations such as a job interview "yeah" sounds unprofessional. Others include "nope," "ya don't say," "no kiddin'?" and "how ya doing?"

Vulgarity and the use of profanity have become commonplace. Relying too heavily on substandard expressions can leave others wondering about the extent of the speaker's vocabulary. Also, swearing and crudeness do affect people's sensitivities and can be offensive so limit or eliminate vulgar and profane expressions. Keep in mind that patterns of expression are difficult to change from one situation to another. An applicant was embarrassed during an interview when he said, "People who don't give a damn annoy me." He later said, "I swear a lot, but I was sure I could control it during a job interview." He learned the hard way that positive language patterns, like all skills, require daily use.

Vocabulary and grammar.   People who are limited in vocabulary and accepted grammar are likely to express themselves poorly. In certain situations, their self-esteem will suffer as a result. I remember a period of time when my daughters and stepsons were in school and proper grammar was not "cool." As a parent and a teacher, I managed to endure "ain't" and "he don't," and even "it don't make no difference" coming from the mouths of intelligent human beings! We purists were competing against the lyrics of music and words uttered by role models of the time.

Although perfection in language skills isn't necessary, effective communication goes hand in hand with the ability to speak a language acceptably. If your vocabulary or grammar skills are poor, you can take advantage of courses or use self-study resources to improve. You might consider a brush-up course in writing skills as well. When you use the best of the language, you are a better communicator.

REVEALING YOURSELF: SELF-DISCLOSURE

Self-disclosure is defined as making the self known by revealing personal information. In doing so, people can know and understand each other. Individuals disclose verbally and nonverbally. The earliest research on self-disclosure revealed

---

A Word (or more) About E-Mail

If you haven't entered the communications arena of electronic mail, the chances are that you will. Because face-to-face paralanguage and body language are nonexistent in e-mail communication, both clarity and effectiveness are at risk. These tips can help.

- Choose your words carefully. Try reading your message aloud if possible. Does it sound like what you want to say?
- Be specific especially about names, places, dates, and times.
- If this is a business message, be brief. Realize that the receiver probably has many messages to read.
- Don't send a message unless you are relatively sure that the receiver will appreciate it or unless it's absolutely necessary. There are far too many forwarded messages circulating.
- Learn e-mail etiquette. For example, using capital letters often comes across as if you are yelling.

A recommended guide is *E-Writing: 20st Century Tools for Effective Communication* (Booher, 2001).

---

that women disclosed more than men. Unmarried participants revealed more to their mothers than to fathers, male friends, or female friends, and married individuals shared more with their partners (Jourard, 1971).

Self-disclosure continues to be the focus of interest. Generally, women enjoy more personal levels of disclosing than do men; this holds true in both opposite-sex and same-sex relationships (Wood, 2001) although personality differences are extremely influential. After learning more about levels of self-disclosing, we will examine the benefits, obstacles, and steps that are involved.

Degrees of Self-Disclosure

Just as all kinds of content can be organized into levels, self-disclosure also has its degrees. Identified by Glaser (1986), the following reveals what can be disclosed.

Basic data refer to biographical and demographic information: I'm 22 years old. I was born in Denver, Colorado. I'm attending college in Columbus, Ohio. I live in an apartment.

Preferences are likes and dislikes, pleasures and displeasures, what one would rather do or not do: I like pizza. I enjoyed going back to Colorado this summer. I'd rather attend a small college. I don't like having two roommates. I love summer.

Beliefs consist of thoughts, opinions, and attitudes: I believe that young adulthood is a challenging time of life. I think that small colleges offer more individualized attention. In my opinion, educators aren't paid enough.

Feelings are disclosures about emotions: I'm proud to be in college. I feel sad when I think about moving to a new city. I was scared when I heard about the accident.

These degrees are arranged in order of least to most difficult to disclose, in general (see Fig. 8–1).

Degrees of
Self-Disclosure

| Basic Data |
| Preference |
| Belief |
| Feeling |

Figure 8-1

In most cases, basic data are risk-free and relatively easy to reveal. Even though preferences can usually be disclosed with little risk, some people will challenge you. For example, have you ever told someone that you liked a certain kind of food and had them reply, "That stuff? How could you like it?" Arguing over preferences seems trivial and unnecessary, yet you will find some people who seem to have difficulty accepting differences even about preferences.

For a number of people, or in certain situations, beliefs may be more difficult to disclose than feelings. Both include a degree of risk and indicate a deeper level of disclosure. Thoughts and opinions, as pointed out in Chapter 7, are often verbalized in the closed style. If the open style were used, beliefs would likely be more acceptable and, consequently, easier to reveal. Emotions can be hidden from others for a variety of reasons. Even if you are in touch with your feelings, they may be difficult to explain.

All relationships benefit from self-disclosure. The levels can be useful in checking out how open you are. Do others reveal all degrees to you? If they don't, do you know the reason? The depth of self-disclosure is generally an accurate reflection of the closeness of two people.

Awareness and Sharing

The Johari awareness model (Fig. 8–2) represents a total person in relation to other persons. (Johari, interestingly, is a combination of Joe and Harry, the first names of its two developers). The divisions, or quadrants, are based on awareness of behavior, feelings, and motivation (Luft, 1969). An explanation follows.

Quadrant 1 (open) refers to what is known to self and to others.
Quadrant 2 (blind) refers to what is unknown to self, but known to others.
Quadrant 3 (hidden) refers to what is known to self, but unknown to others.
Quadrant 4 (unknown) refers to what is unknown to self or to others.

Although the model shows equal-sized quadrants, or windowpanes, each will vary in size because of individual differences, as a result of particular situations, or because of experiences over time. For example, you may be an open person, so your quadrant 1 would be much larger than that of a friend who is rather private. If you are in a situation with strangers, you may choose to reveal little, which means that quadrant 3 is larger. You may develop an annoying habit of which you are unaware and others are; thus, the blind quadrant becomes larger. A change in any quadrant affects the other three. For example, if you reveal a feeling to a friend for the first time, quadrant 3 decreases while quadrant 1 increases. The open quadrant allows for interaction and exchange. Called a "window raised on the world, the smaller the first quadrant, the poorer the communication" (Luft, 1969, p. 14). You increase the open quadrant as you learn about yourself and then share with others.

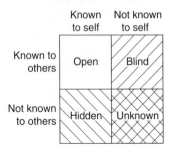

Johari Awareness Window

Figure 8-2

Balance in self-disclosing is healthy. Even though having a large open quadrant can improve communication, you can be too open, overly talkative, and inappropriate. Keeping some things to yourself is healthy. A huge blind windowpane is potentially hurtful or embarrassing: it means that others will know you better than you do yourself. For example, Jerry consistently behaved as if he were spending his last dime. His wife joked about his fumbling for his wallet whenever the bill was delivered to the table. He was oblivious to what was obvious to his family and friends. One day a friend's remark registered, and Jerry realized how his behavior appeared to others. He was embarrassed and hurt; however, his awareness allowed him to change.

Benefits of Self-Disclosure

Matt frowns at Sue when she says, "I wish you'd share more of yourself with me." "Why?" he asks. If Sue is well informed, she will be able to explain the benefits of self-disclosure. One reward has to do with knowing and understanding oneself. Each self-disclosing statement brightens the light of self-understanding. As you reveal, you feel more honest, authentic, and validated. "This is who I am" can be an exhilarating feeling. Self-disclosing is usually a self-esteem builder.

Other benefits are related to the developmental areas of self. In terms of health, a self-discloser seems to benefit. Inhibiting one's thoughts and feelings gradually undermines the immune function, the action of the heart and vascular system, and even the biochemical workings of the brain and nervous system. Not disclosing has been linked to the severity of asthma, diabetes, anorexia nervosa, and even pain thresholds. In an experiment, high self-disclosers showed significant drops in blood pressure compared to low disclosers. (Pennbaker, 1997). Talking to others about disturbing aspects of life is relieving.

Sharing can be relieving. Stress and certain emotions can be managed positively by self-disclosure. Erin described a change.

> I was negative, and now I'm positive. I think it's because I'm being more open and honest. I'm willing to share my "real" self now. I'm glad because people now are starting to look at me from the inside to the outside.

Specific benefits of self-disclosure were identified in a study of lesbians. Degree of disclosure was related to overall levels of social support (Jordan & Deluty, 1998).

Building close relationships is also an outcome of self-revelation. In fact, achieving intimacy is impossible without disclosure of self. **Social penetration theory** (Altman & Taylor, 1973) explains that close relationships develop in terms of increasing self-disclosure. Among dating couples, self-disclosure is a significant predictor of relationship satisfaction (Meeks, Hendrick, & Hendrick, 1998). As discussed in Chapter 5, expression of feeling is beneficial. "None of us who value our relationships can afford to retreat from communication on an emotional level" (Branden & Branden, 1982, p. 66). Self-disclosure has been related to positive outcomes for supervisors in a work setting (Ladany, Walker, & Melincoff, 2001) and perceived understanding in stepchild-stepparent relationships (Martin, Anderson, & Mottet, 1999).

A major plus is that self-disclosure makes relationships interesting. Think how boring life would be if people conversed only on basic data and preference levels. Disclosing affirms the other by saying, "I care enough about you to share my personal self."

Finally, when people self-disclose, the communication process is improved. Individuals can understand and provide feedback to each other and create an open, accepting environment. Self-disclosure is usually reciprocated. There is a relationship between what persons are willing to disclose and what others reveal to them. The openness of one person can begin a sharing process that creates a close relationship.

Obstacles to Self-Disclosure

Even if Sue convinces Matt that the benefits are well worth his consideration, he still may resist self-disclosing or find it difficult. He has a great deal of company in this regard. Why? The most common reason is fear: "I'm afraid that others will laugh at what I believe." "I was hurt before when I revealed how I felt, and I'm not going to let that happen again." "I told her how proud I was of my final grade, and she put me down for bragging." The threat of rejection is frightening. "But, if I tell you who I am, you may not like who I am, and it is all I have" (Powell, 1969, p. 20). Fear of intimacy could be involved. In a study that supported what had been found in heterosexual populations, fear of intimacy decreased self-disclosure among lesbians and gay mean (Greenfield & Thelen, 1997).

Most people receive "parent" messages telling them to not self-disclose. "Don't let others know about your financial situation," "Your sex life should be private," and "What would the neighbors think if they knew?" are common "parent" messages. Thus, many of us grow up believing that silence is golden, and it's often easier to keep quiet. Culture has an effect on self-disclosure. A study found that Asian Indians tend to suppress rather than express. Being exposed to American culture somewhat modified their perceptions and expressive patterns (Hastings, 2000). Gender roles are a part of the culture. As mentioned earlier, the stereotypic masculine role is "at odds" with self-disclosure. Men tend to be less self-disclosing especially about their emotions and weaknesses (Dolgin, 2001) which is unfortunate for both them and their partners.

Personal circumstances and attitudes can be barriers. A study revealed that lonely individuals negatively evaluated deeper levels of disclosure and viewed it as risky and undesirable (Rotenberg, 1997). People with low levels of **interpersonal trust**, defined as the expectancy that another's word or promise can be relied upon,

For Better or For Worse   **by Lynn Johnston**

would likely have more difficulty in self-disclosing. Obviously, after trust is developed, people are more likely to disclose.

Self-disclosure, like all communication skills, is not taught or even encouraged in many cases. Because there is little instruction in how to verbalize beliefs and feelings, attempts are often unaccepted or lead to disagreement. "I told him about my religious beliefs, and he came back with arguments" and "I let her know she hurt me, and she took it personally and got mad" are only two of many such examples. Regardless of the possible obstacles, rewards far outweigh costs.

How to Self-Disclose

After a consideration of the benefits and a removal of obstacles, people who want to feel more authentic and to develop healthy relationships will elect to self-disclose. The critical question for many is how? Before disclosing, honestly answer the questions in "Before You Self-disclose."

Before You Self-Disclose

- Is my level of disclosure appropriate in this situation?
- Do I trust the person to whom I'm disclosing?
- For what reason am I self-disclosing? Is it a positive one, or am I being manipulative, petty, or cruel?
- Are the risks worth my disclosure? What can be gained versus lost? Will my disclosure unreasonably burden another person?
- Is this the most opportune time and place to self-disclose? Is the atmosphere conducive to a positive interchange?

Positive answers give you a "green light" to self-disclosure.

After deciding to self-disclose, the question becomes how to do so. The use of "I" statements is highly recommended. The open style lends itself to positiveness. Body language in harmony with the verbal message is important. Stating that you think open communication is important while maintaining a closed body position is confusing. Being clear, specific, and descriptive are invaluable. Vague disclosures may be worse than more at all. Importantly, telling too much and monopolizing the conversation is very likely to turn off any listener. After disclosing, be ready to accept feedback and keep the exchange open.

GIVING AND RECEIVING COMPLIMENTS

Like breaths of fresh air, **compliments** are comments of admiration and praise; in the TA framework, they are verbal positive strokes. Compliments can initiate a relationship. On his first day at work, Bill was complimented by Rick, a coworker. The expression of praise started a conversation. After a few weeks the two were socializing with each other. Compliments definitely enhance relationships and build a bond between individuals.

Recommendations for Giving Compliments

Are you a compliment giver? Opportunities for expressions of admiration and praise are plentiful; too often, such opportunities are overlooked. Stinginess in compliment giving may come from a tendency to take others for granted or an inability to recognize a situation in which a compliment would be appropriate. Hesitation can come from shyness, embarrassment, or concern about how the compliment will be received. If you have any difficulty, consider how valuable a compliment can be. Jennifer was depressed and had decided to quit school. Then she was complimented about her class participation by an instructor and praised by another student for her note-taking abilities. "Those compliments were like a tonic to me," said. "I had lost faith in myself, and all at once it was restored. I changed my mind about quitting school."

Compliment-giving guidelines.   Raise your awareness level to the point that you notice praiseworthy situations. Everyone has a positive quality. Don't confine your compliments to people you know. A clerk in the department store, a taxicab driver, a waiter or waitress, a person behind the voice on the phone—all are candidates for compliments. Being sincere is important. Phoniness and insincere flattery are likely to be detected and will be disturbing. If you don't truly admire something, you are better off saying nothing.

Vary the reasons for your compliments. People usually compliment others on the basis of appearance. Certainly, people appreciate this type of praise. However, you can also compliment on other qualities and behaviors. "I enjoyed your comments in class," "I thought your work on the project was terrific," "I admire your positive attitude," and "I love your laugh" are generally appreciated by recipients.

When you compliment, check to see that your words, paralanguage, and body language are saying the same thing. Without meaning to do so, you can express a genuine compliment in a tone of voice that sounds negating. Beware of giving "backhanded" compliments. These are comments that start out sounding positive and end with a stinging remark, a question, or a qualifier that implies they aren't wholly true. Some examples are; "You drew a beautiful picture *for a change*," "I *can't believe* your room is clean," and "*How did you manage* to throw such a great party?" Can you see why these need to be reworded or are better left unsaid?

A positive behavior is to be a third-party compliment giver. What can you do if you hear a positive comment about someone? Passing it on to that individual is almost as good as giving it originally. You can also add to it. For example, "Craig said that you're a great golfer. I can see why he thinks so. Shooting par on that hole wasn't easy."

Thinking about yourself as a compliment giver and realizing the benefits of these positive comments can encourage you to increase both their number and their variety. You might want to set a goal of doing so. Your acquaintances, friends, and family members will benefit as will you.

Responding to Compliments

"I enjoy giving compliments, but I feel funny getting them," was Jordan's honest comment. How do you react to a compliment? The comment is, "I really like your suit." Do any of these responses sound like you?

"This old thing? I've had it for years."
"I hate it. I just pulled it out because everything else was dirty."
"Your taste in clothes is slipping."
"Really?" (while wrinkling your nose)

Rejecting or denying compliments is common, and the potential for damage is extensive. A compliment rejection is essentially an insult. It's as if the positive comment is hurled back into the face of the giver. Once rejected, a giver will be reluctant to deliver more compliments. A relationship can be harmed because one individual did not graciously receive what was offered. People with low self-esteem are often guilty of this practice and so do not benefit from a sincere comment of praise. Finally, the communication climate can become negative. Imagine a black cloud settling in because the compliment giver feels diminished.

How to receive.   Receiving a compliment in a positive way is simple. A "thank you" is enough. If you want to add more, some possibilities are "Thank you; I really appreciate that," "Thank you; I've been feeling a little down, and you helped," and "Thank you; I did spend a lot of time on the project."

If you honestly don't agree with the comment, you can choose to keep quiet or you can mention it without a rejection. For example, you really don't like the suit you are wearing, and you receive a compliment. A possible honest response is, "Thank you. I had my doubts about it, and it's nice to know that you think it looks good." You may wonder about returning a compliment with a compliment. In response to "I like your suit," someone could say, "I like your outfit, too." If the response is sincere, no harm will result from a mutual admiration exchange.

CHECKING YOUR PERCEPTION

Picture a person standing on the roof of a house with arms waving over the head. Three people from across the street look at the scene. Later, each tells about the incident.

> Mary to her husband: "This guy was acting really crazy. He was on top of the house and waving his arms like he was trying to scare someone."
>
> Tom to his children: "A man was trying to get my attention by waving his arms at me. I thought he was in trouble, so I came into the house and called 911. I haven't found out yet what was going on."
>
> Ed to a friend: "I didn't have my glasses on, but it looked like a woman up on the roof who was ready to jump. She was yelling really loud, too."

Each person offered a different perception of the situation.

What is perception and how does it affect the communication process? **Perception** is a mental process of creating meaning from **sensory data** that we receive through stimulation of our senses. A message is carried to the brain, which then organizes and interprets the data. In perceiving, our brains are like computers. Once "turned on," we take in data through the senses of sight, sound, smell, taste, and touch. The perception process begins when sensations are received (like raw data being fed into a computer) and continues as the brain quickly interprets. It tries to make sense out of the sensory data (as a computer computes) and attaches meaning to the input.

In differentiating between sensory data and interpretation, think of a courtroom scene. On the witness stand, a person is allowed to give only the facts, or sensory data: "I *saw* the suspect drive away in a red car." If a witness begins to add interpretation such as, "I *thought* that he had come out of the bank and was probably fleeing from a robbery," a good attorney will object. Interpretation is not allowed as evidence.

In interpersonal relationships we receive most information from seeing and hearing, although touching and smelling can also be involved. An individual's perception affects communication and all other aspects of human relationships. If perception were always accurate, several interpersonal difficulties could be avoided. But is perception correct in all situations? At the beginning of this section, three people described the same experience differently. Because of uniqueness, no two people's perceptions are ever exactly the same, and our perception in any given situation can be inaccurate.

Effects on Perception

For what reasons could perception be faulty? What we perceive is affected by such factors as background, self-esteem, personality, values, age, sex, physical condition, mental health, and expectations. For example, read the beginning of the nursery rhyme in these boxes.

Jack and Jill went up the the hill	To fetch a a pail of water.

Look carefully at the nursery rhyme again. If you read it as written here, you used *the* twice in the first box and *a* two times in the second. If you read it as you expected it to be (without the extra words), don't be surprised. Expectations do influence what you actually see. How does this relate to perception of human beings? If you expect to see or hear a certain thing, that may well be your sensory data. A custodian, who was cleaning an office, was facing a window. An office manager came in, sat at her desk, and said, "You're really working late. I'll bet your girlfriend or wife doesn't like that very much." To her surprise, a female voice replied, "Actually it's my husband who minds!" Expecting custodians to be male led to incorrect sensory input.

In addition, the senses and their abilities to gather accurate information differ from person to person. Limitations can lead to errors. Even though well-adjusted people are generally capable of receiving accurate sensory data, that is not a guarantee. Ask a police officer about an investigation of an accident scene! Usually, more than one account is heard. Even if the sensory data are correct, what about comprehension? Have you ever been misinterpreted? Have you misunderstood another person? The potential for errors is enormous. In fact, misperception causes much of the conflict and difficulties in relationships. How often have you heard or said, "That's not what I meant!"

As an example, imagine the following scenario.

> You are in the cafeteria at school or work, and a friend who is usually outgoing walks past your table. She glances at you and then turns away.

You saw what she did, so the sensory data are correct. Recognize, however, that another person might have "seen" it differently. Next is your interpretation. Think of as many possibilities as you can—such "whys" as:

She's mad at me.
She didn't really see me or recognize me.
She just doesn't want to talk right now.
She's stuck-up.

Which is correct? One cannot know at this point, and a person skilled in communication and interpersonal relations will want to clarify it. A first step is to be aware that you don't *know* for sure. Even though evidence may point to one interpretation more than another, the human experience is full of inconsistencies.

Perception Checking as a Communication Technique

When you have doubts about either the accuracy of sensory data or your interpretation or both, a communication technique called **perception checking** can be helpful. This process involves describing the specific sensory data you have received and the interpretations you are making about those data (Glaser, 1986). In cases in which you have no doubts as to accuracy, the technique would be senseless. For example, if someone says, "I don't like you," and punches you in the face, you are receiving a clear message!

Perception checking includes three steps. The first is to describe your sensory data—what you have actually seen and heard or, in some cases, smelled, tasted, or touched. It's important to be specific and descriptive. Secondly, you give an interpretation of the sensory data. What did it mean to you? The third step

---

Perception Checking

1. **Give sensory data**: Exactly what did you see, hear, or smell? Include who, when, and where if possible. Use behavioral terms in your description. Paint a picture in words. Use any of these: I noticed, I saw, I observed, I was told, I heard, I overheard, I smelled, I touched.
2. **Give interpretation**: What did the sensory data mean to you? Interpretation is delivered tentatively, not as if it is the truth or factual. Don't say, "I wonder if." State in a positive way what you think. Use any of these: I thought, it seemed to me, to me it appeared, I took that to mean, I believe, that led me to believe or think.
3. **Check both sensory data and interpretation**: The question checks the accuracy of your sensory data and perception. At this point you are not asking whether the person wants to talk, needs help, or the like; nor do you offer to give help yet. Use any of these: Is that right? Am I correct? Is that how it is or was?

checks out or asks a question to check the accuracy of both. Ideally, "I" statements are used in the first two steps, while the third step is framed as a question.

In using perception checking, certain phrases or ways of asking the question will probably sound more natural to you than another. Or all of the language may seem awkward at first. With use, you will become comfortable with it.

In the situation where your outgoing female friend has glanced at you and then looked away, you can use perception checking as follows:

1. "In the cafeteria this noon when you walked past my table, I saw you glance at me and then look away." (sensory data)
2. "It appears that you were upset for some reason." (interpretation)
3. "Am I right?" (question that checks both)

The friend can then confirm, modify, or deny either your sensory data or your interpretation or both.

You may be wondering why going through all three steps is important. Let's consider other possibilities such as a "why" question. "Why are you mad at me?" This is an assumption that your interpretation is accurate, and it may not be. Also, how do you react to most "why" questions? Generally, people are put on the spot and feel defensive. Also, many "why" questions are not asked to find out the real answer. As one man commented, "Whenever my folks asked 'why,' I knew they didn't approve of what I had done, and I was going to hear about it."

Another poor way to begin a discussion with the friend is what many people do: "You're mad at me, aren't you?" or "You don't like me any more, I guess." An even worse approach would be, "I *know* you are mad at me." These leave out all sensory data and leap directly to conclusions. Instead of checking, you have already made an interpretation, concluded that you are correct, and now the friend is being told the reason for the behavior. In many cases, people just assume that their interpretation is true, become upset, and don't say anything. "I'll treat her just like she treated me" is their way of handling the situation. Too often, relationships suffer because people do not openly share their sensory data and interpretation. Perception checking is direct and honest. Unless you are speaking to a troubled person, perception checking will be nonthreatening. The goal is to clarify a situation, and, in most cases, the person will respond in such a way that this is possible.

USING DIMENSIONS OF AWARENESS

Perception checking is used to clarify your sensory data (sensations) and interpretation (thought): You and your relationships can benefit from sharing even more. Although you may be unaware of them, five key pieces of information are present in a given situation (Miller, Wackman, Nunnally, & Miller, 1988). Let's examine each of them.

- **Sensations:** Verbal and nonverbal input from people's actions, as well as subtleties of what you see, hear, smell, taste, and touch.
- **Thoughts:** The meanings, interpretations, or conclusions from the sensations. Interpretations are not "the way things are." They are the way you put your world together—the way you make sense out of data.

- **Feelings:** Emotional responses, which are important to share in most interpersonal relationships. Review the information about expressing feelings in the section on degrees of self-disclosure.
- **Wants:** Intentions, desires, and wishes for yourself, for others, and for your relationship together.
- **Actions:** Behaviors consisting of past, present, and future actions. These are, or will be, observable, and they indicate commitment.

Confusion between wants and future actions is common. The difference is that intentions do not carry a definite commitment to act and are only desires. You may share what you have done, are presently doing, or will do.

Becoming aware of the five dimensions in any interaction then expressing these to another person indicates a willingness to reveal what you know. Using "I" statements is important. Following is a way to use dimensions of awareness in the situation of the friend in the cafeteria.

(Sensing) This noon as you walked by my table in the cafeteria, I saw you glance at me and then look away.
(Thinking) It seemed to me that you were upset.
(Feeling) I'm concerned about this.
(Wanting) I'd like to straighten this out.
(Acting) In fact, I asked Michele if she knew if something was wrong. She didn't, so I'm checking it out with you.

You may not want to express each dimension in exactly the same way or order presented here. You can begin with any dimension and use wording that is comfortable for you. For example,

> I'm concerned because I noticed that you looked away from me when you walked by my table in the cafeteria this noon. I was sure you had seen me, and it led me to think that you're upset with me. In fact, I even asked Michele if she knew if you were upset and she didn't. I'd like to straighten this out, and I have time to talk about it right now if you do.

If you're thinking that this is too involved and will be time-consuming, ask yourself how worthwhile is clarity. Being partly aware is a major problem in the communication process. You owe it to yourself and to your relationships to become as fully aware as possible.

Thinking about these dimensions can help you discover any areas of self-*un*awareness. For example, you may be able to communicate four dimensions and recognize that your feelings are not clear—even to you. Learning the skills initially is the easiest part; putting them into practice is the most difficult. Usually, it helps to announce that you want to share your dimensions of awareness and would like the other to do so too.

DELIVERING CRITICISM

A life in which criticism is unnecessary may sound wonderful; however, such an ideal world does not exist. Because you will undoubtedly deliver criticism, learning how to do so in a constructive, positive way is advisable. A first step is to ask yourself the reason for criticizing. Is it justifiable? Is it potentially beneficial? Think about whether the criticism is destructive or constructive, and speak only if you believe you can help.

Preparing yourself by thinking about what you will say, and even rehearsing it, is highly recommended. Picking a suitable time and place, if possible, is also a good idea. Be aware of body language and paralanguage. When you deliver a critical remark, use "I" statements. "You" statements will most likely elicit a defensive, combative response. Directing attention specifically and descriptively to behavior or a situation you don't like is more acceptable than being critical of the person. You can choose to use perception checking or, more completely, the dimensions of awareness to increase the chances of a receptive response. Another suggestion has been called the "Mary Poppins rule" (Levine, 1988). Based on the idea that "a spoonful of sugar helps the medicine go down," the aim is to make the criticism more acceptable by prefacing it with a sincere compliment. For example, "Professor Martin, I enjoy your lectures a lot; however, I don't think that the examination policies are as fair as they could be." Using the person's name, also, can be affirming. Check the following steps in criticizing a sloppy roommate.

1. Begin with a sincere positive comment.
   "Rhonda, I really like you and have a lot of fun living with you."
2. Specifically describe the situation and behaviors. Again, draw a picture with your words.
   "We had agreed to keep our apartment clean and neat, yet your clothes are in the living room, and I've cleaned up the mess in the kitchen for the last four days."
3. Acknowledge the other's thoughts, feelings, and personal situation.
   "I realize that you've been so busy and maybe just forgot."
4. Give reasons for your criticism and tell exactly what you want and expect.
   "I'm frustrated, and I don't want this to become a bigger problem. I do expect you to keep our agreement."

Unless Rhonda is an extremely defensive person, this criticism will not offend and will usually get desired results. If it doesn't, you can at least be satisfied that you have expressed your criticism in an open, nonthreatening way.

RESPONDING EFFECTIVELY

Criticism is almost impossible to avoid and can be difficult to receive. If constructive and delivered in a nonthreatening manner, it is easier to handle; however, a sizable number of critical statements are made negatively and for reasons that are not evident. Whether the criticism is deserved or not, a response determines, to a great extent, the course of the exchange and possibly the relationship itself.

Inappropriate Responses to Criticism

Eliminating ineffective or negative responses can clear the way for responses that work in your behalf. In general, individuals respond either aggressively or passively or a combination of the two. An aggressive method is one of counterattack. A person feels wronged, justifiably or not, then lashes out at the perceived attacker. The criticism may be stopped for the moment; however, the aggression is resented, and the situation is only worsened. In the workplace, an aggressive response will probably get you fired.

Passive responses are ones that apologize and acquiesce; they can be delivered verbally or nonverbally. Silence is often a form of surrendering to criticism. If you are a "peace-at-any-price" person, passivity may seem inviting. Nevertheless, the potential damages to your psychological well-being and to the relationship are seldom worth the price. Meek receivers of criticism also invite further attacks.

A combination of the two occurs when an individual responds passively and then acts aggressively at a later time: "Yes, dear, I know I have neglected paying the bills, and I'll make sure it doesn't happen again," is the agreeable response. The bills get paid, and two checks are returned from the bank for insufficient funds. The person who was criticized either purposefully or unconsciously has found a way to get back at the critic. Because this behavior is essentially manipulative and indirect, a relationship can be badly damaged.

Other possibilities are denial and defense. Excuse making is a far too common response. Usually, the criticized person recognizes that the criticism is appropriate, yet still finds it difficult to accept. "Yes, *but*" is an irritating response. Blaming other people or externals is part of excuse making and makes an individual appear immature and irresponsible.

Positive Responses to Criticism

If your goals are to maintain or increase your level of self-esteem, preserve or improve the relationship, and make the situation better for yourself, positive responses to criticism are the key. "The effective way to respond to criticism is to use an assertive style. It doesn't attack, surrender to, or sabotage the critic. It disarms the critic" (McKay & Fanning, 2000, p. 162). The key is to not overreact and make matters worse.

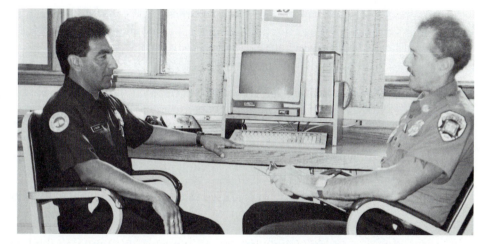

Figure 8-4   During a performance evaluation, constructive criticism is given in a positive way.

Agreement with criticism.   Even if you realize that the criticism is justified, you can still feel somewhat defensive and hurt. Hence, you may respond in a way that will make the situation worse for you. Instead, follow these steps using "I" statements.

1. Agree with the criticism, using such phrases as "I realize," "I agree," "I know," and "I understand."
2. Optional: State the reason briefly and be sure your reason is fact, not excuse. (This step is optional because you may not want to tell the "why.")
3. State what you plan to do to prevent future occurrences or to solve the problem.

Pretend you have been late for work for the past few days, and your supervisor has criticized you. A common reaction is to make an excuse or blame. Refrain from either! Instead, use a response that is refreshing and much more likely to bring about positive results.

1. I know I've been late, and I can understand your concern.
2. I've had several frustrating problems with my car (optional).
3. I'm taking it in to be fixed tonight, and I plan to be careful about my punctuality in the future.

Or, if you don't want to mention your car, skip step 2, and in the third step just say, "I will correct this problem in the future." Dramatically promising that you will *never* be late again is unwise because you might.

You can also agree with part of the criticism. You might understand the person's interpretation and want to clarify. For example, if your supervisor said, "You seem to have lost interest in doing a good job," you can respond, "I can see why you would think that because I have been late the past few days. I haven't lost interest. My being late is due to other factors which I plan to correct."

In certain instances, humor can be used to defuse the situation. When former Nebraska Senator Bob Kerrey was running for Congress, a loud critical voice from the audience said, "I don't know why I should vote for you. During one whole year when you were governor, I don't remember anything you did except entertain that actress, Debra Winger." Kerrey smiled, rubbed the side of his head, and replied, "I know what you mean. Sometimes I don't remember much else about that year either." The crowd broke into laughter, including the critic, and what could have become a negative situation, didn't.

Not understanding the criticism.   Frequently, criticism is vague, and you honestly don't understand what the person means. Emotionally, this is difficult to handle. You are probably inclined to defend even if you don't know the reason for the criticism. Resist the temptation! The following response technique, using "I" statements, is particularly helpful.

1. State your lack of understanding. Use phrases such as: "I don't understand why you think that," "I'm confused as to why you said that," or "I don't know why you have that impression."
2. Tell the person what you need to increase your level of understanding. Use phrases such as: "I'd like for you to explain to me why you think that way," "I'd appreciate your telling me what I've done or not done to lead you to think that," or "I would like to know what you are basing that on."

Now the critic is in the responding position. You have been honest and politely requested what you want while giving yourself time to calm down if needed. You wait for the explanation, which usually gives you enough information to respond specifically. Interestingly, if the critic had used either perception checking or dimensions of awareness, you likely wouldn't need more information. Vague criticism usually doesn't include sensory data.

To illustrate this response, pretend a coworker has said to you, "You don't like to work with me anymore." You have no idea why she believes this because she has not given you her sensory input. You can use a two-step response and say:

1. I don't know why you think I don't like to work with you.
2. I'd appreciate your telling me what has caused you to think that.

You now wait to hear what led to her interpretation, which she has poorly stated as fact. Then you can deal with a concrete description of her sensory data.

Surprisingly, the person may not be able to provide what you have requested. The response may be, "Well, I don't really know. I just don't think you like to work with me." This is frustrating; however, you are wise to continue to behave positively. You can ask key questions such as: "Can you give me some examples?" "Can you specifically describe what I did?" In some cases, you may have an idea of the reason for their criticism and can guess. Be careful about this, however. For example, you respond with: "Is it because I told the supervisor that you hadn't finished your share of the project before you left yesterday?" If you aren't certain that this is known by the coworker, you will be in for a surprise when she says, "No, I didn't know you did that, and now I'm really upset!" If you have probed and still haven't received any useful sensory data, you can conclude by saying, "I don't feel that way; however, until you can give me some specifics, I'm not able to offer more than that."

Not agreeing with the criticism.   Emotionally, the most difficult situation to deal with is one in which you disagree with the criticism. The person has given you sensory data either initially or after you have requested clarification, and you do not agree. A positive response is still the best one.

1. State your disagreement: "I don't agree," "I guess we don't agree on this," or "I don't see it the way you do." Be sure that you are expressing this in a non-threatening way and keeping your voice calm. Usually, a quick "I disagree" sounds aggressive and is not recommended.
2. Either use your own sensory data to give reasons for your disagreement or simply end the conversation. Your choice will depend on what is at stake, what chances you think you have of coming to some sort of an agreement, and other extenuating factors such as fatigue levels and time constraints. You can suggest a future discussion as well as an acknowledgment that disagreement isn't always negative.

Other tactics may be helpful. You may opt to neither agree nor disagree. Instead, you simply acknowledge criticism and let it go. For example, a parent says to you, "Your apartment (or house) is such a mess, I don't know how you stand to live here." You can reply, "Yes, it is a mess," or "It *is* amazing how I stand it." Other useful phrases are: "You *may* be right" and "That could be true." If you feel strongly about the criticism, acknowledgment isn't advisable. However, in many situations, criticism can be like "water off a duck's back" if you allow it to be.

Another choice is to delay. If you are completely surprised by the criticism and, especially, if your reaction is anger, you can express your confusion or surprise and state that you want to think about it for awhile. A good response is, "I'm not sure how to reply. I'm going to think about it, and then I'll get back to you."

> By backing up for a moment to examine our feelings, rather than simply reacting from panic, we can most effectively sort out and respond to the realities of the critical message (Butler, 1992, p. 165).

Positive responses to criticism are not difficult to learn. They lead to a feeling of enhanced self-esteem and of being in control and serve to move relationships in a positive direction. Checking your skills in the communication exercise in Reflections and Applications will help.

Effective Responses to Metamessages

Metamessages, comments with a double-level meaning, were discussed in Chapter 7. Metamessages are usually hidden criticisms, yet they may not be. Recipients of such messages cannot be sure until they check. First figure out what you think it means. The second step is to state what you think the person is saying and ask whether you are correct. Imagine that your mother says, "You are *so* busy these days." The emphasis on "so" creates a metamessage. The statement means more than just that you are busy. Is concern about your welfare being expressed, or does your mother mean that you don't spend enough time with her? Whichever you decide, state it clearly and tentatively: "I wonder if you're worried about me" or "It seems to me that you don't think I'm spending enough time with you." You can phrase it as a question such as, "Do you mean that I'm not spending enough time with you?" Or you can choose to ignore it; however, realize that a relationship based on openness and positiveness is then in jeopardy.

Ways of Responding to Offensive Language Patterns

Being able to respond assertively to offensive language patterns is a worthwhile skill. "I hate it when people make bigoted remarks. I just don't know what to say," said one individual. Because a response is usually preferable to silence, knowing what to say makes a major difference.

- Assertively state your opinion; in doing so, you set limits.

"I don't appreciate profanity."
"I don't approve of those kinds of jokes."
"I don't like to hear others being put down."

- Tell how you feel.

"I feel resentful when you start your sentence with 'Let me tell you.'"
"I get frustrated when you make frequent references to 'when I was your age.'"
"I'm hurt by those kinds of comments."

- Politely challenge with a question.

"Can you clarify that?"
"Is that your opinion or is it based on research?"
"What do you mean?"

- Suggest another alternative.

"As far as I'm concerned, talking positively about people is so much better than being so negative."
"I'd prefer that you didn't say, 'You have no right to feel that way.' I do have a right to my feelings."
"I'd like to talk about something else."

Too often, individuals simply react and respond with whatever happens to come to mind, not realizing what impact their response has on both the communication climate and the interaction. Being prepared with positive responses is an important part of communicating and deserves attention.

Verbal Abuse: What to Do

When a person is told over time that his or her perceptions and feelings are wrong, the challenge is learning to respond to verbal abuse. This type of abuse doesn't leave physical evidence; however, it is just as painful, and recovery takes much longer (Evans, 1996). Prolonged verbal abuse damages the spirit and reduces joy and vitality.

The first step is awareness of verbal abuse. The book *The Verbally Abusive Relationship: How to Recognize It and How to Respond* (Evans, 1996) describes possible

---

Reflect

- See if you can think of your own examples for each of the five levels of content given at the beginning of the chapter.
- Think of different examples of dialect variations.
- What are three benefits of self-disclosure?
- For what reason(s) would you think a significant other no longer cares about you? Be sure you are coming up with sensory data to support your thoughts.
- How many interpretations can you come up with for this situation? You receive a low evaluation on a project at work.

Apply

- Give two sincere compliments to two different people.
- Look and listen, then provide three examples of sensory data beginning with: "I saw," "I noticed," "I heard."
- Ask other people how they would interpret the situation of receiving a low evaluation at work and see how many agree with yours.
- Pretend you have heard something that is offensive. Select a type of response given in the book that you are comfortable using. What exactly would you say?

characteristics and different types of abusers, some of which may surprise you. One not often recognized is verbal abuse disguised as a joke. This kind of abuse "cuts to the quick, touches the most sensitive areas, and leaves the abuser with a look of triumph" (Evans, 1996, p. 93). Some examples are "You couldn't find your way out of a paper sack," "You'd lose your head if it wasn't attached," "What can I expect from a blonde?" The abuser makes a disparaging remark and, if challenged, will often accuse the "victim" of having no sense of humor. Common is a rebuke: "I was just kidding" or "Can't you take a joke?"

Any verbal abuse tactic requires assertive responses. Allowing yourself to be verbally abused is belittling and will lead to more unhappiness in the future. After recognizing a pattern of verbal abuse, you can start to set limits: "I will not accept jokes that put me down or belittle me." The abuser may not honor your limits, but you have other choices. Finding a supportive counselor and asking the abuser to go with you is one possibility. If you decide that the abuse isn't going to end, you are well advised to end the relationship. Handling the abuse with positive, assertive responses may not be the only step you take; however, it is the beginning of finding the respect you deserve.

Whether you are responding to or initiating an exchange, learning about content then practicing can greatly improve what you say. Many people, after gaining awareness of content, say, "I didn't realize so much was involved. I used to just open my mouth and talk. Now I think about it first!" Awkwardness is to be expected initially. Do you recall learning to ride a bicycle, to water ski, or to type? Your first attempts probably felt clumsy, and you may have thought that you would never learn. If you persisted, it was likely you wondered how it could have been so difficult. Learning communication skills is similar. After exposure and practice, less intense thinking is needed, the skills become natural, and you will wonder at your initial lack of ability.

You are now ready to complete the communication exercises in Reflections and Applications. If you do well on the ones in Chapters 7 and 8, you deserve a pat on the back. Keep in mind that content does make a definite difference in all interactions and especially in close relationships, and you influence the course of a relationship by what you say.

LOOKING BACK

- Content consists of verbalized words and sentences.
- What you talk about can be organized into levels ranging from superficial chitchat to deep, intimate communication.
- Communication pitfalls can be avoided by awareness of semantics, dialect, bias-free language, second-language challenges, emotion-packed phrases, disclaimers, slang, colloquialisms, vulgarity, vocabulary, and grammar.
- Self-disclosure, revealing information about yourself, can be organized into degrees or levels that move from basic data through preferences to beliefs and feelings. The Johari Awareness window represent variance in self-disclosure. Individuals vary in their willingness and ability to self-disclose.

- Appropriate self-disclosing has personal and professional benefits. Despite known advantages, an individual may not self-disclose because of obstacles that, with awareness and determination, can be avoided.
- Compliments are comments of admiration and praise given to a person. Increasing the number of sincere compliments you give, doing so in positive ways, and receiving compliments graciously improve relationships.
- Sensation and perception include taking in sensory data and making interpretations. Individuals can err in the accuracy of either the initial input or the meaning they attach to it.
- Techniques such as perception checking and verbalizing dimensions of awareness aid in understanding and clarifying situations.
- Effective responses are usually as important as initial comments. Learning positive responses to criticism, metamessages, and offensive language patterns is a beneficial interpersonal relations skill.
- Handling verbal abuse assertively, which is especially challenging, is necessary in building healthy relationships.
- As with any art, interpersonal communication requires attention and practice.

It is certain that a relationship will be only as good as its communication.

—John Powell

Section Three
Positive Relationships: The Ultimate Achievement

LOOKING AHEAD

After reading this section, you will be able to:

* Explain why your own relationships are important.
* Describe loneliness and what the research shows.
* Give examples of how relationships can be beneficial.

Relationships with others lie at the very core of human existence.
—Ellen Berscheid and Letitia Anne Peplau

Understanding and love of self along with interpersonal communication skills are the foundation of positive relationships. Our exploration of interpersonal relations continues with a look at the benefits of relationships.

For what reasons do people relate to others? "I don't think hermits have much fun, and loners look sad," a student said when I asked this question in class. Another man mentioned that people need others to avoid loneliness which he described as a "bummer." His description was accurate. "Acute loneliness is a terrorizing pain" (Rokach, 1990, p. 41). Loneliness, as defined in one study, is "a feeling of being alone and disconnected or alienated from positive persons, places, or things" (Woodward, 1988, p.4). Besides a dreadful feeling, are there other reasons to be concerned about loneliness? The answer is a definite yes. The book *A Cry Unheard: New Insights into the Medical Consequences of Loneliness* (Lynch, 2000) describes numerous studies linking loneliness to premature death. The author describes loneliness as one of the most lethal risk factors in matters of life and death.

Who is lonely and why? An interesting study looked at both these questions. Loneliness was found in all age groups; however, young adults (19–30 years old) had the highest scores on each of the categories of perceived causes of loneliness. Women scored higher in loneliness than did men (Rokach, 2000). Young children are also lonely, and the causes stem from early family experiences and subsequent peer interactions (Solomon, 2000). As many students will attest, the first year of college is a particularly vulnerable time, especially for those who live away from home. Coining a new term, "*friendsickness*" which means preoccupation with and concern for the loss of or change in precollege friendships, researchers found that it was related to loneliness (Paul & Brier, 2001)

Can people be lonely in the presence of others? The answer is a resounding yes, and the feeling can be dreadful. Julie commented, "You can be in the center of a crowd and be dreadfully lonely." Rita, whose husband had left her, said, "I have periods of loneliness now, but it's nothing compared to how lonely I felt when he was sitting in the same room with me." In fact, **living together loneliness (LTL)**, the result of a perceived discrepancy between expected and achieved contact, has been identified. More than one fourth of married people, the majority of them females, suffer from LTL (Kiley, 1989).

If you experience loneliness on a regular basis, do something about it. One suggestion is to strengthen your level of self-esteem. Finding someone to love is not the solution. Instead, learn to love yourself (Burns, 1985). Cognitive restructuring is useful because thoughts create reality. Behavior techniques also help. Engaging in enjoyable activities is one way of coping. A good idea is to call or visit someone. Ways to create happiness, suggested in Chapter 4, can alleviate loneliness. One of the easiest ways to prevent or end loneliness is to find a group that needs you; volunteer, personal interest, and support groups are everywhere. You will be welcomed. If getting involved doesn't interest you or if you lack the willpower to take the first step, you would be wise to seek counseling. Mistakenly, lonely high school and college students may believe that they just need to get out and do things with large numbers of people. Instead, the time could be better spent deepening and enriching their relationships.

> There is no complete escape from loneliness. It is part of being born, of being human, of living, of loving, of dying. Perhaps there shouldn't be a complete escape. Why would anyone want to be deprived completely of an emotion? To experience the emotions of passion, happiness, grief, love, and loneliness is part of living, part of being human. (Woodward, 1988, p. 85)

Few cases of loneliness persist if the individual tries to live differently.

Other reasons for having relationships are apparent. Pleasure is a prominent one. "We have fun together," and "We just like to be with each other." Jointly participating in activities and just being together are major benefits. Even brief encounters with people can be interesting and stimulating. Additionally, we look to people for favors, help, advice, and support. "My car didn't start, so my neighbor gave me a ride to work," "My buddy loaned me money until payday," and "When I moved, I called everyone I knew to help" are typical descriptions of relationships.

Support is a major benefit of relationships. Being able to share stress, emotional challenges, and problems with someone else decreases their impact. When interviewees were asked to describe their most important relationships, the word "there" kept being used. "She is always *there* for me," "I can count on him to be *there*." Consistently, "thereness" seemed to be the key element in the "why" of their relationships (Josselson, 1992).

The necessity for emotional support struck me a few years ago as I waited for a surgeon to report on my daughter after major surgery. Trying to relieve stress, I wrote my thoughts at that time. These shakily written notes are in my journal.

> Waiting for surgeon and looking around the waiting room and seeing family and friends who have given so much support—my husband, my daughter Lisa, my parents who haven't been in good health themselves, two close friends, and my former husband, who must be as worried as I am. Along with the risk and the pain involved in human relationships is the beauty of emotional support.

Just like a song says, "We all need somebody to lean on." "If I didn't have friends, I'd have given up" is how Ann felt. Do you remember a time when you didn't have anybody near to call upon? If so, you know how reassuring relationships can be.

Having a **confidant**, a significantly close personal friend with whom one can safely share one's deepest concerns and joys, is related to higher levels of well-being, health, satisfaction, and lowered distress (Ornish, 1998). One of the earliest studies on confidants found that older people who had a confidant lived longer than those who didn't (Belsky, 1988). "Close relationships help people weather life's slings and arrows and may even reduce our chances of getting physically ill" (p. 73). Several studies show an increased rate of disease, alcoholism, and premature death associated with a lack of social support. Both receiving and giving love and intimacy are healing (Ornish, 1998).

Our self-concepts benefit from healthy relationships. When individuals feel affirmed, their self-esteem levels increase. Even a friendly hello can lift spirits and spark a feeling of "I matter." Growth can occur as you interact with others. "I learned a lot from that relationship" and "I'm a better person because of her" are statements of growth. "I may not have gone to college if it hadn't been for my friends' influence" shows how relationships can motivate. They also energize.

> Human contact has the power to increase your energy. Human beings need contact with other human beings the way a lamp needs electricity. Contact energizes people and can relieve stress. (Tubesing, 1981, p. 85)

It is clear that we need human contact. In both personal and professional walks of life, being able to interact and get along with others are invaluable. Learning everything possible about relationships is essential if you are to achieve success in your own life. The rest of this book focuses on positive relationships.

Figure III-1   Mother-in-law Lorane Hanna and son-in-law Bob Dinkel found that a positive relationship is a source of joy.

Joy comes to those who succeed in their human relationships.

—Sharon Hanna

9

Building Positive Relationships

LOOKING AHEAD

After completing this chapter, you will be able to

- Name and explain features of healthy relationships.
- Define codependency and recognize that it is not healthy.
- Discuss positive behaviors in relationships and interactions.
- Discuss different types of relationships, including friendships.
- Trace a path from tolerance to appreciation of diversity.
- Define stereotyping, prejudice, and discrimination and explain ways to rid your-self of each.
- Know what is required to approach others, tell how to look for approachability cues and discuss ways to initiate and maintain a conversation.
- Identify factors related to attraction and liking.
- Improve your own relationships.

Humans are conceived within relationships, born into relationships, and live their lives within relationships with others. All human society has a stake in the nature of people's close relationships. We all benefit from the existence of successful relationships and share, at least indirectly, the costs of relationship deficiencies.
—Ellen Berscheid and Letitia Anne Peplau

We are relating beings. "We may almost say that to be is to relate. We relate because we must" (Rubin, 1983). Without self-knowledge, self-love, and positive communication skills, you will encounter difficulty and disappointment in interpersonal relations; with them, you are ready to become even more skilled in building positive relationships.

CREATING HEALTHY RELATIONSHIPS

Not all relationships are good for us. Review the description of a positive one in Section One of this book. The ability to recognize the difference between what are sometimes called healthy and unhealthy relationships is a first step in reducing the chance of becoming involved in those that aren't positive.

Features of a Healthy Relationship

Have you ever been a part of what can be called an unhealthy relationship—one that wasn't good for you? Most unhealthy relationships are sources of frustration and pain. Inevitably, one or both of the participants is hurt. Building a positive relationship is in everyone's best interest.

High self-esteem.   In order for a relationship to be satisfying and nourishing, the people involved must exhibit certain traits. Love for self is a primary one. Genuine self-esteem, as described in Chapter 1, is healthy and allows an individual to reach out positively to others. Both people are in or are committed to achieving an I'm OK, you're OK life position, and they accept and affirm each other.

Freedom from enabling behaviors and absence of codependency.   When two people care about themselves and others, the relationship tends to be balanced. **Enabling** occurs when someone's actions directly, yet unintentionally, allow irresponsible, dysfunctional, or destructive actions of another person to continue. Usually, the enabler is trying to help. Enabling behaviors often lead to codependence, a term that originally was related to substance abuse and is now used in describing various relationships. **Codependency** is often the result of an enabler focusing too much on the needs and behaviors of the other, and both suffer as a result. A codependent is the one who is doing too much. Codependents feel compelled to help others, they do for others what they could be doing for themselves, and they never think they have done enough. People often do not recognize the condition because it is second nature to them. Also, because nurturing and caring, two positive qualities, are typically the bedrocks of codependency, the person usually feels affirmed and justified for his or her sacrifices. In sum, codependents are responsive to the needs of the world to the exclusion of their own needs.

Joanna is one of the kindest individuals in the world. She remembers friends' and clients' birthdays and anniversaries, she is the first to visit someone in the hospital, and she does favors regularly. She used to dote on her two grown sons and grandchildren to the exclusion of her own best interests. She was always there for them as well as everyone else she knew. Stress-related symptoms led her to a therapist, who identified her as a codependent. After several therapy sessions, extensive reading, and soul searching, she is psychologically healthy again.

> Holly, a beautiful young woman expressed codependency so well: "I'm afraid to leave him because he is so dependent on me. I also think that I'm dependent upon his being dependent on me."

Codependency can be related to self-concept. Individuals with low self-esteem are more likely to take extra steps to please others. The stereotypic feminine gender role is often at fault. A nonassertive, appeasing person is more likely to become codependent.

What can be done about codependency? Identifying it and increasing one's level of self-esteem, if necessary, are key elements. Developing an androgynous personality, using the thinking preference in your personality while tempering the tendency to let your feelings control behavior, and assertiveness training will produce results. One of the first to write about codependency was Melody Beattie (1987). In a later book (1989), she points out that because society provides many invitations to be codependent, maintaining firm personal boundaries is necessary. She also reminds a recovered codependent that relapse is possible and describes how to get back on track. In many cases, individual or group counseling is extremely beneficial. It helps to remind yourself that you are not only making these changes for yourself; other people will also benefit. Then you can arrive at a place in which you can say, as did Jean: "I have been so many things to so many people. It's time to be someone for me."

Genuineness.   Besides love for self, androgyny, and assertiveness, which help to eliminate codependency, Carl Rogers (1980) identified four features of a healthy therapist-client relationship, applicable for all types of relationships. One is **genuineness** which means revealing your true self and striving to be honest. This creates trust in the relationship. Honesty between people is more than the absence of lying; openness and authenticity are significant facets. Participants in the relationship feel comfortable showing their true selves. Game playing is unnecessary, and individuals can express what they think and feel. This means that hurt is likely; however, healthy relationships can tolerate some pain.

Warmth.   Another feature that Rogers (1980) calls **unconditional positive regard** is a warm acceptance of each other's personhood. Conditional regard means that conditions are attached to the relationship: "I like you when you do me favors" and "I expect you to be there every time I call" are examples. Unconditional positive regard means that two people appreciate each others' unique personalities and allow for human flaws.

Empathy.   A key element in healthy relationships is **empathy**—the ability to experience another person's perspective. This is the third ingredient identified by Rogers (1980). You are able to participate in another's feelings and ideas. Empathy is related to a high feeling preference on the Myers-Briggs Type Indicator although those with a thinking preference can also empathize as can both sexes.

> Empathetic men become co-beings. They don't talk at you or interrupt. They listen and stand beside you, and in their presence, you have a wonderful feeling that you can be yourself (Keen 1991).

Understanding others and being empathic are challenging. What can help is to accept differences in how people think and feel and not categorize them as right or wrong. Even though you may not have experienced a similar situation, you can still empathize.

Being empathic requires a person to comprehend underlying meanings. Bob talked incessantly to his coworkers about his hospital stay and the results of his laboratory tests. Dave realized that down deep Bob was scared that there was something seriously wrong. He recognized that the nervous chatter was a cover-up for some anxious feelings. He empathized and encouraged Bob to talk about his fear. After the feeling was released, Bob's discussions about his health became fewer.

Self-disclosure.   In order to build and enliven a relationship, individuals share information about themselves. Self-disclosure, according to Rogers (1980), is essential. As discussed in Chapter 8, all relationships require some level of disclosure. In order to develop closer ties, people express on deeper levels. As they reveal more of their hidden selves, a powerful basis for trust can be formed. In some cases, further self-disclosure will indicate that this relationship is not one you want to pursue.

> There are some people who we do not feel are nutritious for us. It doesn't mean they are bad; it only means there isn't a fit. I see no problem with deciding someone is not to your taste once you have explored. This is a continuing experience of meeting, exploring, and choosing. (Satir, 1978, p. 99)

Social exchange.   One way to check the health of a relationship is to ask yourself honestly, "Is it good for me?" If you believe that you are receiving benefits that outweigh costs, yes is the likely answer. **Social exchange theory** maintains that relationships can be assessed by their outcomes, or what the participants are receiving, compared to what they are giving. A study suggested that friendships are more likely to be reciprocal—a give and take—and that those who felt either deprived or advantaged in their relationship reported much more loneliness (Buunk & Prins, 1998).

Think about your friendships. What do you receive and give? Did you once experience a friendship that you no longer have? Relationships can end because one or both are no longer receiving enough from the other. Elizabeth and Courtney shared an apartment. Both were single and pursuing careers. Courtney received a job transfer to a nearby city. "We'll still be close friends," said Courtney. "Oh, yes, it's not that far," agreed Elizabeth. Contact gradually decreased, and within 2 years, the relationship had essentially ended. Their relationship was based on enjoyable daily contact, so when this was no longer possible, neither received enough. The costs exceeded the benefits.

One of the basic principles of the behavioristic approach to psychology is that most people seek pleasure and avoid pain. Although relationships will have elements of displeasure, in those that are positive, rewards either outnumber or are more powerful than punishments. Evaluating a relationship on its rewards is practical and healthful.

Enjoyment.   "I love movies," said one woman, "and I'll go to one alone. But it's so much more enjoyable to go with someone." A healthy relationship will have times of unhappiness, yet the overall vibrations will be those of joy. People enjoy relationships that are encouraging, supportive, and affirming.

Dependability.   In a positive relationship you can count on the other to treat you fairly, and this is reciprocated. Dependability also means that each of you will do what you say unless circumstances prevent it. Trust develops between individuals who can rely on each other to be fair and dependable.

Energizing Feelings.   Being energized means that you leave an interaction feeling "up." Do you have some relationships that drain your energy? In positive relationships, individuals feel fulfilled because each provides sparks of energy. Sue, a close friend of mine since college, and I agree that one reason we enjoy interacting is that when we leave each other, we feel more energized than when we first come together. "The most important thing you can ever do for other people is to leave them feeling better emotionally after being in your presence" (Ellsworth, 1988, p. 115). Be cautious if energy flows out of you and is not restored by the relationship.

Demonstrated mutual interest.   One day I asked students why they no longer had certain relationships. One woman replied, "She just didn't ever seem interested in me. I asked about her life; mine never seemed important to her." You show interest by asking questions such as "What's new in your life?" "What plans do you have for the holidays?" "How are your children doing?" People who show little or no interest in others seem self-absorbed, whereas positive individuals enjoy sharing with others, and they love to be asked about their lives!

Positive Interactions

Think of those with whom you interact? What distinguishes one interaction from another? College students identified several characteristics of positive interactions.

- Acknowledgment (e.g., calling me by my name when greeting)
- Active interest and concern for my feelings
- Willingness to offer help; often before being asked
- Good sense of humor
- Willingness to admit mistakes
- Interesting conversation
- Giving, but not overdoing it
- Willingness to make decisions; doesn't always depend on me to choose activities
- Sharing; will pay their share and contribute in other ways
- Listening skills; will listen openly
- Positive attitude
- Trust; the other will not put me down or embarrass me
- Ability to keep confidences and secrets
- Willingness to stand up for me, if necessary

Figure 9-1   An ordinary interaction is more pleasant when individuals are friendly and positive.

How many of these do you demonstrate in your relationships? How about the other people involved? Can you add to the list?

As human beings rush through busy days, small positive actions can mean so much. Because these are not time-consuming favors or dramatic gestures, their impact may be overlooked. Check the list of "Little Acts of Kindness." How many have you done or experienced? Did any brighten the day for you?

The power of smiles and greetings is often overlooked. A therapist told a story of a client. The young man

Little Acts of Kindness

- When driving, if possible, stop and wait for another car to pull out onto a busy street ahead of you.
- When driving in an area that allows right turns on a red light, pull ahead enough so that a car behind you can pull alongside you and make the turn.
- In a checkout line, when you have several purchases, allow a person behind you with just a few items to go ahead.
- Offer to help someone who is having difficulty carrying a package or crossing the street; hold a door for another person.
- Send a note or card to someone who is not well. Send more than one if the illness is prolonged.
- Congratulate people either verbally or in writing.
- Use the words "thank you" and "please" with clerks, cashiers, cafeteria servers, and others.
- If you smoke, show courtesy to others around you.
- Offer your seat on a bus or in a waiting room to someone who looks as if he or she needs to sit more than you do.
- Smile and greet people, even those you don't know.

believed that nobody cared and had the intention of driving into the base of an overpass and ending his life. He stopped at a traffic light and looked over at a woman in the car next to him. She smiled brightly. At the next corner, he turned around and went back to the therapist's office. He is now living a seemingly happy life.

Making the world a better place by giving of yourself is a rewarding experience. Volunteers are greatly needed. Nursing homes are full of opportunities to reach out. Rewarding feelings and meaningful relationships are probable results. Additionally, being a person who asks for and graciously receives kind deeds and favors helps relationships. Because our society has come to regard dependency as negative, people often find it difficult to take from others; yet, by the act of taking, we solidify relationships. "Borrowing an egg, secure in the knowledge that you will soon lend one in return, can be an act of remarkable power" (Olds, Schwartz, & Webster, 1996, p. 195).

Understanding about healthy relationships and positive interactions can reveal what you have to offer and what you might want to develop. Unless people are aware, they may ruin potentially positive relationships or accept less than nourishing ones.

TA Revisited

"Child" is the driving force within relationships. What would a relationship be without emotion? How could relationships continue without motivation?

"Parent" is full of "do's and don'ts" regarding relationships. Some are wise messages while others are in need of processing.

"Adult" helps us assess relationships and can logically guide us through the building and enriching processes.

EXAMINING VARIOUS TYPES OF RELATIONSHIPS

Relationships vary from casual or informal to close and intimate. They also differ in their **interactions**, those exchanges that occur in face-to-face situations. You may pass a person on the street, exchange smiles and greetings, and continue on your way, possibly not realizing that you have just interacted. You may see someone on a daily basis for a period of time and then not again for months. Because of these variances, several types of relationships emerge.

Acquaintances

Social interactions give people a psychological sense of belonging. "Familiar strangers" are people whom you may not know by name but who have a regular place in your life—a waitress in a restaurant, the postal carrier, a cashier at the grocery store, or a neighbor you occasionally see. You and the other person may just smile or chat briefly. Even though such interactions seem inconsequential, their contributions to positive feelings and self-esteem levels are measurable (Montgomery & Trower, 1988).

Friendships

What does friendship mean to you? You may be surprised to discover that the meaning of friendship varies from person to person. Obviously, some common themes exist. How many of these are part of your image of friendship?

- Fondness and liking
- Continuity over time
- Perceived support and dependability
- Compatibility and help
- Similarities in enjoyable activities, beliefs, and values
- Self-disclosure and sharing of information and stories
- Personal growth
- Understanding, acceptance, and unconditional positive regard

Friendship is almost always high on a person's list of values. "I don't know what I would do if it weren't for my friends. I'd be lost," said a woman. This is probably because to live without friends is a lonely journey (Kasl, 1997). Another reason for valuing a close friendship is personal authenticity. "Only with best friends can we get off the stage, stop the show, quit performing, and allow ourselves to be seen as we are" (Keen, 1991, p. 175). Good friendships provide depth and meaning to life. Friendships, in contrast to acquaintances, take time and effort to develop and maintain; yet, in most cases, the benefits far outweigh the costs. Take advantage of a chance to enrich a friendship by doing the activity in Reflections and Applications.

Figure 9-2 Friendship has rewards throughout a lifetime

Steps in developing a friendship.   You were born into a family, not into a friendship. How does one move an acquaintance relationship to a friendship? Following a first meeting, further encounters are positive and affirming. You enjoy each other's company as you plan and engage in mutually satisfying activities. Self-disclosure at deeper levels occurs, and trust is developed. "Progressive stages of increasing openness can peel off layers of our outer selves like the skins of an onion" (McCarthy, 1988, p. 169). As in all relationships, you may experience conflict and have moments of doubt in the friendship; however, if the social exchange factors are strong enough, differences get resolved. As the relationship progresses, it is easily distinguishable from an acquaintanceship.

Cycles of importance.   Friends are important during all stages of life, yet the extent of significance varies. Friendships become meaningful when an individual enters school and participates in activities outside the family. During junior high and high school, friends typically dominate most aspects of life. Parents aren't far from wrong when they say, "Your friends are your whole world."

As intimate love relationships are formed, individuals usually drift away from reliance on friendships. In fact, a common complaint is, "She doesn't have anything to do with me or her other friends any more since she's involved with him." Significant other relationships and parenthood take precedence over friendships in most people's lives, yet friends often remain important as social companions and confidants. If divorced or widowed, friends usually, again, take center stage.

Types and dilemmas.   The word "friendship" indicates a wide range of closeness. A friend can be a best friend, a close friend, a friend, or just a buddy. How do you differentiate? Usually, this is based on an important gauge of friendship—closeness. A very good friend is often a **confidant**, a person with whom you can be totally open and self-disclose on all levels. Most people reserve this label for only a few.

Long-distance friends can be as emotionally close as ones you see regularly. When you connect, there is a feeling of comfort. I had not seen Ellen for years, and we had been in contact only about three times a year by telephone or letter. Yet, when we came together for a weekend, we felt as if we had not been apart, a typical reaction in long-distance deep friendships. The same is true for my husband and a close high school friend Dan who lives 400 miles away. They pick up as if they have never been separated. "The cadence of friendship is measured in decade-long rhythms" (Keen, 1991, p. 174). It's a wonderful feeling to know that I can telephone or e-mail a number of precious, long-distance friends right now and feel connected and supported as I have been during my recent chemotherapy sessions.

A dilemma related to friendship is enrichment. Even good friends can take each other for granted and not nourish the relationship. Most friendships can survive some neglect; however, investment of time and energy is wise. If you're thinking of a friend with whom you have not been in contact for some time, why not do something to change that? Another dilemma of suitable recognition is probable. At special events, best friends, "just friends," and casual acquaintances are usually not distinguished from one another. A researcher recalled the death of a dear friend. At the funeral she sat in the back of a filled church. In the middle of her grief, she realized that even though she was one of the deceased's closest friends, even closer than one of the siblings, she was being treated the same as a casual acquaintance (Rubin, 1985). The English language provides specific distinctions for family relationships, yet not for friendships.

Sex differences.   Are same-sex friendships different for females than for males? The answer isn't clear. Men do tend to have more "active" friendships, talking about and engaging in more mutually enjoyable activities, many of which are related to sports and outdoor activities while women seem to want to talk more about relationships. Women's friendships tend to be deeper. Although men may care as much for their male friends, they are less likely than women to verbally express or demonstrate their feelings (Wood, 2001). In a study, gender differences were found to be relatively small; both sexes rated equal-power friendships significantly higher than unequal-power ones (Veniegas & Peplau, 1997).

Stereotypic males are less likely to self-disclose and become close to other males. Sue and Marc had been married for 13 years and had several couple friends. When they decided to divorce, both were depressed. Sue suggested that Marc talk with a male friend. He replied. "I don't feel comfortable talking about my personal life with the guys I know." Sadly, until recently this was the case for most men. As gender roles become less stereotypic, the likelihood of being deprived of a same-sex confidant may no longer be a problem. We all share a need for connection. Because friendships offer connection and other significant benefits, both men and women are wise to cultivate them.

> A friend is one
> to whom one can pour
> out all the contents of one's heart,
> chaff and grain together
> knowing that the gentlest of hands
> will take and sift it,
> keep what is worth keeping
> and with a breath of kindness
> blow the rest away.
>
> —*Arabian Proverb*

Support Groups

A major purpose of relationships is to provide solace, encouragement, and advice. A close-knit group is made up of "the priceless people in our lives who help us realize the meaning of our existence. They know the 'real' you; they understand where we've been; and they help us grow" (Johnson, 1986, p. 68). They are your primary support system and contribute immeasurably to self-esteem.

A secondary support system is composed of groups at work, school, church, and within neighborhoods and organizations. Self-help groups are recommended as a way of dealing with challenges. During crises and tragedies, a self-help group can be invaluable as long as the focus is on resolving issues and the emphasis is positive. Being aware of your support systems and how each group affects your self-esteem is important. Any type of relationship that genuinely affirms you is precious.

Caregiving

The special support provided by a person in a caregiving role is of particular value. When individuals are unable to care for themselves, they are either placed in nursing homes or rehabilitation centers for long-term care or someone voluntarily assumes the responsibility. Often, that someone is a significant other. Another common caregiving group consists of adult children who care for aging parents. The term "sandwich generation" applies to those who find themselves caring for both their parents and their own children. The average age of such a person is 46 (Emerson, 2000). The caregiver role is both challenging and rewarding. How to ease stress and maintain a positive relationship between a caregiver and the person for whom care is given deserves attention. One way is to make plans before circumstances demand absolute decisions. Another is to learn and use open communication and other techniques covered in Chapters 6, 7, and 8.

Without a doubt, caregivers need help themselves. Those who tend toward codependency are particularly at risk. A study of caregivers found that those who had more tasks, spent greater amounts of time in their caregiving role, and had lower self-efficacy about self-care and spouse care had a greater number of depressive symptoms and negative health behaviors (Gallant & Connell, 1997).

Solid recommendations are to try to maintain a balance, use stress-coping methods on a regular basis, and develop a broad plan with the help of professionals who specialize in caregiving issues. In recent years a number of resources have become available. Caregivers are not alone (see Resources at end of this chapter). Most importantly, a caregiver has to make sure that he or she stays healthy and well-adjusted.

INITIATING INTERACTIONS

In order for a relationship to begin, someone has to act. Initiating interactions is a valuable interpersonal skill. Your personality will make a difference. If you have an extraverted preference, you are motivated to reach out to a new person, yet, those favoring introversion can be just as skillful. Whatever your preference, particular attitudes and behaviors are necessary.

Open-Mindedness

First impressions, those immediate judgments that people make cannot be avoided. Think of the aspects of a person you might consider when you first meet. Perhaps you have been turned off immediately. If an individual appears too different, negative assumptions are often made. A way to overcome this effectively is to be open when you first meet someone and challenge negative first impressions that form after just "one slice of time."

Ideas expressed by others also can influence your impression. In a classic experiment on expectations and first impressions (Kelley, 1950), students received short differing descriptions about a substitute instructor. Some sketches described the new instructor as "rather cold" while others used the words "very warm." The substitute led the class, and someone else recorded the frequency of participation for each student. Afterwards, the students were asked to write descriptions and ratings of the instructor. A clear difference was evident. Those who had read that the man was "very warm" participated more freely and gave him a higher rating than those who had been given the "rather cold" description.

Any time you form a first impression, analyze it. Whatever the judgment, allow time and involvement to determine how realistic it is. Expectations are powerful. A student had heard that I was a lot of fun in the classroom and told me he was looking forward to a positive learning experience. In fact, I was more humorous and livelier in his class than in others, and he and I both had a great time. What we expect of others frequently becomes a reality.

Tolerance, Acceptance, and Appreciation

Tolerance of people who are different is a worthy, basic goal of interpersonal relations. **Tolerance** can be defined as putting up with something one does not like and not acting against people about whom one feels negatively (Vogt, 1997). Ideally, tolerance will evolve into acceptance, which is more positive. Then the development of appreciation, which requires thought and action, is possible. The following brief coverage can help you examine your attitudes and commit to any necessary positive change. Try to approach this discussion with an open mind and be ready to challenge any preconceived ideas.

Classifying people into groups is a normal mental process called **social categorization**. Unfortunately, it is quite possible to overcategorize and then form a **stereotype**—a fixed belief about the entire category. Stereotyping is thinking in generalities. When you meet a person of a different race, do you have a generalized thought? Even though we may not like to admit that we have such automatic thoughts, awareness of their existence is the first step in eliminating stereotypes.

Stereotyping typically focuses on negative characteristics that are applied to an entire group when, in fact, all people within a group are not the same. Stereotyping of groups then leads to labeling of individuals. A loving individual, according to Leo Buscaglia (1982), does not label others. As a child, Buscaglia himself was bothered by the distancing effect of his label regarding his Italian ancestry.

> They didn't know who I was by calling me a "dago" and a "wop." If you want to know me, you've got to get into my head, and if I want to know about you, I can't say, "She is fat. She is thin. She is a Jew. She is a Catholic." She is more than that. (p. 25)

When labels stick, they become tattoos and, if negative, can damage self-esteem (Hyatt, 1991). Reducing an individual to a category is offensive and misleading (Tannen, 1990).

Actor and comedian Eddie Murphy, appearing on a television show, described a stereotyping experience.

> I was walking out of a grocery store, and I had my head down. Some kids went by and said "Nigger!" They didn't see it was me. That tripped me out because if my head had been up, they would have screamed, "Hey, Eddie!"

Labeling based on what the eye can see limits perceptions. The eye can be the "most inaccurate, most inconsistent, and the most prejudicial organ we have in the body. What is truly essential is invisible to the eye" (Buscaglia, 1982, p. 94).

Assigning labels to family members is common: "That's my good-for-nothing brother." "I have an old-fashioned dad." "He's my lazy kid." These ideas put human beings into boxes; then they usually act out the label.

Even positive stereotypes are a problem, either because they are limiting or they force unrealistic expectations on individuals. The field of sports psychology is well aware of stereotypes that label individuals and then become self-fulfilling prophecies (Horn, Lox, & Labrador, 1998). Don Collins, assistant professor of psychology and student-athlete academic counselor at the University of Findlay, provides insight.

> Unfortunately, students and student-athletes are sometimes labeled as "weak" or "strong" based upon first impressions, gender/racial/ethnic stereotypes, or their records. "Weak" individuals who are performing well may be viewed as lucky or even perceived to be cheating. Those considered "strong" who perform at a "weak" level may be thought of as lazy even if they give much effort. For example, Emily was valedictorian of her high school class and is struggling in her pre-veterinarian courses. Instead of suggesting a tutor, her professor tells her she isn't trying hard enough. Juan, a student from a poor high school that usually has no college-bound students, is getting good grades. His professor is suspicious and is sure that the work is not his. It is essential that we refrain from labeling.

Negative stereotyping and labeling usually lead to **prejudice**, an attitude that others are inferior or less than you in some way. What results is a feeling of dislike or hatred. Prejudice is learned either from others or by generalizing from experiences. Jodi discovered that prejudice has many targets as she acknowledged: "Prejudice is not limited to just race and sex. I've been judging people negatively on looks, clothing, body size, and age. I've now learned that what is inside a person is what's important."

Historically, the American society has experienced myriad problems caused by prejudice. Countless numbers of individuals have suffered. A hope that prejudice was a thing of the past abounded for some time after the Civil Rights Movement in the 1960s. That hope has not become reality, although there are some promising signs. Even though more than half of both white and black youth in a *Time*/CNN poll still consider racism "a big problem," more than a third classified it as "a small problem." A surprising 89 percent of black teens called it "a small problem" or "not a problem at all." Most said that both on a personal level and as a social divisive issue, race is less important to them than it is for adults (Farley, 1997). When Americans were asked in a Gallup poll to identify the most important problem facing the country today, only 4 percent named race relations (Newport, 2001). That does not mean that racial prejudice has disappeared; instead, it has decreased and is more disguised.

Probably more extreme prejudice in recent years has been directed toward gay males and lesbians (Vogt, 1997). A significant number have been targets of verbal abuse, discrimination, and physical assault because of their sexual orientation (Herek, 1996). On a positive note, there has been a gradual improvement in attitudes. From 1992 to 2001 acceptance of homosexuality as an alternative lifestyle has risen from 38 percent to 52 percent with 54 percent saying that homosexual relations between consenting adults should be legal. Over 80 percent of Americans believe that homosexuals should have equal opportunity protection in the workplace (Newport, 2001).

Tragic Aftermath of Hatred

September 11, 2001
As I complete this revision, terrible events sparked by hatred are unfolding. Terrorists have inflicted intense pain on innocent people—an immeasurable depth of anguish and sorrow that nobody should ever have to face. These despicable and horrific acts demonstrate that when hatred and violence prevail, the world suffers, and, ultimately, we all pay a price. The toll of lives taken at the World Trade Center, the Pentagon, and in airline crashes is incomprehensible. This tragedy, more than any in recent times, reminds us of the absolute need to resolve discord that is based on differences and intolerance. Each of us can make a positive difference.

To continue to harbor prejudices against those who are different is insensitive and illogical. In some cases, the stereotypes have a factual basis because a majority of a group exhibit a particular behavior. You can accept a fact and still not apply it to all members of a group. People who feel and act upon prejudice are limiting themselves in terms of relationships. Ira, an African American, volunteered her personal feelings about prejudice in a psychology class. She said, "Prejudice causes people to miss out on the spice of life. To be influenced by prejudice is hogwash. It keeps you from being free within." I would add a challenging question: *Can anyone offer one good reason for a continuation of prejudice and hatred?* Everyone is eventually harmed. Each generation is more diverse than the one before, and by the year 2060 no one racial group will be numerically dominant in the United States (Fonow, 1998). Because of the continual increases in diversity, getting along harmoniously can be considered a necessity.

Discrimination is treating people unfairly. Because discrimination is usually observable behavior, a society can adopt laws against it; this has been the case in recent years. Covert discrimination, that which is hidden or subtle, is still widespread and is commonly based on prejudice. Perceiving others to be evil or inferior often leads to treating them as such. Both prejudice and discrimination cause personal and societal problems. In many states, it is still legal to fire or refuse to hire someone because of sexual orientation (Jones, 1998); in others, civil unions between same-sex partners have been outlawed. We all suffer when individuals are treated unfairly.

Figure 9-3

We can never achieve peace of mind as long as we attack others (Jampolsky & Cirincione, 1990).

Prejudice is learned or develops during one's life. Self-esteem seems to play a part. People with low self-esteem tend to be more critical of themselves and of others (Baumeister, 1997). Tolerance is related to high self-esteem and self-actualization (Vogt, 1997). This doesn't mean that self-esteem leads to or keeps one from prejudice; however, it can be a factor. Having an **authoritarian personality**, a belief that one's ideas are right and others are wrong, is related to prejudice and lack of tolerance (Vogt, 1997).

Authoritarians resist new ideas, tend to think in absolutes, and are dogmatic in their beliefs. **Heterosexism**, the belief that only heterosexuality is right, is a type of authoritarian thinking. Lack of education and experiences with those who are different are also important factors. Ignorance often leads to fear and fear to hatred.

Because prejudice is learned, it can be unlearned, and education is a strong foe of prejudice. Studies show that education increases tolerance and reduces prejudice and stereotyping by giving people new information, changing ways of thinking, altering personalities, and providing new social experiences (Vogt, 1997).

What can be done about prejudice? First, a person must decide to challenge the rigid thinking. Believing that your sex, race, and sexual orientation are the only way to be is an enemy to tolerance. Being open-minded is imperative.

Openness is "at least a first cousin, perhaps even a parent, to tolerance" (Vogt, 1997, p. 148).

Becoming more educated, fostering an androgynous personality, building self-esteem, and ridding oneself of anger and an "always right" attitude are major contributors. Deciding that differences are not frightening or wrong is necessary and leads to feeling enlightened as you learn about multiculturalism and **minority groups**, defined as categories of people who lack power and who are disadvantaged in a society. You can challenge prejudice cognitively, emotionally, and socially by asking the questions in "How to Combat Prejudice."

One of the most effective ways to combat personal prejudices is to use your brain to seriously question and challenge. During a class, I threw out a question: "Where does prejudice come from?" A white student volunteered his story: "I can tell you why I'm prejudiced. When I was a kid, three black kids came into my yard and beat me up. I hated them for it, and I've hated all black people since then." Obviously, he had suffered from a bad experience and had generalized from it. I suggested that he use his imagination and pretend that the three boys had been white. I asked, "Would you now hate all white people because three white boys beat you up?" Critical thinking such as this can help people challenge the generalizations that create and maintain prejudice.

Research supports the value of getting to know individuals and to have pride in one's own group. Close friendships with whites seemed to change negative images and stereotypes held by blacks (Powers & Ellison, 1995). Increased ethnic identity among adolescents contributed to better feelings about one's own group and to those who were members of different groups (Phinney, Ferguson, & Tate, 1997). How many friends do you have from different categories? Only about one-tenth of 1 percent of students' friendships cross the color line, and students

How to Combat Prejudice

Honestly, ask yourself these questions and then reflect on the recommendations that follow.

- *Is my thinking reasonable and rational?* If you take pride in your mental abilities, you will want to reject inaccurate and unreasonable stereotypes. Refuse to accept the idea that all blacks and whites, Catholics and Protestants, old people and young people, and heterosexuals, gay males, and lesbians are one way. "People who think and like to think are more likely to be tolerant" (Vogt, 1997, p. 137). In a compounding of the September 11, 2001 terrorist attacks, a news program reported that a man yelled, "I hate all Arabs, and I always will!"

  Not only is the thinking unreasonable and irrational, hatred will never create a better world. Even if you have an initial negative opinion, you can change it.

- *Am I being fair? How would I feel if I were the victim of prejudice?* Most people are concerned with justice and fairness. Discrimination is unfair, and even the thinking that leads to it can be challenged as unjust. Empathy is a powerful enemy of prejudice and discrimination. A study revealed that feeling empathy for a member of a stigmatized group was found to improve attitudes toward the group as a whole (Batson et al., 1997).

- *Am I basing my impressions on a knowledge of an individual as a person or only as a representative of a group?* Labeling often keeps us from getting to know the "real" person. Moving from a collective analysis, which is a stereotype, to an individual assessment is the key. Being free of prejudice means that you may like or dislike, but your feelings will not be based on an external factor or label. I was delighted when Jennifer, a white student, said, "I have never been around African Americans before because I grew up in a small rural community. Glenn [another student in the class] is the first I've gotten to know. I'm so glad the experience was such a positive one!"

are about a thousand times more likely to have same-race friends as other-race friends (Vogt, 1997). More effort is definitely needed.

Jim, a good friend of mine in graduate school, indirectly taught my children to rid themselves of prejudice. Jim was witty, considerate, and fun. He was always available if someone needed some help—"a great guy," the children said. Jim was like many of our friends except that he was gay. At the time he was still "in the closet," so his sexual orientation wasn't even discussed. Later, the reaction of the children was, "So what? It doesn't matter to us. He's still Jim." I appreciated that they based their opinions on what is truly important—*personhood*.

Donald Kaul (1993) minced no words as he decried prejudice:

The Bible which some religious groups use to denounce gays and lesbians is not meant to serve evil. You can quote the Bible to support just about anything, including polygamy. It was called upon to give moral authority to the institution of slavery. I've never fully understood the deep prejudice against homosexuals. I suppose a lot of people don't know any homosexuals, or think they don't. Ignorance is always bigotry's best ally. It's been my experience that gay people are remarkably like straight people—smart, dumb, kind, vicious, greedy, and generous. Even glum. Ultimately, my position is that human sexuality is so complex and diverse, what's OK with consenting adults is OK by me. (p 6B)

Besides ridding yourself of prejudices, you can help the victims of prejudice and society by asserting yourself in the face of demeaning words and behaviors. A study showed that hearing someone else express strong opinions against prejudice led students to have similar thoughts. The researchers concluded that a few outspoken people who are vigorously antiracist can establish a positive social climate that discourages prejudice (Goleman, 1991). As with any subject, silence is usually interpreted as agreement. Suggestions for responding to prejudicial comments were given in Chapter 8. Taking a stand can increase self-esteem. Rose spoke up loudly and clearly in class, "I don't understand why all the hate toward homosexuals. Of what are we afraid? Why don't people just leave others alone?" Yes, why don't they? Any *good* person would avoid inflicting unnecessary harm on others.

When anyone of us is demeaned, we are all diminished (Blumenfeld, 1992, p 13).

Lack of prejudice does not mean blindness to differences; you simply do not let differences stop you from relating. A positive practice is to view differences as gifts and opportunities.

Embrace the many-splendored colors, revel in the wisdom and the power of a different race and culture. Invite it to spill over us and know that, if our invitation is accepted, it is we who are recipients of an honor. (Schulz, 1988, p. 2)

Getting to know people who are different broadens our perspectives and enriches our lives. This growth then allows us to appreciate human diversity. Sameness can be boring. In comparing the words "variation" and "differentness," Satir (1978) makes an excellent point:

When we see a garden of flowers and notice that there are differences among them, it is easy for us to think of them as variations. When we do this, we experience good feelings. Variation and variety are thought of as positive. When we see a group of people together and notice that they, like the flowers, are different from each other, it somehow brings to mind difficulties and fear, and it is easy to prepare defenses. If we were to think of people as having variation to each other and then have the good feelings that come with that, we could get our interest and discovery buttons turned on. (p. 97)

Would you want a large garden of flowers of just one color, especially if they were all white? Human beings of various colors interacting can be as appealing as a garden of multicolored flowers. Diversity provides opportunities for expansion of self. Multiculturalism benefits individuals as well as societies.

How to Approach and Converse with Others

After a person gets beyond obstacles created by negative first impressions or intolerance, individual traits can block attempts to interact. Shyness is a significant disadvantage when it comes to interacting. People who demonstrate shy behaviors have difficulty initiating or inviting encounters. A book designed to help people defeat shyness, *Shyness: A Bold New Approach* (Carducci, 1999) lets shy people know that they are not alone. Shy people make up almost half the population, and between 75 and 95 percent of people have been shy at some time. What can one do? Stating that inaction is the most common feature of shyness, Zimbardo (1977), who conducted classic studies on the subject, suggests taking specific steps. Being realistic about what is possible to achieve is critical, and dividing a goal into smaller, manageable parts, as recommended in Chapter 3, is part of any sensible behavioral plan. Saying hello to a certain number of new people in a week's time might be a practical goal. Support groups are beneficial, and for severe cases of shyness, therapy is suggested.

"I overcame shyness by telling myself that I have so much to offer to others."
—Wanda, a college student

Even if you aren't shy, you may, in some situations, hesitate to approach because of rejection or embarrassment. It can help to ask yourself, "What's the worst thing that can happen if I'm rejected?" Usually, there is no terrible outcome. Realize that embarrassment isn't the worst thing in the world; letting fears stop you from what could be a satisfying interaction is certainly worse! When you do initiate an exchange, you do not want to do so at an inappropriate time or in an undesirable manner. **Approachability** is a combination of circumstances in which the initiation of contact is likely to be positively received.

Approachability cues. Being observant and looking for cues are helpful in initiating conversation. Begin by realizing that unapproachable situations are best avoided. Can you think of times and situations when people would not be at all approachable or when approachability would probably be diminished? Consider individual moods, physical states, and activities: "I'm a grouch in the early morning, so people know to avoid me." "I hate being disturbed when I'm watching a football game on TV." If you want to initiate contact and realize that the other person is in a hurry, involved, or preoccupied, simply wait for an opportune time and circumstance.

Approachable situations are those in which a person is not preoccupied or absorbed. Such situations are usually indicated by body language. Sitting alone and looking open are good indicators. When people are in waiting situations, such as waiting for a bus, for a class to start, or in a line, they are likely to be approachable. Social occasions are definitely approachable situations.

Approachability checking. Knowledge of a person will give you an advantage; yet you still may be uncertain. In these cases, it is better not to act immediately. Instead, check for approachability. For example, asking a person, "Do you have some time to talk?" or "Are you busy right now?" or "Do you have 5 minutes?" are ways to check. By the way, don't ask for a second or a minute of time when you know you want more!

The checking technique is especially appreciated when the telephone is being used. Has this happened to you? Your favorite television show is on, and you are engrossed. The telephone rings; you answer. Incidentally, you don't have to answer a ringing telephone, yet most people do. A friend, assuming that you are ready to visit because you said hello, begins to talk. You are now in a position of either saying you don't want to talk at this time (whenever you can get a word in, that is) or suffering through the conversation feeling deprived and resentful. To avoid being inconsiderate when you make a telephone call, check approachability with, "Do you have time to talk?" or even "What are you doing?" And be sure to thank people who extend this courtesy to you.

Conversation.   If you know a person, beginning a conversation is usually not difficult. But what about people you don't know and would like to meet? You may have no trouble thinking of just the right thing to say. For a number of people, however, thinking of that "something" can be mind-boggling. "I was tongue-tied," is how one young man described it. "I had wanted to meet her for months, and here she was sitting next to me the first day of class. I couldn't think of one intelligent thing to say, so I kept quiet." Either keeping quiet or saying something "off the wall" puts a damper on interactions.

To initiate conversation in difficult situations, you can use a technique called **search the situation for topics** (Glaser, 1986). Based on the idea that you and the other person share a common environment, you make a comment based on an awareness of what is going on around you. What could the young man in the preceding paragraph have said? The two students had in common the fact that they were sitting next to each other in a class on the first day. Here are some possibilities:

"Have you heard anything about this class?"
"I heard this instructor was a lot of fun."
"Have you ever taken a psychology class before?"
"What year of school are you in?"
"What are your career plans?"

Searching the situation is quite simple; in fact, you probably have already used this technique without realizing it.

Other topics.   Keeping the conversation going is sometimes challenging. Using a bridge or transition to another related topic is sensible and usually simple. In the classroom situation there are several opportunities. Talking about one class or instructor can lead to questions and comments about others. A question about career plans can open up several new topics. One transition leads to another.

Free information.   What seems to be wrong in this conversation between two students?

Student one: Have you heard anything about this instructor?
Student two: No.
Student one: How about the class?
Student two: Not much.
Student one: Have you taken other classes?
Student two: Yes.

> Student one: What are your career plans?
>
> Student two: I don't know.

Like pulling teeth, right? Perhaps the second student is just not interested in talking. Or she or he might not know about **free information**—related additional data. Let's try the conversation again, with the use of free information.

> Student one: Have you heard anything about this instructor?
>
> Student two: No, I haven't because I'm in my first quarter here. I did hear a little about the class from my adviser. He said that it would really help in my major.
>
> Student one: What are your career plans?
>
> Student two: I'm going into marketing.
>
> Student one: So am I.

The conversation is livelier and more interesting. The two people are getting to know each other better. In a job interview, providing appropriate free information increases the possibility of an offer. Of course, too much free information monopolizes the conversation. Combining free information and questions creates a positive interactive climate.

Questions.   Questioning is an excellent way to keep conversations going, to learn more about the people you meet, and to make people feel that you are truly interested in what they are saying as well as in them. Failing to ask questions could indicate self-centeredness or lack of interest. Ann recounts a lunch date.

> We didn't know each other well, and I was looking forward to an opportunity for us to get to know each other and then see if this might develop into a deeper relationship. We were together for 2 hours. Afterwards I thought, "I know almost everything about him, and he knows nothing about me except that I ask questions and am an excellent listener! I don't know if he's stuck on himself or just not interested in me, or both. I don't want to spend another 2 hours with him.

Reflect

- Think of a friendship and the theory of social exchange. What do you receive from the relationship? Compare benefits to costs.
- Pretend you are trying to convince a family member to reject prejudice. What reasons would you give?
- Having just been introduced to a new person at a conference, think of two comments or questions you could use.

Apply

- Tell a friend the benefits you receive from your relationship.
- Make an effort to get to know a person who represents diversity to you.
- Use approachability checking the next time you telephone someone. Don't forget to use it in person, when appropriate

Self-absorption is a major obstacle in communication. Successful conversations are two-way, which means that both participants ask questions and provide information. Different types of questions can be asked.

- Open-ended questions are ones that cannot be answered with one word. Instead of, "What is your major?" ask, "What are your career plans?"
- Focused questions are those that are not too broad to be answered. Instead of, "Tell me all about you," ask, "How did you decide to go into teaching?"
- Specific questions are those that ask for additional details, specific examples, or particular impressions. Examples are "What did you think of the psychology course?" or "When did you leave Denver?"

If you think about people you enjoy, chances are that their interest in you and what is going on in your life is a major factor. Very few people resent questions, and most appreciate them. As long as your questions aren't too probing or inappropriately personal, your relationships can be enhanced by developing and using this skill.

CONNECTING WITH OTHERS

After an interaction takes place, people can choose to build a closer relationship. Why does this happen in some cases and not in others?

Attraction and Liking

If you grow to like another person, you will feel affection or respect or both. These feelings are two fundamental dimensions of liking. **Affection** is based on the way another person relates to you personally and is a feeling of warmth and closeness. **Respect** is liking based on the person's admirable characteristics or actions and is cooler and more distant. (Rubin, 1973)

Why do you like some people and not others? **Attraction**, a force that draws people together or a positive attitude toward another, has been the focus of psychological research. Obviously, physical attractiveness plays a primary part in our impressions. As we get better acquainted the individual becomes attractive for other reasons. Social psychologists have found that attraction and liking are closely linked to certain other factors. As you read about each, relate it to your relationships.

Proximity.   How many friends are from your hometown? Do most of your friends live near you? **Proximity** is physical occupation of the same geographic area. Obviously, in order to meet face-to-face, two people must share proximity. In terms of attraction, physical sharing of space is the means by which you get to know a person. Becoming more familiar could lead to a dislike of the person. More often, though, getting to know someone leads to deeper understanding and liking. In recent years, as a result of the Internet, individuals have established relationships without proximity. Getting to know each other through e-mail communications has established itself. Obviously, safeguards are important if an actual meeting is arranged. Getting together in a public place is a common recommendation along with waiting until you know the person personally before you share addresses and other private information. If the relationship seems promising, eventually, there will be proximity!

Similarities. "Birds of a feather flock together" is an axiom with merit. Differences can be interesting and positive. Yet, for years social psychologists have realized that similarities are strong predictors of attraction (Byrne, 1971) and that people with little in common can repel each other (Rosenbaum, 1986). **Similarities** or being alike in attitudes, interests, degree of intelligence, religion, age, and personality are generally bonding and promote liking. We feel attracted to those who by their attitudes and behaviors confirm our values and beliefs. For example, if equal rights are important, seeing a person actively participate in a rally increases positive feelings. In fact, I recommend to people wanting to meet potential significant others that they participate in causes and activities near and dear to their hearts. Agreement is a powerful force. One word of caution: Even though similarity is comfortable, if we are not aware, it can limit our interactions with those who are different.

Complementarity. A characteristic that is lacking in you can be attractive in another person. This is **complementarity**. And, for practical reasons, it can benefit a relationship. Margaret, one of my college roommates, loved to clean. My interest wasn't keen in that area, so I offered to do errands, and she kept our room immaculate. You may also notice opposite personality traits in two friends. Kent was outgoing and loved to tell jokes. His friend Pat was quiet, except when he was laughing loudly at Kent's stories. Complementing each other was a major factor in these relationships.

Reciprocity. Imagine that you have just met Sarah. You feel neutral toward her; you don't necessarily like or dislike her. As times goes by, Sarah demonstrates a genuine interest in and liking for you. The chances are that you will reciprocate; your feelings will become positive. **Reciprocity** is a tendency to like people who like you. As Rathus (1999) puts it, "If you like me, you must have excellent judgment." This may sound conceited; however, if you genuinely like yourself, you are likely to be attracted to others who share your feelings. When we are liked and admired, we are inclined to return those feelings and behaviors. Conversely, have you ever experienced the realization that another person does not like you? You probably tended to reciprocate and found yourself disliking that person.

Attraction and liking factors contribute to the onset of a relationship and continue to enhance its growth. Wanting to approach someone and then beginning to like that person aren't caused by a mysterious force. Rather, it is fairly easy to predict who will relate to whom and why.

IMPROVING RELATIONSHIPS

You have a choice in the types and quantity of relationships you develop and maintain, and you influence their quality, as well. Certain attitudes and behaviors deserve special attention.

Realistic Expectations of Relationships

Expecting a relationship to be 100 percent harmonious and believing that individuals will always act in certain ways is unrealistic.

> Just as no human being is perfect, neither are relationships. We are none of us ever perfect husbands, wives, children, professionals, teachers, students, employees, employers, fathers, mothers, or friends. We are humanly limited in all these social human roles. (Rubin, 1975, p. 239)

Having unrealistic ideas leads to frustration and disappointment and usually to an end to a relationship. Even with acquaintances, having realistic expectations is helpful. If you're a renter, what is realistic to expect from the property owner? If you own property, are you expecting too much from your tenants?

In all types of relationships, open communication is helpful; in certain cases, written agreements about expectations are appropriate. A common tale of woe concerns roommates. Hannah describes her roommate as a slob, one who doesn't do her share and leaves the apartment a mess. Unfortunately, they had no agreement about task management before they became roommates. Discussing expectations and agreeing to policies, preferably in writing, are more likely to achieve desired objectives than simply expecting things to work out.

Sensitivity and Cooperation

Sensitivity is having an awareness or sense about the perceptions and perspectives of others. In a classroom setting, sensitivity is conducive to learning. When instructors and students understand each other's perspectives, and students are sensitive to one another, the atmosphere is positive. Two older students said that figuring out how to fit in was their biggest challenge. Younger students' sensitivity to their different perspectives was greatly appreciated. Pondering how they would feel coming back to school after several years helped young students to be sensitive.

Cooperation means working with others in a positive way toward a common goal. A printing company had to deliver a large order within a week. The owner called the employees together to discuss how the objective could be accomplished. One person's child was in the hospital awaiting surgery. Others offered to work longer hours to compensate for his time away from the job. The job was accomplished. Wise parents, teachers, and employers incorporate cooperation in the successful completion of tasks.

Assertiveness

Honest, healthy relationships thrive on **assertiveness**—maintaining one's legitimate rights and expressing thoughts and feelings in nonthreatening ways. When someone is passive and allows another to dominate, the eventual outcome is undesirable. Neither the dominator nor the "whatever-you-say" person feels satisfied after a period of time.

Keep in mind that those who don't appreciate assertiveness may not be capable of building positive relationships, and you deserve better. Review the material on becoming assertive in Chapter 2 and realize the benefits extend not only to you but also to all those with whom you interact.

Negotiation Skills

Positive negotiation skills are well worth cultivating because conflict can occur in all relationships. **Conflict** means that disagreement or a difference in thinking is present. Most people have been taught that being right is essential. However, individuals who rate high in interpersonal relations skills are well aware that the need to be right can damage relationships. "You can insist on being right or have a relationship that works, but you can't have both. And the addiction to being right about inaccurate beliefs will destroy any relationship" (Ellsworth, 1988, p. 19).

Once you realize that conflict is not a matter of who's right and who's wrong and that it is caused simply by differences of opinion, you are setting the stage for negotiation. Conflict management is an art like other interpersonal relations skills. Handling conflict in intimate relationships will be covered in Chapter 11; the negotiation skills described in this section are useful, as well.

Not recommended in any relationship is a behavior described as **gunnysacking**. When you "gunnysack," you keep your grievances suppressed or bottled up (Bach & Wyden, 1968). People who hide their grievances do so because of nonassertiveness, fear, and a desire to preserve peace at any cost. Because "gunnysacking" is often the result of a fear of criticizing anyone, the methods for delivering criticism suggested in Chapter 8 are worth learning and using. A "gunnysack" stuffed to its limits is potentially harmful for several reasons. Suppressing annoyances is stressful and can be damaging to health. Keeping quiet about grievances can diminish self-esteem, and relationships suffer terribly. "When complaints are toted along quietly in a gunnysack for any length of time they make a dreadful mess when the sack finally bursts" (Bach & Wyden, 1968, p. 19).

An aggressive style of conflict management is as damaging as "gunnysacking." Closed communication is the norm. An aggressive person tries to dominate and control all issues and will use any steamrolling method available. He or she will turn conflicts into competition and may win on the surface, but the relationship loses. In long-term relationships this is particularly dangerous.

Managing conflict is essentially problem solving. First, the individuals decide to work on an issue. Of benefit is to pick a time and place most conducive to positive results. An agreement can be made that the discussion can be postponed

Figure 9-4

at any time. Conflict is more easily resolved when the participants use open communication and avoid dogmatic, forcing, and grandiose expressions. "I" statements and receptive listening are highly recommended. Pay close attention to the following steps for resolving an issue.

1. Define and describe the issue or problem and all common goals. The use of clear, specific description is critical. Discussion continues until agreement is reached on the specific issue to be resolved with the understanding that related topics can be discussed later.
2. Brainstorm to generate all possible solutions. Creativity and openness are key ingredients at this stage. All ideas are accepted with no judgments.
3. Evaluate each possible solution. Each person has the right to eliminate an idea if it is completely unacceptable. The number of solutions is usually narrowed to two or three.
4. Decide on the best solution at this time. This would be the one that achieves the goals. Flexibility is imperative. You may agree on one choice or concede to another's point of view in order to test its effectiveness.
5. Agree to test the agreed-upon solution and meet again to evaluate.

This last step is especially valuable, as agreeing to treat a solution as tentative will make it easier to gain a consensus to take action. If the solution doesn't work, a different one can be used.

During the third and fourth steps of "Steps to Resolution," a positive communicator will use certain questions and phrases that express openness and encourage participation of all.

- I understand your reasoning, and I'd like to hear how you would go about it.
- What do you think about . . .
- I agree. Have you also considered . . .
- I liked your first idea; however I have a few reservations about . . .

The idea is to be nonthreatening, receptive, and tentative. This method has been called **collaboration** (Cochrane, 1992) and differs from compromise, which means giving up something and ends up being win-lose. Collaboration or resolution is when shared goals are achieved, and everyone wins. Read through the roommate conflict resolution "Resolving an Issue." The situation is based on an actual one described to me by a student who didn't think she could say anything to a roommate who entertained her boyfriend in the bedroom for hours on end. Because of her lack of assertiveness, the student suffered, and a friendship was in jeopardy. Do you see how using collaboration would have made a significant difference?

Especially helpful is for participants to see conflict as an opportunity to learn and grow. Be sure to check how you have improved your relationships (Chapter 9 activity in Reflections and Applications).

Difficult People

"No matter what I do or say, nothing makes any difference. I work for the most difficult person in the world" and "Nobody can get along with her" are de-

Resolving an Issue

Carol, Heather, and Laura have roomed together for 2 months. They have experienced some problems over task management; however, the main issue has to do with Carol's fiancé, Brent, and other friends who visit the apartment. Carol and Laura share a bedroom.

1. *Defining the issue and finding common goals*

Laura: I'm upset because Brent is over here so often, and when you go into the bedroom and shut the door, I don't feel like I should come in, and it's my room, too.

Carol: Well, I don't like doing all the dishes around here.

Heather: I'd suggest we stay on just the one topic for now. We can talk about dishes later. Can we agree that we want to remain roommates and get along? (After affirmation from both) Then I suggest we discuss and, hopefully, resolve what to do about people who come to visit. Is that agreeable?

2. *Generating possible solutions*

Heather: Let's suggest some ideas. No comments from anyone else yet.

Laura: I suggest that the bedroom be off limits to guests.

Heather: My idea is to have certain hours established—some for when guests are to leave and others for when we could be in any of the rooms.

Carol: I prefer that we have the right to have people in any room when we want, and if another person doesn't like it, she can say so—the same with asking guests to go home.

Heather: Any other ideas? If not, let's talk about these.

3. *Evaluating each possible solution*

Carol: I don't like the one about off-limits at all. I have my stereo in the bedroom, and sometimes it's nice to get away from the TV in the living room.

Laura: I guess that off-limits is too much. I think having a reasonable time limit or set hours is a good idea. I know I can tell you that I'm upset, but that's hard to do sometimes.

Carol: How about if I asked you whether it's okay with you before we go in there? And if it's not, I'd understand.

Laura: I like that idea, and we could do the same with other guests. If one of us wants to go to bed or study, we would just agree to do that.

4. *Agreeing on a tentative solution*

Heather: Do we agree that we will check about others being here at all and also being in other rooms?

5. *Setting a testing period*

Carol: How about trying it for 2 weeks and then seeing how we feel?

Laura: Sounds fine. In the meantime, I'm ready to tackle the dishes problem.

The described resolution occurred because the individuals followed the negotiation steps. This discussion progressed ideally, which is not usually the case. Even with some digression, having a method is far better than no discussion or pettiness and dead-end arguments.

scriptions of difficult people. They may be hostile customers, irritable coworkers, passive-aggressive supervisors, or nitpicky neighbors. They could even be family members. Because he couldn't find another book on the subject, Bramson (1988) wrote *Coping with Difficult People*. After reading the list of patterns of difficult behavior, do you recognize anyone? If you see yourself in any of the descriptions, realize that you are probably damaging your relationships.

Before you decide that behaviors are difficult, be sure your expectations are realistic. A person with an introverted preference will probably be reserved. Labeling the person as difficult is unrealistic and unfair. If the problem is definitely because of a difficult individual, certain strategies can help.

Avoidance may be the best solution. This may not be completely possible; however, you might be able to decrease your contact time. Also, putting into practice what you know about personality preferences can be quite useful. For example, I used to become quite frustrated with a staff member who would not leave the matter at hand. "Don't bother me right now. I'm busy," was a common reply. At first, I thought this was rude and showed inflexibility until I realized the person had a strong sensing (S) preference, and being sidetracked was especially bothersome. I learned to wait with patience until I had full attention. We are often uncomfortable with the opposite preference, and, in some cases, those characteristics could be useful to us.

When dealing with a difficult person, cognitive techniques can also be beneficial. Keeping in mind that other people do not control you and aren't able to make you feel, think, or do anything, you can adjust your thinking in various ways. "Just because she was short-tempered (and often is) doesn't mean it's going to ruin my day," changes your reality. The positive responses to criticism from Chapter 8 can help you deal with an aggressive or hostile person who comes off as a critic.

Having an understanding of attribution theory (Heider, 1958) is quite helpful. Discussed in Chapter 5 regarding anger, you use attributions whenever you seek the "why" of behavior. Errors most definitely occur. Social psychologists are quite interested in the common biases we make. For example, if Tim tells a crude joke that demeans women, we might think, "Tim is sexist and rude." The tendency to believe that others' behavior is caused by internal factors such as person-

---

Categories of Difficult People

1. *Hostile-aggressives:* People who try to bully and overwhelm others.
2. *Complainers:* Individuals who gripe incessantly but do not act to improve the situation.
3. *Silent and unresponsives:* Those who respond very little, so aren't helpful.
4. *Super-agreeables*: Reasonable people who either don't produce or act differently when not in your presence.
5. *Negativists*: Pessimists whose favorite reaction is, "No, that won't work."
6. *Know-it-all experts*: Those who think that they know much more than anyone else.
7. *Indecisives*: People who don't seem to be able to make up their minds as well as perfectionists who don't complete tasks.

ality traits, attitude, mood, abilities, or effort is called the **fundamental attribution error** (Ross, 1977). We could have thought, "Tim is a new person who is possibly trying to make an impression on us, and he evidently doesn't understand that this is not the way to do it." In this case, we are recognizing the situation or circumstances as the major factor. Instead, we are more apt to attribute behavior to a facet of the other's self. In our minds, the difficult person is simply difficult.

Why not try to see a situation from the other's perspective? Most people have a reason for being nasty, and if you can figure out accurate underlying causes, your reaction will be less negative. Also be careful not to jump to a conclusion about another's motivation. People are usually more complicated than what is apparent. Being patient, giving people more than one chance, and being empathic are recommended.

Sometimes what is most effective is to change your behavior and reactions toward a difficult person. Invariably, the interactions and relationship also change. Anna's supervisor was, in her opinion, a difficult person. She began to compliment the person and to thank her for advice. Within a few weeks, Anna said to a friend, "What a difference my behaviors have made! At least I can tolerate her now." What Anna did is good medicine for a difficult person. She provided something that was needed by the supervisor. If you can figure out what a person wants and what may be a cause of his or her difficult behavior, you are helping both yourself and the other.

Assertiveness, on your part, is most advisable. Often, difficult people honestly don't realize how they are affecting others. A simple statement of "I didn't like being blamed for missing the deadline when it was your part that came in late, and I'd like to talk about how we can work together more effectively" can help. A book designed to help you deal with people who make your life miserable is *Toxic People* (Glass, 1995). Several ways of identifying these individuals, plus ways to deal with them, are included. To help you assess your involvement with difficult people, as well as unload your "gunnysack," use the Chapter 9 activity in Reflections and Applications. Then, when confronted with a difficult person, use ideas suggested in this book.

> Difficulties are like ocean froth; they can demand your total attention or you can choose to look beyond, to the vast tranquility of the sea. The further view does not do away with the froth, but it places it in perspective. (Keating, 1984, p. 1)

Supportiveness

Picture a roomful of people. One individual is carrying a large, weighty pack on her back, so big and burdensome that it's difficult not to notice. Yet the others mingle about as if they don't see the pack. "How are you?" "Fine." "What do you think of the weather?" Cliché conversation fills the room. They talk about their families and work. They speak of many things but not of the pack on the person's back. Everyone knows that it's there, and it's on each person's mind. Nobody says a thing. Even though the woman sags from the weight and looks as if she could fall, they ignore the heavy pack. We won't discuss it, they think. The woman thinks to herself,

Oh, please talk. Why won't you say his name? I want you to say "Paul." I want for us to talk about his death and his life. Can I say "Paul" and not have you look away and ignore it? For if we don't talk, you are leaving me alone with this dreadfully heavy pack on my back.

People we know will experience crises and tragedies, and they will carry a figurative pack on their backs. If you care, you will want to know how to react at these times. Consider these possibilities.

Marni, a coworker, is diagnosed with cancer.

Todd, a next-door neighbor, dies suddenly. His wife and children are the survivors.

Kari and Jason, a couple you know, are in an accident. She is badly injured.

Are you inclined to do nothing? Do you ignore the pack on the back? A strong recommendation is to show your concern. Completely ignoring another's tragedy sends the message "I don't care." On a rational level, this may be unfounded. "Of course I care," said one man, "I just don't know what to do." On an emotional level, however, saying and doing nothing is hurtful.

People seem to be afraid of a griever's feelings, so they try to ignore or change the subject, or they intellectualize and try to explain away the grief. Some just may not want to be bothered. However, the most commonly given reason for not being supportive: "I just don't know what to do." Closely related is the fear that what is done or said will be wrong. Giving support is another area in which little training is offered. Yet enough has been written on the subject that "I don't know what to say or do" can be seen as an excuse. Being effective in interpersonal relations means that you do respond. It's helpful to be aware of what research has identified as *not* helpful.

- Implied total awareness: "I understand exactly what you're going through." "I know just how you feel," or "I know" used over and over.
- Supplied solutions and reasons for acceptance: "It's better this way." "You'll recover faster than you think." "It'll be just fine." "Just give it time." "He lived a long life; he was ready to go." "Be grateful for—" "It was meant to be." "It was God's will." One author mentioned that she had never met anyone who was comforted by this last statement (Edwards, 1989).
- One-upping comments: "I know what it's like because my grandmother died last year." "You think you've got problems? Wait until you hear mine." "Not only did my sister's husband divorce her, but then—"

Surprisingly, in one study, slightly more than half of all unhelpful comments were made by relatives or friends (Wortman, Battle, & Lemkau, 1997).

Ideally in any situation, we can express caring feelings. Simplicity and sincerity are the key ingredients. Comments such as "I care" and "I'm concerned" are fine. Other possibilities are "I want to do something," and "I remember—" recalling a fond memory of the deceased. If people would realize that they aren't expected to explain the "why," solve the problem, take away the pain, or other such dramatic behaviors, they might be more inclined to express. Research indicates that the most helpful comments are expressions of personal willingness to help or listen; any behaviors that suppress grief or force too much disclosure are not recommended (Range, Walston, & Pollard, 1992). Verbal expression can open a door of relief for a suffering person. Comfort can be found in just talking. You don't have to have the answers; just listening will help (Buckman, 1988). Usually, people don't remain silent long enough for the griever to fully express thoughts and feelings (James & Cherry, 1988). "I just needed someone to talk to and especially a person I believed was truly listening," said a bereaved parent. Empathic and receptive listening skills are especially advisable. A wise suggestion is to let the grieved person be the only one to make evaluative comments such as "It was a blessing."

Sometimes an honest expression of your perception of the situation is best. A comforting comment given to the writer Max Wylie after his daughter had been savagely murdered was, "This did not happen for the best; it happened for the worst." I remember so well a scene in a hospital room at Mayo Clinic before my surgery. I spent a few minutes alone looking into a mirror, realizing that this was the last time I would ever see my left eye. As I was being wheeled into the operating room to have the eye removed, my sister Connie leaned down to give me a loving hug and whispered in my ear, "I love you, and you don't deserve this." My keen thought was, "She knows exactly how I feel right now." Lovingly, she said the same thing before my breast cancer surgery in 2002.

One argument you may hear against talking about the "pack on the person's back" is: "Maybe they are trying to forget the tragedy or not think about their situation. If I say something, it will just remind them of it." Ask yourself whether you believe that people in anguish have forgotten. If you are thinking about their tragedy or problem, don't you believe that they are, too? In situations of anxiety, studies show that conversations do not create new fears. In fact, not talking about a fear makes it bigger (Buckman, 1988).

Several years ago I went to the hospital to see a woman who had been told she was soon to die. Drawing on my experience with cancer and all I had read, I expressed my concern and then asked a question about her treatment. With a look of relief on her face, she disclosed thoughts and feelings. Before I left, she said with a twinkle in her eye, "Thanks, Sharon. I really get tired of talking about the weather. It's not exactly the main thing on my mind."

As was indicated in the scenario at the beginning of this section, usually one of the greatest gifts you can possibly give to a grieving person is to mention the name of the person's loved one and add some memory you have of him or her.

> Most people want their loss acknowledged and the name of their dead loved one spoken, not avoided. They would like to tell callers not to bother if they are going to talk about the weather or how terribly funny their new puppy is. And later on, when they meet, they wish friends and acquaintances wouldn't try so hard to avoid mentioning the subject. The omission is glaring (Ginsburg, 1987).

Writing a note or sending a card can replace verbal expression. Supportive acts are also greatly appreciated. Don't just say, "If you need anything, call." Often, a person won't seek help; in many cases, you can either say what you want to do or just take action. Check the list of specific helping behaviors ("Support: What You Can Do"). Promising to help and then not following through is frustrating, so refrain from idle offers. Don't overlook the supportive impact of your presence.

"People don't have to say a word. If they're here, I know they care," commented a widow. "Of course I'd love a little hug or squeeze on my arm if they could," she added with a tear in her eye. Sharing your sad feelings can also be of comfort. Tears are a by-product of our love and compassion (Edwards, 1989).

Support: What You Can Do

- In the case of a death, address thank-you-for-sympathy cards.
- In any crisis, do errands, such as shopping.
- Clean the person's house.
- Do laundry.
- Mow the person's yard or shovel snow.
- Take the person out for dinner or to a movie.
- Take care of the children, if any.
- Just come by for a visit.

When you show support, another human being is helped, and you, too, benefit. Listening, talking, touching, and doing are what a grieving person probably needs (Donnelley, 1987). Genuine supportiveness strengthens relationships. A poem by Mary Bailey, described by (Vail 1982) as "a lovely lady whose cherished teenage daughter was killed in an accident," eloquently expresses what a person in pain wants.

A Plea from Someone Who Has Been There

Please dear friend
Don't say to me the old clichés
Time heals all wounds
God only gives you as much as you can bear
Life is for the living
Just say the thoughts of your heart
I'm sorry, I love you, I'm here, I care
Hug me and squeeze my hand
I need your warmth and strength
Please don't drop your eyes when I am near
I feel so rejected now by God and man
Just look in my eyes and let me know that you are with me.
Don't think you must always be strong for me
It's okay to cry
It tells me how much you care
Let me cry, too
It's so lonely to always cry alone.
Please keep coming by even after many weeks have passed
When the numbness wears off, the pain of grief is unbearable.
Don't ever expect me to be quite the same
How can I be when part of my being is here no more?
But please know, dear friend, with your love, support and understanding
I will live and love again and be grateful everyday that I have you—dear friend.
—Mary Bailey

Sincere Expression

Willingness to express all sincere emotions can greatly improve your relationships. Besides sorrow, other feelings can be hard to express.

Forgiveness.   Are you one who has difficulty forgiving? Do you know people who bear grudges? Forgiveness, especially when you were truly wronged, is among the most difficult undertakings, and most of us have no idea how or even if to forgive (Flanigan, 1992). The benefits of forgiving are worth the difficulties. Harboring grudges and other bitter feelings can be damaging to psychological and physical health.

Thinking about forgiveness as simply *letting go of the past* may make it more acceptable. To "forgive and forget" is not necessary; you can forgive without forgetting. Erasing a wrongdoing from memory is unrealistic and usually impossible. Neither is forgiving the same as condoning or pardoning. Instead, forgiveness means letting go and moving on. You may not resume the relationship at all, or perhaps it will not be as it was before. However, you are free from the bitterness and pain of negativity.

Forgiveness is easier if you are able to forgive yourself, too. In considering that someone else has wronged you, ask, "Am I perfect? Have I ever hurt somebody else?" The answer to the latter question will likely be that you have. The next question is, "Have I forgiven myself?" If you forgive yourself and learn from the mistake, you will probably find yourself willing to extend the same to another.

To help you forgive, *Forgiveness Is a Choice* (Enright, 2001) and *Forgiving Yourself* (Flanigan, 1996) are excellent resources. Never to forgive means living a life of unending resentment. When you forgive, you decide to move forward with your life. The alternative is not desirable. "The deeply wounded can either change or slowly drown in a deep pool of hatred" (Flanigan, 1992, p. 68). The choice is yours.

Warmth and demonstrated affection.   These particular feelings and behaviors deserve special attention. Touch is the first sense to develop; in order to develop normally, a baby needs to be warmly and lovingly touched. Adults deprived of physical stroking in childhood often develop compulsive, destructive habits such as nail biting, overeating, or smoking. Some speculate that violent behavior may be a result of touch deprivation (Ryan & Travis, 1991). A longitudinal study revealed that adults who had experienced parental warmth and affection as children felt generally happier and less stressed (Franz, McClelland, & Weinberger, 1991). Unfortunately, as people age, touching generally declines. Yet the warmth of body contact and the sensation of strong arms holding us are fundamental. "From the first moments of our life to the last, we need to be held—or we fall" (Josselson, 1992, p. 29). Because touch is so critical, if you don't receive it regularly, self or professional massage is recommended.

Reluctance to behave warmly and affectionately is apparent even in close relationships. Individuals who withhold affection can be filled with regret as evidenced by Matt who said:

A good friend called me one night and said he needed to talk. I lied and told him I was too busy and said I'd get back to him later. The next day I "spaced" it. That night he shot himself. I feel so guilty.

Figure 9-5

A letter to Ann Landers told of a 13-year-old girl who wanted desperately to "belong" but had few friends. She tried to reach out and was rejected. She committed suicide, and the students from her school turned out in droves for her funeral. The letter ended: "Sally left this world believing she didn't have a single friend. If just one of those kids who passed her casket had taken the time and trouble to show her a little kindness, that dear girl might be alive today." Ann's response was to tell people to reach out. Do you know someone you could befriend? In expressing affection and warmth to a friend or loved one, a word to be emphasized is *now*. Because life is tenuous, you can be too late to tell or show someone that you care. Awareness of this can provide the motivation you need. Why not call or write someone for no other reason than just to say, "I love you."

Appropriateness is a key element in demonstrating any emotion. Within close relationships you have more leeway, and warmth and affection can be shown by hugging, kissing, and other physical acts. Among acquaintances, societal guidelines usually direct behaviors. Touch can be a gesture of warmth and concern; however, it may also be perceived as seductive, impertinent, annoying, or degrading. As in other behaviors, being sensitive to individual differences is important. Touching is influenced by culture and gender role socialization. In particular situations, touching is even risky. Teachers are concerned that touching a student might be misinterpreted. Following court action against a male elementary school teacher, a parent in one of my classes expressed this thoughtful opinion.

> I hope that we don't get to the point where people are afraid to touch each other. I have taught my son and daughter to express genuine affection with appropriate touches, pats on the shoulder or back, and hugs. I hate to think that they will go to school and model after human robots fearful of physical contact. Besides, a lot of kids need affirming touches.

Regardless of culture and gender, a study found that people who were comfortable with touching were more talkative, cheerful, socially dominant and nonconforming; those discomforted by touch tended to be more emotionally unstable and socially withdrawn (Thayer, 1988). As people become more aware of the benefits of demonstrating feelings described in Chapter 5, they may touch more freely. "Without the social vocabulary of touch, life would be cold, mechanical, distant, rational, verbal. Deprived of those gestures and their meanings, the world would be far more frightening, hostile, and chilly" (Thayer, 1988, p. 36). Examining the ways in which you express warmth and affection and making an effort to show your feelings appropriately and genuinely will improve your relationships. Do so now.

ANSWERING THE CHALLENGE OF RELATIONSHIPS

Are you willing to risk? All relationships involve risks. Besides the pleasures derived from connecting and interacting, you can expect disappointment and pain. When you exist only to avoid these displeasures, you forfeit all opportunities for the joys of relationships.

Are you committed to spending time, energy, and effort in building positive relationships? Wanting to relate means sacrificing time alone as well as solitary pursuit of your own pleasures. Giving up the extremes of independence and dependence for the nurturance of interdependence is healthy in all close relationships. **Interdependence** means that two people can stand alone, yet prefer to have a relationship with each other and strive to do what's best for both. Education in relating skills can show people how to be interdependent.

> Young people start out without the foggiest notion of how to live in human, personal interaction. I wonder if our educational system would be willing not only to believe, but to prove by their actions that one goal of education is to assist the young person to live as a person with other persons (Rogers, 1972).

Those words are challenging. Although some strides have been made since they were written, most of us are left to seek out relationship training for ourselves. Learning from this book is a major step. Also, check the "Future Intentions" list in Reflections and Applications. You have the opportunity to learn and then act so that you can be enriched by interactions and relationships.

LOOKING BACK

- Because we are human, we relate. Social relationships are needed for self-development.
- Positive relationships are characterized by social exchange. Participants remain in relationships because they receive as well as give, and the benefits outweigh the costs.
- Features of a positive relationship include love for self, absence of codependency, genuineness, warmth with unconditional positive regard, empathy, self-disclosure, enjoyment, encouragement, fairness, dependability, energizing feelings, and mutual interests.
- Various types of relationships contribute to life satisfaction.
- Friendships can have both dilemmas and benefits. Although women and men generally differ in the nature of their friendships, the future holds the promise of deep, nourishing relationships for both. Besides friendships, a variety of support systems are available.

Reflect

- Give an example of a relationship that illustrates one of the attraction factors.
- Recall the last time you behaved assertively.
- Think of a difficult person. Which tactic could you try in order to deal with him or her more positively?

Apply

- Perform a little act of kindness.
- Use the five negotiation steps to resolve a current or future issue.
- The next time you have a chance to provide support, please do so.

- Open-mindedness and tolerance promote a healthy beginning to interactions. Ideally, acceptance and appreciation of diversity will follow.
- Stereotyping, prejudice, and discrimination are not beneficial to individuals or to societies. Because we learn intolerance, we can unlearn and relearn and live productively in a multicultural world.
- In order to connect, shyness needs to be overcome.
- When initiating an interaction, approachability is an important consideration. You can learn to check approachability and then in a positive way initiate and continue conversation.
- Factors related to attraction and liking are physical attraction, proximity, similarities, complementarity, and reciprocity.
- Relationships benefit when the participants have realistic, agreeable expectations of the relationship, along with sensitivity, a cooperative attitude, and assertiveness.
- Conflict will occur. Neither "gunnysacking" nor aggressiveness is recommended. Learning how to negotiate will help in all walks of life. Additional techniques may be needed in dealing with difficult people.
- Among the most difficult behaviors for most people are those of supportiveness. Although ignoring another person's crisis or tragedy is commonplace, it is not recommended. Showing that you care in verbal and nonverbal ways is important.
- Sincere expressions of forgiveness, warmth, and affection significantly improve relationships.
- All relationships involve risks and commitment. A major challenge in relationships is based on the fact that human beings are rarely trained in relating skills. If you want to have the joy and benefits that come from positive relationships, you must be willing to risk, commit, and learn.

The singular life experience I would wish every human being before they die is to feel love for, and be loved by, another. All human beings biologically need to be healthily attached, connected with others.

—Teresa Adams

RESOURCES

Codependents Anonymous. (602) 277–7991. www.ourcoda.org.
Administration on Aging (for health and care providers). www.aoa.dhhs.gov

Southern Poverty Law Center. www.splcenter.org
Anti-Defamation League. www.adl.org
Museum of Tolerance. www.wiesenthal.com

Parents and Friends of Lesbians and Gays (PFLAG). (202) 638–4200. www.pflag.org.

10

Succeeding in Your Career

LOOKING AHEAD

After completing this chapter, you will be able to

- Explain why work is a significant part of life.
- Differentiate between a career and a job.
- Discuss the aspects of self and work orientations related to career and job satisfaction.
- Recognize the importance of wise choices of career and jobs.
- Name several characteristics of a valued employee.
- Recognize the many choices you have regarding career.
- Identify ways you can improve your job search.
- Discuss choices you may have along your career path.
- Describe behaviors that lead to positive work relationships.

We are responsible to ourselves for the quality of our own lives. We can be friends or enemies to ourselves by the choices we make, which in turn make up the lives we lead. Real caring about ourselves is the first step in caring for others and in solving global concerns. May your career choice contribute to your dream of the future.

—Betty Neville Michelozzi

"What do you want to be when you grow up?" is a challenging question to answer when you are 3 years old. At age 18, or sometimes earlier, there comes another one: "Have you decided on a career?" Then be prepared for an inquiry heard over and over before retirement: "What do you do for a living?" Our self-identities are linked to career choices and current jobs, and the workplace serves as the source of much of life's satisfaction or dissatisfaction. A positive professional experience is of prime importance.

When you consider how much time people spend pursuing their careers and actually on the job, it's not surprising that so much of what we think about ourselves is related to work. Additionally, our careers significantly affect all of our relationships. Years ago we were told that with technology, our future lives would offer considerably more leisure time. That "crystal ball" prediction was extremely inaccurate. According to *U. S. News & World Report* (2000), the 40-hour week—about 10,000 days of one's life—has expanded into an average work week of 47 hours!

Even more enlightening is the concept of "24/7," which means that many people find that they are "on call" and are often doing something related to work 24 hours a day, 7 days a week (*U.S. News & World Report*, 2000). More than half of full-time employees—54 percent—put in over 40 hours in a typical week (Saad, 1999), and among those with professional, technical, and managerial positions, 50-hours-plus at work is not uncommon (*Business Week*, 1999). Additionally, a number of people take work home with them. Because of the time and effort spent, what happens with our careers and at work is closely related to life's satisfaction and the quality of our relationships. This chapter will focus on careers, jobs, and interactions at work.

SEEKING SATISFACTION IN CAREER AND JOBS

How do you differentiate between a career and a job? Did you have a job before you selected a career? Most of us did. Maybe you have a job now and either you haven't decided on a career or the job isn't related to what you eventually plan to do. Think of a **career** as a broad field of occupational endeavor that includes a series of work experiences over a span of time. A career path includes planning, training, and dedication of time and talent. Within each career field are numerous job possibilities. A **job** consists of tasks or duties a person does for pay.

Because career and job satisfaction will dramatically affect the quality of your life, learning what makes a difference is time well spent. A Gallup poll showed complete satisfaction with their jobs in only 39 percent of the workers. Complete dissatisfaction was voiced by 14 percent. The most satisfied were self-employed in their own business or professional practice. Of importance is that two-thirds of those who were completely satisfied in regard to job stress, personal recognition, and salary levels were also completely satisfied with their jobs. Those most dissatisfied were unhappy with coworkers, their boss, job security, and opportunities to learn and grow (Saad, 1999). To avoid being discontented and to be counted among the number of satisfied individuals, look over the list "What Makes a Difference?" and then think about what you want.

What Makes a Difference?
(from a Gallup Poll, 1999)

What's Most Satisfying?

- Relations with coworkers
- Physical safety of workplace
- Flexibility of work hours
- Amount of vacation time

What's Most Dissatisfying?

- On-the-job stress
- Salaries and certain benefits
- Lack of recognition for accomplishments

Career Choice

When thinking about satisfaction, it's best to consider career and job separately. Most people select a category or field of interest either before or during college and then seek a job in that area. In the past, many individuals gave little consideration to career choice. For example, Carl farms because his father and grandfather were farmers. Nathan wanted to remain in his hometown, so he took a job in a local bank and made it a career. Tina chose hairdressing because there was a school near her home, and she didn't have other aspirations. People today seem to be more concerned with career selection; however, they can still limit themselves.

As was pointed out in Chapter 2, women, in general, still sell themselves short and opt for lower paying, lower status career fields. Men continue to feel forced to be financially successful and often choose higher paid fields even if they hold little interest. Other men feel pressured to take over a family business. Both sexes can limit themselves by not considering all possibilities. Before you choose a career, it's wise to know yourself. Reading and applying the material in this book will direct you. Now focus on specific career-related aspects of self. The widely read book *What Color Is Your Parachute?* (Bolles, 2001) can lead you through a series of exercises to identify skills you enjoy and those you do best. The key to being able to find pleasure in our work is the sense that we are using our abilities, not wasting them, and that we are being appreciated. (Kushner, 1986).

Most people reply to the question "What do you want to be?" by naming a title or position; this doesn't tell you what is required in a job. The critical challenge, instead, is, "What do you want to *do*?" Does your choice afford you opportunities to do what you enjoy?

An activity in Reflections and Applications can help you link enjoyment and job duties. No matter how much you might enjoy certain tasks and activities, satisfaction is still unlikely if you are not skilled in what is required of you. Greg said he wanted to be a journalist, and his personality type was well suited to that field. However, his writing was stilted, uninteresting, and prone to errors. Unless he improves his skills, his pursuit of journalism would likely lead to frustration and dissatisfaction.

Your values also play a part in the process of choosing a satisfying career. If you highly value money or what it can buy, you cannot expect career satisfaction in lower paid fields no matter how much you enjoy the work. Is prestige important to you? Sociologists have studied prestige statuses of various career fields, and, if this is of concern, acquaint yourself with the status ranking of your career choice. Maybe you value advancement and upward mobility. There is a vast difference between opportunities in the child-care field and a business management career.

Personality type plays a vital role. Do you tend to be more extraverted or introverted? Ask yourself how many interactions you will have on a regular basis. Do you want to provide ideas and possibilities and have variety and flexibility in your work, or are you more comfortable with established procedures and prefer to work with facts and figures? The Myers-Briggs Type Indicator, described in Chapter 2, provides insight into preferred work situations for each personality type. For an insightful approach to career choice related to personality type, two books *Do What You Are* (Tieger & Barron-Tieger, 1995) and *What's Your Type of Career?* (Dunning, 2001) are highly recommended.

How well do you cope? Jon was a laid-back individual who didn't like pressure and externally imposed deadlines. His initial career choice of printing proved to be the wrong one for him. He developed stress-related migraine headaches and ulcers before he realized that he didn't want to cope with the high-speed world of printing technology.

Figure 10-1   Enjoyment of work is priceless

Finally, commitment is a key element. Some career fields require more time, energy, and effort than others. A fire department chief caused a few eyes to widen when he said that a firefighting career means spending one third of your life away from family. It's important to match your career choice with your degree of commitment.

All of this may sound complicated—and it is! However, wise decisions in the beginning can save you years of wasted energy. Even after starting a career, people may realize they have made a poor choice and change directions. Relatively few decisions are as influential in determining the course of life as the choice of a career path. Occupational choices have an impact on several aspects of life, including standard of living, life style, friendships, intimate relationships, how you dress each day, and where you live. For example, my daughters are pursuing careers in California. Even though I applaud their choices, their decisions mean that we will see each other less often, and their life choices will be quite different than if they had stayed in the Midwest. Career decisions are choices about the way we live.

Selection of a Job

After a wise career choice, a specific job selection takes the spotlight. You may liken making a career selection to deciding that you want an ice cream cone. Then you realize that you don't want to limit a selection to vanilla, chocolate, or strawberry, so you go to a specialty store. Now your choice is among any number of flavors! Within a career field are many possible jobs, and anyone looking for the ultimate in satisfaction doesn't just settle for the basic choices. For example, the majority of psychology majors become counselors. Many other possibilities—teaching, research, consulting, training and development, personnel work, and marketing—exist. Take advantage of library and online resources (see list at end of this chapter).

Have you ever had a job you didn't like? Do you know why it wasn't desirable so you can avoid a similar situation? What have you enjoyed in previous or present jobs? Being aware of satisfying factors can be helpful. Using more than your own experiences to make decisions is even more advantageous. In terms of both career and job choices, consider your own work orientation (Derr, 1986). Check the following to see which are significant.

- Valuing upward mobility points to a career field and a job position where you can advance and "move up the ladder."

TA Revisited

"Child" may be tempted by glamorous choices or those that seem fun. "I want to be a truck driver so I can just get behind the wheel and travel and be free as the breeze" is an example of the "child" at work. The student who made this statement, by the way, soon realized that truck driving wasn't that simple!

"Parent" can send messages of "Get a job—any job—just so you're working" or "Get a job that pays well" or "Be a doctor because your father is one."

"Adult" recognizes the wants and feelings of the "child," analyzes the "parent" messages, then thoughtfully and logically selects both a career and a job.

- Being secure means you want job security in a stable industry with an established firm.
- Being free relates to independence and flexibility to "do your own thing" at work.
- Being high signifies that you want excitement and challenge in your career and job, and risks are welcomed.
- Being balanced is harmony between personal and professional life, and you want a career and job that allows time for family and other interests.

The last orientation is a significant one for most people. In fact, the number one career concern of most people is the ability to balance family and work demands (Carrig, 1999). Feeling that your life is out of balance is extremely stressful and a factor in poor job performance. Picture yourself in careers and jobs related to the five identified orientations. Where do you feel most comfortable? Which have little appeal? More than one orientation is possible.

Other ideas can be used to explain satisfaction in the workplace. You may want to apply Maslow's hierarchy of needs discussed in Chapter 4. If you are struggling with survival, money is a critical factor, and you may postpone other ingredients for satisfaction until this basic need is met. Because many individuals are on the self-esteem level, a job that doesn't diminish and, ideally, enhances feelings of self-worth would be important.

Considering how many other life choices are influenced by career and job selection, the relationship between professional and personal satisfaction, and the actual time spent at work, your attention to these choices is imperative. How much satisfaction you get from your career and job will directly influence all other aspects of your life. Choose wisely!

IDENTIFYING DESIRABLE PERSONAL QUALITIES AND WORK HABITS

Pretend you own a business, and you need employees. What qualities would you seek? Certain jobs demand special qualities or abilities, yet a common thread of desirable traits runs through most positions. If you have achieved the objectives presented in this book, you possess several of the positive qualities in Table 10–1 listed by employers and career experts. Check to see how many honestly describe you. If you lack any, go back through the book and seek to develop them.

Of utmost importance are interpersonal skills. For workplaces of the present and the future, publications in the United States (Carrig, 1999) and Canada (*Canadian Manager*, 1999) rate interpersonal skills and communication abilities as essential. Executives who eventually fail do so most often because of an interpersonal flaw, not a technical inability (Gibbs, 1995). Workers are often fired for negative personal characteristics and poor interpersonal skills. An employer remarked, "I can help them improve technical skills; however, I don't know how to change a negative attitude and lack of 'people' skills."

A variety of employers profile the ideal employee. As expected, education, training, and experience related to the job are included. Other characteristics are **transferable assets**, defined as desirable traits and skills valuable in all career fields and useful in almost every job. Owners and managers have identified 10 of these assets.

TABLE 10-1   Positive Personal Qualities and Work Habits

High self-esteem	Understanding of self, including personality and thought-processing
Positive attitude	Freedom from stereotypic thinking
Ability to meet deadlines	Interpersonal communication skills
Ethical character	Ability to feel and manage emotions
Spirit of contributing	Goal orientation and desire to improve
Stress-coping abilities	Sense of responsibility and control
Motivation and action	Ability to give and receive criticism
Ability to see alternatives	Realistic expectations about self and others
A zest for life	Willingness to give positive strokes

Enthusiasm is a quick response. "During an interview, if I don't pick up on some interest and enthusiasm, I won't hire the person, no matter what the other skills are," said an owner of an automotive service business. Demonstrating enthusiasm about the career field and the job itself is recommended.

Desire to exert effort is another. During an employers' panel discussion, a child-development student mentioned that she had detassled corn on a farm (a tedious task on a hot summer day). A director of a day care center shrieked, "Great! When I have applicants who have stuck with that job, I'm convinced that they can work hard—which day care requires." Being a hard worker is a winning quality. Even if you initially lack desired skills, your zest for hard work will compensate, and your efforts will be rewarded.

> Work hard, not only because it will bring you rewards and promotions but because it will give you the sense of being a competent person. Some jobs can afford to be done poorly and no one will be hurt, but none of us can afford the internal spiritual cost of being sloppy in our work. It teaches us contempt for ourselves and our skills (Kushner, 1986, p. 147).

Likability or congeniality, the ability to get along with others, is highly desired. Conflicts will occur; however, people who are congenial and who like others will manage them effectively. Having an appropriate sense of humor is a plus. Qualities such as sensitivity, cooperativeness, and fairness contribute to a positive workplace.

Dependability is invariably a necessity. The fundamental responsibility is getting to work on time on a regular basis. "I have to be able to count on my employees," says a business owner. "My company has a responsibility to the customers, and they can't be served if people don't show up." If you have a positive record of attendance and punctuality, be sure to maintain it and use it to your advantage. Dependability goes beyond physical presence, however. When you are given a job, can your employer count on you to perform? Productivity is the key to success in businesses and organizations, and hardworking employees are almost always productive. Your employer will expect you to do your share, and if you are interested in advancement, you are wise to do even more.

Three additional qualities go hand in hand and are popular with most employers in today's job market: creativity, innovation, and initiative. *Creativity* is the ability to develop good ideas that can be put into action; it is not confined to artistic pursuits. *Innovation* means change and is closely related to creativity. Being imaginative at work could result in a better product or idea, an easier way to perform a task, or a more spontaneous environment. My husband, a business owner, sees a major contrast between employees who can figure out a way to solve a problem and those who seem to have little ingenuity. You may be thinking that creativity and innovation are rare talents. Keep in mind that everyone has a degree of both, that you can employ each in any job, and that many creative, innovative ideas are simple ones. Critical and creative thinking abilities are a definite plus. Individuals who are ambitious and motivated show *initiative*. Instead of standing around waiting to be told what to do next, they seek productive activity. When directing an early childhood center, I was amazed at the differences in initiative among my employees. A few sought new tasks; however, the majority would finish an activity and pause until they received instructions. At times, caution in going ahead is advisable; however, chronic lack of initiative is not appreciated. With almost any job, you can usually find more to do if you look!

Flexibility is like a breath of fresh air. In many work situations, adaptation or adjustment is practical. Jo was considered one of the most valuable employees in an accounting firm, and her flexibility was a major strength. She could adjust her demanding schedule when necessary. During busy times she offered to work overtime or come in early. When new ideas were suggested, she exhibited an open attitude, which made others like her. Being able to "go with the flow" creates possibilities!

"It may seem old-fashioned, but I expect my employees to be loyal," stated a president of a large corporation. *Loyalty* does not necessarily mean that you will never leave a company; however, it does imply that while employed, the employer's best interests will be of concern to you. Speaking negatively about a current or past employer, even if it's deserved, isn't recommended.

In contrast to the work world of years ago, when employees were expected to be "seen and not heard," today's employers want *assertiveness*. At work, you gain little by being overly aggressive or passive. Lori was determined and ambitious. In business meetings she frequently and loudly interrupted. She was intense and hostile whenever she felt challenged. Her aggressive attitude and behavior made her unpopular and, ironically, blocked the advancement she desired so much. On the other hand, Chad was a "yes" person who was meek and humble. His supervisor and coworkers took advantage of him. At his yearly evaluation he was told he wasn't ready to move to the management level.

Assertiveness training would have helped both Lori and Chad. On the job, being able to say no to unreasonable requests is important. Otherwise, you can feel overloaded, taken advantage of, and frustrated. Being assertive during an interview can enhance your chances of being hired. Employers share the belief that behaviors during an interview indicate actions on the job.

Keeping in mind these characteristics of valued employees, a practical way of preparing for an interview is to note the qualities and work habits you possess and emphasize them in résumés, cover letters, and interviews. If you can also document when you have displayed them, you stand an even better chance of being the top applicant.

The more positive qualities you demonstrate, the more likely you are to achieve career success. Because individuals differ in their perceptions, success is difficult to define. If you're a positive person who wants to realize your potential, who sets realistic goals, who takes responsibility for self, who is nonperfectionistic and strives for excellence, you can be successful. Success can be a feeling of having done as well as you could; see it as a process, not as a final destination.

CHOOSING WISELY: FROM THE JOB SEARCH TO RETIREMENT

As in all areas of life, you have, and will continue to have, any number of choices regarding career and jobs. Specific choices are related to the stage of your career.

The Search Itself

You may not recognize that you have a choice about how you will go about the job search itself. The majority of job hunters simply look. They do not prepare and seemingly give little thought to the process. The first step is to know yourself and what you have to offer. To help you, complete the "Assets and Liabilities" exercise in Reflections and Applications. Years ago I designed and taught a career development course which is a requirement for several majors. Convincing students that the course was worthwhile was sometimes a challenge. Yet, does it seem sensible to spend years gaining knowledge in order to get the job you want and then fail to do so because your job-seeking skills are inadequate? Most individuals who are looking for jobs confine their search to the classified ads in a newspaper. Would it surprise you to know that most available jobs on any given day are not advertised? If you only answer ads, you are tapping into a small share of the job market.

According to Pat Sims, a personnel specialist, many job applicants are unprepared. They don't have any idea of what job they want, know nothing about the business, lack the information needed to fill out an application, and don't even bring a pen. "Several bring their babies, and a few even have pets with them!" Their choice, seemingly, has been to approach the job hunt in a lackadaisical way. Employers will be inclined to believe they will handle their jobs similarly.

Being prepared can make the difference between enjoyment or displeasure in your job search and, ultimately, between success or failure in your career. Begin with research into career and job possibilities and expand into the "how-to" of finding a position. An increasingly rich source of information is online. You are also wise to use the In-

I'M LOOK'N FOR A **SOFT DESK JOB**... LIKE YOURS

Figure 10-2

ternet to actually search for openings and to post your résumé and cover letter. In regard to these important written pieces, impressive ways of presenting yourself are essential and worthy of your attention. (Hanna, 2002). See Resources at the end of this chapter for some online recommendations.

Most never actually *learn* how to interview. Being unprepared for a job interview can lead to a stressful situation in which you give a less than positive impression of yourself. A common problem has to do with responses that negate or qualify the interviewee.

> Jamie was nervous. When asked what her work experiences had been, she replied, "Well, uh, I haven't done much except work in a restaurant—really nothing in the secretarial field." The final question was "Why should we hire you over the other applicants?" She blushed and stammered, "Well, I don't think—you know—I'm better than others so I don't really know—uh, I feel I could do a good job, I guess."

Contrast this poor performance with a well-prepared job applicant.

> Jamie faced the interviewer with a smile and a look of confidence. When asked about work experience, she replied, "I have worked for 2 years in a busy restaurant. I developed many interpersonal skills as I waited on customers. I think these skills will be valuable in secretarial work. During college I had simulated office experience, which I really enjoyed." In response to the final question, she replied "I have my secretarial degree and had many hands-on experiences during my training. My work experience has helped me develop many 'people' skills. I am dependable, positive, friendly, enthusiastic about my career, and very interested in this job."

This impressive interview would not have occurred if Jamie had not prepared by anticipating the questions and rehearsing her answers. Going to a job interview with no preparation can be as disastrous as jumping into deep water not knowing how to swim. If you have an opportunity to take a course to help you build confidence, write a better application, prepare a résumé, and learn to interview, take advantage of it. Detailed information is available in books such as *Career by Design: Communicating Your Way to Success* (Hanna, 2002).

Reflect

- What do you want in a job? Think of at least three.
- In what other geographic location would you be satisfied? What type of work would you want to do there?
- How would you reply to an interview question: What are your career goals?

Apply

- Ask someone who has begun her or his career: What is the most satisfying? What don't you like, if anything?
- List five of your transferable assets.
- Write an employment ad that describes job duties you would want.

Because rejection is an inevitable part of most job searches, it is wise to decide how you will handle it. Even though you may be offered the first position you want, for most, what is realistic is to visualize a job search as a series of "no's" finally followed by a "yes." Important to remember is that a "no" is not a rejection of you personally but merely an assessment of a match between you and the position. Thought-changing can do wonders. Rather than think, "Something is wrong with me that they didn't want to hire me," restructure it: "Just because they didn't hire me doesn't mean something is wrong with me. They sure missed an opportunity to have a first-rate employee. It's their loss!" Then choose to move forward to a better job.

Your Career Path

Worth thinking about before you accept a job is where it may lead. Several decisions will be made during your work life that will dramatically influence the direction of your career path.

Career goals.   Just as you couldn't plan a trip without knowing the destination, you are unwise to begin a career unless you know your objective. This decision doesn't have to be made immediately, yet thinking about it can be beneficial. Young people may have aspirations of owning a business or being the head of a company, yet they haven't seriously considered what is required to get there and whether they would like what they will find upon arriving. Ask yourself whether you enjoy being in charge and making final decisions. Are you willing to give the time and effort required to achieve higher positions? Advancement is rewarding, yet sometimes the status achieved isn't worth the price.

Many overlook the need to integrate career and personal plans. Chris started his own business thinking that he would now be his own boss, be in charge of his life, and not have to work so many hours. He soon discovered that he had many bosses—his customers! He found little time to spend with family. Both his business and his personal life began to suffer. He made a difficult decision to sell the business he had recently established and accept a position that didn't interfere with his family life.

Another sound reason to establish career goals is that this is frequently asked in a job interview. Having no goals or poorly defined ones is a liability. Also important is to have goals compatible with what the interviewing employer can offer. "I want to travel on the job, have relocation possibilities, and then eventually start my own business" could be the "kiss of death."

Advancement.   If you decide that you want to advance into different positions, planning becomes significant. First, select employment where promotional possibilities exist. Then do the following.

- Perform as well as you can doing more than what is expected.
- Take advantage of learning and growth opportunities.
- Display professionalism and demonstrate a high degree of ethics.
- Document your accomplishments and keep your résumé updated.
- Research carefully.

The latter is important because promotion just for advancement's sake may lead to job dissatisfaction. Most of us have been convinced that upward mobility is essential, however, this can lead into jobs we either don't like or don't do well. Granted you may be required to take a position with responsibilities that aren't satisfying on the way to one that is. Be sure that your final goal is where you want to be.

The goal-setting techniques outlined in Chapter 3 work well in charting your career path. Action steps are a necessity. Some students write expansive career goals such as, "I plan to make a million dollars and retire within 5 years." The critical question is: "How are you going to do this?"

Keeping records.   Maintaining a personal career file is one of the most practical and worthwhile things you can do, yet many neglect this. One day a frantic former student called: "Did you keep our résumés on file?" My "no" reply resulted in a plaintive outburst, "I threw all my stuff from the class away, and I need a résumé right now!" Another individual missed an application deadline because he didn't have a copy of his transcripts to submit. Poor organization makes the job search more time-consuming and stressful.

Making contacts.   **Networking**, establishing contacts who may be helpful, can help you get a desired job, advance in your career, and change your job or career. Occasionally, a job seeker will balk at the idea of getting a job through contacts. "I don't want to be hired because of whom I know but on the basis of my abilities," a man said. He was assured that even Albert Einstein found a job after graduation only through the father of one of his classmates (Fisher et al., 1977)—a classic example of whom you know being, perhaps, as important as what you know. Besides, you probably won't be hired, even with the best contact, if you aren't qualified. Contacts who can be used as references and sources of job leads, and influential sponsors are tremendous resources throughout your career. Begin building your network immediately. A good idea is to exchange business cards with people and keep them in a file. Almost everyone likes to help others. Cultivating multiple and diverse relationships in order to build a "personal board of directors" is recommended by Linda Hill, Ph.D., Harvard Business School (1994).

Continued learning.   Some students are surprised to realize that their education isn't over when they earn a degree. Take advantage of educational and skills-building opportunities. Lifelong learners are invariably career-success winners. A worthwhile question to ask in an employment interview is what further educational opportunities are encouraged or provided. Even if the employer doesn't pay for these, show that you are determined to continue to learn and grow and then do so. Also, emphasize how important learning is to you.

Leadership.   Training to become a leader will help in several ways. You may then decide that you really don't want to lead, or you may acquire the skills that differentiate effective leaders from poor ones. Being an effective leader is an art that goes beyond successful job performance. Described in a presentation by Brian Tracy, who is a successful business executive, leadership consists of seven qualities: vision, courage, integrity, commitment, responsibility, concentration, and excellence. As ideal as this list sounds, an outstanding leader has even more obvious behaviors: effective communicating, organizing, delegating, seeing that responsibilities are carried out, giving and receiving constructive criticism, praising employees, and promoting teamwork.

As a leader, you will be expected to make tough decisions, including those of hiring and firing. A strong feeling (F) preference on the Myers-Briggs Type Indicator is a hindrance in this regard. Using more of the thinking (T) preference is necessary. Able leadership requires much more than desire. The rewards can certainly be worth the effort it takes to develop the skills.

Challenges at work.   On the job you will periodically face challenges not directly related to the work you do. Prejudice and discrimination based on such factors as age, sex, race, ethnicity, sexual orientation, and disability are possible. **Sexual harassment**—any uninvited and undesired verbal or physical behavior related to sexuality—is of concern in today's work environment. It is important to realize that even though most harassers are men, *most men are not harassers* (Bravo & Cassedy, 1992).

To avoid being a harasser, assume that off-color jokes and sexual advances are not welcomed, recognize that a "no" means just that, and ask how you'd feel if you or someone you cared for was harassed. Because faulty communication is a factor in perceived harassment (Markert, 1999), you can take responsibility for sending and receiving clear messages. To handle harassment, be assertive and let the person know the behaviors are not acceptable, talk to someone about any incident, document both the harassment and your own job performance, seek witnesses, go through appropriate channels, and use the legal system, if necessary (Bravo & Cassedy, 1992).

Being sensitive to others by refraining from degrading comments and language is the fair and decent way to behave. Challenging your own stereotypes and eliminating personal prejudice will make this easier. Acceptance and equal treatment of others are keystones of positive interpersonal relations.

Concerns such as discrimination, equal pay for equal work, comparable worth, maternity and paternity leave, and quality child care have arisen and will continue to be consequential. Controversial issues such as drug testing, disease screening, and smoking policies will necessitate difficult organizational and personal decisions. Stay abreast of new developments, be objective, remain aware of the concerns, and be open to possible solutions.

Career and job changes.   If you are unhappy at work or if a better opportunity arises, you will probably consider a change. Changing jobs is common, and even switching careers is not unusual. The average person can expect to change careers 5 to 7 times and jobs up to 12 times (Shakoor, 2000). A career change demands more thought and planning than a job change and is usually riskier. Look objectively at your present situation and note the costs of a career move as compared with the benefits. Critical thinking is helpful. As with any change, stress is a by-product, and any resulting satisfaction and pleasure are well deserved.

Retirement.   The end of a career seems far away for most people; however, the most effective and productive planning for retirement is started years before a career ends. Those who don't are financially handicapped. Women who have depended on a husband for their financial well-being are especially at risk. More than 80 percent of retired women are not eligible for pension benefits, and only 50 percent of working women have retirement plans. It is no wonder that nearly 75 percent of the elderly poor are women (*Women in Business*, 2000).

Both sexes often avoid planning for a retirement life style that can bring similar rewards to those gained from work. About 63 percent of adults have never discussed retirement needs with a professional financial advisor (Lach, 2000) and about 17 percent of workers in their 40s say they haven't begun to save for retirement (Clifford, 2000). Thoughtful decisions will make the transition from a career orientation to retirement a positive experience. The earlier a person begins to invest, the better. A 22-year-old who saves $50 a week at an 8 percent return will have almost $1 million by age 65. Waiting a year reduces this amount almost $77,000 (Chandler, 2001). Because people are living longer, you are wise to prepare carefully and then continue to be productive throughout the life span.

From the initial career and job selections to retirement, your career path will bring both joy and sorrow, elation and disappointment. Each stage requires choices, and you owe it to yourself to consider all possibilities and make thoughtful decisions about this significant part of your life.

ENJOYING RELATIONSHIPS AT WORK

To whom will you relate as you pursue your career? With whom will you interact on the job? Countless possibilities exist. Let's follow Antonio, a surgical technologist, through part of his workday.

> Antonio said hello to three other employees as he entered the building. In the elevator he exchanged small talk with others. He met briefly with his supervisor and a nurse. He offered a reassuring word to a nervous patient. Later in the morning he had coffee with two coworkers. At lunch he complimented a cafeteria worker on the array of fresh fruit. During the afternoon he met with other members of the surgical team. Before the day was over, he had interacted with approximately 40 people.

In almost any job you will have numerous relationships that are enhanced by your positive behaviors.

Personality Types at Work

An understanding of personality preferences from the Myers-Briggs Type Indicator, discussed in Chapter 2, can help you relate better to others. There are no good or bad types, only different ones, according to the book *Type Talk at Work* (Kroeger & Thuesen, 1993), which profiles personalities in the workplace. Also helpful is the book *Work Types* (Kummerow, Barger, & Kirby, 1997). Both describe temperament types which were covered in Chapter 2. Understanding personality differences and being able to utilize others' strengths will make enjoyment of work more probable.

Positive Relations

If you possess most of the positive qualities of a valued employee described in this chapter and are practicing the skills outlined in previous ones, you will be able to cultivate positive relationships with those in your work environment. Some specific behaviors are especially important.

Give appropriate affirmations.   Positive verbal and nonverbal acknowledgments of others can create a warm atmosphere and be rewarding to you in return. People generally react favorably to a sincere positive stroke. We miss many opportunities to affirm others, and the workplace provides several. In addition to verbal praise, a written or e-mail thank-you, congratulations, or acknowledgment will likely be well received. Praise is a powerful motivator for most people, so if you are in a supervisory position, make it your ally.

Appreciate diversity.   Today's work world is a mosaic composed of various ethnic, racial, religious, and age groups. Review and continue to remind yourself of the recommendations regarding prejudice and appreciation of diversity given in Chapter 9. Except for some educational institutions, the workplace offers the most opportunities for interactions with all types of people. Take advantage of opportunities to meet and get to know those who reflect cultural diversity. Your career will benefit, and your life will be enriched!

Be helpful and supportive.   Opportunities abound to provide help and support to others. Little actions mean a lot. In some cases, more is demanded. If a coworker is ill, handling additional tasks may be in order. Helping new employees learn their duties may take time but will be appreciated. Trish had received some training in family counseling and had excellent listening skills. She spent some lunch hours with Alicia, who was going through a divorce. If your job brings you into contact with people in stressful situations, realize that what you say and don't say and how you behave will make the situation better or worse.

Be friendly and considerate.   Congeniality and regard for others create a more positive work environment and usually bring rewards to the employee. The simple act of greeting may have an impact. Calling a person by name is an added positive behavior. If remembering names is difficult, you might want to try mental association. A man named John had a punctuality problem. Associating him with "Johnny Come Lately" was a simple trick! Another technique is to repeat the person's name. When introduced, say, "I'm happy to meet you, Bob." During the time you are together, call Bob by name as often as practical and use it again when you say good-bye. When you are

Figure 10-3   Positive relationships enhance the workplace

The Power of Support

Personal experiences with health care employees before and after cancer surgery convinced me of the impact they have on a patient. See if you can recognize the helpful and unhelpful, supportive and nonsupportive behaviors in each of the situations.

- The nurse gave me a reassuring smile, and said, "Don't worry. We see many patients with these tumors, and we know what we're doing!" This was such a relief after being told that mine was a rare cancer.
- The world-renowned specialist muttered to himself and to the medical students who were observing the scan of my eye, "Melanoma—doesn't look like it, but I don't know what else it could be." My stress level was at an all-time high. I knew what melanoma cancer was. I kept thinking, "Doesn't he know that I can hear him?"
- The young radiologist greeted me warmly. Before the scans, she calmly explained to me what she was doing and what would happen. I thought that she was wise beyond her years and seemed to be aware of the psychological studies that show that the impact of stress is lessened when people know what to expect.
- The young doctor in residency said a brief hello and then sat behind a desk and looked at what appeared to be my medical records. I was there for a postoperative visit. For 10 long minutes he didn't look at me or say anything except an occasional "Hmmm" as he read and cracked his knuckles! Another stressful situation in which behaviors of a specialist created more tension.
- One of the most positive people I met is Wolfgang Kuss—my eye designer, I call him. When I went to have an artificial eye made, I felt uncomfortable to say the least. Wolfgang immediately set both my husband and me at ease. I laughed more and felt more positive during that hour than I had for months. His attitude made all the difference in the world.
- This story is somewhat humorous now, but at the time nothing about the situation was funny. During a uterine scan after cancer surgery, the technician was unfriendly. The only thing she said was a question: "Did anyone ever tell you that you have two uteruses? It sure looks strange." Then she left and didn't return for another 15 minutes. I lay there fighting terror, knowing that I didn't have two uteruses but wondering what she was seeing. This was a case of poor judgment and an uncalled-for comment. The ending was happy: What she saw was not unusual.

new in a job, you will probably meet several people immediately. In addition to repetition and association, you might write the names, check their names on a company list or directory, and rehearse them mentally. Don't be afraid to ask them to say their names for you again.

Several other gestures are possible. Ask questions and express interest in others. Just be sure you don't go beyond what are sensible inquiries. Consideration means you will be careful to avoid irritating others. In a small office area, Jeff had his radio set on a loud rock-and-roll station. Four employees shared one phone extension, and Rhonda spent several minutes at a time making personal calls. Neither worker was considerate. Approachability checking, recommended in Chapter 9, is appreciated in the work environment. Because time is a valuable commodity, a considerate person does not assume that a coworker or supervisor is available at all times.

Customer relations are considered the "bottom line" by business owners. Employees who turn customers away or even create negative impressions are usually fired. Being a positive salesperson or company representative isn't easy and requires determination, patience, and an understanding of human behavior. As an example, do you like to stand in line for service and then have another customer who just arrived be taken care of first? A sensitive employee would note who was there first or, if necessary, ask. As much as possible, the best employees avoid letting customers wait.

Other tips include treating the customer as if your roles were reversed, greeting individuals with a smile, listening attentively and actively to their request or complaint, handling complaints in an accommodating and cheerful manner, and asking whether your service was satisfactory. All this may sound difficult, and customer relations is definitely a challenge. Remember that you will be rewarded for your efforts. The reward may come not from others but from your own inner self saying, "Great job!"

Interactions with customers or clients are often on the telephone. Modern technology has created some devices that can be helpful yet can also diminish positive impressions. For example, do you recall being put on hold without even being asked whether you wanted to be? Effective telephone skills can be learned and deserve attention. No matter how or when a customer feels slighted or demeaned, the company or organization suffers.

Do your fair share as well as you can.   In most jobs, you are part of a team with a contribution to make. Lazy workers are not wanted, and an inefficient team member is a detriment. While you are at work, your responsibility is to the job at hand. Maria worked in a law office as a word processing specialist. When the attorneys were gone, she used her time to play games on her computer. She was surprised when another employee told her how offensive her behavior was. Be sure not to cheat your employer—and yourself, in the long run—by just getting by.

Be positive and realize the contributions of others.   Employees with positive attitudes are greatly appreciated. Seeing the bright side of a situation helps everyone. In every company or organization, some times are busier and more stressful than others. You may be tempted to think that your job is the most demanding. Picture this scenario: Kent, Roberto, and Anh are on their break in the cafeteria. Let's listen to their conversation:

Kent: I'm so busy I don't know heads from tails. All the quarterly reports I have to do are really getting to me.

Roberto: Just be glad you don't have to fill all the orders that are coming in now. I probably won't even have time to take a break later.

Anh: You think you guys have it rough. If I have to field one more irate phone call, I think I'll find an easier job.

As they're busily trying to "one-up" each other, another employee walks by the cafeteria and thinks, "I don't see how those three have time to take a break. They must not have nearly as much work to do as I do!"

Did you recognize the "one-upping" comments? Realizing that you aren't the only one with a heavy load and acknowledging others' workloads would be a refreshing change from this scene. Receptive listening is as important at work as it is in other situations.

Manage conflict effectively.   Despite your best attempts to create positive relationships, disagreement will occur. You have choices. In several situations, your best bet is to ignore the irritation. Most work environments have at least one annoying employee, and even those who aren't disagreeable will occasionally bother you. Keep in mind that your behavior is not at the mercy of another person's. Only you can determine your actions. Using techniques to defuse your frustration and anger can turn potentially hostile situations into harmless ones.

At other times, avoiding an irritant isn't advisable, and your time is well spent trying to resolve the conflict. Familiarize yourself with the "chain of command." Be honest and address legitimate concerns. Complaining without suggesting alternatives is not advised, although voicing a concern may be advantageous. If perceived mistreatment comes from a supervisor, you are wise to address it; however, don't let your anger control the situation. All that may be needed is an "I" statement describing your annoyance or the perception-checking technique that was explained in Chapter 8. If criticized, using the suggested responses from Chapter 8 can keep the level of conflict manageable. The key is open communication. If more efforts are required, a negotiation strategy, as described in Chapter 9, can create a positive outcome.

Conflict management techniques, discussed elsewhere in Chapters 9 and 11, can be applied to work situations. Understanding is more likely if people recognize personality differences. No type excels at handling conflict; in fact, disagreeable situations can magnify our preferences. I recall explaining to a strong ESTJ type that what she had said to a coworker whose type was ESFP had indeed been insensitive. "Why would anyone be hurt by that?" she asked. Even after accepting that it could have hurt, she considered it a sign of weakness and illogical for her to apologize. The ESFP, in turn, had difficulty accepting that the lack of apology wasn't just a sign of dislike and rudeness.

The section in Chapter 9 on dealing with difficult people can also be helpful. What if the difficult person is your boss or supervisor? How to recognize, understand, and cope with a difficult boss is covered in the book *Coping with Difficult Bosses* (Bramson, 1992). Griping with fellow employees is not recommended. Ask yourself what the person does that is bothersome, what your specific goals or objectives are, and what other people might need to be involved. As you decide on an action plan, you are wise to use a cost versus benefits approach. If you determine after a reasonable period of time that your supervisor is intolerable and you have done all you can to improve the relationship, seek other employment possibilities.

Your degree of satisfaction on the job is greatly influenced by the quality of relationships. The time and effort you spend improving them are well worth it!

LOOKING BACK

- Human beings are typically identified by their career and job choices.
- Career and job satisfaction have a tremendous impact, and thoughtful decisions influence the quality of life.

- Try not to limit your choices, then begin your search by knowing yourself well. Identify your interests, likes, abilities, values, personality, coping skills, and work orientations.
- After career and job choices have been made, possessing and using the personal qualities and work habits desired by employers can make success much more likely.
- Throughout your career you will have choices. Whether and how you prepare for the job search is one of the first ones. A well-prepared job seeker has a much better chance of landing a desired position.
- As you proceed along your career path, you will be faced with many decisions. Recognizing options and making wise choices leads to success.
- Building numerous relationships is common during one's career. Several behaviours can promote positive relations.
- As in all walks of life, if you know yourself well, have a high regard for yourself, demonstrate a positive attitude, gather information, use thought processing, are open and flexible, and can recognize and deal with adversity, you will direct your career path to success.

That which distinguishes the good teachers from the mediocre teachers is primarily not method, style, or personality—but attitude. They consistently project a positive attitude toward each student as an individual and toward the subject being taught. From such teachers, students intuitively receive the message: You are important, and it's important to me that you learn.

—Bob Resz

RESOURCES

Career counseling and placement services at colleges and universities

Service Corps of Retired Executives (SCORE) 800-634-0245 www.score.org (local groups provide free business counseling)

Online sources such as: Bureau of Labor Statistics: http:stats.bls.gov.

The Career Interests Game: http:career.missouri.edu/holland.

Europages, The European Business Directory: www.europages.com

John Holland's Self-Directed Search: www.self-directed-search.com

JobHunters Bible: www.jobhuntersbible.com

JOBTRAK:www.jobtrak.com

Monster Board:www.monster.com

Occupational Outlook Handbook: www.stats.bl.gov/ocohome.htm

O*Net Online: http:online.onetcenter.org

The Riley Guide: www.rileyguide.com

The Salary Calculator at Homefair: www.homefair.com/calc/salcalc_res.html

Salary Wizard:www.salary.com

Small Business Administration: www.sba.gov/starting

11

Developing and Enriching Intimate Relationships

LOOKING AHEAD

After completing this chapter, you will be able to

- Explain the importance of love.
- Recognize obstacles to love and describe addictive behaviors.
- Name and contrast passionate and intimate love.
- Describe components and dimensions of intimate love.
- Explain the relationship growth and needs fulfillment theory, noting how it is related to intimate love.
- Discuss the barriers, benefits, and development of intimacy.
- Define conflict and fighting and describe effective conflict management.
- Discuss barriers to enrichment and tell what couples can do to enhance their relationships.
- Identify ideas for sexual fulfillment.
- Define cohabitation and explain reasons for its use.
- Discuss living together arrangements including success guidelines.
- Explain marriage in terms of definition and images.
- Name and describe different types of marriage.
- Tell how couples can prepare for marriage.
- Explain several factors related to marital success.
- Realize that relationships end and explain how couples can go their separate way in a way that will benefit both parties.
- List some possible benefits of divorce and other relationship endings.

From "I" and "me" to "us" and "we." Your relationships will be as vital and alive as you are. Love is life in all of its aspects And if you miss love, you miss life. Please don't.

—Leo Buscaglia

"I love you" is a statement that is responsible for experiences of joy as well as despair. To love and be loved is desired by well-adjusted human beings. Two intriguing books *Love and Suvival* (Ornish, 1998) and *A Cry Unheard* (Lynch, 2000) present evidence that love and interpersonal relationships are critical elements in health.

To achieve intimacy within a relationship is to realize the deepest meaning of love. How much do you know about love and intimacy? If you had little education in these areas, you're not alone. Intimacy has been either ignored or assumed to be so natural that thinking or talking about it is unnecessary. Or it's been incorrectly defined as sexual relations. Consequently, most people have difficulty with their intimate relationships. This chapter will delve into love and intimate relationships.

You can use it as a springboard to education in what, for most people, are the most important aspects of their lives.

WHAT IS LOVE?

In writing, music, painting, and the performing arts, love is a major theme. In recent years, research has contributed to our understanding of love. Books and courses are available to help people make wise decisions about love and intimacy. Does studying love take away from a relationship? "This doesn't seem very romantic to me," grumbled a woman when she was asked to answer questions about her love relationship. Regardless of one's perception of what is romantic, knowledge and understanding of love and intimacy build a strong foundation for a meaningful relationship.

Love is an art (Fromm, 1956). If you want to have a fulfilling love relationship, first acquire information about love. Meeting the right person doesn't teach us to love. We must learn about love as we learn other skills (Wegscheider-Cruse, 1988). Besides knowledge, a necessary factor is priority. The mastery of love must be a matter of ultimate concern; there must be nothing more important (Fromm, 1956). When I was first "in love" and later as I experienced other love relationships, did I ever study it? Certainly not; I didn't know one could be educated in this area, and, besides who needed it? "Love will conquer all," I thought, along with thousands who believed that the sensation of love was enough.

"What is love?" is an important question. Because love varies from one culture to another, varies in meaning from one era to another, and even shifts within a single relationship as individuals mature, definitive answers may be impossible. However, we can identify obstacles, types and components of love as well as important elements of intimacy.

IDENTIFYING OBSTACLES TO LOVE AND INTIMACY

Individuals can want to love and be loved and still fail miserably. At times, they believe that they are in love, and the results are disappointing and painful. You can shift the odds in the favor of success if you know the potential obstacles.

Low Self-Esteem

The foundation for all love relationships is self-love. The eloquent expressions of other writers concerning the relationship between self-esteem and healthy love for another can benefit anyone who desires a love relationship.

A positive self-image, a sturdy self-esteem, and a love of self sets us free to love others. (Viorst, 1986, p. 55)

The first love affair we must consummate successfully is the love affair with ourselves. Without respect for who I am and enjoyment in what I am, I have very little to give. If I do not feel that I am lovable, it is very difficult to believe that anyone else loves me (Branden & Branden, 1982, p. 40).

One who seeks in another the sense of worth one cannot find in oneself is likely to be disappointed. We cannot find salvation in a relationship (Sternberg, 1987, p. 275).

Why is low self-esteem detrimental? People who don't value themselves tend to create relationships that don't succeed, thus diminishing self-worth even further. Either an individual will be needy and feel helpless in the grips of passionate love or devalue the other. Two women describe low self-esteem problems:

> Luanne: As I grew and changed, he did all he could to knock me down. He was insecure and couldn't stand the thought of my growing and being able to manage without him. I hate to admit that it worked. I easily slipped back to our old roles. I can see now where my low self-esteem allowed him to continue to rule me. After almost 10 years and 2 children, I decided I couldn't take it and left.

> Elizabeth: My relationship with my ex-husband could easily be described as "walking on eggshells." I analyzed my thoughts before speaking and was not negative about anything (due to his low self-esteem). I felt my self-worth being dragged down to his level. This is ironic considering it was my optimism and strong sense of self that drew him to me. I finally realized I had to get out to save "me."

Low self-esteem sets the stage for unhealthy behaviors, including manipulation, unfair fighting, extreme negative reactions to criticism, extended periods of silence, temper tantrums, and abuse. People with low self-esteem feel unworthy of love. They believe that sooner or later, they will lose their lover. Because of their fear of rejection, they frequently bring about the very situation they dread. Their lives become self-fulfilling prophecies (Porat, 1988).

In contrast, high self-esteem creates an attitude that you deserve the finest. This belief influences your behavior and the outcome. Mark confided: "I always said I could never live without her, but I have found that I can. This class has helped me a lot because it has taught me that I deserve better than her." Margaret had a dramatic experience.

> I used to hate myself. I was told that I wasn't good enough, was stupid, and would never amount to anything. In 6 years my ex-husband gave me 27 fractures, killed my second baby in utero, and then started on my daughter when she was less than 2 years of age. In order for him to feel powerful, he would bring me down to his level or lower. Then a "feeling" came over me. It wasn't me who was all these things; it was him. I finally realized I was a worthwhile person. I loved and trusted myself enough not to need his sick love, and I sneaked out with baby in arms.

Margaret learned an essential lesson—that she deserved much better. Being the right person is what's important—not finding the right person (Ornish, 1998). You can eliminate a major barrier to a healthy love relationship by raising your self-esteem level and choosing a partner who values herself or himself.

Extensive Giving and Addiction

"If you love, you give and give and give" is a belief that persists. "Sacrifice is what love is all about" was the resigned explanation of a 56-year-old woman who didn't appear to be loved or loving. Women accepted and lived the sacrificial role more than men. The past influences the present, and in spite of women's quest for equality and independence, the tendency for many women is to give more than men do. These thoughts are reflected in comments from young female students.

> Lisa: I found myself constantly building him up and reassuring him of my love at my expense.
>
> Staci: The part of me that attracted him to me in the beginning I unknowingly gave up. That was ME, my personality, my independence, my self-security. I was, I thought, so much in love, and to show it, I tried to be everything I thought he wanted me to be. In doing so, I was no longer ME, the person he was attracted to.
>
> Jill: I was *so* in love with him that I forgot the things I wanted and focused only on what he wanted.

Addictive and codependent relationships have usually focused on women's loving too much. Men do not necessarily equate this endless giving with love and often grow to resent it. Men don't feel grateful; they feel suffocated (Cowan & Kinder, 1987).

For both sexes, a cultural factor is Americans' preoccupation with obsessive and violent love (White & Bondurant, 1996). Novels, television, movies, and music depict love-crazed individuals who resort to aggression and violent acts in the name of love. Although the obsessed person may call his or her addiction "love," obsessive love has little to do with love (Forward, 1991). One of the greatest stress producers is the feeling of subservience and lack of control which is characteristic of obsessive love.

Relationships that are based on misconceptions of love take their toll. In addition to psychological costs, a pressing concern in American society is abuse—whether it's physical, sexual, or emotional—which is found in addictive and obsessive relationships. An enlightening book on the subject is *When Men Batter Women: New Insights into Ending Abusive Relationships* (Jacobson & Gottman, 1998a). Those who are highly dependent on their partners seem to tolerate more physical violence. Sharon, who entered college at age 41, expressed it candidly:

> Being married to an abusive alcoholic left nothing for "me." There simply was no "me." There was only what he wanted. My basic need was mere survival.

Recent attention has focused on intimate or "common-couple" violence among heterosexuals. This type is engaged in equally by both men and women. The difference is that women are more likely to be injured (DeMaris, 2001). Violence is also present in the relationships of same-sex couples, although incidents are rarely reported (Huwig, 2001). A sobering finding is that battering seldom stops on its own (Jacobson & Gottman, 1998a). Couples who truly care about their relationship do not put it at risk by physically hurting each other.

Even more common is another type of abuse. **Verbal aggression** is verbal or nonverbal communication intended to cause psychological pain to another person or perceived as having that intent. Obsessive love and a verbally abusive relationship share characteristics of inequality, manipulation, hostility, and control. For a review of how to handle verbal abuse, see Chapter 9.

Why would anyone remain in an abusive relationship? The answers are not simple. Some experts believe that women can suffer from what is called **battered woman syndrome**, a type of posttraumatic stress disorder. After so much abuse, they are stripped of self-esteem and falsely believe they need their husbands in order to survive (Jacobson & Gottman, 1998a). Violence at the hands of a partner adversely affects the victim's sense of control (Umberson, Anderson, Click, & Shapiro, 1998), making it extremely difficult to break the cycle. Debra described her experience as follows:

> I gave, and he took. I became his "mother," someone to take care of him and solve his problems. I thought that was what love truly meant, that I would only be important if I was needed by and doing for someone else. My needs or wants never entered my mind. I just plain did not exist. He didn't want me to work, and he "hit on" every female I brought to the house so I stopped associating with my friends. I didn't trust him to care for the children for even an hour on his own so I stayed home. He kept me where he wanted me, and I let him. I despised the fact that even when he hurt me to the point I couldn't see because my eyes were swollen shut or couldn't talk because my jaw was broken, I still didn't have enough courage to move out. It seems now that I never blamed him—only me—which was fine with him. He got fired from one of many jobs, slammed me against a wall, and I packed his bags. He left, and later the hospital called. He had tried to kill himself. I remember going to see him, and the first words I spoke were, "What have *I* done?" I let Debra be destroyed.

Fortunately, Debra became strong enough to leave, return to school, and begin a new life.

To see if you may be involved in an abusive relationship, honestly answer the following questions (Forward & Torres, 1986):

- Does the person assume the right to control how you live and behave?
- Have you given up important activities or people in your life in order to keep this person happy?
- Does the person devalue your opinions, your feelings, and your accomplishments?
- Does the person yell, threaten, or withdraw into angry silence when you displease him or her?
- Do you "walk on eggs," rehearsing what you will say so as not to set the person off?
- Does the person bewilder you by switching from charm to rage without warning?
- Do you often feel confused, off-balance, or inadequate?
- Is the person extremely jealous and possessive?
- Does the person blame you for everything that goes wrong?

If you answered yes to any of these questions, analyze the relationship carefully. If you answered yes to most of the questions, you are in an unhealthy relationship.

Sadly, people often harbor the misguided belief that the other will change, which usually doesn't happen.

Trying to love someone else before you have yourself in tune is as potentially disastrous as beginning a long journey in a poorly equipped, rundown automobile. Positive relationships demand average or better self-esteem and lack of dependency and addiction. Chad's description of a past relationship is an enlightening account of a person's reaction to obsessive love and can serve as a warning to its victims.

> I ended a relationship because she wasn't independent at all. She couldn't make decisions without my advice. She would sit home waiting for me to call while I went out with my friends. She just put her friends out of the picture. Then when I called, she tried to make me feel guilty for having fun without her. She also called me at all hours of the night because she said she just wanted to hear my voice. I wanted to get some sleep! If she hadn't been so obsessive, things might have worked out.

He wrote about his needs in any future relationship; "She must be able to live for herself and not become a person who lives for me. I don't want a person who thinks the world revolves around me." Until obsession and addiction are no longer considered love, people will make tragic mistakes. The challenge is for both women and men to recognize the difference and to resist thoughts and behaviors that spawn these unhealthy relationships.

Love Schemas

What do you expect from a love relationship? A **love schema** is a mental model consisting of expectations and attitudes about love. Six love schemas have been identified by Hatfield & Rapson (1996). See if you can determine which ones represent obstacles to love.

1. *Secure*: comfortable with both closeness and independence
2. *Clingy*: desires a high level of closeness and togetherness
3. *Skittish*: uneasy with closeness; will often run away from intimacy
4. *Fickle*: never satisfied with the present relationship for long
5. *Casual*: enjoys relationships, but doesn't want to be committed
6. *Uninterested*: simply is not interested in any relationship

People formulate ideas about love that usually change over time. Jacob's schema fit the casual category. He enjoyed being with Emily, who, at 25 years of age, wanted to be in a committed relationship. They went their separate ways for 3 years, then resumed dating. This time around Jacob wanted commitment, and within a few years, they were married.

Fear of Risks

Any relationship is risky. Love is even risker. Deep self-disclosure leaves a person vulnerable. Some pain is inevitable, and accepting this reality is healthy. In positive relationships the benefits of loving and being loved will far outweigh the pain. Without risk, individuals reduce their hurts, yet they also decrease potential for happiness. I could decide to stay indoors for the rest of my life because there are risks of getting hurt outside. Wouldn't you question this decision? Resisting a potentially happy relationship because of the possibility of hurt is equally debatable. Instead, you can learn from past hurt, thereby limiting the risks.

Risks of pain are less if you keep self-esteem independent of the relationship. "When our sense of worth—whether we feel lovable or not—depends on the response of some other person to us, we are off balance. We can do nothing but fall" (Kennedy, 1975, p. 94). With self-love, you can separate the end of a relationship from a rejection of self. The idea that you are unlovable because someone no longer wants to continue a love relationship with you is false.

Lack of Knowledge

The assumption that you don't need to know about love, that "it just happens" and then all is well, has pervaded people's thinking. "An individual can get a college degree today without ever having learned anything about how to communicate, how to resolve conflict, and what to do with anger and other negative feelings. Basic, to my mind, is the need for learning to be partners" (Rogers, 1972, p. 216)

Only in recent years have researchers studied love. Difficulty in defining the term was one of the obstacles. There are almost as many definitions of love as people willing to research it (Coleman & Ganong, 1985). When asked to define love, over 60 percent of nearly 400 college students described it strictly in emotional terms. It appears that education about love and intimacy is needed, and if emphasized (which could even mean required training), could provide the necessary understanding of and tools for building satisfying relationships. In the meantime, individuals can seek education on their own and then practice what they learn in developing loving relationships.

RECOGNIZING DIFFERENT TYPES OF LOVE

Love types can be distinguished. Keeping love as simple as possible, we will focus on two general types: passionate love and intimate love. Realize that other researchers and writers may use different words in describing types, such as immature and mature love which are used by Gordon (1996).

Passionate Love

Sensations and unrealistic notions of love are at the heart of **passionate love**. Experts on passionate love describe it as a "hot," intense emotion, sometimes called a crush, infatuation, or being in love; it is an intense longing for union with another (Hatfield & Rapson, 1996). Young people become aware of this type and then define love in terms of sensations: "Love is the feeling of being swept off your feet." "Love is when your heart pounds hard, and you just can't take your eyes off the person." "I love him or her so much I think my heart will burst." "I'm so in love I could just die." Is this love? The individuals sound slightly paralyzed and almost unable to function (Gordon, 1996).

Do you remember the image of love in fairy tales? Love is an overpowering force between an attractive man and woman. He is bold, fearless, and capable of overcoming any obstacle to win her. She is frail and helpless and, of course, extremely beautiful. He rescues her, and together they go forth to live happily ever after. Most of us grow up believing in the magic of "chemistry" between lovers. Love feels exquisite and beyond our control (Cowan & Kinder, 1987).

Although the media do express more realistic versions of love relationships, myths and unrealistic pictures of love are still portrayed. Products even use an image of love to entice consumers. Obsession and other aspects of passionate love are packaged as perfumes and sexy lingerie. Compared to obsession, all other love seems humdrum and mundane, while romanticized versions appear sultry, seductive, and the ultimate in emotionality and sensuality (Forward, 1991).

The Modern "Love" Story

A publishing company sent me guidelines for writing a novel. In order for it to be acceptable, the editor wrote: "The author must create a heartwarming and exciting love story. Get the heroine and hero together, keep them together, make sparks fly, put obstacles in the path of true love, and finally resolve the complications on a high note with a satisfying ending." The guide provided a description of characters as being quite attractive and close to ideal, including a "Mr. Right" who had to be successful in whatever he did. Plenty of sensuous description was to be a part of the novel, and most vital was that sexual attraction to the hero must be recognized early on and should be drawn out to maximum effect. In short, the piece of fiction would be a twentieth-century fairy tale. Incidentally, I chose to write this book instead!

Descriptors of passionate love.   If you were to write an all-consuming romantic novel, what images of love would you present? Hundreds of students have contributed their descriptors of passionate love, or what I call "fluff stuff." Among the most clever ones: "I thought it was going to be an everlasting tingle." "It happens instantly in a flash like a Certs encounter." "Love feels zingy, and you get dingy." The responses are grouped into categories (Table 11–1).

One way to know that these notions are still promoted is to pay attention to music lyrics. Songs from decades ago were full of messages such as "You belong to me" or "Our hearts are on fire." Popular songs today still express an idealized, unrealistic version of love—for example, "I'll do anything for you; I'll even sell my soul for you" and "I'll die without your love." One song even asked: "How do you know if he loves you so?" The answer? "It's in his kiss, that's how you know!" Amazing that you can tell if a man loves you by the way he kisses! And just listen to expressive individuals in the throes of infatuation: "It's a real high." "I feel like I'm on cloud nine."

Dilemmas of passionate love.   So what is the matter with passionate love? The body, in fact, is producing chemicals that contribute to the physical sensations. However, intense sensations aren't enough. Sadly, a song from the past tells us, "Love and marriage go together like a horse and carriage," and individuals with mistaken notions of love do get married in the heat of their passion. "Falling in love is like a space launch, full of flame and fire. Getting married in the fire and flame of the blast-off stage of the relationship is extremely dangerous"

TABLE 11-1   Passionate Love Descriptors

Survival

"I can't live without you."
"I'm nothing without you."
"I just can't get enough of you."
"If you ever leave me, I'll die."

Physical sensations

Walking on air or clouds
Palpitating heart, shortness of breath
Weak knees, dizziness
Can't eat, sleep, think
"I just melt when you look at me."

Perfection

"No one has ever loved like this before."
"It's perfect. You're perfect."
"Nothing will ever go wrong."

Exaggerated promises

"Love conquers all."
"All I need is you."
"I'd do anything for you."
"We'll always be happy (and won't have to even work on it)."
"I'll never look at another man (or woman)."

Exclusivity and possessiveness

"You're the only one for me."
"You're mine."
"You belong to me, and I belong to you."
"I'm jealous and you're jealous, and that means we're in love."
"Just the two of us. Nothing else matters."

(Crowther, 1986, p. 123). Typical dilemmas of passionate love are loving the feeling of being in love more than you do the other person and allowing passions to become destructive.

Mostly love just makes people act silly, but sometimes the afflicted turn violent. Lovers have been known to kill those they love, particularly if the object of their affection is not similarly stricken. If it doesn't work, they either kill themselves or look for another victim. (Chance, 1988, p. 22)

When people are in the throes of passionate love, they are convinced that the wild feelings will last forever. In actuality,

Figure 11-1

they don't. Turbulent emotions become less intense (Hatfield & Rapson, 1996). Passionate love may feel wonderful for awhile, yet is not conducive to long-term happiness. Being responsible and in control of yourself are hallmarks of well-being. In contrast, passionate love often means giving control to the other person. "Ernie always makes me feel terribly alone," wrote a 53-year-old student. "He wants to get married, so he causes me to feel so guilty when I say not now." Love that puts someone else in control has unhappy prospects. "Head over heels is an uncomfortable position for human beings" (Chance, 1988, p. 22).

Lovers become disillusioned when they finally realize that this type of love doesn't last. Those in the throes of passionate love also believe that the other is almost perfect (or at least should be). When reality sets in, these lovers are then disappointed.

> No matter whom we fall in love with, we sooner or later fall out of love if the relationship continues long enough. This is not to say that we invariably cease loving the person . . . but it is to say that the feeling of ecstatic lovingness that characterizes the experience of falling in love always passes. The honeymoon always ends. The bloom of romance always fades. (Peck, 1978, pp. 84–85)

This may sound depressing, yet it doesn't have to be. Most experts believe that the end of the "falling-in-love period" signals the start of a realistic stage when true love can develop. "The most that romance can do is to draw two people together initially, but these feelings tend not to last, and they don't guarantee a satisfying long-term relationship" (Burns, 1985, p. 182). If the psychological attraction isn't there or disappears, the physiological sensations vanish as well. The glue that keeps love intact has a cognitive base.

Do you remember when you bought a new car and the thrill and joy you experienced just looking at it? Later, you still enjoyed the car but in a different way. The newness wore off, so you didn't feel the same "high." The car was familiar, and you felt comfortable and secure with it. Your feelings, including pride, were deep and sure. This experience is similar to the evolution of long-term relationships. The glow is still there; however, it's a different, deeper glow.

Jealousy: A major challenge.   Common to passionate love is **jealousy**, a feeling related to the threat of or actual experience of loss. Usually a blend of fear, anger, hurt, and sadness, jealousy is fueled by irrational thoughts, absolutist "musts," and demands (Ellis, 1996). Hurtful behavior is a typical outcome. More than 33 percent of dating university students said that jealousy was a significant problem in their present relationship (Buss, 2000).

Possessiveness fans the flames of jealousy. "You are mine, and I am yours," a part of passionate-love thinking, usually leads to: "Because you are mine, you will do what I want you to do." This can mean not even looking at another attractive person. Remember the nursery rhyme character "Peter Peter Pumpkin-Eater," who put his wife into a pumpkin shell? In extreme forms of possessiveness, a lover may insist that the other not pursue any outside interests. Violence and abuse are common outcomes of possessiveness.

> Absolute control over another person is neither possible, desirable, nor loving. Instead it destroys what it sets out to protect. (Buscaglia, 1992, p. 142)

Does love mean ownership of your lover? Hopefully, you can answer with no. "A love that inhibits is not love. Love is only love when it liberates" (Buscaglia, 1992, p. 100). Are your expectations unrealistic? It is silly to expect a partner to become blind to others and to react angrily if a "third party" admires one's lover. An affirmative response if your mate finds others attractive is: "I don't mind at all that he or she notices others. In fact, realizing that others are noticed and I am still preferred is a great feeling." What Buscaglia (1984) writes is healthy: "What a grand feeling to have a relationship with someone who is loved not only by you, but by many. That means you've made a good choice" (p. 164).

In addition to damaging a relationship, jealousy has the potential to end it. Joselyn was irrationally jealous of her fiancé, Troy. She couldn't bear his talking to other women, especially when they were apart. Because Troy's job brought him into contact with both sexes, jealousy became a major problem. Joselyn nagged and cried and became suspicious and clinging. Troy felt stifled, and the intensity of their conflicts became unbearable. Eventually, he broke their engagement. "All I did was love you so much!" cried Joselyn, not acknowledging that she had done far more than that. "Love is not expressed by strangulation" (Branden & Branden, 1982, p. 127).

Recognizing the presence of jealousy helps to control it. Some people are chronically jealous. Low self-esteem is usually at fault. Individuals with higher self-esteem and an internal locus of control are generally less jealous and handle it more effectively. Equality is a powerful factor in the prevention of jealousy.

In any relationship, occasional twinges of jealousy can be experienced without damage. These usually occur when, for some reason, the relationship doesn't feel secure or, perhaps, you are suffering from a feeling of insecurity. What can you do? Recognizing the underlying thoughts is helpful because jealousy is related to cognitive appraisals and the meaning attached to an incident. For example, your partner is dancing with an attractive person. Instead of letting jealousy take over, examine your thoughts. If they are: "She or he prefers that person to me" or "This is a threat to our relationship," use rational emotive behavioral therapy to change these irrational thoughts.

If jealousy is based on rational thoughts, it isn't recommended that you suppress the feeling; however, avoid behaviors such as pouting, nagging, threatening, and clinging. Although most people don't like to feel jealous, denying it can cause damage. Much like stress, whether or not you acknowledge its presence, jealousy can wreak havoc on you and the relationship. Instead, using the dimensions of awareness described in Chapter 8 can help the other person understand your perspective. If the relationship is healthy, your partner will understand and help eliminate the reasons for the jealousy. Usually, jealousy lessens as two people become more mature in their relationship. Creating the kind of relationship in which jealousy will have a low survival rate is well worth the effort.

> Everyone who cares and loves feels jealous at one time or another. The essential decision is whether you will allow your jealousy to become an all-consuming monster, capable of destroying you and those you love, or become a challenge for you to grow in self-respect and personal knowledge. (Buscaglia, 1984, p. 129)

Intimate Love

Unlike the "fluff stuff" of passionate love, **intimate love** is a deep, total experience composed of positive thoughts, feelings, and behaviors. Such love is the foundation of a long-term, mutually satisfying relationship. "Love is a process, not just a feeling, of discovery, of development, of growing together" (Solomon, 1988, p. 82). Saying "I love you" and experiencing the sensations are meaningless without actions. Love encompasses attitudes and behaviors such as responsibility, respect, knowledge, giving, and caring. "Love is an activity, not a 'passive affect'; it is a 'standing in,' not a 'falling for.' Love is the active concern for the life and the growth of that which we love" (Fromm, 1956, pp. 22, 26). True love doesn't just happen; two people make it happen.

TA Revisited

"Child" feels passion and love and encourages playful behaviors and spontaneous delight.

"Parent" gives out both positive and negative messages about love and loving relationships.

"Adult" encourages the positive feelings, rejects unwise "parent" messages, considers all factors related to a satisfying love relationship, and makes decisions.

A song from years ago is "Love Is a Many-Splendored Thing." While love may not always be full of splendor, it is a "many-faceted thing," meaning that there are a variety of components and factors that make up intimate love. Let's examine what these are.

Rubin's components of love. Believing that social psychologists had neglected the study of love, (Rubin 1970) developed a scale to measure liking and loving. The scale featured three components of love: attachment, caring, and intimacy (Rubin, 1973).

Attachment has to do with the desire for the physical presence and emotional support of the other person as well as a preference for each other's company. In contrast to the stifling togetherness of passionate love, healthy attachment means enjoyment and involvement in mutually rewarding activities. Enjoying being with each other bonds a couple. Connie, after her divorce, insightfully commented: "A clue I didn't recognize was that Dan and I didn't enjoy activities apart from others. We always double-dated, and after we were married, our social life included other couples. The two of us didn't have fun just being together."

In a marriage-preparation class, a lack of attachment was apparent. A young woman enrolled in the class alone even though she was engaged. Her fiancé bowled on the nights of class. After a discussion of Rubin's components, she said, "I wonder about that. He isn't here tonight because of bowling. Last night was Monday night football, on Wednesday nights he shoots pool, and Thursday and Saturday nights he goes out with his friends. We're together on Friday nights and usually on Sunday when he isn't at a drag race." After I expressed my concern, she remarked, "Well, that's one reason I want to get married. Either he'll change, or at least I'll have more leverage to nag him about it." My expression, I'm sure, was of doubt. I encouraged her to talk with her fiancé. I never knew if she did because she didn't come to class again. Hopefully, she had decided to wait; however, she probably just didn't want to hear reasons to be concerned. Not facing potential problems is another facet of passionate love.

The second component, **caring**, consists of feelings of concern and responsibility for another's welfare, Tenderness, which includes awareness of the other's needs and desires (May, 1969), is related to caring, as is empathy. You will share stressors and experience anxiety and act in extra-thoughtful ways because you love. Often mistaken for caring, while in fact, just the opposite is irrational possessiveness. Consider these examples:

> Jenni was excited when her friend asked her to come to work in a new business. She could finally pursue a career that she had given up 4 years ago. Eric, her husband, said, "You aren't going to work. The kids and I need you at home."

> Raoul received word that his scholarship request had been approved. Although it would mean sacrificing, this was his chance to complete his degree. Amy, his fiancé, protested, "I won't see you much if you have to study and work. And you won't earn as much, so we won't be able to get married as soon."

How caring were Eric and Amy? For whom did they care? Genuine concern means that you consider another's welfare. Blocking personal growth is uncaring behavior. Warm, caring behavior is unconditional positive regard, not the "I'll love you if . . . " ingredient of passionate love.

Intimacy, the third component, is a desire for confidential, close communication. Rubin's concept of intimacy reflects sharing and disclosing on all levels. A love relationship resembles a deep friendship. The term "emotionally divorced" is often used to describe relationships that lack intimacy. Vulnerability is necessary for intimacy, and individuals often fear the risk. Teresa Adams, therapist and author, says, "The crowd thins when it comes to intimacy." This component deserves extra attention and is discussed in a later section.

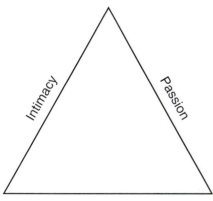

Figure 11-2

Sternberg's love triangle. Picture a triangle with three equal sides of balanced love. Based on his research, Sternberg (1987) identified ingredients of love: intimacy, passion, and commitment.

Similar to Rubin's component with some additions is **intimacy** that includes closeness, sharing, communication, and support. Intimacy is akin to deep friendship. **Passion** is physiological arousal and an intense desire to be united with the loved one. According to Sternberg (1986), the needs for sex and affiliation give rise to passion. For most people, passion is what distinguishes liking from loving. The glue that holds a relationship together is **commitment** that is expressed in dedication to the relationship and faithfulness to each other.

A deeper aspect of Sternberg's theory is that one, two, or all three of the components can be present. A relationship that just has commitment, called empty love, is composed of two people who have been together for a long time with nothing special about the relationship except its longevity. Intimacy by itself is friendship, and passion is physical attraction.

Consummate love consists of all three components. Two people have a strong attraction and sexual desire for each other; they are close, communicative, and supportive; and because of a strong mutual commitment, the relationship is of high priority. Considering these ingredients, do you recognize any of your relationships? Researchers asked heterosexual couples how they experienced intimacy, passion, and commitment. They found overlap in how the three were demonstrated and concluded that even though these components are extremely relevant, love encompasses even more (Marston, Hecht, Manke, McDaniel, & Reeder, 1998).

Ingredients of love.   Using a model of a three-legged stool, Carlton Paine, Ph.D., a clinical psychologist, considers three ingredients to be necessary in a viable, ongoing, intimate relationship. In an interview, he stated that **trust**, which means honesty and dependability, is absolutely essential. He said, "A common way people undermine their relationship is by lying. Not knowing whether or what to believe or whether you can depend on the other is devastating." Having a fondness for each other is **affection**, the second ingredient. This can include passion and emotional comfortableness and, as such, draws a couple together. Completing the foundation is **respect**, an admiration and high regard for another. Paine recognizes that deeply satisfying relationships typically offer more; yet, as he works with couples, he believes that these are fundamental and must be reciprocal.

Examine any love relationship in terms of the various elements that have been identified. If some dimensions you want are missing, express this to your partner. The more open you can be about love, the greater the possibility of achieving a satisfying relationship. Even with all the components present, love can be strengthened by paying attention to other factors.

Relationship growth and fulfillment of needs.   Healthy individuals grow in a positive direction. So do healthy relationships. Individual and relationship growth are associated. If individual growth is stunted, so is the relationship. In order for growth to be positive, individuals have to be free to achieve their potential. Putting one partner into a "pumpkin shell," as described in the nursery rhyme, stifles the relationship. When individuals are committed to their own and each other's positive growth, wonderful things can happen. Each person experiences satisfaction in life, and the relationship is vitalized. Conversely, a person who is deprived of growth has little, or nothing, to offer the relationship except frustration.

> Woe be it unto you if you give yourself totally to another. You're lost forever. Maintain yourself as the others maintain themselves. Then you put "They" together and form "Us." Then work on that "Us," and that "Us" gets bigger and bigger while the "You" and the "I" get bigger and bigger and form these enormous concentric circles that grow forever! And if, by chance, you lose that special "Us"—you still have an "I" and loving memories to build with. (Buscaglia, 1982, p. 162)

Intimate love maintains a balance between partners.

A possible area of concern is the course of individual growth. Individuals can grow, contribute to the relationship, and become closer to each other. Or they can grow apart. A reason why teenage marriages fail at higher rates could be the tremendous surge of individual growth that takes place between adolescence and the late twenties or thirties. Couples who do not experience harmonious growth eventually find themselves worlds apart. Being mindful that change will occur and taking care to direct the course of growth are critical. Love flourishes in an environment of positive growth. When you choose to commit to a relationship, be sure she or he is one with whom you can *live* and *grow*.

Based on social exchange theory, which was covered in Chapter 9, love can be examined in terms of **fulfillment of needs**. A major function of any relationship is to satisfy individual needs. In fact, a predictor of happiness is the degree of difference between what you want and what you think you are getting from a relationship (Sternberg & Whitney, 1991). One relationship cannot fulfill all your needs. However, a love relationship, especially a long-term one, is primary and must satisfy a number of important ones. If you know yourself well, then you know what you need from a relationship.

What Are Your Needs From a Love Relationship?

- Companionship
- Stimulation and excitement
- Affirmation and caring
- Passion and sexual fulfillment
- Emotional support
- Self-awareness and discovery
- Communication and deep self-disclosure
- Demonstrated affection
- Equality
- Loyalty and fidelity
- Tenderness
- Fun and enjoyment
- Trust and honesty
- Commitment
- Intimacy

A specific one identified by a single parent was the need to have a relationship in which the partner would also be a caring stepparent for her children.

After identifying your needs, you are ready for the next step. Deborah has needs for deep communication, demonstrated affection, and honesty. Can you see what would likely happen if Deborah feels a strong attraction for Kurt, who is honest, extremely quiet, and emotionally inexpressive? People who know him describe him as somewhat reclusive and cold. Strange as it may seem, people often fall in love with those who would have difficulty satisfying important needs. "Silent Sam or Sally" won't likely turn into a great communicator overnight. "Boring Bill or Billie" isn't apt to be much fun, and people who are "cold fish" won't find it easy to be affectionate. Some find out in time, as Andrea did: "He showed little caring and didn't share with me. I did 95 percent of the caring. He was jealous and showed it in strange ways. I have learned in this class that I'm glad I got out of it and that there is still hope for me."

Fulfillment of needs requires that you match your needs with a partner who can satisfy them because it is that person who gives to the relationship what you need (see Fig. 11–3). "It's almost like writing a job description," I explained to a class one day. The true "romantics" cringed. I hastened to add that relationships have a better chance of remaining romantic if individuals aren't frustrated by un-fulfilled needs. The needs fulfillment activity at the end of this book can be used for mate selection, premarital assessment, and enrichment of relationships. The key is to communicate personal needs to each other, keeping in mind that the two lists probably won't be exactly the same.

When needs aren't satisfied, what happens? Ideally, one's dissatisfaction is communicated to a partner, and he or she is willing to change. Such was the case with Rosa and Bill. After 33 years of marriage, Rosa said that she would not re-main in the marriage unless her needs for respect and intimacy were met. "Rock-ing the boat" as much as she did definitely made enough waves to open Bill's eyes. He agreed to marital counseling, which guided them into a mutually satisfy-ing relationship. Their story had a happy ending, but what if no changes are made? A sad possibility is that people will just "settle" and try to be content within relationships that aren't nourishing. Unfortunately, this "settling" is quite common and is one cause of what are called empty-shell marriages. Far too many have a dull-but-tolerable coexistence: a kind of death-in-life (Barbach & Geisinger, 1991). The value of a relationship lies in the joy it offers, not in its longevity (Branden & Branden, 1982). Another possibility is infidelity. Many affairs can be traced to an important need not being met in the marriage. A recent challenge, ac-cording to marriage and family therapist Sue Frahm, is an online affair between two people who meet via the Internet. Unmet needs are probably partially respon-sible, and a person owes it to a partner to communicate what is lacking. Finally, when needs aren't being met, another likelihood is to end the relationship. Most endings to relationships reflect unfulfilled needs.

How do you know that a person can or will satisfy you? Even though no guarantee is possible, you can significantly increase your chances by doing the following:

- Use the activity in Reflections and Applications to identify what you want, trying to prioritize as much as possible. What is essential? Be sure that your needs are reasonable. What, if missing, would cause you to be unhappy and possibly end the relationship? Try to specifically describe abstract words such as "honesty." For example, to just say that you want "trust" isn't explaining well. Two partners may have different meanings for the word, and if you aren't sure what trust means, you won't know if it's present or not.

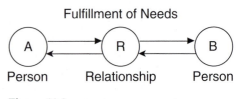

Fulfillment of Needs

A
Person

R
Relationship

B
Person

Figure 11-3

- Communicate your needs to your partner. Describe desired *behaviors*.
- Observe the person you love in the company of others. If you need demonstrated affection, is he or she warm around other people? Affection is difficult to assess, especially in the early stages of a relationship. Even "cold fish" will show passion based on sexual desires. If you're looking for everyday types of affection, the person's behavior with others is a clue. Take note of how your partner's biological family behaves. For example, my husband is a hugger, typical of his entire family. Watching him hug them and others assured me that this was his genuine behavior.
- Be willing to do what is necessary to satisfy the other person's legitimate needs. This may mean behavior changes on your part.
- Don't assume that the other will change after marriage or just because time passes. Behavioral change is possible, yet requires self-motivation. You can only suggest and encourage. The only one you can be assured of changing is yourself. However, a change in one person does alter the relationship.

Two people may not have the same needs, and being compatible in this regard is preferable. For example, if Nicole wants a high degree of togetherness and Kelly prefers personal space, they will have difficulty satisfying each other. This is one reason that similarities are an important attraction factor. In most cases, your needs won't be 100 percent identical; however, equality is of concern. Exchange theory indicates that relationships are more satisfying and stable when outcomes for each partner are more or less equal and when benefits far outweigh costs.

If you find that your needs are unfulfilled and changes in a partner aren't likely, you are hurting yourself, and probably the other person as well, by remaining. Fortunately, unhappy situations can have happy endings. A former student wrote:

> When I thought about needs fulfillment, I talked to my fiancé about our relationship. It was obvious that my needs weren't being satisfied, and he really didn't seem to care enough to change. I gave back the ring and went through a depressing period. Then I met Matt, and the two relationships are like night and day. We really clicked and are getting married next month. How sad it would have been if I had remained in that earlier relationship.

Behaviors of love.   The actions of lovers deserve attention. "Joe loves me. I know because he beats up on anyone who looks at me." Is this love or is it an uncontrollable temper fired by irrational possessiveness? "She loves me because she'll do everything I want." This sounds more like servitude than love. A much more affirming behavior is affection which couples identified as the most important type of interaction in their relationships (Dainton, 1998)

Be aware of how you are treated by a lover. Is it affectionate and loving behavior? In any love relationship, individuals will occasionally demonstrate some less than loving actions. If hurtful behaviors are frequent or occur for poor reasons, and the aggressor feels no remorse and does not act to rectify the situation, you are not being loved. Ask yourself, "Do I feel loved?" If you can honestly answer in the affirmative most of the time, then the relationship is probably positive. "Do I feel affirmed?" is another essential question. Intimate love enhances self-esteem. Be sure to sprinkle love with fun. "Love without laugher is like a car without shocks, jarred by each dip in the road" (Borcherdt, 1996, p. 2). Focusing on all behaviors is a good way to assess the quality of the relationship.

Love is complicated and mysterious, as anyone who has loved knows. Being able to differentiate between passionate and intimate love is a first step in understanding. Taking a close look at intimate love, its components, its potential for contributing to relationship growth and fulfillment of needs, and its behaviors reduces the possibility of mistakes and pain. After you have examined love, you may still wonder whether what you feel is love. In a frank way, Branden & Branden (1982) state: "We suspect that people who ask this question are not in love. In our observation and experience, love reaches a critical point where it tends to generate a clarity of its own" (p. 24).

BUILDING INTIMACY

"The 2:00 a.m. knowledge that you are not alone" is the litmus test of intimacy, according to author and therapist Teresa Adams (1987, p. 95). Both Rubin's and Sternberg's love theories identify intimacy as necessary. What exactly is intimacy, and how do two people create it?

What Is Intimacy?

Intimacy is the pulse of the closest relationships. Intimacy is positively related to individual need fulfillment (Prager & Buhrmester, 1998). Definitions of intimacy, like those of abstract words, vary. To many, intimacy is equated with sexuality. When you consider that retail stores have "intimate departments," which sell lingerie and negligees, it is little wonder that the mind focuses on bedroom scenes. The sexual relationship is only one facet of intimate love. "The most literal meaning of 'intimate' is to really know another" (Rubin, 1973, p. 160). This is an important aspect within intimacy, yet more is involved. Intimacy frees and encourages you to be your own true self and to be accepted and loved because of who you are.

Intimacy has several key elements (Sternberg, 1987).

1. Promoting each other's welfare
2. Experiencing happiness with each other
3. Holding each other in high regard
4. Being able to count on each other in times of need
5. Having mutual understanding
6. Sharing of self and possessions with each other
7. Receiving emotional support from the other
8. Giving emotional support to the other
9. Communicating intimately with each other
10. Valuing each other

Check your own love relationship to see how many of the 10 elements are present.

Development of Intimacy

Building intimacy requires dedication and effort. First, individuals have to be willing to rid themselves of personal postures that prohibit intimacy (Malone & Malone, 1987). Check the list of "Intimacy Blockers." If you see yourself, realize that you have work to do before intimacy is possible.

Intimacy Blockers

- Withdrawal or isolating the self emotionally; possibly becoming overly involved with interests outside the relationship.
- Personal rigidity leading to an unwillingness to allow differences or to compromise.
- Overt self-righteousness and placing the need to be right higher than love.
- Lack of trustworthiness.

The last of the intimacy blockers is of utmost importance. Trust including predictability, dependability, faithfulness, loyalty, and honesty is essential. The essence of trust is emotional safety. "Trust enables you to put your deepest feelings and fears in the palm of your partner's hand, knowing they will be handled with care" (Avery, 1989, p. 27).

In addition to personal characteristics that prevent intimacy is a fear. A study of gay men and lesbians revealed that fear of intimacy, as in heterosexuals, was related to feeling uncomfortable with emotional closeness, low levels of self-disclosure, and relationships dissatisfaction (Greenfield & Thelen, 1997). "We can only be intimate to the degree that we are willing to be open and vulnerable (Ornish, 1998, p. 39).

An obvious deterrent to the development of intimacy is finding a partner to whom one is attracted and who encourages a long-term relationship. This seemed easier years ago when so much attention wasn't being paid to relationship-building. "Dating is easy to do, but finding that 'special someone' seems impossible," lamented a young adult. Where does one look? Two obvious locations are where one attends school and at a place of employment. Other possibilities and recommendations follow.

- Get involved with organizations, professional associations, and volunteer activities. If you have values and beliefs that attract you to certain causes, you will probably find people you can admire.
- Become more active. Join a health club and go to movies, plays, and museums. Spend time doing what you enjoy; you will then find others who like what you do.
- Let others know that you desire a serious relationship. Many people find a significant other through networking.
- Try classified ads or a reputable service that brings people together. A study of college students found that over 60 percent were successful in establishing an online friendship. Interestingly, friendship, not romance or sex, was the primary reason for seeking someone (Knox, Daniels, Sturdivant, & Zusman, 2001).

Regardless of how you proceed to meet someone, remain open to possibility and definitely review features of positive relationships in Chapter 9.

Intimacy can be difficult because of power struggles. Power can be distributed unequally, with either the man or the woman having more control, or power can seesaw back and forth in a continuous struggle. The healthiest type of structure is shared power based on perceived equality. Equal attention and seriousness is extended to the emotions, needs, desires, and roles of both. When equality goes out of a relationship, love follows (Solomon, 1988).

A serious obstacle is stereotypic masculine behavior which destroys potential intimacy. Furthermore, intimacy requires expression of emotions and self-disclosure on all levels. The classic male image denies these behaviors and sets up roadblocks to intimacy (Crose, 1997). The willingness to feel vulnerable—to open your heart—which is difficult for a stereotypic man, is essential to intimacy (Ornish, 1998). Even though many men are changing as they learn the value of intimacy, those who continue in a stereotypic masculine role will face extreme hardships.

Intimacy for all couples is endangered by boredom and the tendency to take each other for granted. Intimacy demands quality interacting time. If, because of relationship longevity or familiarity or both, couples choose to engage in other activities or they simply ignore their relationship, intimacy can be canceled for lack of interest. "To have a long-lasting relationship, we must avoid complacency. More love has been lost on the island of contentment than in any sea of torment" (Buscaglia, 1992, p. 166).

What helps the development of intimacy?

- Androgynous personalities
- Expression of genuine emotions, even unpleasant ones
- During a seminar, Teresa Adams noted that "frozen anger blocks intimacy; thawed anger enhances intimacy."
- Empathic and nurturing behaviors
- Paying attention to each other
- Mutually enjoyable activities
- Communication especially deep self-disclosure
- Commitment

Listed last, commitment is one of the most important aids to intimacy. Feelings of security and stability within a relationship create an oasis for vulnerability that, in turn, allows two people to know each other deeply. Although most research has been conducted on white heterosexual couples, commitment and intimacy are not limited by race or sexual orientation. In a study of African-American lesbians and gay males, intimacy was a significant factor in relationship satisfaction. A majority of the men and women indicated that they loved their partners and had satisfying relationships. As a salute to commitment, they strongly believed that intimacy would continue (Peplau, Cochran, & Mays, 1997).

Building intimacy is one of the most difficult and challenging tasks within a relationship. The excellent chapter "Pathways to Love and Intimacy" in the book *Love and Survival* (Ornish, 1998) provides insight and guidance. The rewards are significant. If a relationship doesn't have intimacy, the partners may not realize what they are missing. If two human beings are truly intimate, their potential for joy is infinite.

> *Intimacy demands the highest risk but yields the richest reward. Intimacy is the driving force which makes the painful grit of life worthwhile. Intimacy is the life-giving beam of light, whereby we discover each other from the inside out, never quite fully, never entirely, but enough to find an exquisite inner oasis that replenishes us on our life's journey.*
> —Teresa Adams

MANAGING CONFLICT

In order to preserve intimacy, couples have to manage conflict successfully. A "just-kiss-and-make-up" philosophy may carry people through the courtship stage, and they probably won't realize the negative impacts of their behavior until later. Years ago, conflict management was not a consideration. The widely held belief was that loving couples did not fight. A disagreement was a sign of weakness in the relationship, so you hurried to patch things up. Important conflict issues were often glossed over for fear that they would spell the end of the relationship. When couples did disagree, they usually did so in an unpleasant, aggressive manner. Then making up was a relief. The crux of the problem was often left untouched.

The Experts and Conflict

Love rarely remains all flowers and sweetness. Disagreements, arguments, and fighting are natural when two people are trying to come together. More important than what you fight about is how you fight (Wegscheider-Cruse, 1988).
The health of a relationship is determined not so much on whether there are conflicts, but whether they are addressed and resolved. Conflict can serve useful purposes (Crowther, 1986).
A fair fight can clear the air and relieve stress. Don't be afraid to fight with ones you love. If you didn't care about each other, you wouldn't bother to fight (Tubesing, 1981).

One of the first and best-known books on the subject of conflict management is *The Intimate Enemy: How to Fight Fair in Love and Marriage* (Bach & Wyden, 1968). My copy is well worn, and I recommend the book as required reading. The premise is that **verbal conflict**, defined as disagreement, between intimates is not only inevitable and acceptable but can be constructive and desirable and the authors provide insight into how to fight. You may inwardly shudder at the word fight. Thinking of **fighting** as a way of handling disagreement may make it more acceptable

Unfair Fighting Styles

Two opposite types of **fighting styles** are identified as unfair. Fight evaders, nonfighters, are "doves." For any number of reasons, these people are fight-phobic and resist fighting. "Gunnysacking," described in Chapter 9, is a common behavior. Two "doves" don't level with each other and often pay the price of emotional divorce. Most would not recognize this as a type of fighting; however, remember that fighting is defined as a way of handling conflict. The opposite are "hawks," or aggressive fighters. They are usually loud, observably angry, and hostile. They use unfair, hurtful tactics and damage their relationship.

Both types experience anger, which is inevitable within an intimate relationship. So when partners don't fight, their anger isn't being expressed and they aren't experiencing true intimacy. Anger is a signal worth listening to. If a person asks, "What am I angry about, what is the problem, and whose problem is it?" anger is potentially constructive. Learning how to fight fairly is essential because the "inability to manage personal conflicts is at the root of the crisis that threatens the structure of the American family" (Bach & Wyden, 1968, p. 31). A key point is that how conflict is resolved is what determines the health of the relationship.

Fair Fighting

What is recommended in conflict resolution between intimates? **Fair fighting** is a process of resolving conflict without hurting each other or the relationship. What is involved? Most experts suggest that, if possible, couples carefully choose the best time, place, and conditions for resolving conflict. Too often, individuals fight when they are tired, under inordinate stress, or after drinking alcohol. Inevitably, these conditions set the stage for unfair fighting. The old adage "Don't let the sun set on a quarrel" which means "Don't go to bed angry" is not wise advice. When tired, couples can create added problems, or, as often happens, one person "gives up" in order to get some rest. The concept of "giving up" and "giving in" places fighting on the level of a wrestling match. Usually, the one who concedes, or "gives in," is left with resentment. Fair fighters can call a time-out, a halt in their discussion, and resume under more positive conditions. Here are a few other criteria by which to determine the extent of fairness.

Winning-losing: If either person "wins," the relationship loses. Getting rid of the win-loss notion is important. The key to win-win is to recognize and satisfy as best as possible each person's highest priorities or most important needs. The health of a relationship takes priority over winning.

Involvement: Have you ever been engaged in a fight that was a monologue? Too often, one person does most, if not all, the talking, and the other simply absorbs or ignores. A behavior that is more often engaged in by men has been described in research as a danger sign (Gottman, 1994b). **Stonewalling** is removing oneself from an interaction and employing a stony silence that conveys disapproval, icy distance, and snugness. As frustrating as it can be, silence equates to power. The amount of information exchanged is decreased with tactics such as the silent treatment and "I-don't-want-to-discuss-it" approaches. In a fair fight the two individuals both talk and listen.

Communication: The use of "I," not "you," statements; active, receptive listening; open, honest, and clear messages from both partners; and no game playing or manipulative techniques are essential.

Injury: Being careful to direct criticism to behaviors, to avoid personal attacks and name calling, and to maintain consideration for the other is necessary. Unfair fighters attack the other in areas of vulnerability.

Directness: Remaining focused in the present and on the subject at hand is difficult to do, yet necessary. If a new topic is presented, the issue can get sidetracked. Agreeing to handle the new topic later is recommended.

Specificity: Clarity and description of behaviors are needed. The use of perception checking and dimensions of awareness help to clarify. Be sure that you aren't arguing simply because of unshared meanings.

Feelings: Frequently, when partners know each other's feelings, they experience empathy and understanding. Be willing to share all emotions.

Responsibility: Both people take a share of the responsibility for the conflict itself and for the process required to resolve it. "It's your fault," "No, it's your fault," will get you nowhere. Conflict is a two-way street.

Humor: As strange as it may seem, if positive humor creeps into a fight, the mood will probably lighten. Obviously, any use of sarcasm or nasty humor would only hurt. Research supports the benefit of a woman's use of humor to soothe a partner (Gottman, Coan, Carrere, & Swanson, 1998).

Figure 11-4   Fair fighting demands the finest communication skills

Another major contribution to conflict management was made by Aaron Beck (1988), a leader in the field of cognitive therapy, with his book *Love Is Never Enough*. Regularly scheduled discussions, what he calls "troubleshooting sessions," give individuals a chance to empty their "gunnysacks." This decreases reasons for nagging. Susan Borkin, a therapist, recommends a 20-minute period for cooling off and digesting the message after one person has expressed anger and displeasure. "Agreement is easier after feelings are vented and allowed to dissipate," she says. Whenever you aren't able to manage anger, you are better off calling for a time-out and refusing to continue the fight. An excellent idea is to tape-record or videotape a fight so each person can see what he or she did to escalate the conflict and how to improve. Learn to assess an unfair fight by reading a description of one in Reflections and Applications.

In addition to paying attention to how partners fight, examine the effects or outcome. Has either partner's self-esteem been diminished? If so, the fight wasn't fair. Do you feel closer, as caring, more intimate? Has the relationship been strengthened or weakened? John Gottman (1994a), a well-known researcher in the field of conflict management, contributes an essential point: No matter how couples fight, they must have at least five times as many positive as negative moments together if their relationship is to be stable.

> Fair fighting is not a sport like boxing. It is an art and a skill like dancing. It takes cooperation and style. In fact, the style of a fight is more important than what you actually fight about. Several days after a fight, you may remember only about 10 percent of the content, but you will probably have almost total recall for the style: whether the fight was fair, how hurt you felt, how strong the emotions were, how satisfied or upset you felt afterward (McKay, Davis, & Fanning, 1983, p. 136)

Fair fighting leads partners along the path of increased closeness and intimacy. Conflict can be viewed as an opportunity to learn about self and your partner. "If you never disagree—never have a conflict of opinion—how can you ever really get to know one another?" was an insightful question by James Parkes, a man from Manchester, England, whom I met in Edinburgh, Scotland, in 1996. At that time, he and his wife, Betty, had been happily married for over 60 years!

Despite the best intentions, lovers do lose control at times and angrily erupt. The value of knowing how to manage conflict positively is that you know and can admit when unfair tactics were used. Apologizing and committing to try harder the next time are signs of maturity. When people refuse to attempt positive change, it may be better to end the relationship. Openness and flexibility are key ingredients in positive conflict management.

ENRICHING A RELATIONSHIP

Pretend you have planted a garden of vegetables and flowers. You pay little attention to the garden. You never fertilize, rarely water, and you don't weed. What will happen? The garden will have little chance of thriving, and even its survival is in jeopardy. Couples who don't take care of their relationship face the same risks. Compare your relationship to a highway that needs to be upgraded, maintained, and even rebuilt; the process is never finished (Sternberg & Whitney, 1991).

Why don't couples enrich their relationships? The primary reasons are simple unawareness and neglect. An assumption in the past was that if you didn't fight much and life was progressing smoothly, your relationship was in good shape. That is not necessarily true.

> Relationships do not typically unravel because of major conflicts. Most relationships die slowly and without the conscious awareness of either party. There is a fine line between a relationship that moves in a positive direction and one that slips silently into apathy or the slow accumulation of disappointments and resentment. (Cowan & Kinder, 1987, p. 5)

Couples have a tendency to "settle." Rather than engage in pleasurable activities such as eating out, attending a movie, dancing, and going on picnics as they once did, a couple will often "settle down" in front of the television or computer night after night. Even the sexual relationship can become predictable. "Sameness" becomes a barrier to enrichment.

Another enrichment obstacle is the destructive habit of criticism. When two people are together often, they seem to find more reasons to criticize.

Why Criticize?
We love others because of what they are—then expect, even demand from them what they are not. (Resz, 1984)

Instead of appreciating the differences they were attracted to in the first place, most partners set out to change each other. (Kinder & Cowen. 1989)

Figure 11-5

Take a Criticism Quiz—True or False?

- Criticizing is a way of helping another improve, so by delivering critical comments, a person is showing love.
- Love can withstand the onslaught of negativism, so criticism won't hurt.
- Criticism is humorous.

All are inaccurate assumptions and false. How well did you do?

Remember that:

- Criticism, at least the way most people deliver it, is not a sign of love.
- Criticism does hurt, and it takes a toll on love.
- Criticism is not funny. Using sarcasm or ridicule to make a critical point is harmful.

Criticism invariably leads to contempt, and the relationship is in jeopardy (Gottman, 1994b). Sadly, lovers often treat each other less kindly than they do friends. In the most loving relationships, there is a minimum amount of criticism.

Picture an intimate love relationship as a large rock. No matter how solid the rock (or the relationship), erosion can take place, and the mass is weakened by a wearing-away process. Resentment from a full "gunnysack" can erode the rock. Criticism, always "being right," and aggressive, hurtful actions chip away at even the most durable rock or relationship.

If neglect has already led to apathy and boredom, or if chronic criticism and hurtfulness have taken their toll, a couple can revitalize the relationship. Couples benefit from deciding that enrichment has a high priority and then committing themselves to achieving it. Improvement in the vital areas of communication and conflict management is enriching Importantly, use any of the following suggestions on a regular basis.

- Set aside a special time to communicate each day if possible. Ideally, you focus on positives, and not use it as a "dumping ground" for negatives. Be sure to self-disclose.
- During this communication time, each can make a list of the other's pleasing behaviors and express appreciation for those.
- Verbally and nonverbally express an interest in each other.
- Give positive strokes on a regular basis. Compliment each other.
- Demonstrate affection by physical contact, words, and deeds. Hug and kiss often, yet don't necessarily do it as a routine. "We kiss each other good-bye" is nice, but don't allow this to replace unpredictable moments.
- Be considerate. Say good-bye when you leave and hello when you come together again. Let each other know where you are and be dependable. Empathize with each other.
- Tell each other "thank you" each day, either for a particular behavior or just to express appreciation for each other and for the relationship.
- Surprise each other with little notes, cards, gifts, and unusual plans. Spontaneity brings delight into a relationship.

- Affirm each other privately and in front of others. Hearing a partner deliver praise about you in the presence of others is like a ray of sunshine on a cloudy day.
- Develop rituals and traditions. Celebrate special days and make everyday events more pleasurable. Provide "pleasers" for each other such as back rubs or a special home-cooked dish.
- Spend time together away from everyday hassles. In spite of best intentions, you may find it difficult to forget the nitty-gritty of daily life. Going away for a weekend or even overnight can be a refreshing and relaxing experience. Even going out for an evening gets you away from the demands of the immediate environment.
- Increase the number and frequency of pleasurable events. Find mutually enjoyable activities and engage in them on a regular basis.
- Express all genuine emotions, the pleasant and unpleasant ones. Sharing true feelings is an enriching experience.
- Laugh with each other at least once a day (more than once is better).
- Talk about your early relationship and what attracted you to each other in the first place. Share other positive memories. Couples who revel in their mutual past are likely to find pleasure in the present.
- Share your hopes and dreams. "Dreams elevate us beyond the mundane. To dream together adds an element of wonder to our relationship and gives us something to look forward to" (Buscaglia, 1984, p. 186).
- Share enrichment ideas with each other. Even if some don't seem feasible, the sharing is enriching.
- Give each other massages and use other types of loving nonsexual touch.

Enrichment vitalizes relationships. A song from the past, "Little Things Mean a Lot," delivers an important message. In our kitchen is a mug inscribed "I love you." Invariably, when my husband brings me coffee or tea, it comes in that mug—a "little thing" whose meaning is far from small.

You and your partner can help each other develop loving behaviors. If you want demonstrated affection, say so. Don't be like Ann, who said, "I know Dave loves me, but he just can't show it." Yes, he can! Learning new behaviors may be necessary. Knowing that hugging and other forms of touching are healthy for individuals and that they also benefit the relationship is motivating. A loving behavior may be to seek counseling. The process of enrichment may uncover areas where professional help could be beneficial. Two intimates are often so close to their situation that they are blinded to underlying problems.

SEEKING SEXUAL FULFILLMENT

"Oh, great, this book has some dirty stuff in it" was the comment of a young student as he looked through a section on human sexuality in his psychology textbook. The equation of sex to dirtiness still exists. Accompanying it are other attitudes that can interfere with sexual fulfillment. Many people seemingly have difficulty conversing about sex without resorting to euphemisms such as "doing it," "humping," "screwing," "getting the groove on," and "getting laid." Discussions about sexuality are frequently filled with jokes (described as "dirty"), innuendos, and insinuating remarks. "There's something wrong with a country that says, 'Sex is dirty, save it for someone you love,'" wrote sex educator and author Sol Gordon (Gibbs, 1993, p. 62). It's ironic that even though most people think that violence is bad and sex is good, parents often do not insist that a child turn off a violent television program. Yet, if that same child were watching sex on Saturday morning, most parents would label it gross or immoral and write a letter in protest (Farrell, 1986). The fact that individuals do succeed in their sexual relationships amid such a negative environment is amazing.

Sexuality is a part of being human, and lovemaking has special meaning within an intimate love relationship. Finding ways to enhance one's own sexuality and to maintain a fulfilling relationship is vital. Because most of our sexual behaviors are learned, possibilities abound. This section will not offer a quick "how-to" course. Fortunately, in today's society, anyone who wants to learn about the sexual act can do so. Excellent books on being sensual, handling sexual dysfunctions, and enriching a sexual relationship, as well as sex therapy, are available. Within this limited space, the importance of one's sex life will be emphasized, and general guidelines will be offered.

Sexual Behaviors

If you don't realize that sexual relations are occurring at an all-time high, you haven't been paying attention. In today's world, the term "premarital sex" isn't even accurate. Why? Individuals who engage in sexual activities may have no intention of marrying, and others who are divorced, widowed or homosexual are certainly not engaging in *pre*marital sex! A Gallup poll found that only 38 percent of U.S. adults think having sexual relations outside of marriage is wrong (Saad, 2001). This lack of diapproval undoubtedly makes nonmarital sex the norm. In a study of college students, 83 percent reported having sexual intercourse (Kelley, Synovitz, Carlson & Schuster, 2001).

Who's Sexually Active?

College students: 78 percent had experienced a casual sexual encounter.
High school students: 49 percent of boys and 48 percent of girls had engaged in sexual intercourse (55 percent of the boys and 72 percent of the girls said they regretted it (*Psychology Today*, 2000).
Before age 13: 8.3 percent had initiated sexual intercourse
(Youth Risk Behavior Surveillance—United States, 1999).

For most people, the best sexual experience occurs within a caring relationship. Sexual fulfillment is a major contributor or deterrent to satisfaction in both heterosexual and homosexual relationships. Marital satisfaction is correlated with sexual satisfaction (Wuh & Fox, 2001), and most of the participants in a study of gay men and lesbians reported satisfying sex lives with their current partner (Peplau, Cochran, & Mays, 1997). In addition to its benefits to the overall relationship, two other interesting findings have emerged. A study reported at the World Stroke Conference showed that men who have three or more orgasms a week are

50 percent less likely to die from coronary heart disease (McCarthy, 2001) while a neuropsychologist who studied 3,500 people for a decade said that regular love-making makes people look younger (*Ebony*, 2001). It appears that a healthy sex life benefits us physically, psychologically, and socially!

Sexual Enrichment

In order to enjoy the benefits of sexual relations, enrichment is especially necessary. Therapists are quick to point out that sexual dissatisfaction in long-term relationships is common, and usually, the underlying cause is not a sexual one. Mark Schwartz, a sex therapist, contends that when clients come to him, he spends 80 percent of the time in relationship therapy and only 20 percent on sexual behaviors. In most cases, he says, each "I" must be fixed before any work can be done on the "we." Incomplete self-disclosure is usually one of the factors; if so, deeper communication is warranted. Sexual problems often stem from other difficulties within a couple relationship which then result in sexual frustration The key is to solve underlying problems.

Even without serious complications, most couples' sexual relationships need attention and nourishment and can be improved. First, even though you think you know all there is to know about sex, you can learn more! Sexual education is an ongoing process. Misconceptions can continue to influence sexual behavior.

> The early sexual learning we get from our parents is mostly negative, usually consisting of "don't." We have very little opportunity of being exposed to and picking up truly accurate information until we are much older, but by then our attitudes to sex and sexual behavior are rigidly fixed, and like all early established beliefs, difficult to change (Williams, 1988, p. 17).

The challenge for couples is to unlearn and relearn.

Sexual myths. Getting rid of sexual myths is part of the education. Realizing that sex and love are not the same would prevent people, like Kate, from erroneously believing she was loved because "he couldn't keep his hands off me and wanted to have sex every time we were together." Unfortunately, equating sexual desire with love often leads to hurt. Young people engaging in sexual relations before they have developed a relationship easily mistake arousal for love. "We thought we were in love because we enjoyed sex. After that wore off, we could see it wasn't love," admitted Kyle.

Another myth is that passion and sex are most important at the beginning of a relationship. Actually, the longer that individuals are together, the more they are likely to

Figure 11-6

benefit. Unfortunately, when people don't understand this, they are apt to let the sexual relationship wane. If you are in a long-term relationship, monitor affectionate behaviors. If you notice a significant decline from the past, decide to show more affection.

A third myth is that the sexual relationship will always stay the same. For example, the length of a marriage negatively affects the frequency of marital sex (Liu, 2000). That doesn't mean it becomes less enjoyable. A common myth is that as people age, their sexual interests and activities die. Is this true and inevitable? No, say the experts, unless you choose this course. Look at these figures from a survey of 1800 Americans 60 and older (National Council on the Aging, 1998).

- Nearly half (48 percent) engage in sexual activity at least once a month. About 40 percent said they would prefer to have sexual intercourse even more often.
- Of those in their 80s, 27 percent of men and 18 percent of women reported sexual activity as compared with 61 percent of men and 51 percent of women in their 60s.

Biological changes occur with age and will alter some aspects of lovemaking. Most important are attitudes that can convert into self-fulfilling prophecies. "It's all over," they say, and it is. "It's not all over," they say, and it isn't. Lovemaking can be better with age. Tenderness and love are powerful sexual motivators.

Satisfaction guidelines.   In order to enjoy a satisfying sexual relationship, a cardinal rule is to communicate openly and honestly with each other. "We don't talk about it . . . we just do it," mumbled a husband in a counseling session. Even among university students, complete sexual self-disclosure was the exception, not the rule. The couples were more likely to disclose about sexuality when there was a high level of self-disclosure about other topics and when they perceived their partner to also be sexually self-disclosing (Byers & Demmons, 1999).

When you openly communicate, you learn about each other's likes, dislikes, needs, and wants. A frank, regularly occurring discussion of your sexual relationship, even if no problems are apparent, is highly recommended. A word of caution is in order. Communicating doesn't mean just complaining about what you don't like. Certainly, you want to be honest and suggest positive changes; yet, put the emphasis on the positive and use communication as a means of enhancing.

A couple is wise to consider sexual intercourse as just one important aspect of the broad scope of love and to enjoy more than the physical act. Also deeply involved are the mental and emotional parts of the selves. "Lovemaking means literally that—interacting physically and emotionally with someone you care about. Arousal, intercourse, and orgasm or ejaculation are nonessential, and simply possible lovemaking options" (Williams, 1988, p. 19). Typically, all the emphasis in lovemaking is placed on the climax phase. Sex therapist Mark Schwartz caused laughter in his audience when he said, "Even foreplay is sometimes seen as unimportant. The word 'foreplay' makes it sound as if all the good stuff is still to come." Lovemaking, in its entirety, is best seen as an ongoing interaction between two loving people.

"Having sex" implies that something happens to you, like having a toothache or a flat tire. It sounds passive and lifeless. "Making love," on the other hand, is creative, not passive. Making love focuses on the sensual expression of closeness between two trusting souls who like as well as love one another, not just the plug-in connection between sex organs. (Castleman, 1989, p. 19).

Probably the most powerful enemy of sexual fulfillment is routine and boredom; it's important to add variety and zest to your sexual relationship. Sameness in time, place, and technique is dull. Couples in the early stages of a relationship are generally more innovative and willing to experiment. Later, they tend to settle into predictable routines. Too much knowledge of each other can actually interfere with arousal, excitement, and enjoyment. Can you determine reasons for boredom in the following heterosexual relationship?

> She: He wants to have sex about 3 times a week, usually on Tuesday, Thursday, and Saturday.
>
> He: I wish she'd wear something to bed besides that old flannel nightgown. It's hard to feel desire even 3 nights a week.
>
> She: He doesn't seem to care about my sexual needs. Our sex is always the same.
>
> He: Another problem is that sometimes I'm tired after watching the late-night talk show.

Was it apparent that their sexual relations predictably took place on Tuesday, Thursday, and Saturday nights at about the same time (after television) and in the same place (bed)? The flannel nightgown added to the doldrums of their sex life.

This situation points out another common problem. If you were asked, "When do most couples make love?" your answer would probably be, "Before they go to sleep." For most people, after a long, busy day, "before sleep" equates to fatigue. The "I'm too tired" is probably not really an excuse. It's fact! Couples benefit by assessing the priority of lovemaking and not always relegating it to the last event of the day.

What can also help is to engage in sexual loving differently from the early relationship phase when strong feelings usually led to passionate behaviors. In contrast, what typically works best in long-term relationships is to first engage in sensual behaviors because passionate feelings almost always follow. In other words, let actions lead into the feelings. Other ideas are to keep in good health, care about your appearance and hygiene, learn how to delight each other, prioritize the sexual relationship, and dare to be spontaneous and creative!

Final guidelines deal with misinterpretations and manipulative uses of sexuality. The myth that love means a constant sexual "turn-on" damages relationships, and it's unfair to think that an occasional lack of interest means lack of love. Commonly, one person may attach a meaning to a behavior that isn't shared by the other, as in the case of this newly-wed couple.

> Marisa (sobbing): You're already tired of me.
>
> Andrew (surprised): What gave you that idea?
>
> Marisa: You usually make a sexual advance, and tonight you turned over and started reading.
>
> Andrew: I was planning to hug you and give you a kiss in a minute because I was close to the end of this book. I noticed that you put on your old

sloppy pajamas instead of one of your gowns, so I assumed you weren't interested in lovemaking tonight.

Marisa: What does what I wear have to do with it?

Several inaccurate assumptions can be detected in this one experience. Did you notice that her expectation seemed to be that he would be the initiator of lovemaking? The myth that only men are interested in lovemaking and should make the first advance decreases spontaneity and freedom within sexual relationships.

"We'll make love if . . . " or "I won't have sex with you if . . . " are manipulative techniques that reduce lovemaking to a game. If the relationship is troubled, you can rightfully refrain from lovemaking. Saying, "I don't want to make love because I don't feel loved (or loving)" is direct and honest. To use sex as a leverage is to demean yourself and the relationship.

Sexual fulfillment is a choice. To achieve satisfaction requires commitment, time, energy, and a great deal of communication. A goal of lovemaking is to relax and enjoy being in close contact with your lover.

LIVING TOGETHER

If you remember the phrase "shacking up," you have firsthand knowledge of how attitudes have changed over time. When a couple was described as "shacking up," it wasn't meant to be positive. Today the name for this is **cohabitation**, two partners living together as if married, and it is no longer viewed in such a negative light.

Who Lives Together and Why?

Research about cohabitation focuses on heterosexual couples. However, gay and lesbian couples also live together in a loving relationship. In fact, the 2000 census counted 601,209 same-sex unmarried partner households in the United States which is likely an undercount (Smith & Gates, 2001). Such relationships are typically enduring, meaningful, and rewarding. As Ruthe describes her committed relationship: "Having spent the past 23 years with Shelly has made me really appreciate what a caring and loving relationship can mean."

For heterosexuals, living together outside of marriage has dramatically increased as a result of a more permissive societal attitude and liberalization of laws. In 2000, 3.8 million couples cohabited (Fields & Casper, 2001). Among young adults surveyed by Gallup, 44 percent had at some time lived with an opposite-sex partner (Whitehead & Popenoe, 2001). Even though cohabitation in heterosexual relationships can serve as a replacement for marriage, usually couples cohabit as a testing ground or as preparation for marriage.

Whether cohabitation can enhance chances for marital success is questionable. Several studies paint a negative picture including cohabitors having more conflict and less relationship satisfaction as well as a higher likelihood of divorce for those who do marry (Terry, 2000). Even though figures show that cohabitation has not improved marriages, the reasons remain elusive. One suggestion is that those who cohabit may be less traditional and more independent in their thinking. Or could it have to do with communication as discussed in "Communication Comparisons."? What do you think the reasons might be?

Communication Comparisons

Picture a group of recently married couples being videotaped as they discuss and try to resolve a problem. When given a problem to discuss and resolve, do you think there would be communication differences between those who cohabited and those who hadn't? Which group do you think were better communicators?

More negative and fewer positive problem solving and support behaviors were demonstrated by the cohabitors. Both partners tried to coerce and control each other. Wives who had cohabited tended to be more verbally aggressive. The researcher, Catherine Cohan, Ph.D., strongly recommends communication-skills training for all couples.

Cohabitation may have a favorable aspect that seems to get overlooked and certainly is worthy of more research. About 40 percent of heterosexuals who cohabit do not marry each other (Terry, 2000). Most cohabitations last for about a year or a little longer then either end in marriage or dissolve (Waite, 2000). It appears that living together does screen out potentially troubled marriages. This, undoubtedly, has lowered the divorce rate. Also beneficial is that living together has led to a postponement of marriage until later ages (Strong, DeVault, & Sayad, 1998). This delay can create better unions.

Few studies look at cohabitation prior to remarriages. A colleague and I were among the first to do so (Hanna & Knaub, 1981). Of 80 remarried couples in the Lincoln, Nebraska, sample, 40 had lived together for at least a month prior to their remarriages while 40 others had not. Unlike studies of cohabitation before first marriage, the cohabiting group scored higher on three measures of marital success, including family strength, marital satisfaction, and their own perception of adjustment.

If either or both is morally opposed to it, cohabitation is not advisable. A hindrance exists if couples "play house" while cohabiting or have stereotypic attitudes about marriage. For example, Sean and Terri lived together happily for 4 years. They married, then divorced 2 years later. Sean had been especially attentive during the cohabitation period then lost interest after marriage. He saw marriage as a bleak life style.

Living Arrangements

If cohabitation has any benefits in terms of testing the strength of a relationship, the attitudes and conditions must be realistic. In addition, giving deliberate thought and action to living together increases the enjoyment of the experience and the likelihood for long-term satisfaction.

A major decision has to do with roles and responsibilities. Who will do what? How will responsibilities be determined? In heterosexual relationships, will you opt for a **traditional arrangement** in which everything is decided on the basis of who is male and who is female? Roles and responsibilities are based on stereotypes so he is primarily the wage earner while she takes care of everything related to housework including the laundry! Or will you choose the **shared or egalitarian arrangement** which means that the partners are equal and roles and responsibilities are not based on their sex? Usually, both are wage earners.

Because roles are flexible and responsibilities are shared, the question arises of who does what. A simple answer is: either or both. The couple uses communication and negotiation in the designation of tasks. A number of criteria can be used. For example, who cooks? The two can share responsibilities, either taking turns or working together in the kitchen. Or couples can consider preference, ability, and convenience. Who cleans the toilet bowls? That's a harder one. For example, I have tried to convince my husband that he does it better. No? That he likes to do it more. No? That it is more convenient for him to do it. Still no? So we share!

Maintaining a truly shared arrangement can be challenging. An unequal division of labor was evident in a study of unmarried opposite-sex roommates and cohabitors. Even though there was no difference in time availability and contributed resources, women spent more time and effort on the majority of tasks (Mikula, Freudenthaler, & Brennacher-Kroell, 1997). Among same-sex partners, the most common division of labor involves flexibility; tasks are either shared or divided according to personal preference (Peplau & Spalding, 2000). In lesbian relationships, when one is the primary breadwinner and the other the homemaker, inequities are more common. The researcher noted that the one in the stereotypic woman's role is often negatively affected by economic dependency (Sullivan, 1996). Negotiating roles and responsibilities and then ensuring that you do your fair share can strengthen a living together relationship. Sharing has other benefits. Egalitarian men who reject stereotypic gender roles are more likely to intend to have a child and less likely to divorce than traditional men (Kaufman, 2000).

What else makes a difference in nourishing a living-together relationship? In a study comparing opposite-sex and same-sex couples, intimacy, autonomy, equality, and constructive problem solving contributed to relationship satisfaction

---

Reflect

- For each of the obstacles to love, write one problem that would likely occur. In other words, give an example of how each one is an obstacle.
- Of the various components of love, which are especially important to you?
- After reading the Teresa Adams quote at the end of the section on intimacy, think of a relationship that comes to mind. Hopefully, it is your own or someone's who is close to you.
- Think of a recent disagreement you have had with another person. How was it resolved? Did you fight unfairly or fairly? If unfairly, what can you do better next time?

Apply

- Listen to a current song about love. Are the lyrics indicative of passionate love, intimate love, or both?
- Look for examples of both traditional and egalitarian behaviors in your own and others' relationships.
- If you are in a love relationship, use one of the enrichment ideas. If you are not, ask someone what he or she does in terms of enrichment.

for both groups. (Kurdek, 1998). For all couples, remembering why you are living together and treating your day-to-day relationship as a precious gift as well as an opportunity for happiness and satisfaction are sound guidelines. In a tribute to my Aunt Jerre after her death in 1999, her husband Louis Garcia said, "Relationships that work do so because there is so much pleasure." Their relationship was a model of love and devotion over a long period of time. Do focus on the pleasure as you love and live together!

CHOOSING TO MARRY

Do love and marriage go together like a horse and carriage? Not necessarily. Should everyone marry? That question is rarely missed on a class examination. Yet, despite a consensus of opinion that marriage isn't for everyone, most heterosexual individuals assume that they will marry, and marriage rates remain high. Nearly 9 out of 10 Americans will marry at least once (Belsie, 2002).

Ideally, marriage is truly a choice. Unfortunately, a feeling persists that unless one marries, life will be meaningless. Since the option of remaining single is more appealing than it once was, getting rid of this notion is beneficial in choosing a happy life, married or not. With no pressure driving individuals to marry, they can be either satisfied with single life or free to decide to marry for positive reasons. If the choice is to marry, thoughtful preparation and knowledge can set the stage for a successful union.

Definitions and Images of Marriage

Too often, couples embark on a marital journey with little or no information except what their own images supply. Looking at a committed relationship through a realistic lens can prove to be extremely beneficial.

What is marriage? Agreement on a general definition, as well as on expectations, is a first step in understanding. In its simplest sense, marriage is a legal institution. Sociologically, **marriage** is a socially approved and legally sanctioned mating arrangement, usually involving sexual activity and economic cooperation. In the United States, marriage is based on **monogamy**, having one mate at a time. For many, marriage is also a commitment based on religious beliefs, personal values, or both.

Currently, marriage is considered a heterosexual institution, and gays and lesbians have been deprived of its legal and monetary benefits. In recent years attempts have been made to allow civil unions for same-sex couples. In 2000, Vermont became the first state to do so which made available more than 300 benefits that had been available only to married couples (Fetto & Lach, 2000).

Commitment, obviously a necessary component of marriage and civil unions, is a declaration of loyalty, loving conduct, and honor and includes mutuality of purpose, a willingness to put forth effort, and a pledge of fidelity. Two people who share this idea of commitment are likely to exert effort and succeed in their relationships. Additionally, being in a state of interdependence in which the partners lose neither their identities nor their sense of autonomy is desirable (Lauer & Lauer, 1985).

Images of commitment have undergone changes. In a 2001 Gallup poll, 94 percent of never-married singles agreed that first and foremost, one's spouse should be a soul mate, a special "someone" who is both lover and friend. In decline were religious, economic and parental reasons for marriage. The survey indicates that individuals are expecting even more from marriage; yet, overwhelmingly, 86 percent said that marriage is hard work and a full-time job (Whitehead & Popenoe, 2001).

Types of Marriage

Marriages vary in a number of ways, and it's important to know what type satisfies you and your partner. Review the two types of living-together arrangements described earlier. In the past, rules for who did what within a marriage were predetermined and inflexible; this marriage is the traditional. Based on a patriarchal framework, the wife defers to her husband. She makes decisions about the home management and the children while he retains final control over family decisions because he is dominant.

This "father knows best" type of arrangement was more common and suited to the society of yesteryear. Although I don't recommend a traditional marriage, it is an option if it satisfies both individuals and if couples can afford to have only one wage earner. In order for it to work, acceptance of the risks is critical. Among these are limitations that sharply defined roles and responsibilities impose on human beings, pressures put on a sole breadwinner, the possibility of low self-esteem if the

---

Are You Willing to Take a Risk?

In the event of divorce:
Rita and Jim were in a traditional marriage for 13 years. He said, "I want you at home taking care of my two boys and not working." She was agreeable, and his business brought them a more-than-adequate livelihood. Suddenly, Jim left, deserting the family. He left neither a forwarding address nor money. Rita, who had never worked before, was able to earn only minimum wage. She had to move from her townhouse because she couldn't make the payments. "I never dreamed that this would happen to me," she said.

In the event of a spouse's death:
Colleen, a 56-year-old, was left with no means of supporting herself after her husband's death. To add to her serious misfortune, 6 months before his death, his job had been eliminated and, along with it, the medical benefits and company-paid life insurance. They were uninsured.

Within a marriage:
Dan and Joan were in their late forties, their children were raised, and they were living in a nice condominium when Dan made a job change. Joan had not pursued a career full time. Soon after the job change, Dan was terminated because of a company downsizing. He sought a professional job with no luck. Without income, they moved in with one of their children for a time. When Dan started work as a security truck driver and Joan took a job at the local hospital, they found a small apartment, similar to one they lived in when they were first married.

homemaker role is not positively recognized, and the frustrations that come from being under someone else's control. The most critical risk for women in a traditional marriage is financial. In the event of divorce or the death of the breadwinner, the risk becomes a stark reality as described in "Are You Willing to Take a Risk?" Couples who choose a traditional marriage are wise to be aware of the potential hazards.

Another type, the complete opposite of the traditional marriage, is the **egalitarian** or **shared** arrangement described earlier. A shared marriage is fair and sensible and fits our current economy and society. Most families today need or want two incomes. Studies on marital success reveal benefits. One found that husbands who did housework were far healthier 4 years later than those who did not (Gottman, 1991). An analysis of egalitarianism, what the researchers call *postgender* marriages, showed that partners enjoyed a balance of power, high emotional quality, and deep friendship (Risman & Johnson-Sumerfod, 1998). Marital satisfaction is related to a perception of equity and satisfaction with division of labor (Huppe & Cyr, 1997). Practical benefits have to do with acquiring a variety of skills and being capable of supporting yourself.

With all its advantages, actually practicing a shared marriage is challenging because of past patterns of thinking and behaving. As is true of most categorization methods, the lines can be fuzzy. Couples today may describe themselves as being in an egalitarian marriage and still engage in behaviors based only on their sex. For example, most women correspond with relatives and send greeting cards. Why? The honest answer is just because they are women. Many husbands drive the automobile, and the wife rides. Why? Again, most often, just because they are men. And couples can forget their commitment to a shared relationship on special occasions. At a holiday dinner in most homes, do you see equal distribution of labor? If it exists, the couple is achieving egalitarianism against the odds

What is today's reality? Even though many couples say they prefer a shared marriage and the majority of women work outside the home, research shows that division of labor is not shared equally in most households. Generally, women continue to carry primary responsibility for household tasks, child care, and care of the elderly even when they work outside the home (Knudsen-Martin & Mahoney, 1998). Taking into account all tasks related to the household, time-diary data from couples showed the following (Bianchi, Milkie, Sayer, & Robinson, 2000):

- Women have cut their housework hours in half since the 1960s.
- Men are doing more housework than they did in the 1960s.
- Wives perform twice as much household labor than husbands especially in the areas of cleaning and laundry.

Times are changing, yet roles and responsibilities seem quite resistant to modification.

What makes a difference in division of household labor? Time availability, relative resources of the spouses, and gender-role beliefs are factors accounting for the gap between husbands and wives (Bianchi, Milkie, Sayer, & Robinson, 2000). Racial diversity corresponds with differences in the participation of males. In off-reservation Navajo Indian families, fathers spent about 75 percent as much time as mothers in household tasks which is more time than for other cultural groups (Hossain, 2001). Similarly, African-American husbands spend more time in household labor than other races (Kamo & Cohen, 1998). From my own experiences and knowledge of other marriages, I believe that what women expect, and in some cases, demand, usually happens.

Reaching agreement about household tasks before making a commitment and then insisting on adherence to the decision are strong recommendations. A study revealed potential problems. Of the 93 percent of teenagers who said they expected to work as adults, 60 percent of boys and half of the girls said their spouse would likely stay home to raise the children (Jackson, 1998). So what will the future hold? Obviously, communication about such a vital part of marriage is in order. Problems are inevitable when people marry without forethought or discussion about marriage type.

Another way of typing a marriage is to look at its quality, rated by perceived satisfaction. Several dimensions are possible. Let's look at two basic groups identified in *Coupleship* (Wegscheider-Cruse, 1988).

- The spirited or centered couple express their satisfaction. Each feels happy and fulfilled. The relationship not only works, it thrives.
- The spiritually dead or estranged couple express dissatisfaction. The partners feel lonely, hurt, and angry. Their relationship is unfulfilled.

Although several marriages can be categorized into one of the two, a third is possibly most common. This couple would be called an "in-limbo couple," whose relationship fluctuates between feelings of satisfaction and dissatisfaction. The partners may be happy in several respects and miserable in others. Consider this relationship:

> To the outside world Nicolas and Karly's relationship looked ideal. They had two children whom they adored and for whom they shared responsibility. They enjoyed sharing interests and participated in social, church, and community activities. They rarely fought, nor did they deeply self-disclose. Karly, at times, expressed, "I wish we were closer and talked and shared more." Nicolas reassured her, "I'm just not that way, darling. I love you, and look at how great our relationship is. We get along well. Don't worry." The bottom fell out of their relationship when they discovered that each was engaged in an extramarital affair. He said he needed to feel admired, and she found someone with whom to communicate and share. The crisis rejuvenated their marriage, and for some time they succeeded in building some intimacy. A few years later Nicolas wanted a divorce because he desired deep self-disclosure and believed that happiness and self-revelation were only possible elsewhere.

Their "in-limbo" relationship had a happy ending for Karly, who discovered new aspects of herself and developed a "spirited or centered couple" relationship with a new partner. Without a doubt, a high-quality couple relationship is what individuals want. The question is how to get it.

Preparation for Marriage

The time to ask serious questions about marriage is before the wedding ceremony. The potential for success is increased when careful examination is followed by a thoughtful decision.

Sadly, lack of any formalized preparation is the norm even though research reveals that couples can benefit a great deal from a premarital education program

(Stanley et al., 2001). Most religious groups either require or offer premarital counseling. However, the value of it lies in the skill of the counseling clergy member, and sound, practical advice based on research may be missing. Premarital counseling by therapists is available yet not commonly sought. Most high schools offer coursework regarding relationships, and almost every college and university has a course in marriage and family.

Unless all students are required to learn how to succeed in long-term relationships, large numbers will remain uneducated. This society demands that you study and pass driving tests before you are given a driver's license. In contrast, a marriage license requires no certainty that individuals know anything about relating. The damage to adults and children that results from unhappy marriages may not be as apparent as damage from careless driving, but the repercussions take an emotional and financial toll.

TA Revisited

"Parent" messages range from "Don't get married. You're not ready" to "You'd better get married soon, or you may never have another chance."
"Child" experiences love and desires marriage because of perceived future happiness and the prospect of pleasure.
"Adult" is needed to process, prepare, and make a conscious choice based on reason.

How to prepare.   Preparation for marriage begins within the self. Chronological age is definitely a factor. Adolescent marriages are especially likely to end in divorce (Strong, DeVault, & Sayad, 1998). The older a woman's age, the longer the marriage is likely to last (National Center for Health Statistics, 2001). The median age for women is about 25.1 years and for men 26.8 years. A young adult is more likely than a teenager to have achieved independence, identity, maturity, and experience. When individuals marry without having had other close relationships, they may wonder what they have missed and are likely to feel restless and dissatisfied.

Do you recall Erikson's psychosocial stages? Regardless of age, establishing identity is needed before intimacy is likely to be successful. People who are divorced or widowed are wise to think about this because identity is easily "lost" after a major life change. Related to identity is independence. Are you able to live on your own? Any healthy relationship is only as strong as its two individual parts. Partners must have a strong sense of "I" to form a successful "we." The symbolism about "two becoming one" may seem romantic; however, a strong "I" and another strong "I" are more likely than an enamored "we" to sustain the stressors of a long-term relationship.

> Love thrives when two people are quite capable of living without each other but choose to live with each other (Peck, 1978).

Clearing away personal litter from past relationships and experiences is important. Bonnie, a friend since grade school, became a clinical psychologist. Reflecting on being raped when she was 16 years old, she said, "Nobody thought of a need for counseling. I was, I guess, just expected to recover over time. I realize now that unresolved issues related to the rape contributed to unhappiness in marriage and then to my subsequent divorce."

Other personal factors related to success are self-esteem, an androgynous personality, and self-created happiness. Desirable behavioral characteristics such as control of temper, assertiveness, and open communication lead to better long-term relationships. In a study designed to predict marital success, one factor that emerged was the male's willingness to accept influence from his wife. For both partners, contempt, belligerence, and defensiveness were destructive patterns (Gottman, Coan, Carrere, & Swanson, 1998). Obviously, a well-adjusted person has a much better chance of having a successful marriage than one who is struggling with personal issues. "You want a partner, not a private nurse, caretaker, or entertainer. Finally, maturity and an understanding of commitment are essential. Each person's "self" determines the success of a marriage. "Your relationships travel the same course that you travel" (Dyer, 1992, p. 114).

> Look for a partner who is also happy, so that you are not burdened with the impossible responsibility of trying to fix someone else (Goulding & Goulding, 1989).

After personal readiness has been achieved, education about long-term relationships is recommended. College courses, personality exploration, marriage-readiness tests, reading, and openly discussing issues with a prospective partner are beneficial. A practical, easy-to-understand book highly recommended for all couples is *Why Love Is Not Enough* (Gordon, 1996). Cohabitation, as discussed earlier, can prepare mature couples for marriage if they live together in a realistic way.

SUCCEEDING IN MARRIAGE AND OTHER COMMITTED RELATIONSHIPS

A thorough discussion of identified success factors can increase the probability of happiness and success in marriage and other long-term relationships. A couple is also advised to consider the opinions of others. Remember the romantic tale of Romeo and Juliet? That story leads us to believe that their families were wrong for objecting. Don't be blinded by this belief. If your family and friends do not think you are making a good choice, at least consider their reasons. Then draw upon research and credible information in making a decision.

Success Factors: Questions to Ask

Either in a preparation program, counseling setting, or by themselves, couples can answer questions and evaluate potential success. If married or already in a committed relationship, many of the questions can be used to assess areas of strength and weakness. Following each question are reasons for their importance as well as recommendations.

- *Have we known each other well for a long enough period?*

Length of acquaintance.   Knowing each other well for at least a year is recommended. This doesn't guarantee readiness; however, giving yourself that amount of time so that you experience the four seasons and all the holidays is revealing. One student remarked, "You need at least a year just to discuss all of these questions!"

- *Why do we want to make a long-term commitment?*

Reasons for marriage or commitment.   Counselors believe that the answer to "Why do we want to enter into a committed relationship?" is one of the best predictors of success. Think of all the possible reasons for marriage. You are likely to come up with a number of poor reasons. Pressure is one. This can come from a lover, family, friends, or society itself. Even age exerts pressure. "I'm almost 27 years old, and I feel like I should be thinking about marriage," said a man. If you feel any kind of pressure, force yourself to resist. Janeen, a student, wrote about her experience:

> We did not look at the "marriage," but listened to the pressure of being married. He was a closed person and a loner. They say opposites attract, but we were too opposite. I also was thinking I had to have someone and not looking at that "someone."

Other reasons come from the child ego state: "Oh, marriage seems like such fun." "It'll be like playing house." "The wedding and honeymoon will be so much fun." "I'm so in love." Even love is not a sufficient reason because satisfying long-term relationships require even more. A need to have someone to feel fulfilled comes from our "child" and is a deficiency-based reason for marrying.

Looking at the advantages and disadvantages of marriage can help you identify the "why" and evaluate costs versus benefits. Some advantages are companionship, caring, sex, learning from and helping each other, financial sharing, legal benefits, and raising a family. Several of these advantages are possible without getting married; however, in this society, marriage is the recognized and legal way of achieving them. Other advantages are related to psychological and physical health. In an international study, marriage increased degree of happiness in 16 of the 17 nations sampled, with the exception being Northern Ireland (Stack & Esheman, 1998). Compared to unmarried people, those who are married tend to have lower mortality, less risky behaviors, more monitoring of health, higher sexual frequency, more sexual satisfaction, more financial savings, and higher wages (Bramlett & Mosher, 2001). The percentage of persons surviving at least 5 years after diagnosis of cancer was found to be greater for married than unmarried persons (Ornish, 1998). Love and intimacy, especially in a socially approved context, apparently contribute to our well-being. Disadvantages include relinquishing personal freedom to a certain extent, added stressors, having to share resources, and the risk of an unhappy relationship as well as possible divorce.

Eliminating all the poor reasons still leaves a question. What is a positive reason for marrying? A couple whose marriage has great potential for success might say, "We are marrying because we are sure that we share an intimate love, we have carefully prepared and considered all known factors, we believe we have an excellent chance of succeeding in marriage, and we want to make a legal and deep commitment to this relationship."

- *What do we expect?*

Expectations about marriage.   This question can yield some intriguing answers. If two partners have incompatible or unreasonable expectations, a red light
should begin to flash. "I expect you to be there for me always. I expect you to satisfy all my needs. I don't expect that we will fight." Even if the two agree on these
expectations, they are being extremely unrealistic. A large gap between what people expect and what actually occurs leads to disappointment and frustration.

Myths about marriage abound. "We will live happily ever after without having to work on the relationship," "Neither we nor our relationship will ever
change," "Fighting is bad for relationship," "What goes on outside of our marriage won't affect us," and "People stay in love forever." Too often, individuals
will look upon marriage as either "a bed or roses" or "a bed of thorns," and neither extreme is accurate. A couple would benefit from dispelling the myths.

An underlying expectation, usually quite subtle, is that marriage will be fan-
tastic for a brief period and then downhill after that. "The honeymoon is over" is a
phrase used to describe a marital relationship after the initial stage. Have you
heard people describe marriage in the following ways?

"They've settled down." (Doesn't this sound inviting?)
"They're an old married couple now." (Probably because they have actually "set-
   tled down.")
"You can tell they're married." (This, if a couple appears bored or uninterested in
   each other)
"They must not be married." (This, if a couple is holding hands or showing affection.)
"They tied the knot." (Ouch!)

When I mentioned his upcoming marriage to a young man, he replied,
"Yeah, I'm going to bite the dust this weekend." He evidently did just that, and in
less than a year was divorced. The "ball and chain" stereotype is apt to lead to unhappy outcomes. Also, if you begin to take each other for granted, either or both
partners suffer. Then negative images can become reality. Checking expectations
is essential. If yours are unrealistic, dismal, or incompatible with your partner's,
either change your thoughts or postpone marriage.

- *What type of marriage do we want and how will we achieve it?*

Possible types of marriage.   As discussed earlier, types of living-together
arrangements are related to roles, responsibilities, and quality. A study of Chinese
young adults provides a reason for an honest discussion. Females were far
more likely than males to believe that household chores and tasks should be
equally shared and that women were entitled to careers (Xie & Lin, 1997).
When one partner desires an egalitarian marriage and the other favors tradi-
tionalism, opportunities for conflict are greatly increased. Differing gender role
beliefs and differing perceptions of role equity significantly affects marital stability (Guilbert, Vacc, & Pasley, 2000). Not only do most women want men who
will share in household responsibilities (Kaufman, 2000), satisfaction with division of labor was a significant predictor of martial satisfaction for both sexes

(Stevens, Kiger, & Riley, 2001). Periodically, checking with each other concerning perceptions of fairness will help prevent resentment and contribute to a more satisfying union.

- *Are we both going to pursue careers and, if so, how will we handle such aspects as work schedules, relocation, and conflict between career and relationship?*

Careers and jobs.   If you opt for a shared marriage, you will probably both be contributing income. Men and women work not only for incomes; often, they prefer having careers and enjoy their work. Even though employment has benefits, dual-career couples can find that issues of relocation and career advancement cause conflict. If couples believe in equality and comparable levels of power, decisions will be made jointly using a costs versus benefits method. The best interests of both will be considered, and either may be expected to make a change. Because of the length of one's career, a few sacrifices aren't devastating.

- *What are our career and personal goals and are they compatible?*

Goals.   If compatible, all goals can have positive effects on a relationship. Two people moving in similar directions can share excitement and challenges. Discussing career goals and personal ones such as homeownership, further education, and travel is important, and doing so with a flexible attitude is essential. Total honesty is imperative. Cynthia sadly mentioned how Rob, before marriage, had talked about his desire to travel. "Since we've been married, all he wants to do is stay home." A positive rate about goals is that higher educated people are more likely to stay married (Armas, 2002).

- *Have we explored our financial situation? Do we know each other's present income and potential, debts, and past financial history? Will we budget? How will we manage our finances? What are our feelings and attitudes about money?*

Financial issues.   Financial incompatibility and struggles can bring even the strongest relationship to its knees. Even with a more than adequate income, couples can face problems if they disagree on how money is to be used and have different attitudes about money. Karen was a saver and would spend money only for essentials. Luxuries weren't important. "The money is better in the bank" was her philosophy. Lee believed in using money and living for today without much thought of tomorrow. "You can't take it to your grave" was his motto. They argued regularly and bitterly about money. The handling of finances covers many areas. Will you keep your incomes separate? Will one or both of you pay bills? How will you make financial decisions? These are practical and necessary issues to resolve.

Another valuable exercise is to assess financial independence so that one isn't overly dependent on the other. Ask yourselves the following (Farrell, 1986).

- Are we committed to sharing all expenses equally? If not, for what reason? (Hopefully, this doesn't indicate a future of financial dependency.)

- Am I able to support myself in the style I prefer?
- If my partner works less than I do, am I comfortable with that?
- If I work less than my partner, am I comfortable with that?

An excellent resource is *Smart Couples Finish Rich* (Bach, 2001), a book designed to create a financially secure future. A frank discussion of finances reveals a great deal about both people and the quality of the relationship.

- *How similar are our values? Religious beliefs? How similar are we in important aspects of life? How will we handle conflicts in these areas?*

Similarities.   Differences are interesting and can be positive; however, relationships are strengthened when partners share similar values and attitudes, have some of the same interests, and share a common life style. Couples who have compatible religious and philosophical beliefs find it easier to be intimate. Strong values and attitudes, if unshared, are especially troublesome. For example, if you are opposed to prejudice and committed to human rights and equality, a partner's bigotry would pose a serious threat to a relationship. Minor differences, which lend spark and variety to a relationship, are acceptable. Major differences, especially in sensitive areas, are disruptive.

Homogamy is the tendency to mate with someone similar. Differences in socioeconomic backgrounds and age are good to examine. Do you feel comfortable in each other's worlds? Do you view the differences as positive or potentially negative? A question for many in today's society has to do with interracial and interethnic marriages. In recent years there has been a substantial increase in rates of interracial marriage especially between black men and nonblack women (Crowder & Tonay, 2000). Asian women have the greatest tendency to marry outside their race. In 2000, nearly 32 percent did so (Gardyn & Lach, 2000). Interracial couples are together for love, affection, and shared values which is no different from same-race couples (Moore, 1999). Understanding the special challenges you face in a world that is still prejudiced and discriminatory is critical. Having several other similarities and a strong intimate love will be instrumental. Realistically, you will be contending with additional obstacles because of your differences. That doesn't preclude you from being successful and, if so, deservedly, with a deep sense of pride.

Race and Ethnic Diversity

	Unmarried couples	Married couples
Black/White	4.3%	1.9%
Black/Asian and Pacific Islander	Zero or rounds to zero	
White/Asian and Pacific Islander	1.8%	1.2%
Hispanic/non-Hispanic	5.8%	3.1%

Source: U.S. Census Bureau, Current Population Survey, March 2000.

- *Do we have common interests? How do we like to spend vacations? How will we use leisure time? How important are our hobbies?*

Interests and leisure time.   People want enjoyment within an intimate relationship. Even though it isn't necessary to have exactly the same interests and hobbies, sharing several and being open to others lead to mutual pleasure. If both generally agree about vacations and holidays and are open-minded when these are being discussed, the relationship benefits.

- *Are our life styles compatible? Do we have some of the same friends? Do we like each other's friends?*

Life styles and friends.   "Amber really likes to party, and when we first started going out, I found her wild ways attractive. As time went by, I realized that I didn't like the drinking scene, the late hours, and all the running around. We fight about this a lot," said Chris. Compatibility of life styles impacts on long-term happiness, and if neither is willing to change, marriage is not the answer. Life style is also reflected in how you demonstrate your socioeconomic status (i.e., large, showy home versus small, average-looking residence) and time allocation (i.e., work before play or fun comes first).

Even though you don't necessarily have to like all the friends of each other, not liking *any* or *few* is a red flag. It's important to explore reasons for liking and disliking; in the process, you will learn more about the other person. Although maintaining friendships throughout life is important, putting friends ahead of a significant other is asking for trouble.

- *Are we independent of our families? What role will our families play in our lives?*

Extended family issues.   Overly strong ties to one's biological family can cause conflict. "He spends more time with his parents than he does with me," complained a young woman. "It seems like they are always wanting him to help them, and he just picks up and goes." Families will remain important, and successful couples usually have positive relationships with extended family members, yet these relationships are to be secondary to the marriage.

What about not liking or not getting along with each other's families? Again, caution is in order. For what reasons don't you like or get along? Are your feelings similar to your partner's? "I don't really get along with two of my brothers, so I don't expect her to like them," said one man. It is true that you aren't marrying a family; however, keep in mind that this person spent many years with family members and has certainly been influenced. Special concerns are families with poor communication, inflexibility, lack of warmth, and unfair fighting patterns. Individuals are wise to assess what they don't like about family members and whether the partner is similar in those areas. Upbringing, while significant, is not necessarily an accurate predictor. What individuals have learned is most important. "People are only victims of the past when they choose to be" (Sternberg & Whitney, 1991, p. 14).

- *Do we want children? If so, have we talked about number, timing, birth-control, and child raising? Have we agreed about responsibilities for child care?*

Having children.   If you didn't do so before, take a close look at your partner as a potential parent. Angela explained why she had made a painful decision to end a relationship: "I concluded that I didn't want him to father my children." Couples are remiss if they don't discuss whether they both want to have children. A bizarre case was related by a miserable woman who had suggested to her husband that she was ready to become pregnant. He looked surprised and said, "I don't want to have kids." Such cases are rare, yet to avoid any surprises, talk about desire for children. Essential is to discuss parenting and all aspects of raising children, covered in Chapter 12, including any stereotypic ideas regarding child care. I enjoyed a comment in a study of dual-earner couples: "If fathers want to romp with their children on the living room carpet, it is important that they be willing to vacuum it regularly" (Hawkins & Roberts, 1992, p. 170). Also, a father would share in caring for the romping children.

- *Have we been open with each other about sexuality? Do we have any attitudes that may cause problems?*

Sexuality.   Couples may or may not have sexual experience before they marry. Current statistics indicate that most will. Regardless, communication about sexual attitudes and desires is highly recommended. This area is not to be avoided because both expect things to work out fine on their own. Dissatisfaction is likely if two people do not share similar attitudes about their sexual relationship. Reading together the earlier section on sexual fulfillment as well as other books on the subject is certainly worthwhile.

- *Do we really know each other, including our habits and faults?*

Knowing each other.   Spending time together under all kinds of circumstances gives each partner an opportunity to truly get to know the other. Annoying habits can seem cute at first, yet over a long period of time, they erode the relationship. The use of drugs must be evaluated. "I realized that he drank a lot when we went out, but I never dreamed he depended on it so much. Now his drinking is ruining our marriage." People are not apt to change their habits after marriage. In a lively public address, Jim Kern, a professional speaker, told of a young woman who bemoaned her fiancé's drinking. "I'm sure he will change after we get married," she said. Kern asked, "How many of you believe that he will?" No hands were raised. "And how many of you think he will find more reasons to drink and blame them all on her?" was the next question. The laughter demonstrated that people know that automatic postmarital changes for the better are rare.

- *Do we have personality differences that may cause difficulties? Do we like each other's personalities and recognize positive traits?*

Personalities.   An extravert and an introvert, as classified on the Myers-Briggs Type Indicator, are likely to report significantly more problems than two who are matched in this category. Creative solutions are in order. One couple decided that they would drive two cars to social events. She, an introvert, wanted to limit her time at such events, while he, an extravert, liked to be a part of the action for the duration. Each returned home at a different time, and both were happy. Personality differences do not necessarily create problems; rather, *un*awareness of the differences causes difficulty. Frequently, a person marries an opposite and then is annoyed when the partner doesn't think and act in a similar way.

Couples who are too much alike can also run into difficulty. If neither has strength in the MBTI sensing preference, for example, the couple will be at a disadvantage in matters such as budgeting and tending to details. Two individuals with strong judging preferences are likely to butt heads when personal plans and schedules do not coincide. Deciding how to manage these areas could prevent serious problems.

Certain characteristics such as being caring, warm, understanding, humorous, and unselfish are desirable for individuals and serve to create a positive environment. Liking and appreciating each other's personalities makes a significant difference in both the success of the marriage and the happiness of each person.

- *Are we flexible and do we communicate in open and effective ways?*

Positive communication and flexibility.   Not surprisingly, communication is a significant predictor of relationship satisfaction (Meeks, Hendrick, & Hendrick, 1998). Communication skills were identified as the most helpful in a premarital education program (Stanley et al., 2001). Listening may be considered "love in action, and nowhere is it more appropriate than in marriage" (Peck, 1978, p. 128).

> Communication is the lifeblood of any relationship, and the love relationship demands communication if it is to flourish. (Branden & Branden, 1982, p. 63).

Even though it is simplistic to say that poor communication leads to low-quality marriages, communication is at the heart of maintaining and enriching a relationship. A mistake is to believe that communication will improve after marriage. I hear individuals say: "We don't self-disclose deeply now, but I'm sure it will get better after we marry." I cringe, remembering that I had the same thoughts before my first marriage, and it didn't get better. If communication and trust aren't established early in the relationship, they are unlikely to develop. Taking an interpersonal communication course before marriage is one of the best possible action steps.

Flexibility influences communication and all other aspects of a relationship. Two rigid persons will not bend, and the marriage is what will break. Similarly, the need to be right is the greatest cause of difficulties and deterioration in relationships (Dyer, 1992). Inflexibility and a controlling personality go hand-in-hand. Controllers go to great lengths to make sure they come out on top and generally do not consider others' feelings or wishes. Controlling methods include criticism, moodiness, anger, threats, and even overprotection. The person may also deny your perception. For example, if you object to a hurtful remark, he or she is likely to say, "You just can't take a joke," even though you are sure it wasn't a joke. Extremely rigid individuals are unlikely to be good partners.

- *How well do we handle conflict?*

Conflict management.   Closely related to communication, the ability to handle disagreement is a pivotal skill in marriage. As discussed earlier in this chapter, two people can "make or break" their chances for a successful long-term relationship by learning about disagreement and fair fighting. John Gottman (1994a), a well-known researcher in this field, says, "If there is one lesson I have learned from my years of research it is that a lasting marriage results from a couple's ability to resolve the conflicts that are inevitable in any relationship" (p. 28). Before commitment, an assessment of conflict management and a willingness to learn and practice necessary skills are highly recommended.

- *Do we enjoy being together and are we good friends?*

Togetherness and pleasure.   Enjoyment of each other's company is essential. Long-term relationships thrive on mutual pleasures. Can the two of you be alone happily while engaging in a variety of pleasurable activities? Can you be alone "doing nothing" and be content?

Friendship.   Being friends and not just lovers is bound to be increase long-term satisfaction. In a survey entitled "What Keeps a Marriage Going?" (Lauer & Lauer, 1985), both women and men listed "My spouse is my best friend" as their top reason, with "I like my spouse as a person" second. All the ingredients of friendship are necessary in intimate love. "We were friends first and then became sexually attracted to each other. I think that's why our relationship is so successful," said one women. Friendship is a much better model for what you need in marriage than the media images of romantic love.

Friendship does not have to be present in the beginning. You can be physically attracted and then become friends. The key is that at some time friendship must develop. "Is friendship essential to love? No, but it is essential to love's lasting for it is the foundation of love" (Solomon, 1988, p. 315). Individuals who can honestly say that their partners are their best friends are quite fortunate. Friendship is the glue that holds marriages together and makes them so fulfilling. Without friendship, intimate love can easily die.

- *How will we help each other during periods of crisis?*

Support during crises.   From firsthand experiences I realize how significant this question is. If you have encountered such crises as a death in the family, a personal health problem, or a family disruption, you already know how the two of you will react. If you haven't, you are wise to discuss possibilities and make some type of commitment to each other. "Being there" for each other is a reasonable expectation and crucial to success in love relationships.

How does the potential partner show support and will that style be helpful to you? A strong thinking preference on the MBTI will immediately begin to problem-solve in a logical way while the feeling type will empathize. Certainly, individuals can offer both types of support, although some offer little. Spending a long time with this person means that you are likely to go through rough times together. A high degree of emotional supportiveness makes all the difference in the world.

- *What else?*

Other questions related to your specific relationship may also be in order. The actual discussion of all questions can reveal potential problems. For example, consider the following:

> Partner A: I'm Catholic, and you're Protestant. Do you think that will be a problem?
>
> Partner B: I hope not, but I won't consider changing.
>
> Partner A: I would like eventually to live on the West Coast.
>
> Partner B: Oh, no, I'd never live there.
>
> Partner A: I like to spend vacations just loafing.
>
> Partner B: It's not a vacation if you don't travel. We're not going to just sit around. That's ridiculous!

Disregarding content, did you notice Partner B's inflexibility? What style of verbalizing was Partner B using? The closed communication style and inflexibility are clearly evident. Partner A would be wise to take heed.

After you read this chapter and consider the success factors, remember that no person or relationship is perfect. You can use a costs versus benefits approach. If both of you share intimate love, have experienced other relationships, and are committed to equality, then apply a 90:10 rule. In considering all factors, if the relationship is 90 percent positive, go for it! Additionally, be sure that the factors in the unfavorable 10 percent aren't the most potentially destructive ones.

Marital Enrichment

Awareness of a high divorce rate and realization that marriage isn't always bliss indicate that **marriage enrichment**, the process of making marriage better, deserves priority. All of the enrichment suggestions offered earlier in this chapter can be used to make a good marriage better and to revitalize one that has declined in quality. For married and other long-term couples, a few areas deserve even more attention.

The sexual relationship over a long duration can easily become an area of benign neglect. Sex therapist Dagmar O'Connor (1985) contrasts lovemaking attitudes and behaviors. Early in a relationship, people describe themselves as being "swept away" by passion and relate the sex act to an "accident that just happened." These feelings usually add to the allure of lovemaking. Over years of togetherness, couples make sex a conscious act that should happen, and then they blame the lack of excitement on being together so long. "That's how it is. After years of being together, the thrill is gone." The thrill in making love does not have to disappear like a puff of smoke. Maintaining a fulfilling sexual relationship is a vital part of couple enrichment.

Another particular challenge has to do with routine and sameness. Too often, couples develop overly predictable patterns of behaving that, along with a lack of creativity, lead to a dreadful state of boredom (Lingren, 1981). Couples get to know each other so well that they prejudge. "I know exactly what his reaction will be" or "She always reacts like that" is what is called the "already known" syndrome (Malone & Malone, 1987). Enrichment relieves the feeling of "being in a rut" and enlivens the relationship.

Enrichment may require therapy. If you decide to see a counselor, go to one recommended by people you trust. Counselors vary in their abilities. Even after you have made your selection, if one of you feels uncomfortable with the therapist, find another one. It's important that each of you feels respected, acknowledged, and valued by the therapist (Weiner-Davis, 1992). Marriage and family therapist Sue Frahm, who has a practice in Lincoln, Nebraska, says that most couples come as a last resort, which makes counseling more challenging. She and her husband, Larry, usually begin by asking individuals on a scale from 0 to 10 how committed they are to the relationship, then they throw out the most critical question: "On a scale of 1 to 10, how willing are you to work on it?" Often, the answers to the two questions are not the same. Sue and Larry favor solution-focused and action-oriented therapy. "We believe that if something is a problem to one person, it's a problem in the relationship. Both then must commit to change."

Think of a marriage or any long-term relationship as an investment. What makes an investment portfolio valuable is having more assets than liabilities. Enrichment adds to the assets. A sad commentary on contemporary life is that people will spend more time maintaining houses, automobiles, and other machines than they do caring for their relationships. An attitude that "our relationship is precious, and we want to keep it that way" can bring a dream of an enriched marriage to reality. Together, couples can choose how rewarding and successful their relationship will be.

ENDING RELATIONSHIPS

"Till death us do part" is no longer a guarantee. The divorce rate since 1960 has more than doubled; the likelihood of divorce now exceeds 40 percent (Raymond, 2001). Contributing to the numbers are certain sociological factors such as divorce being easier to obtain and much more acceptable. Nearly 60 percent of Americans think that divorce is morally acceptable (Saad, 2001). No matter how personally disquieting the idea of ending a committed relationship, thousands of people yearly find themselves faced with a legal ending to their relationship. This section will focus on divorce; however, much of it is applicable to the ending of other intimate relationships.

Reasons for Seeking an End

"We loved each other so much. I don't know what happened" isn't an unusual statement when a relationship ends. Understanding the "why" can help individuals learn from a painful experience. A prime possibility is an inappropriate or poor choice of a partner. An understanding of the needs fulfillment theory, described earlier, will probably reveal unmet needs. One or both partners may decide that the benefits of the relationship are outweighed by the costs. A third person may be involved. As one who does not believe that anyone else breaks up a couple, a recommendation is to examine the weakness in the relationship. Or perhaps, one individual is simply not committed and engages in repeated self-indulgent outside relationships. In that case, the other is better off alone.

Couples can have unrealistic expectations, and disappointment is the likely result. Or realistic expectations may not have been met. "He's almost never home. If he isn't working, he's involved in some community service or leisure-time activity. It's as if I don't exist" is a description of a relationship that falls far short of meeting either a person's legitimate needs or realistic expectations of a marriage. Stephanie explained the ending of her marriage:

> I kept thinking he would change and things would get better. He is so irresponsible and uncaring that I don't even trust him to stay with the children. Now that I'm back in school, I feel like I've seen the light. It's not easy though . . . much like "digging myself out of a swamp." I feel like a consumer trying hard to get rid of a bad product . . . my husband!

Poor communication and lack of conflict management skills are common causes of a break-up. Over a period of time, problems left unexpressed or poorly expressed become insurmountable. Unfair fighting tears couples apart. If one partner engages in repetitive destructive behaviors and is unwilling to change, leaving is probably the best course of action. Being ignored, neglected, or constantly criticized diminishes self-esteem. Attempts by one to control the life of the other are despicable. Charmaine describes her experience:

> I let my husband totally rule my life and take care of everything. How belittling it was. I am a very strong-willed person, and I saw the life being squeezed out of me. I let him take control from the start so he fell in love with some little wimp, which is definitely not me. I fell in love with a man who has no empathy. I want to raise our children in a caring and loving atmosphere. I want them to be the best they can be and to learn to care for and feel for others, not only for themselves. I think they will be fine. I'm fine. I'm getting "me" back, and I like her!

Problems such as sexual infidelity, jealousy, drinking, spending money, moodiness, poor communication, and anger increase the odds of divorce (Amato & Rogers, 1997). A particularly hateful behavior is abuse, either verbal or nonverbal. Habitual serious physical abuse gives separation a green light. Staying with an abuser is, in effect, saying that such behavior is acceptable. In essence, you do both of you a favor by leaving. Leaving a person you have loved and may still have strong feelings for is painful; however, in the long run, an unsatisfying or demoralizing relationship hurts even more.

Counseling as an Alternative

Although ending a relationship can be the best solution, seeking divorce isn't always advisable. Either extreme—"never divorce, no matter what" or "no problem; just divorce when the going gets tough"—is an insult to the dignity and value of nourishing relationships. Before making the serious decision to divorce, be sure that the reasons are sound and that everything possible has been done to revitalize the marriage.

Of great help in doing this is counseling. Even if you think that it is too late, you owe it to yourself to try. You could be like Gina who said, "I would have bet anyone a million dollars that counseling wouldn't work. All I can say now is that I'm really happy I didn't make that bet. Our marriage is wonderful, and we continue to make it more so!" Hopefully, if children are involved, you wouldn't hesitate to use all available resources to repair the damage and develop a stronger marriage. In Chapter 12 there is a section on children and divorce.

Letting Go

When faced with the painful reality of ending a relationship, realize that this is a major stressor. Even if you are the one who initiates the break-up, you can expect to experience unpleasant feelings. If you are the one who doesn't want the divorce, you will sink into one of the "dips" of life. A full gamut of emotions may be experienced, depending on the circumstances.

Depression is common. Research revealed a significant increase in stressful events and depressive symptoms soon after a divorce which then diminished over the next 3 years (Lorenz et al., 1997). Whatever is experienced, remember that you are not alone. In response to the increasing incidence of divorce, books have been written, classes and seminars have been developed, and support groups have been formed. If you divorce, numerous resources are available. One that was especially helpful to me is *How to Survive the Loss of a Love* (Colgrove, Bloomfield, & McWilliams, 1991). Picturing the "healing process as more like a lightning bolt full of ups and downs, progressions and regressions, dramatic leaps and depressing backslides" (p. 36) helped me to remain hopeful in the worst of times. Another book, *Rebuilding: When Your Relationship Ends* (Fisher, 2001), is one that Roz, a student, said "saved my life." Fifteen building blocks are described, and the final one is freedom.

The divorce process, like the grief process, is a series of stages. Six are identified by Gullo & Church (1988):

- Shock, usually ranging in duration from 1 day to 1 month and characterized by numbness, disorientation, and disbelief.
- Grief or a feeling of depression of varying duration.
- Setting blame, generally accompanied by anger.
- Resignation, or the good-bye stage, when you decide to let go, which can be either relieving or draining.
- Rebuilding, when you feel like life is good again.
- Resolution, when peace with the pain is acknowledged and you can look back and see evidence of personal growth.

You can gain strength from seeing where you are in these steps and, after time, how far you have come. Because these stages have been experienced by almost every divorcing person, you can feel assured that you, too, will eventually reach the resolution stage. The "traveling time" for most is about 1 year.

A beneficial step is to change the typical thought that divorce is proof of individual maladjustment and the common feeling of regret that your marriage didn't last forever.

> The value of a relationship lies in the joy it affords, not in its longevity. (There is nothing admirable about two people remaining together, thoroughly frustrated and miserable, for 50 years). The ending of a relationship does not mean that someone has failed. It means only that someone has changed, perhaps for the better. (Branden & Branden, 1982, p. 206)

Following are some recommendations for coping with relationship endings.

- Use this book and others to find coping strategies and behaviors to create happiness and raise self-esteem.
- If you aren't helping yourself, seek counseling.
- Draw upon your support system. You need people. Ideally, talk to people who have gone through the process and feel just fine. Support groups are in almost every community.
- Find a skilled attorney. The legal aspects of divorce require expertise. Learn about current laws so you have input regarding legal decisions. Your future is at stake.
- Be aware of financial consequences. The living standard of the partner who earns the most money rises by about 10 percent while the one who earns the least decreases by about 27 percent (Yip, 2001).
- Pay special attention to your own health and needs.
- Allow yourself all your feelings without getting stuck with any. Prolonged depression and unresolved anger, for example, indicate a need for counseling.
- Resist the temptation to think of yourself as a failure. Instead, realize that the relationship failed. Do, however, examine yourself and make positive changes.
- Let go of any magical quality you assigned to the relationship and recognize that you, as a couple, no longer exist.
- Seek new relationships with both sexes; however, do not try to build an intimate one right away. Keep in mind Erikson's identity stage, which is best to establish again before you are ready for a new relationship. This recommendation is difficult to follow because anyone who has been wounded usually relishes positive attention from the opposite sex. Friendships, at this point, are nourishing. Beyond that, you reduce the potential for success in a future intimate relationship.
- Begin to dream, plan, and live. See the ending as an opportunity, not as a death sentence.

Think of these suggestions as a basic "survival kit." You can add ideas by reading, experiencing, and learning. Self-support and self-respect can be developed by going back to school or taking a course, starting a new project, expanding your network of friends, and becoming involved in a worthwhile organization or cause. Think of each of these as: If I hadn't divorced or ended the relationship, this probably would not have been a part of my life!

During the initial stages, most find it hard to conceive of the possibility of anything positive; however, almost every divorced person can point out several benefits. One is heightened self-esteem after, and often as a direct result of, the divorce. Expanding one's horizons and becoming independent are boosters to confidence and add to the excitement of life. New opportunities present themselves and, if taken advantage of, can lead to positive results. Advanced academic degrees, exciting careers, new or renewed hobbies and interests, and exciting interpersonal relationships can be treasures along the way. If the marriage was painful, the relief from stress and misery is a reward in itself. After their divorces, three individuals expressed their rewards and joy.

> Tammy: Now that I have a chance to go to school, I'm learning about myself as well as preparing for a profession. I needed this more than words can say. My grandma used to say, "Every dark cloud has a silver lining." Now I understand. Losing a husband is hard, but finding yourself is wonderful.
>
> Shirley: From divorce I have learned: to love myself, to not forget me and to think of myself, to live for today, to be an independent person, to make my own happiness, to accept my mistakes, to make my own choices, and, most importantly, that life is up to me. In my marriage I gave all of me. I didn't even know who I was. I am now a happier, wiser person and am still growing. I realize I have so much to learn . . . so many miles to travel before I sleep.
>
> John: It wasn't easy to have someone I loved leave me; yet the feelings I have today are worth it. I now realize that there was even more pain when we were together.

All relationships end at some time. Divorce is an ending that was precipitated by a decision. Whether one person likes the decision or not, understanding the process and electing to move toward a positive ending are beneficial.

An ending such as a divorce is not a failure of self; usually, it just indicates unwise choices. Objectively, individuals can accept a share of the responsibility and resolve to be wiser in the future. They can become optimistic about future relationships and willing to risk new experiences. The ability to let go and say goodbye is a sign of a well-adjusted person. A quote from Dale Carnegie is apt here: "When fate hands us a lemon, let's try to make lemonade."

LOOKING BACK

- Love and intimacy are important in most people's lives. Although education would be very beneficial in the areas of loving, marrying, and divorcing, unfortunately, it is not required. Love as an art requires attention, skill, practice, and priority.
- Passionate love is the "fluff stuff" of which dreams may be made yet usually not realized. Several problems materialize in a passionate-love relationship; a major challenge is jealousy.
- In contrast, intimate love is renewing and rewarding and can serve as a strong foundation for a long-term, mutually satisfying relationship. Components of intimate love have been identified.

- Examination of relationship growth and needs fulfillment reveals a great deal. Intimate love expands as the individuals grow in compatible directions and as the relationship fulfills primary needs.
- Intimacy includes the freedom to be one's genuine self within a relationship and the development of psychological closeness with another person.
- Building intimacy is challenging. Removing barriers is the first step. The rewards are well worth all efforts.
- Conflict management deserves special attention because the harm caused by mishandled conflict is a major source of relationship dissatisfaction and dissolution. Conflict or disagreement is inevitable in intimate relationships. The key to couple success lies in how the conflict is managed. Fair fighting is highly recommended.
- Enrichment is the exception, not the rule. Without attention and priority, love and intimacy can gradually erode. Enriching attitudes and behaviors are essential for long-term successful relationships.
- Despite an increase in numbers of sexually active individuals, people can be woefully ignorant about healthy sexual behaviors. Enrichment makes a difference.
- Both heterosexual and gay/lesbian couples choose to live together as partners. Successful long-term relationships pay consideration to living arrangements and all aspects of couple satisfaction. Cohabitation is defined as living together in a committed relationship. Whether cohabitation influences the probability of marital success is questionable.
- If one chooses to marry, an understanding of marriage helps foster a positive commitment. Shared and traditional types of marriage based on roles and responsibilities are possible, and individuals are wise to agree on the type they prefer.
- Couples can benefit from marriage preparation. Self-examination comes first. Success factors, as identified by research, can be the basis of relevant, important questions. The discussion of the answers may reveal personal characteristics that are damaging to relationships. For partners who are already in long-term relationships, the questions can serve as guideposts for positive changes.
- In spite of the best intentions, love relationships can end. Divorce rates are high. For those who divorce, resources are available, and people can learn how to end relationships in less hurtful ways. Pain is inevitable as one passes through predictable stages, yet divorce can lead to personal growth, happiness, and an extremely satisfying future.

Intimate love is manifested by giving, receiving sharing, and growing—two vital individual forming a strong "We."

—Sharon Hanna

RESOURCES

Association for Conflict Resolution. (202) 667–9700. www.mediate.com

American Association for Marriage and Family Therapists. (202) 452–0109. ww.aamft.org.

National Board for Certified Counselors. (336) 547–0607. www.nbcc.org

Collaborative Divorce. (415) 383–5600. www. collaborativedivorce.com

Fisher's Rebuilding Seminar. www.fisherseminars.com

Classes and workshops on love, relationships, communication, and conflict management offered through community colleges and university continuing education programs.

12

Strengthening Family Relationships

LOOKING AHEAD

After completing this chapter, you will be able to

- Define family, realizing that there are several types of families.
- Recognize the significance of parenting, as well as realize that there is a lack of formal required training.
- Make thoughtful decisions about parenting and preparation.
- Describe areas in which education is beneficial.
- Discuss parenting responsibilities.
- Define discipline, explain three styles, and give reasons that democratic discipline is recommended.
- Describe positive parenting behaviors.
- Discuss grandparenting and the benefits of its many roles.
- Describe family diversity.
- Understand ways to help a child cope with parents' divorce.
- Describe the challenges and benefits of dual-earner, gay and lesbian, divorced, single parent, and stepfamily households.

When "I-other" relationships work, then families work. When families work, societies work; when societies work, nations work; when nations work, nature works; and when nature works, the universe works.

—Thomas and Patrick Malone

Take a moment and reflect on the momentous influences a family has on a person's life. Your family gave you a name, a geographic home, and a societal position, and most important, family members contributed to your self-concept, learned attitudes, values, behaviors, and personality. The family, for most people, is the most determining factor in the quality of an individual's life. Family in the field of sociology is called a **primary group**, one that is small, intimate, and enduring.

Diversity is the best descriptor of families today. This chapter focuses on one of a family's most critical functions, that of raising children. A variety of family types will be discussed with the emphasis on the importance that families play. The strengths of diverse families will be evident, and recommendations for building even stronger families will be given.

EXPLORING FAMILIES

What is a family? Responses from college sociology students range from the all-encompassing "a group of people who love each other" to the traditional, biological definition of "a mother, father, and child(ren)." According to the 2000 census, only 24.1 percent of households fit the traditional definition (Fields & Casper, 2000). Check your own idea of family by completing the "Family Picture" in Reflection and Applications. Sociologists have long agreed that a **family** is a relatively small domestic group of kin (related by biology, marriage, or adoption) who function as a cooperative unit. The concept of family among professionals has broadened to include other groups in a committed relationship. Families are expected to provide financial support, affection, companionship, and the important task of **socialization**, transmitting the culture from one generation to another.

Quality of family life is worthy of attention. Even though children can overcome family patterns, they are better off not having to do so. When one considers the tremendous influence a family has on self-esteem, self-efficacy, self-fulfilling prophecies, personality development, happiness, emotionality, values, goal achievement, and interpersonal communication, there is no doubt that a person's life can be positively or negatively affected. While no family is perfect, some function at a much higher level than do others. High-quality families are open and flexible. Family members respect and allow fulfillment of one another's needs and rights, support the mental, emotional, and spiritual growth of each individual, and allow and encourage personal growth. Within such families, the following occurs.

- Individuals are treated with dignity and perceived as equally deserving of respect.
- Personal freedoms are upheld; boundaries are maintained.
- Problems are acknowledged and resolved.
- Flexibility is evident.
- Love and affection are present.
- Communication is open and nonjudgmental.
- Mistakes are forgiven and viewed as learning tools.

Even if this doesn't sound like your family of origin, know that individuals are not destined to suffer permanent, adverse effects from family backgrounds. An invaluable benefit of achieving the objectives of this book is that you will be capable of developing a strong family.

PARENTING IN A POSITIVE WAY

"The biggest responsibility in the world." "The hardest job you could imagine." "Stressful, joyful, and challenging . . . I wouldn't trade it for the world." These are a few of the responses I have received to the question "What is parenting?" A consensus of opinion is that parenting is a difficult task. A few erroneously believe that the hardest part is giving birth. After that, they think that raising a child will just come naturally. "I know what to do. I was a kid once," said a young parent. You may be able to "parent"; however, positive parenting doesn't come naturally.

Positive parenting means doing everything possible to learn about and raise a child with a goal of **optimum development**. This includes the best possible prenatal and postnatal environments. Love, nurturance, and commitment are required. One point is clear: even though parents are not the only factors in a child's life, they are most significant and, as such, bear a high level of responsibility.

Figure 12-1

The scope of parenting cannot be covered in one chapter, or even in an entire book. In presenting a brief treatment of the subject of positive parenting, I take comfort in the realization that everything you have learned and gained thus far from this book will make you a better parent. If your self-esteem is high, you will be more successful. In learning how to create happiness, express feelings, manage stress, cope with crises, transmit values, communicate, manage conflict, and give and receive criticism, you have developed strategies for positive parenting. Hopefully, you will learn more through other resources and formal training. This chapter will simply open the door to positive parenting and helpful strategies for success in different types of families. The rest is up to you. Raising children deserves priority and training.

The Decision to Parent

You did not select your parents; however, you can choose whether or not to become a parent. This decision will probably be the most important one you will ever make. If you are already a parent and didn't give it a great deal of forethought, you are not alone and certainly it is not wise to berate yourself. Your choice now is to learn how to be a positive parent. And, you can encourage others to make thoughtful decisions.

Again, the ego states from transactional analysis (TA) are applicable. The "child" will emotionally want a baby and will, perhaps, see raising a child as pure pleasure. The "child" could also react selfishly and not want to parent responsibly. Your parent ego state may contain messages such as, "You'd better have a baby soon. Your biological clock is ticking" or "You can't be truly fulfilled if you don't have a child." A 19-year-old student told me that her grandmother wanted her to get married and quickly have a baby so that she could be a great-grandmother before she died. Ideally, parenting is a decision for your "adult." One suggestion is to read books about becoming a parent and child raising before you decide.

Factors to consider.   Adults who are alcoholic or dependent upon other drugs, codependent, abusive, rigid, punitive, overly judgmental, unloving, or extremely needy are not deserving of a parental role. A primary factor is the psychological health of the two adults.

Then, before having children, it is best if a couple's relationship is stable and time-tested. Bringing a baby into a new relationship isn't advisable, and having a baby to strengthen a weak couple relationship is one of the poorest reasons imaginable. A baby doesn't deserve the responsibility of saving a relationship; furthermore, this repair attempt invariably doesn't work. The transition to parenthood usually strains a couple. Keeping the relationship healthy continues to be important. A study showed that parenting satisfaction was significantly higher for adults whose marriages were of high quality (Rogers & White, 1998).

A critical question to answer is "Why do we want to have a child?" A list identifying advantages and disadvantages usually reveals more cons than pros. What comes to your mind when you think of the disadvantages? A typical immediate answer is sacrifice. What types of sacrifice?

Couples are realistic when they acknowledge that time, energy, a great deal of effort, and money are required. The estimated cost of raising a child born in 2000 until he or she is 17 is $121,230 for families under $38,000 annual before-tax income, $165,630 for families under $64,000, and for those above $64,000 income, the amount is $241,770. Expenses include housing, food, transportation, clothing, health care, education, child care, and miscellaneous (U.S. Department of Agriculture, 2001). A wise financial consideration also has to do with how many children are desired. Besides finances, parents' other resources of time and energy are reduced with each child.

What about the positives? Parenting can be one of the most rewarding of human experiences. The benefits of having children include: giving and receiving of love, adding interest to life, increasing life's enjoyment, opening additional avenues of pleasure and relating, and making life meaningful. "Realizing that I have given life to a person who is enjoying life and contributing to this world is the greatest reward possible," said a parent of a young adult.

Having a realistic picture of parenting and family life hopefully will cause one to think and hesitate. You may choose to be one who doesn't have children, an option that has become increasingly more common. Because of the importance of the decision, you owe it to yourself and to a child to be careful and deliberate. Unlike other statuses you may choose, this one cannot be undone. After a thoughtful decision has been made, make another one—to educate yourself.

Parent Education

In the movie *Parenthood*, a teenage boy talks about the irony of requiring fishing licenses to fish, hunting licenses to hunt, and driving licenses to drive, yet having no licensing requirement to become a parent. Society requires less to become a parent than to take on other statuses. Even marriage usually requires a blood test.

The good news is that parent education classes and workshops are offered, organizations and support groups focus on family issues, and books and audiovisual aids are available. Importantly, these resources do work. Even with the number of offerings and the reported successes, the tragedy is that parents do not avail themselves of the educational opportunities they have. "Canceled for lack of registrants" is a common frustration of those who offer parent courses. The assumption may be that such classes are canceled for lack of interest. Actually, the reason

---

What Positive Parents Can Learn

- Influences on the very important prenatal environment
- Erikson's stages of development and ways of helping children successfully achieve tasks at each stage
- Cognitive development stage theory as conceptualized by Jean Piaget (Piaget & Inhelder, 1969) including exploration within a child-safe environment and different ways that children learn and think
- Self-esteem and self-efficacy enhancement
- Child-raising techniques and methods

---

is more complex. Most parents are interested, yet are either unaware of how helpful education can be or don't think that they need training. Most parents-to-be take childbirth classes, but not child-raising courses.

What specifically is good for parents to learn? Check the list in "What Positive Parents Can Learn." This knowledge will not only help the child but will also make parenting less burdensome and more enjoyable

If parents practice open communication and handle conflict positively, they will, by example, teach priceless skills. Additionally, children often model their relationships after adults in their lives. Simply stated, as a parent, whatever you learn and live will be evident to a child. Another advantage of parenting education is that the more you know, the more secure you can be as a parent. "The security of the parent about being a parent will eventually become the source of the child's feeling secure about self" (Bettelheim, 1987, p. 13).

Goals of Child Raising

One of the most valuable lessons I learned about parenting was from Deanna Eversoll, a University of Nebraska professor. "What do you want your child to be like at the age of 21?" she asked our class. After receiving several answers—responsible, honest, loving, happy, confident, independent—she challenged us: "Do you know what to do, and what not to do, to help bring these about?" Parents are certainly not the only influence, yet they contribute immeasurably to the lives of their offspring.

In thinking about what you want, general ideas are preferable. Think "I want my child to be satisfied in a career," rather than "I want my child to be a doctor." This allows for flexibility and uniqueness. "I always wanted my child to get a 4-year degree," one of my students said, "But he seems perfectly happy learning automotive technology at a community college."

> Whenever we try to push our children to become the people that they may be in our heads, we become less effective as parents (Glasser, 1984).
> Enabling children to discover who they want to be and then helping them to become people who are satisfied with life is a worthy goal (Bettelheim, 1987).

In contrast to parents 60 or 70 years ago, modern parents seem to have different goals for their children. They are more likely to want their offspring to think for themselves, accept responsibility, show initiative, and be tolerant of opposing views. These characteristics replace such traits as obedience, conformity, and respect for home and church.

One student, in reply to the question about desired qualities in a child, said, "I want for us to be friends." Because parenting is a lifelong commitment, developing a deep friendship with an adult child is rewarding. Liking a child for the person he or she has become is a wonderful feeling. One of my cherished possessions is a framed verse from my daughter: "How lucky we are, how fortunate I've been—that you are my mother and also my friend!"

Responsibilities of Parenting

If you were to write a job description for parenting, what would you include? One weary-looking mother in a parenting workshop answered, "Drive them here and there and everywhere." Transportation is only one responsibility. The number of parental tasks is almost overwhelming, with some responsibilities being more important than others.

Developing love and trust.   Children deserve to live in loving environments. According to Erikson's (1963) developmental theory, trust precedes the other stages, and the early years are critical. The most valuable parenting behavior during the first year is to demonstrate love by being responsive, warm, and nurturing. A child not touched enough will not develop properly; a child touched in a disturbed way will suffer. Adults who were maltreated as children include John Wilkes Booth, Lee Harvey Oswald, James Earle Ray, and Sirhan Sirhan, all convicted of assassinations (Older, 1982). Other outcomes are less dramatic, yet still unfortunate.

Even withdrawing from an infant has repercussions. In comparing styles of mothering, babies of withdrawn mothers showed less optimal interactive behavior and had lower mental scores at 1 year (Jones et al., 1997). A convincing 36-year study, ending when the subjects were 41 years old, showed that those who had been raised with the most parental warmth and affection were more likely to have long and relatively happy marriages and close friendships and report greater happiness and less stress (Franz, McClelland, & Weinberger, 1991). Other studies support the benefits of parental warmth and closeness in the areas of physical and psychological health years later (Ornish, 1998). Demonstrated affection by cuddling, hugging, and other physical contact is meaningful at all ages.

When children are loved, they more easily develop an optimistic attitude. An additional help is the book *The Optimistic Child* (Seligman, 1995). Love continues to be the foundation of positive parenting. As with intimate love, the focus should be on loving behaviors—those that foster positive personal growth and promote personal responsibility.

Figure 12-2   Trust develops through loving, supportive experiences.

Encouraging wellness.   Obviously, parents are responsible for feeding and overseeing other behaviors related to health. Almost all take care of children's physical well-being. However, positive parenting calls for more. Among the tasks are seeing that children are physically active, that they get adequate rest, and that they are strongly encouraged to develop healthy nutritional habits. Research reveals that children who ate breakfast had 40 percent higher math grades and were less apt to be absent or tardy from school from those who didn't. The latter were more likely to be hyperactive and have a variety of psychosocial problems (Carper, 2000). Often, parents must be firm. "What can I do?" asked one. "I try to get them to eat healthy, but they just won't." In such cases, wise parents don't give children a choice. For example, my daughters had only what we called "special juice," a blend of apple and grape juice instead of the extremely popular sugar-laden drinks. The examples parents set in this regard are also significant. A child's degree of wellness is greatly influenced by parental choices.

Building self-esteem and self-efficacy.   Two all-important responsibilities are the encouragement of children's high self-esteem and the fostering of self-efficacy. The most important task of parenthood is how the authors of *Self-Esteem* (McKay & Fanning, 2000) describe helping a child develop high self-worth. In the course of constructing self-esteem, a child is likely to develop an internal locus of control and other positive behaviors discussed earlier in this book. During the early childhood stages, wise parents help their children develop what Erikson (1963) called autonomy and initiative. Encouraging a child to develop skills and talents and to teach "I can do that" instead of "I can't" helps foster the beliefs that lead to self-efficacy expectancies.

Adults are teachers of and models for self-esteem, and they can't teach or model what they don't know. Before parenting, building your own self-esteem, as discussed in Chapter 1, is highly recommended. If you became a parent before your own self-esteem was high, do all you can to elevate it. Also important are your parenting behaviors. The language and nonverbal behaviors you use with a child are building blocks of self-image and self-worth. "Every day, in the hundreds of interactions you have with your children, you mirror back to them who they are. Like a sculptor's tools on soft clay, your words and tone of voice shape their sense of self" (McKay & Fanning, 2000, p. 293).

Offering positive comments for being capable and for doing well helps to build self-esteem and strengthens self-efficacy. In the TA framework, giving positive strokes is a primary parenting behavior. The "how" of praising is important, and descriptive recognition is recommended. The words tell about a specific event and the parent's specific feelings; a child can then draw a general conclusion about personality and character (Ginott, 1969). Here is an example of descriptive recognition: "I really appreciate your helping clean house. I especially like the job you did in your own room. I'm relieved that such a big job is done." An example of evaluative praise, which is not recommended, is "You're an angel. I couldn't ask for a sweeter daughter. I don't know what I would do without you." When you allow the child to infer positives from your descriptions, the message is stronger. "Our words should be like a magic canvas upon which a child cannot help but paint a positive picture of self" (Ginott, 1965, p. 42).

Praise does not have to be present-oriented. If a child isn't doing much now to deserve descriptive recognition, recall past situations. Additionally, positive offerings just for being alive are rare and, as such, are precious gifts of unconditional positive regard and deep love. Expressing joy for a child's birth and existence is like giving a gift for no special reason. Priceless is the assurance that what a child *is* counts more than what he or she does.

As valuable as praise is, it can be detrimental when it's unrealistic and lavish praise. Overpraising is often uncomfortable for children and may put pressure on them to try to live up to an unrealistic standard (McKay & Fanning, 2000). Telling children over and over that they are perfect, wonderful, and angelic will probably be rejected and may even be behaviorally refuted later. Parents are wise to encourage achievement which builds self-esteem. Children then can prove to themselves that they are worthy. A strong recommendation is to avoid backhanded compliments, ones that mix praise with insult (McKay & Fanning, 2000). Examples are "I like the way you cleaned your room . . . for a change" or "I just can't believe you did so well on your math test." Like adults, children can be hurt by the implied criticism and are better off without any praise at all.

Positive parents will deliver small quantities of criticism in nonhurtful ways. As discussed earlier, criticism delivered with "I" statements and directed toward undesirable behavior will get a better reception and, more importantly, is unlikely to damage self-esteem. A skillful parent will set boundaries and limits and enforce these in consistent ways. One expert describes it as a delicate balance of casting out a fishing line while still holding the rod and reel (Vinton, 1998).

Destructive language styles are to be avoided. These include generalizations (the grandiose type of closed communication) and vague or violent threats such as, "Try that again and you'll find out how mad I can get" or "If you do that one more time, I'll spank you so hard you won't be able to sit down." Body language and paralanguage are also potentially damaging. Facial expressions of disgust and anger and sarcastic tones of voice, among others, are potentially detrimental. Not addressing issues of concern and playing the "silent game" are also not recommended (McKay & Fanning, 2000).

Constructive criticism points out improvement possibilities and omits any negative remarks about the child's personality (Ginott, 1965). Matt inadvertently spills a glass of milk. His parents' criticisms are not constructive.

"You are old enough to know how to hold a glass! How many times have I told you to be careful!"
"He can't help it—he's so clumsy. He always was and always will be."

Consider that Matt spilled a few cents' worth of milk, yet the caustic remarks are likely to cost much more in terms of self-regard. Instead, milk spilling and other accidents can be handled by a calm, "Accidents happen. Use the sponge on the sink to clean the table."

Children who are spoken to abusively learn to verbally abuse others. These four steps are recommended when correcting a child (McKay & Fanning, 2000):

1. Describe the situation or behavior in nonjudgmental language. ("I notice that you haven't cleaned your room yet.")
2. Give a reason for wanting behavior to change. ("I'm frustrated when you procrastinate.")
3. Acknowledge the child's feelings and thoughts. ("I know how busy you have been" or "I realize that schoolwork has been stressful lately.")

Figure 12-3   Copyright Universal Press Syndicate. Reprinted with permission.

4. State a clear expectation. ("I want the room cleaned before you go out tonight.")

Parents who place unrealistic expectations on a child do not contribute to either self-esteem or self-efficacy. "I know you can do better," a parent says looking at a report card with mostly Bs. Maybe a B is the best a child can do. Unrealistic expectations, especially about behavior, are frequently the result of what is called "adultism," which occurs when adults forget what it is like to be a child. They then expect and require a child, who has never been an adult, to think, act, understand, and do things as an adult (Glenn & Nelson, 1989). Instead, parents do well if they know their children well and are then realistically encouraging.

"What can I do to help my son rid himself of 'can'ts'?" asked a parent. As discussed in Chapter 4, a "can't" is extremely limiting and an enemy to the development of self-efficacy. First, model and encourage children to resist using the word "can't." Then provide opportunities for them to demonstrate what they can do and praise appropriately. According to Erikson (1963) if young children have developed autonomy and initiative, they will be working on industry. During all three stages, a parent can encourage self-efficacy in children.

Positive parenting behaviors and interactions contribute to **attachment**, the positive emotional bond that develops between a child and another person. The self-image of adolescents was found to be significantly strengthened by attachment to parents (O'Koon, 1997). In essence, when children develop high self-esteem and self-efficacy, the other responsibilities of parenting are easier, and, most importantly, a parent has served a child well.

Developing emotional well-being.   An entire chapter of this book is devoted to the emotional self. The value of teaching children how to feel and express is obvious. Children are affected by their parents' emotional state. Thus, an essential task for parents is to develop positive emotional selves so that they will be able to teach and model healthy emotionality. Children with emotionally competent parents are calmer, less whiney, better able to cope, better able to focus their attention, much less negative when playing with friends, less stressed, and more likely to try new things (Gottman, 1997). In addition to using the material presented earlier, a few specific points can be beneficial.

Sometimes as a result of unawareness, parents use the common emotional weapons of guilt and intimidation. These can have grave psychological consequences (Bloomfield, 1996b). The **martyr parent** seeks to instill guilt in children: "How could you do this to me?" "I don't deserve this kind of treatment." "I've given you everything." "I went without so you could have all the nice things." If you recognize any of these messages, because you once received them or because you now give them, realize that the child translates the message as "Being who I am hurts my parent" and "I'm not good or nice enough."

The **dictator parent** has the same motive as the martyr parent: to control the child's life even after the child is an adult. The method is intimidation. Fear-inducing statements and temper outbursts are common: "I'm the boss around here, and you do what I say." "Don't you dare talk back to me." "You do that again, and I'll smack you hard." "Do it or else. Remember, I'm your mother." The child remembers quite well. The reason given for the threats and abuse is that the parent knows what's best and is acting in the child's interests: however, the parent is actually inflicting great harm. Trying to produce fear in order to control is the parent's objective; the result is a fearful child.

Do you know any parents who "overparent?" A potentially damaging behavior is the compulsion to help and direct others and do for them what they could be doing for themselves. Such behavior does not serve the best interests of children. In adulthood, they may find it hard to take care of themselves. Playing either the martyr or dictator role or overparenting are not positive parenting practices.

Worrying can be passed down from generation to generation because it is learned behavior. "I'm a worrywart just like my mom" may be true. How sad that a parent taught a child to worry. To avoid this, ideally, you, as a parent, won't be such a worrier. If you are, let children know that they didn't cause it. Messages like "I can't help worrying. That's what parents do," "I love you so much, and you cause me so much worry" are hard on young people. Children placed in this position almost always grow up to be worriers. The truth is that the adults undoubtedly worried before the child was born and are now using the child as a scapegoat. Instead, a positive parent teaches a child to look critically at worries and to challenge them. He or she teaches the joy of problem solving rather than the anguish of fretting.

As discussed in Chapter 5, one's family is a powerful influence on emotional expression. Cold, unemotional children and young adults frequently come from cold, unemotional parents. If children are raised in a "sick" emotional climate, they become victims of victims. In such an environment, people frequently feel one way and act another, experience few positive emotional expressions, and are subject to hysterical, manipulative outbursts (Rubin, 1998). A healthy emotional climate is maintained by parents who know that:

> Love doesn't hurt, it feels good. Loving behavior nourishes your emotional well-being. When someone is being loving to you, you feel accepted, cared for, valued, and respected. Genuine love creates feelings of warmth, pleasure, safety, stability, and inner peace. (p. 324)

Knowing what not to do is important; additionally, learning what to do can result in an emotionally intelligent child. EQ (emotional quotient) was discussed in Chapter 5, and parents can contribute to their own child's abilities. How to do so is explained in the book *The Heart of Parenting* (Gottman, 1997). As emotional coaches, parents do the following:

1. Be aware of your child's emotions, including the most subtle clues.
2. View emotions as an opportunity for intimacy or teaching.
3. Listen empathically and validate a child's feelings.
4. Assist a child in verbally labeling her or his emotions.
5. Help solve a problem by setting limits. For example, "It's okay to be mad at her for not sharing a toy; it's not acceptable to just take it from her."

Teaching a child to manage angry feelings is a vital aspect of discipline. Some suggestions are to instruct them in deep breathing and visualization of peaceful settings, counting to 10, working off tension with physical activity, and communicating verbally or through writing (Ginsburg, Fein, & Johnson, 1998). Parents can be effective teachers and trainers in emotional development, which profoundly influences all aspects of life.

Developing positive social relationships.   Social development begins when life does. As pointed out, trust is the cornerstone of psychosocial development. In all stages, parents play significant roles; knowing what and how to encourage is beneficial.

The identity stage is one of the most challenging stages for both adults and children. It usually begins and is in "full bloom" during adolescence. The more you know about typical adolescent behavior the better parenting skills you will have and the more you will enjoy your teenager. The book *You and Your Adolescent* (Steinberg & Levine, 1997) is a good resource. The authors assure us that the horror stories about adolescence are false and point out that 9 out of 10 teenagers do not get into trouble. The book is full of accurate information about adolescent development, plus enjoyable ways to enhance the relationship. Trusting children by assuming the best and treating them with the same respect parents extend to total strangers are worthy recommendations. Positive parents help an adolescent achieve independence and don't put them in a double bind by steering them toward independence and then objecting to how they do things.

Children of all ages learn from their families how to be social creatures. Even though families are not the only socializing agents, we still develop much of our social selves at home. In terms of relationships, love and intimacy are taught or not taught in the family. Parents have a tremendous responsibility to model intimate adult relationships and to help children feel connected to others.

Showing an active interest.   Being actively interested in what your child does shows love and respect. A study of 10,000 high school students revealed another benefit. Parents who were more involved in their adolescents' schooling had offspring who performed better in school (Bogenschneider, 1997). One might think that interest and involvement would automatically be demonstrated; yet, too often, parents seem indifferent. "My folks never came to school events," said Shelly. "Even when I was a homecoming queen finalist, they weren't there." I listened in astonishment, recalling the endless numbers of piano recitals and band concerts my father, who had no interest in music, endured. He and my mother were always there showing their interest and support. When I taught sixth grade years ago, parents usually had perfect attendance at important school events. Times may have changed; however, the need for demonstrated interest and support remains as strong as ever. With increasing numbers of career responsibilities and other activities and interests, parents who make the time and effort are to be commended.

A Special Word to Fathers

As a champion of shared parenting responsibilities, I hope that a special section for fathers will seem ridiculous in the near future. In the past, a mother was responsible for child raising while the dad was often seen as someone who came and went. Or he was the heavy disciplinarian. That has changed for many. Today, fathers are more equal to mothers in caring for children, especially on weekends. They also are involved in a variety of the children's activities beyond play and companionship. One factor that made a difference was the mother's contribution to family income (Yeung, Sandberg, Davis-Kean, & Hofferth, 2001). Another was the attitude the father had regarding gender roles. A study showed that egalitarian men not only want children more than traditional males, they also want to share with their partners and be involved in caring for their children (Kaufman, 2000). Fathers appear to be as important as mothers in the traditionally feminine role of emotionality (Cummings & O'Reilly, 1997). They're important in all other aspects as well. A study of dual-earner couples showed that shared parenting was associated with both closeness to children and marital satisfaction (Ehrenberg, Gearing-Small, Hunter, & Small, 2001).

Interestingly, common understandings of "to mother" and "to father" are quite different. While the former brings forth an image of nurturing, "to father" means to impregnate. Happily, fathering is enjoying a broader meaning with the benefits of being fathered, as well as mothered, becoming widely recognized. Entire books are devoted to fathering (Hawkins & Dollahite, 1997), and studies on infant temperament and emotionality include both mothering and fathering effects (Park, Belsky, Putnam, & Crnic, 1997). Yet the attitude that a mother is the primary parent is sometimes subtle and resistant to change. This was demonstrated in class when a woman commented that her husband was home baby-sitting. She was asked if her husband was the children's father. He was. "Then why call it baby-sitting?" asked another student. "Do you call it baby-sitting when you stay home with them?"

Only recently has society acknowledged gay fathers. Contrary to popular stereotypes, children of gay fathers are no more likely to be gay, no more likely to be sexually abused, and not at any significant disadvantage when compared with children of heterosexual fathers (Patterson & Chan, 1997). A study showed that 91 percent of adult sons of gay fathers were

Figure 12-4   Fathers play an invaluable part in their children's development

heterosexual. Those who were gay had actually lived with their fathers fewer numbers of years than the heterosexual offspring, adding to the belief that environmental conditions are not responsible for one's sexual orientation (Bailey, Bobrow, Wolfe, & Mikach, 1995). Eric, in his generous, loving way, adopted a child who had been abandoned by her single mother. "My only concern is any repercussions my daughter might face because I'm not accepted by many in the society because I'm gay," he said during a class panel on parenting. Hopefully, there will be none, and she is lucky to have such a loving father.

Fathers have great impact and are as important as mothers in the overall development of children. Societal attitudes that support the role of men in the lives of children need strengthening while fathers who want to be involved in an affirmative way are advised to learn as much about positive parenting as they can. For the most part, fathers today want more involvement and are taking parental responsibilities seriously. In a book of optimism, hope, and success that tries to lift the cloak of invisibility surrounding black fathers, Hutchinson (1992) sums it up well: "Black fathers want their sons to smile into the camera on the sidelines of football games, wave, and say, 'Hi, Dad'" (p. 17). My stepson Greg, who is a wonderful hands-on dad, said, "Being a dad is the most tremendous feeling in the world. I can't imagine life without my children."

Beginning at the earliest stages of life, a child's entire being is in the hands of the caregiving adults. Each child deserves and profits from the love, warmth, and support of both parents.

Discipline and Its Multifaceted Dimensions

An area in which education is sorely needed is discipline. Ask adults to define discipline, and you get such answers as "making a child mind you," "correcting a child," or "teaching a child right from wrong." Ask children and you are likely to hear "getting punished" or "not being allowed to watch TV." Sadly, parents often use only punishment to accomplish what they think discipline is.

A broader definition of **discipline** is the entire process of teaching and guiding children from infancy to adulthood. The word discipline means "to teach," not "to punish" or "to hurt." Discipline that is loving is an essential ingredient in child rearing (Ginsburg, Fein, & Johnson, 1998). The parent has a role of leader and teacher, and the children are learners. Thus, discipline is multifaceted, and parents use a variety of child-raising techniques to guide children. What you want your child to be like become the goals of discipline.

When people think about discipline, they don't usually picture anything positive. The broader concept of discipline is affirmative rather than negative. Punishment may be used, but if so, then sparingly and as a last resort. Inappropriate punishment, which is harsh, unreasonable, violent, or harmful, is never recommended. Parents use such punishment because (1) it brings about immediate change, (2) they are not sure of what else to do, (3) they fear losing their authority, (4) and they have not been taught other methods. If you picture discipline as a pie, *appropriate* punishment is the smallest possible slice. The rest of the pie is filled with various techniques and methods described later. This concept of discipline has unlimited potential!

Styles of discipline.   An understandable model describes three styles of raising a child (Albert & Einstein, 1983). The **authoritarian style**, the norm of yesteryear, puts the parent in total control as the boss. As such, a parent is dictatorial, strict, and inflexible. The child is to obey or else. Harsh punishments are commonly used. The home atmosphere is tense and rigid and feels restrictive. The parent-child relationship is characterized by fear, distance, coldness, and rigidity. The closed communication style is used; values are moralized. The dictator parent (described earlier) is in charge.

Exactly the opposite is the **permissive style**, in which the parent is a bystander and servant while the child is powerful and in control. The parent is indecisive, yielding, and inconsistent. The atmosphere is uncontrollable and chaotic. In several families, discipline shifts quickly between the two extremes, and children are kept off balance.

Research reveals several negative effects of these two types. Methods commonly used in authoritarian discipline are harsh physical punishment and verbal abuse. These have been directly related to greater perpetuation of violence against an intimate partner in later life (Swinford, DeMaris, Cernkovich, & Giordano, 2000), to behavior problems (Brenner & Fox, 1998), and to cruelty to animals (Flynn, 1999).

Recent studies have focused on **corporal punishment**, the use of physical force with the intention of causing pain but not injury for purposes of coercion or control (Straus & Yodanis, 1996). The common habit of spanking is a form of corporal punishment and used by all types of parents. To spank or not to spank? This is a dilemma for most parents. About 10 percent spank and see nothing wrong with it, about 20 percent never spank, and about 70 percent do and wish they hadn't (Severe, 1997). For children younger than 2 years or for adolescents, social scientists generally agree that spanking should not be used (Gunnoe & Mariner, 1997). Beyond that and confusing to parents is the disagreement among the experts. Some are adamantly opposed to any use of corporal punishment while others say that light spanking probably does no harm. Almost all argue against harsh punishments. One study found a direct link between frequency of spanking and slapping during childhood and future problems with anxiety disorder, alcohol abuse, and other problems (MacMillan, 1999). Others recommend that parents be trained in alternative strategies of discipline (Day, Peterson, & McCracken, 1998).

In order to sort it out, parents can seek a readable account of research and experts' advice in a *U.S News & World Report* article, "When to Spank" (Rosellini, 1998) as well as an enlightening chapter in the book *How to Behave So Your Children Will, Too!* (Severe, 1997). Whether one believes that spanking may be harmless, a strong recommendation is that parents realize that there are dozens of alternatives to any use of corporal punishment. Sparing a child by sparing the rod is in everyone's best interests.

Another reason for rejecting the authoritarian style is that, like moralizing values, it usually doesn't work. Punitive discipline often leads to disobedience. Also, few desirable qualities are developed with authoritarian discipline. The chances of being loving with high regard for the self are slim. Honesty? Wouldn't you learn to be a good liar if you were faced with harsh punishment? A parent may be fooled into thinking that authoritarian methods work because, especially at young ages, children can be forced to mind a parent. Long-term consequences, however, are frightening. The adage "We reap what we sow" is true.

Permissive discipline has its sad effects as well. When parents are permissive, children often feel insecure and do not understand the meaning of cause and effect. Permissiveness isn't likely to lead to responsible adult behavior and probably encourages selfishness and self-indulgence. In considering these two styles, you may be thinking, as did one man, "My parents were authoritarian, and I turned out okay." Certainly individuals survive harshness, just as children who are raised in a permissive atmosphere can turn out fine. Ask yourself whether the present "you" could have been improved and whether life wouldn't have been happier if you had been raised in different way.

The recommended **democratic style** fits the broader definition of discipline and is used in positive parenting. The parent is a leader, guide, and teacher. As such, she or he is approachable, reasonable, flexible, and affirming. A child is encouraged to think, contribute, and cooperate. Power is not a major issue and is shared as much as possible. Each person has a voice and feels empowered. Open communication is the norm. The atmosphere is relaxed and consistent, and the parent-child relationship is close, open, and sharing. Democratic discipline emphasizes positiveness. Can you think of affirmative ways to guide a child? How about praise and positive strokes? Most children respond readily to praise and encouragement. Too often, instead of giving positive strokes, many parents don't comment on behavior until they reprimand. "No" in most households is said louder and more often than "yes." In fact, during the first 18 years of life the average person is told "no" or what one cannot do about 148,000 times (Helmstetter, 1989).

Positiveness is helped by a change in vocabulary. "Rules" is one of the "bummer" words identified in Chapter 4. Using the terms *guidelines* or *policies* instead sounds more positive. Who establishes these guidelines? The most powerful aspect of democratic discipline and why it is so effective is that input regarding guidelines and consequences comes from all who are able to contribute. Young people are more likely to adopt family attitudes and norms when their voices are heard (Brody, Moore, & Glei, 1994). If you are an employee, aren't you more likely to comply with policies if you have been involved in their formation? Children react similarly in usually cooperative ways. Periodically, the family can evaluate the guidelines and the consequences. Some may be obsolete or need updating. Specific democratic methods follow.

Openly communicate.   One of the most powerful tools of discipline is open communication. How strange that parents forget to use it! Verbalizing openly and listening actively and receptively may be all that is required in changing a child's behavior. The use of "I" messages and active listening will make a major difference. When our children were asked about discipline on a television program, I was heartened to hear them say, "We were hardly ever grounded or punished. Instead we talked things out."

Model the behavior you want.   Realizing that parents will have adult privileges that children do not have, discipline includes the positive examples you set. As in transmitting values, your actions will speak louder than words. Children are quite susceptible to watching and then doing. For example, children's tobacco and alcohol use is associated with parents' use (Jackson, Henriksen, Dickinson, & Levine, 1997). Parents also model how to express feelings. In fact, parents discipline simply by the way they live their lives.

> **Time-Out Prescription** (Azerrad, 2001)
>
> Assume that your daughter has hit another child. Follow these steps.
>
> 1. Say to her, "We do not hit other people." Say nothing more.
> 2. Take her by the hand and seat her in a small chair facing a blank wall. If she attempts to leave, immediately return her to it.
> 3. Make sure she stays there for three minutes. Ignore *all* of her behaviors such as screaming, crying, or hitting the wall. Say nothing.
> 4. After three minutes, keep her in the chair until she is quiet and well-behaved for five more seconds. Then tell her she has been good and may leave the chair.
> 5. Say nothing about time-out except that "We do not hit other people."

Apply behavior modification techniques.   Learning theory offers a variety of tools. The ones that will be effective depend on the age and personality of a child. With young children, changing the environment by **redirection**, either attracting them to an alternate location or by diverting their attention, is often sufficient. For example, a 2-year-old is naturally curious (and stubborn!) and will likely attempt to open a cupboard door against your wishes. You can simply get the child involved elsewhere. If a child isn't in danger and not likely to be harmed or hurt others, ignoring misbehavior can be effective because children do misbehave to get attention. In fact, studies show that problem behavior is typically the result of misplaced adult attention. In other words, parents tend to pay too much attention to a child who is misbehaving (Azerrad, 2001).

Time-out means moving a misbehaving child to a neutral (nonentertaining) location for a brief period of time. A child psychologist (Azerrad, 2001) recommends that an adult first ignore minor misbehavior, pay more attention to children when they behave well, and reserve time-out for particularly immature or potentially injurious behaviors. Highly recommended is Azerrad's "Time-Out Prescription".

Time-out doesn't work all of the time with all children, and it can be overused. And some children enjoy it. "My nephew loves time-out. He sits with his head down and hums, whistles, and smiles." In this case, the method doesn't deter misbehavior.

Rewarding desired behavior can work miracles. **Positive reinforcement** is presenting a positive stimulus in an attempt to increase or strengthen behavior. Adults relish rewards; so do children. After reading a book on behavior modification, a mother shared a success story:

> My 4-year-old girl misplaced her shoes daily. When we got ready to go somewhere, we had to look for shoes. I scolded and even spanked occasionally with no luck. From a book, I got a new idea. I put a large box in her room and told her that this was her special shoe box. Each night I counted the number of shoes in the box, and she received stickers for each shoe, which she could later use for treats. She has not misplaced a shoe for a month.

The stickers were powerful positive reinforcers. Unfortunately, parents forget to apply an important principle of learning theory which is that human beings generally seek pleasure or rewards. Verbal awards may be more beneficial than material ones as these can lead children to become motivated only by external factors. Large doses of verbal praise are preferable.

As children get older, different behavior modification methods are more effective. Positive reinforcement continues to be effective. In addition, parents can use **contracting** in which an agreement about specific behaviors is developed. A negotiation process is effective with adolescents. Involving teenagers in discussions about their behaviors shows respect and acknowledges that they can be responsible.

Use logical consequences.   In order to be prepared for adulthood and responsibility, it's important that a child experience consequences. For a child who is old enough to understand, the use of logical consequences as a method of discipline is amazingly effective. The consequences can be natural ones. If a child carelessly breaks a toy, it is no longer available. As in values development, allowing natural consequences to occur is hard on a loving parent, yet invaluable in developing responsibility. Consequences can also be created. A key element is including the child in formulating consequences. Some descriptions of effective and fair consequences follow (McKay & Fanning, 2000).

Reasonable: If a child is 45 minutes late coming home after a movie, an earlier time could be set the next time. Grounding someone for a week is not reasonable. In fact, grounding is a consequence (sometimes a punishment for unrelated misbehavior) that can be overused. And it is often as hard on the parents as it is on the child!

Related: If children are careless in completing a task, they are expected to do it over rather than have television privileges suspended. Making the consequences relate to the misbehavior makes sense.

Timely: If grades are unusually low, and the consequence is imposed study time, the time to start is that day. Waiting too long to impose consequences makes them irrelevant.

Consistent: How many times have you heard a parent say, "If you do that one more time, . . ." and the behavior continues? If the consequence for hitting a sibling is time-out, then a parent imposes the consequence until the behavior is changed. If time-out isn't working, change the consequence.

Understandable in advance: If children have input, they will know the consequences before they misbehave. If a bicycle left outside is stolen, the child will already know that money will have to be earned to replace it. Unforeseen situations may occur; a parent can then impose reasonable consequences or involve the child in the process.

One of my favorite consequence stories concerns my stepson Greg, who was quite even-tempered. However, a phone conversation with a girl got the best of him. He hit the stairwell wall, making a hole in it. "The wall has to be fixed," was our reaction. He paid for, patched, and even painted the entire stairwell! Greg assures me that he hasn't used his fist on a wall since. The use of consequences teaches responsibility and prevents parents from having to nag, scold, and use other punitive measures. A child's self-esteem usually remains intact, and the feeling of responsibility can even give it a boost.

Provide structure.   Planning with children how the household will operate is an excellent strategy. Having an established system and designated tasks decreases the number of times a parent feels a need to intervene.

A family meeting is a good forum to use. A parent can introduce the idea by saying, "I want to include everyone in deciding how our household is going to function. A family is a team: a home requires care and maintenance. Let's first decide what needs to be done and how often, and then how it will be accomplished." For excellent tips on family meetings, read *Positive Discipline* (Nelsen, 1996), a book written for both parents and teachers. Meetings are best if used for positive reasons more than for problem ones. For a first meeting, plan a family outing or trip. Regarding tasks, my stepfamily used a system in which the children had daily and weekly duties designated by number. I still smile when I think of the neighbors' reaction to one child's yelling to another, "Come on in. It's time for you to do number 2!" The system was not foolproof, and consequences were a part of it. However, it saved hours of complaining and nagging.

Performing tasks and assuming responsibility are beneficial to children; however, most parents build in their own obstacles: "She's too young to do that." "I couldn't let her iron her clothes; she won't do a good job." Is she really too young? My younger daughter Lyn started doing her own laundry when she was 7 years old. That came from my personal rebellion after the remarriage. There was not only laundry from three females, but what seemed like an avalanche of dirty clothes from three males. "I quit!" I exclaimed. "From now on we can all do our own laundry." Lyn was probably the most enthusiastic of the group. Years later, a reward was in store for me. Both Lyn and Greg said that doing their own laundry all those years was a "good deal" because they were self-sufficient in that area As for quality, whether a child does as good a job as you can do is only as important as you make it.

Advantages of the democratic style.   Contrast the democratic style with the other two. In considering what parents want children to be like as adults, what is probable with permissive discipline? Most picture a spoiled, irresponsible, and demanding individual. What about the authoritarian style? Several possibilities exist. A young adult may be fearful, obedient, and yielding to any authority figure. Frequently, however, a rebellious, aggressive attitude is the result. What do you envision under the democratic style? Check your ideas with "The 'Why' of Democratic Discipline."

The "Why" of Democratic Discipline

- Decreases the likelihood of developing negative traits and behaviors while establishing a fertile ground for the development of positive ones.
- Involves children in such a way that it promotes self-discipline.
- Teaches children how to live peacefully and cooperatively.
- Enhances loving parent-children relationships.

Sensitivity to cultural differences reveals that democratic discipline may not achieve the goals that are valued by all parents. A Chinese female reacted in class with: "That would not work with my parents. They want obedience, not democracy!" Even in the North American society, cultural variation is evident. African-American parents are more apt to use firm discipline as a way of preparing their children for an antagonistic environment (Bradley, 1998).

Freeing yourself from past restrictions and deciding what method of discipline you want to use are important choices. No matter how long you have parented, you can switch to democratic discipline. A recommendation is to bring the family together and discuss the new approach. Hopefully, you will echo the sentiments of one excited parent: "After the parenting seminar, we explained to our children that we were changing our approach to discipline. They were somewhat doubtful at first; however, that was a month ago, and things are so much better now that we are all fans!"

Positive Parenting Behaviors

Obviously, what a parent does and doesn't do plays an important role in a child's development; yet parents often forget to focus on their own actions. Positive parents practice the following:

Admitting a mistake.   You may wish to be an ideal parent, yet perfection isn't possible. A stress-reducing aspect of positive parenting is that parents are allowed to make mistakes. Those who are able to admit an error and apologize to their children are to be commended, because children then learn a valuable lesson. "I never heard either of my parents apologize—to each other or to us kids. I would have respected them so much more if they had. I find that I have difficulty saying, 'I'm sorry,' but I'm working on it," said one man. When you apologize to your children, you teach them to trust their feelings and perceptions. "You are right. I did act unfairly." Then, taking responsibility for your mistakes puts the "icing on the cake." A sincere apology is a sign of love.

Spending quality time with children.   I'd love to have a dollar for the number of times I've heard people say, "I wish I had spent more time with my children. The years went by so fast." Wouldn't it be wonderful if nobody had those regrets? Happily, modern parents are spending four to six more hours a week with their children than did previous generations. Especially affirming is that working mothers are spending even more time (26.5 hours a week) with their children as stay-at-home moms did in 1981 (26 hours) (Wingert, 2001). Positive parenting means you have fun with children. Laughing together is stress reducing and promotes bonding. "Appreciate the child within you and each other. Especially in families, let the child in each of you romp. Having fun together is positive bonding (Satir, 1988, p. 330).

Communicating openly.   Most important are communicating with and showing genuine interest in children as individuals. Talking and listening to your child are probably the most positive and rewarding parenting experiences of all.

Figure 12-5 A warm hug is good for both parents and children.

Open communication is preferable. As discussed previously, a poor communication habit is to ask "why" questions, especially those that concern personal feelings and motivations. Interestingly, parents feel justified asking a child, "Why were you late?" and resent the same question asked of them by a child. "Why did you break that dish?" is a poor question unless you honestly believe a child did so deliberately, which usually isn't the case. A feeling of discomfort or defensiveness is a typical response to a "why." Open communication is a hallmark of positive parenting!

Demonstrating warmth and affection. Positive parents are warm and affectionate expressing feelings nonverbally and verbally. The importance of demonstrativeness has been repeatedly pointed out in this book and deserves special emphasis between parents and children. Wouldn't you want your children to have high self-esteem, and when they are young adults, be more capable of congenial relationships? A longitudinal study showed that these were the outcomes when parents demonstrated high levels of warmth and affection (Franz, McClelland, & Weinberger, 1991). Children whose parents are physically affectionate and warm have a definite advantage.

Some parents tend to refrain from physical expressions of love, especially with older children. "I knew my dad loved me, but I would have loved to hear him say it—just once," said a student. Generally, when peers become important, a child shuns demonstrated affection from parents, especially big hugs and kisses. Parents can still hug children in private and find other ways to show their love. If demonstrating warm feelings is personally difficult for you, attack the problem. In order to develop a jogging regimen, an adult may have to say, "I will run 5 miles each day." The same adult can say, "I will hug my child at least once today."

Showing appreciation and consideration. Being polite, saying "thank you," and showing appreciation seem simple, yet many don't practice these within the family. Parents and children take for granted the kind deeds of family members and neglect courtesies they extend to other people. A positive parent makes a point of expressing gratitude on a regular basis. Children then learn from observation and benefit from feeling respected.

Teaching and modeling a core values system. The foundation of a child's values is built in the family. As discussed in Chapter 3, parents have a powerful influence especially during the early, formative years. Neither moralizing nor permissiveness is recommended, and you are advised to review the chapter and the methods that seem to produce the most positive results. Rather than try to instill several specific values in a child, a wise course of action is to teach and model a broad-based core set. Especially important are beliefs in human dignity and freedom to live in harmony with one another coupled with values on self, health, and continued learning. "My folks never told me exactly what to do or not to do. Instead, they helped me realize that respect for others and peaceful interactions are essential. I weigh many of my values decisions on those basics," a student shared.

Exhibiting fairness and equality.   After a presentation, I was asked by a woman, "What can be done about my children's fighting with each other?" No easy answer was forthcoming. I recommended books on the subject and an excellent chapter in *Raising Good Kids* (Ames, 1992). In most cases, children benefit from settling their own disputes. When a parent intervenes, being fair and explaining the "why" of decisions are desirable. A mother wanted to be fair with her young daughters, Nicole and Cindy. To her, this meant keeping everything equal. When one received anything, so did the other. Their needs were different because Nicole was 3 years older. Yet she was expected to wait until Cindy was ready for such things as a bicycle. This led to her extreme resentment of Cindy. Understanding children's different developmental levels and explaining to them why they were not being treated exactly the same could have solved the problem. Children also differ in what they perceive as love. One may want more togetherness while another wants more privacy. Equal does not necessarily mean "same." Making one child overly responsible for another can also lead to resentment. "I had to take my little brother everywhere. It got so I hated him," commented Sara.

As mentioned in Chapter 1, parents frequently compare siblings and set up undesirable competitive feelings. Comments such as, "I wish you'd be more like your sister" or "Your brother never gives us any trouble" cultivate rivalry and resentment which can damage both a child and the sibling relationship. "Upon hearing these 'loving' comments, there is a desire to drop-kick a sibling into the next century" (Lang, 1990, p. 116). A positive parent treats children democratically and instills a cooperative, not competitive, attitude.

Emphasizing uniqueness and freedom from stereotypic restrictions.   Each child is unique. Unconditional love means loving children for who they *are*, not for what they do. This doesn't mean you accept or like all behaviors; you love them no matter what.

Do you believe that your children will be exactly like you? Hopefully, you realize that each will be unique. Knowledge of personality differences in preferences and types, as discussed in Chapter 2, can be helpful. A must-read in this area is *Nurture by Nature; Understanding Your Child's Personality Type—and Become a Better Parent* (Tieger and Barron-Tieger, 1997). The authors believe that all four preferences are apparent by age 3 or 4 and with some, by age 2. Kari sounded relieved as she told a class: "My mom is really extraverted. For years she told me I had a depression problem because I wanted to be alone in my room quite often. Now I know and can tell her that it's just because I have a strong preference for introversion. We're complete opposites!" Knowing your child's type will also provide insight into discipline. With my older daughter, who is sensing and thinking, clear logical communication was a necessity; because my younger one is intuitive and feeling, appealing to her emotional side was effective.

Reflect

- Which of the characteristics of a high-quality family describe your family of origin?
- If you were asked, "How were you disciplined as a child?" which style would it most fit?
- From your past, think of an example of learning from logical consequences.

Apply

- Ask someone who is a parent to describe their parenting behaviors.
- Write a brief description of what you would want a child of yours to be like at the age of 21. Importantly, if you have a child or if you plan to become a parent, make a commitment to raise a child in a way that this is likely to happen.
- Set up a simple behavior modification program based on rewards to change something about yourself. If you have children, do the same with them.

As discussed earlier, stereotypic gender-role restrictions and expectations are limiting and unwise. "I expect the woman to wait on me. My mom always waited on my dad" and "I'll get married and have him support me like my dad did my mom" are unrealistic ideas. An interesting study reveals that a mother's gender role attitudes when children are young and parental division of housework when children are adolescents predict children's ideal allocation of housework at age 18. During all stages of growing up, maternal gender role attitudes appear to influence adult children's attitudes (Cunningham, 2001).

In a plea to parents, two authors (Levant & Brooks, 1997) make some salient points:

> Child rearing may be a pivotal force in the reshaping of the culture itself. Just as there needs to be continued emphasis on helping young girls become better able to access instrumental and competitive skills, there must be corollary shifts in emphasis for young boys with a greater emphasis on interpersonal connection and the ability to interact cooperatively. Boys' activities will need to become less gender-stereotyped with less devaluation of "feminine" activities. Interpersonal sensitivity, empathy, and compassion can receive greater emphasis as emotional skills for young boys (p. 265).

Rather than encouraging stereotypic roles, parents who wish to be gender-fair and encourage the best in their sons and daughters would do well to adopt an androgynous gender-role orientation and encourage the same in their children. Studies have shown that families with one or more androgynous parents generally score higher in parental warmth and support (Witt, 1997). Realizing the numerous benefits of an androgynous personality, one can conclude that parents who model and teach androgyny are helping their children and preparing them for a satisfying life.

Equally important, young people in today's world do not benefit from the locked-in mentality of bigotry, nor does a society. Even if parents aren't free from prejudice, they do a child and the world a service by keeping these attitudes to themselves. Those who model acceptance of all races and cultures are setting the stage for a child to live harmoniously in today's world.

Applying reality therapy. Behaviors described in reality therapy (Glasser, 1965) can be very useful. One suggestion is to laugh and have fun with a child and avoid any criticism during play times. If parent and child are playing tennis for enjoyment, this isn't the time for the parent to be a critic. The world doesn't end if a mistake is made, and helping a child learn this is positive. I would add a postscript. A positive comment may not be welcomed if it's unrealistic. I recall playing golf with my dear mother when I was a preteen. I hit the ball about 2 feet; Mom said, "Great, honey, it went straight!" Somehow that wasn't comforting.

Reality therapy emphasizes choices and responsibility for one's own actions. A positive parent offers realistic choices, while authoritarian discipline offers none, and permissiveness provides unlimited choices. Giving young children choices, such as selecting among three different outfits for the day, helps them learn to choose within limits. Wise parents don't give options in all situations. "Do you want to go home now?" is a poor question if you, as the adult, have decided to go. Later, choices become more numerous and frequently more challenging for both child and parent. Courage is in order. Children need practice with decision making, yet parents are apt to be impatient or unwilling to allow the pain of seeing them fall on their face (Spezzano, 1992).

Reality therapy also suggests not to accept excuses. Teaching a child that excuses don't solve problems and are only temporary forms of relief, as discussed in Chapter 4, is important. An excellent book *Raising a Responsible Child* (Dinkmeyer & McKay, 1996), says that the democratic approach to discipline works best because children have choices and are involved in decisions. A final ban from reality therapy is on hurting others which includes yelling, hitting, and imposing excessive restrictions. Parents are powerful examples. "Don't yell at me," the mother screams. "But you've been yelling at me," protests the child. The usual response is, "I'm the parent, so I can yell." Honestly, does that make sense?

Managing conflict successfully.   All families experience conflict. If a child doesn't disagree with a parent, something is wrong. The child is either fearful or incapable of independent thought. The conflict management recommendations discussed in previous chapters work well in the parent-child relationship as well. How disagreement is handled is the key. Conflicts over power and control are especially prevalent during adolescence. A teenager strives for self-identity, independence, and separation from home. A normal adolescent will disagree, sometimes unrealistically. Parents can agree with a child's perception while maintaining their own. Saying, "I can see why you think that" or "You have a good point" shows respect and affirmation. Almost all adolescents care about their parents and want to be cared about, so conflict can be managed positively.

In the parent-child relationship, as in any relationship, giving in is not healthy. When children become angry and resentful, a loving parent sometimes caves in to stop these negative feelings or for the sake of peace. Sometimes it's much better to suffer painful emotions if you, as a parent, believe that the chosen course of action is heading in a positive direction. If conflict is managed fairly, emotional outbursts will be minimized in both number and intensity.

Even when children leave home, there is potential for conflict. This could be a carryover from unresolved hurts or newly emerging areas of disagreement. "My mom still thinks that everything I do is wrong, including how I handle my children," said a young woman. "We just don't get along," said a mother of an adult child. Breaking the cycle of negative patterns of behavior, opening up lines of communication, and forgiveness are discussed in the book *Making Peace with Your Parents* (Bloomfield, 1996b).

Positive parenting is a challenge and a commitment. Education, love, and dedication are required. A realization that you are not only parenting but also, in essence, *training the next generation of parents* is sobering. If you are or plan to be a parent, be sure to do the activity on "Parenting Behaviors" in Reflections and Applications. The choice of learning and practicing positive parenting behaviors is among the most significant, and potentially rewarding, ones you will ever make.

ENJOYING THE ROLE OF GRANDPARENT

"I enjoyed being a parent. I absolutely love being a grandparent!" is a commonly heard remark. Many people progress from parenting into special grandparent-grandchild relationships. Grandparents are different from yesteryear in that they are generally healthier, more educated, and more affluent. Because of a longer life span, the role of grandparent can last for many years. Possible roles of a grandparent are caregiver, educator, living ancestor, family historian, mentor, role model, playmate, and friend.

Grandparenting is increasingly becoming a subject of research. An overwhelming number of grandparents in an American Association of Retired Persons survey (Baker, 2001) said they are delighted in their role with less than 1 percent reporting dissatisfaction. One confided, "All my troubles, aches, and pains go away when I'm with them. They fill me with so much love." They most commonly keep in touch by telephone and wish that they were together more. The most difficult part of grandparenting is keeping up with the energetic children. A survey of 11,000 grandparents by AARP (Baker, 2001) found the most satisfying parts (see "What is Most Satisfying about Being a Grandparent?").

Another study questioned grandchildren from ages 16 to 37. Emotional closeness was reported by 73.1 percent. The "close" group depicted a loving, nurturant grandparent whose devotion and attachment were evident. These grandparents were also described as a valuable source of family history, as well as good listeners—someone to whom anything could be told. The closeness was related to the grandparent's interest in and appreciation for the grandchild, as well as availability for help and support (Boon & Brussoni, 1998)

What Is Most Satisfying about Being a Grandparent?

- Unconditional love without the burden of discpline
- Watching children grow and develop
- Seeing their faces light up when we come together
- Passing on family and religious values

Figure 12-6   Families have certainly changed!

UNDERSTANDING AND APPRECIATING FAMILY DIVERSITY

Just as diversity is the norm in society, so it is with families. Although a concept of family may be "father who works, mother who is a full-time housewife, and at least one child," this represents only a very small portion of families today. Even if both parents work outside the home, married couples with their own children make up only about one-fourth of households in the United States (Fields & Casper, 2000). Respecting the wide diversity of families and concentrating on how families can contribute to the quality of life are worthy pursuits.

> Families come in different sizes and ages and varieties and colors. What families have in common the world around is that they are the place where people learn who they are and how to be that way. Families don't have to look any certain way. Any of the people in any of the families can improve the quality of the living experiences they are offering to each other. (Clarke, 1982, p. 1)

Positive parenting works in all kinds of families. This section focuses on common societal changes and structural variations in the family.

Dual-Earner Households

A change affecting most families is the reality of dual-earner couples. Depending upon the age of a child, the percentage of mothers who work outside the home ranges from 59 percent to 73 percent (U. S. Census, 2000). In 2000, both parents were employed in 64.2 percent of families with children under 18 (Bureau of Labor Statistics, 2001). When both parents are employed, the common question is "How does this affect a child?" As with many questions, studies don't necessarily agree. One showed that paternal employment was not consistently related to child outcomes (Harvey, 1999). Another looked at just maternal employment and noted a negative cognitive effect on white, but not on African American or non-Hispanic white, children (Han, Waldfogel, & Brooks-Gunn, 2001). A major study (National Institute of Child Health and Human Development, 2001) showed mixed results (see "Effects of Early Childhood Care").

One point is clear. Parents will continue to work outside the home, and quality child care does make a positive difference. A study followed children over the first 7 years of their lives. Higher quality care was related to better mother-child relationships; lower probability of insecure attachment; fewer reports of problem behaviors; and higher cognitive performance, language ability, and level of school readiness in the children. The opposite results were found when the care was of low quality. Family characteristics and the quality of the parent's relationship with the child were stronger predictors of children's development than the child-care factors (Peth-Pierce, 1998).

Within the family, what will help is a fair division of household labor and child-care responsibilities. Of utmost importance is one's use of time. A comparison between full-time mothers and ones who worked found no support for the idea that young children fare best when they have a mother at home full time. They concluded that full-time mothering is not critical to good child outcomes. What did make a significant difference was the time spent with the children (Bianchi & Robinson, 1997). Making the reality of dual-earner families a positive experience is of paramount importance.

Gay and Lesbian Households

Another type of family, usually composed of two employed adults and included in the broader family definition, is headed by a gay or lesbian couple. One or both of the adults may have already been a parent or the couple may choose to adopt or give birth. With the increase in cases of donor insemination comes an increase in lesbian-headed families. In 1998, children lived in 17 percent of same-sex female households (Kantrowitz & Wingert, 2001).

What do we know about families of gays and lesbians? In the face of more prejudice, discrimination, and oppression when compared with those headed by heterosexuals, these families show positive adjustment in supportive environments (Patterson, 2000). Except for social stigma, no other significant differences in self-concept development, behavioral problems, intelligence, and psychiatric evaluations

---

Effects of Early Childhood Care

- Of children who were in child care for more than 30 hours per week, 17 percent were regarded as being aggressive toward other children compared with 6 percent in child care for less than 10 hours per week.
- Children who spent more time in child-care centers, as opposed to other types of child care, were more likely to display better language skills and have better short-term memory.

have been found. Children raised in homosexual households almost always develop a heterosexual orientation; typically, they do not have problems with gender, emotional, and social development nor in relationships with others. Researchers conclude that the children mature in a positive manner, and they do not consider the sexual orientation of their parents as a meaningful predictor of successful child development. In fact, many children benefit from being taught increased empathy, tolerance, and respect for differences (Fitzgerald, 1999). A short story told by two women who each gave birth to one boy (Wingert & Kantrowitz, 2000):

> One of our sons Jacob told a little girl at preschool that he had two moms. Later she told one of the moms, "I have two granddads, so I guess that Jacob can have two moms."

A Loving Family

The two parents took turns rocking 8-month-old Nicole, their precious daughter, during our informal interview. It was obvious that Dee and Shelly, a same-sex couple, share a stable, intimate love relationship and that their love for Nicole is unconditional and unlimited. "We've been together 6 years," they said. "We talked about having a child but wanted to wait until we were sure that our relationship was stable." When a couple chooses artificial insemination, it is a conscious decision. Putting the child first means that you will be sure of yourself and of the relationship."

When asked how they decided who would give birth, Dee with her quick wit, answered, "That was easy. I can't handle pain!" Shelly added that age and family history were also important factors. Another decision had to do with the sperm donor. They considered a male friend but decided there were too many possible complications and opted for an anonymous donor from a highly reputable sperm bank. Seven attempts and thousands of dollars later, Shelly became pregnant.

In response to any negatives associated with the experience, they described a nonsupportive doctor and the muted feelings of joy related to pregnancy. "We felt a bit of shame at the first clinic. It was if we were doing something selfish so we went to another doctor and found support and acceptance. As to the pregnancy itself, our gay/lesbian friends didn't relate to it, our families were still struggling to accept our relationship; we just didn't feel as much validation as most parents do." An issue of concern is lack of legal recognition of their family because the state in which they reside does not allow civil unions. "I have no legal rights as a parent," Dee said, "and this is scary."

As for the positives, Shelly said, "There are so many." They then mentioned the ultimate joy of having a child, an enrichment of their lives, an emotional bonding, and a solidification of their relationship. "Our lives are child-centered right now, and we love it," they said.

Looking at Nicole who appeared so at peace in Dee's arms, I asked, "And what about her when she gets older?" Shelly said, "My worst nightmare is that she will be hurt by people who don't accept her." Dee quickly added, "Yet some of my best traits have come from being hurt. We will raise her in love and nurture her self-esteem and hope that these will shield her." The three of them represent all the finest in strong, healthy families. My wish, and I hope yours, is that Nicole will never experience hurt as a result of having two loving parents who just happen to be the same sex.

In addition to unreasonable intolerance that can be directed against gays, lesbians, and their children, another major challenge has to do with lack of legal recognition and rights. Some progress has been made in terms of public acceptance. As compared with 1977 when 43 percent of respondents said that homosexual relations should be legal, 54 percent in 2001 said the same (Newport, 2001). Adoption by a same-sex partner is allowed in some states although only 39 percent of the general public is in favor of adoption rights for gay partners (Wingert & Kantrowitz, 2000). Perhaps, if those who are opposed come to understand that, as in all families, it is the quality of the relationships, not the structure, that makes a difference, the level of acceptance will rise.

Adoptive Households

Compared to years ago when 80 percent of babies born out of wedlock in the United States were given up for adoption, the rate is only 2 to 3 percent. Still there are at least 150,000 children adopted each year (Dunkin, 2000). While dealing with unique issues such as explaining the adoption and the probable desire of a child to learn about biological parents, adoptive families compare quite favorably with biological units (Borders, Black, & Pasley, 1998). In one study adoptive mothers reported spending more time with their children and having higher family cohesion than did mothers from other family types (Lansford, Ceballo, Abbey, & Stewart, 2001).

Challenges include a societal assumption that biology equates to more love than is possible in an adoptive situation, emotional uncertainties, and, in many cases, an unknown genetic history. Yet, as Alison commented, "I have the best of two worlds—adoptive parents with whom I share a deep love and biological parents who made a very wise decision in my behalf."

Divorced Households

Divorce, a challenge for individuals, discussed in Chapter 11, can be a process of family change if children are involved. A **binuclear family** is one in which marital separation has occurred (Ahrons, 1994). One reason for this term is to lessen the social stigma and deviant view. The phrase "child of a broken home," in contrast, is a negative label that conjures images of something that is faulty, unworkable, and unable to be fixed. The term "binuclear family" also shows that even though a marriage ends, a family consisting of two biological parents continues.

Divorce occurs regularly in the United States. Since 1960, the divorce rate has more than doubled (Raymond, 2001). Obviously, millions of children are affected. No matter how positive the end results may be, divorce of parents is an extremely painful experience for children.

> I held my 10-year-old in my arms as she wept. "I miss Daddy so much," she cried. This was 2 hours after he had left following a weekend visit. Who knows how much pent-up agony had finally been expelled. I assured her it was okay to miss him, that it showed how much she loved him, and that I was sure Daddy was very sad, too. I suggested she write to him and make a tape recording. I told her she could call him that night. It's easy to forget how terrible it must be for a 10-year-old or any child

who loves both divorced parents, especially when one leaves to go home 500 miles away with 13 long weeks before the next visit.

The tightness in my throat reminds me that these are exact lines from my journal describing my daughter, Lisa, in 1977. Lyn, 4 years younger, experienced her painful reaction a few years later. Perhaps no greater adjustment challenge exists than helping children cope with their parents' divorce. A positive beginning is to consider options to an adversarial legal battle such as mediation or a collaborative divorce (Thayer & Zimmerman, 2001) in order to focus on the children's best interests.

Divorce is a different experience for children than it is for adults. They feel rejected, angry, powerless, lonely, and guilty. They didn't ask for divorce yet are forced to being a part of a battle between two people they love, according to the authors of a recommended book *The Co-Parenting Survival Guide* (Thayer & Zimmerman, 2001).

> Loyalty conflicts, sometimes flipping from one parent to the other and back again, are common for children of divorce. Children often conceptualize divorce as a fight between two teams with the more powerful side winning the home turf, and will root for different teams at different times. (Wallerstein & Blakeslee, 1989, p. 13)

Adolescents have a different experience than younger children; more challenges exist because of their multiple developmental changes. Negative effects can be alleviated by a positive parent-adolescent relationship (Hines, 1997). Adult children are frequently shocked and may react in extreme ways. "I couldn't believe it when my parents who have been together for 36 years said they were divorcing. I wanted to blame one or the other and force them to stay together. I finally realized that I was thinking only of myself and not about their well-being," confided Diane. Hopefully, reading this section will motivate all children of divorce to make the effort to heal any old hurts.

How divorce affects children has been the source of numerous research studies. More recent studies have focused on predivorce conditions as a factor in the outcome. Prior to their parents' divorce, male and female adolescents had more academic, psychological, and behavioral problems than did their peers whose parents stay married (Sun, 2001). Children's long-term welfare was linked to conditions both before and after their parents' divorce (Furstenberg & Kiernan, 2001). Obvi-

Figure 12-7   Children feel a keen sense of loss when their parents divorce.

ously, how divorce itself directly affects children is still unknown. An important consideration is how an unhappy living situation impacts child development.

> There is no evidence that children need two parents in order to grow into healthy adults. But there is a great deal of evidence that children raised in an environment of tension, conflict, and abuse either reenact these behaviors in adulthood or become withdrawn and depressed and take on the role of the victim (Forward & Torres, 1986, p. 260).

Even if tension, conflict, and abuse do not exist, an environment lacking an intimate love relationship between two parents isn't an optimum one for children. They learn about relationships and marriages within a family, and those who witness an emotionally dead marriage aren't gaining healthy messages about love.

The key to how well children do is in the hands of the divorcing parents. A challenge for all loving parents is to do everything possible to ensure that children do not suffer any more than necessary. A positive memory from my divorce is Lisa and Lyn's father saying, "We had a good marriage. I'd like to see us have an even better divorce." He, too, was committed to the goal of lessening the children's pain as much as possible. Children are helped by realizing that self-esteem isn't based on someone else's love for you; instead, it comes from within. Watching parents cope positively with divorce teaches valuable lessons.

Just as people are not trained to be married, they have little or no education in divorce. Society is making some efforts to correct this deficit by requiring post-divorce counseling and offering classes and seminars for divorcing parents and children. I try to rarely use "should"; however, the following statement deserves it. Divorcing parents *should* be required to learn how to help children cope. Ideally, individuals would seek all available resources because a well-handled divorce alleviates much of a child's pain. Left-over hurt from divorce continues largely because of parental attitudes and behaviors. Children whose parents are committed to doing a better job with their divorce than they did with their marriage are fortunate. Following are some important guidelines.

Leveling.   Divorcing parents can make the crisis easier for children by talking with them about the divorce. The child's age will influence the content of the discussion. Preferably, both parents will participate. Children then feel that both will continue to act as parents, and they aren't as likely to take sides. At this time, and on a regular basis thereafter, children need reassurance that parental love continues and that the divorce, while painful to them, is the result of an adult relationship that didn't work. Make sure that the message is clear that the children are not in any way at fault. The fulfillment of needs theory, discussed in Chapter 11, can be used with children old enough to understand. The marriage failed to meet individual needs, and neither parent is seen as the cause of the divorce.

Expressing.   Intense feelings surrounding divorce are best vented. No matter how much it hurts parents to experience a child's pain and anger, such disclosures are to be freely encouraged. Divorce leads to a feeling of loss, and grieving is in order. Parents may feel a need to suppress their own emotions in front of a child. Being out of control is not recommended; however, an honest, "I'm scared sometimes, too" or "I hurt, too" can be beneficial.

Normalizing.   It's best to keep life as normal as possible and avoid other major changes. Both parents can help by keeping children involved in activities and continuing to show an active interest. If a change is in order, you can make it easier by informing the children about it and listening to their input. You may need to be strong enough to hold fast against their objections. Eight months after my separation, I decided to leave Illinois and return to Nebraska to attend graduate school. Lisa, a strong-willed 10-year-old, protested, "I won't go. I'll stay here and live with Dad." Fortunately, I was able to tell her that her father and I had discussed the decision, and even though I cared about her feelings, we were moving. Within a few months she felt fine about her new home.

Forming a positive parenting coalition.   When divorcing partners do not get along, fathers especially tend to distance themselves (Doherty, Kouneski, & Erickson, 1998). Thus, being able to co-parent in a positive way greatly benefits a child. Developing a "temporary alliance for the purpose of accomplishing a project" is how my good friends Emily and John Visher (1988) described a parenting coalition. The Vishers, authors, therapists, and stepfamily adults, founded Stepfamily Association of America, an organization dedicated to educating and supporting stepfamilies. A coalition involves both divorced parents cooperating and staying involved in raising the children; later, it can also include stepparents. Even though a coalition approach is challenging and often frustrating, loving parents who want to serve their children best find that it is a wise investment of their time, energy, and efforts. In fact, it may be central to the welfare of a child.

Do you have to be a good friend with the other parent? The answer is no. An ideal situation is to have a high friendship and low preoccupation with that person. If being friends isn't possible, maintaining a cordial, businesslike relationship is highly recommended. A skeleton of connection with an "ex" will always be there because of a common bond to a child; yet, creating emotional distance is healthy.

Children are the real winners when their parents get along. A basic step that divorced parents can take is to agree on a general "want" for the children, such as "We *want* the children to be spared as much pain as possible" or "We *want* to do what is best for the children." In developing a working relationship as co-parents, use the following steps from the book *Between Love and Hate: A Guide to Civilized Divorce* (Gold, 1996).

1. Be businesslike and relate to each other as people do in the workplace. Focus on solutions and use teamwork to reach objectives. Use businesslike communications throughout the process.
2. Separate how you feel about your ex-spouse from how you relate to the person as a parent.
3. Focus on what the children need.

Other recommendations are to use open communication, describe desired behavioral changes, and don't assume. One parent's interpretation is no more correct than is that of the other parent.

What not to do.   Parents can help children by eliminating all too common negative behaviors.

- *Don't* criticize the personhood of the other parent. Keep negative comments to yourself. Children perceive themselves as half of each parent, so berating your former spouse is hurtful and damaging to the child. "It feels like an arrow going right through me," said one child. If you are critical, direct your comment to the behavior of the person, as recommended for all criticism.

- *Don't* place a child in the middle of two warring camps. Children of divorce often speak of feeling torn. Parents add to the burden by setting up situations in which children are pulled in different directions: "Whom would you rather live with?" "Do you want to spend the holidays here or with your dad?" You may wish to offer a child alternatives, but be aware that having to make such decisions is difficult.

- *Don't* pump a child for information: "Who is your mom dating?" "How much money did your dad spend on you?" Putting a child on the spot is cruel.

- *Don't* use a child as a messenger. Closely related to pumping for information is to ask a youngster to relay a message: "Tell your dad that the child support check is late." "Ask your mom if she wants you to come this summer." The adults can communicate for themselves in an "adult" manner. If this seems impossible, communicate through the mail or through another person, not through the child.

- *Don't* add to a child's already weakened emotional state. "I'm so unhappy. If only you lived with me, I'd be much better" will only burden a child more. Or, if a child is angry at the other parent, don't increase the pain level. Instead, encourage the child to talk the problem over with the person. If the other parent hurts the child by not being in contact or forgetting special days, listen to the pain and confine your comments to: "I don't understand why this happens. Someday he or she is likely to regret not being a part of your life." You may inwardly feel justified by a child's resentment; however, don't feed the unpleasant emotional fire. Children don't benefit from feeling unloved and unwanted by either parent.

- *Don't* create more stress for the child. If finances are worrisome, for example, find a friend in whom to confide. Not recommended is to use child support and visitation as weapons in a struggle with the other parent. Paying support on time is in the best interests of a child. The reality is that only 48 percent of mothers receive the full amount that is due; the rest receive some, and others get nothing (Doherty, Koueski, & Erickson, 1998). Even though fathers typically pay support, noncustodial mothers bear equal responsibility. Spending quality time in a safe environment with a parent is in a child's best interests; to deny this to get back at the other person is childish and selfish. Both custodial and noncustodial parents can deprive and damage children. Loving parents do neither.

Parents who work together to set up custody arrangements and a reasonable, flexible schedule of visits are helping a child. A key guideline is to do what is in the best interests of the child. A father asked me once, "What do you think of this idea? My wife and I have joint custody, and we're thinking of having our 3-year-old live with her for 1 year in Montana and then a year with me in Nebraska and just keep trading off." My negative reaction was honest. Designed to make parents happy, it would likely make the child miserable.

Children typically appreciate being consulted about moving back and forth between households. The best course of action is to provide them with a number of choices that are acceptable to both parents and that do not indicate a preference for one or the other. The child's input should be neither judged nor criticized. Because parental conflict and distress can impair a child's adjustment, flexibility, congeniality, and cooperation are key elements in doing the best you can.

Ideally, both parents will remain actively involved in a child's life. Consistency and dependability about spending quality time with a youngster are essential to well-being. If one parent has custody and the child spends the most time there, that person can keep the other parent informed about the child's school progress, activities, health, and so on. If parents have difficulty in this area, a third party is the answer, and mediation is highly recommended.

Mediation is a neutral forum in which a trained person serves as mediator and helps the family make the transition in the child's best interests. Counseling may be needed for an adult or child who is emotionally unstable or severely depressed. A good suggestion is to opt for family counseling instead of sending just the children so that there is no indication that the child is the problem. Most family service agencies provide help on a sliding fee scale. The choice for divorcing parents is clear. Divorce can be handled badly and cause injuries to children. Or parents can learn and apply strategies that not only help children survive divorce, they also contribute to their positive growth.

Single-Parent Households

Even though a family endures as long as its members are alive, its structure may be changed by circumstances. Any serious examination of families today includes the alterations brought about by death of a parent, desertion of a parent, or parental divorce. The numbers of households headed by a single parent have doubled since 1970. Even though a larger percentage of these families are headed by women (26 percent), the number of single-father families is 5 times greater than it was in 1970 (Fields & Casper, 2000).

An expectation is that more than half of the children born in the 1990s will spend time in a single-parent home (Kantrowitz & Wingert, 2001). In fact, about 35 percent of Hispanic, 66 percent of black, and 20 percent of white children now live with one parent (Demo, 2000). The most common type of **single-parent family** is one in which a divorced parent has the children in his or her care. This type is also known as a *binuclear* family. Terms such as custodial and noncustodial parents are used to identify physical and, typically, legal custody. Joint custody is becoming more prevalent. In the United States, in at least 40 states shared custody is written into law (Gillenkirk, 2000). More fathers today are seeking their full parental rights. Research finds few differences between children living in either a single mother or single father family (Downey, Ainsworth-Darnell, & Dufur, 1998).

Individuals who do not live with their children are considered noncustodial parents. A study indicates that both sexes appear to have difficulty staying actively involved in their children's lives (Stewart, 1999). Still uncommon is the mother in a moncustodial role. Negative societal attitudes make the role difficult. Karen, the mother of my stepsons, led a workshop for mothers without custody. Her objective was to encourage people to accept and empathize with women in this difficult role. "I have suffered because of others' opinions of me," she admits, "and I have some regrets. I do know that my relationship with my sons is loving and close, and I honestly don't think it could have worked out as well if all this had not happened the way it did." The acceptance of mothers as loving noncustodial parents will be a step forward. Perhaps a simple statement made by Irene will put this in perspective: "I did not give up my child. She just lives with her father more than with me."

Regardless of whether the custodial parent is female or male, single parenting is a challenge. "It's the hardest job in the world, no doubt about it" and "I feel I have to be all things to all people" are typical thoughts. Deciding to be the custodial parent requires objectivity and a great deal of thought. Too often, mothers assume custody just because society expects them to do so. An individual is wise to assess honestly what is in the best interests of the children. Of course, in cases of desertion or death, a parent has no choice. And if never married, the parent has always been custodial.

Difficulties include the inordinate stress of trying to assume multiple roles and attempting to handle all the children's pain; one's own feelings of guilt, anger, and depression; time management; and finances. For women especially, the latter is usually quite challenging.

A common concern of single parents has to do with the welfare of children without a same-sex parent in the household. In a comprehensive evaluation of research on this subject, no evidence was found for a benefit of living with a same-sex parent (Powell & Downey, 1997). An interesting study of African-American children found that at lower socioeconomic levels, students in single-parent families actually scored significantly higher on academic tests than did those from dual-parent families (Battle, 1998). Having another caring adult to share the load is helpful; however, democratic discipline and other positive parenting strategies can be used effectively by one as well as by two. Support groups are major sources of help. Classes and seminars can offer practical advice and encouragement to parents floundering in their new (or old) role.

The benefits and rewards of single parenting can diminish the impact of the problems. Most parents without partners proudly acknowledge:

- Heightened self-esteem and feelings of pride in all the accomplishments of single parenting
- Close, meaningful relationships based on shared coping, emotional expression, and deep communication
- Self-respect and the pride of being self-sufficient
- Freedom to make solitary decisions on child raising

A study showed many strengths including flexibility and adaptability to change; less adult conflict and tension; and more warmth, cooperation, and cohesiveness (Morrison, 1995).

Contrary to what is implied by the stigma of single-parent families, children can do extremely well. Ryan was described by a high school counselor as an outstanding scholar, athlete, and all-around student—one of the most well-liked kids in his large California high school. He said, "I know of no other student, past or present, whom I would most like to have as my own child than Ryan." This remarkable young man earned athletic and academic scholarships and graduated from Stanford University. In a letter of recommendation, his college baseball coach wrote:

> I have never had a student athlete that I have been more impressed with than Ryan Turner. He has an enthusiasm for everything he does that is contagious. He proved to be one of the most, if not the most, exceptional young men I have ever been associated with in my 21 years of collegiate coaching. Ryan is first class in every respect!

Figure 12-8   Proud single-parent mom Connie and son Ryan after the College World Series game victory.

Ryan, now in his thirties, added to his laurels by being the first player signed by the Colorado Rockies and then earned an MBA from Harvard Business School. This fine young man, who could be described as the "product of a broken home," was raised since age 5 by his single-parent mother Connie. Both son and mother deserve a great deal of credit.

Parents without custody also play a significant role in a child's life. As indicated earlier, children want and profit from a positive relationship with both parents. Successful noncustodial parents make parenting a high priority. Showing your love and concern, while resisting a temptation to spoil a child, is highly recommended. The ones who do an excellent job get to know their children even better and often develop a closer relationship than they had before. They don't cause problems for the other parent; instead, they are cooperative and flexible and attempt to make the most of their special role.

Noncustodial parenting can be frustrating. "I want to be involved, but she won't allow it," said one father in reference to his former spouse. "I have no idea what's going on with my two children except what they tell me every other weekend. I can't get information from their father or their school," said a frustrated mother. Obviously, the parent with custody can do a great deal to encourage positive participation of a child's other parent. Even without that positive involvement, children can do quite well. "Every child needs to feel that at least one adult is crazy about him or her" (Spezzano, 1992, p. 72). The love of both biological parents is even better. With all of its challenges and frustrations, single-parenting is special and rewarding. Growing up in a binuclear family or with one surviving parent has its difficulties, yet the benefits can outweigh the costs. As with all of life's challenges, individuals create their own realities.

Stepfamily Households

What is a stepfamily? Definitions vary even among the families themselves. The broadest concept of a **stepfamily** is a couple with one or both having at least one child from a previous relationship. The child or children may or may not live in the household with the couple. One or both of the partners may have been married before. About 75 percent of those who divorce marry again (Hatfield & Rapson, 1996). Divorce is the typical reason for the end of the former relationship, although stepfamilies also form after the death of a parent. A stepfamily also forms when a previously unmarried person with a child does marry. Are you a member of a stepfamily? You could be and not realize it. For example, 40 percent of all families include stepgrandparents (Szinovacz, 1998).

Stepfamilies come in many varieties, and the situation can be complicated. Both adults may have custody of children; one parent can have custody and the other can be a noncustodial parent; both can be noncustodial parents; or a stepparent may not have any biological children. The couple may add their own biological child to the existing family. As one who is familiar with the configurations, explanations are still difficult! If you are not yet married, you could join increasing numbers of people who become stepparents in their first marriages. "Instant parent" is what they are sometimes called. Glen, a former student, wrote me a note: "Would you believe that I'm marrying a woman with two children? After hearing you talk about stepfamilies, now I'm going to be in one!"

Men and women form stepfamilies for the same reasons they marry. They love each other, and they want to commit to a lasting relationship. For anyone considering stepfamily living, what is important is to take the time to "stop, look, listen, and learn." Preparing for a first marriage is important, and if you're going into a stepfamily; prepare, prepare, and prepare. Even though stepfamilies have existed throughout history, the 1990s produced more research than in the previous 90 years (Coleman, Ganong, & Fine, 2000). The studies unveiled the challenges, the strengths, and the ways to succeed.

For stepfamilies, a major challenge lies in overcoming society's image that spills over into how individuals perceive their family. What do you think when you hear the word "stepmother"? Most think of Cinderella or the wicked stepmother in the story of Sleeping Beauty. The image is powerful, and stepfamily stereotypes form early. A 3-year-old who had an excellent relationship with her soon-to-be stepmother asked on the day of the wedding, "As soon as you get to be my stepmother, will you beat me?" People presume that the stepfather will be cruel, the stepmother wicked, and the stepchildren poor maligned waifs. "To interact in the middle of such a dark cloud is crippling to many stepfamilies" (Visher & Visher, 1979, p. 6).

In one of the first studies of remarriage, **attitudinal environment**, perceived support from the general society as well as specific people, was identified as a

---

Images of Stepfamilies

- A stepfamily is somewhat like a Cecil B. DeMille production—a cast of thousands (Westoff, 1977).
- The numbers of people involved and the subsequent myriad of relationships that are created contribute to the complexity of a stepfamily (Knaub, Hanna, & Stinnett, 1984).
- Being in a stepfamily ends one's fear of living a dull life. Stepfamilies that are born in pain can grow into joy (Adams, 1987).

contributing factor to the success or failure of stepfamilies (Bernard, 1956). A favorable environment was found to be significantly related to family strength (Knaub, Hanna, & Stinnett, 1984). My stepson Greg pinpointed it well in a video program: "If you feel accepted from the outside, it helps you to accept yourself and the stepfamily from the inside." Support and involvement are needed from the extended family, including grandparents. "Grandparents are in an excellent position to build bridges or build walls between stepfamily members" (Visher & Visher, 1982, p. 120). The educational system can play a major part in imparting accurate information about families and in encouraging an acceptance of the merit of all types of families (Pasley & Ihinger-Tallman, 1997).

Attitudes today are more accepting, and many adults and children perceive their stepfamilies as positive. Researchers are paying more attention to strengths. In 1989, only 4 of more than 50 self-help books contained a mention of potential strengths (Coleman & Ganong, 1989); most research emphasized only problems (Ganong & Coleman, 1996). My graduate thesis (1980) and subsequent articles (Hanna & Knaub, 1981; Knaub & Hanna, 1984; Knaub, Hanna, & Stinnett, 1984) were among the first to concentrate on the positives of remarriage and stepfamilies. Stepfamilies are strengthened in the same ways as other families are: communicating, showing appreciation, doing things together, handling conflict effectively, and perceived support (Knaub, Hanna, & Stinnett, 1984).

> The stepfamily is a courageous and positive new family unit. It is not second-class. We are a different kind of family and we face different kinds of problems than other families. But we will survive and provide a second chance of happiness for millions of adults and children. (Getzoff & McClenahan, 1984, p. 142)

Because of stepfamily uniquenesses, special challenges are best handled before they lead to insurmountable problems. Following are solid recommendations from the Stepfamily Association of America (2001), an organization that has educated and supported stepfamilies for over 20 years. Elaborations of the recommendations follow the list.

- Nurture and enrich the couple relationship.
- Have realistic expectations.
- Develop new roles.
- Express and understand emotions.
- Seek support and see the positive.

Expectations must be closely examined. People entering into stepfamilies may have unrealistic ideas, representing opposite ends of a continuum. Some adults believe that because they love, the stepfamily will automatically succeed. "I love you, and you love me, and I know the children and we will love each other, too." Realistically, love, if it develops at all between stepparent and stepchild, takes time and effort. Both may have to settle for a feeling of care and concern.

> The belief that parents should love all their children equally and that children should love both parents equally is not a reasonable expectation for stepfamilies. In fact, such injunctions can produce guilt and may inhibit the development of a caring relationship. (Kelley, 1992, p. 585)

Stepparents are advised to stop worrying about whether or not they love their stepchild and focus on establishing caring, openly communicative relationships. In this environment, love can grow (Bloomfield, 1993).

The opposite expectation is a sour idea that stepfamily life will be the pits. Some parents begin by thinking, "I just know it's going to be a terrible struggle," and it's not unusual for children to say, "I know I'll hate my stepparent." Neither is realistic. Stepfamily success is clearly possible, but not guaranteed.

A common mistake is expecting a stepfamily to be like a biological one. A stepfamily is different, and "different" doesn't mean deficient. In a workshop the question was asked, "How are stepfamilies different?" A loud male voice boomed, "Blood!" He meant that the biological basis is missing for the stepparent and stepchild. When this is acknowledged and not considered as negative, a positive relationship can develop. Other expectations include "shoulditis." For example, "Mike, you should love the kids; after all, they're mine," or "Mary, you need to be a real mother to my kids," and "Son, you should respect Mike because he's my husband and your stepfather." As with all forcing words, the reaction is usually negative. Expressing a realistic expectation as a "want" is healthier.

It is realistic is to realize that stepparenting is not like being a biological parent; nor is it equivalent to adopting a child. Realistically, the stepparent is likely to be resented at first, be somewhat feared, and be compared, usually unfavorably, to the biological parent. Stepchildren are apt to be jealous of a stepparent's place of affection in their parent's life. A former spouse can magnify these feelings and make the situation even more uncomfortable. A stepparent can expect to hear, "You're not my parent, and I don't have to love you." A suggested reply is, "I know I'm not your biological parent, and you don't have to love me. I am your stepmom (or stepdad); and I would like to have a positive relationship with you." It's best to contain negative reactions and continue to let the child know that you are concerned and that you care.

Within a stepfamily, each person assumes new **roles**, behaviors within a status. The **status**, or position, of stepparent is considered to be an achieved one because it is earned by individual effort. Lack of training for biological parents is the norm, and only recently have the roles of stepfather, stepmother, stepchild, and stepsibling been examined. This lack of role definition is positive in a sense, because it allows the development of a role that fits the particular situation. If you are the stepparent of a 2-year-old whose biological father is dead, you will play a different part in the child's life than you would if you were the stepparent of a child whose biological parents are divorced. In the former case, your role will be similar to that of the typical father. In the latter, your role would be as an additional significant adult in the child's life. Trying to replace the other biological parent is not recommended. Children do better if they are encouraged to have a tie with a biological parent that is different from their relationship with the stepparent.

Figure 12-9

The stepparent's role will vary, too, depending on the living arrangements. Noncustodial stepparents can act more like just a friend, while a stepparent in the home will assume a parental role. Roles also differ depending on the age of the stepchild, his or her personality, and individual preferences. For example, a 6-year-old who is somewhat insecure may want a strong parental figure, while a strong-willed 16-year-old will prefer one who is flexible and friendly. A recommendation is to move slowly into a certain role. Stepparents who "come on like gangbusters" are usually resented. Shared or egalitarian marital roles work best. Resentment is likely when individuals feel that inequities exist. Research indicates that women in second relationships do a smaller proportion of housework than others because the man contributes more in this area (Sullivan, 1997).

Emotions are generally more intense, and often confusing, in a stepfamily. A full range of feelings is probable as people progress through stages of stepfamily life. People in stepfamilies are likely to have their share of hurt, disappointment, jealousy, fear, and anger. Freedom in expression and open communication are especially helpful. Empathy is sorely needed. Of utmost importance is for a stepparent to demonstrate warm and nurturing behavior, as much as possible.

For a biological parent outside the stepfamily, acceptance of a new significant adult in your child's life is difficult. "When I heard my sons talking about their stepmother," one divorced parent said, "I wanted to scream that she isn't any kind of mother to you. She's just the one who married your dad!" Stepparents, too, may have jealous or resentful feelings of the children's other parent. Keeping in mind what is best for the children is critical. Additional love and caring adults in their lives are bonuses. "No healthy stepcouple blocks a child from loving a natural parent" (Adams, 1987, p. 46). Additionally, no healthy parent blocks a child from loving a stepparent.

Jealousy and resentment related to a spouse's former mate are common. "I wish she would just go away," one stepparent said of her husband's ex-wife. "She calls and monopolizes his time, and what is so maddening is that he allows it!" Positive communication skills can enable partners to express these feelings in non-combative ways. And learning effective, businesslike ways of parenting with a former spouse, as discussed in a previous section, could alleviate these problems.

In a number of stepfamilies, as noted before, one person is not remarried. In a workshop, a young woman raised her hand and said, "I would like a different term instead of 'remarriage.' This is my first marriage." Because of increased numbers of unmarried births, a high divorce rate, and marriages occurring at later ages, she has a lot of company. More than ever, first marriages today mean becoming an immediate parent. First-marrieds in the stepfamily face some different challenges from those that confront remarried persons. Their emotional concerns may be acute as they deal with the role of stepparenting someone else's children when they have never parented before. Education and support are strongly advised.

A number of potentially stressful issues confront stepfamilies. Discipline and finances topped the list of identified problems for 80 stepfamilies (Knaub, Hanna, & Stinnett, 1984). Strongly recommended is to begin a new family system based on positive parenting principles and the style of democratic discipline described earlier. The use of the authoritative style, which is quite similar to democratic discussed earlier, is supported by research (Fine, Ganong, & Coleman, 1997). The authoritarian style isn't healthy in biological families, and in stepfamilies it becomes a time bomb. Stepchildren do not usually accept a stepparent as an enforcer of limits, at least not initially. Having the biological parent take the lead at first is wise. Both adults working together and being supportive of each other are highly desirable.

If children move back and forth between households, binuclear family issues, identified in a previous section, need attention. A positive finding is that the proportion of children who report good relationships with their noncustodial fathers is higher in stepfamilies than in those where the mother does not have a partner (White & Gilbreth, 2001). The extended family becomes more extended in that stepfamilies have additional sets of grandparents and other relatives involved. How and where a stepfamily will spend holidays is an issue. Flexibility and compromise are necessary. In stepfamilies, people learn that holidays are not dates; instead, they are special times when family members can be together, regardless of the date. Other issues include who pays for what and for whom and in what ways are resources such as child support used; of utmost importance, is estate planning. Developing a parenting coalition that includes stepparents is a wise investment of time and energy. Advantages are more resources and people to deal with issues and events, less tension, more information about the children, less manipulation, and positive feelings for all concerned (Bloomfield, 1993)

A major challenge for stepfamilies is the higher divorce rate of 60 percent for remarriages (Marano, 2000) Various reasons have been suggested. "Dealing with stepchildren and ex-spouses, complex finances, the demands of two careers, and the need to meld two distinctive ways of doing things can create stresses that challenge the best of relationships" (Stuart & Jacobson, 1985, p. 230). Because of all the challenges, the interpersonal relations suggestions in this book are highly recommended.

One reason for lack of success is at the heart of all the others. When people in stepfamilies are neither educated nor prepared to meet the challenges, they find themselves hopelessly frustrated. "Stepfamilies must be built with more than good intentions, dreams, and hopes. Awareness, skills, and realistic expectations can provide a stable structure that permits the stepfamily to achieve its potential" (Einstein, 1982, p. 2)

In order to succeed, learning about this unique family type takes center stage. First, because stepfamily adjustment and integration take time, patience is encouraged. Books, workshops, classes, and programs about remarriage and stepfamilies are valuable educational resources. The Stepfamily Association of America, mentioned earlier, has local chapters throughout the United States. A step-by-step program manual for stepfamilies titled *Stepfamilies Stepping Ahead* (Burt, 1989) is an invaluable help, as are numerous other books and tapes available through the organization (see Resources at the end of this chapter).

Are the benefits worth the challenges? Thousands of stepfamily members would say they are. The "pluses" can include the following:

- Additional caring relationships within the stepfamily and the extended family
- Opportunities for learning and growing derived from other role models and from challenging situations
- Diversity of people and interesting situations
- Emphasis on deep communication and problem solving
- Focus on give-and-take, compromise, and sharing

- Living within intimate love relationships and happy marriages
- Satisfaction from succeeding in spite of challenges
- Joy from being cared for (and maybe even loved) by people who are not biologically related

Many stepfamilies do quite well. Family strength, marital satisfaction, and positive perceptions of family adjustment were found in an early study of 80 step-families (Knaub, Hanna, & Stinnett, 1984). Within two or three years after step-family formation, most children adapt quite well (Demo, 2000). With no biological buffer of love, individuals can learn to care. Susie, a student, wrote that she had a stepfather and then added, "He's several *steps* above what I had." She described their relationship as very loving.

The absolute joy of being affirmed and loved by children who were not born to you is worth all the stressors along the way. Successful stepfamilies prove that human beings are capable of reaching out and developing long-term nurturing and loving family relationships that are not based on biology.

In tracing family diversity, a painful loss and ending can herald the beginning of a new and diverse type of family. The first is usually a single-parent or binuclear family. Life can be stressful and challenging, yet full of potential rewards. A step-family is possibly the next family type. Complexities and challenges are hallmarks of stepfamily life. Education and support can be of great help. Or a family can be di-verse from its inception such as an adoptive family or one headed by same-sex par-ents. Asking the question of whether family structure matters, researchers found that processes—the relationships and what actually happens within families—are much more important than the type of family (Lansford, Ceballo, Abbey, & Stewart, 2001). Perhaps, an author in a celebration of family diversity expresses it best:

> More important for children's development are close, involved relationships with a rich variety of family members and kin-support networks. Children are not disad-vantaged by living in nontraditional family structures; rather, they are victimized by cultural intolerance and a reluctance to accept, embrace, and celebrate family diver-sity. (Demo, 2000)

If you know and value yourself, you are well equipped to meet the multiple challenges involved in parenting and developing strong families. The rewards are bountiful. Unique types of families who succeed illustrate excellent interpersonal relations. Such nourishing relationships are among the finest expressions of love.

LOOKING BACK

- A family is a primary social group and has tremendous influence on the lives of its members.
- A family can be defined as a relatively small domestic group (related by biology, marriage, or adoption) who function as a cooperative unit. For some, any kinlike, cooperative group can be a family.

Reflect

- Of the positive parenting behaviors, which did your parents use? If you are a parent, which are you using?
- What do you think or know would be painful for a child when parents divorce?
- Think of both possible challenges and benefits of being in a stepfamily.

Apply

- Watch a current television program or a movie with special attention to how families are portrayed.
- Write three tips for divorcing parents in regard to children.
- Ask someone who has had stepfamily experience about both the positives and the negatives

---

- Today's society includes several types of families. Identified high-quality family characteristics describe loving, successful relationships.
- Parenting is a major responsibility for which no formal training is mandated. Even though educational resources are available, adults do not typically take advantage of them. Ideally, adults will become educated and make a thoughtful decision about becoming parents.
- Parental responsibilities are numerous. Love and trust are basic to a child's healthy development.
- Fathers are becoming more involved in caregiving; their role is considered as significant as mother's.
- Discipline, defined broadly as the entire process of guiding and teaching a child from infancy to adulthood, has many dimensions. Two styles, authoritarian and permissive, are not recommended. Families can benefit by using democratic discipline.
- Positive parenting behaviors include admitting mistakes, spending quality time with children, demonstrating warmth and affection, showing appreciation, emphasizing uniqueness and freeing children from the restrictions of stereotypes, allowing choices, and managing conflict successfully.
- The role of grandparent is usually extremely enjoyable and satisfying, and relationships between grandchildren and grandparents are typically very loving.
- Today's typical family is no longer the "Father Knows Best" variety. Dual careers characterize the majority of families. Diversity in families is represented by gay and lesbian households, adoptive households, divorced households, single-parent households, and stepfamily households. Research has demonstrated that the quality of family relationships rather than the type is critical in the positive adjustment of its members. Children can flourish in any type of loving environment.
- A major challenge faced by many parents is helping their children cope with divorce. Recommendations, if followed, can make divorce easier on

children. If two biological parents are alive, children are best served by positive experiences with both. Developing a positive parenting coalition with a former spouse is often difficult, yet definitely in the children's best interests.

- A binuclear family is one in which children have biological parents in different households. Regardless of custody arrangement, both parents have responsibilities. Children who are single-parented can adjust positively, and adults can enjoy many rewards.

- A stepfamily consists of a couple and at least one child from a prior relationship. Stepfamilies are rapidly increasing in numbers. Usually formed as a result of death or divorce, they can be complex and challenging.

- Education and support are invaluable helps for stepfamilies. Overcoming a negative societal image, having realistic expectations, developing new roles and relationships, handling all kinds of emotions, and dealing with unique issues are major tasks of stepfamily members. The high divorce rate for stepfamily couples would likely be lower if education about and preparation for stepfamily life were the norm.

- Successful stepfamily relationships develop through application of personal and interactive skills and exemplify what this book emphasizes: positive interpersonal relations.

The family has a special place in thinking about close relationships. Family relationships are central to human existence, health, and happiness.

—Elaine Berscheid and Letitia Anne Peplau

RESOURCES

Family Service America (local agencies in most communities). (800) 221–2681. www.fsanet.org.
Parenting classes and help available through:
    American Red Cross
    Community colleges/university continuing education programs
    Cooperative Extension

Parent Effectiveness Training (PET)
Systematic Training for Effective Parenting (STEP)
YWCA
Divorce help for children and teens;
    www.childrenanddivorce.com
    KidsPeace.www.teencentral.net
Parents Without Partners (local chapters in many communities).

www.parentswithoutpartners.org
Stepfamily Association of America, Inc. (provides education and support with local chapters in many communities and has books and resources for sale). (800) 735–0329 or (402) 477–7837. www.stepfam.org

References

*ADAMS, T. (1987). *Living from the inside out*. Self-published. 1331 Philip St., New Orleans, LA 70130.

ADLER, J., & RAYMOND, J. (2001, Fall/Winter). Fighting back with sweat. *Newsweek*, 35–41.

AGARWAL, S., & VENKETESHWER RAO, A. (2000). Tomato lycopene and its role in human health and chronic diseases. *Canadian Medical Association Journal, 163*(6), 6.

AHMAD, K. (2000). Anger and hostility linked to coronary heart disease. *Lancet 355* (9215), 1621.

*AHRONS, C. (1994). *The good divorce: Keeping your family together when your marriage comes apart*. New York: HarperCollins.

*ALBERT, L., & EINSTEIN, E. (1983). *Dealing with discipline*. Available from Stepfamily Association of America, Inc., 650 J St., Suite 205, Lincoln, NE 68508. Toll-free: 800–735–0329.

*ALBERTI, R., & EMMONS, M. (1975). *Stand up, speak up, talk back*. New York: Pocket Books.

*———. (1995). *Your perfect right: A guide to assertive living*. San Luis Obispo, CA: Impact.

ALBRECHT, K. (1979). *Stress and the manager*. Englewood Cliffs, NJ: Prentice Hall.

ALCOHOL RESEARCH & HEALTH. (2000). Prenatal exposure to alcohol, *24*(1), 32–41.

ALLSOP, S., SAUNDERS, B., & PHILLIPS, M. (2000, January).

The process of relapse in severely dependent male problem drinkers. *Addiction, 95*(1), 95–106.

ALTMAN, I., & TAYLOR, D. A. (1973). *Social penetration theory: The development of interpersonal relationships*. New York: Holt, Rinehart & Winston.

ALTSHUL, S. (2001, September). Protect yourself against HIV. *Prevention, 53*(9), 178–181.

ALZHEIMER'S ASSOCIATION. (2001). Frequently asked questions. Retrieved September 15, 2001 from http://www.alz.org.

AMATO, P. R., & ROGERS, S. J. (1997). A longitudinal study of marital problems and subsequent divorce. *Journal of Marriage and the Family, 59*(3), 612–624.

AMERICAN CANCER SOCIETY (2001). *American Cancer Society predicts US cancer burden for 2001*. Retrieved July 15, 2001 from EBSCOhost database.

*AMES, L. B. (1992). *Raising good kids: A developmental approach to discipline*. Rosemont, NJ: Modern Learning Press.

ANDERSON, B. L., FARRAR, W. B., GOLEN-DREUTZ, D., KUTZ, L. A., MACCALLUM, R., COURTNEY, M. E., & GLASER, R. (1998). Stress and immune responses after surgical treatment for regional breast cancer. *Journal of National Cancer Institute, 90*(1), 30–36.

ANDERSON, D. A., & WADDEN, T. A. (1999). Treating the obese patient. *The Journal*

of the American Medical Association, 8*, 156–167. Retrieved June 13, 2001 from http://www.ama-assn.org.

ANDERSON, K. E., CARMELLA, S. G., YE, M. BLISS, R. L., CHAP, L., MURPHY, L., & HECHT, S. S. (2001). Metabolites of a tobacco-specific lung carcinogen in nonsmoking women exposed to environmental tobacco smoke. *Journal of the National Cancer Institute, 93*, 378–381.

ANDREWS, J. D. (1989). Psychotherapy of depression: A self-confirmatory model. *Psychological Review, 96*, 576–607.

ANYANWU, E., & WATSON, N. (1997). Alcohol dependence: A critical look at the effects of alcohol metabolism. *Review of Environmental Health, 12*(3), 201–213.

ARDELT, M. (2000). Still stable after all these years? Personality stability theory. *Social Psychology Quarterly, 63*(4), 392–405.

ARMAS, G. C. (2002, February 8). Second marriage up, census says. *Associated Press*. Retrieved February 15, 2002 from Electric Library database.

ARNOLD, K. (1995). *Lives of promise*. San Francisco: Jossey-Bass.

ASCHWANDEN, C., & CEDERBORG, L. (1999, October). Run from your nasty habit. *Prevention*, 22.

AUCHINCLOSS, K. (2001, September 24). We shall overcome. *Newsweek*, 18–25.

*An asterisk indicates recommended reading.

AVERILL, J. R. (1997). The emotions: An integrative approach. In R. Hogan, J. Johnson, & S. Briggs (Eds.), *Handbook of personality psychology* (pp. 513–537). San Diego: Academic Press.

AVERSA, S. L., & KIMBERLIN, C. (1996). Psychosocial aspects of antiretroviral medication use among HIV patients. *Patient Education and Counseling, 29*(2), 207–219.

AVERY, C. S. (1989, May). How do you build intimacy in an age of divorce? *Psychology Today,* 27–31.

AXTELL, R. E., BRIGGS, T., CORCORAN, M., & LAMB, M. B. (1997). *Do's and taboos around the world for women in business.* New York: John Wiley & Sons.

AZERRAD, J., & CHANCE, P. (2001, September/October). Why our kids are out of control. *Psychology Today,* 43–48.

BACH, D. (2001). *Smart couples finish rich: 9 steps to creating a rich future for you and your partner.* New York: Broadway Books.

*BACH, G., & WYDEN, P. (1968). *The intimate enemy: How to fight fair in love and marriage.* New York: Avon.

BAILEY, J. M., BOBROW, D., WOLFE, M., & MIKACH, S. (1995). Sexual orientation of adult sons of gay fathers. *Developmental Psychology, 31,* 124–129.

BAKER, B. (2001, April). Grandparents speak out. *AARP Bulletin,* 31–32.

BAKER, K., BEER, J., & BEER, J. (1991). Self-esteem, alcoholism, sensation seeking, GPA, and differential aptitude test scores of high school students in an honor society. *Psychological Reports, 69,* 1147–1150.

BANDURA, A. (1977). *Social learning theory.* Englewood Cliffs, NJ: Prentice Hall.

———. (1986). *Social foundations of thought and action: A social-cognitive theory.* Englewood Cliffs, NJ: Prentice Hall.

BARBACH, L., & GEISINGER, D. L. (1991). *Going the distance: Secrets to lifelong love.* New York: Doubleday.

BARBOR, C. (2001). The science of meditation. *Psychology Today, 34*(3), 54–58.

BARON, R. A. (1990). *Understanding human relations: A practical guide to people at work.* Boston: Allyn & Bacon.

———. (1998). *Psychology.* Boston: Allyn & Bacon.

BARTOLOMEO, J. (2000, March). Sweat away the stress. *Women's Sports and Fitness,* 108–109.

BATSON, C. D., POLYCARPOU, M. P., HARMON-JONES, E., IMHOFF, H. J., MITCHENER, E. C., BEDNR, L. L., KLEIN, T. R., & HIGHBERGER, L. (1997). Empathy and attitudes: Can feeling for a member of a stigmatized group improve feelings toward the group? *Journal of Personality and Social Psychology, 72*(1), 105–118.

BATTLE, J. J. (1998, July). What beats having two parents? *Journal of Black Studies, 28*(6), 783–801.

BATTY, D. (2000, December). Does physical activity prevent cancer? *British Medical Journal, 321*(7274), 1424–1425.

BAUMEISTER, R. F. (1997). Identity, self-concept, and self-esteem: The self lost and found. In R. Hogan, J. Johnson, & S. Briggs (Eds.), *Handbook of personality psychology,* 681–703. San Diego: Academic Press.

*BAUMEL, S. (1995). *Dealing with depression naturally.* New Canaan, CT: Keats.

*BEATTIE, M. (1987). *Co-dependent no more.* New York: Harper/Hazelden.

*———. (1989). *Beyond codependency and getting better all the time.* San Francisco: Harper & Row.

*———. (1991). *A reason to live.* Wheaton, IL: Tyndale House.

BECHMAN, J. C., BURKER, E. J., LYTLE, B. L., FELDMAN, M. E., & COSTAKIS, M. J. (1997). Self-efficacy and adjustment in cancer patients: A preliminary report *Behavioral Medicine, 23*(3), 138–142

*BECK, A. (1988). *Love is never enough.* New York: Harper & Row.

BELSIE, L. (2002, February 8). America's on/off relationship with wedlock. *Christian Science Monitor,* 3.

BELSKY, J. K. (1988). *Here tomorrow: Making the most of life after fifty.* Baltimore: Johns Hopkins University Press.

BEM, S. L. (1974). The measurement of psychological androgyny. *Journal of Consulting and Clinical Psychology, 42*(2), 155–162.

———. (1975). Sex role adaptability: One consequence of psychological adaptability. *Journal of Personality and Social Psychology, 31,* 634–643.

———. (1993). *The lenses of gender.* New Haven, CT: Yale University Press.

BENET-MARTINEZ, V., & JOHN, O. P. (1998). *Los Cinco Grandes* across cultures and ethnic groups: Multitrait multimethod analyses of the Big Five in Spanish and English. *Journal of Personality and Social Psychology, 75,* 729–750.

*BENSON, H. (1975). *The relaxation response*. New York: Avon.

———. (1987). *Your maximum mind*. New York: Random House.

———. (2001). Mind-body pioneer. *Psychology Today, 34*(3), 56–59.

BERGLAS, S., & JONES, E. E. (1978). Drug choice as a self-handicapping strategy in response to noncontingent success. *Journal of Personality and Social Psychology, 36*, 405–417.

BERK, L. S. (1996). The laughter-immune connection: New discoveries. *Humor and Health Journal, 5*(5). Retrieved July 15, 2001 from http://www.drleeberk.com.

BERK, L. S., FELTEN, D. L., TAN, S. A., BITTMAN, B. B., & WESTENGARD, J. (2001, March). Modulations of neuroimmune parameters during the eustress of humor-associated mirthful laughter. *Alternative Therapies, 7*(2), 62–66.

BERNARD, J. (1956). *Remarriage: A study in marriage*. New York: Russell and Russell.

BERNE, E. (1962). Classification of positions. *Transactional Analysis Bulletin, 1*, 23.

———. (1972). *What do you say after you say hello?* New York: Bantam.

BERRY, D. S., PENNEBAKER, J. W., MUELLER, J. S., & HILLER, W. S. (1997). Linguistic bases of social perception. *Personality and Social Psychology Bulletin, 23*(5), 526–537.

BERTHIAUME, M., DAVID, H., SAUCIER, J. F., & BORGEAT, F. (1996). Correlates of gender role orientation during pregnancy and the postpartum. *Sex-Roles, 35*(11–12), 781–800.

*BETTLELHEIM, B. (1987). *A good enough parent*. New York: Random House.

BIANCHI, S. M., & ROBINSON, J. (1997). What did you do today? Children's use of time, family composition, and the acquisition of social capital. *Journal of Marriage and the Family, 59*(2), 332–344.

BIANCHI, S. M., MILKIE, M. A., SAYER, L. C. & ROBINSON, J. P. (2000, September). Is anyone doing the housework? Trends in the gender division of household labor. *Social Forces, 79*(1), 191–228.

BILYEAU, N. (1998, April). Walk 45 minutes a day. *Health*, 73–75.

BLACK, S. (2000, December). A wake-up call on high-school starting times. *Education Digest, 66*(4), 33–37.

*BLOOMFIELD, H. H. (WITH FELDER, L.). (1996a). *Making peace with yourself*. New York: Ballantine.

*———. (1996b). *Making peace with your parents*. New York: Ballantine.

BLOOMFIELD, H., & GOLDBERG, P. (2000). *Making peace with your past*. New York: HarperCollins.

*BLOOMFIELD, H. H. (WITH KORY, R). (1978). *The holistic way to health and happiness*. New York: Simon & Schuster.

*———. (1980). *Inner joy: New strategies for adding (more) pleasure to your life*. New York: Wyden.

*———. (1993). *Making peace in your stepfamily*. New York: Hyperion.

BLUM, D. (1998, April). What makes Troy gay? *Health*, 82–87.

*BLUMENFELD, W. J. (1992). *Homophobia: How we all pay the price*. Boston: Beacon Press.

BOGENSCHNEIDER, K. (1997). Parental involvement in adolescent schooling: A proximal process with transcontextual validity. *Journal of Marriage and the Family, 9*(3), 718–733.

*BOLLES, R. N. (2001). *What color is your parachute?* Berkeley, CA: Ten Speed Press.

*BOOHER, D. (2001). *E-writing: 21st century tools for effective communication*. New York: Pocket Books.

BOON, S. D., & BRUSSONI, M. J. (1998). Popular images of grandparents: Examining young adults' views of their closest grandparents. *Personal Relationships, 5*, 105–119.

BORCHERDT, B. (1996). *Head over heart in love: 25 guides to rational passion*. Sarasota, FL: Professional Resource Press.

BORDERS, L. D., BLACK, L. K., & PASLEY, B. K. (1998). Are adopted children and their parents at greater risk for negative outcomes? *Family Relations, 47*, 237–241.

*BORTZ, W. M. (1991). *We live too short and die too long*. New York: Bantam.

BOTHWELL, R., & SCOTT, J. (1997). The influence of cognitive variables on recovery in depressed inpatients. *Journal of Affective Disorders, 43*(3), 207–212.

BOWER, B. (2001). Healthy aging may depend on past habits. *Science News, 159*(24), 373.

BOWLIN, S. J., LESKE, M. C., VARMA, A., NASCA, P., WEINSTEIN, A., & CAPLAN, L. (1997). Breast cancer risk and alcohol consumption: Results from a large case-control study. *International Journal of Epidemiology, 26*(5), 915–923.

BRADLEY, C. R. (1998). Cultural interpretations of child discipline: Voices of African American scholars. *Family Journal, 6*(4), 272–278.

BRAMLETT, M. D., & MOSHER, W. D. (2001, May 31). First marriage dissolution, divorce, and remarriage: United States. Retrieved August 25, 2001 from http://www.cdc.gov/nchs.

*BRAMSON, R. M. (1988). *Coping with difficult people*. Garden City, NY: Anchor/Doubleday.

*———. (1992). *Coping with difficult bosses*. New York: Carol.

*BRANDEN, N. (1983). *Honoring the self*. Los Angeles: Tarcher.

*———. (1992). *The power of self-esteem*. Deerfield Beach, FL: Health Communications.

*BRANDEN, N., & BRANDEN, E. D. (1982). *The romantic love question and answer book*. Los Angeles: Tarcher.

*BRAVO, E., & CASSEDY, E. (1992). *The 9 to 5 guide to combating sexual harassment*. New York: Wiley.

*BRENNER, V., & FOX, R. A. (1998, June). Parental discipline and behaviour problems in young children. *Journal of Genetic Psychology, 159*(2), 251–256.

*BRIGGS, D. C. (1970). *Your child's self-esteem*. Garden City, NY: Doubleday.

———. (1977). *Celebrate yourself: Enhancing your own self-esteem*. New York: Doubleday.

BRINK, S. (2000, January 17). Weighing alcohol's benefits. *U.S. News & World Report, 128*(2), 62.

———. (2001, May 7). Your brain on alcohol. *U.S. News & World Report, 130*(18), 50–57.

BRODY, G. H., MOORE, K., & GLEI, D. (1994). Family processes during adolescence as predictors of parent-young adult attitude similarity: A six-year longitudinal analysis. *Family Relations, 43*, 369–373.

BROOKS, G. R. (2001). Masculinity and men's mental health. *Journal of American College Health 49*(6), 285–287.

BUNTAINE, R. L., & COSTENBADER, V. K. (1997). Self-reported differences in the experience and expression of anger between girls and boys. *Sex Roles, 36*, (9–10), 625–637.

BUREAU OF LABOUR STATISTICS. (2001). Employment characteristics of families in 2000. Retrieved September 6, 2001 from http://www.bls.gov/news.release/famee.txt.

*BURKA, J. B., & YUEN, L. M. (1983). *Procrastination: Why you do it, what to do about it*. Reading, MA: Addison-Wesley.

BURKE, E. (1999). Test-anxious learners. *Adults Learning, 10*(6), 23–24.

*BURNS, D. D. (1980). *Feeling good: The new mood therapy*. New York: New American Library.

*———. (1985). *Intimate connections*. New York: Morrow.

*———. (1989). *The feeling good handbook*. New York: Morrow.

*BURT, M. (1989). *Stepfamilies stepping ahead: An eight-step program for successful stepfamily living*. Available from Stepfamily Association of America, Inc., 650 J St., Suite 205, Lincoln, NE 68508. Toll-free: 800-735-0329.

*BUSCAGLIA, L. (1982). *Living, loving, and learning*. New York: Ballantine.

*———. (1984). *Loving each other*. Thorofare, NJ: Slack.

*———. (1992). *Born for love: Reflections on loving*. Thorofare, NJ: Slack.

BUSINESS WEEK. (1999, April 12). Who's stressed out at work? 26.

BUSS, D. M. (2000, May/June). Prescription. *Psychology Today*, 54–61.

BUTCHER, J. (2000). Sleep deprivation. *Lancet, 356*(9245), 1907.

*BUTLER, P. E. (1992). *Self-assertion for women*. New York: HarperCollins.

BUTLER, R. N. (2001, Fall/Winter). The myth of old age. *Newsweek*, 33.

BUTTON, E. J., LOAN, P., & DAVIES, J. (1997). Self-esteem, eating problems, and psychological well-being in a cohort of schoolgirls aged 15–16: A questionnaire and interview study. *International Journal of Eating Disorders, 21*, 39–47.

BUUNK, B. P., & PRINS, K. S. (1998). Loneliness, exchange orientation and reciprocity in friendships. *Personal Relationships, 5*, 1–14.

BYBEE, J., LUTHAR, S., ZIGLER, E., & MERISCA, R. (1997). The fantasy, ideal, and ought selves: Content, relationships to mental health, and functions. *Social Cognition, 15*(1), 37–53.

BYERS, E. S., & DEMMONS, S. (1999, May). Sexual satisfaction and sexual self-disclosure within dating relationships. *Journal of Sex Research, 36*(2), 180–189.

BYRNE, D. (1971). *The attraction paradigm*. New York: Academic Press.

CALABRESE, K. R. (2000, November). Interpersonal conflict and sarcasm in the workplace. *Genetic, Social and General Psychology Monographs, 126*(4), 459–495.

CANADIAN MANAGER. (1999, Summer). Meeting the people challenge, 20–24.

*CANFIELD, J., & SIICCONE, F. (1993). *101 ways to develop student self-esteem and responsibility*. Boston: Allyn & Bacon.

CARDUCCI, B. J. (WITH GOLANT, S. K.) (1999). *Shyness: A bold new approach*. New York: HarperCollins.

CARL, H. (1980, December). Nonverbal communication during the employment interview. *ABCA Bulletin*, 14–18.

*CARLSON, B., & SEIDEN, O. J. (1988). *Healthwalk*. Golden, CO: Fulcrum.

CARLSON, R. (1999). *You can be happy no matter what: Five principles for keeping life in perspective*. California: New World Library.

CARMAN, M. B. (1997). The psychology of normal aging. *Psychiatric Clinics of North America*, 20(1), 15–24.

CARPER, J. (2000). *Your miracle brain*. New York: Harper Collins.

CARRIG, M. (1999). Interpersonal skills are key in office of the future. *TMA Journal*, 19(4), 53.

*CARTER-SCOTT, C. (1989). *Negaholism: How to recover from your addiction to negativity and turn your life around*. New York: Villard.

*CASTLEMAN, M. (1989). *Sexual solutions*. New York: Simon & Schuster.

CEJKA, M. A., & EAGLY, A. H. (1999). Gender-stereotypic images of occupations correspond to the sex segregation of employment. *PSPB*, 25(4), 413–423.

CENTERS FOR DISEASE CONTROL AND PREVENTION. (1999). Youth risk behavior surveillance—United States, 1999. Retrieved August 20, 2001 from http://www.cdc.gov.

———. (2000). HIV/AIDS Update. Retrieved September 15, 2001 from http://www.cdc.gov.

———. (2001a). Tobacco information and prevention source. Retrieved September 15, 2001 from http://www.cdc.gov/tobacco.

———. (2001b). Teen pregnancy. Retrieved August 20, 2001 from http://www.cdc.gov/nccdphp/teen.

CERVONE, D. (2000). Thinking about self-efficacy. *Behavior Modification*, 24(1), 30–57.

CHANCE, P. (1988, February). The trouble with love. *Psychology Today*, 22–23.

CHANDLER, M. (2001, August 11). Gen Xer's saving habits vary. *Lincoln Journal Star*, 4A.

*CHAPMAN, E. N. (1993). *Your attitude is showing*. Chicago: Science Research Associates.

CJEM, Z. Y., & KAPLAN, H. B. (2001, February). Intergenerational transmission of constructive parenting. *Journal of Marriage and Family*, 63, 17–31.

CHIU, L. H. (1997). Development and validation of the school achievement motivation rating scale. *Educational and Psychological Measurement*, 57(2), 292–305.

CHOI, C. (2001, January 30). Women with high-profile jobs, ratings but still hold few top positions. Retrieved January 31, 2001 from http://www.DiversityInc.com.

*CHOPICH, E. J., & PAUL, M. (1990). *Healing your aloneness: Finding love and wholeness through your inner child*. New York: HarperCollins.

CLARK, B. J. (1997). The fun kids club: Developing an effective school-based program for children at risk. *Journal of Psychohistory*, 24(4), 361–369.

*CLARKE, J. I. (1982). *Self-esteem: A family affair*. Minneapolis: Winston.

CLARKSON, P. (1992). *Transactional analysis psychotherapy: An integrated approach*. London: Tavistock/Routledge.

CLASSEN, C., KOOPMAN, C., ANGELL, K., & SPIEGEL, D. (1996). Coping styles associated with psychological adjustment to advanced breast cancer. *Health Psychology*, 15(6), 434–437.

CLIFFORD, L. (2000, August 14). Getting over the hump before you're over the hill. *Fortune*, 145–150.

COCHRANE, D. L. (1992). *Work-related conflict can be productive*. Chicago: Dartnell.

COCOLA, N. W., & MATTHEWS, A. M. (1992). *How to manage your mother: Skills and strategies to improve mother-daughter relationships*. New York: Simon & Schuster.

COHEN, D. A., & GELFAND, R. M. (2000). *Just get me through this!* New York: Kensington Books.

COHRAN, S. V., & RABINOWITZ, F. E. (2000). *Men and depression: Clinical and empirical perspectives*. San Diego, CA: Academic Press.

COLEMAN, M., & GANONG, L. H. (1985). Love and sex role stereotypes: Do macho men and feminine women make better lovers? *Journal of Personality and Social Psychology*, 49(1), 170–176.

———. (1989). Stepfamily self-help books: Brief annotations and ratings. *Family Relations*, 38, 91–96.

COLEMAN, M., GANONG, L., & FINE, M. (2000, November). Reinvestigating remarriage: Another decade of progress.

Journal of Marriage & the Family, 62(4), 1288–1307.

*COLGROVE, M., BLOOMFIELD, H. H., & MCWILLIAMS, P. (1991). *How to survive the loss of a love.* Los Angeles: Prelude.

CONGER, J. J., & PETERSON, A. C. (1984). *Adolescence and youth: Psychological development in a changing world.* New York: Harper & Row.

CONSUMER REPORTS ON HEALTH. (2001, February). Check your anger. *13*(2), 7.

COOKSEY, E. C., & FONDELL, M. M. (1996). Spending time with his kids: Effects of family structure on fathers' and children's lives. *Journal of Marriage and the Family, 58*(3), 693–707.

COOPERSMITH, S. (1967). *The antecedents of self-esteem.* San Francisco: Freeman.

COSTA, P. T., & MCCRAE, R. R. (1997). Longitudinal stability of adult personality. In R. Hogan, J. Johnson, & S. Briggs (Eds.), *Handbook of personality psychology* (pp. 269–285). San Diego: Academic Press.

*COUSINS, N. (1979). *Anatomy of an illness.* New York: Bantam.

*———. (1983). *The healing heart.* New York: Avon.

*———. (1989). *Head first.* New York: Penguin.

*———. (1991). *The celebration of life.* New York: Bantam.

*COWAN, C., & KINDER, M. (1987). *Women men love, women men leave.* New York: Clarkson N. Potter.

COWLEY, G. (2001, January 29). The skin-cancer scare. *Newsweek,* 58.

*CROSE, R. (1997). *Why women live longer than men and what men can learn from them.* San Francisco: Jossey-Bass.

CROTHERS, M., & WARREN, L. W. (1996). Parental an-

tecedents of adult codependency. *Journal of Clinical Psychology, 52*(2), 231–239.

CROWDER, K. D., & TOLNAY, S. E. (2000). A new marriage squeeze for black women: The role of racial intermarriage by black men. *Journal of Marriage & the Family, 62*(3), 792–807.

CROWTHER, C. E. (1986). *Intimacy: Strategies for successful relationships.* Santa Barbara, CA: Capra.

CUMMINGS, E. M., & O'REILLY, A. W. (1997). Fathers in family context: Effects of marital quality on child adjustment. In M. E. Lamb (Ed.). *The role of the father in child development* (pp. 49–65). New York: Wiley.

CUNNINGHAM, M. (2001, February). The influence of parental attitudes and behaviors on children's attitudes toward gender and household labor in early adulthood. *Journal of Marriage and Family, 63,* 111–122.

CURRENT HEALTH 2. (2000, February). *If you don't snooze, you lose, 26*(6), 2. Retrieved June 18, 2001 from EBSCO-host database.

CULTER, B. (1989, September). Are you an average person? *Reader's Digest,* 189–195.

DAINTON, M. (1998, Summer). Everyday interaction in marital relationships: variations in relative importance and event duration. *Communication Reports, 11*(2), 101–109.

DANIEL, A. G. F. (1998, October 26). Success secret: A high emotional IQ. *Fortune,* 293.

DANNER, D. D., SNOWDON, D. A., & FRIESEN, W. V. (2001). Positive emotions in early life and longevity: Findings from the nun

study. *Journal of Personality and Social Psychology, 80*(5), 804–814.

DAUGHERTY, P. W., RANDALL, K. P., & GLOBETTI, E. (1997). Psychological types among women senior student affairs officers on college and university campuses. *Journal of Psychological Type, 41,* 28–32.

*DAVIS, D. L. (1991). *Empty cradle, broken heart.* Golden, CO: Fulcrum.

DAVIS-PACKARD, K. (2000, August 15). Why the number of teen mothers is falling. *Christian Science Monitor, 92*(185), 1.

DAWSON-THREAT, J., & HUBA, M. E. (1996). Choice of major and clarity of purpose among college seniors as a function of gender, type of major, and sex-role identification. *Journal of College Student Development, 37*(3), 297–308.

DAY, R. D., PETERSON, G. W., & MCCRACKEN, C. (1998). Predicting spanking of younger and older children by mothers and fathers. *Journal of Marriage and the Family, 60*(1), 79–94.

DEFFENBACHER, J. L., LYNCH, R. S., OETTING, E. R., & KEMPER, C. C. (1996). Anger reduction in early adolescence. *Journal of Counseling Psychology, 43*(2), 149–157.

DEGAETANO, G., & SIMINI, B. (2001). Drink in moderation, says consensus panel. *Lancet, 357*(9267), 1511.

DEMARIS, A. (2001). The influence of intimate violence on transitions out of cohabitation. *Journal of Marriage and the Family, 63*(1), 235–246.

DEMO, D. H. (2000). Children's experience of family diversity. *National Forum, 80*(3), 16–20.

DERR, C. B. (1986). *Managing the new careerists The diverse career success orientations of today's workers*. San Francisco: Jossey-Bass.

DESPELDER, L. A., & STRICKLAND, A. L. (1999). The last dance: Encountering death and dying. Mountain View, CA: Mayfield.

DEVLIN, B., DANIELS, M., & ROEDER, K. (1997, July). The heritability of IQ. *Nature, 388*(31), 468–471.

DEVRIES, B., DAVIS, C. G., WORTMAN, C. B., & LEHMAN, D. R. (1997). Long-term psychological and somatic consequences of later life parental bereavement. *Omega: Journal of Death and Dying, 35*(1), 97–117.

DIEGO, M. A., & FIELD, T. (2001). HIV adolescents show improved immune function following massage therapy. *International Journal of Neuroscience, 106*(1–2). 35–45.

*DINKMEYER, D., & McKAY, G. D. (1996). *Raising a responsible child*. New York: Simon & Schuster.

DOHERTY, W. J., KOUNESKI, E. F., & ERICKSON, M. F. (1998). Responsible fathering: An overview and conceptual framework. *Journal of Marriage and the Family, 60*(2), 277–292.

DOLGIN, K. L. (2001). Men's friendships: Mismeasured, demeaned, and misunderstood? In T. F. Cohen (Ed). *Men and masculinity*. New York: Wadsworth.

DONALDSON, L., & SCANNELL, E. E. (1986). *Human resource development: The new trainer's guide*. Reading, MA: Addison-Wesley.

*DONNELLEY, N. H. (1987). *I never know what to say*. New York: Ballantine.

*DONNELLY, K. F. (2000). *Recovering from the loss of a parent*. New York: Berkely.

*———. (2001). *Recovering from the loss of a child*. New York: Berkley.

*DOWLING, C. (1991). *You mean I don't have to feel this way?* New York: Charles Scribner's Sons.

DOWNEY, D. B., AINSWORTH-DARNELL, J. W., & DUFUR, M. J. (1998). Sex of parent and children's well-being in single-parent households. *Journal of Marriage & the Family, 60*(4), 878–893.

DOYLE, J. A., & PALUDI, M. A. (1998). *Sex and gender: The human experience*. Boston: McGraw-Hill.

DUNKIN, A. (2000, February 21). Adopting? You deserve benefits, too. *Business Weekly*, 160.

DUNNING, D. (2001). *What's your type of career?* Palo Alto, CA: Davies-Black Publishing.

DUVANDER, A. Z. E. (1999). The transition from cohabitation to marriage. *Journal of Family Issues, 20*(5), 698–717.

*DYER, W. (1976). *Your erroneous zones*. New York: Funk & Wagnalls.

*———. (1990). *The sky's the limit*. New York: Pocket Books.

*———. (1992). *Real magic*. New York: HarperCollins.

EDER, R. A., & MANGELSDORF, S. C. (1997). The emotional basis of early personality development: Implications for the emergent self-concept. In R. Hogan, J. Johnson, & S. Briggs (Eds.), *Handbook of personality psychology* (pp. 209–324). San Diego, CA: Academic Press.

EDMOND, T., RUBIN, A., & WAMBACK, K. G. (1999). The effectiveness of EDMR with adult female survivors of childhood sexual abuse. *Social Work Research, 23*(2), 103–116.

*EDWARDS, D. (1989). *Grieving: The pain and the promise*. Salt Lake City: Covenant.

EHRENBERG, M. F., GEARING-SMALL, M., HUNTER, M. A., & SMALL, B. J. (2001). Child-care task division and shared parenting attitudes in dual-earner families with young children. *Family Relations, 50*(2), 143–153.

*EINSTEIN, E. (1982). *The stepfamily: Living, loving, and learning*. Boston: Shambhala.

EKMAN, P. (1994). Strong evidence for universals in facial expressions: A reply to Russell's mistaken critique. *Psychological Bulletin, 115*, 268–287.

EKMAN, P., DAVIDSON, R. J., & FRIESEN, W. V. (1990). The Duchenne smile: Emotional expression and brain physiology. *Journal of Personality and Social Psychology, 58*, 342–353.

ELIOT, R. S., & BREO, D. L. (1984). *Is it worth dying for?* New York: Bantam.

ELLIS, A. (1977). The basic clinical theory of rational-emotive therapy. In A. Ellis & R. Grieger (Eds.), *Handbook of rational-emotive therapy* (pp. 3–34). New York: Springer.

———. (1984). The essence of RET. *Journal of Rational-Emotive Therapy, 2*, 19–25.

———. (1993). Reflections on rational-emotive therapy. *Journal of Consulting and Clinical Psychology 61*(2), 199–201.

———. (1996). The treatment of morbid jealousy: A rational-emotive behavior therapy approach. *Journal of Cognitive Psychotherapy, 10*(1), 23–33.

ELLSWORTH, B. A. (1988). *Living in love with yourself.* Salt Lake City: Breakthrough.

EMERSON, J. (2000). The sandwich generation. *DollarSense,* 8–10.

ENRIGHT, R. D. (2001). *Forgiveness Is a choice.* Washington, DC: American Psychological Association.

ERIKSON, E. (1963). *The challenge of youth.* New York: Norton.

———. (1968). *Identity: Youth and crisis.* New York: Norton.

ERNST, F. H. (1973). *Who's listening?* Vallejo, CA: Addresso' set.

ETTER, J. F., BERGMAN, M. M., HUMAIR, J. P., & PERNEGERI, T. V. (2000). Development and validation of a scale measuring self-efficacy of current and former smokers. *Addiction, 95*(6), 901–914.

EVANS, K. (2000, April). Is stress wrecking your mood? *Health,* 118–129.

*EVANS, P. (1996). *The verbally abusive relationship: How to recognize it and how to respond.* Holbrook, MA: Bob Adams.

EYRE, L., & EYRE, R. (1993). *Teaching your children values.* New York: Simon & Schuster.

EYSENCK, H. J. (1988, December). Health's character. *Psychology Today,* 23–35.

FARLEY, C. J. (1997, November 24). Kids and race. *Time,* 88–91.

*FARRELL, W. (1986). *Why men are the way they are: The male-female dynamic.* New York: McGraw-Hill.

*FAST, J. (1970). *Body language.* New York: M. Evans.

FAVA, G. A., RAFANELLI, C., GRANDI, S., CONTI, S., & BELLUARDO, P. (1998, September). Prevention of recurrent depression with cognitive behavioral ther-

apy. *Arch Gen Psychiatry, 55,* 816–820.

FELDMAN, R. S. (2000). *Development across the life span.* Upper Saddle River, NJ: Prentice Hall.

FERRARI, J. R. (1991). Compulsive procrastination: Some self-reported characteristics. *Psychological Reports, 68,* 455–458.

FERRENCE, R., & ASHLEY, M. J. (2000). Protecting children from passive smoking. *British Medical Journal, 321*(7257), 310–311.

FETTO, J., & LACH, J. (2000, June). With this ring. *American Demographics,* 14–15.

FIELD, T. M. (1996). Touch therapies for pain management and stress reduction. In R. J. Resnick & R. H. Rozensky (Eds.), *Health psychology through the life span: Practice and research opportunities* (pp. 313–321). Washington, DC: American Psychological Association.

FIELDS, J., & CASPER, L. M. (2000). America's families and living arrangements. Retrieved August 23, 2001 from http://www.census.gov.

FINE, M. A., GANONG, L. H., & COLEMAN, M. (1997). The relation between role constructions and adjustments among stepfathers. *Journal of Family Issues, 18,* 503–525.

FINE, M. A., & OLSON, K. A. (1997). Anger and hurt in response to provocation: Relationship to psychological adjustment. *Journal of Social Behavior and Personality, 12*(2), 325–344.

*FISHER, B. (1992). *Rebuilding: When your relationship ends.* San Luis Obispo, CA: Impact.

FISHER, C. S., JACKSON, R. M., STUEVE, C. A., GERSON, K.,

JONES, L. M., & BALDASSARE, M. (1977). *Networks and places: Social relations in the urban setting.* New York: Free Press.

FITZGERALD, B. (1999). Children of lesbian and gay parents: A review of the literature. *Marriage & Family Review, 29*(1), 57–75.

*FLANIGAN, B. (1992). *Forgiving the unforgivable.* New York: Macmillan.

*———. (1996). *Forgiving yourself: A step-by-step guide to making peace with your mistakes and getting on with your life.* New York: Simon & Schuster.

FLETT, G. L., HEWITT, P. L., & DEROSA, T. (1996). Dimensions of perfectionism, psychosocial adjustment, and social skills. *Personality and Individual Differences, 20*(2), 143–150.

FLYNN, C. P. (1999, November). Exploring the links between corporal punishment and children's cruelty to animals. *Journal of Marriage and the Family, 61*(4), 971–981.

FOLSOM, A. R., & KUSHIT, L. H. (2000, January). Physical activity and incident diabetes mellitus in postmenopausal women. *American Journal of Public Health, 90*(1), 134–139.

FONOW, M. M. (1998). Difference and inequality. In M. M. Fonow (Ed.), *Reading women's lives* (pp. 101–106). Needham Heights, MA: Simon & Schuster Custom Publishing.

*FORWARD, S. (WITH BUCK, C.). (1989). *Toxic parents: Overcoming their hurtful legacy and reclaiming your life.* New York: Bantam.

*———. (1991). *Obsessive love.* New York: Bantam.

*FORWARD, S., & TORRES, J. (1986). *Men who hate women and the women who love them.* Toronto: Bantam.

FOZARD, J. L. (1999). Epidemiologists try many ways to show that physical activity is good for seniors' health and longevity. Review of special issue of journal of aging and physical activity: The evergreen project. *Physical Fitness, 25*(2), 175–183.

FRANZ, C. E., MCCLELLAND, D. C., & WEINBERGER, J. (1991). Childhood antecedents of conventional social accomplishment in midlife adults: A 36-year prospective study. *Journal of Personality and Social Psychology, 60,* 586–595.

*FRIEDAN, B. (1993). *The fountain of age.* New York: Simon & Schuster.

FRIEDLAND, R. P. (1998). Exercise throughout life may provide protection against Alzheimer's. *Modern Medicine, 66*(6), 56.

*FROMM, E. (1956). *The art of loving.* New York Harper & Row.

FUMENTO, M. (1998, May June). Weight after 50: Is there too much on our plate? *Modern Maturity,* 34–41.

FURSTENBERG, F. F., & KIERNAN, K. E. (2001). Delayed parental divorce: How much do children benefit? *Journal of Marriage and the Family, 63*(2), 446–457.

THE FUTURIST. (1999). The dangers of passive smoking, *33*(1), 7.

GAGER, C. T., COONEY, T. M., & CALL, K. T. (1999). The effects of family characteristics and time use on teenagers' household labor. *Journal of Marriage and the Family, 61*(4), 982–994.

GALLANT, M. P., & CONNELL, C. M. (1997). Predictors of mammography use in the past year among elderly women. *Journal of Aging and Health, 9*(3), 373–395.

GANONG, L. H., & COLEMAN, M. (1996). A comparison of clinical and empirical literature on children in stepfamilies. *Journal of Marriage and the Family, 48,* 309–318.

GARDNER, H. (1983). *Frames of mind: The story of multiple intelligences.* New York: Basic Books.

GARDYN, R., & LACH, J. (2000). Love is colorblind . . . or is it? *American Demographics, 22*(6), 11–13.

———. (1999). *Intelligence reframed: Multiple intelligences for the 21st century.* New York: Basic Books.

GERIATRICS. (2000). Alzheimer's: It's more than normal forgetfulness. *55*(2), 22.

*GETZOFF, A., & MCCLENAHAN, M. (1984). *Stepkids: A survival guide for teenagers in stepfamilies.* New York: Walker.

GIBBS, N. R. (1993, May). How should we teach our children about sex? *Time,* 64–71.

———. (1995, October 2). The EQ factor. *Time,* 61–68.

GILLENKIRK, J. (2000, November 4). A revolution in American fathering. *America, 183*(14), 18–21.

GILLIGAN, C. (1982). *In a different voice.* Cambridge, MA: Harvard University Press.

GINOTT, H. (1965). *Between parent and child.* New York: Macmillan.

*———. (1969). *Between parent and teenager.* Toronto: Macmillan.

*GINSBURG, G. D. (1987). *To live again: Rebuilding your life after you've become a widow.* Los Angeles: Tarcher.

GINSBURG, K. R., FEIN, J. A. & JOHNSON, C. D. (1998). Violence prevention in the early years. *Contemporary Pediatrics, 15*(4), 97–110.

GLASER, S. (1986). *Toward communication competency.* New York: Holt, Rinehart & Winston.

GLASSER, W. (1965). *Reality therapy: A new approach to psychiatry.* New York: Harper & Row.

*———. (1984). *Control theory: A new explanation of how we control our lives.* New York: Harper & Row.

GLASSMAN, A. H., & SHAPIRO, P. A. (1998). Depression and the course of coronary artery disease. *American Journal of Psychiatry, 155*(1), 4–11.

GLENN, H. S., & NELSEN, J. (1989). *Raising self-reliant children in a self-indulgent world.* Rocklin, CA: Prima.

GOFFMAN, E. (1959). *Presentation of self in everyday life.* New York: Anchor.

*GOLD, L. (1996). *Between love and hate: A guide to civilized divorce.* New York: NAL Dutton.

GOLDBERG, H. (1979). *The new male.* New York: Signet.

GOLDBERG, K. (1993). *How men can live as long as women: Seven steps to a longer and better life.* Fort Worth, Texas: The Summit Group.

GOLDSTEIN, L., & CONNELLY, M. (1998, April 30). Today's American teens worldly, devoid of cynicism, poll finds. *Lincoln Journal Star,* p. 7A.

GOLEMAN, D. (1991, November 26). New way to battle bias: Fight acts, not feelings. *New York Times,* pp. C1, C8.

*———. (1995). *Emotional intelligence.* New York: Bantam Books.

GOLEMAN, D. (1997). Affective and nourishing emotions: Impacts on health. In D. Goleman (Ed.), *Healing emotions* (pp. 33–46). Boston: Shambhala.

———. (1998). *Working with emotional intelligence*. New York: Bantam Books.

GOODMAN, E. (2001, July 30). Women slighted by Bush plan. *Lincoln Journal Star*, 4B.

GORDON, S. (1996). *Why love is not enough*. Boston: Bob Adams.

GORRELL, C. (2000, November/December). Live-in and learn. *Psychology Today*, 16.

———. (2001, September/October). Finding fault. *Psychology Today*, 24.

GOTTFRIED, A. E., FLEMING, J. S., & GOTTFRIED, A. W. (1994). Role of parental motivational practices in children's academic intrinsic motivation and achievement. *Journal of Educational Psychology*, 86, 104–113.

GOTTMAN, J. M. (1991). Predicting the longitudinal course of marriages. *Journal of Marital and Family Therapy*, 17, 3–7.

*———. (1994a). *Why marriages succeed or fail . . . and how you can make yours last*. New York: Simon & Schuster.

———. (1994b). *What predicts divorce? The relationship between marital processes and marital outcomes*. Hillsdale, NJ: Lawrence Erlbaum Associates.

GOTTMAN, J. M., COAN, J., CARRERE, S., & SWANSON, C. (1988a). Predicting marital happiness and stability from newlywed interactions. *Journal of Marriage and the Family*, 60(1), 5–22.

GOTTMAN, J. M., COAN, J., CARRERE, S., & SWANSON,

C. (1988a). Predicting marital happiness and stability from newlywed interactions. *Journal of Marriage and the Family*, 60(1), 5–22.

*GOTTMAN, J. M. (WITH DE-CLAIRE, J.). (1997). *The heart of parenting: Raising an emotionally intelligent child*. New York: Simon & Schuster.

*GOULDING, M. M., & GOULDING, R. L. (1989). *Not to worry*. New York: Morrow.

GREENBERG, M. (1997). High-rise public housing, optimism, and personal and environment health behaviors. *American Journal of Health Behavior*, 21(5), 388–398.

GREENE, R. (1998, January 12). Political interest among freshmen hits new low, survey finds. *Lincoln Journal Star*, p. 3A.

GREENFIELD, S., & THELEN, M. (1997). Validation of the fear of intimacy scale with a lesbian and gay male population. *Journal of Social and Personal Relationships*, 14(5), 707–716.

GROSSMAN, A. H., & KERNER, M. S. (1998). Self-esteem and supportiveness as predictors of emotional distress in gay male and lesbian youth. *Journal of Homosexuality*, 35(2), 26–39.

GUILBERT, D. E., VACC, N. A., & PASLEY, K. (2000). The relationship of gender role beliefs, negativity, distancing, and marital instability. *Family Journal*, 8(2), 124–132.

*GULLO, S., & CHURCH, C. (1988). *Loveshock: How to recover from a broken heart and love again*. New York: Simon & Schuster.

GUNNOE, M. L., & MARINER, C. L. (1997). Toward a developmental-contextual model of the effects of parental spanking on children's aggression. *Archives of Pediatrics & Adolescent Medicine*, 151(8), 768–775.

HAGGA, D. A., & STEWART, B. L. (1992). Self-efficacy for recovery from a lapse after smoking cessation. *Journal of Consulting and Clinical Psychology*, 60, 24–28.

HAKIM, A. A., PETROVITCH, H., BURCHFIEL, C. M., ROSS, G. W., RIDRIGUEZ, B. L., WHITE, L. R., YANO, K. CURB, J. D., & ABBOTT, R. D. (1998). Effects of walking on mortality among nonsmoking retired men. *New England Journal of Medicine*, 338(2), 94–99.

HALL, E. T. (1969). *The hidden dimension*. New York: Anchor/Doubleday.

———. (1973). *The silent language*. New York: Doubleday.

HALL, P. D. (1999). The effect of meditation on the academic performance of African American college students. *Meditation*, 29(3), 408–416.

HALLORAN, J., & BENTON, D. (1987). *Applied human relations: An organizational approach*. Englewood Cliffs, NJ: Prentice Hall.

*HALLOWELL, E. M. (1997). *Worry: Controlling it and using it wisely*. New York: Pantheon.

HALPERN, D. F., & CROTHERS, M. (1997). Sex, sexual orientation, and cognition. In L. Ellis & L. Ebertz (Eds.), *Sexual orientation: Toward biological understanding* (pp. 181–197). Westport, CT: Praeger.

HAMER, D., & COPELAND, P. (1998). *Living with our genes*. New York: Doubleday.

HAN, W. J., WALDFOGEL, J., & BROOKS-GUNN, J. (2001). The effects of early maternal employment on later cognitive and behavioral outcomes. *Journal of Marriage and the Family*, 63(2), 336–354.

HANNA, S. L. (1980). The strengths within families of remarriage: A descriptive study. Master's thesis, University of Nebraska, Lincoln.

———. (2002). *Career by design: Communicating your way to success*. Upper Saddle River, NJ: Prentice Hall.

HANNA, S. L., & KNAUB, P. K. (1981). Cohabitation before remarriage: Its relationship to family strengths. *Alternative Lifestyles*, 4(4), 507–522.

HANSON, M., STEWARD, V., LUNDWALL, L. K., HIGGINS, M. J., & EL-BASSEL, N. (1997). Correlates of aftercare attendance by socially disadvantaged alcoholics. *Alcoholism Treatment Quarterly*, 15(2), 15–29.

HARJU, B. L., & BOLEN, L. M. (1998). The effects of optimism on coping and perceived quality of life of college students. *Journal of Social Behavior and Personality*, 13(2), 185–201.

HARRIS, J. R. (1998). *The nurture assumption*. New York: The Free Press.

HARRIS, S. (1982, April 3): When your leading role models are entertainers, what kind of a society will you have? *Lincoln Journal Star*, p. 6.

*HARRIS, T. (1969). *I'm ok, you're ok*. New York: Harper & Row.

*HARRIS, T. A. & HARRIS, A. B. (1985). *Staying ok*. New York: Harper & Row.

HARTSTEIN, N. B. (1996). Suicide risk in lesbian, gay, and bisexual youth. In R. P. Cabaj & T. S. Stein (Eds). *Textbook of homosexuality and mental health* (pp. 819–833). Washington, DC: American Psychiatric Press.

HARVARD HEALTH LETTER. (1999, April). Moderate activity keeps heat, waistline in shape, 24(6), 4–6.

———. (2000, September). Five new treatments, 25(11), 2–3.

HARVEY, E. (1999). Short-term and long-term effects of parental employment on children of the National Longitudinal Survey of Youth. *Developmental Psychology*, 35, 445–459.

HASTINGS, S. O. (2000). Asian Indian 'self-suppression' and self-disclosure. *Journal of Language and Social Psychology*, 19(1), 85–109.

HATFIELD, E., & RAPSON, R. L. (1996). *Love and sex: Cross-cultural perspectives*. Boston: Allyn & Bacon.

HAWKINS, A. J., & DOLLANITE, D. C. (1997). *Generative fathering: Beyond deficit perspectives*. Thousand Oaks, CA: Sage.

HAWKINS, A. J., & ROBERTS, T. (1992). Designing a primary intervention to help dual-earner couples share housework and child care. *Family Relations*, 41, 169–177.

*HAY, L. L. (1991). *The power is within you*. Carson, CA: Hay House.

HEALTH. (1997, July/August). No wonder health officials are down on Joe Camel, 48.

———. (1998, July/August). A strong vote for B vitamins, 15.

———. (2000, June). Vital statistics, 24.

HEIDER, F. (1958). *The psychology of interpersonal relations*. New York: Wiley.

*HELMSTETTER, S. (1989). *Predictive parenting: What to say when you talk to your kids*. New York: Pocket Books.

HENDERSON, C. W. (2000, May 20). Depression associated with increased risk for heart disease in men and women. *Women's Health Weekly*, 11.

*HENDLIN, S. J. (1992). *When good enough is never enough*. New York: Putnam's.

HENRY, D. B. (2000). Peer groups, families, and school failure among urban children: Elements of risk and successful interventions. *Preventing School Failure*, 44(3), 97–103.

HENSRUD, D. D. (2001, March 30). How to live longer. *Fortune*, 143(9), 210.

HEREK, G. M. (1996). Heterosexism and homophobia. In R. P. Cabaj & T. S. Stein (Eds.), *Textbook of homosexuality and mental health* (pp. 101–111). Washington, DC: American Psychiatric Press.

HICKLING, L. (2000, November 17). Study: Hearty laughter may be good for the heart. *Health News*. Retrieved July 15, 2001 from http://drkoop.com/news/stories/2000/nov/17_laughter.html.

HILL, L. A. (1994). *Managing your career* (Note 9–494–082). Boston: Harvard Business School Publishing.

HINES, A. M. (1997). Divorce-related transitions, adolescent development, and the role of the parent-child relationship: A review of the literature. *Journal of Marriage and the Family*, 59(2), 375–388.

HOFFMAN, R. M., & BORDER, L. D. (2001). Twenty-five years after the Bem Sex-role Inventory: A reassessment and new issues regarding classification variability. *Measurement & Evaluation in*

Counseling & Development, 34(1), 39–55.

HOLMES, T. H., & RAHE, R. R. (1967). The social readjustment rating scale. *Journal of Psychosomatic Research, 11,* 213–218.

*HOPSON, D. P., & HOPSON, D. S. (1990). *Different and wonderful.* New York: Simon & Schuster.

HORAN, J. J. (1996). Effects of computer-based cognitive restructuring on rationally mediated self-esteem. *Journal of Counseling Psychology, 43*(4), 371–375.

HORN, T. S., LOX, C., & LABRADOR, F. (1998). The self-fulfilling prophecy theory: When coaches' expectations become reality. In J. M. Williams (Ed.), *Applied sport psychology: Personal growth to peak performance* (pp. 74–91). Mountain View, CA: Mayfield.

HOSSAIN, Z. (2001). Division of household labor and family functioning in off-reservation Navajo Indian families. *Family Relations, 50*(3), 255–261.

HOWARD, G., WAGENNECHT, L. E., BURKE, G. L., DIEZ, R. A., EVANS, G. W., McGOVERN, P., NIETO, F. J. & TELL, G. S. (1998). Cigarette smoking and progression of atherosclerosis: The atherosclerosis risk in communities (ARIC) study. *Journal of the American Medical Association, 279*(2), 119–124.

HUPPE, M., & CYR, M. (1997). Division of household labor and marital satisfaction of dual income couples according to family life cycle. *Canadian Journal of Counselling 31*(2), 145–162.

HURDLE, D. E. (2001). Social support: A critical factor in women's health and health promotion. *Health and Social Work, 26*(2), 72–79.

HUSTON, M., & SCHWARTZ, P. (1996). Gendered dynamics in the romantic relationships of lesbians and gays. In J. T. Wood (Ed.); *Gendered relationships* (pp. 163–176). Mountain View, CA: Mayfield.

*HUTCHINSON, E. O. (1992). *Black fatherhood: The guide to male parenting.* Los Angeles: Impact.

HUTCHINSON, K., & COONEY, T. M. (1998). Patterns of parent-teen sexual risk communications: Implications for intervention. *Family Relations, 47*(2), 185–194.

HUWIG, P. (2001, March). A look at lesbian domestic violence. *Lesbian News, 26*(8), 52.

HYATT, R. (1991, March). Self-esteem: The key to happiness. *USA Today,* 86–87.

ISHII-KUNTZ, M., & COLTRANE, S. (1992). Remarriage, stepparenting, and household labor. *Journal of Family Issues, 13,* 215–233.

JACKSON, C., HENRIKSEN, L., DICKINSON, D., & LEVINE, D. W. (1997). The early use of alcohol and tobacco: Its relation to children's competence and parents' behavior. *American Journal of Public Health, 8*(3), 359–364.

JACKSON, M. (1998, May 7). Working moms frustrated with trying to do it all. *Lincoln Journal Star,* p. 1.

*JACOBSON, N. S., & GOTTMAN, J. M. (1998a). *When men batter women: New insights into ending abusive relationships.* New York: Simon & Schuster.

———. (1998b, March/April). Anatomy of a violent relationship. *Psychology Today,* 60–64, 82.

*JAMES, J. W., & CHERRY, F. (1988). *The grief recovery handbook.* New York: Harper & Row.

JAMPOLSKY, G. G. (1979). *Love is letting go of fear.* Millbrae, CA: Celestial Arts.

JAMPOLSKY, G. G., & CIRINCIONE, D. V. (1979). *One person can make a difference.* New York: Bantam.

JANG, K. L., McCRAE, R. R., ANGLEITNER, A., RIEMANN, R., & LIVESLEY, W. J. (1998). Heritability of facet-level traits in a cross-cultural twin sample: Support for a hierachical model of personality. *Journal of Personality and Social Psychology, 74*(6), 1556–1565.

JARET, P. (1998, May/June). Only 5 a day. *Health,* 78–85.

———. (1999, January/February). Move the body, heal the mind. *Health,* 48–50.

*JASPER, J. (1999). *Take back your time.* New York: St. Martin's Griffin.

*JEFFERS, S. (1987). *Feel the fear and do it anyway.* New York: Fawcett Columbine.

*JEFFRIES, W. C. (1991). *True to type.* Norfolk, VA: Hampton Roads.

JEMMOTT, J. B., & JEMMOTT, L. S. (1996). Strategies to reduce the risk of HIV infection, sexually transmitted diseases, and pregnancy among African American adolescents. In R. J. Resnick & R. H. Rozensky (Eds.), *Health psychology through the life span: Practice and research opportunities* (pp. 395–422). Washington, DC: American Psychological Association.

JEVNE, R. (2000). *Hoping, coping, & moping.* Los Angeles: Health Information Press.

JINKS, J., & MORGAN, V. (1999). Children's perceived

academic self-efficacy: An inventory scale. *Clearing House*, 72(4), 224–231.

JOHNSON, D. R., & SCHEUBLE, L. K. (1995). Women's marital naming in two generations: A national study. *Journal of Marriage and the Family*, 57(3), 724–732.

*JOHNSON, H. M. (1986). *How do I love thee?* Salem, WI: Sheffield.

JOHNSON, L. G., SCHWARTZ, R. A., & BOWER, B. L. (2000). Managing stress among adult women students in community colleges. *Community College Journal of Research and Practice*, 24(4), 289–301.

JOLLEY, R. P., ZHI, Z., & THOMAS, G. (1998). The development of understanding moods metaphorically expressed in pictures: A cross-cultural comparison. *Journal of Cross-Cultural Psychology*, 29(2), 358–376.

JONES, N. A., FIELD, T., FOX, N. A., DAVALOS, M., MALPHURS, J., CARAWAY, K., SCHANBERG, S., & KUHN, C. (1997). Infants of intrusive and withdrawn mothers. *Infant Behavior and Development*, 20(2), 175–186.

JONES, M. (1998, June 14). Gays and lesbians have plenty to celebrate this month. *Lincoln Journal Star*, p. 7D.

JORDAN, K. M., & DELUTY, R. H. (1998). Coming out for lesbian women: Its relation to anxiety, positive affectivity, self-esteem, and social support. *Journal of Homesexuality*, 35(2), 41–63.

JOSSELSON, R. (1992). *The space between us*. San Francisco: Jossey-Bass.

JOURARD, S. M. (1971). *The transparent self*. New York: Van Nostrand Reinhold.

JUNG, C. G. (1921). *Psychological types*. Princeton, NJ: Princeton University Press.

———. (1968). *Analytical psychology, its theory and practice*. New York: Vintage.

KAMO, Y., & COHEN, E. L. (1998). Division of household work between partners: A comparison of black and white couples. *Journal of Comparative Family Studies*, 29, 131–145.

KANTROWITZ, B. (2001, May 21). Parents today make more time for quality time. *Newsweek*, 53.

KANTROWITZ, B., & WINGERT, P. (2001, May 28). Unmarried with children. *Newsweek*, 46–55.

*KASL, C. S. (1997). *A home for the heart: Creating intimacy and community with loved ones and friends*. New York: HarperCollins.

KAUFMAN, G. (2000). Do gender role attitudes matter? *Journal of Family Issues*, 21(1), 128–144.

KAUL, D. (1993, January 1). Gen. Powell's stand disappointing. *Lincoln Journal*, p. 6B.

*KEATING, C. J. (1984). *Dealing with difficult people*. Ramsey, NJ: Paulist Press.

*KEEN, S. (1991). *Fire in the belly: On being a man*. New York: Bantam.

*KEIRSEY, D., & BATES, M. (1978). *Please understand me*. Del Mar, CA: Prometheus Nemesis.

KELLER, M. B., MCCULLOUGH, J. P., KLEIN, D. N., ARNOW, B., DUNNER, D. L., GELENBERG, A. L., MARKOWITZ, J. C., NEMEROFF, C. B., RUSSELL, J. M., THASE, M. E., TRIVEDI, M. H., & ZAJECKA, J. (2000). A comparison of nefazodone, the cognitive behavioral-analysis system of psychotherapy, and their combination for the treatment of chronic depression. *The New England Journal of Medicine*, 342(20), 1462–1469.

KELLEY, H. H. (1950). The warm-cold variable in first impressions of persons. *Journal of Personality*, 18, 431–439.

KELLEY, P. (1992). Healthy stepfamily functioning. *Families in Society*, 73, 579–587.

KELLEY, R. M., SYNOVITZ, L., CARLSON, G., & SCHUSTER, A. L. (2001). Sexual behaviors of college students attending four universities in a southern state. *Research Quarterly for Exercise and Sport*, 72(1), A-31.

KELLNER, M. H., & BRY, B. H. (1999). The effects of anger management groups in a day school for emotionally disturbed adolescents. *Adolescence*, 34(16), 645–651.

KELLY, W. E., & MILLER, M. J. (1999). A discussion of worry with suggestions for counselors. *Counseling and Values*, 44(1), 55–67.

*KENNEDY, A. (1991). *Losing a parent: Passage to a new way of living*. New York: HarperCollins.

*KENNEDY, E. (1975). *If you really knew me, would you still like me?* Niles, IL: Argus.

KESSLER, D. A. (1995). Nicotine addiction in young people. *New England Journal of Medicine*, 333, 186–189.

KEYES, K. (1975). *Handbook to higher consciousness*. Coos Bay, OR: Living Love.

KHAW, K., BINGHAM, S., WELCH, A., LUBEN, R., WAREHAM, N., OAKES, S., & DAY, N. (2001). Relation between plasma ascorbic acid and mortality in men and women in Epic-Norfolk

Prospective study: A prospective population study. *Lancet, 357*(9257), 657–663.

KILBOURNE, J. (1995). Beauty and the beast of advertising. In P. S. Rothenberg (Ed.), *Race, class, and gender in the United States: An integrated study*. New York: St. Martin's.

*KILEY, D. (1989). *Living together feeling alone*. New York: Prentice Hall.

*KINDER, M., & COWAN, C. (1989). *Husbands and wives*. New York: Penguin.

KIRCHMEYER, C. (1996). Gender roles and decision-making in demographically diverse groups: A case for reviving androgyny. *Sex Roles, 34*(9–10), 649–663.

KLINGER, R. L., & STEIN, T. S. (1996). Impact of violence, childhood sexual abuse, and domestic violence and abuse on lesbians, bisexuals, and gay men. In R. P. Cabaj & T. S. Stein (Eds.), *Textbook of homosexuality and mental health* (pp. 801–815). Washington, DC: American Psychiatric Press.

KNAUB, P. K., & HANNA, S. L. (1984). Children of remarriage: Perceptions of family strength. *Journal of Divorce, 7*(4), 73–90.

KNAUB, P. K., HANNA, S. L., & STINNETT, N. (1984). Strengths of remarried families. *Journal of Divorce, 7*(3), 41–55.

*KNAUS, W. J. (1998). *Do it now! Break the procrastination habit*. New York: Wiley.

KNOX, D., DANIELS, V., STURDIVANT, L., & ZUSMAN, M. E. (2001). College student use of the Internet for mate selection. *College Student Journal, 35*(1), 158–157.

KOBASA, S. C. (1979). Stressful life events, personality, and health: An inquiry into hardiness. *Journal of Personality and Social Psychology, 37*(1), 1–11.

KOHLBERG, L. (1963). The development of children's orientations toward a moral order I: Sequence in the development of moral thought. *Vita Humana, 6*, 11–35.

KOWALKSI, K. M. (2001, April/May). Debunking myths about alcohol. *Current Health 2, 27*(8), 6–11.

*KROEGER, O., & THUESEN, J. M. (1993). *Type talk at work*. New York: Delacorte.

KUBANY, E. S., RICHARD, D. C., BAUER, G. B., & MURAOKA, M. Y. (1992). Verbalized anger and accusatory "you" messages as cues for anger and antagonism among adolescents. *Adolescence, 27*, 505–516.

*KÜBLER-ROSS, E. (1969). *On death and dying*. New York: Macmillan.

KUMMEROW, J. M., BARGER, J. J., & DIRBY, L. K. (1997). *Work types*. New York: Time Warner Books.

KUNKEL, A. W., & BURLESON, B. R. (1999). Assessing explanations for sex differences in emotional support. *Human Communication Research, 25*(3), 307–340.

KURDEK, L. A. (1998). Relationships outcomes and their predictors: Longitudinal evidence from heterosexual married, gay cohabiting, and lesbian cohabiting couples. *Journal of Marriage and the Family, 60*(3), 553–568.

*KUSHNER, H. (1986). *When all you've ever wanted isn't enough*. New York: Pocket Books.

LACH, J. (2000). Asset analysis. *American Demographics, 22*(6), 15–17. Retrieved August 7, 2000 from EBSCOhost database.

LADANY, N., WALKER, J. A., & MELINCOFF, D. S. (2001). Supervisory style: Its relation to the supervisory working alliance and supervisor self-disclosure. *Counselor Education and Supervision, 40*(4), 263–276.

LANG, D. (1990). *Family harmony*. New York: Prentice Hall.

LANSFORD, J. E., CEBALLO, R., ABBEY, A., & STEWART, A. J. (2001). Does family structure matter? A comparison of adoptive two-parent biological, single-mother, stepfather, and stepmother households. *Journal of Marriage & the Family, 63*(3), 840–851.

LARKINS, M. (1999). Walking sharpens some cognitive skills in elderly. *Lancet, 354*(9176), 401.

LAUER, J., & LAUER, R. (1985, June). Marriages made to last. *Psychology Today*, 22–26.

LAUERMAN, C. (2001, August 7). Saving your skin. *Lincoln Journal Star*, 1D.

———. (1981, July). Little hassles can be hazardous to your health. *Psychology Today*, 58–62.

*LEBOEUF, M. (1979). *Working smart: How to accomplish more in half the time*. New York: McGraw-Hill.

LEE, I. M., PAFFENBAARGER, JR., R. S., & HENNEKENS, C. H. (1997). Physical activity, physical fitness and longevity. *Aging Milano, 9*(1–2), 2–11.

———. (2001). Physical activity and coronary heart disease in women: Is "no pain, no gain" passe? *The Journal of the American Medical Association, 285*(11), 1447.

LEE, J. (1985, May 20). One less for the road. *Time*, 76–78.

LEE, I. M., REXRODE, K. M., COOK, N. R., MANSON, J. E., & BURING, J. E. (2001). Physical activity and coronary heart disease in women: Is "no pain, no gain" passe? *Journal of the American Medical Association, 285*, (11), 1447.

LENARDUZZI, G., & McLAUGHLIN, T. F. (1996). Working on grade point average, test accuracy, and attendance of high school students. *Psychological Reports, 78*(1), 41–42.

*LESHAN, E. (1997). *It's better to be over the hill than under it.* New York: Newmarket.

LEV, E. L. (1997). Bandura's theory of self-efficacy: Applications to oncology. *Scholarly Inquiry for Nursing Practice, 11*(2), 21–37.

LEVANT, R. F., & BROOKS, G. R. (1997). *Men and sex: New psychological perspectives.* New York: Wiley.

LEVINE, M. (1988). *Effective problem solving.* Englewood Cliffs, NJ: Prentice Hall.

LEVOY, G. (1988, July/August). Tears that speak. *Psychology Today,* 8–10.

LEVY, B. (1996). Improving memory in old age through implicit self-stereotyping. *Journal of Personality and Social Psychology, 71,* 1092–1107.

LINCOLN JOURNAL STAR. (1998a, May 5). Survey shows steroid use even among 10-year-olds, p. 4A.

———. (1998b, May 21). Wasted time, p. 1C.

LINGREN, H. G. (1981, March). Strengthening the couple relationship. *NebGuide F-2.* Lincoln, NE: Cooperative Extension Service Institute of Agriculture and Resources.

LIU, C. (2000, May). A theory of marital sexual life. *Journal of Marriage and the Family, 62*(2), 363–373.

LONG, V. O., & MARTINEZ, E. A. (1997). Masculinity, femininity, and Hispanic professional men's self-esteem and self-acceptance. *Journal of Psychology, 131*(5), 481–488.

LONGMORE, M. A., & DEMARIS, A. (1997). Perceived inequity and depression in intimate relationships: The moderating effect of self-esteem. *Social Psychology Quarterly, 60*(2), 172–184.

LONGSHORE, D., STEIN, J. A., & ANGLIN, M. D. (1997). Psychosocial antecedents of needle/syringe disinfection by drug users: A theory-based prospective analysis. *AIDS Education and Prevention, 9*(5), 442–459.

LORENZ, F. O., SIMONS, R. L., CONGER, R. D., ELDER, G. H., JOHNSON, C., & CHAO, W. (1997). Married and recently divorced mothers' stressful events and distress: Tracing change across time. *Journal of Marriage and the Family, 59*(1), 219–232.

LUBAR, J. F. (1997). Neocortical dynamics: Implications for understanding the role of neurofeedback and related techniques for the enhancement of attention. *Applied Psychophysiology and Biofeedback, 22*(2), 111–126.

LUFT, J. (1969). *Of human interaction.* Palo Alto, CA: Mayfield.

*LUKAS, C., & SEIDEN, H. M. (1997). *Silent grief: Living in the wake of suicide.* New York: Bantam Books.

LYNCH, J. J. (2000). *A cry unheard: New insights into the medical consequences of loneliness.* Baltimore, MD: Bancroft Press.

MACCOBY, E., & JACKLIN, C. (1974). *The psychology of sex differences.* Stanford, CA: Stanford University Press.

MACMILLAN, H. L. (1999). Slapping and spanking in childhood and its association with lifetime prevalence of psychiatric disorders in general population sample. *The Journal of the American Medical Association, 282*(21), 1990.

*MALONE, T. P., & MALONE, P. T. (1987). *The art of intimacy.* New York: Prentice Hall.

MALTZ, M. (1960). *Psychocybernetics.* New York: Pocket Books.

MANGUM, A. (2000, July). Walk your way to great health! *Prevention, 52*(7), 122–132.

MARANO, H. E. (2000). Divorced? *Psychology Today, 33*(2), 56–61.

MARKET, J. (1999). Sexual harassment and the communication conundrum. *Gender Issues, 17*(3), 18–21.

MARKHAM, R., & WANG, L. (1996). Recognition of emotion by Chinese and Australian children. *Journal of Cross Cultural Psychology, 27*(5), 616–643.

MARKUS, H. R., & KITAYAMA, S. (1998). The cultural psychology of personality. *Journal of Cross-Cultural Psychology, 29*(1), 63–87.

MARSH, P. (1988). Making eye contact. In P. Marsh (Ed.), *Eye to eye: How people interact.* Topsfield, MA: Salem House.

MARSTON, P. J., HECHT, M. L., MANKE, M. L., McDANIEL, S., & REEDER, H. (1998). The subjective experience of intimacy, passion, and commitment in heterosexual loving relationships. *Personal Relationships, 5,* 15–30.

MARTIN, M. M., ANDERSON, C. M., & MOTTET, T. P.

(1999). Perceived understanding and self-disclosure in the stepparent-stepchild relationship. *Journal of Psychology, 133*(3), 281–290.

MASLOW, A. (1968). *Toward a psychology of being.* New York: D. Van Nostrand.

MASTEKAASA, A. (1997). Marital dissolution as a stressor: Some evidence on psychological, physical, and behavioral changes in the pre-separation period. *Journal of Divorce and Remarriage, 26*(3–4), 155–183.

MATTHEWS, L. S., WICKRAMA, K. A. S., & CONGER, R. D. (1996). Predicting marital instability from spouse and observer reports of marital interaction. *Journal of Marriage and the Family, 58*(3), 641–655.

MAY, R. (1953). *Man's search for himself.* New York: Dell.

———. (1969). *Love and will.* New York: Norton.

MAYER, J. D., CARUSO, D. R. & SALOVEY, P. (1999). Emotional intelligence meets traditional standards for an intelligence. *Intelligence, 27*(4), 267+.

MCCARTHY, B. (1988). Friends and acquaintances. In P. Marsh (Ed.), *Eye to eye: How people interact* (pp. 169–173). Topsfield, MA: Salem House.

MCCARTHY, K. (2001, March/April). Getting healthy in bed. *Psychology Today, 34*(2); 16.

MCCLANAGHAN, M. E. (2000). A strategy for helping students learn how to learn. *Education, 120*(3), 479–487.

MCCORMACK, A. S. (1997). Revisiting college student knowledge and attitudes about HIV/AIDS: 1987, 1991 and 1995. *College Student Journal, 31*(3), 356–363.

MCKAY, J. R., ALTERMAN, A. I., CACCIOLA, J. S., RUTHERFORD, M. J., O'BRIEN, C. P., & KOPPENHAVER, J. (1997). Group counseling versus individualized relapse prevention aftercare following intensive outpatient treatment for cocaine dependence: Initial results. *Journal of Consulting and Clinical Psychology, 65*(5), 778–788.

*MCKAY, M., DAVIS, M., & FANNING, P. (1983). *Messages: The communication book.* Oakland, CA: New Harbinger.

*MCKAY, M., & FANNING, P. (2000). *Self-esteem.* Oakland, CA: New Harbinger.

*MCKAY, M., FANNING, P., & PALEG, K. (1994). *Couple skills: Making your relationship work.* Oakland, CA: New Harbinger.

MEAD, G. H. (1934). *Mind, self, and society.* Chicago: University of Chicago Press.

MEGARGEE, E. I. (1997). Internal inhibitions and controls. In R. Hogan, J. Johnson, & S. Briggs (Eds.), *Handbook of personality psychology* (pp. 251–611). San Diego: Academic Press.

MEHRABIAN, A. (1968, September). Communication without words. *Psychology Today,* 53–55.

———. (1981). *Silent messages.* Belmont, CA: Wadsworth.

MENEC, V. H., & CHIPPERFIELD, J. G. (1997). Remaining active in later life: The roles of locus of control in senior's leisure activity participation, health, and life satisfaction. *Journal of Aging and Health, 9*(1), 105–125.

MENNINGER LETTER. (1994, July). Steroids influence moods, actions, p. 7.

MERTON, R. K. (1948). The self-fulfilling prophecy. *Antioch Review, 8,* 193–210.

MESCHKE, L. L., BARTHOLOMAE, S., & ZENTALL, S. R. (2000). Adolescent sexuality and parent-adolescent processes: Promoting healthy teen choices. *Family Relations, 49*(2), 143–154.

MESSINA, J. J. (1982). *Basic communication skills handbook.* Tampa, FL: Advanced Development Series.

MICHAUD, E. (2000, February). When worrying becomes deadly. *Prevention, 52*(2), 134–42.

MIKULA, G., FREUDENTHALER, H. H., & BRENNACHER-KROELL, S. (1997). Division of labor in student households: Gender inequality, perceived justice, and satisfaction. *Basic and Applied Social Psychology, 19*(3), 275–289.

*MILLER, E. E. (1978). *Feeling good: How to stay healthy.* Englewood Cliffs, NJ: Prentice Hall.

*MILLER, S., NUNNALLY, E. W., & WACKMAN, D. B. (1979). *Talking together.* Littleton, CO: Interpersonal Communication Programs.

*MILLER, S., WACKMAN, D. B., NUNNALLY, E. W., & MILLER, P. A. (1988). *Connecting with self and others.* Littleton, CO: Interpersonal Communication Programs.

MILLIGAN, R. A. K., BURKE, V., BEILIN, L. J., RICHARDS, J., DUNBAR, D., SPENCER, M., BALDE, E., & GRACEY, M. P. (1997). Health related behaviors and psycho-social characteristics of 18-year-old Australians. *Social Science and Medicine, 45*(10), 1549–1562.

MINTON, L. (1993, March 7). Gay sensitivity sessions: Readers speak out. *Parade,* p. 12.

MISRA, R., & MCKEAN, M. (2000). College students' academic stress and its relation to their anxiety, time management, and leisure satisfaction. *American Journal of Health Studies, 16*(1), 41–51.

MITCHELL, T. (2001, August 17–19). Maximize your liquid assets. *USA Weekend,* 4.

*MITCHELL, W. (WITH LEMLEY, B.) (1997). *It's not what happens to you, it's what you do about it: Taking responsibility for change.* Denver, CO: Phoenix Press.

MOCHARNUK, R. S. (2001). Lung cancer screening and prevention: Quit smoking! Retrieved August 12, 2001 from http://oncology.medscape.com/Meds.

MONTAGU, A. (1990, January-February). Reaching the child within us. *Utne Reader,* 87–90.

MONTGOMERY, B. M., & TROWER, P. (1988). Friends and acquaintances. In P. Marsh (Ed.), *Eye to eye: How people interact* (pp. 164–169). Topsfield, MA: Salem House.

MOORE, A. (1999). This time the news is good: TT helps ease arthritis pain. *RN, 62*(1), 16.

MOORE, K., BABYAK, M. A., WOOD, C. E., NAPOLITANO, M. A., KHATRI, P., CRAIGHEAD, E., HERMAN, S., KRISHNAN, R., & BLUMENTHAL, J. A. (1999). The association between physical activity and depression. *Journal of Aging and Physical Activity, 7*(1), 55–61.

MOORE, R. M. (1999). Interracial dating as an indicator of integration. *Black Issues in Higher Education, 15*(26), 120.

MOORE-EDE, M. (1993). *The twenty-four-hour society.* Reading, MA: Addison-Wesley.

MORRISON, N. C. (1995). Successful single-parent fami-

lies. *Journal of Divorce and Remarriage, 22,* 205–219.

MONOW, L. (1993, March 8). The strange burden of a name. *Time,* 76.

MOTTE, P. (2000, May). Medical news: Easing pain with an embrace. *Health,* 98.

*MOYERS, B. (1993). *Healing and the mind.* New York: Doubleday.

MURRAY, H. A. (1938). *Explorations in personality.* New York: Oxford University Press.

*MYERS, D. G. (1992). *Pursuit of happiness.* Dresden, TN: Avon.

MYERS, D. G., & DIENER, E. (1995). Who is happy? *Psychological Science,* 10–19.

MYERS, I. B. (1980). *Introduction to type.* Palo Alto, CA: Consulting Psychologists Press.

*MYERS, I. B. (WITH MYERS, P. B.) (1995). *Gifts differing.* Palo Alto, CA: Consulting Psychologists Press.

NAHOM, D., WELLS, E., GILLMORE, M. R., HOPPE, M., MORRISON, D. M., ARCHIBALD, M., MUROWCHICK, E., WILSDON, A., & GRAHAM, L. (2001). Differences by gender and sexual experience in adolescent sexual behavior: Implications for education and HIV prevention. *Journal of School Health, 71*(4), 153–158.

NAJEM, G. R., BATUMAN, F., SMITH, A. M., & FEUERMAN, M. (1997). Patterns of smoking among inner-city teenagers: Smoking has a pediatric age of onset. *Journal of Adolescent Health, 20*(3), 226–231.

NAMEROW, P. B., KALMUSS, D., & CUSHMAN, L. F. (1997). The consequences of placing versus parenting among young unmarried women.

Marriage and Family Review, 25(3–4), 175–197.

NAPIER, K. M. (1998, July). Lose pounds for good. *Prevention,* 98–104.

NATIONAL CENTER FOR HEALTH STATISTICS. Life expectancy. Retrieved August 16, 2001 from EBSCOhost database.

NATIONAL COUNCIL ON THE AGING. (1998). Sex and aging. *Patient Care, 32*(20), 14.

NATIONAL DEPRESSIVE AND MANIC-DEPRESSIVE ASSOCIATION. (2001). Diagnosis, treatment and support. Retrieved July 28, 2001 from http://www.ndmda.org.

NATIONAL HIGHWAY TRAFFIC SAFETY ADMINISTRATION. (2001). Alcohol-related percentages. Retrieved September 15, 2001 from http://www.nhtsa.dot.gov.

NATIONAL INSTITUTE OF CHILD HEALTH AND HUMAN DEVELOPMENT. (2001). The NICHD study of early child care. Retrieved May 23, 2001 from http://www.hichd.nih.gov/publications/pubs/early_child_care.htm.

NATIONAL INSTITUTE OF MENTAL HEALTH. The numbers count. Retrieved July 23, 2001 from http://www.nimh.nih.gov.

———. (2001). Depression. Retrieved July 28, 2001 from http://www.nimh.nih.gov.

NATIONAL STRATEGY FOR SUICIDE PREVENTION. (2001). Retrieved May 22, 2001 from http://www.mentalhealth.org/suicideprevention/.

*NELSEN, J. (1996). *Positive discipline.* New York: Ballantine.

*NEWMAN, M., & BERKOWITZ, B. (1974). *How to be your own best friend.* New York: Ballantine.

NEWPORT, F. (2001, February 5). Morality, education, crime, dissatisfaction with government head list of most important problems facing country today. *Gallup Poll Analyses*. Retrieved August 13, 2001 from http://www.gallup.com/poll/releases/pr010205.asp.

NEWPORT, F. (2001, June 4). American attitudes toward homosexuality continue to become more tolerant. *Gallup Poll Analyses*. Retrieved August 14, 2001 from http://www.gallup.com/poll/releases/pr010604.asp.

NICHOLAS, D. R. (2000). Men, masculinity, and cancer: Risk-factor behaviors, early detection, and psychosocial adaptation. *Journal of American College Health*, 49(1), 27–33.

*NORRIS, P. A., & PORTER, G. (1987). *I choose life*. Walpole, NH: Stillpoint.

*NORWOOD, R. (1985). *Women who love too much*. Los Angeles: Tarcher.

OBISESAN, T. O., HIRSCH, R., KOSOKO, O., CARLSON, L, & PARROTT, M. (1998). Moderate wine consumption is associated with decreased odds of developing age-related macular degeneration in NHANES-1. *Journal of American Geriatric Society*, 46(1), 1–7.

*O'CONNOR, D. (1985). *How to make love to the same person for the rest of your life and still love it!* Toronto: Bantam.

O'KOON, J. (1997). Attachment to parents and peers in late adolescence and their relationship with self-image. *Adolescence*, 32(126), 471–482.

OLDER, J. (1982). *Touching is healing*. New York: Stein and Day Publishing.

*OLDS, J., SCHWARTZ, R. S., & WEBSTER, H. (1996). *Overcoming loneliness in everyday life*. New York: Birch Lane Press.

OMAHA WORLD HERALD. (2001, June 26). Divorced women surpass widows in number, poverty risk, p. 2.

ORNISH, D. (1998). *Love and survival: The scientific basis for the healing power of intimacy*. New York: HarperCollins.

OSOFSKY, J. D. (1995). The effects of exposure to violence on young children. *American Psychologist*, 50(9), 782–788.

OTHMER, S., PHILLIPS, J., & ROOST, A. (2001). The promise of neurofeedback. *San Diego Psychologist*, 10(4), 1–5.

PACKARD, M. (1992). *An investigation of family relations courses taught in high schools in the United States*. Unpublished master's thesis, University of Nebraska, Lincoln.

PARK, S. Y., BELSKY, J., PUTNAM, S., & CRNIC, K. (1997). Infant emotionality, parenting, and 3-year inhibition: Exploring stability and lawful discontinuity in a male sample. *Developmental Psychology*, 33(2), 218–227.

PASLEY, K., & IHINGER-TALLMAN. M. (1997). Stepfamilies: Continuing challenges for the school. In T. W. Fairchild (Ed.), *Crisis intervention strategies for school-based helpers*. (pp. 60–100). New York: Scribner.

PATIENT EDUCATION MANAGEMENT. (2001). Get patients to tune into their brain: Monitor physical signals to teach stress reduction, 8(4), 43–44. Retrieved June 19, 2001 from EBSCO-host database.

PATTERSON, C. J., & CHAN, R. W. (1997). Gay fathers. In M. E. Lamb (Ed.), *The role of the father in child development* (pp. 245–260). New York: Wiley.

PATTERSON, C. J. (2000). Family relationships of lesbians and gay men. *Journal of Marriage and the Family*, 62(4), 1052–1069.

PAUL, E. L., & BRIER, S. (2001). Friendsickness in the transition to college: Precollege predictors and college adjustment correlates. *Journal of Counseling and Development*, 79(1), 77–89.

*PEARSALL, P. (1988). *Super joy*. New York: Doubleday.

*PECK, M. S. (1978). *The road less traveled*. New York: Simon & Schuster.

PEDEN, A. R., RAYENS, M. K., HALL, L. A., & BEEBE, L. H. (2001). Preventing depression in high-risk college women: A report of an 18-month follow-up. *Journal of American College Health*, 49(6), 299–306.

PEDERSEN, B. K., RHODE, T., & ZACHO, M. (1996). Immunity in athletes. *Journal of Sports Medicine and Physical Fitness*, 36(4), 236–245.

PEDIATRICS. (2001). Tobacco's toll: Implications for the pediatrician. 107(4), 794–798. Retrieved September 15, 2001 from EBSCOhost database.

*PENNEBAKER, J. W. (1997). *Opening up: The healing power of expressing emotions*. New York: Guilford.

PENNEBAKER, J. W., MAYNE, T. J., & FRANCIS, M. E. (1997). Linguistic predictors of adaptive bereavement. *Journal of Personality and Social Psychology*, 72(4), 863–871.

PENNEBAKER, R. (1992, June). Go ahead, say it! *Parents*, 71–77.

PENNINX, B., GURALNIK, J. M., PAHOR, M. FERRUCCI, L., CERHAN, J. R., WALLACE, R. B., & HAVLIK, R. J. (1998). Chronically depressed mood and cancer risk in older persons. *Journal of the National Cancer Institute*, 90(24), 1888–1893.

PEPLAU, L. A., COCHRAN, S. D., & MAYS, V. M. (1997). A national survey of the intimate relationships of African American lesbians and gay men: A look at commitment, satisfaction, sexual behavior, and HIV disease. In B. Greene (Ed.), *Ethnic and cultural diversity among lesbians and gay men* (pp. 11–38). Thousand Oaks, CA: Sage.

PEPLAU, L. A., & SPALDING, L. R. (2000). The close relationships of lesbians, gay men and bisexuals. In C. Hendrick & S. Hendrick (Eds.), *Close relationships: A sourcebook*. Thousand Oaks, CA: Sage.

*PERT, C. B. (1997). *Molecules of emotion: Why you feel the way you feel*. New York: Scribner.

PETH-PIERCE, R. (1998). *The NICHD study of early child care*. Washington, DC: National Institute of Child Health and Human Development.

PETRESS, K. (1999). Listening: A vital skill. *Journal of Instructional Psychology*, 26(4), 261–262.

PHELPS, S., & AUSTIN, N. (2000). *The assertive woman*. California: Impact Publishers.

PHILLIPS, J. M., & GULLY, S. M. (1997). Role of goal orientation, ability, need for achievement, and locus of control in the self-efficacy and goal-setting process. *Journal of Applied Psychology*, 82(5), 792–802.

PHINNEY, J. S., FERGUSON, D. L., & TATE, J. D. (1997). Intergroup attitudes among ethnic minority adolescents: A causal model. *Child Development*, 68(5), 955–969.

PIAGET, J., & INHELDER, B. (1969). *The psychology of the child*. New York: Basic Books.

*PIPHER, M. (1994). *Reviving Ophelia: Saving the selves of adolescent girls*. New York: Putnam

PITZER, R. L. (2002). What does research say about the effects of physical punishment on children? Retrieved February 26, 2002 from http://www.extension.umn.edu.

*PITTMAN, F. (1998). *How taking responsibility can make you grow up*. New York: Golden Books.

PLUTCHIK, R. (1980). *Emotion: A psychoevolutionary synthesis*. New York: Harper & Row.

PODELL, R. M. (1992). *Contagious emotions: Staying well when your loved one is depressed*. New York: Pocket Books.

*PORAT, F. (1988). *Self-esteem: The key to success in work and love*. Saratoga, CA: R & E.

*POTTER, L. L. (1979). *When someone you love dies: A book to share feelings*. Self-published. Available from Tom Potter, 1800 Memorial Drive, Lincoln, NE 68502.

POULSON, R. L., EPPLER, M. A., SATTERWHITE, T. N., WUENSCH, K. L., & BASS, L. A. (1998). Alcohol consumption, strength of religious beliefs, and risky sexual behavior in college students. *Journal of American College Health*, 46(5), 227–232.

POWELL, B., & DOWNEY, D. B. (1997). Living in single-parent households: An investigation of the same-sex hypothesis. *American Sociological Review*, 62, 521–539.

*POWELL, J. (1969). *Why am I afraid to tell you who I am?* Niles, IL: Argus.

*———. (1976). *Fully human, fully alive*. Valencia, CA: Tabor.

POWERS, D. A., & ELLISON, C. G. (1995). Interracial contact and black racial attitudes: The contact hypothesis and selectivity bias. *Social Forces*, 74, 205–226.

PRAGER, K. J., & BUHRMESTER, D. (1998). Intimacy of social and personal relationships. *Journal of Social and Personal Relationships*, 15(4), 435–469.

PREBOTH, M. (2000). Clinical review of recent findings on the awareness, diagnosis and treatment of depression. *American Family Physician*, 61(10), 3158–3161.

PRENTICE-DUNN, S., JONES, J. L., & FLOYD, D. L. (1997). Persuasive appeals and the reduction of skin cancer risk: The roles of appearance concern, perceived benefits of a tan, and efficacy information. *Journal of Applied Social Psychology*, 27(12), 1041–1047.

PROVINI, C., & EVERETT, J. R. (2000). Adults mourning suicide. *Death Studies*, 24(1), 1–19.

PRYOR, J. B., DESOUZA, E. R., FITNESS, J., HUTZ, C., KUMPF, M., LUBBERT, K., PESONEN, O., & ERBER, M. W. (1997). Gender differences in the interpretation of social-sexual behavior: A cross-cultural perspective on sexual harassment. *Journal of Cross-Cultural Psychology*, 28(5), 509–534.

PSYCHOLOGY TODAY. (2000, November). Behind closed doors. 6–15.

*QUINN, P. O. (2001). *ADD and the college student: A guide for*

high school and college students with attention deficit disorder. Washington, DC: Magination Press.

RADECKI, C. M., & JACCARD, J. (1996). Gender-role differences in decision-making orientations and decision-making skills. *Journal of Applied Social Psychology, 26*(1), 76–94.

RADKOWSKY, M., & SIEGEL, L. J. (1997). The gay adolescent: Stressors, adaptations, and psychosocial interventions. *Clinical Psychology Review, 17*(2), 191–216.

RALOFF, J. (2000, April 22). Boning up on calcium shouldn't be sporadic. *Science News,* 260–261.

RANGE, L. M., WALSTON, A. S., & POLLARD, P. M. (1992). Helpful and unhelpful comments after suicide, homicide, accident, or natural death. *Omega, 25*(1), 25–31.

RATHUS, S. A. (1999). *Psychology.* Fort Worth, TX: Harcourt Brace Jovanovich.

RAUSCHER, F. H., KRAUSS, R. M., & CHEN, Y. (1996). Gesture, speech, and lexical access: The role of lexical movements in speech production. *Psychological Science, 7*(4), 226–231.

RAYMOND, J. (2001, Feburary). The ex-files. *American Demographics,* 60–64.

*REAL, T. (1997). *I don't want to talk about it: Overcoming the secret legacy of male depression.* New York: Scribner.

*RESZ, R. (1984). *Bits and pieces.* Lincoln, NE: Southeast Community College Press.

RICHARDS, J. M. & GROSS, J. J. (2000). Emotion regulation and memory: The cognitive costs of keeping one's cool. *Journal of Personality and Social Psychology, 79*(3), 410–424.

RIOS, D. M. (1993, August 23). Now the blame falls squarely on men. *Lincoln Journal,* p. 6.

RISMAN, B. J., & JOHNSON-SUMERFORD, D. (1998). Doing it fairly: A study of postgender marriages. *Journal of Marriage and the Family, 60*(1), 23–40.

*ROGERS, C. (1961). *On becoming a person.* Boston: Houghton Mifflin.

*———. (1972). *On becoming partners: Marriage and its alternatives.* New York: Delacorte.

———. (1978). The necessary and sufficient conditions of therapeutic personality change. In E. A. Southwell and M. Merbaum. (Eds), *Personality readings in theory and research.* Monterey, CA: Brooks/Cole.

*———. (1980). *A way of being.* Boston: Houghton Mifflin.

ROGERS, S. J., & WHITE, L. K. (1998). Satisfaction with parenting: The role of marital happiness, family structure, and parents' gender. *Journal of Marriage and the Family, 60*(2), 293–308.

ROKACH, A. (1990). Surviving and coping with loneliness. *Journal of Psychology, 124,* 39–54.

———. (2000). Perceived causes of loneliness in adulthood. *Journal of Social Behavior and Personality, 15*(1), 67–84.

ROSENBAUM, M. E. (1986). The repulsion hypothesis: On the nondevelopment of relationships. *Journal of Personality and Social Psychology, 51,* 1156–1166.

*ROSENBERG, E. (1983). *Growing up feeling good.* New York: Beaufort Books.

ROSENBERG, M. (1979). *Conceiving the self.* New York: Basic Books.

ROSENTHAL, R., & JACOBSON, L. (1968). *Pygmalion in the classroom: Teacher expectations and student intellectual development.* New York: Holt, Rinehart & Winston.

ROSS, L. (1977). The intuitive psychologist and his shortcomings: Distortions in the attribution process. In L. Berkowitz (Ed.), *Advances in experimental social psychology,* 10. New York: Academic Press.

ROSS, S. E., NIEBLING, B. C., & HECKERT, T. M. (1999). Sources of stress among college students. *College Student Journal, 33*(2), 312–318.

ROTENBERG, K. J. (1997). Loneliness and the perception of the exchange of disclosures. *Journal of Social and Clinical Psychology, 16*(3), 259–276.

ROTTER, J. B. (1972). *Applications of a social learning theory of personality.* New York: Holt, Rinehart & Winston.

———. (1975). Some problems and misconceptions related to the construct of internal versus external control of reinforcement. *Journal of Consulting and Clinical Psychology, 43*(1), 56–57.

———. (1990). Internal versus external control of reinforcement. A case history of a variable. *American Psychologist, 45*(4), 489–493.

ROTTER, J. B., CHANCE, J. E., & PHARES, E. J. (1972). *Application of a social learning theory of personality.* New York: Holt, Rinehart & Winston.

ROUILLARD, L. (1993). *Goals and goal setting.* Menlo Park, CA: Crisp.

RUBIN, L. B. (1985). *Just friends: The role of friendship in our lives.* New York: Harper & Row.

———. (1975). *Compassion and self-hate: An altenative to despair.* New York: Ballantine.

———. (1983). *One to one: Understanding personal relationships*. New York: Pinnacle.

*RUBIN, T. I. (1988). *The angry book*. New York: Macmillan.

RUBIN, Z. (1970). Measurement of romantic love. *Journal of Personality and Social Psychology, 16*, 265–273.

———. (1973). *Liking and loving*. New York: Holt, Rinehart & Winston.

*RYAN, R. S., & TRAVIS, J. W. (1991). *Wellness: Small changes you can use to make a big difference*. Berkeley, CA: Ten Speed Press.

SAAD, L. (1999, September 3). American workers generally satisfied, but indicate their jobs leave much to be desired. *Gallup Poll Analyses*. Retrieved August 14, 2001 from http://www.gallup.com/poll/releases/pr990903.asp.

———. (2001, May 24). Majority considers sex before marriage morally okay. *Gallup Poll Analyses*. Retrieved August 16, 2001 from http://www.gallup.com/poll/releases/pr010524.asp.

SALMELA-ARO, K., & NURMI, J. E. (1996). Uncertainty and confidence in interpersonal projects. Consequences for social relationships and well-being. *Journal of Social and Personal Relationships, 13*(1), 109–122.

SALZBERG, S., & KABAT-ZINN, J. (1997). Mindfulness as medicine. In D. Goleman (Ed.), *Healing emotions* (pp. 107–144). Boston: Shambhala.

SALT, R. E. (1991). Affectionate touch between fathers and preadolescent sons. *Journal of Marriage and the Family, 53*, (3), 545–554.

*SANDERS, C. M. (1992). *Surviving grief and learning to live again*. New York: Wiley.

SATCHER, D. (2001). Why we need an international agreement on tobacco control. *American Journal of Public Health, 91*(2), 191–193.

*SATIR, V. (1972). *Peoplemaking*. Palo Alto, CA: Science and Behavior Books.

*———. (1976). *Making contact*. Millbrae, CA: Celestial Arts.

*———. (1978). *Your many faces*. Millbrae, CA: Celestial Arts.

———. (1983). *Conjoint family therapy*. Palo Alto, CA: Science and Behavior Books.

*———. (1988). *The new peoplemaking*. Mountain View, CA: Science and Behavior Books.

SAVIN-WILLIAMS, R. C. (2001). *Mom, dad, I'm gay: How families negotiate coming out*. Washington, DC: American Psychological Association.

SCHACHTER, S., & SINGER, J. E. (1962). Cognitive, social, and physiological determinants of emotional state. *Psychological Review, 69*, 379–399.

SCHEFLEN, A. E. (1972). *Body language and social order*. Englewood Cliffs, NJ: Prentice Hall.

*SCHMIDT, J. A. (1976). *Help yourself: A guide to self-change*. Champaign, IL: Research Press.

SCHULZ, B. (1988, March/April). Finding time. *The World*, 2–3.

SCHULZ, R., BOOKWALA, J., KNAPP, J. E. SCHEIER, M., & WILLIAMSON, G. M. (1996). Pessimism, age, and cancer mortality. *Psychology and Aging, 11*(2), 304–309.

SCREENING FOR MENTAL HEALTH, INC. (2001). National depression screening day. Retrieved July 28, 2001 from http://www.nmisp.org/depression.htm.

SEGALL, R. (2001). Sleep on it. *Psychology Today, 34*(2), 18.

*SELIGMAN, M. E. P. (1995). *The optimistic child*, Boston: Houghton Mifflin.

*———. (1998) *Learned optimism*. New York: Pocket Books.

SELYE, H. (1974). *Stress without distress*. Philadelphia: Lippincott.

———. (1976). *The stress of life*. New York: McGraw-Hill.

SENIOR, K. (2001). Should stress carry a health warning? *Lancet, 357*(9250), 126.

SEVERE, S. (1997). *How to behave so your children will, too!* New York: Viking.

SHAKOOR, A. T. (2000). Career success in the new millennium. *Black Collegian, 30*(2), 60.

SHAPIRO, F., & FORREST, M. S. (1997). *EMDR: The breakthrough therapy for overcoming anxiety, stress, and trauma*. New York: Basic Books.

SHAVER, P., & SCHWARTZ, J., KIRSON, D., & O'CONNOR, C. (1987). Emotion knowledge: Further exploration of a prototype approach. *Journal of Personality and Social Psychology, 52*(6), 1061–1086.

SHERMIS, M. D., & LOMBARD, D. (1998). Effects of computer-based test administrations on test anxiety and performance. *Computers in Human Behavior, 14*(1), 111–123.

SHIFREN, K., & BAUSERMAN, R. L. (1996). The relationship between instrumental and expressive traits, health behaviors, and perceived physical health. *Sex Roles, 34*(11–12), 841–864.

SHIKANY, J. M., & WHITE JR., G. L. (2000). Dietary guidelines for chronic disease prevention. *Southern Medical Journal*, 93(12), 1138–1152.

SHIMONAKA, Y., NAKAZATO, K., & HOMMA, A. (1996). Personality, longevity, and successful aging among Tokyo metropolitan centenarians. *International Journal of Aging and Human Development*, 42(3), 173–187.

*SIEGEL, B. S. (1986). *Love, medicine, and miracles*. New York: Harper & Row.

SIMMONS, W. W. (2000, December 26). When it comes to having children, Americans still prefer boys. *Gallup Poll Analyses*. Retrieved August 16, 2001 from http://www.gallup.com/poll/release/pr001226.asp.

SIMON, S. B., HOWE, L. W., & KIRSCHENBAUM, H. (1991). *Values clarification: A handbook of practical strategies for teachers and students*. New York: Warner.

*SIMONTON, O. C., MATTHEWS-SIMONTON, S., & CREIGHTON, J. (1978). *Getting well again*. New York: Bantam.

*SIMONTON, S. M. (1984). *The healing family*. New York: Bantam.

SIMS, D. (1985). The grief process. *The Compassionate Friends Newsletter*, 8(2), 1, 6.

SINATRA, S. T. (1999). *Heartbreak and heart disease: A mind/body prescription for healing the heart*. New Canaan, CT: Keats Publishing, Inc.

SINGH, B. R. (1996). The genetic environmental influences on individual cognitive function or IQ. *Educational Studies*, 22(1), 41–56.

SKAALVIK, E. M. (1997). Self-enhancing and self-defeating ego orientation: Relations with task and avoidance orientation, achievement, self-perceptions, and anxiety. *Journal of Educational Psychology*, 89(1), 71–81.

SKINNER, B. F. (1953). *Science and human behavior*. New York: Macmillan.

———. (1987). *Upon further reflection*. Englewood Cliffs, NJ: Prentice Hall.

SMARR, K. L., PARKER, J. C., WRIGHT, G. E., STUCKY, R., RENEE, C., BUCKELEW, S. P., HOFFMAN, R. W., O'SULLIVAN, F. X., & HEWETT, J. E. (1997). The importance of enhancing self-efficacy in rheumatoid arthritis. *Arthritis Care and Research*, 10(1), 18–26.

*SMITH, S. (1993). *Succeeding against the odds*. Los Angeles: Tarcher.

SMITH, D. M., & GATES, G. J. (2001, August 22). Gay and lesbian families in the United States: Same-sex unmarried partner households, 1–4. Retrieved September 1, 2001 from http://www.hrc.org.

SMITH-WARNER, S. A., SPIEGELMAN, D., YAUN, S. S., VANDENBRANDT, P. A., FOLSOM, A. R., GOLDBOHM, R. A., GRAHAM, S., HOLMBERG, L., HOWE, G. R., MARSHALL, J. R., MILLER, A. B., POTTER, J. D., SPEIZER, F. E., WILLETT, W. C., WOLK, A., & HUNTER, D. J. (1998). Alcohol and breast cancer in women: A pooled analysis of cohort studies. *Journal of the American Medical Association*, 279(7), 535–540.

*SMOLIN, A., & GUINAN, J. (1993). *Healing after the suicide of a loved one*. New York: Simon & Schuster.

SMYTH, J. M. (1998). Written emotional expressions: Effect sizes, outcome types, and moderation variables. *Journal of Consulting and Clinical Psychology*, 66(1), 174–184.

*SOLOMON, R. C. (1988). *Love: Reinventing romance for our times*. New York: Simon & Schuster.

SOLOMON, S. M. (2000). Childhood loneliness: Implications and intervention considerations for family therapists. *Family Journal*, 8(2), 161–164.

SPANGLER, L. (1995). Gender-specific nonverbal communications: Impact for speaker effectiveness. *Human Resource Development Quarterly*, 6(4), 409–419.

*SPEZZANO, C. (1992). *What to do between birth and death: The art of growing up*. New York: Morrow.

SPIEGEL, D. (1993). *Living beyond limits: New hope and help for facing life-threatening illness*. New York: Times Books.

———. (1996). Cancer and depression. *British Journal of Psychiatry*, 168(30), 109–116.

———. (1999). Healing Words: Emotional expression and disease outcome. *The Journal of the American Medical Association*, 281(14), 1328.

STACK, S., & ESHLEMAN, J. R. (1998). Marital status and happiness: A 17-nation study. *Journal of Marriage and the Family*, 60(2), 527–536.

STAKE, J. E. (2000). When situations call for instrumentality and expressiveness: Resource appraisal, coping strategy choice, and adjustment. *Sex Roles: A Journal of Research*.

STANARD, R. P. (2000). Assessment and treatment of adolescent depression and suicidality. *Journal of Mental Health Counseling*, 22(3), 204–217.

STANLEY, S. M., MARKMAN, H. J., PRADO, L. M., OLMOS-GALLO, P. A., TONELLI, L., ST. PETERS, M., LEBER, B. D., BOBULINSKI, M., CORDOVA, A., & WHITTON, S. W. (2001, January). Community-based premarital prevention: Clergy and lay leaders on the front lines. *Family Relations, 50*(1), 67–76.

STATE OF OUR NATION'S YOUTH. (2001). Retrieved September 16, 2001 from http://www.horatioager.com.

*STEARNS, A. K. (1984). *Living through personal crisis*. Chicago: Thomas More Press.

*STEINBERG, L., & LEVINE, A. (1997). *You and your adolescent*. New York: HarperCollins.

*STEINEM, G. (1992). *Revolution from within: A book of self-esteem*. Boston: Little Brown.

STEINER, C. (1974). *Scripts people live*. New York: Bantam.

STEPFAMILIES. (1999, Summer). Our stepdad, our hero, 5.

STEPFAMILY ASSOCIATION OF AMERICA. (2001). Facts & FAQs—Stepfamily. Retrieved September 9, 2001 from http://www.saafamlies.org.

STEPHAN, W. G., STEPHAN, C. W., & DEVARGAS, M. C. (1996). Emotional expression in Costa Rica and the United States. *Journal of Cross-Cultural Psychology, 27*(2), 147–160.

STEPHEN, A. (1999, April 2). Bigger and better here: Road rage. *New Statesman, 129*(4430), 1.

STERN, S. B. (1999). Anger management in parent-adolescent conflict. *American Journal of Family Therapy, 27*(2), 181–193.

STERNBERG, R. J. (1986). A triangular theory of love. *Psychological Review, 93*, 119–135.

————. (1987). *The triangle of love: Intimacy, passion, commitment*. New York: Basic Books.

————. (1998). *Love is: A new theory of relationships*. New York: Oxford University Press.

*STERNBERG, R. (WITH WHITNEY, C.). (1991). *Love the way you want it*. New York: Bantam.

STEVENS, D., KIGER, G., & RILEY, P. J. (2001). Working hard and hardly working: Domestic labor and marital satisfaction among dual-earner couples. *Journal of Marriage and the Family, 63*(2), 514–526.

STEWART, S. D. (1999, November). Nonresident mothers' and fathers' social contact with children. *Journal of Marriage and the Family, 61*(4), 894–907.

STODGHILL, R. (1998, June 15). Where'd you learn that? *Time*, 52–59.

STONE, A., SMYTH, J. M., KAELL, A., & HUREWITZ, A. (2000). Structured writing about stressful events: Exploring potential psychological mediators of positive health effects. *Health Psychology, 19*(6), 619–624.

*STONE, H., & STONE, S. (1993). *Embracing your inner critic*. New York: HarperCollins.

STONEY, C. M., & ENGEBRETSON, T. O. (2000). Plasma homocysteine concentrations are positively associated with hostility and anger. *Life Sciences, 66*(23), 2267–2275.

STOWERS, D. A., & DURM, M. W. (1996). Does self-concept depend on body image? A gender analysis. *Psychological Reports, 78*(2), 643–646.

STRAUS, M. A., & YODANIS, C. L. (1996). Corporal punish-

ment in adolescence and physical assaults on spouses in later life: What accounts for the link? *Journal of Marriage and the Family, 58*(4), 825–841.

STRONG, B., DeVAULT, C., SAYAD, B. W. (1998). *The marriage and family experience: Intimate relationships in a changing society*. Belmont, CA: Wadsworth.

STUART, R., & JACOBSON, B. (1985). *Second marriage*. New York: Norton.

STURM, W. (2000, February). Does obesity contribute as much to morbidity as poverty or smoking? *Healthcare for Communities*. Retrieved June 13, 2001 from http://www.hsrcenter.ucla.edu/hcc/viewallhccp.html.

SUEDFELD, R., & PENNEBAKER, J. W. (1997). Health outcomes and cognitive aspects of recalled negative life events. *Psychosomatic Medicine, 59*(2), 172–177.

SUITOR, J. J., & CARTER, R. S. (1999). Jocks, nerds, babes and thugs: A research note on regional differences in adolescent gender norms. *Gender Issues, 17*(3), 87–101.

SULLIVAN, M. (1996). Rozzie and Harriet? Gender and family patterns of lesbian co-parents. *Gender and Society, 10*(6), 747–767.

SULLIVAN, O. (1997). The division of housework among "remarried" couples. *Journal of Family Issues, 18*, 205–223.

SULLUM, J., & CLARK, M. M. (2000). Predictors of exercise relapse in a college population. *Journal of American College Health, 48*(4), 175–181.

SUN, Y. (2001). Family environment and adolescents' well-being before and after parents' marital disruption: A longitudinal analysis. *Journal of Marriage and the Family, 63*(3), 697–713.

SURGEON GENERAL. (2001). Youth violence. Retrieved May 22, 2001 from http://www.sugeongeneral.gov.

SWARTZLANDER. (1998, June 15). Health statistics separate the men from the boys—and the women. *Lincoln Journal Star*, p. 1D.

SWINFORD, S. P., DEMARIS, A., CERNKOVICH, S. A., & GIORDANO, P. C. (2000). Harsh physical discipline in childhood and violence in later romantic involvements: The mediating role of problem behaviors. *Journal of Marriage and Family, 62*(2), 508–519.

SZINOVACZ, M. E. (1998). Grandparents today: A demographic profile. *Gerontologist, 38*, 37–52.

TANGNEY, J. P., MILLER, R. S., FLICKER, L., & BARLOW, D. H. (1996). Are shame, guilt, and embarrassment distinct emotions? *Journal of Personality and Social Psychology, 70*, 1256–1279.

TANNEN, D. (1990). *You just don't understand: Women and men in conversation.* New York: Ballantine.

———. (2001). *I only say this because I love you: How the way we talk can make or break family relationships throughout our lives.* New York: Random House.

TAYLOR, E., & OLSWANG, S. G. (1997). Crossing the color line: African Americans and predominantly white universities. *College Student Journal, 31*(1), 11–18.

TERRY, S. (2000, April 10). The unexpected consequences of living together. *Christian Science Monitor*, 1.

THARINGER, D., & WELLS, G. (2000). An attachment perspective on the developmental challenges of gay and lesbian adolescents: The need for continuity of caregiving from family and schools. *School Psychology Review, 29*(2), 158–172.

THAYER, S. (1988, March). Close encounters. *Psychology Today*, 30–36.

THAYER, E. S., & ZIMMERMAN, J. (2001). *The co-parenting survival guide.* Oakland, CA: New Harbinger Publications.

THOMAS, B. S. (1997). Direct and indirect effects of selected risk factors in producing adverse consequences of drug use. *Substance Use & Misuse, 32*(4), 377–398.

THOMAS, V., & OLSON, D. H. (1993). Problem families and the circumplex model: Observational assessment using the clinical rating scale (CRS). *Journal of Marital and Family Therapy, 19*, 159–175.

THORTON, J. (2000, July). Cheat and run. *USA Weekend*, 6–7.

THUN, M. J., PETO, R., LOPEZ, A. D., MONACO, J. H., HENLEY, S. J., HEATH, C. W., & DOLL, R. (1997). Alcohol consumption and mortality among middle-aged and elderly U.S. adults. *New England Journal of Medicine, 337*(24), 1705–1714.

TICE, D. M., & BAUMEISTER, R. F. (1997). Longitudinal study of procrastination, performance, stress, and health: The costs and benefits of dawdling. *Psychological Science, 8*(6), 454–458.

*TIEGER, P. D., & BARRON-TIEGER, B. (1995). *Do what you are: Discover the perfect career for you through the secrets of personality type.* Boston: Little, Brown.

*———. (1997). *Nurture by nature: Understand your child's personality type—and become a better parent.* Boston: Little, Brown.

TIGGEMANN, M. (2001). The impact of adolescent girls' life concerns and leisure activities on body dissatisfaction, disordered eating, and self-esteem. *Journal of Genetic Psychology, 162*(2), 133–142.

TIME. (1982, January 15): We're going down, Larry, 21

*TRICKETT, S. (1997). *Anxiety and depression: A natural approach.* Berkeley, CA: Ulysses Press.

TROCKEL, M. T., BARNES, M. D., & EGGET, D. L. (2000). Health-related variables and academic performance among first-year college students: Implications for sleep and other behaviors. *Journal of American College Health, 49*(3), 125–131.

TUBESING, D. A. (1981). *Kicking your stress habits: A do-it-yourself guide for coping with stress.* New York: New American Library.

UMBERSON, D., ANDERSON, K., GLICK, J., & SHAPIRO, A. (1998). Domestic violence, personal control, and gender. *Journal of Marriage and the Family, 60*(2), 442–452.

U.S. CENSUS BUREAU. (2000). Working, single and teen moms. Retrieved May 7, 2001 from http://www.census.gov.

———. (2000, March). Current population survey. Retrieved July 8, 2001 from http://www.census.gov.

U.S. DEPARTMENT OF AGRI-
CULTURE. (2001). Expendi-
tures on children by families.
Retrieved September 4, 2001
from http://www.usda.gov/
cnpp/Crc/Crc2000.pdf.

*VAIL, E. (1982). *A personal guide
to living with loss*. New York:
Wiley.

VANDERVOORT, D. (2000). Social
isolation and gender. *Current
Psychology*, *19*(3), 229–336.

VELLA, M. L., PERSIC, S., &
LESTER, D. (1996). Does self-
esteem predict suicidality
after controls for depression?
Psychological Reports, *79*(3, Pt.
2), 1178.

VENIEGAS, R. C., & PEPLAU,
L. A. (1997). Power and the
quality of same-sex friendships. *Psychology of Women
Quarterly*, *21*(2), 279–297.

VERLOOP, J., ROOKUS, M. A.,
VANDERKOOY, K., & VAN-
LEEUWEN, F. E. (2000). Physical activity and breast
cancer risk in women aged
20–54 years. *Journal of the National Cancer Institute*, *92*(2),
128–136.

VERNAREC, E., & PHILLIPS, K.
(2001). How to cope with job
stress. *RN*, *64*(3), 44–49.
Retrieved

VERSCHUEREN, K., MARCOEN,
A., & SCHOEFS, V. (1996).
The internal working model
of the self, attachment, and
competence in five-year-
olds. *Child Development*,
67(5), 2493–2511.

*VINTON, E. C. (1998). *How to set
limits: Defining appropriate
boundaries of behavior for your
children—from infants to teens*.
Lincolnwood, IL: Contemporary Books.

VIORST, J. (1986). *Necessary
losses*. New York: Ballantine.

*VISHER, E., & VISHER, J.
(1979). *Stepfamilies: Myths

and realities*. Secaucus, NJ:
Citadel.

———. (1982). *How to win as a
stepfamily*. Chicago: Contemporary Books.

*———. (1988). *Old loyalties, new
ties*. New York: Brunner/
Mazel.

*VOGT, W. P. (1997). *Tolerance
and education: Learning to live
with diversity and difference*.
Thousand Oaks, CA: Sage.

*VON OECH, R. (1983). *A whack
on the side of the head: How to
unleash your mind for innovation*. New York: Warner.

WADE, T. J. (1996). The relationships between skin color
and self-perceived global,
physical, and sexual attractiveness, and self-esteem for
African Americans. *Journal of
Black Psychology*, *22*(3),
358–373.

WADE, C., & TAVRIS, C. (2002).
Invitation to psychology.
Upper Saddle River, NJ:
Prentice Hall.

WAITE, L. J. (2000). The negative effects of cohabitation.
The Responsive Community,
10(1). Retrieved from http://
www.gwu.edu/~ccps/rcq.

WALKER, V., & BROKAW, L.
(1998). *Becoming aware*.
Dubuque, IA: Kendall/Hunt.

WALLERSTEIN, J. S., & BLAKES-
LEE, S. (1989). *Second chances:
Men, women and children a
decade after divorce*. New
York: Ticknor & Fields.

WAMPLER, K. S. (1990). An update of research on the couple communication program.
Family Science Review, *3*(1),
21–40.

WARD, C. A. (2000, October).
Models and measurements of
psychological androgyny: A
cross-cultural extension of
theory and research. *Sex Roles:
A Journal of Research*, 529.

WARREN, C. W., KANN, L.,
SMALL, M. L., SANTELLI, J. S.,
COLLINS, J. L., & KOLBE, L. J.
(1997). Age of initiating selected health-risk behaviors
among high school students
in the United States. *Journal of
Adolescent Health*, *21*(4),
225–231.

*WEGSCHEIDER-CRUSE, S.
(1988). *Coupleship: How to have
a relationship*. Deerfield Beach,
FL: Health Communications.

WEIDNER, G. (2000, May). Why
do men get more heart disease than women?: An international perspective. *Journal
of American College Health*,
48(6), 291–294.

*WEIL, A. (1995a). *Health and
healing*. Boston: Houghton
Mifflin.

*WEIL, A. (1995b). *Spontaneous
healing*. New York: Fawcett
Columbine.

*WEINER-DAVIS, M. (1992).
*Divorce busting: A revolution-
ary and rapid program for staying together*. New York:
Simon & Schuster.

WELLS, A. J. (1998). Heart disease from passive smoking
in the workplace. *Journal of
American College of Cardiology*,
31(1), 1–9.

WESTOFF, L. A. (1977). *The second time around*. New York:
Viking

WHEELER, P. (2001). The
Myers-Briggs Type Indicator
and applications to accounting education research. *Issues
in Accounting Education*,
16(1), 125–150.

WHITE, H. R. (1997). Alcohol,
illicit drugs, and violence. In
D. M. Stoff & J. Breiling
(Eds:), *Handbook of antisocial
behavior* (pp. 511–523): New
York: Wiley.

WHITE, J. W., & BONDURANT,
B. (1996). Gendered violence

in intimate relationships. In J. Wood (Ed.), *Gendered relationships* (pp. 197–210). Mountain View, CA: Mayfield.

WHITE, L., & GILBRETH, J. G. (2001). When children have two fathers: Effects of relationships with stepfathers and noncustodial fathers on adolescent outcomes. *Journal of Marriage and Family*, 63(1), 155–167.

WHITEHEAD, B. D., & POPENOE, D. (2001, June 27). Singles seek soul mates for marriage. *Gallup Poll Analyses*. Retrieved August 23, 2001 from http://www.gallup.com/poll/releases/pr010627basp.

*WHITFIELD, C. L. (1987). *Healing the child within*. Deerfield Beach, FL: Health Communications.

*WHITLOCK, K. (1989). *Bridges of respect: Creating support for lesbian and gay youth*. Philadelphia: American Friends Service Committee.

WILLIAMS, J. G., & COVINGTON, C. J. (1997). Predictors of cigarette smoking among adolescents. *Psychological Reports*, 80(2), 481–482.

WILLIAMS, J. M., & HARRIS, D. V. (1998). Relaxation and energizing techniques for regulation of arousal. In J. M. Williams (Ed.), *Applied sport psychology: Personal growth to peak performance* (pp. 219–236). Mountain View, CA: Mayfield.

WILLIAMS, R. L., & LONG, J. D. (1983). *Toward a self-managed life style*. Boston: Houghton Mifflin.

*WILLIAMS, W. (1988). *Rekindling desire: Bringing your sexual relationship back to life*. Oakland, CA: New Harbinger.

WILLIAMSON, A. M., & FEYER, A. M. (2001). Moderate sleep deprivation produces impairments in cognitive and motor performance equivalent to legally prescribed levels of alcohol intoxication. *Professional Safety*, 46(1), 17.

WILSON, S. A., BECKER, L. A., & TINKER, R. H. (1995). Eye movement desensitization and reprocessing (EMDR) treatment for psychologically traumatized individuals. *Journal of Consulting and Clinical Psychology*, 63(6), 928–937.

WINGERT, P., & KANTROWITZ, B. (2000, March 20). Gay today: The family. *Newsweek*, 50–53.

WINGERT, P. (2000, June 12). Young and overweight. *Newsweek*, 52.

WINGERT, P. (2001, May 21). Parents today make more time for quality time. *Newsweek*, 53.

WITHERSPOON, K. M., SPEIGHT, S. L., & THOMAS, A. J. (1997). Racial identity attitudes, school achievement, and academic self-efficacy among African American high school students. *Journal of Black Psychology*, 23(4), 344–357.

WITT, S. D. (1997). Parental influence on children's socialization to gender roles. *Adolescence*, 32(126), 253–259.

WOLVIN, A., & COAKLEY, C. G. (1988). *Listening*. Dubuque, IA: Wm. C. Brown.

WOMEN IN BUSINESS. (2000, July–August). Money wise: Saving for retirement vital for women, 42. Retrieved August 7, 2000 from EBSCOhost database.

WOO, T. O., & MIX, P. (1997). Self-enhancing reactions to performance feedback in an academic setting. *Journal of Social Behavior and Personality*, 12(2), 481–500.

WOOD, J. T. (2001). *Gendered lives: Communication, gender, and culture*. Belmont, CA: Wadsworth.

WOOD, K. C., BECKER, J. A., & THOMPSON, J. K. (1996). Body image dissatisfaction in preadolescent children. *Journal of Applied Developmental Psychology*, 17(1), 85–100.

*WOODWARD, J. C. (1988). *The solitude of loneliness*. Lexington, MA: Heath.

WOOLLAMS, S., & BROWN, M. (1979). *TA: The total handbook of transactional analysis*. Englewood Cliffs, NJ: Prentice Hall.

WORCHEL, S., & SHEBILSKE, W. (1989). *Psychology: Principles and application*. Englewood Cliffs, NJ: Prentice Hall.

WORLD HEALTH ORGANIZATION. (1998). Passive smoking does cause lung cancer, do not let them fool you. Retrieved from http://www.who.ch.

WORTMAN, C. B., BATTLE, E. S., & LEMKAU, J. P. (1997). Coming to terms with the sudden, traumatic death of a spouse or child. In R. C. Davis, A. J. Lurigio, & W. G. Skogan (Eds.), *Victims of crime* (pp. 108–133). Thousand Oaks, CA: Sage.

*Wuh, H. C. K., & Fox, M. (2001). *Sexual fitness*. New York: G. P. Putnam's Sons.

XIE, X., & LIN, S. (1997). Gender differences in perceptions of family roles by Chinese university students. *Perceptual and Motor Skills*, 84(1), 127–130.

YEUNG, W. J., SANDERG, J. F., DAVIS-KEAN, P. E., & HOFFERTH, S. L. (2001, February):

Children's time with fathers in intact families. *Journal of Marriage and the Family, 63*, 136–154.

YIP, P. (2001, September 15). Divorce will also bring financial repercussions. *Lincoln Journal Star*, 6A.

YOUTH RISK BEHAVIOR SURVEILLANCE—UNITED STATES. (1999). Retrieved August 20, 2001 from http://www.cdc.gov.

*ZIMBARDO, P. G. (1977). *Shyness: What it is, what to do about it*. New York: Jove/HBJ.

REFLECTIONS AND APPLICATIONS

This section of the book is intended to involve you in looking at yourself and your relationships. We gain more by thinking and writing than just by reading. Be honest and strive for a deeper understanding of your life—and enjoy the process!

SELF-APPRAISAL

Before you read the book and complete the other activities in this section, use the following scale and rate yourself honestly in these areas. Each reflects the potential benefits of learning from this book and continuing to improve your interpersonal skills.

5 = Perfect (couldn't improve)
4 = Very good (almost to the desired level)
3 = Average (could be improved)
2 = Below average (could be much better)
1 = Poor (needs a great deal of improvement)

1. _____ How well do I really know and understand myself?
2. _____ How much regard do I have for myself?
3. _____ What do I think about my ability to change?
4. _____ How effectively do I manage stress?
5. _____ How well do I cope with crises?
6. _____ How do I rate my personal relationships (friendships, significant other)?
7. _____ How do I rate my family relationships?
8. _____ How do I rate my work or school relationships?
9. _____ How well do I handle my emotions?
10. _____ How happy am I?

Total your scores and divide by 10 to get an average score. If you have less than a 5.0 average, this book will help you. If you scored a 5.0 (perfect), you can benefit from learning what this book has to teach about perfectionism.

Honestly reflect on what you hope to gain from this book, then write your ideas below and on the back of this sheet. Be specific. After you have read the book, come back to what you wrote and see what you have accomplished.

CHAPTER 1

SELF-CONCEPT INVENTORY

Complete the inventory about yourself (two sides) and have at least two other people (preferably a male and a female) fill out similar inventories *about you*. One two-sided inventory for another person is provided from which you can make copies.

Descriptors: Describe yourself in the following four areas of self using at least four different descriptors for each (specific words, phrases, or sentences).

Physical (appearance, condition of body, health):

Mental (abilities, preferred ways of learning, attitude or mental outlook):

Emotional (usual feelings or typical ones in certain situations, mood):

Social (my statuses, behaviors around others, preferences of social activities and interactions):

If I were to achieve my ideal self, would these descriptors be different, and, if so, in what ways? Use other paper, if needed.

Physical:

Mental:

Emotional:

Social:

Complete the following sentences.

Some relationships that are important to this person are

Two of this person's skills or talents are

Two characteristics or behaviors this person appreciates about him- or herself are

One thing about self this person would like to improve is

One thing about self this person is proud of is

One of this person's goals is

What does this person value? Name at least four values.

For the next 3 questions, use other paper if you want.

During an average weekday, specifically how does this person spend her or his time?

What would this person do with one million tax-free dollars?

If this person had only 1 to 3 months to live, what would he or she do during that time?

Thinking of attitude as a broad outlook on life, place an X on the continuum to describe this person.

Very negative   Negative   Average   Positive   Very positive

Thinking of self-esteem as a value placed on self or genuine regard for who one is, what is this person's current level of self-esteem?

    1 = very low   2 = low   3 = average   4 = high   5 = very high

THANK YOU VERY MUCH FOR YOUR HELP!

COPING WITH STRESS

Identify sources of stress in your life.

- A major life change

- A common hassle or everyday irritant

- Internal or self-imposed

    List the ways you handle stress.

    How else could you cope with stress in your life?

Breathing to Relieve Stress and Anxiety

How do you breathe? Proper breathing comes from the diaphragm, the thin muscle that separates the lung and abdominal cavities (Williams & Harris, 1998). To relieve stress, try deep breathing several times during the day. Inhale slowly and deeply through your nose, hold briefly, then exhale through your mouth. To check if you are breathing deeply, place your hands (outstretched middle fingers lightly touching each other) over the area of your diaphragm/abdomen. Inhale. Did your middle fingers separate slightly? If not, you are not breathing deeply. Deeply inhaled air will move the diaphragm down slightly, thus pushing the abdomen out creating a vacuum in the lungs. This fills up the lungs from the bottom (Williams & Harris, 1998). In most situations, a few of these deep breaths can relieve stress and anxiety. To use a relaxation technique, get into a comfortable position and use several deep breaths to lower your body's state of arousal.

REMEMBER TO USE DEEP BREATHING THE
NEXT TIME YOU WANT RELIEF!

CHAPTER 2

PERSONALITY: THE CORE OF SELF

- Drawing from mental, emotional, and social descriptors of self as well as common behaviors, describe your personality using five or more words or phrases.

- In what ways, if any, is your personality similar to the personality of family members? Identify the person and the characteristics. If your personality is not at all like that of anyone in your family, speculate or explain why it isn't. Use other paper if necessary.

- Disregarding chronological age, in which of Erikson's psychosocial stages do you think you are? Why?

- What challenges or difficulties have you encountered or are you encountering in any of the stages?

- Give an example of when you behaved from these ego states. Describe what you did or said.

    (1) "parent"

    (2) "child"

    (3) "adult"

- Monitor both positive and negative strokes given and received for a few days. Give examples of any or all types. Describe briefly what you learned from doing this.

- Circle what you think (or know) your four MBTI preferences to be. For each preference describe some of your behaviors that support it. If you have none that do, explain why you think you tend to be more the opposite preference.

Extraversion	Introversion
Sensing	Intuition
Thinking	Feeling
Judgment	Perception

- Identify a personality trait about yourself you especially like and one that is related to one of the MBTI preferences. Identify the preference. Describe how it helps you and for what reason(s) you like it.

- Do the same with a personality trait about yourself you would like to change. Be sure to identify the MBTI preference.

- In which of the following areas would your life have been (or will be) different if you had been born the opposite sex? Put a check in the blank.

_____ Career choice	_____ Education	_____ Sports/other activities
_____ Household tasks	_____ Marriage and child raising	_____ Self-esteem
_____ Self-efficacy	_____ Independence	_____ Assertiveness
	_____ Emotions	

- Pick one category you checked and explain how you think it would have been different.

- Answer the following as Yes, No, or Unknown (neither yes nor no).

  1. _____ I usually express my anger.
  2. _____ I am generally self-sufficient and independent.
  3. _____ I am a caring person.
  4. _____ I often demonstrate affection.
  5. _____ I am usually assertive rather than passive or aggressive.
  6. _____ I want and intend to achieve success.
  7. _____ I usually show fear when I experience it.
  8. _____ I let others know I love them.
  9. _____ I laugh *and* cry when appropriate.
  10. _____ I am capable in several areas.
  11. _____ I can solve problems and take care of others.
  12. _____ I can financially support myself.

  "Yes" answers indicate an androgynous personality.

- Either list examples of recent assertive behavior or identify situations in which assertive behavior on your part would have been advantageous.

CHAPTER 3

VALUES AND CHOICES

Use the same four values you identified in the Chapter 1 activity and describe as follows:

Value   *Received by Which Method(s)*   *Influence*

My 10-year decade was _____.

What significant event(s) occurred at that time and how were you influenced?

What significant event has influenced you in the past 5 years? How were your values affected?

Give any examples of values being transmitted to you by:

Moralizing

Laissez-faire or *hands-off*

Identify any of the recommended ways your values were developed.

As a parent, what are you doing or will you do to transmit values?

HEALTH CHOICES

Complete the following sentences.

A poor choice I have made regarding my health was

A wise choice I have made regarding my health was

A wise choice I will make about my health is

DECISION MAKING

An important decision I have made was

I made the decision in the following ways:

I used more of my _____ (thinking or feeling) preference.

GOALS

Develop a list of "wants" allowing your child ego state complete freedom. No matter how unrealistic your "wants" are, DREAM. Then select one and make it a goal.

One of my short-term goals is _____.

Check the following if you can answer "yes."

_____ Is the goal mine, not someone else's?

_____ Is the goal in accord with my values?

_____ Is the goal a priority of mine?

_____ Is the goal realistic?

Identify specific action steps, pinpointing as much as possible. Be sure to mention exactly what action you will take with a specific way to measure it as well as a date of completion for each step. When completed, be sure to pat yourself on the back!

TIME MANAGEMENT

On a scale of 1 (excellent) to 5 (poor), how well do I manage my time?

One time-management tip I can use is _____.

CHAPTER 4

HAPPINESS—IT'S UP TO ME!

Finish these statements.

On a scale of 1 to 5 (1 = very unhappy, 2 = unhappy, 3 = moderately happy, 4 = happy, 5 = very happy), currently I rate myself _____.

In order to be satisfied, I need

An example of a time when life seemed especially wonderful was

An example of a time when life seemed extremely difficult was

From the rest of your life (80 percent for most readers of this text), describe a time when you created your own reality by making the situation happier or unhappier.

Decide to create your own happiness by:

Initiating Pleasure and "Smelling Roses"

In the first column, write a pleasurable activity and/or ways of "smelling roses" in your life. Then fill in the other columns. Continue on a sheet of paper, as this can be quite an eye-opening exercise.

PLEASURE	HOW OFTEN DO I DO?	WHEN DID I LAST DO?

An example of the last time I enjoyed the "present" or "now" was

Use yourself, someone you know, or make up an example of:

"futurizing"

"pasturizing"

Giving to Others

One way I "give to life" is

A nourishing, rewarding relationship I have is with

The last time I let her or him know how much I value this relationship was when I

Thinking and Acting Positively

Write an excuse you have made or one you could have made. Then reword it to reflect the truth.

Catch yourself using "can't/couldn't" when not literally true. Write how you used it and what is actually true. Do the same for "should/shouldn't" (or "have to," "must," "need to" or "ought").

Decrease the number of "bummer" words you use and increase the positive. Fill in the following blanks:

Instead of saying _____, I did (or can) say _____.

Briefly describe a situation or event in your past or present life. Show that you can consider alternatives by listing several choices you had or have. Don't evaluate a choice at this time and don't think "I can't do that."

Briefly describe a problem or bothersome situation from your past. List any positive action steps you took in an effort to solve or change it. If you took no action, what *could* you have done?

The last time I procrastinated was

This was an example of procrastination that was (positive or negative) because

CHAPTER 5

EMOTIONAL MONITORING AND LEARNING

- Over a period of a week, keep an emotional diary. Whenever you become aware of a particular feeling, list the emotion, the reason for it, your physiological arousal (if apparent), and the way you expressed the emotion (verbally, nonverbally, or both).

- List two emotions you commonly experience, then describe how you express them.

- With whom do you feel most comfortable expressing these emotions? If you experience discomfort expressing them, with whom does this occur?

Finish these statements.

When I'm slightly annoyed, I usually

When I'm angry, I usually

I show my affection to _____ by

When I'm happy, others know it because I

When I'm proud, I usually

I am afraid of

I show fear by

When I'm sad, I usually

I get sad when

I don't show affection to _____ because

As a result of your gender role, what idea did you receive regarding emotional expression?

From the following sources, list one message (verbal or nonverbal) you received concerning emotional expression.

Family

Peers

Ethnic group and/or religion

RATIONAL EMOTIVE BEHAVIORAL THERAPY

Fill in the A, B, C boxes regarding an event in your life.

The Way It Was

Activating Event	*Belief*	*Consequences* (emotions and behaviors)

The Way It Could Have Been Using Thought-Changing

Activating Event	*Belief*	*Consequences* (emotions and behaviors)

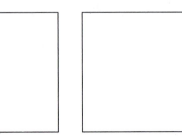

Practice using REBT at least once a day and enjoy the results.

BEHAVIOR CHANGES

- Describe a situation in which you could have or did change your behavior which resulted in a change in emotion or mood?

- As silly as it might seem, try changing your facial expression and see if your emotion or mood changes. Especially, try smiling when you aren't particularly happy or in a good mood. Don't give up too soon!

- List ways in which you can usually elevate your mood. Check the ones that work the best and then don't forget to use them!

CRISIS

Draw a path of life for yourself identifying major ups and downs.

Which of the coping mechanisms/behaviors recommended in this chapter have you used?

CHAPTER 6

HOW WELL DO YOU LISTEN?

Using the scale, answer the following questions:

5 = Almost always   4 = Usually   3 = About half the time

2 = Sometimes   1 = Hardly ever

1. _____ I am interested in other people.
2. _____ I ask questions about other people's interests.
3. _____ The opinions of others are of interest to me.
4. _____ I am able to focus my attention on what someone is saying.
5. _____ I put aside my thoughts and feelings and concentrate on what is being said.
6. _____ I try to create a positive listening environment by getting rid of distractions and other obstacles.
7. _____ I realize I have a psychological filter and check it periodically so that it doesn't interfere with my listening.
8. _____ I approach others with the idea that they have something of value to contribute to a conversation.
9. _____ When listening, I face the person who is talking.
10. _____ I keep an open body position.
11. _____ When listening, my body is relaxed yet attentive.
12. _____ I maintain eye contact at least three quarters of the time. When I look away, I quickly bring my eyes back to the speaker's face.
13. _____ When listening, my facial expression registers what I am thinking and feeling.
14. _____ My facial expression changes during a typical conversation.
15. _____ When listening, I nod my head affirmatively an appropriate number of times.
16. _____ During conversation I am comfortable with appropriate touching.
17. _____ When listening, I use brief verbal responses which show interest.
18. _____ I ask encouraging questions of the speaker.
19. _____ When listening, I try to find ways to clarify the speaker's point.
20. _____ I avoid negative listening behaviors.

Total your score. Give yourself a grade as follows:

95–100 = A +   90–94 = A   85–89 = B+   80–84 = B

75–79 = C+   70–74 = C   65–69 = D+   60–64 = D

59 or below = Unsatisfactory

Most importantly, what can you do to improve your listening?

Observe two other people who are in a listening role. Briefly describe and evaluate their listening behaviors.

Listen for and then describe these types of listening.

Empathic:

Receptive:

Directive:

What has been especially helpful to you in Chapter 6?

CHAPTER 7

IDENTIFYING CLOSED COMMUNICATION

Use the following letters to identify closed types. If the statement has more than one type, use more than one letter.

D = Dogmatic   C = Commando   G = Grandiose

1. _____ That man has an obnoxious personality.
2. _____ He needs to listen more to other people's opinions.
3. _____ Jane always thinks of other's feelings.
4. _____ I think you should quit that job.
5. _____ It seems to me that he will never learn good money management skills unless he has his own income.
6. _____ Nobody appreciates what I do.

USING OPEN COMMUNICATION

Re-write each of the statements above in the open style.

1. _____

2. _____

3. _____

4. _____

5. _____

6. _____

Listen for any example of closed communication, write it, then reword it in the open style.

Ask someone to listen to you for any uses of fillers.

UNDERSTANDING PARALANGUAGE AND BODY LANGUAGE

While listening to a conversation, be aware of examples of paralanguage and body language. Describe some of these. Disregarding what was actually being said as much as possible, briefly explain what could be interpreted from the paralanguage and body language examples.

Pretend you are writing a script for a play. Write a short scene between two or more characters. Write the lines to be said and after each describe briefly the paralanguage and body language you want the characters to demonstrate.

Carry on a conversation with someone and try not to vary your body language during the time (same posture, facial expression, etc.). Hopefully, you will see how this creates a negative communication environment.

CHAPTER 8

SELF-DISCLOSURE

Using the following, identify each self-disclosing statement.

BD = Basic data   P = Preference   B = Belief   F = Feeling

_____ I was concerned when he was late coming home.

_____ I thought he might have had an accident.

_____ My opinion on that candidate is a positive one.

_____ I graduated from high school last year.

_____ I voted in the last election.

_____ I enjoyed the concert.

_____ I am disappointed because you don't want to go with me.

_____ I don't think that was a wise choice.

_____ I didn't like that restaurant.

_____ I was quite proud of my grade.

Now write one statement disclosing about yourself on each level.

BD _____

P _____

B _____

F _____

Fill in the blanks about your self-disclosure.

I enjoy sharing preference statements with _____ because
_____.

I am comfortable disclosing about my beliefs with_____.

One person who shares beliefs with me is _____, while
_____ seems reluctant to do so.

My feelings in most situations are easy to disclose to _____

because _____.

One person who discloses feelings to me is _____.

A person who doesn't reveal feelings to me is_____.

SENSING, INTERPRETING, OR FEELING?

Tell which is provided in the statements using the following code.

S = Sensing   I = Interpretation   F = Feeling

_____ It seems to me that she is upset.

_____ I'm happy.

_____ I think that taking time to visit her was good for me.

_____ I heard what he said.

_____ I noticed that she didn't talk to him.

PERCEPTION CHECKING

Write what to say using perception checking. Because each scenario contains only sensing *or* interpretative information, you are to make up what is missing.

Your friend Jack tells you that he has seen your roommate and another person looking at apartments. Use perception checking in talking to your roommate about this.

1.

2.

3.

You think that your supervisor at work is unhappy with your performance. Use perception checking to speak to him or her about this.

1.

2.

3.

FEELING STATEMENT

Write a feeling statement about the supervisor situation described above. Remember that your feeling is related to your interpretation.

GIVING CRITICISM

A family member disturbs you by telling very negative, derogatory stories about a minority group. Write what you would say using recommendations for delivering criticism.

POSITIVE RESPONSES TO CRITICISM

Your employer has said to you, "You don't seem to care about your job." First, write the two-step response if you *understand the reason* for the criticism.

1.

2.

Then write the two-step response if you *do not understand the reason* for the criticism.

1.

2.

DIMENSIONS OF AWARENESS

Read the scenario regarding Terri and Matt in the Fair Fighting activity in this section of Reflections and Applications for Chapter 11. Pretend you are Matt before the fight begins. Write statements of awareness that he could have used in discussing the situation with Terri. You can then do the same for Terri's dimensions of awareness.

Sensing

Thinking

Feeling

Wanting

Acting

You might also try doing the same for Terri's dimensions of awareness. Use a separate sheet of paper.

Indicate several ways you can improve in the area of content (what you say) related to this chapter.

CHAPTER 9

FRIEND-TO-FRIEND

With a friend, talk about the following, then write a short summary of your discussion in each category.

Social Exchange

What does each of us receive from our friendship? What more, if anything, would we like to receive from this friendship?

Attraction Factors

Describe briefly how any of the following are involved in your friendship.

Proximity

Similarities

Complementarity

Reciprocity

Characteristics and Behaviors

How would each of us describe a best friend? Which of the behaviors and characteristics do we possess? What do we like about each other?

Expectations

What do we expect of each other in this friendship?

IMPROVING RELATIONSHIPS

Identify any situation in which you have or could have demonstrated the following positive characteristics.

Tolerance, acceptance, or appreciation of diversity

Empathy

Sensitivity

Cooperation

Assertiveness

Negotiation skills

Complete the following sentences.

To me, a person is being difficult when he or she

I usually deal with this by

An effective way to deal with it might be to

I probably am "difficult" to others when I

Unload Your Gunnysack

Using "I" statements, describe a resentment, then tell how you feel and what you want.

Resentment	Feeling	Want
(I resent it when you)	(When this happens, I feel)	(I want you to)

Future Intentions

In the future, I would like to:

_____ Call or write a note when someone needs support.

_____ Tell someone that I have been concerned about him or her and I care.

_____ Visit someone in the hospital or nursing home.

_____ Actually do something to assist a person or family during a crisis.

_____ Be a courteous driver.

_____ Help someone by opening a door, offering to let the person go ahead of me, etc.

_____ Smile and greet someone.

_____ Do a favor for another person.

_____ Say thank you and please. Show appreciation.

_____ Forgive someone.

_____ Demonstrate warm and affectionate behavior.

CHAPTER 10

ASSETS AND LIABILITIES

Your assets are what you have to offer a potential employer. These are strong points that will help you get and keep a job. Your liabilities are drawbacks or limitations that could hinder you from getting or keeping a job. Consider the following categories.

Interests	Education	Work Experience	Personality
Skills	Goals	Volunteer Work	Work Habits

In each of the areas, list assets, then liabilities. Use other paper and make long lists. Consider ideas from Chapter 10 (i.e., the table of positive personal qualities and work habits and the characteristics employers have identified as positive).

Now looking back, write about any of your needs that were not fulfilled in a past relationship. Or do so for a present relationship. Use your own paper.

FAIR FIGHTING

Read the following scenario, then using the fair fighting criteria described in Chapter 11, identify all the ways in which this was an unfair fight. Jot these down in the margin.

Matt and Terri, who are engaged to be married, had attended a wedding and reception together. At the reception Terri spent a great deal of time talking with friends of hers from high school whom Matt did not know and then she danced a few times with a former boyfriend. After the reception they have the following conversation.

Terri: You're mad, I can tell.

Matt: No, I'm not.

Terri: Come on, Matt. You've been quiet since we left the reception. I know you are.

Matt: I'm surprised you even noticed.

Terri: What's that supposed to mean?

Matt: You were so busy having a great time.

Terri: What else are you supposed to do at a reception . . . sit alone and not talk to anyone like you do?

Matt: Like I do, huh? You weren't exactly the friendliest person in the world when we went to my class reunion last summer!

Terri: No wonder. They were all so boring. At least my high school friends are fun.

Matt: You looked like you were having a *lot* of fun dancing with Paul.

Terri: So that's it! You are so insecure sometimes. I can't believe you would be jealous just because I danced with him. Remember when you danced with several old girlfriends at your reunion? Did I get jealous? No!

Matt: You wouldn't ever get jealous because you think you're so much better than anyone else. Besides that, you don't show me enough affection. I give and give and don't get a lot in return unless you happen to be in the mood to really pay attention to me. You talk to your other friends more than you do to me and seem to enjoy their company more. You don't act like you're ready to get married; in fact, you don't even seem to really be in love with me. And every time we fight, you want to have the last word.

Terri: You sure seem to have a lot of complaints! And of course there's *nothing* wrong with you. Why don't you just find someone else?

Matt: Maybe I will! I hope you're satisfied that you've won another one.

Could you write this scenario using positive, open communication and fair fighting suggestions?

CHAPTER 12

FAMILY PICTURE

Using any figures you want (human-like, stick figures, circles, squares, etc.), draw a diagram of your family. Label each figure with the person's name and relationship to you.

If possible, compare your diagram to others and think about how your concept of family is similar or different.

PARENTING BEHAVIORS

What do you want or would you like your child to be like when he or she is a young adult? First list or describe the characteristic in the left-hand column, then describe what would be advisable for you to do or not do in terms of parenting behaviors. Use other paper if necessary. **Use this as a guide now or in the future**.

Description of Young Adult	Parenting Behaviors

Write a brief summary of how applying the concepts, techniques, and skills from this book can make someone a better parent.

Index